Warraparna Kaurna!

Reclaiming an Australian language

This book is available as a free fully-searchable ebook from
www.adelaide.edu.au/press

Warraparna Kaurna!

Reclaiming an Australian language

by

Rob Amery

Department of Linguistics
The University of Adelaide

THE UNIVERSITY
of ADELAIDE

UNIVERSITY OF
ADELAIDE PRESS

Published in Adelaide by
University of Adelaide Press
Barr Smith Library
The University of Adelaide
South Australia 5000
press@adelaide.edu.au
www.adelaide.edu.au/press

The University of Adelaide Press publishes externally refereed scholarly books by staff of the University of Adelaide. It aims to maximise access to the University's best research by publishing works through the internet as free downloads and for sale as high quality printed volumes.

© 2016 Rob Amery

This work is licenced under the Creative Commons Attribution-NonCommercial-NoDerivatives 4.0 International (CC BY-NC-ND 4.0) License. To view a copy of this licence, visit http://creativecommons.org/licenses/by-nc-nd/4.0 or send a letter to Creative Commons, 444 Castro Street, Suite 900, Mountain View, California, 94041, USA. This licence allows for the copying, distribution, display and performance of this work for non-commercial purposes providing the work is clearly attributed to the copyright holders. Address all inquiries to the Director at the above address.

For the full Cataloguing-in-Publication data please contact the National Library of Australia: cip@nla.gov.au

ISBN (paperback) 978-1-925261-24-0
ISBN (ebook) 978-1-925261-25-7
DOI: https://doi.org/10.20851/kaurna

Book design: Rob Amery
Project coordinator: Julia Keller
Cover design: Emma Spoehr
Cover image: © 2015 Katrina Karlapina Power, used with permission

Table of Contents

Table of Contents — v
    Maps, Plates, Graphs and Tables — viii
Preface to this Edition (2016) — x
    Revised Kaurna Spelling — xii
Additional References — xiv
Foreword to the 2000 Edition — xix
Preface to the 2000 Edition — xxii
Acknowledgements — xxiii
Abbreviations — xxx
Conventions and Terminology — xxxii

Chapter 1: Locating the Study — 1
    Who are the Kaurna? — 3
    Kaurna territory — 4
    Kaurna neighbours — 5
    Kaurna people today — 7
    A Kaurna linguistic and cultural renaissance — 11
    The relationship between Kaurna and Nunga English — 13
    Prospects for the revival of Kaurna — 16

Chapter 2: Language Reclamation — 19
    Language reclamation: preliminaries — 19
    'Dead' or 'sleeping' languages? Terminology does matter — 20
    Revival of a 'dead' language: is it really possible? — 23
    What do we need as a basis for reviving a language? — 24
    What is being revived? — 27
    Natural vs. artificial languages — 28
    Language reclamation: the method — 31
    Assembling the language sources — 32
    Archival research — 33
    Philology and comparative/historical linguistics — 34
    Language typology and language universals — 36
    Language modernisation — 37

Chapter 3: An Ecological Approach to Language Revival   41
   Language ecology   41
   On the nature of language   45
   Communicative vs. symbolic functions of language   47
   Esoteric vs. exoteric languages   49
   Language as cultural artefact   50
   Language planning issues   52

Chapter 4: A Sociolinguistic History of Kaurna   56
   First contacts   57
   Invasion of Kaurna lands: colonisation, 1836   61
   Christianising and 'civilising'   64
   The German missionaries   65
   Decline of the Kaurna and loss of the Kaurna language   73
   Surviving the 'dark ages'   78

Chapter 5: Kaurna Sources   85
   The sources   86
   Language contact and contact languages   104
   Recent compilations of Kaurna material used as resources   104
   Grammar   106
   Kaurna texts   110
   Kaurna Dreaming stories   113
   Kaurna songs   118

Chapter 6: Restoring and Transforming the Kaurna Language   128
   Recovering the sounds of Kaurna   129
   Restoring the lexicon   137
   Lexical semantics   143
   Grammar and syntax   146
   Variation   151
   Recapturing the genius of the language   152
   The reintroduction of aspects of traditional culture   155
   Kaurna in the twenty-first century   156
   Authenticity and integrity   162
   Development of Kaurna language materials   166
   Summary and conclusions   168

Chapter 7: Kaurna Language Programs   172
   Precursors of Kaurna programs in the education sector   172
   Language ecology in the education sector   174
   Kaurna language programs   180
   Teacher training and in-service   183
   Curriculum development   183
   Approaches and methods   187

Evaluation   193

Chapter 8: Kaurna in Society   203
    Names and naming   203
    The public function of Kaurna   210
    Cultural tourism   221
    Language use within the Kaurna community   228
    Summary and discussion   230

Chapter 9: Kaurna Language Revival: The Formulaic Method   234
    A revival of Kaurna as a spoken language?   234
    Approaches to language revival   235
    The Formulaic Method   237
    Introducing the language into the Kaurna community   241
    'Artificial pidgins' and Ngarrindjeri 'language renewal' 245
    The relationship between minority and majority languages 247

Chapter 10: Sociopolitical Dimensions of Kaurna Language Revival   250
    The construction and reconstruction of identity   255
    The struggle for recognition, empowerment and reconciliation 261
    The sociopolitical backdrop for Kaurna language revival 262
    Whose language is it? Ownership and copyright issues   266
    The role of linguistics   272

Chapter 11: Into the Twenty-first Century: Developments since 2000   280
    Kaurna sources   281
    Restoring and transforming the Kaurna language   282
    Revised Kaurna Spelling (2010)   283
    Kaurna language programs   285
    Kaurna in society   286
    Kaurna on the web   287
    Media coverage   288
    International profile   289
    Sociopolitical dimensions of Kaurna language revival   291

Chapter 12: Summary and Conclusions   295

Bibliography   307

Index   338

Maps, Plates, Graphs and Tables

List of Maps

Map I: Kaurna Native Title claim	xxvi
Map II: Kaurna territory and neighbouring languages	xxvii
Map III: Thura-Yura languages	xxviii
Map IV: Main localities referred to on the Adelaide Plains	xxix
Map 7.1 Location of Kaurna language programs, 1990-1997	180
Map 8.1: Prominent Kaurna names appearing on current maps	204
Map 8.2: Kaurna sites of cultural significance in the metropolitan area	223

List of Plates (between pp. 202 and 203)

Plate 1: Clamor Schürmann
Plate 2: Christian Teichelmann
Plate 3: Kadlitpinna 'Captain Jack'
Plate 4: Ivaritji (Amelia Taylor)
Plate 5: The *Kuri* (RS Kurdi) and *Palti*
Plate 6: A page from Kartanya's copybook, 1840
Plate 7: Letter written by Pitpauwe, 1843
Plate 8: Letter written by Wailtyi, 1843
Plate 9: Group Letter written to Gawler (penned by Itya Maii), 1841
Plate 10: Ten Commandments and Gawler's speech, 1840
Plate 11: Lewis O'Brien and Georgina Williams KL&LE launch
Plate 12: Nelson (Snooky) Varcoe teaching Kaurna at KPS, 1992
Plate 13: Dr Alitya Wallara Rigney at KL&LE launch, 1997
Plate 14: Cherie Warrara Watkins, steps of Parliament House, 1996
Plate 15: Alma Ridgway and Vicki Hartman, 1996
Plate 16: First Kaurna workshop, KPS, 1990
Plate 17: Nola Foster and children out the front of KPS
Plate 18: Tauondi students on excursion
Plate 19: Julie Hodgkinson and children at KPS
Plate 20: Nelson Varcoe and PWAC singers, 1995
Plate 21: Kevin Duigan, Cherie Watkins and KPS children, 1997
Plate 22: Singing group in Tarntanyangga (Victoria Square)
Plate 23: Smoking ceremony at PWAC
Plate 24: Kevin Duigan and KPS children, 26 May 1999
Plate 25: Nelson Varcoe at Journey of Healing, 26 May 1999
Plate 26: Lester Irabinna Rigney, 26 May 1999
Plate 27: Kaurna Radio Shows team, 2010
Plate 28: CKLR team
Plate 29: Kaurna media team (Steve and Taylor) on location at Brighton
Plate 30: Jack Kanya Buckskin and daughter Mahleah Kudlyu
Plate 31: KWP members, 4 December 2014

Plate 32: Signing of MoU between KWP and the University of Adelaide, 2013
Plate 33: Return of Kaurna letters from Germany
Plate 34: Kaurna TAFE Certificate III course, 2012
Plate 35: TAFE Certificate III graduates, December 2013
Plate 36: University of Adelaide Kaurna Summer School excursion, Warriparinga, January 2013
Plate 37: Steve Gadlabarti Goldsmith at Kaurna Learner's Guide launch, Tandanya, December 2013
Plate 38: Jack Kanya Buckskin and *Kuma Kaaru* dance troupe
Plate 39: Kaurna street signs
Plate 40: Kaurna Coast public artwork
Plate 41: Tindo solar bus
Plate 42: Kaurna graffiti art under Southern Expressway

List of Graphs

Graph 7.1: Enrolments and graduates of Tauondi Kaurna course, 1993-1997	197
Graph 8.1: Kaurna speeches in public, 1991-1997	211
Graph 8.2: Number of individuals giving Kaurna speeches in a given year	213
Graph 8.3: Performance of Kaurna songs in public, 1992-1997	215

List of Tables

Table 5.1: 'Traditional' Kaurna songs	121
Table 5.2: Kaurna hymns written in the early 1840s	123
Table 5.3: Kaurna sources making an original contribution	126
Table 5.4: Secondary Kaurna sources	127
Table 6.1: Kaurna consonants	130
Table 6.2: Nukunu consonant system	131
Table 6.3: Some variant spellings in T&S	132
Table 6.4: Borrowings from Aboriginal languages, 1990-1997	138
Table 6.5: Prominent lexical gaps in Kaurna fauna terminology	141
Table 6.6: Gaps in the fauna domain addressed so far	142
Table 6.7: Examples of Kaurna neologisms developed in the 1990s	159
Table 7.1: Kaurna language programs: a chronology	181
Table 11.1: KWP Projects funded by Commonwealth Government Grants (2005-2015)	292

Preface to this Edition (2016)

This book, *Warraparna Kaurna!*, is a revised paperback edition and ebook of the hardcover book *Warrabarna Kaurna!* originally published in Lisse, The Netherlands, in 2000. It is the chronicle of the early stages of the revival of a language that ceased to be spoken many years ago. This revival is based on historical documents, most of which were recorded in the period 1836-1858. Taking an ecological perspective, I trace the history of the language and all known sources. Since 2000, a few more minor sources have come to light and there is always the possibility of discovering something more in the future.

My analysis of Kaurna language revival here focuses primarily on the period 1990-1997 when I undertook intensive research for my PhD project completed in 1998. Kaurna language revival began with the writing of six songs in 1990. Since then, the language has developed considerably; Kaurna programs have been established and expanded across several institutions catering for a range of learners; increasingly, the language is being used in public by members of the Kaurna community; the range of functions for which the language is being used continues to expand; and there are early signs that the language is beginning to take root within Nunga households.

The study is part of a long-term ongoing project, where the ground is continually shifting. The use of and interest in the Kaurna language is gathering momentum and much has happened since 1997. Kaurna language reclamation is an exciting collaboration between Kaurna people, educators, linguists and others. This collaboration was solidified with the formation of Kaurna Warra Pintyandi (now Kaurna Warra Pintyanthi) (KWP) in 2002 and an incorporated Aboriginal organisation, Kaurna Warra Karrpanthi (KWK) in September 2013. Partnerships with a number of organisations have been formalised and agreements reached. Considerably more Kaurna language resources are now available to the learner or teacher of Kaurna. Developments since 2000 are discussed in more detail in Chapter 11 (pages 281-295).

Despite all these developments, we are still in the very early stages of Kaurna language revival. Will the Kaurna language take the 'great leap forward' and emerge as an everyday language within the Kaurna community? The signs that this might actually happen are certainly more positive than they were back in 2000. The Kaurna language has transformed the lives of several young Kaurna people who are teaching the language, developing resources and passing the language on to their own children. Two young Kaurna provided quotes for the national curriculum Framework for Aboriginal Languages and Torres Strait Islander Languages released in 2015. Jack Kanya Buckskin says in the explanatory 'What is the Framework' section:

> *Ngaityu warra ngathaitya ngai. Ngaityu warra yaintya yarta-ana tarraitpayinthi.*
> *Warraitya tampinthi yaintya yarta tampi-apinthi.*

> My language is more than just a way to converse with me. It is my identity and the doorway to understanding my culture as a whole. Understanding my language helps me to understand the place around me and connects me to this country.
> Vincent 'Jack' Buckskin, Cultural Mentor, Tauondi College and Kaurna language leader.
> (http://www.australiancurriculum.edu.au/languages/framework-for-aboriginal-languages-and-torres-strait-islander-languages/what-is-the-framework)

Taylor Power-Smith writes in the Rationale:

> *Ngathaitya, ngathu Kaurna Warra nguthu-atpama, ngai tidna kuinyunta yartangka ngatpanthi. Naku'athu, yailty'athu ngana ngai tiyati. Ngai kararrinthi ngaityu warraku, ngaityu tapa purrunaku kuma. Ngai padlurninthi ngaityu warra pirrki-apititya ngapidluku, ngana padlurninthi yuringkarnititya, tirkatitya, kumangka ngathaityangka padnititya.*
> To me, teaching Kaurna means sinking my toes into this sacred soil and embracing who I am. It means being so proud of my language and culture that I want to share it with whoever wants to listen, learn and be a part of my journey.
> Taylor Power, Kaurna language teacher, Gilles Street Primary School, with Kaurna translation assistance from Rob Amery, Head of Linguistics, University of Adelaide.
> (http://www.australiancurriculum.edu.au/languages/framework-for-aboriginal-languages-and-torres-strait-islander-languages/rationale)

Whatever the ultimate outcome, the Kaurna language movement has already been a success in the eyes of the Kaurna community, within the education sector, and, to some extent, in the eyes of the public.

This study is breaking new ground. In the Kaurna case, very little knowledge of the language remained within the Aboriginal community. Yet the Kaurna language has become an important marker of identity and a means by which Kaurna people can further the struggle for recognition, reconciliation and liberation. This study challenges widely held beliefs as to what is possible in language revival and questions notions about the very nature of language and its development.

A major revision of Kaurna spelling was adopted in 2010. Prior to that the spellings used by the German missionaries Teichelmann and Schürmann (1840) were used by the Kaurna language movement. The spelling of Kaurna words in current use in this edition have been changed to conform to the revised spelling system, though historical spellings are retained as they appear in the original source material. Historical spellings will be retained in all quotations and will be the default spelling in Chapters 4 and 5, whilst revised spelling will be the default in the remaining chapters. Where necessary, revised spellings in brackets may be used alongside historical spellings, as for example with the personal name Mullawirraburka [RS Murlawirrapurka]. Historical spelling is continued for placenames, with the revised spelling noted once in brackets as in the example given above. In the ebook version, historical spelling appears in blue font, whilst Revised Spelling (RS) appears in red, in keeping with the practice adopted in Kulurdu Marni Ngathaitya, the Kaurna Leaners Guide published in 2013.

Revised Kaurna Spelling (adopted by KWP in 2010)

The following letters make up the Kaurna Alphabet:
a, aa, ai, au, dl, dlh, dly, dn, dnh, dny, i, ii, k, l, lh, ly, m, n, ng, nh, ny, p, r, rd, rdl, rdn, rl, rn, rr, rt, t, th, ty, u, ui, uu, w, y.

These letters represent the distinctive sounds of the Kaurna language. There are many digraphs and trigraphs in the Kaurna Alphabet. Just as *sh* in English 'wi*sh*ing' is not simply an *s* followed by an *h*, in the same way **dl** is not simply a *d* followed by an *l*. The letters **dl** represent a single sound described further below.

Vowels
There are actually just three short vowels in Kaurna: **a i u** and their long counterparts **aa ii uu** plus the diphthongs **ai au ui**.

a	as in the English words: m**a**ma, p**a**pa, vis**a** or Maori h**a**ka
i	as in the English words: b**i**t, p**i**t, s**i**t
u	as in the English words: p**u**t, b**u**tcher
aa	as in the English words: f**a**ther, B**a**rt,
ii	as in the English words: t**ea**, k**ey**, sk**i**
uu	similar to the vowel in the English words: c**oo**ler, fl**u**, S**ue**
ai	as in the English words: p**ie**, sp**y**, ch**ai**
au	as in the English words: p**ow**er, t**ow**n, M**au**i
ui	similar to the vowel in the English word: b**oy**

Consonants
The Kaurna consonant sounds **l m n w y** are pronounced much the same as the same English letters.

Voicing
The Kaurna spelling system uses **p t k** (as opposed to *b d g* in Ngadjuri and Narungga). The pronunciation of **p** is sometimes [*p*] and at other times closer to [*b*]. Similarly the pronunciation of **t** often sounds like [*d*] and **k** often sounds like [*g*].

Interdentals
Kaurna has sounds made with the tongue in between the teeth (interdental).

th	is like the d in the English word: wi*d*th, but unlike the *th* in *th*ink, this, wi*th* or la*th*e
nh	is like the n in the English word: te*n*th
lh	is like the l in the English word: fi*l*th

The *d*, *n* and *l* in width, tenth and filth are interdental because they anticipate the following interdental fricative th sound, but the sound written *th* in English is not the same as the Kaurna **th**. No air passes through the mouth with Kaurna **th**. It is a true stop.

Retroflex Sounds

The Kaurna retroflex sounds **rl**, **rn** and **rt** do not occur in English and are pronounced with the tongue tip curled slightly back from where it occurs when saying the English sounds l n t. This same sound is common in Indian-English and many other Aboriginal languages.

Alveopalatal Sounds

These sounds are produced with the blade of the tongue placed against the palate, and with the tip down behind the bottom and top teeth.

- **ty** is similar to the sound in English words: *ch*ur*ch*, bu*tch*er, *j*u*dg*e and go*t-y*ou,
- **ny** as in the middle of the English words: Bu*n*yan, o*n*ion
- **ly** is similar to the sound in the English words: mi*lli*on, wi*ll-y*ou

Prestopping

l-sounds and n-sounds in Kaurna may be prestopped. These prestopped sounds pattern as single consonants. Prestopping is often in free-variation with their non-prestopped counterparts. For instance the word for 'house' is both wa**rl**i and wa**rdl**i. 'Fire' is both ka**rl**a and ka**rdl**a. Notice that the *rd* here is part of the trigraph **rdl** and is totally different to **rd,** which is the flapped or tapped r-sound discussed below.

The Velar Nasal, ng

The **ng** sound in Kaurna occurs at the beginning of words and syllables, but is exactly the same sound as the *ng* in English.

- **ng** as in the middle and end of the English words: ri**ng**ing, si**ng**er,

Rhotics or r-sounds

There are three 'r' sounds in Kaurna: **r**, **rd** and **rr**.

- **r** is exactly the same as in Australian English: **r**oaring
- **rd** is a quick flap or tap (similar to the *tt* when said quickly in English bu*tt*er it).
- **rr** is 'rolled' or 'trilled' like the 'r' sound in Scottish English, Italian or Indonesian.

Spelling of placenames

Kaurna placenames often end in the locative suffixes **–ngka** or **–ila** 'in, at, on'. When these suffixes occur on common nouns they are spelt **–ngka** and **–ila**. However, when they occur on a proper noun (an actual name) they are spelt **–ngga** and **–illa**. So the two words **nurlungka** 'on the curve' and **Nurlungga** 'at Nurlu = Noarlunga' are pronounced exactly the same but spelt slightly different. You will see placenames spelt in many different ways, but increasingly councils are adopting the new spelling illustrated in this book.

Spelling of personal names
Some Kaurna people prefer to use their own spelling or keep the old T&S spelling in their own names. Others have adopted the new spellings used here. Kaurna people are free to choose the spelling of their own names.

Stress
The first syllable in Kaurna words as always stressed. In longer words, the third syllable receives secondary stress. Stress the bold syllables in **Ngang**kipa**ringga.**

Sounds at the start of words
Kaurna words can only commence with i, k, m, n=(nh), ng, p, t=(th), w or y. Note that when Kaurna words commence with the letters n and t, these sounds are actually interdental nh and th. In reduplicated words like tadlithadli 'frypan' the t at the beginning and th in the middle are exactly the same sound pronounced in exactly the same way.

Additional references
Much has been written on the Kaurna language since the publication in 2000 of *Warrabarna Kaurna! Reclaiming an Australian Language*. These additional references have been integrated into the previous Bibliography. The Bibliography in this volume is up to date with respect to the Kaurna language, though recent developments, of which there are many, within the field of revival linguistics are not captured here.

Tampitirkanthu, Kaurna Warra tirkatitya!
'Read in order to understand the Kaurna language.'

Amery, Rob (2000). The First Lutheran Missionaries in South Australia and their contribution to Kaurna language reclamation and the reconciliation movement. *Journal of Friends of Lutheran Archives,* No. 10, October 2000, 30-58.

Amery, Rob (2000). Reclaiming the Kaurna Language. In *Footprints in the Sand*, compiled by Yvonne Allen, Holdfast Bay Reconciliation Group (pp. 30-40). (Includes a section on Kaurna placenames and Kaurna words used elsewhere in the booklet).

Amery, Rob (2001). Round pegs in square holes: Formalising the teaching of Australian Indigenous languages. In the *MLTASA Newsletter*, Spring 2001. Paper presented at the AFMLTA Conference, Canberra, 7-10 July 2001.

Amery, Rob (2001). Language planning and language revival. *Current Issues in Language Planning* 2(2&3): 141-221.

Amery, Rob (2002). Indigenous language programs in South Australian Schools: Issues, dilemmas and solutions. Paper prepared for the NSW Board of Studies, March 2002.

http://www.boardofstudies.nsw.edu.au/aboriginal_research/pdf_doc/indig_lang_sa_amery.doc

Amery, Rob (2002). Weeding out spurious etymologies: Toponyms on the Adelaide Plains. In Luise Hercus, Flavia Hodges and Jane Simpson (Eds), *The land is a map: Placenames of Indigenous origin in Australia* (165-180). Canberra: Pacific Linguistics.

Amery, Rob (2002). Marginalised relics or dynamic modern languages? Emerging issues when Australia's Indigenous languages modernise. *Babel* 37(2): 10-15; 37-38. Paper presented at the Indigenous Languages Panel, AFMLTA conference, Canberra, 10 July 2001.

Amery, Rob (Ed.) (2003). *Warra Kaurna: A resource for Kaurna language programs.* 3rd ed. revised and expanded. Kaurna Warra Pintyandi, c/- University of South Australia. Reprinted September 2005, Image & Copy Centre, The University of Adelaide.

Amery, Rob (2004). Beyond their expectations: Teichelmann and Schürmann's efforts to preserve the Kaurna language continue to bear fruit.[1] In Walter F. Veit (Ed.) *The struggle for souls and science. Constructing the Fifth Continent: German missionaries and scientists in Australia.* Strehlow Research Centre, Alice Springs: Occasional Paper No. 3, 9-28.

Amery, Rob (2004). Early Christian missionaries — Preserving or destroying Indigenous Languages and Cultures? Commissioned paper written for *Holy Holy Holy* exhibition, Flinders University, 2004. In Vivonne Thwaites (Ed.), *Holy Holy Holy*, Flinders University City Gallery, 36-45.

Amery, Rob (2009). Phoenix or relic? Documentation of languages with revitalization in mind. *Language Documentation & Conservation (LD&C)* December 2009 issue (Volume 3, Number 2). Online at: http://nflrc.hawaii.edu/ldc/

Amery, Rob (2009). Kaurna language reclamation and the Formulaic Method. In Wesley Y. Leonard & Stelómethet Ethel B. Gardner (Eds), *Language is Life. Proceedings of the 11th Annual Stabilizing Indigenous Languages Conference*, 10-13 June 2004 at University of California at Berkeley. Report 14, Survey of California and other Indian Languages, 81-99. Online at: http://linguistics.berkeley.edu/~survey/resources/publications.php

Amery, Rob (2010). Monitoring the use of Kaurna, the language of the Adelaide Plains. In John Hobson, Kevin Lowe, Susan Poetsch & Michael Walsh (Eds) *Re-awakening languages: Theory and practice in the revitalization of Australia's Indigenous languages.* Sydney: Sydney University Press, 56-66.

Amery, Rob (2012). Four Dresdners in South Australia in the early-mid nineteenth century: A lasting legacy for Kaurna, Ngarrindjeri and Barngarla peoples. *Zeitschrift für Australienstudien* 26.

Amery, Rob (2012). Taking to the airwaves: a strategy for language revival. In M. Ponsonnet, L. Dao & M. Bowler (Eds), *Proceedings of the 42nd*

---

[1] This paper is based on an earlier paper entitled 'The First Lutheran Missionaries in South Australia: Their contribution to Kaurna language reclamation and the reconciliation movement', which was published in the *Journal of Lutheran Archives* No. 10, October 2000: 30-58.

Australian Linguistic Society Conference — 2011. Australian National University Canberra ACT, 5-6 December 2011. ANU Digital Collections. http://hdl.handle.net/1885/9280

Amery, Rob (2013). Authenticity and correction of errors in the context of language reclamation. *History and Philosophy of the Language Sciences.* http://hiphilangsci.net/2013/08/28/authenticity-and-the-correction-of-errors-in-the-context-of-language-reclamation

Amery, Rob (2013). A Matter of interpretation: Language planning for a sleeping language, Kaurna, the language of the Adelaide Plains, South Australia. *Language Problems and Language Planning* 37(2): 101-124.

Amery, Rob (2014). Reclaiming the Kaurna language: A long and lasting collaboration in an urban setting. *Language Documentation and Conservation.* 8: 409-429. {*The Role of Linguists in Indigenous Community Language Programs in Australia.* Special issue edited by John Henderson. http://www.nflrc.hawaii.edu/ldc http://scholarspace.manoa.hawaii.edu/bitstream/handle/10125/4613/amery.pdf?sequence=3

Amery, Rob (2014). A New Lease of life: 25 years of reclaiming and re-introducing a forgotten language in metropolitan Adelaide, South Australia. 2014 Tâi-Uân Gí-giân Kap Kàu-ha̍k Kok-tsè Ha̍k-sut Giân-thó-huē: *Proceedings of the 10th International Symposium on Taiwanese Languages and Teaching,* Chengkung University, Tainan, Taiwan. Vol. 1: 1.1 – 1.26 (Invited Keynote address).

Amery, Rob (2015). Kaurna. In Nicola Grandi & Livia Körtvélyessy (Eds), *Edinburgh Handbook of Evaluative Morphology* (423-429). Edinburgh: Edinburgh University Press.

Amery, Rob (forthcoming). The trail of discovery of Kaurna Language Source Material. To appear in a Special Issue of the *Australian Journal of Linguistics* edited by Ian Green.

Amery, Rob (forthcoming). The application of Dual Naming to Kaurna toponyms. Australian National Placenames Survey 2011 Workshop, Adelaide, 2 September 2011.

Amery, Rob & Jack Buckskin (2012a). A comparison of traditional Kaurna kinship patterns with those used in contemporary Nunga English. *Australian Aboriginal Studies* 1: 49-62.

Amery, Rob & Jack Buckskin (2012b). Handing on the teaching of Kaurna language to Kaurna Youth. *Australian Aboriginal Studies* 2: 31-41.

Amery, Rob & Jack Kanya Buckskin (2013). Having it both ways: Towards recognition of the Kaurna language movement within the community and within the university sector. *Proceedings of FEL XVII Endangered Languages Beyond Boundaries: Community Connections, Collaborative Approaches, and Cross-Disciplinary Research.* The Seventeenth Conference of the Foundation for Endangered Languages: Ottawa, Canada. October 2013.

Amery, Rob & Mary-Anne Gale (2008). Language Revival in Australia. In William McGregor (Ed.), *Encountering Aboriginal languages: Studies in the history of Australian linguistics,* Canberra: Pacific Linguistics, 339-382.

Amery, Rob & Mary-Anne Gale (2014). They came, they heard, they documented: The Dresden missionaries as lexicographers. *Australex Adelaide: Endangered Words, and Signs of Revival,* 25-28 July 2013. http://www.adelaide.edu.au/australex/publications/amery_and_gale.pdf

Amery, Rob & Peter Mühlhäusler (2006). Koeler's Contribution to Kaurna Linguistics. In Peter Mühlhäusler (Ed.), *Hermann Koeler's Adelaide. Observations on the language and culture of South Australia by the first German visitor.* Unley, SA: Australian Humanities Press, 25-48.

Amery, Rob & Dennis O'Brien (2007). Funeral liturgy as a strategy for language revival. In Jeff Siegel, John Lynch & Diana Eades (Eds), *Linguistic Description and Linguistic Applications: Studies in Memory of Terry Crowley.* John Benjamins, 457-467 (Chapter 34).

Amery, Rob & Alice Wallara Rigney with Nelson Varcoe, Chester Schultz & Kaurna Warra Pintyandi (2006). *Kaurna Palti Wonga — Kaurna Funeral Protocols.* (book, CD & Sympathy Cards) Kaurna Warra Pintyandi, Adelaide.

Amery, Rob & Alitya Wallara Rigney (2007). Collaborative Language Revival — the work of Kaurna Warra Pintyandi (Adelaide Plains, South Australia). *FEL XI Working Together for Endangered Languages: Research Challenges and Social Impacts.* The Eleventh Conference of the Foundation for Endangered Languages: Kuala Lumpur, Malaysia. Rumah University, University of Malaya 26-28 October 2007 (paper delivered by Rob Amery & Jack Buckskin 26 October 2007).

Amery, Rob & Lester Irabinna Rigney (2006). Recognition of Kaurna cultural heritage in the Adelaide Parklands: A linguist's and Kaurna academic's perspective. Proceedings of The Adelaide Parklands Symposium: A balancing act: past — present — future. University of South Australia, Adelaide, 10 November 2006, 12-26.

Amery, Rob & Simpson, Jane (1994). Kaurna. In Thieberger & McGregor (Eds), 144-172.

Amery, Rob & Jane Simpson (2013). *Kulurdu Marni Ngathaitya! Sounds Good to me! A Kaurna Learner's Guide.* Kaurna Warra Pintyanthi in association with Wakefield Press, Kent Town.

Amery, Rob, Watkins, Cherie & Lester Rigney (1997). Tape transcripts. A series of weekly lessons with accompanying tape for self-instruction. Prepared for the Kaurna Language & Language Ecology course, University of Adelaide.

Amery, Rob & Georgina Yambo Williams (2002). Reclaiming through renaming: The reinstatement of Kaurna toponyms in Adelaide and the Adelaide Plains. In Luise Hercus, Flavia Hodges and Jane Simpson (Eds), *The land is a map: Placenames of Indigenous origin in Australia,* 255-276. Canberra: Pacific Linguistics, 2002.

Buckskin, Jack Kanya, Mary-Anne Gale, Rob Amery, Cherie Warrarra Watkins & Jane Wilson (2013). *Kaurna alphabet book second edition.* Adelaide: Kaurna Warra Pintyanthi, University of Adelaide.

Chittelborough, J. (1906). 'Primitive Adelaide' in *The Register*, 27/28 December 1906 (article includes a short Kaurna wordlist).

Gale, Mary-Anne (2012a). Summary Report TAFE Certificate III 'Learning an endangered Aboriginal language (Kaurna Language)', workshop held at the University of Adelaide 10-14 April & 25 April 2012.

Gale, Mary-Anne (2012b). Summary Report TAFE Certificate III 'Learning an endangered Aboriginal language (Kaurna Language)', workshop held at Relationships Australia SA, Hindmarsh, 9-13 July 2012.

Gale, Mary-Anne (2012c). Summary Report TAFE Certificate III 'Learning an endangered Aboriginal language (Kaurna Language)', workshop held at Wilto Yerlo, University of Adelaide 24-28 September 2012.

Gale, Mary-Anne (2012d). Summary Report TAFE Certificate III 'Learning an endangered Aboriginal language (Kaurna Language)', workshop held at Relationships Australia SA, Hindmarsh, 17-21 December 2012.

Gale, Mary-Anne (2013). Summary Report TAFE Certificate III 'Learning an endangered Aboriginal language (Kaurna Language)', workshop held at Port Adelaide TAFE 15-19 April 2013.

Mühlhäusler, Peter (Ed.) (2006). *Hermann Koeler's Adelaide. Observations on the language and culture of South Australia by the first German visitor*. Unley, SA: Australian Humanities Press.

Schultz, Chester (forthcoming). Ask the right question, then look everywhere: Finding and interpreting the old Aboriginal place-names around Adelaide and Fleurieu Peninsula. Australian National Placenames Survey 2011 Workshop, Adelaide, 2 September 2011.

Schultz, Chester (forthcoming). *Feet on the Fleurieu*.

Watkins, Cherie Warrara & Mary-Anne Gale (2006). *Kaurna alphabet book*. Kaurna Plains School, Elizabeth.

Foreword to the 2000 Edition

As an Indigenous Australian I take honour in writing the foreword for this book. My honour is shared in two ways. Firstly, to the further advancement such writing makes to the liberation struggle of my people. Secondly the theoretical contributions it makes to the disciplines of Indigenous Education and Linguistics.

I find comfort in its pages as a Narungga, Kaurna, Ngarrindjeri man who has worked in the Kaurna language revival movement for several years. For here is a story of a journey that needed telling. A story of Indigenous and non-Indigenous peoples working diligently to revive and maintain Indigenous Language. From the contents of these pages we see determined people who want to make Kaurna language a functional part of their daily lives.

However, the languages of colonised peoples cannot be meaningfully discussed outside the context of imperialism, colonialism and neo-colonialism. Therefore, the story of the Kaurna Language Revival movement is a counter-story to early western ideas and beliefs regarding Indigenous cultures.

Colonial interruption in language transmission from older to younger generations has done violence to the survival of Indigenous languages, identities and cultures. Such genocidal interruption meant that very little knowledge of the language remained within the Kaurna community.

The scars of systematic suppression of Indigenous languages and cultures map the Indigenous terrain of languages revival and maintenance. Moreover, it is to the process of colonial imposition and elevation of English whilst subjugating our languages that we as colonised peoples remain defiant.

Documented in the pages of this book are real lives in real struggle. Language is not simply about words or the lexicon. It is about people. *Warrabarna Kaurna!* reflects the challenges, the celebration and the struggles facing Kaurna peoples today in reclaiming and maintaining our language.

The book seeks to inform the reader of the strategic transformation process of Kaurna language from the historical record to the hearts, minds and vocal chords of my peoples. What makes this study unique is that Kaurna is at the far end of the continuum of language revival activities. Seemingly insurmountable odds had to be overcome.

- Colonial forced silence of language leaves no fluent speakers
- Fluent Kaurna not used as an everyday language for well over a century
- No sound recording of language as it was spoken last century
- Kaurna population a small minority spread across several communities

As a longitudinal study nine years in the making, this book brings clarity to the dual processes needed for such delicate surgery. The author's methodological approach and his use of various theoretical positions highlight the need to firstly reclaim and develop language. Such a technical pursuit involves archival research, philology, linguistics and language planning.

The second process is largely a complex matter of sociolinguistics. In other words, the nature of language revival and its role within the Kaurna community.

It is the analysis and extensive investigation of the latter that make a substantial contribution to the discipline of Linguistics in terms of understanding the politics of knowledge, language and identity. Uncovering the inherent dilemmas and contradictions a community faces when engaging in struggle to revive language is indeed very rare within the literature. By illuminating how language revival intersects with Kaurna lives and the greater push for the possibility of a non-colonial future, the book offers insights for Indigenous groups whose languages are in a similar position. The book is timely in this regard.

The result is a persuasive exposé of the unique and proactive nature of an ecological approach to language and the sociological aspects that surround language revival research. In these ways this study is of crucial value to Indigenous and non-Indigenous linguists, language practitioners, and Indigenous education policy and practice. The progress we have made is phenomenal and is testimony to the courage and strength of all those involved. Similarly, it highlights what can be achieved when the commitment of the people and its supporters are strong.

The broader agenda of this book is located in the context of a growing debate of endangered languages and linguistic rights. Therefore its value and contribution to linguistics, sociolinguistics, history, anthropology, sociology, environmental studies and education extend well beyond the Australian context. Its value as a scholarly text is indicated by the contribution it makes to the emergence of Ecological Linguistics as a field of study. It attempts to move beyond 'orthodox' Linguistics, in turning the gaze to human agency whilst seeking long-term sustainable solutions to the complexities of language revival.

By drawing on studies of Cornish, Hebrew, Irish, Maori, Hawaiian and Indigenous languages of North America the author uncovers similarities, differences and further nuances. It is these nuances that teach us important theoretical, sociolinguistic and sociopolitical dimensions of language revival.

Language revival, within the context of Australia's Indigenous Languages, is a very recent phenomenon. Therefore, this work is a major contribution to the field. Attempts to reclaim, relearn and revive colonial-suppressed Indigenous languages are relatively uncommon. Whilst a number of similar attempts are under way in South Australia (e.g. Diyari and Barngarla), and in the United States (e.g. Esselen and Huron), it seems that Kaurna is on the cutting edge of language reclamation activities and provides a key site to develop productive collaborations between linguists and Indigenous communities. In this regard this book is compulsory reading for all engaged in this area.

A final word to methodology and non-Indigenous researcher involvement with Indigenous peoples. Indigenous peoples and their cultures in Australia have been and continue to be a playground for many researchers. Indeed, it is upon this foundation that many academic careers have been built. For example, in my own work I offer a critique of research epistemologies and ontologies and their implicit dispossession of Indigenous knowledges from the custodians. This is not to say that Indigenous peoples reject outright research and its various methodological practices. Indeed, some research has benefited the emancipation of Indigenous communities. However, we as Indigenous peoples now want research and its designs to contribute to self-determination and liberation struggles as defined by us and our communities. A fundamental feature of this book is the author's willingness to reflect on his own practices and speaking position in relation to Kaurna language revival. Rob gives valuable insight into the tensions and contradictions implicit in disciplinary research protocol.

In a shrinking world and with increasing globalisation, Indigenous languages are under far more threat of extinction than ever. With the passing of the last speakers of Indigenous languages, time is of the essence.

Lester-Irabinna Rigney

Preface to the 2000 Edition

This book is the chronicle of the early stages of the revival of a language that ceased to be spoken many years ago. This revival is based on historical documents, most of which were recorded in the period 1836-1858. Taking an ecological perspective, I trace the history of the language and all known sources.

However, as this book goes to press, an additional early German source has just come to light. Dr Hermann Koeler visited South Australia in 1837 and 1838 and published a list of approximately 150 words and eight Pidgin Kaurna sentences, together with observations on the customs of the Kaurna people and the state of the colony, which await translation. This source is a significant find, with the potential for adding several words to the known lexicon and helping to refine our knowledge of the meanings and pronunciation of some words. The Pidgin Kaurna sentences appear to correlate closely with sentences recorded by Williams and Wyatt (analysed by Simpson, 1996), providing further confirmation of the existence of a Pidgin Kaurna language. It is possible that further research in the German archives will unearth additional documents in the future.

My analysis of Kaurna language revival focuses primarily on the period 1990-1997. Kaurna language revival began with the writing of six songs in 1990. Since then, the language has developed considerably; Kaurna programs have been established and expanded across several institutions catering for a range of learners; increasingly, the language is being used in public by members of the Kaurna community; the range of functions for which the language is being used continues to expand; and there are early signs that the language is beginning to take root within Nunga households.

The study is part of a long-term ongoing project, where the ground is continually shifting. The use of and interest in the Kaurna language is gathering momentum and much has happened since 1997. Kaurna language reclamation is an exciting collaboration between Kaurna people, educators, linguists and others.

However, we are still in the very early stages of Kaurna language revival. Will the Kaurna language take the 'great leap forward' and emerge as an everyday language within the Kaurna community? Experience elsewhere tells us that the prospects for this to happen are slender. However, the programs have already been a success in the eyes of the Kaurna community and within the education sector.

This study is breaking new ground. In the Kaurna case, very little knowledge of the language remained within the Aboriginal community. Yet the Kaurna language is becoming a marker of identity and a means by which Kaurna people can further the struggle for recognition, reconciliation and liberation. This study challenges widely held beliefs as to what is possible in language revival and questions notions about the very nature of language and its development.

Acknowledgements

It has been a privilege to work on this topic. I thank the Kaurna community for their enduring support for this work on their language. In particular, Auntie Alice Wallara Rigney, Uncle Lewis O'Brien, Cherie Warrara Watkins, Lester Irabinna Rigney and Georgina Yambo Williams were patient in answering questions, discussing issues and reading drafts of chapters. Their enthusiasm for Kaurna language reclamation has sustained me in the arduous task of compiling this material and grappling with the difficult issues. Numerous others within the Nunga community, including Snooky Varcoe, Auntie Josie Agius, Auntie Veronica Brodie, Paul & Naomi Dixon, Fred Warrior, Vince Branson, Frank Wanganeen, Auntie Pearl Nam, Auntie Phoebe Wanganeen, Katrina Power, David Wilson, Garth Agius, Kath Burgemeister, Cherylynne Catanzaritti, Klynton Wanganeen and Karl Telfer made a direct contribution to this study. I also acknowledge the interest of KACHA in this project.

Many people including Alice Rigney, Chrissy Hill, Kathryn Gale, Tony Wakefield, Antonio Mercurio, Lea Stevens, Ruth Smiles, Wendy Teasedale-Smith, Sylvain Talbot, Greg Wilson, Mike Gray, Georgina Williams, Tim Goldsmith and Peter Mühlhäusler were instrumental in establishing the Kaurna programs. I acknowledge especially fellow members of the Kaurna language teaching teams at Para West Adult Campus and Elizabeth City High School including Snooky Varcoe, Cherie Watkins, Jennifer Simpson, Leigh Hughes, Yvonne Robertson and Cheryl Uren. I thank them all for their cooperation and willingness to be part of the research process. The staff and students of Kaurna Plains School and Kaurna Plains Early Childhood Centre always welcomed my presence, shared information and invited me into their classes. They include Alma Ridgway, Eileen Wanganeen, Pathma Iswaran, Jenny Burford, Kevin Duigan, James Parkin, Nola Davis, Pilawuk White, Maurice Wheatley, Julie Hodgkinson, Vicki Hartman and Liz Loan. Mike Gray, Pat Kartinyeri and Kevin O'Loughlin at Tauondi were always willing to volunteer information and lend support.

I thank the students at Para West Adult Campus, Tauondi and the University of Adelaide for their willingness to share their thoughts and experiences. In particular Jenny Burford and Helen Reilly shared their interview transcripts, with the permission of interviewees. Peter Gale gave me access to unpublished data from a previous study.

Dot Davy and Greg Ryan at the Adelaide City Council, Bill Watt and staff of the Department of Environment and Natural Resources, Malcolm Lane of Belair National Park, Mike and Jean Brown of the Blackwood Reconciliation Group and Don Chapman of the Marion City Council invited me to work in collaboration on their projects.

Brian Kirke sparked my initial interest in language revival work by inviting me to participate in workshops and other activities. Since then, my relationship with the Nunga community has developed. I thank them for their acceptance of me, a non-Indigenous linguist, and allowing me to become involved in their languages, regarded by many as an 'insider' domain. I trust that I have reciprocated by imparting linguistic skills and understandings that empower them to reclaim their own languages. My former employers, Batchelor College, the Northern Territory University and the Senior Secondary Assessment Board of South Australia supported my early forays into Kaurna language revival initiatives. They funded my efforts to convene workshops and supported initial work with the school programs.

Many individuals and institutions have been of assistance in locating archival materials. They include staff of the Mortlock Library, in particular Jenny Tonkin, Valmai Hankel & Anthony Laube; the South Australian Museum, especially Kate Allport, Philip Clarke, Philip Jones and Neva Wilson; Andrew Wilson and others at State Records; Lyall Kupke of the Lutheran Archives; Donald Kerr of the Auckland Public Library and Arlene Fanarof of the South African Public Library, Cape Town. I am particularly appreciative of the efforts of Reinhard Wendt who obtained access to the Lutheran Archives in Leipzig, Germany, on my behalf and located precious Kaurna materials which he hand-delivered to me here in Adelaide. Philip Baker also obtained valuable material from the Methodist archives in London, whilst Heidi Kneebone procured a copy of Koeler's papers in Berlin.

Letters written by Kaurna children have been reproduced here in good faith. Descendants of their authors are not able to be located.

Margaret Young, Sue Murray and Chris Crothers in the Geography Department at the University of Adelaide assisted in preparing the maps and Graeme Fussen assisted in scanning illustrations.

I thank my supervisors, Peter Mühlhäusler and Jane Simpson, who both took a keen interest in this project, providing guidance and comments on earlier drafts. Peter shared his broad knowledge of language planning phenomena and his personal library. His ecological approach to linguistics gave me a firm basis on which to proceed. Jane's critical eye on matters of detail, and her knowledge of Kaurna and related languages, provided an excellent balance.

Chester Schultz, Guy Tunstill, Greg Wilson and others have always lent a listening ear and passed on information and observations. Most of all I thank my partner Mary-Anne Gale for her support and patience, allowing me to discuss experiences and formulate ideas. She also copy-edited many chapters. Thank you, too, Jemima and Miriam for being so patient during the final stages of writing of the original manuscript.

The Faculty of Arts provided financial support to convert the thesis into publishable form, whilst Robin Eaden edited and formatted the original manuscript and created the index.

Since the publication of Warrabarna Kaurna in 2000, many more, both Kaurna and non-Kaurna, have become part of the story. In particular, I thank the members of KWP and KWK for their ongoing support and collaboration. Dr

Acknowledgements

Lewis Yerloburka O'Brien and Dr Alitya Wallara Rigney continue to provide leadership, support and direction. Copies of the additional chapter (Chapter 11) were circulated for comment. I also express my gratitude to the KWP team based at the University of Adelaide, especially Steve Gadlabarti Goldsmith, Taylor Tipu Power-Smith and Jack Kanya Buckskin, who is now based at Tauondi College. They are now such a central and integral part of the Kaurna language movement. Paul Finlay, who has provided mentoring and support for Steve, Taylor and Katrina, also provided numerous photos of recent events. I thank Gerhard Rüdiger for organising and hosting the visit to Germany by Ngarrpadla Alitya Rigney, Karl Telfer, Verna Koolmatrie and myself in 2011, and his efforts to pursue further archival research in Germany. Gerhard also did much of the groundwork to establish KWK.

I thank Taylor and Francis for granting me the rights to republish and Adelaide University Press for taking on the task so that this work is more readily available and more accessible to Kaurna people. Brigitte Sloot assisted greatly with the layout by providing me with a useful tutorial on the process. Bill Watt (Geographical Names Unit) provided the Kaurna Native Title Map, while Katrina Karlapina Power provided the magnificent artwork for the cover.

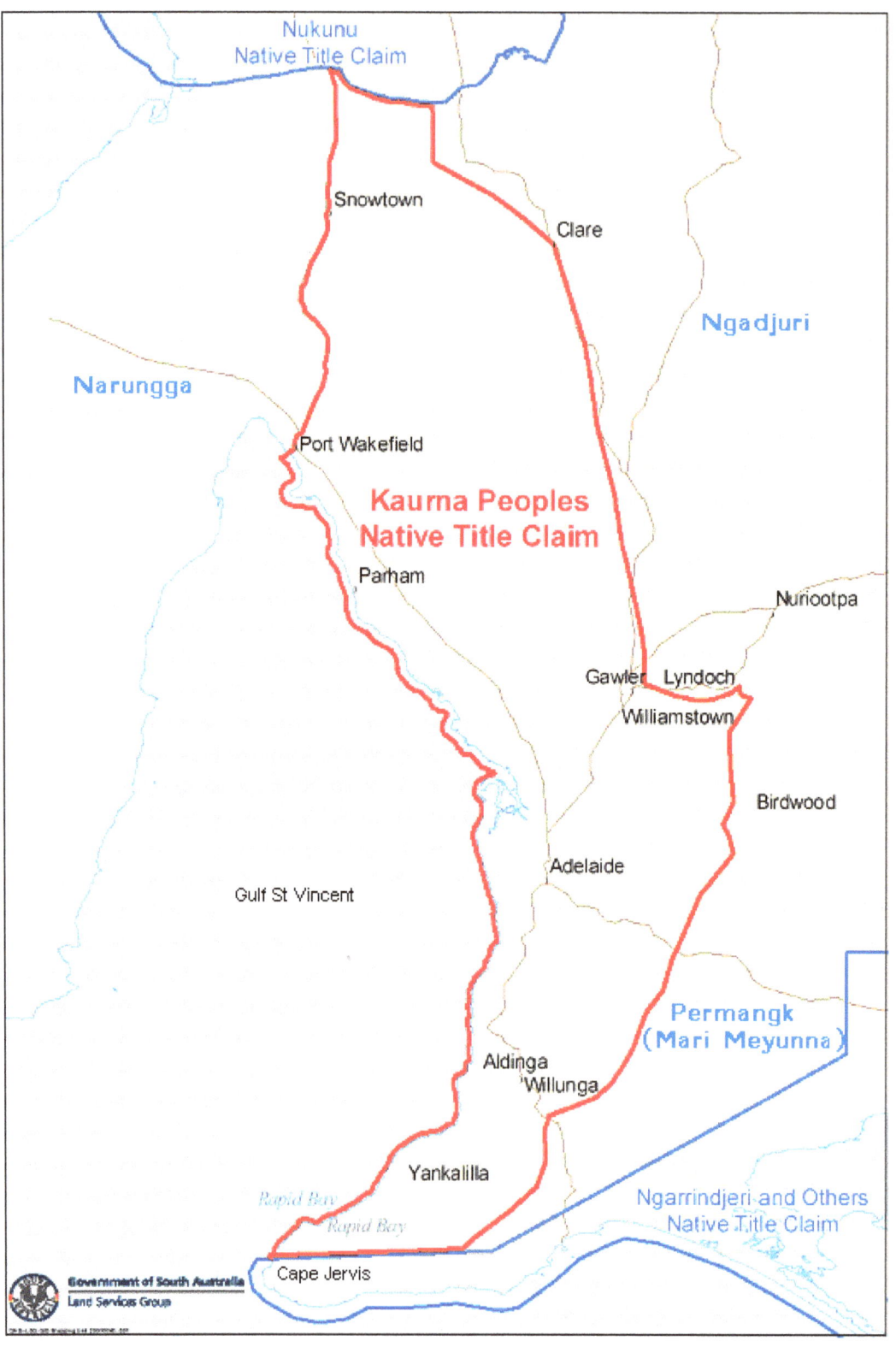

Map I: Kaurna Native Title claim

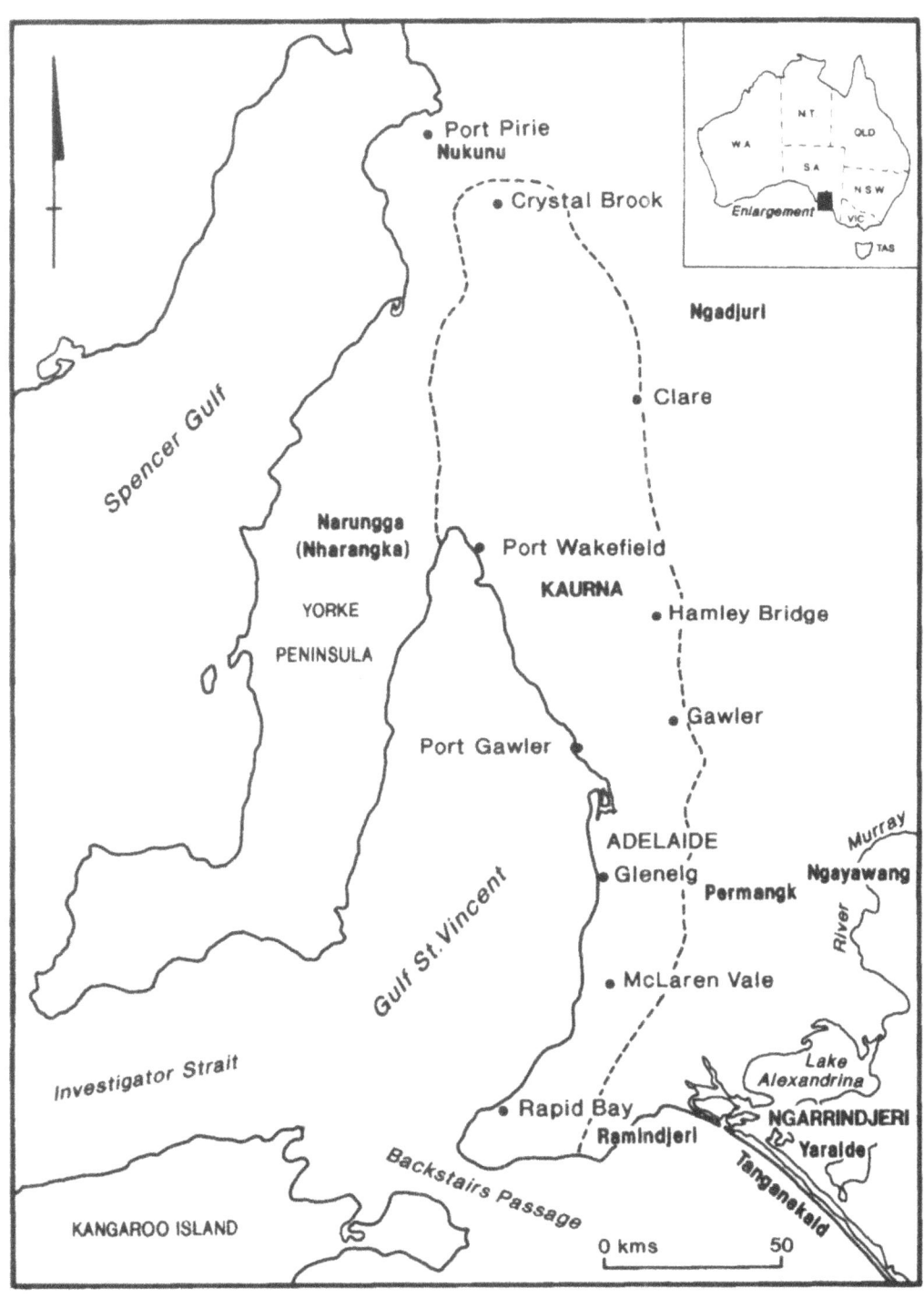

Map II: Kaurna territory and neighbouring languages

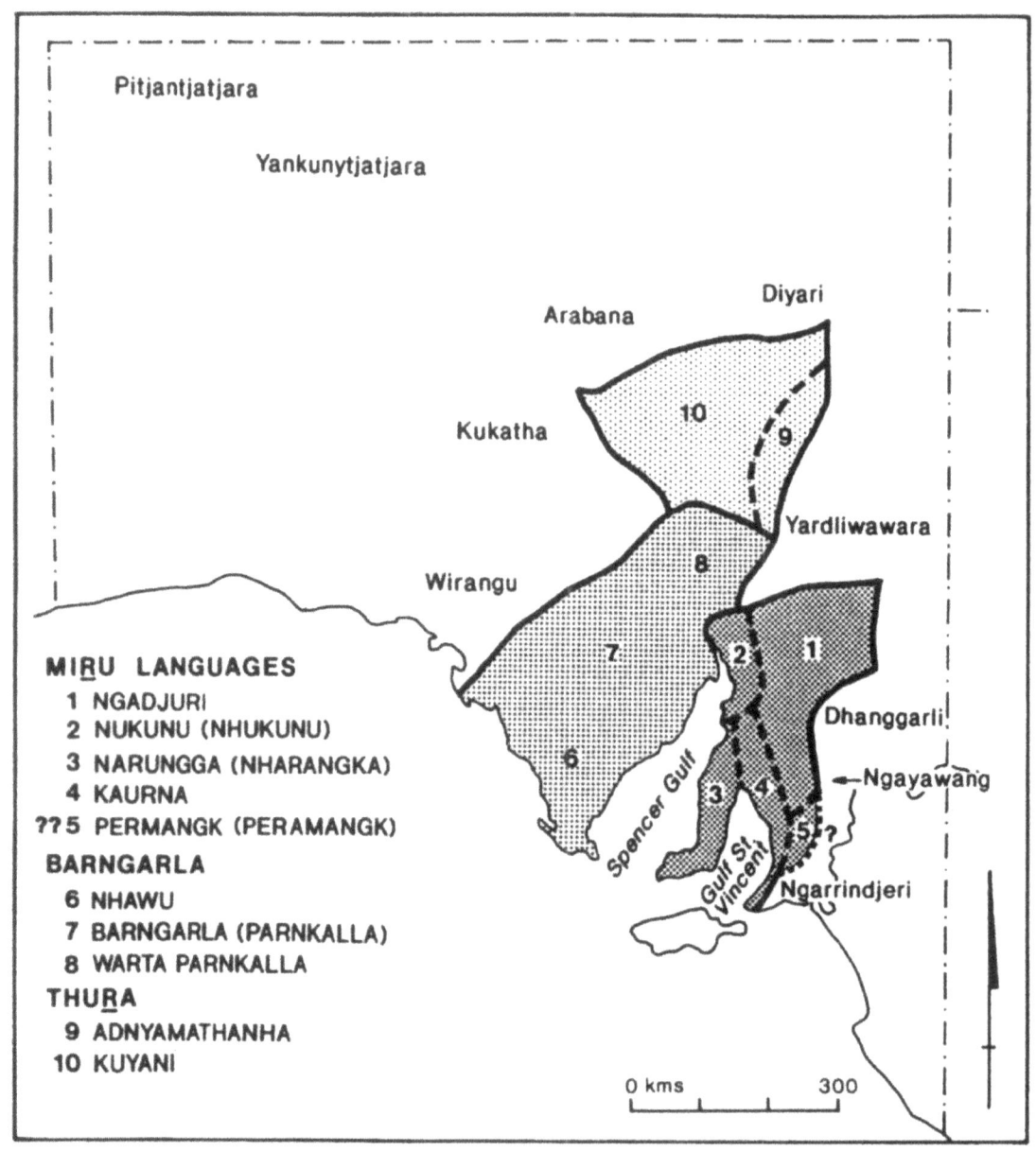

Map III: Thura-Yura languages (Note that Wirangu should also be included following work by Simpson and Hercus, 2004)

Maps xxix

Map IV: Main localities referred to on the Adelaide Plains

Abbreviations

General

ACC	Adelaide City Council
AERT	Aboriginal Education Resource Teacher
AEW	Aboriginal Education Worker
AIATSIS	Australian Institute of Aboriginal and Torres Strait Islander Studies
AILF	Australian Indigenous Languages Framework
ALL	Australian Language Levels
ARI	Adelaide Research and Innovation
ATSIC	Aboriginal and Torres Strait Islander Commission
ATSILIP	Aboriginal and Torres Strait Islander Languages Initiatives Program
BBC	British Broadcasting Commission
CASM	Centre for Aboriginal Studies in Music (University of Adelaide)
CKLR	Consolidating Kaurna Language Revival
CSO	Childrens Services Office
DECD	Department for Education and Child Development[2]
DECS	Department for Education and Children's Services
DEET	Department of Employment, Education and Training
DEETYA	Department of Employment, Education, Training and Youth Affairs (formerly DEET)
DETE	Department of Education Training and Employment
ECHS	Elizabeth City High School
EDSA	Education Department of South Australia
EWAC	Elizabeth West Adult Campus (now PWAC)
HS	High School
ILS	Indigenous Languages Support
IPA	International Phonetic Alphabet
KACHA	Kaurna Aboriginal Cultural and Heritage Association Incorporated
KL&LE	'Kaurna Language & Language Ecology'
KPECC	Kaurna Plains Early Childhood Centre
KPS	Kaurna Plains School

---

[2] During the period in which research was conducted, the South Australian state government department responsible for education changed its name six times as follows:

prior to 1993	Education Department of South Australia (EDSA)
1993	Department of Education, Employment and Training (DEET)
end of 1993	Department of Education and Children's Services (DECS)
Oct. 1997	Department of Education Training and Employment (DETE)
1999	Department of Education and Children's Services (DECS)
since Feb. 2012	Department for Education and Child Development (DECD)

I use the title relevant to the period of discussion and DECD if referring to ongoing activities.

KWK	Kaurna Warra Karrpanthi
KWP	Kaurna Warra Pintyandi/ Kaurna Warra Pintyanthi
LOTE	Languages Other Than English
LOTEMAPP	Languages Other Than English Mapping and Planning Project
MOOC	Massive Open Online Course
MoU	Memorandum of Understanding
NAIDOC	National Aboriginal and Islander Day Observance Committee
NALP	National Aboriginal Languages Program
NAPLAN	National Assessment Program — Literacy and Numeracy
ORIC	Office of the Registration of Indigenous Corporations
PWAC	Para West Adult Campus (Inbarendi College, Elizabeth)
PS	Primary School
RS	Revised Spelling
SACAE	South Australian College of Advanced Education (now the University of South Australia)
SACE	South Australian Certificate of Education
SAL	School of Australian Linguistics
SASSL	South Australian Secondary School of Languages
SSABSA	Senior Secondary Assessment Board of South Australia
TAFE	Technical and Further Education
T&S	Teichelmann & Schürmann (1840)
TMs	Teichelmann (1857)
YWW	Yaitya Warra Wodli, South Australia's Aboriginal Language Centre

Abbreviations used in interlinear glosses

1	First Person
2	Second Person
3	Third Person
ABL	Ablative
ACC	Accusative
ALL	Allative
CAUS	Causative
ERG	Ergative
FUT	Future
GEN	Genitive
IMP	Imperative
INCH	Inchoative
INDEF	Indefinite
INST	Instrumental
LOC	Locative
NOM	Nominative
NOML	Nominalizer
PERF	Perfective
Pl ~ PL	Plural
PRES	Present
PST	Past
REDUP	Reduplication
Sg ~ SG	Singular

Conventions and Terminology

Unless otherwise specified, Kaurna words are taken from Teichelmann & Schürmann (1840) or Teichelmann (1857) or formed according to word-building patterns laid down in these sources. Language materials produced in association with school programs or community events all employ these spellings.

Unless otherwise specified, contemporary Kaurna neologisms, new expressions, translations and other Kaurna language products cited were developed by me, typically within a classroom or workshop situation where Kaurna people have been present and have been part of the process. Often the Kaurna texts are negotiated and always open to change and revision, subject to feedback from members of the Kaurna community.

Neologisms not in the historical sources are identified with an asterisk*. Inflected or derived forms, e.g. *kangkutha* 'will look after' or *narna-ana* 'to the door', many of which will not be found as such in the historical sources, have not been identified in any special way as their formation is predictable. Borrowings from other languages have been identified with ° before the word.

I use italics for words taken from Indigenous languages as they appear in their original sources. Phonetic and phonemic representations of Kaurna words are written without italicisation within square [ ] and slash / / brackets respectively. Names are written without italicisation as in general usage.

Language names are spelt according to local community preferences. A range of spellings of these names are to be found in the literature. The preferred spelling of Narungga has changed recently from Narrunga, which appears in a number of quite recent publications and DETE Aboriginal Studies materials.

I privilege the use of Indigenous terms. I refer to Kaurna individuals by their Kaurna names, where these are known. For instance, I use Kadlitpinna rather than 'Captain Jack', even though he is almost always referred to by his English name in the literature. Similarly, I use Piltawodli, Bukkiyana and Raukkan in preference to 'Native Location', Point Pearce and Point McLeay respectively. This often results in a disparity between the names as they appear in my text and in quotations. Local Aboriginal people from Adelaide and surrounding areas are often referred to as Nungas, their term of self-ascription. The term Nunga covers Aboriginal people belonging to a range of southern South Australian language groups, including Kaurna, Narungga and Ngarrindjeri. Non-Aboriginal people are sometimes referred to as Gunyas (also spelt Goonya) in accordance with local use, a term used in opposition to Nunga.

The designations Auntie and Uncle are used as a mark of respect for senior figures, in accordance with use at KPS and within the Nunga community. The terms Indigenous, Elder and Dreaming are spelt with an initial capital letter out of respect in accordance with current Indigenous protocol.

It is often difficult to find neutral terms. Many times I have been forced to use value-laden terms in accordance with the literature. For instance, the term 'Protector' is hardly an appropriate title in the light of the actions of these individuals and subsequent historical events. Still I am forced to use the term.

The terms 'full descent' and 'mixed descent' are occasionally used when there is a need to distinguish. These terms, imposed by colonial administrations and governments to divide and subjugate Indigenous peoples, are no longer acceptable. Unfortunately, I have not been altogether able to avoid using them in relation to historical matters.

1
Locating the Study

Some people have described Kaurna language as a dead language. But Kaurna people don't believe this. We believe that our language is a living language and that it has only been sleeping, and that the time to wake it up is now and this is what we're doing.

(Cherie Watkins in *Warranna Purruna* video DECS, 1997)

This book tells the story of the renaissance of the Kaurna language, the language of Adelaide and the Adelaide Plains in South Australia. It is based on a longitudinal study conducted between 1989 and 1997, which resulted in a PhD thesis submitted to the University of Adelaide in June 1998. It chronicles and analyses the efforts of the Nunga[1] community, and interested others, to reclaim[2] and relearn a linguistic heritage on the basis of mid-nineteenth-century materials. In particular the study focuses on a small Aboriginal school in the northern suburbs of Adelaide and the adjoining secondary school, and the work of several committed and hard-working Nunga language specialists. This longitudinal study documents in detail the very earliest stage of the attempted revival of a language long considered 'dead' or 'extinct'. The Kaurna language has probably not been used as an everyday language of communication for well over a century. As far as is known, the 'last speaker', a woman known as Ivaritji or Amelia Taylor, died in 1929 (Gara, 1990: 100). There are no sound recordings of the language as it was spoken last century, though limited print-based materials do exist. Kaurna people are a small minority dispersed across a large metropolitan city and throughout surrounding country towns and Aboriginal communities. On the face of it, reclamation of the Kaurna language is undertaken against seemingly insurmountable odds, yet with positive results, at least according to some criteria.

I cannot in any sense claim this to be a neutral account of the reclamation of the Kaurna language, since, as a non-Aboriginal Australian, I am one of the main protagonists of the language revival efforts and have been involved with it on a practical level since 1989. However, the study does claim to be an informed one. I have attempted to take differing perspectives into account and to represent the full spectrum of views expressed to me and to other observers, but I admit I am partisan in the views I express. It is essentially a linguistic and sociolinguistic study, but by necessity draws upon a number of disciplines including history, anthropology, language-teaching pedagogy and Aboriginal studies.

This book traces the history of the Kaurna language from the earliest descriptions of the language and its speakers, made by European observers last century, through to current efforts to reclaim and relearn it during the 1990s. Most of the information contributing towards this study comes from two short eras — the first years of the South Australian colony (1836-1858) and the contemporary period (1989-1997). Very little was recorded or developed in relation to Kaurna in the intervening period.

The work draws on all known sources, and all known uses to which the language is put in the contemporary period, but additional sources, of which I am unaware, may exist. Likely locations for such material include Captain Grey's collection now held in the South African Public Library, Cape Town, and in Auckland, New Zealand; mission archives in Germany; the logs of American sealing and whaling vessels; journals, letters and other papers held in private collections, both in Australia and overseas; or remnants of the language remaining within certain Aboriginal families. It is evident that in many Nunga families there is a body of linguistic and cultural knowledge, some of which is shared with outsiders, but some of which is retained as 'family secrets'. This knowledge is passed down from generation to generation when the recipients are deemed responsible to possess that knowledge and not divulge it. It is possible that certain Kaurna linguistic and cultural knowledge has been retained in this way beyond the knowledge of the writer.

More extensive oral history relating to Kaurna sites and genealogies does remain within the Nunga community, much of which has not been documented. Comparatively few words unique to Kaurna have survived in oral form. Almost all Kaurna words known are place names appearing on maps[3] or common words shared by neighbouring languages. A considerable amount of sign language still remains within the Nunga community, but because it was never documented in the early period, it is impossible to say from which language group it originates or if indeed it was shared by Kaurna and neighbouring languages.

Kaurna as spoken in the nineteenth century, like the New South Wales Pidgin and the Sydney language studied by Troy (1994a, 1994b), can be known only from the records of non-Aboriginal (or Gunya) observers, though contemporary Aboriginal oral history can sometimes provide useful insights. Of course many aspects of Kaurna were never documented and they remain unknown and unknowable.

Reclamation of the Kaurna language is taking place within the context of a broader Aboriginal linguistic and cultural renaissance and the re-emergence of a distinctive Kaurna social, cultural and political identity over the last few decades. Developments in relation to the Kaurna language in the modern period began in 1989-1990 with a Commonwealth-funded language revival project in Ngarrindjeri, Narungga and Kaurna, the three most important languages belonging to Nungas living in Adelaide. Most of the activity generated by that project centred on Ngarrindjeri and Narungga, reflecting the main area of interest of the Nunga community at the time. In fact, little of the work of the 1989-1990 Project touched on Kaurna. In a songbook produced at the end of the project, only seven of the 33 songs were devoted to Kaurna. Yet, with the exception of the naming of places, institutions and people with Kaurna names, and the inclusion in some publications of words and phrases taken directly from the historical sources, this was the first work undertaken in Kaurna language reclamation.

From this small beginning, in less than a decade, Kaurna teaching programs have been established and expanded across several institutions catering for a range of learners of different ages. Increasingly, the language is being used by members of the Kaurna community, albeit in limited ways, chiefly in public forums and in cultural tourism. Use of the language in this way draws on the symbolic value of the language. Significantly, the range of functions for which the language is being used continues to expand. There are some early signs that the language is beginning to take root within certain Nunga households and extended families.

Who are the Kaurna?

The Kaurna people are the Indigenous inhabitants of the Adelaide Plains (see Map I), Adelaide being the capital of South Australia. Within the nineteenth-century literature they were generally referred to as 'the Adelaide Tribe', though a number of other names were employed at times. Last century the Kaurna language was known as 'the Adelaide language', though it is now known as 'Kaurna', usually pronounced by Nungas as [ga:na], sometimes [gauna] or [gau̱na] and occasionally [kʰa:na] depending on the background and origins of the speaker.

The term 'Kaurna' does not appear within the main sources of the Kaurna language: Teichelmann & Schürmann (1840), hereafter T&S, and Teichelmann (1857), hereafter TMs. Most likely it comes from the Ramindjeri or Ngarrindjeri word *kornar* 'men; people'. It appears to have been used first in the literature by Wyatt (1879) in reference to 'Encounter Bay Bob's Tribe' and was popularised in the 1920s by Norman Tindale of the South Australian Museum. It is likely that Encounter Bay Bob was actually a Ramindjeri man, as the next entry listed by Wyatt appears as 'Meeyurna — Onkaparinga Jack's Tribe', the implication being that Encounter Bay Bob belonged to a different group. Onkaparinga Jack, known to the missionaries as Mullawirraburka or 'King John', was one of their main sources for information on the Kaurna language, whilst *meyunna* [RS *miyurna*] 'people' is the direct Kaurna equivalent of Ramindjeri *kornar*.

Perhaps a more suitable name for the Kaurna might be *Miyurna*, a point recognised by Lewis O'Brien (pc 1997), a Kaurna Elder with a long interest in the language. *Meyu* [RS *miyu*] 'man; person' is distinguished from corresponding terms in neighbouring languages: Nukunu *mi̱ru*; Ngayawang *meru* (*mera* 'men'); Ngarrindjeri *korni*; and Narungga *nipu*. *Miyurna* then would define the Kaurna-speaking region. However, the term 'Kaurna' has been widely adopted by Kaurna people themselves and is used universally in twentieth-century publications to refer to the people of the Adelaide Plains. I, too, use the term in accordance with popular usage.[4]

Kaurna territory

Nineteenth-century sources identify the territory of the 'Adelaide Tribe' as a localised tract of country centred on Adelaide. However, as Hemming (1990) points out, such early references probably referred to the territory of the local group rather than the lands of the Kaurna-speaking peoples as a whole. Tindale defined a territory much more extensive relating to a larger 'nation' sharing a common language and culture. In *Aboriginal Tribes of Australia* he provides the following lengthy description:

> Kaurna
> Loc.: Cape Jervis to Port Wakefield along eastern shore of Gulf St.Vincent; inland to near Crystal Brook, Snowtown, Blyth, Hoyleton, Hamley Bridge, Clarendon, Gawler, and Myponga; from the east side of the Hummock Range to Red Hill where northern hordes were sometimes known as Nantuwara. Inland the Jultiwira or stringybark forests of the Mount Lofty Ranges marked their boundary. The Kaurna were the southernmost tribe to perform the initiatory rite of circumcision. Their territory was very correctly indicated as 2800 square miles (7200 sq. km.) with a population of 650 in the South Australian Register of 30 January 1842. Ivaritji, the last woman survivor[5], who died in 1931[6], provided much of our scanty knowledge of the Kaurna. A southern horde spoke a slight dialect at Rapid Bay. Tunkalilla Beach, 12 miles (20 km.) east of Cape Jervis, was given as the actual ['keinari] or boundary with the Ramindjeri. East (1889) incorrectly included the related Yorke Peninsula people, the Narangga, under his term Padnayndie. This is in the form Padnaindi, a hordal term for the folk living between Hamley Bridge and Crystal Brook. (Tindale, 1974: 213, footnotes added)

This definition of Kaurna territory, extending from Crystal Brook to Cape Jervis (see Map I), is generally accepted in Museum and Education Department publications and within the Nunga community. However, Berndt & Berndt (1993) establish a set of very different boundaries for the Kaurna and their neighbours. They claim that the whole of the Fleurieu Peninsula as far north as Noarlunga is Ramindjeri territory. They worked with Ngarrindjeri people, especially Albert Karloan, in the 1930s and 1940s. Their comments about the Ramindjeri and their territories are especially insightful:

> Karloan's knowledge was most detailed in relation to his own dialectal unit, Yaraldi ...
> The material is relatively complete for all the Kukabrak [Ngarrindjeri] dialectal units, except for the Wakend and Ramindjeri. As regards the latter two, we considered when we recorded the information that this was a remarkable feat on the part of Karloan and some others, especially since this area was the first to have borne the brunt of European contact. Moreover, the information on this dialectal unit and its clans demonstrates that the area its members occupied was much larger than had previously been suggested. However, the extension towards Willunga, Clarendon, Noarlunga and the surrounding country could have been brought about through the trade routes which linked the Kukabrak to northern peoples. Undoubtedly, that expansion must be seen in the light of the fascination with European settlements. (Berndt & Berndt, 1993: 312)

Here we have confirmation of a relatively recent westward and northward expansion of the Ngarrindjeri nation and a warning as to the tentative, second-hand information upon which Berndt and Berndt's analysis and description of Ramindjeri territory is based.[7]

In a recent paper (Amery, 1998b) I discuss the southern limits of Kaurna territory, on the basis of linguistic and historical evidence, and suggest that Kaurna territory may have extended as far eastward as Encounter Bay and that the occupation of Encounter Bay by the Ramindjeri in the late 1830s may have been a response to the activities of whalers in the area. It would appear that the 'Encounter Bay' people referred to by Colonel Light and other members of his party at Rapid Bay in 1836 were Kaurna speakers.

Kaurna neighbours

Neighbouring languages are important in the study of Kaurna. They contribute to an understanding of the ecology in which Kaurna existed in the 1830s and 1840s and in which the Kaurna language exists today. Knowledge of neighbouring languages, especially closely related ones, is used to a significant extent in the reclamation of the Kaurna language.

The languages to the immediate north and west are the closest relatives of the Kaurna language. Writers have long recognised the affinity between Kaurna and Narungga of Yorke Peninsula. East (1889) argued that the peoples of Yorke Peninsula and the Adelaide Plains belonged to one nation. Mathews (1900), who called this nation the *Adjadurah,* reasoned:

> Owing to the similarity of the dialects of the Yorke Peninsula and Adelaide tribes, the prevalence of circumcision and other customs, together with the fact of their being adjoining neighbours, seems to me to justify the assumption that they were practically the same people. I have therefore included these two tribes in one nation.
> (R.H. Mathews, 1900: 86; in Hemming, 1990: 129)

This affiliation is also recognised by present-day Kaurna and Narungga people. Unfortunately, little of the Narungga language remains within the conscious memory of Narungga people and little of the language was recorded. Despite this, Narungga identity is strong and is centred on Bukkiyana (Point Pearce)[8], an Aboriginal Community and previously a mission station located on the central west coast of Yorke Peninsula.[9]

Nukunu, to the immediate north and extending to Port Augusta, is the next most closely related language to Kaurna. Some Nukunu recordings were made by Luise Hercus between 1955 and 1971, collated with earlier sources and published in a dictionary (Hercus, 1992). This material has proved particularly useful, especially in terms of reconstructing Kaurna phonology.[10]

Ngadjuri, to the north-east, is also a closely related language, though, like Narungga, it has been poorly documented (see Berndt & Vogelsang, 1941). In late 1996, an interim Ngadjuri committee was formed by Fred Warrior who was then a leading member of the Kaurna Aboriginal Community and Heritage Association (henceforth KACHA). A number of people, like Fred, have both Kaurna and Ngadjuri ancestry.

Together, Kaurna, Narungga, Nukunu and Ngadjuri form a subgroup known as the Miru languages, which, together with Barngarla from Eyre Peninsula and Adnyamathanha from the Flinders Ranges, form the Thura-Yura subgroup[11] (see Map II).

To the immediate east of Kaurna lay the lands of the Permangk people, previously known as the 'Mount Barker Tribe'. They were known to the Kaurna as the *Mari Meyunna* [RS *Marri Miyurna*] 'east people'. So little is known about the Permangk language that it is impossible to even classify. Most writers, including myself, have assumed that Permangk is closely affiliated with Ngarrindjeri. However, I am now of the opinion that it is more likely that it was mutually intelligible with Kaurna.[12]

Further east, the Ngayawang language extends up the Murray River, according to Moorhouse (1846: title page) from Wellington on the Murray, as far as the Rufus. The Ngayawang were known to the Kaurna of the 1830s and 1840s as the *Pitta Meyunna* [RS *Pita Miyurna*] 'goose people'. In contemporary Australia it seems that practically all the Murray River districts in South Australia identify as Ngarrindjeri country, though many people also have Western Desert links as a result of a number of people being shifted from Ooldea to Gerard (Sapinsky, 1997: 24). School-based or community-based language programs choose Ngarrindjeri or Pitjantjatjara, never Ngayawang, despite the existence of reasonably comprehensive Ngayawang materials compiled by Weatherstone (1843) and Moorhouse (1846). Ngayawang, whilst being a very different language, seems to share some features with Kaurna and other features with Ngarrindjeri.

To the south-east of Kaurna lay the lands of the Ngarrindjeri nation. The Ngarrindjeri, also known as the Kukabrak (Berndt & Berndt, 1993) comprise a large number of clans including the Ramindjeri from Encounter Bay and the Yaralde from Raukkan (Point McLeay). The Ngarrindjeri clans from the Lower Murray were known to the Kaurna as the *Parnka Meyunna* [RS *Parnka Miyurna*] 'lake people' whilst the Ramindjeri from Encounter Bay were known as the *Wirramu Meyunna* [RS *Wirramu Miyurna*] after the Kaurna name for Encounter Bay. The Ngarrindjeri language is very different from Kaurna. Few vocabulary items are shared by the two languages and Ngarrindjeri phonology exhibits some marked deviations from the majority of Pama-Nyungan[13] languages. Linguistic differences notwithstanding, at the time of colonisation, the Ramindjeri people at least were close allies of the Kaurna. It would appear that these strong cultural ties were long-standing. An analysis of place names also shows evidence of linguistic diffusion, with frequent use of the locative suffix (*-ngga* or *-illa*) in Kaurna place names owing to the influence of languages of the Ngarrindjeri nation (Hercus & Potezney, 1999).

The Ngarrindjeri are still a strong and powerful people and are perhaps the most numerous Indigenous group in South Australia today. Whilst fluent speakers no longer exist, a significant amount of linguistic and cultural knowledge has been retained within the Ngarrindjeri community, despite its proximity to Adelaide and the effects of colonisation and various government and mission policies. Most Aboriginal people living in districts along the entire South Australian stretch of the Murray River and the Coorong identify as Ngarrindjeri, as well as a great number living in Adelaide. Ngarrindjeri language and culture programs have been operating in certain schools in the Murraylands and in Adelaide since the mid-1980s.

Kaurna people today

Until comparatively recently, most Kaurna people thought of themselves primarily as Nunga or Aboriginal people, or perhaps as Narungga or Ngarrindjeri people. Few thought of themselves as a 'Kaurna person', though this is now changing. Kaurna people today, as distinct from other Nunga peoples, define themselves primarily on the basis of genealogical links to the people who formerly inhabited the Adelaide Plains[14], relying on the boundaries of Kaurna territory as laid down by Tindale (1974).

It seems that the Kaurna, who witnessed the destruction of their most important sites, and whose population base was seriously undermined by the ravages of disease, had largely abandoned Adelaide itself by 1847, having been displaced by Europeans and the more numerous, more powerful Murray River peoples. A number of young Kaurna were shipped to Poonindie as the core of Archbishop Hale's 'Native Training Institution' (see Chapter 4). Some Kaurna, however, remained in Kaurna country at Cleland into the early 1860s and, according to oral tradition, others lived at Port Adelaide until about 1890, though they are invisible in the official records after 1853. Remaining Kaurna people were absorbed into the neighbouring Narungga and Ngarrindjeri peoples living respectively at Bukkiyana and Raukkan though some attempted to maintain contact with their country. Police records of the 1890s show continual eviction from Adelaide (see Foster, 1998).

As a result, information about connections to the Adelaide Plains was often not detailed or specific and was eclipsed by other Narungga or Ngarrindjeri connections, in whose territory they lived. Still, on their return to Kaurna lands, initial connections to the people of the Adelaide Plains were made through oral traditions transmitted from generation to generation within Nunga families.

Some Nunga families have maintained a keen interest in family history and have kept old photographs and papers. Doreen Kartinyeri is such a person with a keen personal interest. In 1979 she was encouraged by Lewis O'Brien to pursue this interest in a more formal way to record Raukkan and Bukkiyana genealogies (Kartinyeri, 1983: xv). As a result, the family history project at the South Australian Museum was born. Doreen's work, based largely on Tindale's unpublished materials and photographs held in the museum and her own knowledge within the Nunga community, has been particularly influential in shaping the identity of the Kaurna people. The Kaurna genealogies published for the opening of Tandanya, the national Aboriginal cultural institute located in Adelaide (Kartinyeri, 1989), identify five full blood Kaurna ancestors[15] from whom a number of large families are descended. They are as follows:

- Kaurna woman[16] (of Clare region) married to John Armstrong (white man)
- Rebecca Lartelare (Kaurna? Ngarrindjeri?) married to George Spender
- Kaurna woman[17] married to John Wilkins (Russian Finn)
- Kudnarto (Kaurna woman from Crystal Brook) married to Tom Adams
- Rathoola (Kaurna woman from Rapid Bay) married George Solomon

(extracted from Kartinyeri, 1989)

Of these five Kaurna women, four were married to white men, whilst the fifth married a Ngarrindjeri man, George Spender, from the Coorong.

Kartinyeri identified 50 living descendants of these five women who were over the age of 60 in 1989. Whilst she intended this list to be exhaustive, she acknowledged the possibility that she might have 'accidentally missed some links and omitted some people' (Kartinyeri, 1989: 3). The extended families identified in these genealogies are large. Kartinyeri (1989: 4) claims that the Wilkins family 'has more living descendants than any other South Australian family of Aboriginal descent'.

It is worth noting that none of these five women are connected directly to the Tarndanya clan, or the prominent Kaurna *burka* [RS *purka*] 'Elders' from whom Schürmann and Teichelmann recorded the Kaurna language. Kudnarto and Armstrong's wife came from the northern extremities of Kaurna territory. Rathoola and Wilkins' wife came from the southern districts (Cape Jervis and Rapid Bay). Lartelare's daughter, Laura Glanville, was born at Port Adelaide. Lartelare is believed to have been the sister of Ivaritji (Brodie & Melvin, 1994: 2), who was the daughter of Tangkaira, from the Clare district, and Ityamaiitpinna 'King Rodney' (Gara, 1990: 64). See Brodie (2002) for more details.

Since the publication of the Tandanya Souvenir Program, more information has come to light. For instance, Kath Burgemeister discovered another Kaurna link in her genealogy on her mother's side (pc Kath Burgemeister, March 1998) in addition to a connection on her father's side of the family, made known to her in 1993 through a telephone call from Veronica Brodie (*The Advertiser*, Saturday 19 July 1997: 1).

It is also known that the Kaurna woman, Kalloongoo, who was taken to Kangaroo Island, Portland, Bass Strait and finally Port Phillip, has descendants in the Portland district (see Amery, 1996d). It is likely that Emma or Emue, also living in Bass Strait at the same time, has descendants in Tasmania and Victoria, but these are unknown to Kaurna people in Adelaide.

Kaurna people began returning to the Adelaide Plains before World War Two. After the 1967 referendum, this process accelerated as Aboriginal people were able to move back into Adelaide of their own volition, no longer subject to the 'Act' (see p. 70). Upon arrival in the city, Nungas began to pursue their connections with the Adelaide Plains, their ancestral lands. It seems that some had always been aware of these links with Adelaide and with the Kaurna people through oral history passed down within the family. Georgina Williams was perhaps the first to actively pursue and voice her Kaurna identity. She had long been aware of her Kaurna ancestry on her mother's side, through Kudnarto, but she had heard little about her father's side and began to question him about it. She began to explore her links with Kaurna country by taking her father by car to places he had been taken as a boy. She learnt that her father had links to Kaurna country south of Adelaide. Lewis O'Brien actively pursued his Kaurna identity by research in the archives, after it was brought to his attention by the late Gladys Elphick when he moved to Adelaide. Lewis, like many other Kaurna people, had 'grown up with Narungga' as the focus of his identity. The Adams, Goldsmith, Spender and Wilson families were identified by Gladys Elphick as being of 'Kaurna descent', contrasting with the Edwards, Hughes and

Sansbury families who were said to be of Narungga descent (in Mattingley & Hampton, 1988: 201).

For many older Kaurna people, their primary identity remains Narungga or Ngarrindjeri, depending on whether they grew up at Bukkiyana or Raukkan respectively. For others, especially young people who have grown up in Adelaide, Kaurna identity is all-important. The number of people who identify primarily as Kaurna is growing, as people explore their history and genealogies.

The Kaurna community is dispersed throughout the metropolitan area and beyond. Today, Kaurna people are spread across a broad socio-economic spectrum. Some are tertiary educated with postgraduate qualifications. They fill a range of occupations, though most Kaurna are located in the lower socio-economic strata and many are dependent on social welfare. Unemployment, lifestyle-related illnesses, drug-taking and a loss of hope due to the processes of colonisation are taking their toll on the community as reflected in an extraordinarily high death rate over the past few years.[18]

Perhaps equally important as genealogical connections with the people of the Adelaide Plains are connections with sites of significance and Kaurna Dreamings.[19] The Tjilbruke Dreaming, in particular, is a major Dreaming trail which follows the creation of numerous sites within metropolitan Adelaide itself and along the coast to the south as far as Cape Jervis.

Georgina Williams, employed by the South Australian Museum in 1981 to research the trail, had a somewhat different agenda from that of the pre-existing committee, which simply wanted to record the trail for posterity. She explains:

> ... at that time the Kaurna people are an extinct [sic] people. This was what was said. The Kaurna people are no more ... We need to put up the John Dowie sculpture ... There were good white people who wanted to remember these things. I wanted more than a memory. I wanted an association. I wanted to be able to access the spirit of the place for myself and I wanted also to be able to pass that on to others. This has been my life's work. I don't get paid for it. I just do it. Because Tjilbruke was to me an example of the law of my people and of the law related to the land and the places along the coast.
> (Georgina Williams, guest lecture in KL&LE, University of Adelaide, 21 August 1997)

The Tjilbruke Dreaming is more than just a creation story to the Kaurna people. For some it has the status of a religion. It provides the meaning for life, a set of rules to live by and has a deep spiritual dimension to it. A number of the sites on the Tjilbruke trail are believed to be special sites of deep spiritual significance, with the spirit still living in the earth today. Kaurna Elder, Lewis O'Brien explains:

> ... councils started to ... wanted to rub out all these sites and that disturbed me. Because how could you rub something out that we know from a lot of different angles is 6000 years old. It's probably the oldest story in the world and you want to rub it out. It's older than the pyramids and anything you want to name. It's here on our land. It's affected all our people. And it's affected every people that's come here. It's powerful. It shows that because people have gone out of their way to protect these sites.
> Because our people had a statement about that. You walk this land and you will be affected the same as what we are. And they have been ... Because if you've got all these Dreaming spirits are lying in this earth, they're going to affect you, whether you like it or not.

> We haven't protected all the sites, but other people have. They know about them. And they sense the strength of the things that are there that's embedded in the earth. You can't rub it out in lots of ways because it's real. It exists. And that the power of the Dreaming is at its most powerful here.
> (Lewis O'Brien, guest lecture in KL&LE, University of Adelaide, 21 August 1997)

On their return to the Adelaide Plains, many Kaurna people have been deeply affected by the land through a series of spiritual or mystical experiences. For instance, Georgina Williams was 'drawn' to sites of significance, to places of which she had no prior knowledge. She says 'in accessing those places, the voices of the past spoke to me and said in that 150th year to "Go wake the people up" — my people, our people' (guest lecture, KL&LE, University of Adelaide, 21 August 1997). Georgina believes that the spirit of Tjilbruke came to her and spoke to her (without words) and instructed her to warn the people that imminent death was at hand. She explained: 'and that was why I had to bring Tjilbruke back, because we were being absorbed by the dominant culture' (pc 26 May 1998).

The Kaurna Aboriginal Community and Heritage Association (KACHA) is recognised as the representative body acting on behalf of all Kaurna people. Identification and protection of sites has been the main preoccupation of KACHA since its formation. However, its terms of reference are wide, making specific mention of the language. The first two of 16 'objects' of the Association are:

> 3.1 To provide opportunities for the advancement of the economic, educational, social, artistic, cultural, linguistic, spiritual, psychological, emotional and physical wellbeing of the Kaurna community.
> 3.2 To establish, acquire, maintain and control social, cultural and study centres and other projects to further the economic, educational, social, artistic, cultural, linguistic, spiritual, psychological, emotional and physical wellbeing of the Kaurna community.
> (Kaurna Aboriginal Community and Heritage Association Incorporated Constitution)

KACHA, previously known simply as the Kaurna Heritage Committee, grew out of the Tjilbruke Track Committee[20] based at the South Australian Museum. In 1981, after a period of inactivity, the Committee was reconvened by John Moriarty, the Director of the South Australian Department of Aboriginal Affairs. The committee was restructured, giving Kaurna people more power and control over their heritage. They became centrally involved in the day-to-day activities of the committee:

> The power of decision making on the committee was given to 'Kaurna' descendants and Georgina Williams (a 'Kaurna' descendant) was employed along with Suzi Hutchings (an anthropologist) to work, based at the SA Museum, on the research aspect of the project. Other 'Kaurna' descendants involved with the committee included Doris Graham and Lewis O'Brien. (Hemming, 1990: 135)

In the 1980s Kaurna identity was focused on the Tjilbruke Dreaming and associated sites through the work of the Committee. KACHA now encompasses much broader issues. Naomi Dixon elaborates:

Locating the Study 11

> I suppose then [1986], it was really just the interest in Tjilbruke. And you know, Georgina believed that ... she told us that she was told to go out and wake the people up. And I think she did that very successfully ... Tjilbruke was the main instigator for us too ... but since then, our interest has grown much bigger than just Tjilbruke. Because we've sort of learnt that too, that Tjilbruke is important to give us a set of guidelines, but it's much bigger than that now. It's about all of the culture, you know.
>
> (Interview transcript, 21 November 1996)

In 1996, there were 22 Kaurna extended families represented in KACHA. In addition, there are other Kaurna families outside the committee who are perhaps less politically inclined but nonetheless strongly identify as Kaurna people and take an interest in Kaurna affairs. Some Kaurna extended families are highly organised and are legally incorporated.

A Kaurna linguistic and cultural renaissance

Half a century ago, a number of Kaurna people, of their own volition and in their own ways, began exploring their roots. One of the first to start lines of enquiry beyond the Nunga community was Lewis O'Brien. Lewis explains:

> ... that's what I've been fascinated with all along about reviving this [Dreaming of the Kaurna], because that's been a thought of mine when I was a young lad. I came to the city when I was quite young, leaving the mission when I was about six. And then when I was about 17, I kept going back and forth all the time to the mission. And I kept hearing these numbers all the time — Block number 346. And so we had that property up at Clare around North Auburn in 1848. And here it is 1947, and the family still knew that number orally. So I found it very interesting. They remembered. They never wrote it down. So I went to the library in 1947.
>
> (Guest lecture, KL&LE, University of Adelaide, 21 August, 1997)

The journey of rediscovery of Kaurna identity in the modern period probably begins with these enquiries made by Lewis O'Brien in 1947 about this block of land which once belonged to his ancestor Kudnarto [RS Kudnartu], but which had been resumed by the government despite deputations and protests from her husband and descendants (see O'Brien, 1990 and O'Connor, 1998 for details). Lewis recollects:

> I thought for a long time, that I was a Narrunga person but I found out, through tracing history, that there were some survivors of the Kaurna — including myself — and now there's probably a thousand of us Kaurna descendants who can trace their ancestry back to a number of Aboriginal women who had children. It pleased me to think that we were survivors and that we are still here and still doing things.
>
> (O'Brien, 1990: 117, 119)

In recent times more and more people have been seeking out their roots and connections with the people of the Adelaide Plains.

Concurrently, there was some interest in the Indigenous culture of the Adelaide Plains among non-Aboriginal researchers and antiquarians who regarded the Kaurna as 'extinct'. They often had no contact with and made no reference to the Nunga community. Even for those non-Aboriginal researchers, such as Norman Tindale and the Berndts, who did have extensive contact with the Nunga community, their interest was in documenting a 'dying' or 'dead' traditional culture, ignoring much of a more contemporary nature. Tindale certainly had no interest in reviving the culture. On the contrary, much of the motivation for his ethnographic research was to lay scientific parameters for the swift assimilation of Aboriginal people, and he saw little place for people of 'mixed ancestry'. Certainly the work of Tindale, the Berndts and others provided invaluable information, especially for the Ngarrindjeri, on which Nungas can now draw, but their work was quite independent of the current linguistic and cultural renaissance.

However, in the 1970s and 1980s a number of people working within the education sector and institutions such as the South Australian Museum acted as intermediaries and catalysts, making connections between research and the Nunga community. Over the past two decades, Kaurna Elders and community leaders have been active in preserving Kaurna heritage and promoting Kaurna culture and history through the development and implementation of Aboriginal Studies curriculum, notably *The Kaurna People* (EDSA, 1989). Kaurna people, like Lewis O'Brien, the late Gladys Elphick, Georgina Williams and Alice Rigney, had a major impact on the education system, ensuring that Aboriginal perspectives were introduced into this curriculum. In addition, some have published life stories, articles, poems and other materials (see, for instance, Graham & Graham, 1987; O'Brien, 1990, 1991; G. Telfer, 1984; Williams, 1986, 1997; K. Telfer, 1997; Brodie, 1991, 2002; Agius & Gale, 1994; Agius, 1994; A. Rigney, 1994; L. Rigney, 1995, 1996a, 1996b).[21] They are the driving force behind a cultural revival and have been strong supporters of the Kaurna language movement. Accordingly, most are central within this study.

In many ways, Kaurna language revival has been a natural progression of earlier developments in Aboriginal Studies curriculum. As a non-Indigenous researcher my interests have coincided with the directions in which the Kaurna community was already moving. Members of the Kaurna community have inspired my research. In turn, my research has acted as a catalyst for the development of programs in the education sector and stimulates interest in the language within the community. Both feed off each other in a mutually beneficial relationship, though the initial impetus came from the community.[22]

Whilst Kaurna people were cut off from their ancestral lands and cultural traditions, most grew up at Bukkiyana and Raukkan where they were exposed to varying aspects of Narungga and Ngarrindjeri cultural traditions respectively. A number of Dreaming stories from these places are remembered. Tracking and hunting skills, string games, weaving skills and artefact manufacture are still practised and knowledge of a range of cultural practices and beliefs is maintained to varying degrees, along with a strong sense of Aboriginality. It has been from this base that Kaurna people have been seeking out a unique Kaurna culture.

In recent years there has been a marked increase in the use and display of traditional skills, such as weaving and artefact manufacture. Some of these skills had lain dormant for some time, now rekindled by renewed ethnic pride, the introduction of Aboriginal Studies in schools and a developing Aboriginal cultural tourism industry. Kaurna people, too, are engaged in these activities. For instance, Paul Dixon, when he was Chair of KACHA and living at

Warriparinga, an important site at the start of the Tjilbruke Trail in metropolitan Adelaide, cut several shields from large red gums there.

The situation is complex. Kaurna culture of the nineteenth century is only partially known, from the writings of outsiders — missionaries, government officials and other interested observers. This 'traditional' culture is of interest to Kaurna people today who live in an entirely different world to their forebears. There is a strong desire to revitalise aspects of this inheritance, including the dances and ceremonies (pc Lester Rigney, 1997; Georgina Williams, 1996; 1997). Georgina's son, Karl Telfer, who is a dancer and musician, has already begun to draw on Kaurna traditions, incorporating Kaurna language into his performances.

Work has begun on a 'reviving the dreaming' project under the auspices of KACHA. Some Kaurna people are interested in drawing on the knowledge of past funeral practices with a view to incorporating some elements of past rituals into modern practices in an effort to promote healing within the community. Smoking rituals have recently been reintroduced. The 'Kaurna Blessing' as performed by Cherie Watkins is part of a smoking, cleansing ritual which honours the four directions: *kauanda* [RS *kawanta*] 'north', *mare* [RS *marri*] 'east', *patpa* [RS *patpa*] 'south' and *wongga* [RS *wangka*] 'west' by blowing smoke in that direction and uttering the Kaurna words (pc Cherie Watkins, November 1997).

This then is the cultural context in which Kaurna language reclamation and its incipient revival is taking place. Rebuilding the Kaurna language goes hand in hand with rebuilding the Kaurna culture. The language is seen by some as the means of reviving the culture and unlocking the past. However, relatively few Kaurna are actively involved in the formal language programs themselves. Logistical problems, work commitments, family commitments and other barriers prevent this. Amongst the adults, it tends to be the community leaders, Elders, intellectuals[23] and professionals within the Kaurna community who are most actively involved in the Kaurna language movement. Yet, there is a growing sense of pride in the language and recognition of the Kaurna language programs. This pride and recognition are widespread, if not universal, within the Kaurna community.

The relationship between Kaurna and Nunga English

A distinctive variety (or varieties) of English, generally referred to as Nunga English, is spoken as an in-group language by Aboriginal people in Adelaide and surrounding communities. Whilst major studies have been conducted on Aboriginal English spoken elsewhere in Australia (Kaldor & Malcolm, 1982; Malcolm & Kaldor, 1991; Harkins, 1994; Eades, 1982, 1983, 1988), until recently little attention was given by linguists to researching these varieties in South Australia. The most detailed study to date is that by Wilson (1996) which investigated English used by Nunga children at Alberton Primary School, a school which has recently been engaged in performing Kaurna songs in public. Philip Clarke, in the course of his work with the Anthropology Division of the South Australian Museum and as an adjunct to his PhD (Clarke, 1994a), has, over the course of a decade, compiled a reasonably comprehensive database of terms, mostly drawn from local Indigenous languages, which are used in distinctive ways by Aboriginal people in southern South Australia from Port Lincoln to Mount Gambier (see Clarke, 1994b).

The relationship between Kaurna and Nunga English is tenuous. The majority of terms of Indigenous origin used in Nunga English come from Ngarrindjeri, though there are many from languages on the west coast and some from Narungga. Comparatively few terms originate from Kaurna. Even those that do come from Kaurna are seldom recognised as such. Of the 900 or so terms recorded by Clarke (1994b), approximately 60 bear similarities to Kaurna words as recorded in the historical sources, but only four of these: *bandabri* 'gun', *guna-wadli*[24] 'toilet', *pinyata:wi*[25] 'sugar' and *Tandanya* 'a cultural institution', are identified by Clarke as having exclusive Kaurna origins. There are at least six additional terms with Kaurna counterparts frequently used by Nungas which have been omitted from Clarke's wordlist.[26]

Clarke also noted the 'attributed language', which is believed by most informants to be the source of the word. Significantly, only three words, *Kaurna, Tandanya* and *Tjilbruke* are attributed to 'Adelaide', though as Clarke points out, two of these most likely have Ngarrindjeri origins. Of the four words identified by Clarke as having exclusive Kaurna origins, most informants said *bandabri* has Aboriginal English origins, *guna-wadli* is from Yorke Peninsula and *pinyata:wi* is Ngarrindjeri, leaving *Tandanya* as the only word attributed to Adelaide which does in fact have its origins in Kaurna. However, Tandanya is known as the name of an institution established in 1989, and as such is different from other terms documented by Clarke.[27] It is probably not a retention, but rather has been relearned recently.

Undoubtedly Kaurna is the source of a number of words in Nunga English. *Nantu* 'horse', *kapi* 'tobacco', *bandabri* 'gun', *tulya*[28] 'police' and *wardli* ~ *wurley* 'house' almost certainly come from Kaurna, even though they are not recognised as such within the Nunga community. With other words such as *mara* 'hand' or *yuri* 'ear' it is difficult to say which language is the source, since they are shared by so many languages.

Nunga English emerged as the language of Aboriginal peoples thrust together on the missions. Contemporary Nunga culture is an amalgam of the traditions of a number of peoples and elements of languages, including Ngarrindjeri, Narungga, Kaurna, Kukatha, Wirangu and others, with a heavy overlay of European culture, especially that rooted in the mission experience. So Nunga English came to represent a larger group identity for Indigenous peoples from across southern South Australia. It has also been influenced to some extent by notions of pan-Aboriginality, by other 'traditional' Aboriginal cultures such as Pitjantjatjara and to some extent by Indigenous cultures from outside Australia.

There are now moves to 'unpack' Nunga culture, to separate out the contributing linguistic and cultural traditions and to reinstate a range of specific cultural practices. With increased awareness of history and heritage and the emergence of a distinctive Kaurna identity, a distinctive 'Kaurna culture' will probably emerge as a combination of contemporary Nunga culture and 'traditional' Kaurna culture.

Although Nunga English is an important element within the contemporary Kaurna language ecology today, it is unclear how the languages might coexist. There seem to be a range of differing opinions. Lester Rigney sees a possibility for the relexification of Nunga English, whereby distinctive varieties emerge such as Kaurna English, Narungga English, Ngarrindjeri English, which use only lexemes drawn from the respective heritage languages along with English. These distinct Nunga English varieties would then be spoken by those respective groups within their respective territories (Lester Rigney, interviewed by Jenny Burford, 21 October 1997).

Others, such as Lewis O'Brien and Georgina Williams, would like to see Kaurna eventually replace Nunga English, which they consider to be the product of oppression. Lewis is tolerant of Nunga English, but does not want to see it promoted within education:

> Well I think Nunga English is like a second grade step. It doesn't explain to you why you do what you do. To me, I always believe that you've got to go to the source. You've got to learn your Kaurna language or whatever Aboriginal language you learn and you'll find out why you speak like you do. It gives you the structure and that's why I think you need to know. And that's why I never like people to learn in a course Nunga English. I don't mind them using Nunga English. But don't do it as a subject. It's like a second grade fall back. And everyone does that, but I think it's a bad thing to learn. I'd rather learn Kaurna. If you want to learn a language learn your own.
> (Lewis O'Brien, interview transcript, 8 December 1997)

I do not envisage that Kaurna culture will replace Nunga culture, but rather that Kaurna culture will continue to emerge from within it.[29] Ngarrindjeri people at one level adhere to the same Nunga culture in common with Kaurna and Narungga people, but at another level the Ngarrindjeri have their own stories, history and aspects of language that belong to them and form a contemporary Ngarrindjeri culture. The same is true of Narungga and to some extent of Kaurna, with research into and promotion of the Tjilbruke story, aspects of Kaurna history and oral traditions. There are certain knowledges and certain clues within the language that reinforce continuing traditions and provide foundations to build on or seeds to propagate. Needless to say, the development of Kaurna culture is something for Kaurna people to work out for themselves.

Prospects for the revival of Kaurna

One might argue, and many will, that revival of the Kaurna language is a lost cause as it is an impossible task. And perhaps it is, if this question is viewed in terms of reviving Kaurna as a language of everyday communication. But, as governments and government agencies such as departments of education are discovering, issues of Indigenous rights and the survival of Indigenous peoples will not go away and sink into oblivion. Rather, Indigenous people are becoming more vocal and making more demands regarding Indigenous rights and issues.

Although the revival of the Kaurna language is just one small element within that larger discourse on Indigenous rights and Indigenous survival, it is not a passing fad in which people will soon lose interest. Already the profile of the Kaurna language has been lifted from that of an obscure 'extinct' language, of which almost nothing was known, to a credible, worthwhile pursuit within the school system. Efforts over the past eight years have already proved a success. Nunga students who have taken Kaurna language workshops and courses have reported favourably on their experiences. For some it has provided a new, positive view of themselves as Nungas, engendering a new found pride and a knowledge and motivation for working with other Aboriginal students and teaching Aboriginal Studies. They have found that language is an important element in their social identity. For some Nungas at least, a knowledge of ancestral languages, such as Kaurna, is filling a gap and contributing to the healing of a people who have been marginalised, oppressed and disenfranchised of their heritage; a people who have often been the butt of racism and ridicule. There are signs that several Kaurna extended families are taking the Kaurna language seriously and are attempting to learn it for communication within the family.

The possibilities for the revival of Kaurna must be viewed within a long-term time frame. We are still in the very early stages of Kaurna language revival. This book documents in some detail the nature of revived Kaurna, the situations in which it is being used and the context in which this incipient revival is taking place. In the interests of brevity, it has not been possible to include all the detailed analysis. For additional examples and in-depth discussion, see Amery (1998a): volume II includes a wide range of historical documents, sample materials and documents associated with Kaurna language programs and activities.

Only time will tell whether or not the Kaurna language will take the 'great leap forward' and be used to any great extent within the community outside the formal programs. The experience of language revival programs elsewhere tells us that the prospects for this to happen are slender. Nevertheless, already the programs have been a success in the eyes of the Kaurna community, within the formal education sector and on many other social and political levels.

Notes

[1] Nunga, pronounced [nʌŋgə], is a term of self-ascription used by Aboriginal persons in the southern parts of South Australia, contrasting with Gunya, pronounced [gʊɲə], used to refer to non-Aboriginal persons. Nunga seems to have originated from Wirangu, a language from the west coast of South Australia (Wilson, 1996: 6-7). It is used in the same sense as Koori or Koorie in NSW and Victoria, Murrie in Queensland, Palawa in Tasmania, Nyungar or Noongah in the south-west of Western Australia and Yura in the Flinders Ranges.

[2] This term is defined as 'efforts to relearn a language on the basis of historical documentation and archival material' (SSABSA, 1996a: vii). It is discussed further in Chapter 2 and explicated in detail in Chapter 6. The term has since been adopted by a number of writers, notably McKay (1996).

[3] Consequently, some Kaurna place names are known generally throughout the wider community.

[4] Since this paragraph was originally written, a meeting of interested Kaurna people was held in April 2013 to discuss the possible name change from Kaurna to Miyurna. Non-Kaurna people were excluded from the meeting, which resolved to continue with the use of Kaurna as the name of the people and language of the Adelaide Plains.

[5] Ivaritji was a survivor of the 'invasion' and the first dispossession of Kaurna lands. Tindale's views are coloured by the notion that 'traditional' Aboriginal people of 'full descent' are the only 'real' Aboriginal people, a view wholeheartedly rejected by the author and by Kaurna people today.

[6] This date appears to be incorrect. See Gara (1990: 64, 98). It seems that Ivaritji died of pneumonia on Christmas Day 1929.

[7] Recent post-invasion movements of peoples are found elsewhere in the country. It is of interest to note that the Antekerrenye wordlist in Taplin (1879) is of an Arandic language. According to the location given by Taplin the Antekerrenye wordlist was obtained from deep inside current Western-Desert speaking areas. The Antikirinya today, centred around Oodnadatta, speak a language which is a variety of Western Desert. There have been early eastward movements of Western-Desert speaking peoples as a result of the presence of the 'doggers' who paid a bounty for dingo scalps. It is unclear whether language shift took place in the Oodnadatta region or whether Arandic speakers were replaced by Western Desert speakers.

[8] Bukkiyana, also written as Bookayana, is the Indigenous name for Point Pearce and is used in this thesis in accordance with Nunga preferences, even though Point Pearce is better known and used more widely.

[9] The local Point Pearce School is engaged in the delivery of a Narungga language program. Some schools in Adelaide also teach elements of the Narungga language from time to time.

[10] Several families living in Port Augusta identify as Nukunu and a Nukunu language awareness program was commenced within Port Germaine Primary School in 1995.

[11] These subgroups are labelled after the word for 'person' in the respective languages. Nukunu has *miṟu*, Kuyani has *thuṟa* while Adnyamathanha and Barngarla use *yuṟa* (Hercus, 1992: 1-2).

[12] The colony of South Australia was centred on Adelaide. In the 1830s and 1840s, the colonial authorities were keen to establish the number of languages needed to communicate with the Indigenous population. Following the publication of grammars of Kaurna (T&S), Ramindjeri (Meyer, 1843) and Barngarla (Schürmann, 1844), Grey ordered Moorhouse to write a grammar of Ngayawang (Moorhouse, 1846). In the Preface, Moorhouse writes 'the Europeans had been several years in contact with Natives speaking four dialects, and Vocabularies of three dialects had been prepared ... it was thought desirable ... to have the fourth placed on record'. Had Permangk been significantly different from Kaurna, a grammar would most likely have been prepared earlier. Furthermore, we learn from Teichelmann's journals (5 January 1840) that he was able to communicate with 'the Marri Mejus', presumably in Kaurna.

[13] Pama-Nyungan languages cover 4/5 of mainland Australian and include all South Australian languages. They are grouped together on the basis of typological similarity (strictly suffixing), and named after the words for 'man; person' in Cape York and south-west Western Australia.

[14] Although genealogy may be the primary criterion that Kaurna people use to distinguish themselves from other Nungas, this does not diminish the importance of other aspects of identity, including the relationship with the land, the Dreaming, the Law, the songs, language and other aspects of culture.

[15] Since this was written, another three Kaurna ancestors have been identified (see Gale, 2012a: 10).

[16] On the basis of oral history, Kartinyeri (1989: 1) believes that this woman may have been the sister of Ivaritji's mother, though there are conflicts in the available evidence.

[17] In the Wilson family genealogies (Kartinyeri, 1990), Wilkins' wife is identified as Nellie Raminyeramin. However, correspondence from Wilkins (SA State Records GRG 35/1/374/1860) written in about 1860 and other papers relating to Kangaroo Island (Log Books & Early Journals, Trinity Board & Miscellaneous Papers, SA State Records) record his wife's name as Mary Monatto, using the Kaurna birth-order name. According to the Sub-Protector (11 March 1862) she left Kangaroo Island for Yankalilla in March 1861 (SA State Records GRG 35/1/374). Perhaps Wilkins had two wives.

[18] In July 1997, Georgina Williams (Launch of KL&LE) noted that over the previous few months '43 people [in the Nunga community], 20 of them at least of which are known to me, have died'.

[19] The Dreaming, originating in Spencer & Gillen (1898), is a problematic term. In most Australian languages the 'Dreaming' bears little relationship to the bodily function 'to dream'. Still the term is well-established, thus I too use it.

[20] The Tjilbruke Track Committee grew out of the Tjilbruke Monuments Committee, established in 1971 by Robert Edwards of the South Australian Museum, the sculptor John Dowie and staff of the *Sunday Mail*. Hemming (1990) provides details in his discussion of the emergence of Kaurna identity.

[21] Several people are working on the life story of the late Gladys Elphick, a prominent Kaurna Elder within the cultural revival movement in the 1980s, based on tapes recorded by Betty Fisher.

[22] It seems that Kaurna people and linguists started looking into the Kaurna language independently. Jane Simpson was working on Kaurna of her own volition in the late 1970s onwards, whilst Kaurna people began searching the archives for material. Alice Rigney, for instance, made enquiries at the Lutheran Archives in the mid 1980s (pc April 1998).

[23] By the term 'intellectual' I refer not just to those with formal tertiary education qualifications, but also to the 'thinkers' in the community and those who engage in philosophical and intellectual discussion.

[24] The Kaurna counterpart of this word is recorded as *kudnawodli* [RS *kudnawardli*] 'toilet' with a prestopped nasal. Whilst undoubtedly of Kaurna origin, this term appears to have been assimilated to Ngarrindjeri, Pitjantjatjara or west coast languages which have the word *kuna* 'faeces'.

[25] *Pinyata:wi* 'sugar' probably has its origins in *pinyatta* [RS *pinyata*] 'honey from the grass tree; sugar' + *kauwe* [RS *kauwi*] 'water'.

[26] These include *barti* [RS *parti*] 'witchetty grub', *kappi* [RS *kapi*] 'tobacco', *kari* [RS *kardi*] 'emu', *kondolli* [RS *kuntuli*] 'whale', *yambo* [RS *yampu*] 'dolphin', *parnka* [RS *parnka*] 'lake' (used to refer to Ngarrindjeri people) and *biltamasta* 'spirit bird bringing death' (? < *pilta* [RS *pirlta*] 'possum'. Cf. *possumaster ~ posamaster* 'spirit bird' (Clarke, 1994b: 102)).

[27] Numerous other Kaurna place names and institution names not listed by Clarke are known and used within the Nunga community. *Tandanya* seems out of place here in the absence of these other terms.

[28] *Tulya* ultimately comes from the English word 'soldier', but was documented as *tulya* [RS *tulya*] by T&S. *Tulya* was probably borrowed into neighbouring languages from Kaurna at a very early stage with the expanding frontier.

However, some Kaurna people possibly do want to see Kaurna culture replace Nunga culture. Georgina Williams sees Nunga culture as a stifling thing, resulting largely from the mission experience (pc Georgina Williams, KL&LE lecture, 11 September 1997).

2

Language Reclamation

Now I don't see it as something that has been written by goonyas, therefore we shouldn't embrace it. It is there. It's ours. It has been recorded for us and indeed in some of those recordings our people are talking to us. But we need to decode it.

(Lester Irabinna Rigney, interviewed by Jenny Burford, 21 October 1997)

Language reclamation: preliminaries

I use the term **language reclamation** specifically to refer to language revival in situations where the language is no longer spoken and little is known orally within the community (Amery, 1994: 146; SSABSA, 1996a; Mercurio & Amery, 1996: 48). The term refers to attempts to relearn a language from material recorded in another era, when the language was spoken. The term reflects the politics of Indigenous rights. As the quotation above indicates, such a revival is associated with the reclaiming of identity and culture from which a people have been dissociated. The term 'language reclamation', used in this way, was coined by Mary-Anne Gale and myself in 1992. Prior to that I had been using the term **language resurrection** in relation to Kaurna, but rejected this term because of its inherent view of such languages as 'dead' or 'extinct', and its unwelcome religious overtones. Perhaps others have used the term independently of my usage, even before 1992.[1] Dick & McCarty (1997) use both 'reclaiming' and 'renewal' in relation to Navajo[2] in the title of their paper. Van Heerden (1991) talks of militant Black writers in South Africa 'reclaiming' Afrikaans 'as their personal language' and as 'the language of Liberation', in a conscious effort to break the stigma of apartheid.[3] This use is quite different from my own.

Some writers (e.g. Paulston et al., 1994: 92) use the term **language revival** in a narrow, restrictive sense:

> We intend the literal meaning of language revival; that is, the giving of new life to a dead language, or the act of reviving a language after discontinuance, and making it the normal means of communication in a speech community.

I use it, however, as most other writers do, as a cover term both for situations in which a language is undergoing a resurgence and for measures taken to extend the domains of usage of a language, increase the number of speakers or indeed to reintroduce a language after it has ceased to be spoken.

The term **resuscitation** is sometimes encountered and seems to be used in reference to attempts to revive a language which no longer has speakers. Dixon's (1989: 31) 'resuscitation' seems to be equivalent to Paulston's (1994) use of 'language revival'. Note, however, that Edwards (1984: 285) speaks of the failure 'in resuscitating spoken Irish among the population at large', which conflicts with Dixon's usage.

In my usage, the term 'language reclamation' contrasts with **language renewal**, which I use to refer to efforts to revive a language that has no fluent speakers, but where a significant amount of the language is known within the community. Language renewal efforts draw mainly on this remaining oral heritage as opposed to historical documentation. I restrict the use of the term **language revitalisation** for revival efforts where some fluent speakers of the language remain, as is the case for Maori and most language revival movements discussed in the literature.

Little of substance has been written about attempts to relearn or revive so-called 'dead' or 'extinct' languages. In fact, linguistics has generally ignored, dismissed or discredited such activities, usually in the space of a single sentence. This is because the discipline of linguistics has been constrained by certain assumptions about the nature of language and languages.

This book proposes and explicates a method for reviving so-called 'dead' languages where reasonable records exist. The language reclamation approach utilises a range of linguistic techniques to retrieve, piece together, develop and transform the language into a form capable of being relearnt and used for a range of contemporary purposes. Whilst this chapter focuses on the research and technical aspects of language revival, we should remember that language reclamation begins with the community and the language is continually shaped in response to community needs and sensitivities. Otherwise the application of techniques advocated here is an empty intellectual exercise, without any point or purpose. This chapter focuses primarily on corpus-planning aspects of the process whilst the next focuses more on status planning.

'Dead' or 'sleeping' languages? Terminology does matter

This study concerns a language which, according to the criteria invoked by most linguists, would be described as well and truly 'dead' or 'extinct'. However, the Indigenous people central to the Kaurna language movement see Kaurna very differently. They see it as having been 'dormant' or 'sleeping' but nonetheless 'surviving'.

According to the Concise Oxford Dictionary definition, a **dead language** is 'one no longer ordinarily spoken'. In Australia, most people think of Latin and Sanskrit as prototypical 'dead' languages. Yet these languages did not 'die' in the same sense that many Indigenous languages of Australia, North America and other parts of the world are said to have 'died'. Latin and Sanskrit changed and evolved over the centuries giving rise to a number of 'daughter' languages, such as Italian, French, Spanish and Hindi, Urdu, Marathi etc. Latin and Sanskrit are referred to as 'dead' languages for two main reasons. Languages descended from them are referred to by quite different names, so they are thought of as completely different entities. Also, Latin and Sanskrit continued to be used in written form or for restricted religious purposes after the everyday language had diverged to a considerable extent. Old English, Old German or proto-Indo-European are not usually referred to as 'dead' languages though they are comparable in all other ways to Latin and Sanskrit.

As it turns out, both Sanskrit and Latin have made a comeback in certain situations. Pandharipande (1996) discusses the increasing role of Sanskrit as a lexical 'base for the emergence of Sanskritised registers of Modern Indian languages' in official registers used in government, literature and the media, as well as its continued use as a religious register. Pandharipande (1996: 196-198) also discusses the new use of Sanskrit as a medium of communication in radio news broadcasts and in creative literature where the language is undergoing structural changes and is being modernised 'in order to maintain itself'. David (1997: 7) reports that Sanskrit is now used as the everyday language in two Brahmin villages in Karnataka's Shimoga district in western India. The reintroduction of Sanskrit took place following a visit by a head of the Pejawar Math who 'exhorted the people to revive the tongue'. The challenge was taken up by a group of priests who offered classes in Sanskrit. The response was reportedly overwhelming, the cause being taken up by housewives, farmers and doctors alike.

Latin held a central place within the Catholic Church until the Second Vatican Council in 1962, which extended the use of national languages and vernaculars in church liturgy (Mullarney, 1987: 357). Since then the knowledge and use of Latin has rapidly declined everywhere, except in China, 'where up to 8 million Catholics cling to Latin' (Mullarney, 1987: 359). The cause of spoken Latin has been promoted by a Finnish Professor, Jukka Ammondt, who recently released a compact disk of Latin translations of many of Elvis Presley's most famous songs including *Tenere me ama* 'Love Me Tender' and *Nunc hic aut humquaum* 'It's Now or Never'. Two years previously he recorded Finnish tangos in Latin. Since 1989, the Finnish Broadcasting Company has broadcast weekly Latin news bulletins[4] (Schwarz, 1995: 67). Contrary to popular belief, Latin, at least for some, is not an unchanging language. Latin has incorporated words for 'helicopter' and other recent inventions. Schwarz discusses the resurgence of spoken Latin in the 1990s and includes excerpts from Latin translations of *Asterix* comics. A phrasebook *Latin for All Occasions* (Beard, 1991) which incorporates a number of neologisms such as *orbem rigidum* 'hard disk' has recently been published.

Whilst there are major differences between the circumstances of Latin or Sanskrit and a language like Kaurna, there are still important lessons to be learnt from attempts to revernacularise them.

By contrast with Latin and Sanskrit, many Indigenous languages in Australia have 'died' because all their speakers have died, or because all the speakers have adopted other languages such as English, a creole or another Indigenous language. Most of Australia's Indigenous languages have 'died' as a result of language shift and not as a result of language change. Accordingly, some linguists, such as Jean Aitchison (1991: 197), exclude languages like Latin from their discussion of 'language death'.

Thomason (1982), cited by Paulston et al. (1994: 93), defines a **dead language** as one which: (1) has no native speakers, (2) is not used in everyday communication by a speech community, and (3) does not undergo normal processes of change. Sasse (1992: 18), essentially agreeing with Thomason's definition, provides further illumination:

> For the present purpose my proposal is to define the final point of language death as the cessation of regular communication in the language ...
>
> A dead language may leave residues of various kinds. It may continue as a ritual language, as a secret language, as a professional jargon, etc. It may leave a codified version, which in turn can be used for ritual or other purposes. It may finally leave a substratum influence (especially lexically) in the dialect of T [target language] which the former speech community of A [abandoned language] continues to speak.

This definition is formulated strictly from a linguist's perspective, which is at odds with the perceptions of members of the speech community of the abandoned language (see p. 41). Auxiliary languages[5] that are still in use would not normally be regarded as 'dead' and the 'residues' are seen within the Nunga community as 'living' and 'strong'. For Sasse (1992: 21) 'language death' results in a discontinuity.[6] Anything that might be attempted after that is artificial and not the same language:

> any total interruption of language transmission results in language death; any revitalization after total interruption of language transmission results in the creation of a new language.
> From Phase III [following language death] on, only artificial revitalization on the basis of thesaurus-like, codified material is possible. The most conspicuous example of such an event is Ivrith, Modern Hebrew, which was created on the basis of the codified holy texts after more than 2000 years of interruption of regular language transmission.

The views of many linguists and scholars resonate with those of Sasse. For instance, a well-known sociolinguist sees revived Cornish as contrived and artificial:

> The revived Cornish is a somewhat piecemeal and quite artificial creation of antiquaries, and some Celtic scholars have been quite critical of it. But it is this variety that is used whenever 'Cornish' is used today and it is on this variety that those who see a future for the language and possibly too for a Cornish nation have pinned their hopes. The Cornish that exists today is really to be found only among those who seek to bring about a revival of the language along with a revival of a Celtic ethnic consciousness.
> (Wardhaugh, 1987: 75-76)

Terminology is important, as are the ways in which we view languages and language planning initiatives. If we adhere to the view held by Sasse, we are defeated before we start. Anything that we attempt will be characterised as artificial and bearing no connection with the previous language. By contrast, Kaurna people emphasise survival and continuity. A strict linguistic approach, as taken by Sasse, does little to promote healing within communities dispossessed of their linguistic and cultural heritage.

The terms used draw on metaphors of various kinds, many of which serve to devalue, marginalise or question the authenticity of language revival efforts. I attempt to avoid labels which work against the interests of Indigenous peoples and to seek neutral or more positive metaphors which will inspire action rather than dismissal.

I prefer to use the terms 'no longer spoken' or 'no longer spoken right through'. Use of the terms 'dead' or 'extinct' invoke a certain hopelessness about the situation, implying that nothing can be done. Similarly, I prefer to use the terms 'threatened' or 'endangered' rather than 'dying', 'obsolete' or 'moribund'.

The health or body state metaphor applied to languages in regard to their contemporary status is misleading. Languages are not the same as living organisms, though there are parallels. Do languages really 'die' in the sense that a living thing dies?[7] In what senses are languages 'alive'? Certainly a 'living' language changes continually. It is dynamic, whereas a 'dead' language is considered static. That is where the analogy ends.

In contrast to writers such as Thomason, Sasse, Dixon and others, Denison, in a paper written two decades ago, at least considers the possibility of the continued existence of languages no longer spoken, but notes that it runs counter to the prevailing attitude of linguists:

> we might wish to say that a language exists — or, metaphorically, 'lives' — as soon as and for as long as it can be considered to be fully or partially codified and described ... By this criterion, one might well be prepared to issue a death certificate for Etruscan without too much scruple, whereas ancient Egyptian could not be pronounced wholly dead — at best it might be felt that it would be 'healthier' if we had a better description of it. However, such a view offends the general feeling that a language must be considered 'dead' if it is no longer spoken by anyone (? as a native language). It runs counter to the statement often made by linguists ... that a language must be regarded as dead as soon as it stops developing (that is, changing; in other words as soon as its performance can be generated on the strength of its codified rules alone). On both of these counts, Hebrew would have been judged at least to have been feigning death before it was restored to life in Israel. (Denison, 1977: 13-14)

Revival of a 'dead' language: is it really possible?

Just as life can exist as relatively inert spores in a bottle, languages, too, can exist in a static unchanging form as words written in a book, or indeed as sounds recorded on a tape, or even accompanied by images on video and film. Given the right conditions the spores can be activated and burst into life. In fact, a recent publication (Comrie et al., 1996: 214) appeals to the DNA metaphor in a similar fashion:

> Just as plants and animal species can be preserved and recreated by preserving their DNA, the sounds, grammar, and vocabulary of languages can be stored on tape and disk for posterity and even for later resuscitation.

Whilst several linguists have considered the 'theoretical' possibility of reviving 'dead' languages, its actualisation seems to be regarded, even by these writers, as remote. They envisage the need for vast amounts of archival material before the task is even contemplated:

> For each threatened language X that still has not been documented, a team of linguists and anthropologists might need to spend ten years collecting data and processing. After that work is done, if X stops being spoken, there will be a theoretical possibility of reviving it or creating an approximation to it.
> ('The Conservation of Endangered Languages', reporting on seminar at Bristol University Philosophy Department, 21 April 1995.
> http://www.bris.ac.uk/Depts/Philosophy/CTLL/article.html)

Ken Hale sees language revival, based on written, audio, video and electronic records, as being an increasingly common and feasible undertaking in the future, further underscoring the need for comprehensive documentation of endangered languages for the benefit of future generations affiliated to them (Endangered Languages discussion, Australian Linguistics Institute, July 1994). In 1996, Hale was quoted as saying that:

> The next 35 years of linguistics [will see] the restoration of a significant number of endangered languages to the communities in which they were once fully functional. Investigations of language acquisition have begun in a number of restoration programs. The human and intellectual importance of the movement is unquestionable, because without it as many as 95 percent of the world's existing languages will die out in the next two centuries.
> (Hale, 1996: 8)

I would argue that, given the right conditions and support systems, it is possible to regenerate languages from written records, even where these records are modest and incomplete.

What do we need as a basis for reviving a language?

For many writers, language revival assumes the existence of native speakers. They simply do not admit the possibility that a language no longer spoken might be revived. Even Fishman (1991: 12) who says that 'there is no language for which nothing at all can be done' seems not to include languages like Kaurna in his graded typology of threatened languages. The most advanced stage of social disruption is described as follows (Fishman, 1991: 88):

> Stage 8 on the GIDS (Graded Intergenerational Disruption Scale): most vestigial users of Xish are socially isolated old folks and Xish needs to be re-assembled from their mouths and memories and taught to demographically unconcentrated adults.

From his subsequent discussion, it is clear that Fishman has in mind situations where there are at least 'rememberers' or semi-speakers of the language.[8] For instance:

> 'Stage 8 contexts yield individuals who are well recognized as informants by folklorists and by linguists who are concerned with saving even the last few remnants of language-in-culture already in the most advanced stages of attrition'.
> (Fishman, 1991: 88)

In the Kaurna case, there are no vestigial users, semi-speakers or 'rememberers' of the language[9], though it could be argued that there are still some 'last few remnants of language-in-culture already in the most advanced stages of attrition'.

In my conceptualisation of language reclamation, it requires minimally a sketch grammar and a reasonable vocabulary, or at least records of a number of genetically related languages which can be used to generate a distinctive vocabulary according to the principles of comparative linguistics.

If all that is available are wordlists, as is the case with a great many languages no longer spoken, then if the goal is to revive the language as a spoken language, the alternatives are to graft the material available into English grammar, to graft it onto the grammar of another Indigenous language still spoken or better described, or to develop some kind of putative grammar of the protolanguage which is believed to have given rise to the language in question. A grammar has to be developed in much the same way as Esperanto grammar was formulated, or it must be borrowed from somewhere. Whilst I do not wish to belittle the grafting of vocabulary onto the grammar of another language, especially in circumstances where there is no other option, I will exclude these activities from my definition of language reclamation.

Apart from the specific literature on Hebrew and Cornish, the sociolinguistic and, more specifically, language revival literature makes little mention of attempts to reclaim (revive, resurrect or resuscitate) 'dead' languages. For many linguists, language revival implies the existence of native speakers. The 'dead' languages end of the spectrum is not considered. Even the term 'language resurrection' is used by some with the same assumption that native speakers still exist. For instance:

> Where language resurrection plans are feasible, it is necessary that some persons must be available who still know the language but who rarely, if ever, use it. In Pacific northwestern North America there are a number of older American Indians who know their respective native languages but who seldom have an opportunity to use them. A language resurrection plan is particularly feasible in this context.   (Eastman, 1979: 216)

Fishman (1991: 362-363) also discusses 'heritage languages', languages no longer in regular use but 'utilized for specific and delimited ethnicity-encumbered "special events"'. Fishman paints a pessimistic picture of such usage gradually shrinking and becoming less relevant:

> it will be little more than a relic of bygone days in societal terms because, like various other recondite subjects, it has no real functional validity outside the school which is entrusted with its instruction. Long-term prospects for intergenerational continuity under such circumstances are not good, precisely because of the extreme attrition of heritage languages vis-à-vis most aspects of home and neighbourhood functioning at the very same time that respect for the memory of such functioning in the past is their only claim to church (stage 6) or school (stages 5 or 4a) attention. As that memory fades with time, so, inevitably, does that attention.   (Fishman, 1991: 363)

The prospect of a 'heritage' language like Kaurna actually being introduced and gaining some of those institutionalised heritage functions in addition to some functions in the home and neighbourhood seems not to have been contemplated by Fishman. As we shall see in Chapter 8, Kaurna is not simply an historical relic, but is beginning to be used in limited ways to address here and now concerns in the 1990s.

Much of the earlier literature is dismissive of attempts at language revival per se. Edwards (1985: 86-87), whilst briefly considering Cornish and other cases of successful revival cited by Ellis and Mac A'Ghobhainn (1971), ends up supporting Nahir's (1977) view that 'all language revival efforts have failed, with the exception of that of Hebrew'. According to Edwards, Nahir lists Irish, Welsh, Provençal and Breton amongst his list of unsuccessful attempts at language revival. However, many contemporary observers are more positive towards language revival efforts, even towards Irish.

As might be expected, the literature is even more dismissive of attempts to revive languages which have ceased to be spoken. Some linguists (e.g. R.M.W. Dixon, 1989: 31, 1991; Cooper, 1989) have argued that it is not possible to 'resuscitate' languages in circumstances such as these. In a recent article, Spolsky (1995:178) says that:

> With all the problems involved in language maintenance, the most difficult is that concerned with control of the passing of a language from parents to children as a 'mother' tongue. This phenomenon, labelled formally as 'intimate' or 'informal intergenerational transmission', is clearly the central feature of maintenance. If the chain is once broken, to repair it takes not just a major effort but, if not a miracle, then the rare and largely fortuitous co-occurrence of language-and-nationality ideology, disciplined collective will and sufficient societal dislocation from other competing influences to make possible a relatively *rapid and clean break with prior norms of verbal interaction*.
>
> (Fishman, 1991: 291; italics in original)

Further, Spolsky (1995: 178) still accepts Cooper's view that the revival of a 'dead' language is impossible and goes on to quote Cooper (1989: 19-20):

> ... The term Hebrew revival is a misnomer. Hebrew is no exception to the rule that once a language has passed out of all use whatsoever, it remains dead. The 'revival' of Hebrew refers to its resuscitation as a vernacular, as a language of everyday spoken life.

Parallels between Hebrew and Kaurna are partial. The two situations are very different. The other case of revival of a 'dead' language frequently referred to in the literature is Cornish (see Ellis, 1974), which is considerably closer to the Kaurna situation. Still there are many differences. Closer parallels are found in North, Central or South America where the colonial experiences have been similar. Indeed, current attempts to revive some Californian languages (Hinton, 1994), and plans to revive languages such as Wampanoag (also known as Natick or Massachusett), Naragansett, Paugusett and Pequot on the east coast or Huron in Quebec, Canada (Abley, 1992; Sioui, 1996) have much more in common with the revival of Kaurna. There are also a range of attempts to revive Australian languages, some of which are in a similar position to Kaurna. See Amery (1998a: 92-103) for details.

What is being revived?

In cases where attempts are made to revive languages no longer in regular use, it is essential to ask the question 'What is it exactly that is being revived?' Is the 'revived' language the same language as the original language? Certainly the 'revival' metaphor implies that it is. Or is the 'revived' language essentially something new? These are both linguistic questions and socio-political questions, and there are no clear-cut answers. Language enthusiasts and Nungas are likely to stress continuities with the past, whilst linguists are likely to stress discontinuities and draw attention to change, as we saw in Wardhaugh's views towards Cornish (see p. 20).

Bentahila & Davies (1993) address this very question, claiming that whilst the 'revivalist dream' is 'restoration of the language to its former position', the reality is a process of 'transformation' with the promotion of the language into new domains of use. They argue that once the community realises that language revival is not simply a matter of 'turning back the clock ... there remain many possible avenues through which a declining language may nevertheless be carried on towards the future' (Bentahila & Davies, 1993: 371). Fettes (1997: 312), writing in regard to Indigenous languages in North America, warns that:

> reweaving of the language braid will not produce the old language, as the Elders remember it and speak it. If it is successful, a new language will arise, one with deep roots in its traditional heritage but equally reliant on the urge of its speakers to use the language for everyday purposes and in everyday contexts far removed from the traditional ones. This can be disappointing, even disillusioning, for those who see the old language as something sacred, a rock of stability in a sea of confusion. But the dilemma cannot be escaped. A commitment to primary discourse requires a willingness to accept and foster change.

We shall see, in Chapter 6, that in linguistic terms Modern Kaurna draws heavily, almost exclusively, on the original language in terms of its vocabulary and to a large extent in its grammar. Its phonology, semantic or conceptual structure and its discourse structure are necessarily less closely aligned, though efforts are made to draw to the maximum extent on remaining records and our knowledge of other Australian languages. Most norms of usage are yet to be established. At present, Kaurna is almost devoid of any form of unmonitored speech. All spoken Kaurna is in the form of interlanguage[10] used by learners of the language, most of whom are at an elementary stage of language proficiency.

Our task is to transform Kaurna from an historical relic, a cultural artefact (see pp. 44-46) in a very literal sense, into a dynamic 'living' entity that serves the symbolic and possible future communicative needs of the Kaurna community today. This entails restoring the functional links and support mechanisms that sustain the language. These matters will be taken up in Chapters 3 and 9 in some detail. As we shall see, Kaurna reclamation goes hand in hand with a struggle for recognition, self-determination and liberation. It is both a linguistic and a social process.

The Kaurna case study is pushing the boundaries of what is possible, feasible and acceptable in relation to the revival of languages no longer spoken. Perhaps the 'impossible dream' could even become reality. The 'miracle' might just take place. We have seen that whilst the attempted revival of Kaurna is unusual, it shares many attributes with a range of language planning activities, so-called 'artificial' languages and classical languages.

Natural vs. artificial languages

The charge that Kaurna is an 'invention' and a 'whitefella creation' must be addressed. Therefore, it is necessary to explore the 'natural' vs. 'artificial' dichotomy in more detail. Many writers see 'natural' vs. 'artificial' and 'dead' vs. 'live' as simple oppositions[11] — if a language is not a natural language, then it is artificial; a language is either dead or alive. However, I prefer to view these parameters as continua.

Most linguists regard 'invented spoken languages' such as Esperanto, and computer languages, such as Basic, as 'artificial' languages which contrast with 'natural' languages, for which the following criteria are generally invoked:

1) spontaneous creation
2) continuous tradition
3) existence of native speakers
4) existence of a speech community

Most weight is placed on the first criterion: that of spontaneous creation. However, this criterion makes many assumptions about the way in which languages come into being. Jouko Lindstedt[12] points out that there are problems with all four criteria and concludes that '"natural language" is a surprisingly ill-defined concept with unclear ideological background.'

Relevant to my purposes here is Larry Trask's response[13] to Lindstedt's discussion of 'natural languages'. Trask supplied the following definition and ensuing discussion which I quote at length because of the detail supplied and the clarity of the argument developed:

> A natural language is any language which is, or once was, the mother tongue of a group of people ...
> By this criterion, then, English, Swahili and Isthmus Zapotec are natural languages, because they are mother tongues today, and Latin, Etruscan and Cornish are natural languages, because they were mother tongues once.
> American Sign Language is a natural language for the same reason, ... So is Israeli Hebrew. I can see not the slightest difficulty here in reaching this last decision; what is problematic about Israeli Hebrew is the nature of its relation to Biblical Hebrew, but this question is neither here nor there in the present context. And, by my criterion, the Esperanto spoken by native speakers (if these exist) must also be a natural language. The non-native Esperanto of other people is a different matter, but then, when I declare that Spanish is a natural language, I certainly don't have in mind my own halting Spanish.
> On the other hand, pidgins, Volapuk, Glosa, the official written Turkish of the Ottoman Empire, and probably even the stilted and neologistic high Basque used by Basque television newsreaders, all fail to be natural languages by my definition ... but many of these things would certainly fall under Lindstedt's definition.
> I absolutely can't see that either the origin of a natural language or the length or continuity of its tradition is of any significance. Creoles, ASL, Israeli Hebrew, native

> Esperanto — all of these have what we might consider unusual origins, but so what? We might like to think that English is directly descended from an unbroken line of ancestors stretching back to the origins of human speech, but we don't know that this is true — for all we know, PIE [proto-IndoEuropean] itself might have descended from a very ancient creole. Once a natural language exists it is indistinguishable from any other natural language.

Just as plants can be grafted, organs transplanted, prostheses applied and artificial blood products, valves, joints etc. introduced into the body, languages, too, can be grafted and artificial elements can be introduced. New languages can be formed from the amalgamation of a number of different languages or they may be created through the deliberate actions of an individual, as in the case of so-called artificial languages like Esperanto, which now has a considerable body of speakers and an extensive literature. For Trask, the origins of a language are not important. Rather its current or former status and use decides whether a language should be designated as 'natural' or 'artificial'.

So, the distinction between natural and artificial languages is not as clear-cut as it may seem to be at first. All languages are cultural artefacts. They are the collective creation of their speakers. All languages have artificial elements in them. Words are continually being created consciously and introduced deliberately by individuals, be they language planners, writers, politicians or children. People, especially children, play with language, thereby introducing new elements. Even in traditionally-oriented Indigenous societies, whole languages appear to have been invented for special purposes. A good case in point is Damin, a speech style formerly used only by initiated Lardil men from Mornington Island in the Gulf of Carpentaria. Damin has an extremely aberrant phonology with several sounds found nowhere else in the world leading the phonetician Catford to 'perhaps hypothesize that [Damin's] sound system is a deliberately invented one' (Dixon, 1980: 67). While some languages, such as English, more readily adopt foreign elements than others, such as Mandarin, all languages are profoundly influenced by languages with which they come into contact.

Esperanto
Esperanto is a 'planned' language[14] invented last century to serve as a world-wide auxiliary language. It does not seek to replace ethnic and national languages currently spoken (Harry, 1992: 25). Rather, it is seen as a second, additional language available to all people for the purpose of cross-cultural communication. According to literature produced by the Esperanto Association, it is now spoken by 10 million people and is studied in over 100 universities.

Esperanto is not the first, or the last, attempt to invent and propagate a language, but it is the best known and most successful of such endeavours. Other attempts include Volapük, Ido, Occidental, Interlingua and Latino Sine Flexione (Golden, 1987: 362). Dulicenko (1989: 51) lists 917 language projects of universal and international languages between the second and twentieth centuries, with interest peaking in the early part of the twentieth century.

However, few ever attain a 'sociolinguistic status', as Dulicenko (1989: 58) puts it.[15]

Esperanto was devised in 1887 by Dr L.L. Zamenhof. In its original formulation, it consisted of a two-page grammar which included 16 rules and 900 roots from which numerous words could be derived through regular processes.[16] One hundred years later, the grammar had grown to some 600 pages of discussion in the *Complete Analytical Grammar of Esperanto*, whilst the number of roots had multiplied to 16,000 published in the *Complete Illustrated Dictionary of Esperanto*, 1970. Since its original inception as a rarefied linguistic system, Esperanto has developed as a sociolinguistic system. Of late, 'normal' processes of language change have taken over with the lexicon expanding rapidly as Esperantists write and communicate. Dulichenko (1988: 149) claims that:

> Esperanto has shown, for example, that the principle of 'one word, one meaning' ... is entirely unrealizable, because the active 'living' function of a language requires polysemy, the development of synonyms, heterogeneous means of expressing antonymous relations and so on.

In addition to its use as an international auxiliary language, Esperanto is growing as a home language and as a first language. There are now some 350 families in which 'Esperanto is spoken between at least two members as the chief language for every kind of communication' (Corsetti, 1996: 265). There are a small number of children who grow up speaking Esperanto as a first language alongside of their own ethnic or national language.[17] Such users speak of a 'dual identity' and of being 'bicultural'.[18]

Although the Esperanto movement claims to be independent of any language, religion, culture or ethnic affiliation, the language draws heavily on European languages for its vocabulary. Zamenhof relied on languages that he knew best. These included Latin, French, English, German, Polish, Russian, Yiddish and Volapük. The Slavic languages had a strong formative influence on the grammar of Esperanto, but are less important as sources of vocabulary. Because of its origins and the location of most of its users, Esperanto has a strong European bias. Indeed, one linguist (Janton, 1977), described it as essentially a modernisation of Latin (in Tonkin, 1987: 266).

In contrast to Esperanto, which seems to borrow lexemes freely, Kaurna people have been very reluctant to borrow. The early Kaurna sources document many new derivations but few borrowings for new concepts.[19] Modern Kaurna has resumed this practice.

<u>Is Kaurna an 'artificial' language?</u>
Certainly Kaurna that is being taught at KPS, Inbarendi College and elsewhere in the 1990s is not identical to what was spoken on the Adelaide Plains in the 1830s and 1840s. It does, however, strive to maintain the integrity of the language as it existed back then, and be as true as possible to it. But everybody involved understands that most of the time our utterances are a 'best guess' based on what we know of the Kaurna language in particular and Australian

languages in general. Kaurna, as being learnt in the 1990s, certainly has incorporated some 'artificial' elements and perhaps does have an 'artificial' flavour to it. Dulicenko (1989: 59-60) assembles a list of six prerequisites for the successful functioning of any ethnic language which are not shared by planned languages at the initial stage. Like planned languages, Kaurna lacks at least four, if not five of these six prerequisites. So according to Dulicenko's criteria, Kaurna currently has much more in common with 'planned' or 'artificial' languages like Esperanto than it does with ethnic languages.

But it would be unfair to describe Kaurna in the 1990s as an 'artificial' language. In sociological terms Kaurna is far-removed from those entities commonly referred to as 'artificial languages'. Esperanto and Kaurna are at opposite ends of the spectrum. Esperanto seeks to be a universal language that belongs to no-one. Kaurna is a small language which is closely tied to an ethnic group. Its main reason for being is as an expression of ethnicity and identity and as a vehicle for a specific localised heritage. Esperanto facilitates communication across speakers of many different languages. Yet communication, in the narrow sense of the word, is a very minor, almost non-existent purpose for which Kaurna is being used. Ideologically, they are indeed poles apart.

However, in functional terms, both Esperanto and Kaurna are auxiliary languages[20], used for a specific set of more limited purposes in addition to another language. The purposes for which the two languages are used are different of course.

There are many similarities, too, in terms of the ways in which the two languages are being created and developed and the ways in which they are introduced and taught. Planned languages, in functional terms, appear first in aesthetic domains (Dulicenko, 1989: 59) because, according to Dulicenko, emotional expressiveness is more essential than transmission of information and because creativity is essentially an individual act. As we shall see, the use of Kaurna, too, is more frequent in aesthetic domains.

The characterisation of languages as 'natural', 'artificial', 'dead' or 'extinct' is not particularly helpful. Whilst for certain purposes linguists may choose (with good reasons) to study so-called 'living' or 'natural' languages, the summary dismissal or denigration of so-called 'dead', 'extinct' or 'artificial' languages denies a social and political reality. They are the products of legitimate social movements as people strive to re-assert their identities and rebuild their cultures, or to foster a sense of 'internationalism' as the case may be. What is often overlooked is the fact that every standard language, including English, has many artificial elements. As written languages, rarefied by a set of prescriptive rules, many are spoken by no-one. Yet they escape the stigma of artificiality.

Let us now look in more detail at the language reclamation process.

Language reclamation: the method

The language reclamation approach uses language materials, primarily in the form of a grammar, vocabularies and texts obtained from a variety of historical sources, as the basis of a spoken language taught and learnt in the contemporary context. Historical sources are analysed according to the principles of philology and comparative linguistics. Each source is analysed for internal consistency, compared with other sources and with neighbouring related languages. A knowledge of the typology of the language family or subgroup provides further direction for making sense of incomplete historical records.

In this section I am attempting to sketch out some general principles to follow in applying the language reclamation method, but this is exceedingly difficult because circumstances will vary enormously from one language to another, depending on the nature and extent of records remaining. In the Kaurna case there are no sound recordings, but conceivably in other situations there may be reels of archival film, wax cylinder recordings, reel to reel tapes or even more modern tape or digital sound recordings. Attempting to revive a language which has been spoken until recently is a vastly different enterprise from attempts based solely on mission records from centuries past.

In the Kaurna case, historical/comparative linguistics and language typology facilitate the construction of a modern language of a distinctly Australian type, which still adheres closely to the original sources. The nineteenth-century sources remain the ultimate authority at this time.

The language reclamation approach is not an armchair or ivory tower approach to language revival. It makes no sense to artificially construct and develop the language divorced from its social context. Understandings of the language, which has lain dormant in historical records, evolve slowly and are tempered by the contemporary culture of its owners or custodians. Knowledge of the language develops through use within particular social contexts. Teachers of Kaurna continually return to the sources to ensure maximal integrity of the newly constructed spoken language.

Various strategies are pursued to fill in the gaps in the historical sources. Some words are borrowed from closely related languages, whilst many others are rendered as compounds or derivations. A number of new terms for new concepts are developed from time to time as required. Almost all of these neologisms are constructed using the productive word-forming processes inherent in the language.

Finally, the construction of this new spoken Kaurna is tempered by perceptions and attitudes held by the Kaurna community, owners and custodians of the language. Certain words are avoided out of respect for linguistic taboo. A word might sound similar to a known rude word within Nunga English and is thus avoided. See Haas (1951) for a discussion of this phenomenon. Other words are considered sacred or too precious to warrant their use for everyday purposes in a compound or with an extended meaning.

Assembling the language sources

Language reclamation as a linguistic process begins with identifying and locating sources on the language. It is probably wise to begin by assessing what is still known within the community and identifying those with most knowledge of the language and culture and those having a strong interest in the language itself.

Little data may be remembered at first, and more may only emerge days or weeks later after much thought and reflection. Various methods may be used to trigger memories. Photos, archival materials, visits to places of significance and talking about old times may be useful. It is often fruitful to bring several people together, as they may stimulate each others' memories. In the Kaurna case, after a decade of working with historical materials in the absence of anything much remembered in the community, some individuals have emerged who appear to have had some knowledge told to them when they were young, though they did not recognise its significance at the time.

Hypnosis, meditation and trance (whether induced by ritual and ceremony or mind-altering substances) may offer means of bringing to the surface memories and language long forgotten and buried deep in the subconscious. However, I have no experience or expertise whatsoever in the use of these methods, so I leave this as a possibility for others to consider.

Archival research

In some cases, material lodged in archives may constitute the main sources on the language. This material may have already been examined by historians or other researchers who may not recognise the significance of language material embedded in the records. A linguist will view these documents from another perspective. Other researchers can often provide hints and clues about where best to look. Sharing of information between disciplines works in everyone's favour. Archival research is a time-consuming and often hit or miss affair. It is difficult, if not impossible, to predict in advance what archival research might yield.

Many early records compiled by missionaries, explorers and adventurers were recorded in languages other than English. Materials relating to Australian languages have been written in German, French, Spanish and Italian. A knowledge of German in particular in the Australian context is a distinct advantage. We cannot afford to bypass or overlook records, simply because they were written in other languages.

The study of Kaurna sources is based on archival research retrieving published and manuscript materials on the Kaurna language itself and neighbouring languages, as well as other sources which provide insights into the language ecology at the time the Kaurna language was recorded and still spoken on a daily basis. In the pursuit of an understanding of this language ecology, a variety of sources have been drawn upon, including government records, mission records, personal memoirs and journals, newspapers and various historical and anthropological works relating to this early period in South Australia.

I made searches for Kaurna materials primarily in the Mortlock Library of South Australiana, the Lutheran Archives, South Australian Museum and the Public Records Office. Some sources were located further afield. Once I had a good idea of the kinds of Kaurna language materials that the German missionaries had created or recorded I made a list of these items and placed a small notice in the *Friends of Lutheran Archives Newsletter*. Some months later, the archivist notified me that he had located some of these materials. I sought the assistance of researchers and librarians in Germany, the United Kingdom, New Zealand and South Africa to help track down materials, with some positive results. Various lines of enquiry were pursued, searching under the names of individuals known to have been associated with the Kaurna or the Office of the 'Protector' of Aborigines, or to have pursued an interest in Aboriginal culture in the early years of the South Australian colony. Leads were followed from one source to the next. Other sources were hit upon more or less by accident. Some were so obscure that methodical archival research would have been of no use in locating them. Details of the Kaurna materials recovered appear in Chapter 5.

Philology and comparative/historical linguistics

Philology is a dominant methodology underpinning language reclamation. Goddard (1973:727) explicates the discipline as:

> ... subject[ing] records to examination and interpretation in order to gain information about the languages in which these records are cast. It is written records that are the principal objects of study, but sound recordings are becoming increasingly important in philological investigations.

The discipline of comparative philology boomed in the nineteenth century as links between distantly related languages were discovered and pursued. With the advent of modern linguistics and the use of the International Phonetic Alphabet (henceforth IPA), field linguistics largely replaced philology. Philology was abandoned and even disparaged by some linguists as it was felt to be inexact and unscientific in the light of modern linguistic techniques. Goddard (1973:728) cites Michelson, writing in 1912:

> It is simply a waste of time to attempt to unravel the vagaries of the orthography of the older writers in the case of dialects existing today.

In the early part of this century, linguistics, as a scientific discipline, was generally seen to have replaced philology. Linguists focused primarily on oral language gathered first hand and transcribed onto paper. The first linguistic analyses were severely hampered by the limits of human memory and thus focused on word lists in citation form and on short sentences. The invention of sound recording equipment enabled many of these early limitations to be overcome. With the advent of linguistics, less notice was taken of earlier written records, and languages which ceased to be spoken were written off as 'dead' or 'extinct' and ignored or perhaps only examined for the purposes of comparative linguistics. However, in the last few decades there has been a revival of interest in philology on the part of linguists, discussed by Koerner (1997).

Now, comparative philology is precisely the methodology required to make sense of historical texts, the prime — almost sole — source of information on the Kaurna language. Goddard (1973) and Haas (1975) signalled the return of philological procedures in the study of North American languages as linguists began to take more notice of historical materials. Many linguists in Australia, too, are drawing increasingly upon historical texts in the production of dictionaries and grammatical sketches of Australian languages. Note Troy's (1994b) description of the Sydney language; Blake's (1991) description of Woiwurrung, the Indigenous language of Melbourne; Crowley & Dixon's (1981) sketch of Tasmanian and the dictionary of Nyungar compiled from historical sources (Bindon & Chadwick, 1992), and so on. Earlier linguistic work on Australian languages tended to draw exclusively on information recorded first-hand, ignoring historical work. Austin's (1981) grammar of Diyari is a good case in point: it was written on the basis of limited knowledge possessed by a number of second-language speakers, and largely ignored voluminous historical materials compiled by German missionaries in the last century. These German mission materials for Diyari are currently under scrutiny by Cynthia Rathjen and Heidi Kneebone in Peter Mühlhäusler's mission linguistics project, and by Chris Nobbs of the South Australian Museum.

Philological procedures provide the tools to assess and interpret historical materials. This is the preliminary work which must be done prior to the application of the techniques afforded by comparative and historical linguistics. An overriding concern is to clarify the orthography and phonetic details of the materials. In some cases, the author has provided a key to the orthography. Most Kaurna sources, however, provide no indication as to how the words should be pronounced.

Crystal's (1994: 297) definition of philology in the *Dictionary of Language and Languages* explains the relationship between philology and linguistics:

> philology Traditionally, the study of language history, sometimes including the historical study of literary texts; also called comparative philology when the emphasis is on the comparison of the historical states of different languages. The subject overlaps substantially with historical linguistics, but there are several differences of emphasis, both in training and subject matter. The philological tradition is one of painstaking textual analysis, often related to literary history, and using a fairly traditional descriptive framework. The newer linguistic approach tends to study historical data more selectively, as part of the discussion of broader issues in linguistic theory, such as the nature of language change.

Philological procedures include an examination of the written sources for internal consistency. Working with the source alone, the philologist notes whether spellings are consistent and, if not, notes the variants, attempting to identify and rectify typographical errors as distinct from true variants.

Comparative/historical linguistics is closely allied to philology, but provides more powerful techniques. Related languages are systematically compared to identify shared inheritances, as distinct from borrowings or chance similarity. Of particular importance is the identification of regular sound correspondences between related languages. Historical linguistics is closely allied to comparative linguistics and involves the reconstruction of an earlier stage of a language based on evidence drawn from its 'daughter' languages — languages which are believed to have all descended from an earlier proto-language. The comparative method is explained in detail in numerous textbooks on comparative/historical linguistics. See, for instance, Jeffers & Lehiste (1979), Bynon (1977) and Hoenigswald (1960).

The methods afforded by comparative/historical linguistics provide insights into aspects of the Kaurna language as it was recorded. Further, these methods allow some of the gaps in the language to be filled in sound and well-motivated ways, drawing on the available evidence from the Kaurna sources themselves and those of neighbouring languages. Where a lexical gap exists, for instance, in some cases a proto form can be reconstructed for the Yura subgroup of languages to which Kaurna belongs, and the expected reflex of this proto-form in Kaurna can be reconstructed. This reconstructed Kaurna reflex may or may not have actually existed in the Kaurna language. It may well have been part of the repertoire of speakers in the 1830s and 1840s, but for one reason or another observers simply failed to record it. Of course it is quite possible that Kaurna had an entirely different word for the particular concept when compared with neighbouring languages, there is simply no way of knowing.

Comparative/historical linguistics has only limited applications in the Kaurna context due to limited records of neighbouring closely related languages. The inland territories associated with Adnyamathanha and more distant Pitjantjatjara, which are still spoken, are vastly different from the Adelaide Plains, so that much of the fauna and flora found in Kaurna country does not have counterparts in those languages. However, in other situations, the comparative method may assist greatly to help fill in gaps in the historical records. Comparative/historical linguistics has most to offer in situations where related languages have been better documented than the language under study and where identifiable sound changes have occurred in the target language. Words may then be generated, which have their own distinctive identity, in keeping with the sound patterns of the language — words which may well have actually occurred despite the absence of records.

Language typology and language universals

Language typology refers to features shared by a subset of languages which may or may not be related. Language universals, on the other hand, refer to properties shared by all languages; see Comrie (1981) and Shopen (1985). An understanding of the broad typological features of other Australian languages, particularly those most closely related to Kaurna, aids in the interpretation of the historical materials and in the construction of the Kaurna language as it is used in the 1990s. A knowledge of typological features is especially useful in the interpretation and reconstruction of Kaurna grammar and syntax. Dixon (1976), Dixon (1980) and Blake (1987) are especially useful sources on the typology of Australian languages. Grammatical descriptions of individual Australian languages also prove to be useful points of reference.

Language universals come into play in situations of uncertainty. It makes sense to develop a language which behaves like other languages rather than develop highly unusual or aberrant features not actually found in the world's languages.

The modern construction of the Kaurna language is somewhat similar to the reassembly of dinosaurs on the basis of remnant and often incomplete fossilised bones. The dinosaur itself is reconstructed on the basis of the bones and other clues left in the rocks, using a knowledge of anatomy and physiology. The reconstructed dinosaur is the animal that best fits all the known data. The modern 'living' dinosaurs that appear in movies such as *Jurassic Park* or series like *Walking with Dinosaurs* are undoubtedly wrong in some details. Indeed, in the past many dinosaurs were reconstructed as quadrupeds that stood on all four limbs. Recently this has been revised and some of these same dinosaurs are now believed to have been bipeds and more like birds in stature. In the same way, the modern construction of a language which is being pieced together from written records will necessarily be different in some details from its predecessor. Various assumptions made about aspects of its grammar will need to be rethought as new evidence comes to light or as additional information is taken into account.

Language modernisation

Minority Indigenous languages spoken throughout the world are adapting to changed circumstances as they are forced to accommodate a dominant majority culture. As a result, they are being used in a range of new domains, notably in education, health and government. But even life in the home has undergone a radical transformation with the introduction of new foods, utensils, clothes, living arrangements and values. Languages still spoken have had some time to adapt and change in response to these new circumstances, often by borrowing new words and associated concepts, though sometimes relying on their own resources.

In the context of language reclamation, however, where the language has lain dormant for an extended period of time, the need for vocabulary to talk about common everyday objects and notions that people wish to express is heightened. This was a major issue in the revival of Hebrew, despite a vast body of literature, a vocabulary of 20,000 words catalogued by Ben Yehuda and comprehensive grammars. Furthermore, Hebrew had served as the language of science, medicine, philosophy and poetry in Europe in the Middle Ages.

Despite this, Hebrew changed little over a period of 1700 years. Fellman draws attention to the difficulties faced by Ben Yehuda. Vocabulary for even the most common household objects and foodstuffs was absent:

> At the time, Hebrew lacked precisely those vital terms necessary for the performance of daily household tasks. Devora [Ben Yehuda's wife] did not speak Hebrew and even Ben Yehuda himself was unable to express himself fluently and with ease. . . when Ben Yehuda wanted Devora to pour him a cup of coffee with sugar, he was at a loss to communicate words such as 'cup', 'saucer', 'pour', 'spoon', and so on, and would say to his wife, in effect: 'Take such and such, and do like so, and bring me this and this, and I will drink.'
> (Fellman, 1973: 37-38)

The Hebrew literature, apparently, lacked vocabulary for natural species as Josef Klausner and Meir Medan note:

> In all of the ... writers of the period, there is no flower but the rose and the lily, no bird but the dove, nightingale, cuckoo, rooster and chicken. There is no individual delineation ... of colours, there is only red, black, green and blue.

(Klausner quoted in Fellman, 1973: 62)

> There was a wealth of words for all matters pertaining to religion, to emotion and to abstract thought, but none for some of the most elementary accessories of modern living: newspaper, dictionary, street pavement, railway, train, airplane, screw-driver, corkscrew, and the like. Numerous animals and plants had no Hebrew names, while certain nouns pertaining to the animal and vegetable kingdoms — and there were many of these — were used with a confusing lack of discrimination. A common term ... , when a difficulty of this kind was encountered in writing, was a 'kind of bird', 'a kind of vegetable', 'a kind of fowl'. Needless to say, terms for the machines, appliances and forms of organization of the new age were completely wanting.

(Medan quoted in Fellman, 1973: 62-63)

Kaurna language reclamation can be informed by the methods used by Hebrew revivalists to modernise the language. It is wise to take particular note of unsuccessful practices. Some of the earliest new terms introduced were long, cumbersome and unwieldy periphrastic constructions. Hebrew now enjoys considerable official support and is boosted by concerted language planning efforts (see Fellman, 1976; Rabin 1976). There is an extensive literature, much of it written in Hebrew, on efforts to modernise Hebrew (see, for instance, Alloni-Fainberg, 1974; Fellman, 1973; Saulson, 1979 and Kutscher, 1982).

Maori serves as another particularly good case from which we can draw inspiration for the development of new terms. In 1996 Te Taura Whiri i te Reo Maori, the Maori Language Commission, produced a dictionary *Te Matatiki Contemporary Maori Words*, which includes over 2000 previously unpublished terms, some of which do not appear in any general dictionary of Maori. It includes numerous terms in the field of mathematics and computers, which have been developed by a team of Maori mathematicians. It also includes the Maori names of government agencies, days of the week, months of the year and international place names, most of which are borrowings assimilated into the Maori sound system. In addition, a Maori man, Peter Keegan, maintains a website of new and technical terms in Maori.[21] The Maori have taken a highly puristic approach. They resist borrowing from English, preferring to draw on Maori words and constructions for the development of new terms. See Harlow (1993) for details.

Kaurna, like other Aboriginal languages, was unwritten prior to the coming of Europeans. Ironically, until recently, the Kaurna language has existed almost entirely in written form. Much of this record was written in the first few years of contact with the colonists.

The world has changed considerably since the 1840s. If the Kaurna language is to be used to address everyday needs in the 1990s, there is a need for modernisation of the language, specifically for the development of terms for modern technology and everyday items which did not exist last century. There are various means for accomplishing this, discussed in Amery (1993).

Other Australian languages provide useful examples which serve as models for Kaurna terminology. Similarly, approaches taken by language planners and language revivalists in similar circumstances are also insightful. Hebrew, Maori, Cornish and some North American languages have proved useful in this regard.

The reclamation of Kaurna will be analysed in more depth in Chapter 6, in an attempt to demonstrate the application of the method. Whilst the circumstances of another language will be quite different, many of the principles and methods applied to Kaurna will be able to be replicated.

This chapter has dealt primarily with the corpus planning aspects of language reclamation — the methods we use to identify, shape, fill out and give voice to the substance of the language on the basis of historical records. The next chapter engages primarily with issues of status planning by which we establish a place for the reclaimed language within contemporary society.

Notes

[1] Ihimaera (1993) as editor of a volume of Maori writings includes 'Reclaiming the Reo [language]' as a section heading, in reference to a language still having native speakers.

[2] Navajo is a North American language with hundreds of thousands of speakers, though many younger generation Navajo do not speak the language. A number of bilingual and immersion programs operate in Navajo. Thus amongst Indigenous languages, Navajo and Kaurna are at opposite ends of the spectrum.

[3] Van Heerden's use of 'reclaiming' a language refers to a very different entity, though the underlying politics bear some similarity.

[4] Also discussed in an unidentified newspaper article titled 'Latin lovers flock to Finland'.

[5] An auxiliary language is one used in addition to one's first language to facilitate communication within restricted domains. Esperanto, pidgins, Latin within the Catholic church and English at international conferences are often regarded as auxiliary languages.

[6] Some Nungas claim that the Kaurna language has survived, and most stress continuities with the past. For instance, Katrina Power, Chair of Tandanya, in a radio interview with 5UV on 23 April 1997 said 'It's [Kaurna language] still alive and well ... it's developing and it's strong and it's growing stronger every day,' and further in response to a proposition that the language used today is quite different to what it used to be she said 'I don't know that that's entirely correct. It does remain strong and fairly intact ... The base for it is very much there and very much strong.'

[7] Even in the biological world 'death' is an ill-defined notion with advances in medical technology, life-support systems, suspended animation and cryonics. There is the hope of being able to restore life into dead bodies at some time in the future.

[8] Earlier Fishman (1991: 13) notes that: 'Some Amerindian languages are already in such disarray, and have been neglected for such a length of time, that it is necessary to piece their grammars and vocabularies together first, from various oral and written sources, before any efforts on behalf of active spoken use, by either adults of children, can be undertaken'. Whilst this statement is compatible with the Kaurna situation, his later discussion indicates that he has not thought through these issues in terms of languages like Kaurna.

[9] To place Kaurna at Fishman's Stage 8, one would have to go back in time to the 1920s or earlier, prior to Ivaritji's death.

[10] I use the term 'interlanguage' in relation to learners' attempts to speak Kaurna, though I realise that the situation is quite different from that of, say, second-language learners of English.

[11] Sasse (1992: 21) has extended the 'natural' vs. 'artificial' distinction into language revival and makes a sharp distinction between 'natural revitalization' and 'artificial revitalization'.

[12] E-mail from Jouko Lindstedt to LINGUIST List, 23 September 1996.

[13] E-mail from Larry Trask to LINGUIST List, 1 October 1996.

[14] Esperanto is often referred to as an 'artificial' language, though Esperantists prefer to use the term 'planned' language (see Blanke, 1987, 1989).

[15] As Dulicenko observes, planned languages, consisting of an idiolect used only by the inventor, are unfunctional in their project stage.

[16] Esperantists take pride in the fact that it is an easy language to learn because the morphology is transparent and there is no allomorphy. Any word stems may be combined and given any grammatical function. Any combination is permitted provided that it makes sense.

[17] In this respect they are similar to children growing up as Cornish-English bilinguals who exist as more or less isolated first language-speaking individuals in a dominant English-speaking environment.

[18] Jouko Lindstedt, e-mail communication, 1996. See also Fettes (1996).

[19] However, this may not reflect the actual situation, as borrowings may have been deliberately purged from materials compiled (see Chapter 6, p. 141).

[20] Many Nungas would view the relegation of Kaurna to the status of auxiliary language as being too restrictive and short-sighted. Many Kaurna people would like very much to see the revival of Kaurna as a full language used for everyday purposes, spoken in the home and the community. They point to the changes in attitudes and behaviour in the past decade. Some have a vision for the future which includes Kaurna as a spoken language.

[21] http://www.nzcer.org.nz/kimikupu

3
An Ecological Approach to Language Revival

> *With all the problems involved in language maintenance, the most difficult is that concerned with the control of the passing of a language from parents to children as a 'mother' tongue ... If the chain is once broken, to repair it takes not just a major effort but ... a miracle.*
>
> (Spolsky, 1995: 178)

To this point we have looked at language in isolation. However, language revival is fundamentally a social process. Our main task in reviving a language 'no longer spoken' is to reunite the language with its community. An ecological approach lends itself to addressing this task.

Almost all writers view the attainment of 'intergenerational transmission' as the main, if not sole criterion for success of language revival efforts.[1] I would argue that more modest goals, such as reintroducing formulaic expressions, public speeches, signage and so on, are important steps along the way. Even if intergenerational transmission is never achieved, programs might be judged highly successful and the progress made might be highly meaningful within the context of the language community. Whilst some like Fishman (1991: 397, 408) might devalue or condemn these lesser goals for diverting attention away from the 'main game', in the case of languages 'no longer spoken' they could be viewed as remarkable achievements in their own right.

In fact, the lesser goals are the 'main game' for a language like Kaurna, at least at this stage. The establishment of formal language programs in schools, using the language in cultural tourism etc. are achievable goals. The reestablishment of 'intergenerational transmission' is desired, but everyone realises that this is a more distant, less achievable goal. There are many hurdles to be overcome first, including the need to develop the language to a point whereby it can function in these contexts. Nor would people feel defeated if this ultimate goal were never realised.

Language ecology

The notion of language ecology, a useful and insightful metaphor, is a major theoretical construct underpinning the approach taken to reviving Kaurna. It not only aids in our understanding of the language as it was spoken in the nineteenth century, but also underpins the task of language reclamation in the 1990s. In order to attempt to maintain or revive a language, an understanding of the wider context in which the language exists is helpful. It is simply not enough to know all there is to know about the language per se.

Haugen (1972: 325) coined the term **ecology of language** in a paper first presented in 1970. He defined it simply 'as the study of interactions between any given language and its environment' and defines the environment of a language in the following way:

> The true environment of a language is the society that uses it as one of its codes. Language exists only in the minds of its users, and it only functions in relating these users to one another and to nature, i.e. their social and natural environment. Part of its ecology is therefore psychological: its interaction with other languages in the minds of bi- and multilingual speakers. Another part of its ecology is sociological: its interaction with the society in which it functions as a medium of communication. The ecology of a language is determined primarily by the people who learn it, use it, and transmit it to others.
> (Haugen, 1972: 325)

The language reclamation process brings the language into existence in Haugen's terms, transforming it from purely a written record, a material cultural artefact, into a living, dynamic entity in the minds of people. As Haugen aptly points out, the very nature of the language will be shaped by the learners, and, in the case of Kaurna, by linguists working with them to reclaim and reassemble the language. It is worth distinguishing between the psychological and sociological dimensions as Haugen does. The ecological approach, then, unlike 'orthodox' linguistics (see, for instance, Hudson, 1981), focuses on human agency in shaping the language. Haugen further illuminates his concept of 'language ecology' through a series of pertinent questions:

> For any given 'language', then, we should want to have answers to the following ecological questions:
> 1) What is its classification in relation to other languages? This answer would be given by historical and descriptive linguists.
> 2) Who are its users? This is a question of linguistic demography, locating its users with respect to locale, class, religion or any other relevant grouping;
> 3) What are its domains of use? This is a question of sociolinguistics, discovering whether its use is unrestricted or limited in specific ways;
> 4) What concurrent languages are employed by its users? We may call this a problem of dialinguistics, to identify the degree of bilingualism present and the degree of overlap among the languages;
> 5) What internal varieties does the language show? This is the task of a dialectology that will recognize not only regional, but also social and contactual dialects;
> 6) What is the nature of its written traditions? This is the province of philology, the study of written texts and their relationship to speech;
> 7) To what degree has its written form been standardized, i.e. unified and codified? This is the province of prescriptive linguistics, the traditional grammarians and lexicographers;
> 8) What kind of institutional support has it won, either in government, education, or private organizations, either to regulate its form or propogate it? We may call this study glottopolitics;
> 9) What are the attitudes of its users towards the language, in terms of intimacy and status, leading to personal identification? We may call this the field of ethnolinguistics;

10) Finally we may wish to sum up its status in a typology of ecological classification, which will tell us something about where the language stands and where it is going in comparison with the other languages of the world. (Haugen, 1972: 336-337)

These questions are all pertinent in relation to the Kaurna language, both in terms of its status in the nineteenth century, and its incipient revival in the 1990s. We have addressed some of these questions which deal with the corpus of the language already in Chapter 2. Others are more relevant to this chapter, especially 2, 3, 4, 8 and 9. For Kaurna, questions of identity are paramount, thus question 9 takes on heightened importance.

Moreover, Haugen's questions stimulate consideration of a number of more specific issues in relation to the particular ecology of the Kaurna language. Especially important to consider in the nineteenth-century ecology is the disruption brought about by disease, environmental degradation, population movements, desecration of sacred sites and the undermining of Kaurna social institutions and political structures. In addition, the ecology was shaped by the policies of the colonial administration and the efforts of the German missionaries.

In the 1990s, important elements of Kaurna language ecology include historical documents, neighbouring and related languages, government and education policies, the Kaurna language teaching programs, KACHA, the nature of Kaurna society (especially demography and residence patterns), attitudes to the language within the Kaurna community and within the wider community, public and private domains of language use, the World Indigenous Peoples Movement and the reassertion of Kaurna rights, current events such as the Native Title debate, Nunga politics, KPS, Tauondi and the role of key individuals. These are just a few facets of contemporary Kaurna language ecology.[2]

In the linguistic ecology of a 'dormant' language we need to think more in terms of 'potential users' of the language and in terms of persons connected to the language. In Haugen's formulation there is no specific question about territory, but this is fundamental to Kaurna language ecology. As Harré et al. (1999: 164) point out, Haugen's questions are concerned with interrelationships and largely ignore the nature of the habitat or environment needed for languages to survive. A more specific set of additional questions we need to ask in this context might read:

- What is the territory associated with the Target Language (henceforth TL)?
- Who are the owners or custodians of the TL?
- What is known of the neighbouring Indigenous languages and how are they related to the TL?
- What Indigenous placenames survive? What can they tell us about the TL?
- How can the TL be used as a key for understanding the environment, geography and early contact history associated with territory of the TL?
- How can a knowledge of the TL aid in developing understandings of its associated culture, religion, ceremonial practices and Dreamings?
- How can ancient knowledges be transformed so as to have relevance in the present time?

- How do we ensure authenticity, integrity and acceptance of the TL by members of the TL community?
- Who are the potential users of the TL?
- For what purposes will the TL be used? By whom?
How can networks be set up between learners and users of the TL?
- What is the relationship between the TL and the dominant language?
- What is the relationship between the TL and the social dialect (e.g. Nunga English) spoken by the owners or custodians?
- How can ownership and control of the TL be reasserted by its owners or custodians?
- How can we ensure access to the TL by all members of the TL community?
- What role can outsiders play in support of language reclamation efforts?

Whilst some of Haugen's concerns have been addressed by sociolinguists, it is only recently that his ecological model has been taken up in a concerted and systematic fashion. The emergence of ecological linguistics as a field of study has been promoted primarily by Peter Mühlhäusler in a series of papers (Mühlhäusler, 1992, 1994) culminating in the publication of the book *Linguistic Ecology* (Mühlhäusler, 1996a).

Both Haugen and Mühlhäusler indicate the proactive nature of an ecological approach to language. Rather than simply being objective observers of languages, linguists are encouraged to become actively involved:

> One may even venture to suggest that ecology is not just the name of a descriptive science, but in its application has become the banner of a movement for environmental sanitation. The term could include also in its application to language some interest in the general concern among laymen over the cultivation and preservation of language. Ecology suggests a dynamic rather than a static science, something beyond the descriptive that one might call predictive and even therapeutic. What will be, or should be, for example, the role of 'small' languages; and how can they or any other language be made 'better', 'richer', and more 'fruitful' for mankind? (Haugen, 1972: 329)

Mühlhäusler (1996a: 2) takes this one step further:

> The ecological metaphor in my view is action oriented. It shifts the attention from linguists being players of academic language games to becoming shop stewards[3] for linguistic diversity, and to addressing moral, economic and other 'non-linguistic' issues.

However, while the role of the linguist in language reclamation is a vital and legitimate one, as Crawford (1996: 64) warns, 'language shift cannot be reversed by outsiders, however well-meaning. ... If language preservation efforts are to succeed, they must be led by indigenous institutions, organizations, and activists'. This theme will be taken up in more detail later in the book.

A linguist, Mark Fettes (1997; forthcoming) in his work with Indigenous peoples in Canada, has attempted to apply an ecological approach to language revival. Fettes talks of 'reweaving the 'triple braid' of language renewal', where three strands, 'critical literacy', 'local knowledges' and 'living relationships' are developed concurrently. Language revival involves reshaping the language ecology through a process of consciousness-raising and rebuilding relationships. The process advocated by Fettes begins with people. The language itself is a secondary concern. Although Fettes has in mind languages like Inuktitut, Mohawk or Maori, which are still spoken, many of the points he raises resonate well with my own experiences of working with Kaurna and other Indigenous languages of South Australia.

An ecological approach to language planning seeks long-term sustainable solutions. In the Kaurna case, this means rebuilding the support systems for the language and carving out niches[4] in which the language performs useful functions and fulfills needs in the lives of those who care to learn it. It means creating situations and establishing networks within which the language can be used. It means changing behaviour.

On the nature of language

In order to further understand the ecological approach, it is important to explore the nature of 'language' itself. Although languages are traditionally viewed as objective, tangible entities which exist independently of their users (Coulmas, 1997: 42-43), Coulmas and integrational linguists denounce this perspective. As Toolan (1996: 2) observes:

> The majority view within linguistics [adheres to] ... an understanding of languages as coherent and complete systems, essentially autonomous of direct influence from other mental, social or cultural influences, enabled by the arbitrariness of the sign (the sound-meaning nexus), and structured by complex patterns of rules.

Toolan goes on to argue that the notion of a 'language' which the majority of linguists appeal to is in fact a second-order construct, though they consistently treat it as a first-order one (see also Grace, 1981: 15). Viewing language as a first-order construct allows linguists and others to regard language as 'natural'. However, the 'natural' characteristics of language are simply a result of its having been fostered long enough within a culture for it to be regarded as 'natural' (Toolan, 1996: 12). Yet there is nothing very 'natural' about any language. All are created by humans. All are cultural constructs. As Coulmas (1997: 43) says:

> every language is the result of human language-work ... every individual word in every language traces back to an individual act of coining.

This view is reiterated by Toolan (1996: 318-319):

> Too often, linguistics uncritically attributes 'possession' of the language to the community, neglecting the fact that the community is in essence an aggregation of individuals of finite life span. It is the individual who creates language, and it is the individual who, in dying, ceases to do so; it is not, ultimately, in the power of the community either to 'give' language to the individual or to take it away.

As Coulmas (1997: 43) points out, the contribution of each individual is 'more conspicuous in demographically small languages whose continuation is threatened than in language communities numbering in the millions'. In the case of newly invented languages, such as Esperanto, the role of individuals is far-reaching and decisive, as it is for languages subject to intervention in the form of standardisation, or making a language conform to a particular ideology as in Turkish under Ataturk (Landau, 1993), and for 'revived' languages such as Hebrew. The case of Kaurna, too, brings the contributions of individuals sharply into focus. Up to this point practically every user of Kaurna is known, practically everything written in the language is known and the majority of utterances made in the language are known to me. The contributions of these individuals are identifiable. Practically every new word and every new usage can be tracked down to specific individuals and to specific events and occasions. The circle of language users, enthusiasts or adherents is much smaller in the Kaurna situation than in most others.

In keeping with the view that languages are autonomous and exist independently of their users, linguists have often taken a dim view of the efforts of language planners and language enthusiasts who might 'meddle' with languages, attempting to influence their course of development, labelling languages like Katharevousa, Norwegian, Cornish etc. as 'artificial inventions' or 'fabrications' (see, for example, Hall, 1950). Attempts to create new artificial languages such as Esperanto or Volapük have been damned outright. Linguists have traditionally taken a strict 'hands-off' stance in relation to language, seeing their role to be objective observers and analysts, free of any particular ideology or value system. A recent example of this is Ladefoged's (1992) response to the 'endangered languages' issue raised by Hale (1992), Krauss (1992) and others.

By contrast, within an ecological approach language is seen as a 'dynamic, ever changing set of interrelationships' and an 'entire ecological system of communicative strategies rooted in time and place, history, and the land' (Fettes, 1997: 302). In the context of language revival, this tends to shift attention away from language to people and their society.

Ecological approaches are much more in keeping with Nunga perspectives on language. Indigenous peoples tend to view languages holistically, as an integral part of their culture and way of life. In the Kaurna context, there is extreme reluctance to disassociate the language from issues of land, heritage, the Dreaming etc.[5] Whilst linguists see a language primarily as an autonomous, coherent and complete system where the grammar is more important or more central than the lexicon (Chomsky, 1982: 14), it is evident that Nungas hold onto a very different notion of what a language is. It is not uncommon to hear Nungas claim 'I speak Ngarrindjeri' or 'I speak Narungga', meaning not just that they are a Ngarrindjeri or Narungga person or that they identify with the Ngarrindjeri or Narungga language, but they actually believe that they speak Ngarrindjeri or Narungga. Their use of Ngarrindjeri or Narungga is in fact limited to the use of words from those languages within English.

In a survey conducted by Peter Gale in 1991, out of 14 Nunga parents who responded to the questionnaire, most with Point Pearce origins or affiliations, ten claimed to speak Narungga, seven claimed to speak Ngarrindjeri, four Pitjantjatjara, two Kaurna and two another Nunga language. However, when asked 'Could you write a letter in any of these Nunga languages?' only one respondent claimed to be able to write a letter in Narungga, whilst none claimed to be able to write a letter in any other Indigenous language. Contrary to appearances, this discrepancy is to be accounted for by a lack of language competency rather than a lack of literacy skills.

It is interesting that Gale's Narungga informants claimed the Narungga language as the high point or the strength of Narungga culture, admitting to having lost other aspects of their culture: 'we lost the song and the dance ... the body painting and all that, but I think that other stuff is still strong, the language' (Interview in Gale, 1991: 194). Point Pearce School runs a Narungga language and culture program. They speak in all seriousness, in the context of choosing a program type from amongst the AILF categories, of their program being a language maintenance program. In reality it is basically a language awareness program, but to Nungas, being able to use some words of a language is to be able to speak it. In this respect their views contrast sharply to those of linguists and to a lesser extent with views held by the general public.

Nungas generally do not see their languages as 'dead'. As noted earlier, people now refer to Kaurna as having been 'sleeping' (Cherie Watkins in *Warranna Purruna* video; Alice Rigney, interview with Jenny Burford, 29 October 1997). On a radio interview, a young Kaurna woman claimed that:

> It's still alive and well and thanks to lots of committed people in terms of retrieving the language program. The basis of the Kaurna language as it was documented by the early German missionaries in South Australia is very strong.
> (Katrina Power, interview on 5UV, 23 April 1997)

Communicative vs. symbolic functions of language

When an ethnic group loses its traditional mother tongue, the language may still play an important role in the group's sense of identity. In Ireland, despite the 'failure' of language revival, the Irish language is still an enduring emblem of Irish identity. Language may sometimes be relegated to the status of a material artefact as in a grammar book or dictionary, but the knowledge that 'this is ours; this is our language, even if we don't know it and can't speak it' may still be a very potent force. Even the knowledge of the language name and knowing that the group once spoke a distinctive language may be an important pillar of identity. Eastman & Reece (1981) and Eastman (1984) refer to this symbolic aspect of language as 'associated language', which they see as a durable aspect of ethnic identity. Eastman argues that ethnic identity has two aspects, the primordial belief component and the social behaviour aspect, which includes language use. According to Eastman (1984: 271):

> the language we name as an emblem of our ethnic identity when we associate ourselves with a group of people does not change, as long as it remains an aspect of the belief level of our identity.

Furthermore, 'a change in primordial beliefs can only change over a long period of time' (Eastman, 1984: 272). I question this latter assertion. The situation in Belize (see Le Page & Tabouret-Keller, 1985) and the current developments amongst Aboriginal people of Adelaide demonstrate that not only behavioural aspects of identity but the very belief systems themselves are capable of changing rapidly. Certainly behaviour is more readily suppressed and changed, but beliefs can also change surprisingly quickly.

According to Jordan (1984: 274) 'Aboriginal people assert that a crucial contemporary problem for them is the need, after centuries wherein their culture has been destroyed, to build Aboriginal identity'. Jordan (1988a: 109) quotes sociologists, Berger & Luckman, who claim that 'identity is formed by social processes. Once crystallized, it is maintained, modified, or even reshaped by social relations'. Many Aboriginal identities are in a state of flux and are currently being redefined and transformed in response to new-found rights and freedoms obtained since 1967. As a result, the experiences of younger generations of Aboriginal people are radically different from those of the older generation. This theme will be taken up in detail in Chapter 10.

In accordance with Eastman & Reece's 'associated language', Edwards (1984, 1985) argues that languages have both 'communicative' and 'symbolic' value. These values coexist in majority language situations, though, according to Edwards, in certain minority language contexts, the two are separable and it is possible that the communicative value of a language may be lost whilst its symbolic value persists.

The question should be asked, 'Are we attempting to revive the 'symbolic value' of the language or are we trying to revive communication functions or both?' Edwards argues that a failure to make this distinction can result in misdirected efforts. He elaborates:

> Ignorance of the communicative-symbolic distinction can lead to lack of clarity and misdirected effort. If language revivalists or restorationists conceive of language in communicative terms alone, and if their appeals are directed towards groups in which communicative shift has occurred, then they may (a) be unsuccessful in their attempts to promote language use; (b) reintroduce, under the mantle of pluralism, a sort of anomie ... ; (c) promote a cynical view of any and all efforts on behalf of group identity.
> (Edwards, 1984: 290)

In the reclamation of Kaurna, the symbolic functions of language are coming back first. The communicative value of Kaurna is a more distant goal, more elusive and more difficult to achieve.

Fettes (1997: 309), too, acknowledges the importance of religious and symbolic functions as key areas for beginning language revival:

> Religious or, more broadly, spiritual discourses seem often to hold on to the language longest; they may also be where it can also most readily be brought back. Names can provide another focus of resistance... formulaic expressions and ceremonial texts can be deliberately reintroduced in appropriate settings, including everyday acts such as greetings, welcomes, introductions, and so forth.

These observations are confirmed by the Kaurna experience. Bentahila & Davies (1993: 368, 372) also suggest that use of the language in new domains in symbolic ways is a much more achievable goal than immediate intergenerational transmission (366).[6]

Esoteric vs. exoteric languages

Societies differ in the ways in which they regard their own languages and the languages of others. These attitudes may change substantially over time as societies become more open or closed, as the case may be, to outside influences.

Thurston (1987, 1989) first proposed the esoteric-exoteric dichotomy, following work on Anêm, spoken in West New Britain in PNG (Thurston, 1982: 11). Anêm is virtually a secret language, considered too difficult for neighbouring people to learn, and further complicated by the deliberate creation of 'secret code lexemes' for common items.

Esoteric languages like Anêm belong solely to insiders. Typically there is a strong sense of ownership. An esoteric language is regarded as property. The language community may resist outsiders learning or using it, and permission may need to be sought to teach it.

Exoteric languages on the other hand are not regarded as belonging to any particular individuals or groups. Anyone is free to learn or speak an exoteric language with impunity. Major world languages are highly exoteric, with English being the exoteric language par excellence.[7] No one minds if people learn English. In fact, there is great pressure on speakers of other languages to do so. Nor is anyone concerned about the ethnicity of those who teach English.

Of course, every language has areas of vocabulary and usage which are relatively esoteric. Within the English language there are professional jargons which are used, sometimes deliberately, to exclude non-members of the profession. There are varieties of English which are associated with certain minority groups or subcultures, which are also used to exclude non-members.[8]

Australia's Indigenous languages are generally located toward the esoteric end of the spectrum. But even amongst Australian languages there is a wide range, and within each language community there are different views expressed. Some members of the language community may encourage outsiders to learn the language, others resent this.

Last century, Japanese was a highly esoteric language. To teach Japanese was a capital offence (Mühlhäusler, 1996c: 259). Now, of course, with the opening up of Japan to the West, Japanese lies towards the exoteric end of the spectrum with the Japanese government actually promoting and funding the teaching of Japanese outside of Japan. Kaurna has shifted in the opposite direction. Sentences recorded by Teichelmann (1857) indicate that the Kaurna were keen for Europeans to learn and use Kaurna. Note for instance:

> *Ngadluko warra nindo paianintyidla nindo, warra meyu pulyunnurlo wonggai'nki.*
> RS *Ngadluku warra ninthu payarnintyidla ninthu warra miyu pulyunurlu wangka-inki*
> 'Whenever you understand the black man's language, then you must speak in it.'

> *Ngaii tangka waierendi manti ninna wongganintyerla.*
> RS *Ngai tangka wayarrinthi manti niina wangkarnintyarla*
> 'I am sorry that you cannot speake <sic> (the language)'

As we shall see, there is now considerable resistance towards outsiders learning and using Kaurna. The more languages are threatened the further they shift towards the esoteric end of the continuum. The profane becomes sacred and the language tends to be regarded more and more as a tangible cultural artefact. The portion of the language which is accessible only to the initiated may expand when the language is threatened.

Much of the prevailing language planning, language policy and linguistic literature has failed to take this dimension into account. The Draft Declaration on Linguistic Human Rights formulated in Barcelona in 1996 makes no mention of the rights of Indigenous minorities to restrict access to their languages. This is a major failure of the Declaration. Progressive and enlightened authors, such as Skutnabb-Kangas & Phillipson (1994) have similarly ignored this dimension. The reader is referred to Mühlhäusler's (1996c) review of this otherwise informative and insightful work.

An understanding of the esoteric-exoteric dichotomy helps explain Indigenous peoples' attitudes and behaviours towards their languages. These attitudes are a major component of the language ecology and drive Nunga language politics. Language ownership and copyright issues will be addressed in Chapter 10.

Language as cultural artefact

In 1968 Einar Haugen wrote an article titled *The Scandinavian Languages as Cultural Artifacts* (Haugen, 1972) in which he noted the role played by language in the social fabric of Scandinavian nations, in forging distinctive political entities within the respective nation states and in embodying separate identities. In the use of the term 'cultural artifact', Haugen was paying attention to the high level of conscious activity that contributed to the development of standard languages in Scandinavia:

> By the time a norm has been codified and elaborated by its users, it has become virtually impossible to identify its base. It has become an independent artifact in the culture, one of the devices by means of which a particular group, usually a power elite, manages to maintain or assert its identity and, when possible, its power.
>
> ....
>
> If we adopt the metaphor of the traditional family tree for languages, SLs [Standard Languages] are artifacts that result either from pruning or grafting the tree. The gardeners are a special priesthood of taste and learning, who are entrusted by society with the codification and elaboration of a code that is part of the conscious heritage of the social establishment. (Haugen, 1972: 266)

Within the context of language revival in Aboriginal Australia, I view language as a cultural artefact in a different, though related way. Australian languages are owned, in the same way that art designs are owned by particular groups or clans. Certain senior individuals are recognised as the owners or custodians of the language. For instance, one generally needs to obtain their permission to teach the language within a language course.

In some parts of Australia, there is strong resistance towards non-Aboriginal people learning Aboriginal languages or even having access to them. In Tasmania, the position of the Tasmanian Aboriginal Centre, as enunciated by its spokesperson Jim Everett in 1993, is that the 'Tasmanian language' should not be taught in schools. The Tasmanian Aboriginal community wishes to keep the language for itself. Only when it is known by, and secure within, their community will consideration be given to its being taught more widely (Minutes AILF National Steering Committee meeting, 1 April 1993).[9]

A number of recent dictionaries have been kept in-house. For instance, the Butchulla Dictionary, recently produced with funding from the *Dictionaries for Reconciliation* project, has not been released for general consumption. Rather its circulation has been restricted to the Butchulla community in south-east Queensland (Jeanie Bell, pc 1995).

Aboriginal people in Adelaide talk about their languages having been 'stolen' and linguists and anthropologists are sometimes accused of 'stealing' by virtue of having recorded the languages and deposited the wordlists, linguistic descriptions, tapes etc. in a museum or archive. Linguists and anthropologists like Tindale have been blamed for taking the languages away. In the contemporary era of language revival and language retrieval, some people talk of their resentment at having to 'buy back' their linguistic heritage in the same way that they are having to buy back artefacts from museums overseas.

There is a certain uneasiness about borrowing words from other Aboriginal languages into Kaurna, for fear of offending the owners and custodians of the source language. Where words are borrowed, there is a felt need to seek permission first. Of course borrowing and diffusion of lexemes is a process that occurs between practically all languages in contact with each other, whether or not those languages are related or not. All Aboriginal and Torres Strait Islander languages spoken today have borrowed large numbers of words from English, and English has borrowed a number of words from these languages (see Dixon et al. 1990). Furthermore, Australian languages have borrowed a significant number of words from each other. See, for instance, Heath's (1978) study of *Linguistic Diffusion in Arnhem Land*. People, even within the Arnhemland context, don't normally seek permission to borrow a word from a neighbouring language. It is something that just happens, and people are mostly quite unaware of the process even at the time of borrowing. In a situation like reclaiming the Kaurna language, however, language use is highly monitored and all decisions about lexical choice are made consciously during this early phase. In fact, it is highly likely in the climate of language revival and retrieval that Kaurna people would indeed be accused of 'stealing' if, for instance, they borrowed well known Ngarrindjeri icons such as *ponde* 'Murray Cod' or *pilaki* 'callop' and started using them within their Kaurna speech and Kaurna language materials.[10]

Written language, especially that on signs, in books and elsewhere in the public eye is something tangible. In the language revival context, languages take on qualities similar to other artefacts (e.g. woomeras, boomerangs, paintings, carvings etc.) and the tangible language products are viewed as cultural artefacts in much the same way as other artefacts.

Language as artefact manifests itself in the purposes to which the Kaurna language is being put. Kaurna is often used within a public display of Kaurna culture. Songs, speeches of welcome, signs, names (of institutions, organisations, programs, magazines and journals etc.), posters, books and other material language products are particularly important. In fact, these are far more important outcomes of the Kaurna language program than is communicative competence at this stage in its delivery within Inbarendi College.

Aboriginal people's attitudes to copyright issues, as we shall see in Chapter 10, also serve to reinforce the notion of language as cultural artefact. Suggestions have been made by some Kaurna people that the entire language should be copyrighted under heritage legislation. If this were possible, it would be done word by word, including all known spelling variants appearing in historical materials. It is not seen as appropriate for non-Aboriginal people to write and produce materials in Aboriginal languages and even less appropriate for non-Aboriginal people to copyright such materials, unless in collaboration with Indigenous authors. Copyrighting the materials is often viewed as copyrighting the language itself.[11] There is also a perception that linguists and anthropologists have made a significant amount of money out of Aboriginal languages, money which is not considered rightfully theirs as the languages do not belong to them.

So within the context of language revival in Aboriginal Australia, I am referring to language as a cultural artefact in a much more direct and literal way than Haugen.[12]

Language planning issues

As mentioned earlier, the main task confronting us in language reclamation is to reunite the dormant language with owners, custodians and potential speakers. But who are the potential speakers and what rights do they have to the language? What rights do I have, as a non-Indigenous linguist, to shape and promote the Kaurna language? These are immediate issues confronting us as language planners. Obviously some kind of accommodation must be reached which recognises the right of the owners and custodians to control the process, but also acknowledges the skills and expertise that outsiders may bring to the enterprise. This collaboration is crucial.

I am mindful of my role as a 'language maker' and as a 'lame' (see below). As a 'language maker' (to use a term promoted by Roy Harris, 1980) I am in a similar position to Jay Powell in the development of the Quileute 'artificial pidgin', Aasen with Norwegian, Ben Yehuda with Hebrew, Korais with Katharevousa and Mihalic with Tok Pisin to mention just a few individuals who have had a major role in deciding the shape of specific languages. Added to these are the many missionaries over the past few centuries who have had a major influence on the development of many Indigenous languages.

Many of those mentioned above, such as Ben Yehuda, are members of the speech community and ethnic group associated with the language in question. Others, such as Jay Powell and most missionaries, are outsiders like myself. As an outsider, there are added responsibilities. I must recognise the primacy of Indigenous ownership over the language and the right of the group to have the final say as to how the language should develop. I can present various options and offer advice, but in the final analysis I must work at the direction of the Kaurna Elders and Kaurna community.

On the one hand, I am at the very centre of the Kaurna language revivalist efforts, and in many ways responsible for the ways in which the language is developing and being used. On the other hand, as a non-Indigenous person, I am an outsider. Unlike the kind of participant research carried out by an anthropologist in Papua and New Guinea, I do not live in a Nunga household. Whilst I am involved to some extent in Nunga social and political activities, I am not a member of the Nunga or Kaurna community. The nature of my research would be quite different if I were a Kaurna person.

My situation leads to a rather extraordinary kind of participant observation. I am generating much of the subject matter of the research, whilst at the same time being an outsider. Labov (1972: 255-292) discusses 'The Linguistic Consequences of Being a Lame'. A 'lame' is an outsider, an isolated individual, who speaks the vernacular code but not quite in the same way that insiders or full group members do. Labov applies the concept to linguists who often use themselves as 'informant' and use their own intuitions as data and gives us a salutary warning:

> To refine the intricate structure of one's own thoughts, to ask oneself what one would say in an imaginary world where one's own dialect is the only reality, to dispute only with those few colleagues who share the greatest part of this private world — these academic pleasures will not easily be abandoned by those who were early detached from secular life. The student of his own intuitions, producing both data and theory in a language abstracted from every social context, is the ultimate lame. (Labov, 1972: 292)

I am in a position where I am 'producing both data and theory in a language abstracted from every social context', though not in the same way that Labov originally intended when he wrote this passage. I am a 'lame' in a double sense: that of a non-Aboriginal outsider and that of a linguist generating and abstracting Kaurna language data in a situation somewhat divorced from its community.

In this role, I bear considerable responsibility for my part in the development of the Kaurna language, which in turn has an impact on the construction of Kaurna identity and Kaurna culture. This could potentially have far-reaching implications for the future, not only for the Kaurna community, but for the role of Indigenous languages in formal education and the relationships between black and white Australians in Adelaide. As Jordan says:

> Academics must take responsibility for their part in the construction of Aboriginal worlds and for the directions in which their writings and their deliberation unwittingly contribute to Aboriginal identity by the very way in which their research topics are conceptualised. (Jordan, 1988a: 128)

Under these circumstances, it is imperative that I continually refer back to the Kaurna community. I must be prepared to listen and take direction from them and defer to the Kaurna Elders, particularly in relation to matters of cultural significance.

As a general principle, language planning measures that work with, rather than against, societal trends are far more likely to succeed. Therefore, we need to be clear about the ways in which Kaurna people are making use of the language on their own initiative, and work in those directions. We need to watch how the community reacts to various initiatives and pursue those which are well-received and be prepared to abandon others.

Status planning strategies are central within an ecological approach. Kaurna language enthusiasts have been working on multiple fronts to seek recognition for the language and, conversely to some extent, use the language to gain recognition for the Kaurna as a separate identity with links to their ancestral lands on the Adelaide Plains. The language has been actively promoted within education (see Chapter 7 for a detailed discussion) and a range of public domains (see Chapter 8). As a result, during the 1990s Kaurna has gained widespread recognition within Nunga society and is becoming better known within mainstream society.

A range of specific language functions, such as conducting weddings, christenings and funerals in the target language, might be promoted, as is the case with Cornish and Breton for instance. More traditional ceremonies might be reinstituted and likewise conducted in the target language. But it would not be wise to proceed too hastily down this path without widespread support and involvement from members of the target language community.

Use of the target language in new domains necessarily entails language development and often coinage of neologisms. Too much haste in these areas, however, runs the risk of alienating the language from the community. The situation needs to be carefully managed. Understandings about the nature of language and language change need to be cultivated within the community by means of forums and workshops that allow people to voice their opinions and concerns.

There is a constant tension between viewing the target language as a static, historical relic and seeing it as a dynamic resource for the future. It is essential, therefore, that we proceed carefully to ensure that these two aspects are kept in balance to ensure both authenticity and relevance.

Notes

[1] Dorian (1987), whilst still adhering to this view, points to the value of language programs, such as East Sutherland Gaelic, which are unlikely to succeed in these terms.

[2] Even though the Kaurna language movement is small and most of the use of Kaurna is known, the ecology is still very complex. There are many more factors than we can control or adequately account for.

[3] Mühlhäusler notes that the 'shop steward' metaphor is used in contemporary discourse on environment issues.

[4] Fettes (1997: 307) writes of the need to create a 'discursive space' within the 'invading language' for the use of the Indigenous language.

[5] Indeed, I have been criticised at times for focusing too much on the language and ignoring or paying insufficient attention to other aspects of culture and identity. Guest lectures delivered by Kaurna Elders typically draw on much broader perspectives than the set topic would seem to warrant from an academic perspective.

[6] It was noted earlier that Fishman (1991) downplays the importance of the symbolic use of language in the institutional domain.

[7] Whilst the roots of English are widely known and its original territory recognised by the general public as the United Kingdom and ultimately Denmark and Northern Germany, it now has many focuses, with ever-increasing numbers of new indigenised varieties emerging, such as Singlish or Singaporean English.

[8] There is a body of literature on 'secret English' relating to some Aboriginal perceptions that they are being denied access to the 'real' English, the language of power (see Martin, 1990).

[9] There has been much debate within the AILF project as to whether Australian languages should be taught to non-Indigenous Australians or not, and whilst the general consensus has been that they should be open to all, the decision will be made on a local level as to whether a particular language should be taught and to whom it should be offered. In teaching the languages, there are some concerns within the local Nunga community of a subtle takeover by the system, the schools, the government, linguists and the dominant society.

[10] It would, however, be expected for Kaurna to borrow such words from Ngarrindjeri were the languages fully viable as *ponde* and *pilaki* are riverine species of fish prominent within the Ngarrindjeri environment, diet and mythology. However, these species were probably not found in Kaurna territory itself, hence the motivation to borrow them.

[11] Strictly speaking according to Australian law, copyright applies only to the particular arrangement of words, not the language itself, but Aboriginal people do not always see it in these terms.

[12] We have already seen how linguistics has treated language as an 'object' through its approach to linguistic description. Now we see Aboriginal people treat language as an object in quite a different sense, through its being likened to an artefact or relic.

4

A Sociolinguistic History of Kaurna

> *Taking the things we need to survive as a race of people with us for our children NOW, we may still have life TOMORROW. Without a Cultural Identity we will be lost, with no sense of place; our spirit will die and we will enter into the Dreaming of the White Man's Nightmare.*
> (Georgina Williams, 1984: 24, in Mattingley & Hampton, 1988: 155)

The Kaurna's is a remarkable story of survival, re-emergence and transformation of an identity and culture that was largely shattered by European invasion of their lands more than 160 years ago. The population was decimated by disease and the people were forced off their lands, but the roots were not completely severed.

In recent times, the Kaurna have regrouped and are forging a distinctive Kaurna identity which is shaped by their past history. The Kaurna in the 1990s are characterised by both continuities and discontinuities with the past. This is reflected in the attention given to archaeology and prehistory by Kaurna people themselves. The Kaurna draw on a long-standing connection with the Adelaide Plains, which has only recently been disrupted by the European invasion.

Early observers of the Kaurna[1] sometimes wrote glowing reports in the tradition of the 'noble savage'. They were described as 'superior' to other Aboriginal groups. Colonial officials tried to present a picture of peace and harmony and of the Kaurna people welcoming the colonists to their lands. Later reports, however, pointed to the 'degraded' nature of the Indigenous peoples of the Adelaide Plains, after many apparently resorted to begging and prostitution following the theft of their lands. By the late 1840s, the Kaurna were portrayed as a weak remnant of a once proud people. As early as 1850, some writers were claiming that the Kaurna were virtually 'extinct'.

From 1850 onwards, the scant references to the Kaurna typically refer to some surviving remnants of the former 'Adelaide Tribe'. For instance, Cawthorne knew of the existence of just five Kaurna individuals belonging to one family in 1861 (Hemming, 1990: 132). Even Teichelmann, who had spent so much effort in documenting the language, referred in 1858 to the Kaurna as no longer existing.[2] The few later nineteenth-century references invariably refer to the 'Adelaide Tribe' as 'extinct' (e.g. Woods, 1879: ix; Stephens, 1889), and this belief was general among Europeans at the turn of the twentieth century.

There was a brief reassertion of the existence of Aboriginal people with links to the Adelaide region with the 'discovery' of Ivaritji in 1919 by Daisy Bates. Ivaritji was then living at Bukkiyana. Little interest was taken in the Kaurna in the years following her death in 1929; the Kaurna or 'Adelaide Tribe' were again said to have ceased to exist.

Throughout the twentieth century there is an evolving change in the discourse on Kaurna people, from the 'last survivor' (e.g. *Advertiser*, 8 Decmber 1927) and an 'extinct people' (e.g. Howchin, 1934; Edwards, 1972; Brunato, 1973) to a gradual recognition of their continuing existence and survival. In the 1980s, those who were aware of them generally referred to these survivors as 'Kaurna descendants'.[3] Only recently have the Kaurna been rehabilitated to the status of 'a people'. Of course one still finds numerous references to 'descendants' and occasionally to the 'extinct Kaurna people', but there is a growing recognition of their existence as a people in their own right.[4]

First contacts

First contacts between the Kaurna and Europeans occurred rather late in Australia's colonial history. The colony of South Australia was not established until 1836, half a century after New South Wales. Exploration of Kaurna waters was also relatively late, and it seems that explorers such as Flinders and Baudin who entered Kaurna waters in 1802 made no contact with Kaurna people. The first Europeans to make contact with the Kaurna were probably American sealers and whalers who may have visited Kangaroo Island and Kaurna lands even before 1800.

Possibly the first long-term European visitors on Kangaroo Island were six sealers led by Joseph Murrell in 1806 (Clarke, 1994a: 4). Kangaroo Island became a permanent base for gangs of sealers who were able to hunt the then numerous seals and trade skins with passing ships in return for provisions and women, brought initially from Tasmania. However, it wasn't long before the sealers were raiding the nearby mainland for Indigenous women, who were useful not only for their sexual favours, but also for hunting and skinning seals and processing skins. They were adept at living off the land and provided for the sealers. As Kangaroo Island was unoccupied by Aboriginal people, women could be captured and taken there without fear of reprisals from their husbands or other kin. The sealers and whalers were active around Kangaroo Island up until the establishment of the colony of South Australia.

Several authors (Pope, 1989: 13; Clarke, 1994a: 7) assume, wrongly, that most of the contact between the sealers and whalers on Kangaroo Island and Indigenous peoples of the mainland was with the Ngarrindjeri. But the sealers' main point of entry onto the mainland from Kangaroo Island was the Rapid Bay–Yankalilla region where the seas were calmer. Indeed, two early wordlists obtained from women originating from this region are both Kaurna. The earliest Kaurna wordlist was recorded in 1826 from Harry and Sally, members of a sealing party, then in King George Sound (Gaimard, 1833; Amery, 1998b); another was recorded from Kalloongoo, abducted from the region probably in the early 1820s (Amery, 1996d).[5] Such evidence suggests that it was the Kaurna who bore the brunt of the activities of the sealers and whalers in South Australia. Ngarrindjeri women were indeed involved, but the known cases where identities can be proved beyond doubt involve Tasmanian and Kaurna women. This matter is discussed at length in Amery (1996d).

Records are sketchy on how many Kaurna people were involved with sealers and whalers before 1836. The sealers, or 'straitsmen', as they were known, were mostly illiterate. Some were escaped convicts and fugitives from the law and would not want to write about their exploits. Aboriginal people often joined whaling and sealing ships, but seldom listed in the ships' crews, they were largely invisible in any records. Even so, several reports of Aboriginal women living with sealers on Kangaroo Island were made by passing ships. One of the earliest was made by Captain Sutherland in 1819 when he noted that there were several Europeans living on the island who:

> have carried their daring acts to an extreme, venturing on the mainland in their boats and seizing on the natives, particularly the women, and keeping them in a state of slavery, cruelly treating them on every trifling occasion.
> (Sutherland, cited in Cumpston, 1970: 51)

There was a constant passage of ships which transported the sealers and their women to various locations between Bass Straits and King George Sound and sometimes as far as Mauritius. Aboriginal women from the mainland opposite Kangaroo Island, probably Kaurna women, were known to have been taken to New Zealand in the early 1820s. References to two such women are to be found in Cumpston (1970: 63, 66).

Some years later, the sealer John Jones sailed from Launceston in the *Henry* to Kangaroo Island in July 1833 and reported in 1835 that:

> He met a tribe of natives on Cape Jervis, consisting of ten families. Five of the men worked for him occasionally, and two were with him constantly for near five months. To the two who remained with him long he gave pistols, powder, and shot; to the others slop-clothing. He saw their women and children only at a distance, and saw no other natives on the rest of the coast along Gulf St. Vincent; but their fires were very numerous.
> (Jones, cited in Clarke, 1994a: 13)

This report suggests that by 1833, the Kaurna were wise to the activities of the sealers. The men were prepared to work for them in exchange for goods, but kept their women at a distance. It is likely that Ngarrindjeri women were more prominent in these later years of sealing, as the Kaurna became more wary. Sealers were known to have walked from Yankalilla to the Murray Mouth in search of women.

Aboriginal women living with the sealers had a high mortality rate. They were made to carry out the dangerous sealing work such as swimming out to wave-lashed rocks to club seals. The children born of liaisons between sealers and Aboriginal women were often killed at birth, sometimes by the sealer and occasionally by the woman herself (Clarke, 1998: 10, 36). Children were often regarded as a hindrance, though other sealers recognised their future potential as labour. The women were seen as expendable and easily replaced through direct raids or purchase, especially in the early days of sealing. Some sealers, such as

Meredith, engaged in a regular trade of captive women for sale to other sealers: he was responsible for the capture of Emue from Cape Jervis (Plomley, 1987: 366).

The activities of the sealers and whalers may well have had a much greater impact on the Kaurna nation, particularly the southern Kaurna clans who inhabited the Cape Jervis, Rapid Bay and Yankalilla areas, than has been acknowledged. Repeated raids over several decades could have reduced the population significantly. In terms of our knowledge of the Kaurna language, Harry and Sally (Amery, 1998b) and Kalloongoo (Amery, 1996d) are important in providing two totally independent wordlists, the earliest records of the language.

When the colonists arrived in 1836, most Kaurna were aloof at first, choosing to observe the strangers from a distance and to get on with their own lives. Most likely they never expected the colonists to stay. After all, they had seen numerous sealers and whalers and several explorers come and go and perhaps thought that the best way of dealing with such intrusions into their country was to avoid them.

The Colonial Secretary, Robert Gouger, reported on early interactions with Aboriginal people in a 13-page letter in 1837, effectively the first year of the colony. He begins:

> Though I landed in South Australia without any feeling of fear of the natives, I nevertheless felt great anxiety respecting them. I knew full well that if the first encounter with them should be unfriendly, that the effect might be truly deplorable.
>
> (in Gouger, 1838: 46)

Gouger and other 'founding fathers' of the South Australian colony were well aware of the atrocities committed by colonists in other parts of the continent, especially in Tasmania and New South Wales, and were anxious that 'our province would be unstained by native blood' (Gouger, 1838: 46). He comments favourably on the good relationships established by Light's party and Aboriginal people at Rapid Bay.[6]

Some Kaurna, such as Sally who lived with sealers on Kangaroo Island, were exceedingly forward, outgoing and self-confident in the presence of the colonists. By 1836, Sally was already well-travelled. She had spent the best part of two years in Western Australia, living with an abandoned group of sealers, left there in 1826. In 1828 she was sent to Sydney for the trial of sealers in connection with murders they committed at King George Sound. In 1831, her help was sought to investigate the disappearance of Captain Collet Barker at the Murray Mouth by members of his party who recognised her from King George Sound. In 1836, she met passengers and crew of the *Africaine* which had pulled in to Kangaroo Island before landing at Holdfast Bay on the mainland. Her services were again enlisted to help find six passengers who became lost when they attempted to walk across Kangaroo Island. See Amery (1998b) for details.

In the initial phase of colonisation, sealers often acted as intermediaries and cultural brokers between the Kaurna and the colonists. Colonel Light's survey party engaged three or four sealers from Kangaroo Island, taking them to Rapid

Bay in September 1836. One, named Cooper, brought his two wives with him. Almost a year later, Cooper acted as interpreter for Aborigines at Glenelg whose belongings had been stolen by two white sailors named Hoare and Moon (*South Australian Register,* 8 July 1837: 4). The four male Aboriginal plaintiffs were living at Glenelg and had erected a house in imitation of the European dwellings. It is highly likely that these men were Kaurna, as these events occurred well before reports of the movement of Aborigines from other districts into Adelaide. So it seems that Cooper had gained a good working knowledge of Kaurna through his association with Kaurna people on Kangaroo Island and the southern Fleurieu Peninsula. Unfortunately, there are no known records of Cooper's Kaurna.

Whilst many colonists were apprehensive and avoided contact with Aboriginal people, a few such as William Williams and James Cronk, both passengers aboard the *Africaine,* actually sought out Kaurna people and succeeded in establishing friendly relationships with them. According to Mary Thomas, a fellow passenger, Williams met by accident with a man and a boy about five miles inland from Glenelg on 1 December 1836 (Hope, 1968: 115f), a little more than two weeks after their arrival. Gouger's description of the first encounter with Aboriginal people at the new settlement at Holdfast Bay undoubtedly also refers to Williams:

> About a fortnight or three weeks after landing at Glenelg, one of the settlers, who was out shooting, saw at a distance a native man and boy employed in making a fire; he prudently withdrew his sporting charge, and put a bullet into each barrel in case of being obliged to defend himself. Having taken this precaution, he advanced silently until within a short distance, and then laughed heartily. The natives immediately seized their spears; but as he continued laughing, and held a biscuit to them, they put down their spears and approached him. They then embraced, and he succeeded in bringing them down to the settlement. (Gouger, 1838: 47)

However, James Cronk, in a letter written to his mother on 2 November 1837, claimed to be the 'first person as ventured over the hills in search of them'. Like Williams, Cronk just happened to stumble across a party of four Kaurna men whilst out hunting. The four men were enticed with sugar and biscuits to visit the European settlement. A few days later, Cronk, laden with biscuits and sugar, went out in search of the Kaurna and found a party of 35, about 18 miles from Glenelg, including the four men they had met a few days before. After hunting and camping with them for two days, he persuaded the group to come down to their encampment at Holdfast Bay. His letter portrays the nature of relationships that he had established with the Kaurna:

> The next morning I persuaded them to come down to our tents: the women objected to this at first; I then made motions to them that I would give them plenty of sugar and biscuit, then they consented to come; but when the women saw the ships in the bay they stared with astonishment to look at them. They stopped close to my tent that night, the next day they went away: they came down again in about a fortnight afterwards, and had several corrobborees; but now they stop about the town, and fetch wood and water for the people for some bread. They now bring me in young cockatoos and opossum-skins for which I give them bread in return. ... The natives, just before I wrote these few lines to you, asked me to go with them about a hundred miles in a north-east direction, and asked

me to take two kangaroo dogs with me ... the natives that way are very frightened of us, for they were a coming to have a look at us, when there was a ship a coming in fired two big guns, which frightened them so they turned back again.

(Cronk, in Gouger, 1838: 100f)

Cronk assessed his own ability to speak Kaurna as follows:

I have been a good deal about the country since I have been here, and had a good deal of intercourse with the natives. I begin to talk their language very fair for considering the short time I have been here. (Cronk, in Gouger, 1838: 100f)

Invasion of Kaurna lands: colonisation, 1836

A number of histories of the colonisation of South Australia have been written (see Kwan, 1987; Richards, 1986; Jaensch, 1986; and Gibbs, 1995). Several authors have focused on the impact of the invasion and relationships between Aborigines and the colonists (see Hassell, 1966). Mattingley & Hampton (1988) in *Survival in Our Own Land* have attempted to provide an Aboriginal perspective on South Australia's history. Pope (1989) in *Resistance and Retaliation* has portrayed the Aboriginal response to invasion, whilst Foster (1993) in a PhD thesis titled 'An imaginary dominion: The representation and treatment of Aborigines in South Australia', makes a detailed study of references to Aborigines in historical documents. All these sources focus on the Kaurna in the early phase of colonisation, for it was the Kaurna who bore the brunt of the invasion. However, little attention is given in any of these sources to language issues. It is the language ecology, and policies which impacted on that ecology, that I wish to focus on here.

By the 1830s the British government was painfully aware of the breakdown of relationships between the colonists and the Indigenous inhabitants in New South Wales and Tasmania, and indeed in other colonies throughout the world. The planners of the South Australian colony wished to establish a peaceful settlement in which black and white could live side by side as brothers and where Aboriginal people could be 'civilised' and Christianised and partake in the 'benefits' that England had to offer. The original South Australian Act tabled in 1834 was rejected by the House of Commons because it did not make sufficient provision for the Indigenous inhabitants of South Australia.

Land rights and compensation for the use of Aboriginal lands were issues that were taken seriously. Some colonists tried to force the Governor and the South Australian Company to act in the interests of Aboriginal people. Robert Cock, in a letter to the Protector, reminded the government of the pledge of the Colonisation Commissioners to set aside 20% of the lands 'for the support and advancement of the natives'. Accordingly, he sent the Protector £3 16s 6d, which he calculated as 10% interest on the purchase price of one fifth of his property as rent for the land. Cock concluded his letter with the statement: 'I disclaim this to be either donation, grant, or gift, but a just claim the natives of this district have on me as an occupier of those lands' (Letter by A. Tenant [Robert Cock] in *Southern Australian,* 15 September 1838: 3). Wyatt, as interim Protector, then wrote to the Colonial Secretary and the Governor pointing out the need for some permanent support for Aborigines 'whose future means of existence is ... seriously threatened by the tide of Emigration' (quoted in Kwan, 1987: 23). The matter was taken up with Lord Glenelg by the Acting Governor, George Stephen, on 5 October 1838 when he suggested that the rental from a certain portion of land in each district would provide a continual source of support (Kwan, 1987: 23).

George Fife Angas argued passionately at the Select Committee enquiry into South Australia, in March 1841, in favour of Indigenous rights to the land. He vehemently attacked the notion of *terra nullius* and attempted to point out the flaws in the South Australian Act of the British Parliament which established the colony. The Minutes of Evidence Taken at the Select Committee enquiry shows the strength of Angas's argument:

> it is owing to a deficiency of the Act that no measures for their amelioration have been adopted. With respect to the Act, I conceive that those words in the preamble, which declare that South Australia consists of waste and unoccupied lands, clearly exclude the aborigines from any advantage whatever arising from the land; it does not even recognise their existence. They have no existence in a legal point of view, therefore no provision could be made for them by the commissioners. The natives cannot purchase and hold land. The commissioners are to declare, according to the Act, that all the lands of the said province are public lands, open to purchase by British subjects; consequently the natives can hold no property. In the next place, no grant of land can be legally made to the aborigines, because in the sixth section of the Act it is stated, that all lands are public lands open to purchase, and that the said public lands shall be sold in public for ready money.   (G.F. Angas evidence given at the Select Committee on
> South Australia, British Parliamentary Papers, Vol. 2, 1841: 210)

Angas argued further that some of the best land, up to 10% of all unsold land, should be set aside in perpetuity for the benefit of Aboriginal people (British Parliamentary Papers, 1841: 217-218). However, the interests of business and white landholders won the day.

The official instructions given to William Wyatt on his appointment to the position of interim Protector of Aborigines were aimed at 'civilising' and encouraging European habits of work and fixed residence through offering rewards and incentives. Any form of compulsion was specifically rejected. These instructions include a number of points which demonstrate the centrality of Indigenous languages in the role of Protector:

> With a view to the attainment of the first of these objects [ascertaining the number, strength, and disposition of the various tribes, especially those in the vicinity of the settled districts], and to facilitate intercourse between yourself and the Aborigines generally, you are authorised to engage an interpreter, who will take instructions solely from yourself, and whose whole time will be considered at your disposal. . . You are recommended to endeavour to attach one or two of the most docile and intelligent of the natives particularly to your person, who should habitually accompany you in your excursions...
>
> No time should be lost in acquiring a knowledge of their native tongue, and it appears also desirable that the Aborigines, and especially their youth, should learn the English language. By communicating with them in their own tongue, and by giving them a knowledge of our language, you will readily enable them to appreciate our modes and habits, our moral and political laws, and our intentions towards themselves ...
>   (Robert Gouger, Colonial Secretary in *South Australian Gazette and*

Colonial Register, 12 August 1837: 1)

It is clear from the above that language policy was central to government policy in relation to the Indigenous inhabitants of South Australia. Both Indigenous languages and English were seen as tools for achieving assimilation and spreading English civilisation. Wyatt and Moorhouse both had an interest in Kaurna and other Indigenous languages in part because it was one of their official duties to do so.

In the early years of the colony, Kaurna people were taken seriously and treated with a certain amount of respect. Efforts were made by some to learn about Kaurna culture and to learn the Kaurna language because they were genuinely interested. Cawthorne is a good case in point, as we shall see in Chapter 5. Aboriginal people were initially tolerated within the city of Adelaide. In fact, they were even encouraged by the Protector to come to Adelaide from outlying districts to see for themselves that Aborigines and colonists could live side by side in peace. South Australia's second Governor, George Gawler, was favourably disposed towards the Indigenous inhabitants. On the day Gawler was instituted as Governor he addressed a crowd of Kaurna people through an interpreter and continued this practice throughout his period of governorship.

The Kaurna soon realised that the colonists were there to stay. Game, such as possums and kangaroos, soon became scarce in Adelaide and surrounding areas and the Kaurna expected food and blankets from the colonists in return, as their right, to compensate for the losses incurred. Many Kaurna became dependent on handouts. Some tried to adapt their lives to the colony. Many sought employment and proved themselves to be diligent and hard-working. According to Teichelmann (Diary, 24 April 1840) one of the first Kaurna to embrace employment in the European world was Milte-widlo [RS Milthi-widlu]. Teichelmann's observations are insightful:

> On 24th April in the evening a young native came to me selling brooms. The first example of an Aborigine copying the industry of a European. Milte-widlo has already been working for Snooke and Co. for more than a month ... (this man stayed with that merchant for 18 months, was fully civilised and then returned completely to his naked life-style. Then he made several journeys as a sailor on a ship, came back, divided the wealth he had gained amongst his countrymen, went around completely naked on the third day and was worse than before. In Singapore he had seen black people who were slaves, living on atrocious food-stuffs and now says: 'Would not I be a fool to take on a life like that! These people are half-starved and at the end of the week they get 1/2 crown, ... while I live here in comfort and can eat meat whenever I like. And what have I earned after all that? Nothing!' (Teichelmann Diary, 24 April 1840)[7]

One young Kaurna woman gained employment in Government House, and a young Kaurna man went to Tasmania in 1841 where he worked in various occupations for five years 'in a Corn Mill ... at sea, in whaling and coasting vessels' (Protector's Report, Second Quarter 1846, 15 April 1846, cited in Pope, 1989: 29). The government was also in the practice of taking Kaurna men and boys as guides and intermediaries in their efforts to explore the surrounding districts, and in tracking down suspected criminals.

Initially the colonists seemed willing to give food and money to Aboriginal people as a small measure of compensation for the use of their lands. However, it wasn't long before vices, such as begging, prostitution and drunkenness were widespread and a strong resentment of the very existence of the Aboriginal population emerged. Violence resulting from conflict over land, women and labour characterised relations on the frontier, though few acts of open violence between the colonists and Aborigines in Adelaide are recorded. The position of Protector of Aborigines was soon seen by the colonists as being responsible for protecting their own interests from Aboriginal people and he was held responsible for any crimes committed by Aboriginal people.

In the initial phase of colonisation, the ability to speak Kaurna was valued and admired by other colonists. As we have seen, the government made use of sealers with a command of the language, and their women, as guides, interpreters and intermediaries. They also engaged those colonists who had shown an aptitude and interest in acquiring Kaurna. The Kaurna language played a pivotal role in the colonisation of South Australia.

Cronk and Williams were engaged as interpreters on the basis of the language skills they had acquired. On 1 November 1838 they both assisted Wyatt during Governor Gawler's initial meeting with Indigenous peoples:

> Mr Wyatt, the Protector, also attended, and was assisted on the occasion by James Cronk, the interpreter, and William Williams, the deputy storekeeper, both great favorites of the natives, and tolerably versed in their language and customs.
> (*South Australian Gazette and Colonial Register*, Saturday 3 November 1838: 4)

A number of Kaurna leaders, such as Kadlitpinna [RS Kadlitpina] (Captain Jack) and Mullawirraburka [RS Murlawirrapurka] (King John) developed friendly and lasting relationships with several colonists. Their stories are told in detail by Gara (1998). They assisted the European newcomers in various ways — by maintaining law and order within their own community, and by teaching interested colonists various aspects of their culture and the Kaurna language. Kadlitpinna, Mullawirraburka and several others were co-opted by the colonial authorities and appointed as police constables in early 1838 (Gara, 1998: 12).

Piltawodli, literally 'possum home', was chosen as the site of the 'Native Location' in April 1837 by Kaurna people themselves, who led Captain Walter Bromley, South Australia's second interim Protector, to a spot about a mile down river from the allocated area. Bromley built himself a hut and supervised the Kaurna in 'the construction of half a dozen "commodious wigwams" as he called them' (Foster, 1990a: 12; see R. Harris (1999) for further details).

Christianising and 'civilising'

Piltawodli [RS Pirltawardli] was the first in a planned system of reserves[8], designed to settle Aboriginal people in a confined space in order to open up the land for systematic colonisation. The government was keen to promote a sedentary existence and develop skills useful to the colonists in a captive labour force. A dozen huts to accommodate Kaurna families, a garden, schoolhouse, storehouse and residence for the interpreter were established by 1838. From the outset, the colonial authorities had planned for schools, as an integral part of the reserve system and policy of 'protection'. However, serious delays were encountered in finding a teacher. These delays were in the interests of the Kaurna language, as the school did not get under way until the Lutheran missionaries arrived and had spent over a year acquiring Kaurna. Thus the first school for Aboriginal children in South Australia used Kaurna as the medium of instruction.

Piltawodli is highly significant in a study of the Kaurna language. Almost all sources and especially the main ones, were recorded from Kaurna people, who resided at or frequented the site, by Europeans who lived there or were closely involved with the establishment. Williams, Wyatt, Teichelmann, Schürmann, Klose, Moorhouse and Cawthorne all come into this category. All known letters written in Kaurna by Kaurna people had their origins there. The only substantial material not associated with Piltawodli consists of three short wordlists compiled by Gaimard, Robinson and Piesse, all recorded from southern Kaurna people. The Kaurna sources will be investigated in detail in Chapter 5.

The German missionaries

Missionary activity amongst the Kaurna commenced on October 14, 1838 with the arrival of **Clamor Wilhelm Schürmann** and **Christian Gottlieb Teichelmann** who were sent to South Australia by the Dresden Missionary Society under the patronage of the wealthy philanthropist, George Fife Angas. Fortunately, governor-elect Lieutenant Colonel George Gawler was aboard the same ship. On the journey out, Gawler asked the missionaries to tutor his 14-year-old daughter in the German language and a good relationship developed. He invited the missionaries to his table and lent them books (Schurmann, 1987: 21), including Threlkeld's grammar of Awabakal.[9] Amongst other things, they discussed issues relating to missions and government policy towards the Indigenous inhabitants of South Australia. Gawler informed them that their activities in relation to Indigenous people would be controlled by the Protector of Aborigines. Schürmann's journals record revealing conversations about his early attitudes to Indigenous languages:

> Surprisingly, His Excellency said that the best way to educate the natives would be to bring them nearer the larger towns. Naturally I spoke against such an idea, and so did Teichelmann. If the natives blended with the Europeans, the language of the natives could be lost. His Excellency and Mr Hall then agreed, and stated they would do everything possible to preserve the native language.
> (Journal, June 1838 quoted in Schurmann, 1987: 21)

Evidently, Gawler pursued this topic further:

> There was further discussion on the extent to which the missionary wished to preserve the natives' language, and on whether that had been ordered by the Mission Society. He answered that he believed the Society would naturally expect the retaining of the language, because in his instructions he had been told that as soon as he could master it, he should translate the Bible. Well then, would he encourage the natives to learn English?

> Individuals, yes, but not the people as a whole. In church and school I would introduce their own language, and when they had education and ability, I would encourage them to learn their own language to perfection. (Schurmann, 1987: 26)

So, both the missionaries and Gawler had thought about the issue of language preservation. Perhaps the missionaries helped the Governor towards a more positive attitude towards Indigenous languages. In any event, Gawler did demonstrate his willingness to make use of Kaurna through having a number of his speeches translated, and encouraging the retention and use of Indigenous place names.

Teichelmann and Schürmann were eager to begin learning the Kaurna language and set about eliciting Kaurna material on their first day in Adelaide: 'I asked some of them their words for the sun, and different parts of their bodies, etc., and they were very willing to answer' (Schürmann's journal, 14 October 1838; in Schurmann, 1987: 30).

In their introduction (T&S, 1840: v) they provide some insights into the circumstances under which they learnt and recorded the Kaurna language:

> Eighteen months is but a short period for the study of an unwritten language, where no means of instruction exist, and where all information must be gleaned from casual and trivial conversation. To this must be added, the uncommon rapidity, abbreviation, and carelessness with which the Aborigines speak; their extreme reluctance, for a long time to inform the inquirer; their natural inability to answer grammatical questions; together with their situation for the study of the language. These things considered, the reader will be enabled to form some idea of the difficulties which were to be overcome.

Many Kaurna used Piltawodli as a base, whilst in Adelaide, but there was a high level of mobility, with people coming and going all the time. For instance, Schürmann noted that on 10 June 1839, 'not a single soul of them remains' (Schurmann, 1987: 42), as people had gone hunting or north for a funeral. The missionaries did establish close relationships with a number of Kaurna men. On 7 December 1839 Schürmann wrote: 'It seems that the natives realize that we want only the best for them, and they are becoming attached to us. They appreciate the fact that we are learning their language' (in Schurmann, 1987: 76).

Schürmann's journals provide some indication of his progress in establishing relationships with Kaurna people and in his attempts to learn the Kaurna language and culture. There are only a few references to Aboriginal people in his journal entries during the first month after his arrival. The only mention of Kaurna people is of 'King John' and 'Captain Jack', attending the dinner given by Governor Gawler on 1 November, but there is no indication that Schürmann actually spoke with these men at the time. Unfortunately, there is a long gap in Schürmann's journal between 17 November, 1838 and 30 May, 1839 — the early period of intensive language learning.

The first named Kaurna source in Schürmann's journal is Munaitya Wattiwattitpinna [RS Munaitya Watiwatitpina], who told Schürmann certain information about Kaurna mythology and 'men's business', information to which women or children were not privy. Wattiwattitpinna preferred to accompany

Schürmann home so that he could tell him 'in secrecy and on my promise not to tell it to any native' (Journal, 5 June 1839). Schürmann regarded this event as a major breakthrough, writing the next day, 'Yesterday evening I had great pleasure in getting important insight into the religious imaginings of the natives' (Journal, 6 June 1839), and proceeded to teach them about the Creation and the 'main principles of the Christian religion'.

On 17 June, Wattiwattitpinna began building a house next to Schürmann's, giving some further indication of the depth of their relationship. Wattiwattitpinna is mentioned on a number of occasions in the ensuing weeks and months, having conversations with Schürmann late at night about aspects of Kaurna religion. He is last mentioned in the journals on 23 January 1840.

Schürmann indicates several times in his journal that he engaged Kaurna boys to help around the house and share his lodgings. For instance, on 29 October 1839: 'The native Nanto Kartammeru, Kariru <sic>[10] Warinya [RS Nantu Kartamiru Karnu Warrinya] decided today to live with me. He is a young man of 22 to 24 years, very lively, sometimes wild and obstinate, but I hope to keep him as he is useful around the house.'

Schürmann made rapid progress in learning Kaurna, writing to the Aborigines' Protection Society in London, 12 June 1839:

> I can say without pride or praise of myself, that I now know more, if not of the language, at least of the notions and manners of the natives, than any person in the colony ...
>
> ... Although my knowledge of the native language is increasing slowly and as yet very limited, the number of words (not including compound words, which are very frequent) in my possession not being upwards of a thousand, yet I can make myself understood on many subjects.

Schürmann wrote these remarks a mere eight months after arriving in South Australia. By that time, according to this letter, he had developed close relationships with the Kaurna, some of whom referred to him as 'brother'.

One of the high points in Schürmann's attempts to learn Kaurna was a five-day hunting trip (9 to 13 September 1839) to which he and Teichelmann had been invited by two young men, Tuitpurro [RS Tuitpuru} and Kudnaipiti [RS Kudna-ipiti]. Schürmann records valuable information about Kaurna hunting and food preparation practices and their camping arrangements. He also refers to collecting some 'rhymes they used in their own language' (quoted in Schurmann, 1987: 64). On the first night it was dark when they arrived at their camping spot, so, to the delight of the missionaries, they shared the fire and hut of a Kaurna person. On the second evening, Schürmann built his own hut, but found that the young people decided to camp very close to him. On the third and fourth nights Schürmann mentions sharing a hut with 'his brother Tuitpurro'. Schürmann was obviously very pleased with the outcome of this hunting expedition:

> I couldn't close this account of these five days in the bush without some added remarks. My anticipated hopes from this journey — a better knowledge of their way of life and language — were entirely fulfilled. There was progress in learning new words in their language and in the more fluent use of ones I already knew, and especially the discovery

> of a modus conjunctivus. I have also enjoyed the gracefulness and decency evident among the natives, and particularly the obedience of the young men toward the older ones.
> (Quoted in Schurmann, 1987: 66-67)

Schürmann's language learning progressed so well that he was able to open a school on 23 December 1839.[11] He was engaged as an interpreter in April 1840 at the trial of a 'Northman' who was accused of taking part in the murder of a shepherd. On 25 May 1840, he acted as interpreter for Governor Gawler at the Queen's Birthday celebrations, where he translated the Governor's speech address to the Indigenous inhabitants and read the Ten Commandments.

Just when Schürmann's facility in the Kaurna language was beginning to flower and he was beginning to make use of it in public forums, his attention was directed further afield to Encounter Bay, where he expected to take up a post in the near future. Even as he was still learning and describing Kaurna, he was gaining instruction in Ramindjeri from Tammuruwe Nankanere ('Encounter Bay Bob'). By early 1840 he observed that 'the Natives from the Murray were astonished and delighted when I spoke to them in their own language' (Journal, 10 February 1840). In September 1840 Schürmann was sent to Port Lincoln where he learnt and documented Parnkalla (now known as Barngarla), publishing a sketch grammar and vocabulary in 1844.

It is evident from his journals that Schürmann made use of every opportunity to Christianise and 'civilise'. Even during the hunting trip, he records telling the young Kaurna camping nearby about 'the creation, heaven, hell, and the future judgement' (quoted in Schurmann, 1987: 65). Although the missionaries succeeded in learning Kaurna and using it within the church and the school, they did not succeed in their goal of translating the Bible. However, they did translate the Ten Commandments and German hymns into Kaurna, and composed a school prayer (see Chapter 5).

Teichelmann was some years older than Schürmann and tried to exert his authority over him, resulting in some tension and a falling-out between the two, even as they journeyed from England to South Australia. He seems to have had a far more rigid personality, a man whose 'outlook was dominated by his religious views of what ought to be' (Kennedy, 1989: v). As a result, he often 'rubbed people up the wrong way'. This may have contributed in large part to Schürmann's willingness to relocate to Encounter Bay and eventually to Port Lincoln.

Following its discovery, Teichelmann's diary (1839-1846) was translated into English. By comparison with Schürmann's journal it contains few Kaurna personal names or other Kaurna words. In addition to the journal, some correspondence between Teichelmann and Angas, other official correspondence and articles prepared by Teichelmann that were published in the newspapers at the time have survived.

Teichelmann refers in his diary (24 November 1839, 5 January 1840) to the Kaurna deliberately withholding the language from him and (29 July 1844) avoiding his efforts to minister to them. Teichelmann remained in Adelaide after Schürmann departed for Port Lincoln and for a while continued his association with Piltawodli. However, the day-to-day running of the school was left in the hands of missionary Klose, Schürmann's replacement.

Teichelmann seems to have made a habit of visiting the Kaurna in their dwellings each Sunday and attempted to assemble them in order to preach 'God's Word'. He was forthright in his efforts to Christianise the Kaurna and challenge their beliefs to the point of inducing an angry reaction. His diaries record a number of occasions when he deliberately set out to undermine the Kaurna culture. But whilst he may not have valued many aspects of Kaurna culture, Teichelmann did have a deep respect for the Kaurna language. He writes:

> His Excellency [Governor Grey] ... expressed his favourite idea, to speak to the natives only in English. Br Meyer agreed and said to my no small amazement that the language is so lacking in abstract concepts that it would be more advisable to use the English language, even in religious instruction because one could never express anything in their language. In order not to start an argument I simply said that our Adelaide language had enough abstract concepts for them to be instructed in christendom; that in no way was I opposed to teaching the children in the English language in everything except religion. It saddened me that Br Meyer expressed his opinion during this evening when I had no opportunity to counter it in this situation, an opinion however false in itself, agreed to only because it fits into the Governor's plan, is seized upon by him and used as authoritative but which must strike to the disadvantage of our Mission. Mr Meyer's reasoning goes like this: because I have not the necessary abstract concepts ergo they are not in the language ergo it is better to give up using the language altogether. Later I gave him a host of important expressions for the teaching of the reconciliation in our dialect and outlined on them how the natives apply them.
> (Translation of Teichelmann Diary, Wednesday, 18 December 1844)

Teichelmann used his knowledge of Kaurna at every opportunity, even amongst speakers of other languages. He observes that the Kaurna language served as a passport[12] and was an instrument of power.[13] However, he was aware of his limitations and lack of knowledge, often admitting to his inability to understand[14], especially when people spoke quickly.

In November 1842, Teichelmann moved to Happy Valley, where he attempted, with the support of Governor Grey, to set up a mission called Ebenezer. He hoped that a number of Kaurna would follow him there. Several were with him for short periods but Teichelmann had limited means to provide for them in addition to his own family. The *South Australian Register* reported on 17 May 1843:

> It is not we think generally known that a section of land has been procured by the German missionaries at Happy Valley and that a Mission Station has been established with a view to the benefit of the aborigines. Mr Teichelmann has been residing there and preparing the section for cultivation for some time past; principally by the aid of the natives. At the date of our last information from Happy Valley, one of the natives had been industriously employed by Mr Teichelmann for the last eight weeks, and another for three. Of course an attempt is made to instruct them, not only in the arts of civilisation but also in the doctrines of Divine Truth. All that prevents a permanent and continued effort, is the difficulty of providing the natives with food, the whole onus of which, as far as we can learn, falls in the meantime on the missionaries.
> (Quoted in Kennedy, 1989: 10)

Kennedy goes on to say:

> This newspaper article might as well have been an obituary for the Ebenezer experiment. Small and disappointing as the native participation had been at Piltawodli their recruitment and retention at Happy Valley was even more so, due to their wandering habits and the ease with which food could be scrounged in Adelaide without having to work.
> (Kennedy, 1989: 10)

Teichelmann moved back to Adelaide in early 1846 and from there in 1847 to a farm in Morphett Vale. In 1856, Teichelmann moved to Salem on the Bremer River near Callington where he ministered to a group of German settlers newly arrived in the district. Whilst there he finished his Kaurna vocabulary (TMs) and grammatical notes (Teichelmann, 1858) which he sent to Grey, then living in Cape Town, South Africa. This is the last mention of any connection between Teichelmann and the Kaurna language.

Samuel Klose arrived in Adelaide on 9 August 1840 with another missionary, H.A.E Meyer; Meyer went straight to Encounter Bay, while Klose took up his duties at Piltawodli, principally the running of the school. A body of correspondence between Klose and the Dresden Mission Society, recently made accessible by the Lutheran Archives and translated into English, reveals there was little interaction between Klose and Kaurna adults, though he did visit the gaol regularly. Klose seems to have been particularly focused on the children, with whom he developed close relationships. He soon developed a high opinion of his students and their ability to learn. After 12 months learning Kaurna, Klose himself was beginning to feel more confident of his ability to communicate the gospel in Kaurna, though his ability to speak Kaurna was still limited, particularly, it seems, in discussing abstract or theological issues (20 August 1841).

After nearly three years, Klose reports preaching in Kaurna and successfully communicating his message, despite his inadequate language ability:

> On the second Sunday after Trinity I told them the story of the great banquet: Luke 14,16, explained to them what God wanted to be understood by it and made as an application that we too had come to invite them to this great feast. Br. Schürmann sat among the adults and gathered from them that they understood me clearly. Even though my language was still broken, so I was delighted, and was encouraged to continue. The children would have understood me better, because they are better acquainted with the story of the Old Testament. The bible pictures you sent me are very helpful ...
> (Letter, 7 July 1843)

Like his fellow missionaries, Klose used every opportunity to Christianise the Kaurna. An anecdote reveals how the missionaries were working to break down the traditional belief systems:

> The children saw a small lizard (Tarrutarru [RS tarutaru]) about 4 inches long come out of a mousehole and crawled to the fireplace. They immediately called me and said that the grown-ups say that that is the creator who made man and woman. I asked, 'What do you believe?' They all laughed; one boy named Mannara [RS Manarra] said, 'It cannot possibly be the creator because it has a mother who is probably still in the hole.' These examples are very valuable because the answers are not merely formalities from the lessons but rather convictions. From these you can see that God's word has found an opening into their hearts, which in its own good time will flourish.
> (Letter, 3 September 1844)

Klose found running the school at Piltawodli frustrating because of the irregular attendance of the children, and was dismayed at the ease with which they abandoned 'civilised' habits when they returned to the bush. Children were 'bribed' to attend school with the provision of food, and blankets were distributed to adults whose children attended. Klose had a genuine affection for the Kaurna, especially the children and was particularly concerned at the prostitution and abuse of the girls which took place at Piltawodli. In June 1843, the government instituted a kind of dormitory system at Piltawodli largely as a measure to counteract prostitution. A woman was employed to care for the girls and to instruct them in cooking and washing. Soon after, the boys slept in the schoolhouse. These measures did in fact result in more regular attendance.

Early in 1844, Klose introduced English alongside of Kaurna, 'because later on they will have to make their living among the English, and it is therefore unavoidably necessary' (Letter, 3 September 1844). Klose remained at Piltawodli until March 1846 when he was dismissed by the Governor because he, and the Lutheran Missionary Society in Dresden, insisted that they maintain control over religious education in the school (Klose letter, 6 February 1846), terms which were unacceptable to Governor Robe (see Kennedy, 1989: A3-11).

Whilst the activities of the German missionaries gained considerable government support and goodwill in the early phase, in the mid-1840s their activities were increasingly restricted and monitored. The government intervened to assume direct responsibility for Aboriginal education in 1844 with the establishment of the Walkerville School for the Murray River children. In July 1845 the Native School Establishment on Kintore Avenue opened, amalgamating the Walkerville and Piltawodli schools. This was the end of the Kaurna language for educational purposes in the nineteenth century. Its use as the medium of instruction was brief, lasting from December 1839 to July 1845.

The Native School Establishment in Kintore Avenue operated until 1852, when it was closed due to a lack of Aboriginal children remaining in Adelaide. Throughout its operation, the Kaurna were a minority at the school, which included a dormitory run by a Mr Smith. The children from the Murray districts, who were the majority, had separate dormitories from the Kaurna from Piltawodli. The dormitory system has been identified as a 'major factor contributing to the demise of numerous Aboriginal languages' (Schmidt, 1990: 12) and along with the English-only education introduced at the Native School Establishment, it was undoubtedly a powerful force leading to the rapid loss of Kaurna.

Kudnarto, the ancestor of many contemporary Kaurna people, was amongst those educated at the Native School Establishment. Her story is told in *The Kaurna People* (EDSA, 1989: 185-205) and in more detail by O'Connor (1995; 1998).

In 1850, the Anglican Archdeacon Horatio Hale established a total training institution for Aboriginal youth at Poonindie, near Port Lincoln in Barngarla country. This institution, like the Kintore Avenue establishment, was strictly English only and totally assimilationist in orientation. Initially, the majority of recruits came from the Native School Establishment in Adelaide. During its first two years, Hale had a strict policy of taking only young people 'who had been to a European school and had a knowledge of reading, writing and Christianity' (Brock & Kartinyeri, 1989: 15). There were three major intakes from the Adelaide school, a group of 11 early in 1850, a second group in October 1850 and a third in June 1851. Brock & Kartinyeri note further that:

> After his last large intake of children from the Adelaide school in 1852, the seven children remaining there absconded from the school to return to their people on Yorke Peninsula. As a result the school was temporarily closed for lack of children and in the ensuing months there were so few children in Adelaide it was never reopened.
>
> (Brock & Kartinyeri, 1989: 15)

Few of the initial recruits, though sent from Adelaide, were actually Kaurna people: most originated from the upper Murray River districts (Brock & Kartinyeri, 1989: 24). They refer to three Kaurna people amongst these early recruits by name:

- Pitpowie [RS Pitpauwi], referred to in Hale's diary entry on 14 July 1852 (Brock & Kartinyeri, 1989: 22). This is undoubtedly the same as Pitpauwe, a signatory to the 1841 letter to Gawler and author of one of the Kaurna letters sent to Dresden in 1843 (see Chapter 5).
- Maria, who spent four months at Poonindie before being dismissed for 'disreputable habits of life'. Her baby son Charlie of 'mixed descent' remained at Poonindie, but died in a boating accident in 1872 (Brock & Kartinyeri, 1989: 20). Maria had worked many years at Government House and was probably the girl referred to in Moorhouse's 8 July 1843 report (cited in Pope, 1989: 29-30).
- Monaitya [RS Munaitya], who had spent five years at the Adelaide school, was said to have been a 'disruptive influence on the mission' and was dismissed in April 1851. He returned to Adelaide and then to the bush. (Brock & Kartinyeri, 1989: 19-20)

By 1854, only four of the 53 Aboriginal people at Poonindie were said to come from Adelaide (Brock & Kartinyeri, 1989: 25). The mortality rate at Poonindie was very high in the first ten years mainly from tuberculosis. It is not clear whether any of the young Kaurna sent to Poonindie who had attended school in Adelaide have any living descendants. However, two Aboriginal women married to white men, whose children were sent to Poonindie, do have numerous descendants. These women, the aforementioned Kudnarto from the Clare district and Rathoola from Rapid Bay, are both identified as Kaurna women (Kartinyeri, 1989). These were the first two legal marriages between Aboriginal women and white men in South Australia, permission having been granted by the Protector.

Following Kudnarto's death in 1855, her husband, Tom Adams, was no longer in a position to care for their two sons, Tom and Tim, and applied to send them to Poonindie. George Solomon, whose wife Rathoola died in 1858, was left in a similar position. His sons George, John and Emanuel were sent to Poonindie in 1858, 1860 and 1870 respectively. It is also possible that other Kaurna were sent to Poonindie at a later date. Early white residents of the Aldinga area report that Bishop Short sent some Aboriginal people from Aldinga scrub to Poonindie, apparently ending Kaurna occupation of the area.[15]

With the closure of Poonindie, most residents were relocated to Bukkiyana (Point Pearce) in Narungga country and a smaller number were sent to Raukkan (Point McLeay) in Ngarrindjeri country. A few, including John Solomon, remained in the Port Lincoln district to apply for leases and take up farming. A strong Poonindie identity had developed by the 1890s, but following the move to Bukkiyana and Raukkan, these latter mission identities came to the fore. Brock & Kartinyeri (1989: 77) explain:

> Poonindie lands did not survive as Aboriginal lands. The institution did not survive after its closure in 1894 but Poonindie people survived, although they did not retain their identity. Most of them became Point Pearce or Point McLeay people.

Decline of the Kaurna and loss of the Kaurna language

The Kaurna language declined in use and status in an extraordinarily short time. The major contributing factor must have been the demise of the people themselves, the rapid destruction of their culture and the breakup of family structures. Within ten years of the establishment of the colony of South Australia, Kaurna lands had been totally occupied, the Kaurna were considered by the colonists as a defeated people and by many as a minor nuisance factor. By 1850, some writers were claiming that the Kaurna were virtually 'extinct'. Oates & Oates (1970: 93), in their survey of Australian languages, wrote under the Kaurna entry that 'this tribe was extinct by 1850' (quoted in J. Harris, 1990: 328); and the Commissioners of Belair National Park wrote in 1909: 'A Lost Tribe — The Adelaide Tribe of natives disappeared with incredible rapidity. In 1860 — not twenty five years after the first white settlement — they were all gone' (from the booklet *The National Parks of South Australia*, quoted in Cordes, 1983: 2). Whilst these pronouncements were premature, certainly by the 1850s the Kaurna were small in numbers, scattered and no longer recognised by the majority population; 'When the majority of the remaining young people were taken to Poonindie late in the same year, the Kaurna as a social group effectively disappeared' (J. Harris, 1990: 328). Yet there was no war, and by comparison with other colonies both in Australia and overseas, there was little violence between the colonisers and the colonised within Kaurna lands, though there was considerably more violence in outlying districts such as the Rufus River and Eyre Peninsula. So how did this situation come about?

We are unable to provide satisfactory answers to this question for want of adequate records[16], but in the rest of the chapter I shall attempt to outline what happened to the Kaurna people, culture and language in the latter half of the nineteenth century.

The Kaurna were never a large group, compared with neighbouring groups such as the Ngarrindjeri. A report prepared by Teichelmann & Moorhouse that was read to the Statistical Society in December 1841 noted that 'In an area of 2800 square miles, that is a distance of 80 miles to the north, and 60 to the south of Adelaide, running parallel with the coast 20 miles, there are 650 natives; or one in every 4 1/2 square miles' (in Foster, 1990b: 46). The area specified corresponds roughly to Kaurna territory as mapped out by Tindale (1974), the area generally acknowledged as Kaurna country today. The figure of 650 is perhaps reasonably accurate for the Kaurna population in 1841, by which time it was already in decline. Over the previous two years, Teichelmann & Moorhouse (1841) recorded 14 births and 36 deaths.

The Kaurna population is likely to have been considerably higher before the European invasion and the introduction of European diseases. Shortly after the establishment of the First Settlement at Sydney Cove, a smallpox epidemic broke out in 1789 killing vast numbers of Indigenous people in the Sydney region. This first epidemic possibly reached the Kaurna by being communicated from one group to the next down the river systems into South Australia, though opinion is divided on this. What is certain is that the second smallpox epidemic of 1829-1830 did affect the Kaurna and the Ngarrindjeri, as well as other groups along the Murray in South Australia, with disastrous consequences. T&S provide an illuminating entry on the subject in their vocabulary:

> Nguya, s. pustule; the disease of small-pox, from which the aborigines suffered before the Colony was founded. They universally assert that it came from the east, or from the Murray tribes, so that <it> is not at all improbable that the disease was at first brought among the natives by European settlers on the eastern coast. They have not suffered from it for some years; but about a decennium ago it was, according to their statement, universal; when it diminished their numbers considerably, and on many left the marks of its ravages, to be seen at this day. They have no remedy against it, except the nguyapalti <smallpox song>. (T&S, 1840: 34)

Before the smallpox epidemics the Kaurna population may well have numbered several thousand people. Whatever the case, by the time the colony was established in South Australia in 1836, it was probably no more than 700. The colonists brought with them additional diseases, notably syphilis, gonorrhoea, tuberculosis, typhoid, measles, whooping cough, typhus and influenza. These are known to have resulted in high mortality rates in Indigenous populations worldwide because of their lack of resistance to them.

The rapidly growing township of Adelaide put much stress on the local environment. Within a short period of time, the Torrens became heavily polluted, especially through tanneries upstream pouring their effluent directly into the river. Pope (1989: 40) writes that 'Pollution of the Torrens from sewerage and tanning works effluent probably contributed to an outbreak of typhoid fever in 1843'. The effects of this typhoid outbreak on the Kaurna would have been especially severe. Those living at Piltawodli were totally dependent on water from the Torrens, by contrast with colonists who were able to turn to wells that had been sunk. Accurate figures on the effects of these diseases are not available, but disease is probably the biggest single factor in the massive and rapid decline of the Kaurna population.

Curiously, several observers note an under-representation of females in the Kaurna population, as in a report prepared by Teichelmann & Moorhouse (1841): 'The proportions of the sexes gives a peculiar predominance to the males; out of the number 650 there are 280 males, 182 females, and 188 children - it may be observed that there is about one child to each female' (in Foster, 1990b: 46).

Pope (1989: 25) notes that 'Among about 3000 Europeans in 1840, there lived almost 100 Aborigines — 47 men, 20 women and 26 children.' These figures relate to the immediate Adelaide township, but reflect the same pattern. An article in the *Register* (17 January, 1844) noted that, as 'respects the Adelaide tribe, the proportion of men is nearly seventy per cent in excess of the women and children' whereas in neighbouring groups to the north and east there were equal proportions of men, women and children. This disparity may have been due in part to single men drifting into Adelaide from outlying areas. However, it could well be an indication of the activities of the sealers in the preceding few decades.[17] It is unlikely to have been the result of diseases such as smallpox or influenza, which would be expected to affect the population more uniformly, though sexually transmitted diseases such as syphilis and gonorrhoea introduced by the sealers, whalers and colonists may have contributed to this pattern. Whatever the cause, a population profile which included few women of child-bearing age was disastrous for the Kaurna.

Whilst disease was undoubtedly the major cause of the population decline, it was not the only cause. The historical record frequently points to peaceful co-existence and friendly relations between the colonists and the local Adelaide Aboriginal people, but, the possibility that numbers of Kaurna were secretly killed by colonists, especially in the northern areas of Kaurna territory, should not be ruled out. Following the hanging of four members of the 'Kapunda Tribe' in June 1861 for their alleged carrying out of the Rainbird Murders, it appears that a large-scale massacre of the 'Kapunda Tribe' took place because the local white population were incensed that the four had been hanged in private behind the walls of the Adelaide Gaol and not in public at Kapunda. Peter Liddy, a criminologist and lawyer, who has recently researched the Rainbird Murders mentions the discovery in 1915 of a mass grave just north of Auburn in the mid-north, the area to which the remaining 'Kapunda Tribe' had moved (Liddy, 1993: 85-86).

The prevailing view was that the Aboriginal population should be left alone, as they would soon disappear. The missionaries, whilst gaining some official support in the early years, were heavily criticised by many colonists:

> The cry was raised 'Leave the blacks alone. You are only wasting your time, and money, and talent. They are doomed to extinction, and the sooner they are extinct, the better. With their loitering in the parklands, and their 'beastly corroborees', and their petty thieving, they are nothing but a nuisance.' (Brauer, 1956: 155)

Teichelmann and Klose responded to the criticism by asking:

> Who is responsible for their acquisition of the white man's vices and diseases? Is it not the depraved whites who infect them morally and physically? Why are they doomed to extinction? Is it not largely because of the bad habits some white people teach them, and because of the diseases they transmit to them? Who must take the greater blame for their degradation and acquired corrupt practices, the benighted blackfellow himself, or the vicious white men upon whom the light of reason and the blessings of civilization have been shed in vain? Why are many of the natives not taking kindly to the teachings of the white man? Among other reasons also because they lose confidence in the white man, when they see some of their number abused and ill treated by white men, and their wives and sisters and relatives becoming the victims of the most loathsome diseases which formerly were utterly unknown to them. (Quoted in Brauer, 1956: 155)

The Kaurna were quickly outnumbered by Aboriginal people from the Murray River who remained for extended periods in Adelaide. Fights broke out between the two groups and the Kaurna leaders resented the uninvited presence of the Murray peoples on their land. They correctly attributed their presence to the Europeans and appealed to the government to prevent them from coming. It could be that numbers of Kaurna women were taken off by men from the Murray who had perhaps come to Adelaide unaccompanied, leaving their own women behind.

We can only assume that with different language groups coming into unprecedented long and sustained contact with each other, and with the breakdown in Aboriginal family groups and accompanying alcohol abuse and prostitution, there must have been high rates of black on black violence, resulting in a considerable number of deaths. This view is supported by an article in a newspaper in 1847:

> it is commonly said that the whites have driven away the Cowandilla or Adelaide natives from the city. No such thing. This now small tribe have been driven away, their wives and daughters seized on, and their men killed almost before our eyes, by hordes of wild Murray and even Darling natives, who at this moment infest our streets, and who were never seen on this side of the mountains before the whites came.
> (*Southern Australian*, 15 June 1847: 2)

Some Kaurna may have merged with neighbouring groups and their Kaurna identities been lost. There is a suggestion that Kadlitpinna ('Captain Jack') was living at Raukkan with the Ngarrindjeri people in the later part of his life (Simpson, 1998: 8).[18] A few Kaurna, such as Kalloongoo and Emma or Emue (see Amery, 1996d), were known to have remained elsewhere in the pre-colonial sealing era. Kalloongoo was last reported at Port Philip in 1842 and it seems that Emue remained in Bass Strait. Other Aboriginal people who left the colony through employment on ships or with overlanders may have remained in other colonies or even overseas, though attrition of the population in this way after 1836 is not likely to have been high.

In 1850, there were reported to be 300 Aboriginal people in the Adelaide district and a further 300 in the Encounter Bay to Yankalilla district. Many of these people were undoubtedly Ngarrindjeri or Ngayawang from the Murray River districts, but nonetheless, the figures indicate that there was still a significant Aboriginal presence in the Adelaide district.

As we have seen, there was little direct violence against the Kaurna, at least in the vicinity of Adelaide, but government policies were clearly directed towards imposing English 'civilisation' and obliterating Indigenous cultures as quickly as possible. Whilst they tried to preserve the language, the missionaries also contributed in a major way to this cultural genocide. We have seen how they attempted to challenge and break down the Kaurna belief systems and to set the young against their Elders. Both the missionaries and the government were responsible for instituting a dormitory system, cutting children off from their families. Finally, government policies served to remove Kaurna peoples from their lands and to institute forced marriages at Poonindie in disregard of kinship prohibitions and family alliances, the backbone of Kaurna culture.

Important Kaurna sites were violated. It appears that the Tarnda Kanya[19] 'red kangaroo rock' site was quarried to provide stone to build many of the substantial early buildings on North Terrace. Portatangga 'Ochre Cove', a sacred men's site to the south, was mined to supply hundreds of tons of red ochre to the paint industry in England up until the 1940s (Campbell, 1983: 6). Graves were desecrated and bodies and skeletons were deposited in museums both here and overseas.[20]

Game quickly became scarce as the colonists occupied Kaurna lands and set up agricultural and pastoral industries; the Kaurna were reduced to a state of dependency, and as a consequence, were soon treated with contempt.

Kaurna leaders died in the prime of life. According to the *Register* (6 January 1845) Mullawirraburka was only 35 years when he died, probably as a result of tuberculosis (Gara, 1998: 29). According to this report he was survived by only two of his four wives and three of at least nine children. This, no doubt, further contributed to loss of hope and cohesion within the group. Some Kaurna people refer to this period as the 'holocaust' or the 'initial holocaust' (pc Georgina Williams, March 1998).

It would appear that language shift from Kaurna to English took place in an exceedingly short time following colonisation. In the early years colonists made efforts to learn Kaurna and there is some evidence that a jargon or pidgin Kaurna developed briefly (Simpson, 1996). Soon after Schürmann arrived in South Australia he reported that Aboriginal people from other districts quickly learnt and used Kaurna when they came to Adelaide (Report attached to letter, 21 June 1839). So it seems that Kaurna was to some extent a prestigious language. However, this pattern probably did not persist for long as the population balance changed.

After the school at Piltawodli closed in July 1845 there is no evidence that Kaurna continued to play any role whatsoever in public life. Grey, as Governor, forbade Teichelmann to preach in Kaurna and there are no further references to singing and praying in Kaurna, which were previously a frequent occurrence. All the newly developed language functions, the speeches, hymns, sermons, prayers and literacy had been abandoned or prohibited. The services of Kaurna-English interpreters were no longer needed. The status of the language had plummeted.

The dislocation of Kaurna peoples from their lands, the population collapse and subsequent minority status, the dormitory system and English-only education must all have been instrumental in promoting the shift to English. On 4 August 1845, just after the relocation of the school from Piltawodli to Kintore Avenue, Klose remarked 'The language which has been introduced into the school is English, which the children also use amongst themselves' (Letter, 29 August 1845).[21] When the Kaurna children went to the Kintore Avenue school, they were a minority mixing with children who spoke a language that was not mutually intelligible.[22] A lingua franca was needed and in the context of an all-English school, it seems that English came to serve that function. Of course the Murray River children had been previously schooled in English in the Walkerville school.

Kaurna children, it appears, had also acquired some knowledge of English informally from their interactions with the colonists and by 1845 were well versed in singing hymns and reciting prayers in English. Their understanding of English, however, was probably limited. A few months earlier, Teichelmann had tried to test their understanding by asking them to translate passages from an English reader into Kaurna:

> ... in an English reader that contained moral and biblical sections and [I] had the bigger ones read a few of the short sections which they were then to translate into their own language. Apart from the remarkable fact that those who were most advanced in their own language read worst as opposed to the young ones who read well, I was again shown that the children while they read well do not understand it since none could translate what was read into their own language (Teichelmann Diary, 27 April 1845)

The children's apparent inability to translate the English passages may well have been due to resistance to Christianity or an unwillingness to try to render unfamiliar and foreign concepts into their own language, rather than evidence of not understanding English. The English colonists strongly disfavoured the use of Indigenous languages in education. Klose's introduction of some English into his program early in 1844 was probably partly an accommodation to the colonists' wishes, though Klose himself saw the need for English if the Kaurna were to survive within colonial society.

But the shift in government policies which imposed English-only education and forbade the missionaries to preach in Kaurna, together with plans to relocate the Kaurna away from their lands and settle them in a mixed community at Poonindie, with a pervading all-English ethos, sealed the fate of the Kaurna language. Survival for the Kaurna meant life in this all-English environment, merging with neighbouring language groups at Raukkan and Bukkiyana or eking out a living on the fringes of small country towns. The support systems for the language had been destroyed. The remaining Kaurna had been thrust into new situations requiring the use of other languages, and into situations which were hostile to Kaurna.

Surviving the 'dark ages'

Claims of 'extinction' made in the 1850s and 1860s were indeed premature. It seems, for instance, that a group of Kaurna maintained a continual presence in the Port Adelaide area up until 1890 (Brodie & Melvin, 1994: 25). A group camped near the western end of the Jervois Bridge were moved in about 1890 to make way for the CSR sugar factory. Port Adelaide was probably one of the last refuges for the remaining Kaurna, even into the twentieth century. A white resident, Fred Miller, recalls from his father's time:

> They [Aboriginal people] lived along Hawker's Creek in wurlies, round the path of Hawkers Creek. There were quite a few of them. When I was a boy [1907-1912] there were still some old Aboriginals living round the swamp at Buck's Flat near where the Le Fevre Boys High School is now. They were the very old Aboriginals, the sort that was dying off. In those early days women used to do a lot of working to keep house and they used to get the blacks to come and do their housework to save them the hard labour of it. Hart owned right to the river. He owned practically everything. It was all absolutely open in those days, there was nothing here at all and the Aboriginals did live around the rim of the swamp. (Quoted in Brodie & Melvin, 1994: 30)

One old 'full-blood' man is remembered by a number of people as living in the Glanville area until about 1930. Other historical sources say that the last Kaurna male of 'full descent', James Phillips, died in 1897 (Hemming, 1990: 80).

Nevertheless, the number of Kaurna persons alive in the latter part of the nineteenth century must have been few indeed. Certainly, by contrast with the early days of the colony, the Kaurna were practically invisible. Those that remained were probably scattered over a wide area. Some lived at Port Adelaide, aloof perhaps from the troublesome Murray peoples who outnumbered them in Adelaide. Others seem to have lived in nearby small country towns such as Clarendon and Kangarilla, and some drifted to Bukkiyana[23], as Brock & Kartinyeri indicate above. And of course there were the Kaurna youth who were sent to Poonindie.

It would seem that a Kaurna woman from Gawler was amongst a small group of Aborigines rounded up in the city and sent to Raukkan in 1912. She was known as 'Warrette (Emma Pritchard). "Last of the Gawler Tribe"' (Mattingley & Hampton, 1988: 155).[24] Under the 'Aborigines Act' of 1911, the Protector was granted powers to remove the few Aboriginal people remaining in the city. On the 10 January 1912 he issued the following order to the Commissioner of Police:

> I have the honor to request that the following Aborigines who are a nuisance in and around the City must be mustered up and conveyed by a Police Officer to Point McLeay, on Friday next; George Donnelly, Wilson Hack, Jennie Hack, Emma Pritchard and Susan Campbell. (in Mattingley & Hampton, 1988: 7)

As a result of these measures, in 1913 the Chief Protector reported that 'The aborigines who used to infest the city and suburbs have all been removed and placed on Point Mcleay, where they are kept and provided for under the Act. They are quite happy there and behave themselves well' (in Mattingley &

Hampton, 1988: 6). This would appear to be the end of an Aboriginal presence in Adelaide.

Having been removed to the missions, Kaurna people grew up with mission identities, though some still retained a knowledge of their ties with Kaurna country. On the missions the Kaurna intermarried with the Ngarrindjeri, Narungga and other groups and took on 'Point Pearce' and 'Point McLeay' mission identities. They tended to identify closely with the place and the lifestyle in which they grew up.

Some Kaurna people may have been on the missions at the time of their establishment, Point McLeay in 1859 and Point Pearce in 1868 respectively. It is likely that in the face of the expansion of the colony and the threat of being removed to Poonindie the few remaining Kaurna people merged with the neighbouring Ngarrindjeri and Narungga peoples at Raukkan and Bukkiyana by drawing on their kin ties and in-laws.

Gara (1990) has traced the life story of one important Kaurna identity in this period, namely Ivaritji. She is believed to have been the last Kaurna person of 'full Aboriginal descent' and possibly the last fluent speaker of Kaurna. She moved with her family to the Clarendon area in the 1850s. After the death of her parents in the early 1860s she was adopted by a white family in the district. However, she later lived for some time at both Raukkan and Bukkiyana, where she was living in 1919 when Daisy Bates visited. In the intervening period she may also have lived for a while at Poonindie. Ivaritji was the daughter of Ityamaiitpinna ('King Rodney').[25] Ivaritji died in 1929, though she seemed to remember only a little of her language in the last years of her life.

Throughout this period at least some people, it seems, tried to keep in touch with Kaurna country by visiting Kaurna places whenever possible. However, life on the missions was strictly controlled and movement in and out was at the discretion of the Superintendent and the Protector of Aborigines. Nevertheless, the mission offered a sense of community and a sense of security. A number of Nunga people comment that it wasn't until they left the mission environment that they realised they 'were different' and experienced the direct effect of personalised racism (see Rigney, 1995).

It needs to be pointed out that Aboriginal people in South Australia were subject to 'The Aborigines Act' of 1911, which remained in place with some minor alterations until 1962. Under 'The Act', as it was known, their lives were subject to severe restrictions. They were a captive workforce, as movement was controlled and other civil liberties curtailed:

> The Act gave the Chief 'Protector of Aboriginals' wide powers over families, children, property, rights of movement and freedom of access. Under the Act the Chief 'Protector' became the 'legal guardian of every aboriginal and every half-caste child' until we reached the age of twenty-one, regardless of parents or relatives. He could 'undertake the general care, protection, and management of the property of any aboriginal or half-caste'.
>
> He had the power to 'cause any aboriginal or half-caste to be kept within the boundaries of any reserve or ... institution', or to be removed or transferred to another. Our people could be ordered to move their camps from any municipality, town or township. Such places could be proclaimed 'prohibited areas'. Any one of us could be arrested for

> loitering. Entry to reserves was restricted and any person 'who removes an aboriginal, or causes, assists, entices or persuades an aboriginal to remove, from a reserve' was guilty of an offence.
> (Mattingley & Hampton, 1988: 45)

Mattingley & Hampton (1988) provide ample graphic description of life under 'The Act' from a Nunga perspective. On the missions a strong Aboriginal identity developed in the relative isolation from mainstream society. Ceremonial life was suppressed and as a result most 'traditional' cultural practices were lost. However, many aspects of kinship did survive, notably the centrality of the extended family.

Before the 1960s and the granting of full citizenship rights, there were very few Aboriginal people resident in Adelaide. The Commonwealth census figures show 30 'half-castes' in Adelaide in 1921, 95 in 1933, 241 in 1944 and in 1954 (Inglis, 1961: 201), though it appears that many of these were transient.[26] No doubt these figures under-represent the true situation to some degree and probably exclude numbers of people whose appearance allowed them to merge with the general population, even though some may have continued to associate with and identify with the Nunga population. Prior to 1954 the growth of Adelaide's Indigenous population was slow. According to F. Gale (1972: 74), most resident in Adelaide at that time had come during World War II and had remained. Aboriginal people from the Northern Territory and northern South Australia made up the bulk of this population. In the 1950s, there were only a dozen or so people drawn from Bukkiyana and Raukkan. However, Kaurna people were amongst the first Aboriginal people to return to Adelaide.

After 1954 the South Australian government adopted a policy of assimilation, which intentionally moved people away from the crowded missions and reserves, where the population was increasing, into mainstream Australia. More people were issued with exemption certificates and were thereby forced to cut their ties and move to the city[27] — usually those whom it was thought would more easily blend with the European population, either because of their appearance or their lifestyle and propensity to obtain employment. As a result of this policy, many people were moved from Bukkiyana and Raukkan into Adelaide, actively encouraged and assisted to migrate by the Department of Aboriginal Affairs.

The relaxation of laws in the 1960s and the granting of full citizenship with the 1967 Referendum resulted in a full-scale migration to the city. The reasons were many and varied; important amongst them were the desire to escape restrictions imposed by the mission, and to experience new-found freedom. No doubt many people moved to Adelaide to join relatives, for health reasons or for their children's education. Mattingley & Hampton (1988, Chapter 6) provide numerous excerpts from interviews with Aboriginal people, including Mary Cooper, mother of Georgina Williams.

People with ties to Raukkan have become numerically dominant, since 1961, with the Ngarrindjeri emerging as the biggest Indigenous group in Adelaide. Both Inglis (1961) and F. Gale (1970) draw attention to the strength and resilience of family ties and Aboriginal culture amongst Nungas from Bukkiyana and Raukkan living in Adelaide, in contrast to the peoples now generally referred to as the 'stolen generation' living in institutions and foster homes. Inglis refers to these Bukkiyana and Raukkan people as the 'insiders'. Those at the forefront in promotion of the Kaurna language are generally secure in their Aboriginality and feel comfortable about who they are and where they are from. Moreover, they demonstrate a strong commitment to developing this sense of Aboriginal identity amongst the younger generation. A strong identity is seen as an inner strength, a protection for a minority people growing up within a dominant, and sometimes openly negative and racist majority culture.

Fay Gale discusses identity issues at a time when a distinctive Nunga community was just beginning to form in Adelaide. Her discussion, grounded in detailed demographic data, is invaluable in understanding the roots of a modern Kaurna identity, and I quote Gale at length:

> Aborigines born in Adelaide have little group or kinship identity. Those now old enough to be married, grew up in a period when there were few other Aborigines in the city and they were forced to become assimilated into the general community. Therefore most of the adult Aborigines who were born in Adelaide have now married Europeans. Whether this will happen in the next generation is not so certain. It may well be that in the future there will be sufficient numbers of Aborigines living in strong enough social groupings to enable marriage to take place within the Aboriginal community rather than outside of it. The Aboriginal population is growing rapidly both in numbers and in group solidarity. Aborigines in the city are becoming increasingly conscious of an identity separate from that of the white community. Aborigines who once considered themselves to be completely assimilated are now beginning to identify with other Aborigines. Now that it has become socially acceptable to be known as an Aboriginal and there is a sufficiently large community to identify with, people who once 'passed' as European are now referring to themselves as Aborigines. If this process of group identification continues it is likely that the amount of intermarriage with Europeans will diminish and more Aborigines will marry within their own community in the future. It also means that new Aboriginal social groups are forming which are no longer based on kin affiliation. Furthermore, the population in Adelaide is increasing, not just because of the increasing rate of immigration to the city but also because of the people who were once 'white' but now call themselves Aboriginal. There is thus a social as well as a natural increase in population taking place in the city. (F. Gale, 1970: 323)

Aboriginal people living in Adelaide in the 1960s identified very strongly with their community of origin. According to Jordan:

> Aboriginal people interviewed in the city saw the reserve they were brought up on as 'home' and, while having a comprehensive knowledge of their own relations, often had no knowledge of other Aboriginal families outside these groupings. They saw themselves as Point McLeay people or Point Pearce people. (Jordan, 1984: 281)

Peter Gale (1991), on the basis of interviews conducted with Nungas who had all migrated to Adelaide in the 1960s, concludes that for some members of the older generation this 'mission' identity is still important:

> For some older Nunga people who had lived most of their lives on the missions the land continued to have a higher level of cultural significance, and there remained strong feelings for the land associated with the mission. This was most clearly expressed in the desire to be buried on the mission land, and they would defend that 'right' of burial.
> (P. Gale, 1991: 154)

These observations accord with my own made over the last decade. The identification with Bukkiyana or Raukkan is still paramount for most older Nungas, despite the fact that they have been living in Adelaide for three decades or more. All Kaurna people today relate to these two missions, either because they grew up there themselves or because their parents or grandparents did. Most Kaurna people still make frequent visits to one or other (perhaps both) of these missions and refer to these visits as 'going home station'.

However, there is also a reawakening and a yearning for knowledge of culture and language that go beyond childhood memories. To some extent the forging of new identities is focused on languages which ceased to be used on a regular basis many years ago. These matters are taken up in Chapter 10.

Notes

[1] The term Kaurna was not used in reference to the people of the Adelaide Plains in the nineteenth century. They were usually referred to as the 'Adelaide Tribe', though a number of other terms were also occasionally used.

[2] Teichelmann writes 'of the Aborigines who once inhabited the district round about Adelaide; for they have disappeared to a very few ... the Tribe has ceased to be' (Letter to Grey, 18 January 1858 (Item 56, section 40. Supplement: Southern Australian Languages), in Bleek's catalogue of Sir George Grey's collection, South African Public Library, Cape Town).

[3] Many Aboriginal people resent being referred to as a 'descendant', interpreting this as meaning that they are not 'real' Aboriginal people.

[4] It is now commonplace for public events in Adelaide to be opened by Kaurna Elders and for Indigenous visitors to acknowledge that they are visiting and standing on Kaurna land.

[5] The wordlists themselves will be discussed in detail in Chapter 5.

[6] See also Gouger (1898: 199-200).

[7] The additional information in brackets in this entry appears to have been added at a later date.

[8] Though Piltawodli was set aside for Aborigines, they were never granted title to the land. In the 1840s the 'Native Location' at Piltawodli consisted of 14 acres.

[9] In a letter to Dresden (10 December 1838) Schürmann writes: 'Although we had in London copied the grammar compiled by Threlkeld at the Wellington School, New South Wales, it was most gratifying to be offered by the Governor [Gawler] a copy of his printed version to study.'

[10] 'Kariru' in the English translation should be 'Karnu' ('mountain'). See original entry. In the published version, this name is given as 'Nanto Kartammera' <sic> (Schurmann, 1987: 72).

[11] It seems that Teichelmann doubted the possibility for success of the school at this stage for he writes: 'I have always considered this step premature because the parents, on whom the children are totally dependent, still lead their old nomadic life. If it succeeds, however, not a little will have been won. Schürmann's undertaking crowned and my view totally disproved; which would really please me' (Diary, 26-27 December 1839). Despite his misgivings, Teichelmann assisted in the venture by preparing a set of alphabet cards.

[12] On a trip to the Murray River, Teichelmann observes 'All of them are very trusting, and so much more so when I gave them to understand that I spoke a language of the natives, even though they spoke a different one' (Diary, 22 October 1840).

[13] Teichelmann writes 'Our influence on them appears to be growing ... once we have their language in our power, the Lord will through his word perform signs and wonders on these natives, however, low they have sunk' (Diary, 18 January 1840).

[14] For instance, after more than six years in Adelaide, Teichelmann says 'I assembled the old natives (men only) to talk to them and to find out what they really thought about our work amongst them and what opinions thay <sic> had about the truths we had presented to them. But

I could reach no conclusion, partly because they spoke evasively, partly because I could not understand them' (Diary, 2 March 1845).

[15] Campbell (1981: 4) writes 'Yet some small family groups of Aborigines continued to live in the more isolated areas, such as the Aldinga Scrub. It was here that the presence of a few wurlies worried Bishop Short sufficiently for him to organise the removal of their owners to Poonindie ... This appears to have marked the end of the local Kaurna people, for recollections of early residents interviewed in 1979 indicate that whilst Aborigines were present in the vicinity of the Scrub until late in the nineteenth century, these people were from Goolwa.'

[16] Reports about the Kaurna or 'Adelaide' people in the historical record after 1845 are fragmentary and sketchy. Few articles appeared in the newspapers of the period. A number of colonists made observations about their dealings with Aboriginal people in their journals. Some observers just made a passing comment, perhaps relating to a single event. Information can also be gained from official letters and reports, especially to and from the Protector of Aborigines.

[17] Plomley attributes the gross disparity in the sexes amongst some north-eastern Tasmanian Aboriginal groups which George Augustus Robinson observed to the capturing of women by the sealers. Amongst one group of about 80 people, Robinson found just three women compared with 72 men and made no mention of any children (Plomley, 1966: 439).

[18] Taplin refers to a man called 'Captain Jack' with a Ngarrindjeri name 'Tooreetparne', which translates as 'wild dog', as does *kadli* the root of Kadlitpinna.

[19] Tandanya, the name for the land upon which Adelaide was built, appears to be a contraction of *tarnta* 'red kangaroo' and *kanya* 'rock'. Numerous quarries were located on the southern bank of the Torrens, and it is likely that *Tarnta Kanya* referred to one or more rock formations which no longer exist.

[20] There is a reference in the Tindale papers to two bodies sent from Adelaide to the Royal College of Surgeons in England by Governor Grey in 1845. Photos of the embalmed bodies are to be found in Tindale's box of ephemera relating to the 'Adelaide Tribe'. Tindale also believed that the smoked body of Ityamaiitpinna [RS Ityamai-itpina] 'King Rodney' is held in the Berlin Museum (Kaurna or Adelaide Tribe Data, Tindale Collection, South Australian Museum) though enquiries by museum staff revealed that the body in question probably originated from Queensland (Gara, 1990: 73).

[21] Klose made this remark just five years after his earlier observations that people from other districts quickly acquired Kaurna, and less than ten years after the arrival of the colonists.

[22] Three years earlier Klose reported that the Murray children 'understand neither English nor the local native language' (Letter, 26 April 1842).

[23] Bukkiyana was the destination for children absconding from the Adelaide school, presumably because their families had already moved there.

[24] The caption appears on a photo held in the South Australian Museum. Warrette is probably the same as the birth-order name Warruato [RS Warru-artu] 'second-born + female'.

[25] Ivaritji's childhood name was possibly Itya Mau (Gara, 1990: 64) or more likely Itya Maii [RS Itya Mai]. Itya Maii was the writer of several Kaurna letters.

[26] F. Gale's (1972) figures reveal that between 150 and 200 Aboriginal people were resident in Adelaide between 1950 and 1954.

[27] Under the Act those issued with exemption certificates were no longer able to remain on the missions and reserves or visit their family there without permission.

5

Kaurna Sources

> *...[I]it is hoped that the reader will not expect a complete specimen of the language. Eighteen months is but a short period for the study of an unwritten language, where no means of instruction exist, and where all information must be gleaned from casual and trivial conversation. To this must be added, the uncommon rapidity, abbreviation, and carelessness with which the Aborigines speak; their extreme reluctance for a long time, to inform the inquirer; their natural inability to answer grammatical questions; together with their unfavourable situation for the study of the language.* (T&S, 1840: v)

> *Now I don't see it as something that has been written by goonyas, therefore we shouldn't embrace it. It is there. It's ours. It has been recorded for us and indeed in some of those recordings our people are talking to us. But we need to decode it.*
> (Lester Irabinna Rigney, interviewed by Jenny Burford, 21 October 1997)

The vast bulk of documentation of the Kaurna language was recorded in the early years of the colonisation of South Australia, from 1836 to 1845, by a number of different observers, themselves of differing linguistic background including German, English and French. A short wordlist was even recorded a decade earlier in Western Australia.

Almost no new Kaurna material was recorded in the latter half of the nineteenth century. Some material was published or compiled in that period, notably Teichelmann (1857, 1858) and Wyatt (1879), but most, if not all, of this material was probably collected before 1845. No further original work seems to have been undertaken, post Teichelmann, until the twentieth century, when Daisy Bates (1919), John McConnell Black (1920) and Norman Tindale worked with Ivaritji, who was said to be the last remaining speaker of the Kaurna language (see Gara, 1990: 82). Tindale also recorded a few words from Alf Spender. This more recent material is indeed valuable, but it is not nearly as extensive as the work carried out last century. In addition, both Tindale and the Berndts recorded information about the Adelaide Plains and Kaurna traditions from Ngarrindjeri and Ngadjuri informants.

Tapes made more recently by the late Gladys Elphick and late Auntie Kumai (Rebecca Harris) could possibly reveal additional information. Gladys Elphick's life story is currently being written on the basis of these interviews, but the tapes and transcripts are not available to me at present. As mentioned earlier, there is always the possibility that some residual Kaurna language might be handed down orally from one generation to the next within certain Nunga families, who may not wish to make this information public.

This chapter introduces the Kaurna sources, the material we have to work with in the reclamation of the language. Primary and secondary sources are summarised in Tables 5.3 and 5.4 at the end of the chapter. The first section introduces the respective researchers and observers and their records of the language, focusing on vocabulary. Many observers simply recorded a wordlist and nothing else. Other aspects of the language — grammar, texts, Dreaming stories and songs — are addressed in separate sections. Sources on these aspects of Kaurna are limited and are better discussed together, relative to each other, than with the author or compiler.

The sources

The historical sources include both primary sources, recorded from Kaurna speakers, and secondary sources, where one author has taken material recorded by another and reshaped it in his[1] own publication, often introducing errors in the process. A number of sources include both primary and secondary material and are hard to classify. Historical sources include several writers from the early twentieth century who recorded some material from Ivaritji.

The Kaurna sources vary greatly in their accuracy, reliability and depth. The German mission sources, T&S and TMs, comprise by far the best and most comprehensive sources on the Kaurna language. T&S also provide the only grammar. These two sources are the foundation upon which the teaching of Kaurna and its attempted revival in the 1990s is based.

The 'Adelaide School'
The German missionaries gained some followers in Adelaide who adopted their orthography and their methods. Weatherstone (1843), a Wesleyan lay preacher, used their orthography to compile a vocabulary of Ngayawang at Swan Reach on the Murray River. Moorhouse (1846) also modelled his grammar of Ngayawang on work produced by the missionaries and appears to have incorporated Weatherstone's vocabulary, without acknowledgement, into this publication. Simpson (1992: 410) puts forward the notion of an 'Adelaide School of language researchers' who exchanged information and learned from one another. She identifies Teichelmann, Schürmann, Meyer and Moorhouse, under the patronage of Governor Grey and Governor Gawler before him. To this group should be added the names of Klose and Weatherstone. Whilst Klose, as far as we know, produced little original linguistic research himself, he did use the vocabulary, grammar and hymns written by Teichelmann and Schürmann and employed their orthographic system in teaching literacy at Piltawodli. Others also adopted T&S spellings and used their materials.

Upon their arrival in Adelaide, **Teichelmann** and **Schürmann** immediately set about learning the Kaurna language for the purpose of Christianising and 'civilising' the Indigenous inhabitants. They had been instructed to translate the Bible as soon as practicable. For the period, they were reasonably well-prepared to research Aboriginal languages. They had been instructed in Latin, Greek,

English, Hebrew and even a little Chinese in seminaries in Germany, and, whilst they were frustrated in their attempts to learn Kaurna, they made good progress. Schürmann's journals (Schurmann, 1987: 101) reveal that the manuscript for T&S was completed early in April of that year, just eighteen months after their arrival in the colony. This was an outstanding feat. However, the authors make its shortcomings and deficiencies explicit in the introduction and in a letter sent by Schürmann to Angas on April 3, 1840: 'we ourselves do not think it to contain one half of the riches of forms and ideas which may probably be hidden in the language' (in Schurmann, 1987: 91).

T&S consists of a 24-page sketch grammar, a vocabulary of some 1816 head entries, a phraseology of 141 entries, two short passages illustrating dialect differences and five short song lines. The major deficiency lies in the absence of any substantial texts. The missionaries had Threlkeld's (1834) grammar and studied it on the ship on their journey to Australia (cf. p. 57 above). Whilst undoubtedly influenced by it, they did not simply copy the same format.

The vocabulary section of T&S is more than a list of words and their meanings. Many entries demonstrate a level of sophistication, including different senses in which a word is used plus illustrative examples. Consider, for instance, the entry for *yaitya*:

> Yaitya, adj. proper; own; native; fresh; as yaitya warra, one's own language; yaitya meyu, countryman; yaitya kauwe, proper (ie fresh) water. The reverse is kuma, or pindi.

Other entries provide ethnographic or historical information, as in:

> Pangkarra, s. a district or tract of country belonging to an individual, which he inherits from his father. Ngarraitya paru aityo pangkarrila, there is an abundance of game in my country. As each pankarra has a peculiar name, many of the owners take that as their proper name, with the addition of the term burka; for instance, Mulleakiburka (Tam O'Shanter), Mullawirraburka (King John), Kalyoburka, Karkulyaburka, Tindoburka, &c. Another mode of giving names to themselves is to affix the same term, or itpinna, to the surname of one of their children; as Kadlitpinna (Captain Jack), Wauwitpinna, Wirraitpinna, &c.

Cf. also Nguya, referred to on p. 65.

The Phraseology section contains a range of sentences, some of which are useful for everyday communication, including simple question and response routines. The sentence examples given illustrate utterances T&S heard Kaurna people produce, as opposed to elicited or constructed material. These sentences thus contrast sharply with religious texts such as the Ten Commandments or the translations of Gawler's speeches, which are probably far removed from native speaker utterances. T&S have attempted to represent Kaurna speech sounds in a regular and consistent fashion, though they do not entirely achieve this objective. Unlike most other observers in the nineteenth century, they attempted to explain their orthography. These matters are taken up in Chapter 6.

After the publication of T&S, Teichelmann continued working on the Kaurna language. In 1857 he sent his handwritten manuscript 'Dictionary of the Adelaide Dialect' to Captain George Grey, South Australia's third Governor, who was by then resident in Cape Town, South Africa. Shortly afterwards he sent an annotated copy of T&S and additional grammatical notes (Teichelmann, 1858), discussed below (p. 95, 'Grammar').

TMs contains almost 2500 words, somewhat more than T&S. However, Teichelmann compiled his dictionary, to some degree, as a companion to T&S. Some of the most common words such as *kuya* 'fish' and *warto* 'wombat' are not included in TMs, though they are in T&S. Simpson (1992: 412-413) observes that the semantic content of TMs entries shows greater sophistication and more hierarchical organisation. The various senses of many terms are elucidated more fully and many more example phrases and sentences are provided.

The spelling system is essentially the same as in T&S, though minor changes, such as the addition of some diacritics, are evident. One of the most noticeable differences is that *e* occurring after *y* in T&S is often spelt as *ä* in TMs. Teichelmann realised there were deficiencies in the spelling system, for he writes in the letter accompanying his manuscript (18 January 1858):

> I do not entirely approve of the orthography of the native language, as we have spelt it, but it is useless now to alter any thing in it after the Tribe has ceased to be.

The two sources T&S and TMs complement each other. They employ essentially the same spelling system and there are few areas of conflict between them. They have been integrated into a combined 'Kaurna Wordlist organised by topic or subject area' in Amery (1995c, 1997), about 2700 words in total.

In addition to their major works and papers on the Kaurna language, the German missionaries include some Kaurna in correspondence to the Dresden Mission Society. Both Teichelmann and Schürmann kept journals, but these are more useful for an understanding of the language ecology than as a source on the language per se.

Schürmann's journals contain about 40 vocabulary items, most of them culture-specific and associated with a discussion of Kaurna religious concepts. All of this vocabulary is known from T&S, though the journals provide invaluable contextual information. In addition, about 30 Kaurna personal names, a number of group names for neighbouring clans and language groups, and some place names are also included, together with several short Kaurna sentences and two Kaurna songs, one of which is recoverable only from this source. The journals were published by Schürmann's great-grandson (Schurmann, 1987). Unfortunately, a Kaurna song line and several other snippets of Kaurna language, including several sentences, were omitted in this publication. It should be noted that the typescript version of Schürmann's journals contains numerous errors, no doubt arising from misreading his handwriting, which are perpetuated in the published version. For instance, *Parnka Meyunna* 'lakes people' (i.e. Ngarrindjeri people) has become *Parakameyunna*; *Yura* 'rainbow serpent' has become *Tura; kakirra* 'moon' has become *kakirro* etc.

In a letter dated 19 January 1839[2], Schürmann includes almost 20 Kaurna words, again mostly associated with Kaurna religion. He also refers to the hangings which took place on the north parklands in May 1839 and the manner in which the Kaurna wept for the deceased by saying '*ngaitjarli ngaitjarli* (my father my father) or *ngaityo panjapi ngaitjo panjapi* (my brother, my brother)'.[3]

In 1840, Schürmann began researching the Barngarla language in Port Lincoln, publishing *A Vocabulary of the Parnkalla Language* in 1844[4]. His journals reveal that he used his knowledge of Kaurna in his initial interactions with the Barngarla (Journal, 8 October 1840) and drew comparisons between the two languages. Interestingly, Schürmann (1844: 23) documents a Barngarla word 'Kurru midlanta, national name for the Adelaide natives'.[5]

Teichelmann's diary (1839-1846) has only recently been discovered and translated. Its 65 typescript pages include seven personal names, about 15 words, mostly concerning Aboriginal religion, several place names and the phrase '*Kartammeru, ngadluko yunga ninna*.'Kartammeru, you are our older brother" (Diary, 2 August 1844).

Samuel Klose arrived in Adelaide in August 1840, replacing Schürmann at the Piltawodli school. His letters contain several Kaurna names, words and phrases. More importantly, however, they contain two Kaurna letters, several pages from the children's copybooks and six Kaurna hymns, discussed below. He also makes brief references to aspects of Kaurna grammar, discussed in the next section.

Klose's *mannara* 'a crow', given as a boy's name is at variance with Eyre's *mannara* 'crow's nest'. Klose also clarifies the meaning of several other words and introduces several previously unknown phrases or usages. For instance, he identifies *Tarrutarru* as 'a small lizard about 4 inches long'. T&S (1840: 45) refer to 'Tarrotarro, a species of lizard; a fabulous person said to have made male and female, or divided the sexes'. Despite the slight difference in spelling, the two sources obviously refer to the same entity, for Klose continues 'They [the children] immediately called me and said that the grown-ups say that this is the creator who made man and woman' (Letter to Dresden, 3 September 1844). He also mentions that a group of Kaurna told him that 'they were going to the *Kuiya yertanna* (fish country)'[6] (Letter to Dresden, 7 July 1843); and he recorded various group names including *Tarralye Meyunna* 'Stockade Men' and *Wito Meyunna* 'Reed Men' (Letter to Dresden, 3 September 1844). These terms were unknown before the discovery of Klose's letters.

H.A.E. Meyer also arrived in August 1840. He went at once to Encounter Bay where he learnt and recorded the Ramindjeri language, a variety of Ngarrindjeri, publishing a grammar and vocabulary. He lists a number of place names, noting that:

> Several of these names, especially of those in the vicinity of Adelaide, belong to the Adelaide language, as their terminations show; and, indeed, are known only to a few individuals who have been in the habit of visiting the Adelaide tribe, and who can speak both languages. (Meyer, 1843: 50)

At least one entry is identified as an Adelaide word: 'pappauwe, *s* (Adelaide word) same as kainyani'[7] (Meyer, 1843: 90). *Pappauwe* seems to be the Kaurna word *pappa* 'youth who has undergone the ceremony of circumcision' (T&S, 1840: 36) with the Ramindjeri genitive suffix *-auwe*. Some words seem to refer specifically to Kaurna artefacts. Others are identical to Kaurna words, and at least some appear to be borrowings from Kaurna. For instance, *kape* 'tobacco' (Meyer, 1843: 69) is said to be derived from *kappendi* 'to vomit' (T&S, 1840: 9), suggesting that when Meyer encountered the word at Encounter Bay it was recently borrowed.

A bundle of Meyer's letters has been returned to the Lutheran Archives in Adelaide and await translation. It is possible that they may contain further insights into Kaurna.

John Philip Gell, Principal of Queen's School, Hobart, was a leading member of the Tasmanian Society, of which William Wyatt was also a corresponding member. Gell was greatly impressed by the work of Schürmann and Teichelmann and prepared a paper entitled 'South Australian Aborigines: The Vocabulary of the Adelaide Tribe', based almost entirely on T&S. Teichelmann read Gell's initial paper and made a number of comments which Gell inserted as footnotes attributed to Teichelmann. These provide additional ethnographic notes and elucidate certain culture-laden Kaurna terms, some of which can only be gained from Teichelmann's comments contained in Gell's paper. It is therefore best regarded as an additional Teichelmann source. The paper was translated into German by Schayer (1844).

Sir George Grey, South Australia's third governor (1841 to 1845), had already taken an interest in Kaurna when he was in Western Australia, where he carried out explorations and wrote a grammar and vocabulary of Nyungar. Grey was keen to look for similarities between the two languages. In an appendix to his grammar (1840a: 143-144) he published nine Kaurna nouns and 12 verbs which showed similarities with the Swan River and King George Sound dialects of Nyungar. These same words, together with *tin-dee* 'sun' and *kauw-ee* 'water' are published in his journals of exploration (Grey, 1841: 211, 212, 214). Grey's spellings of Kaurna words are mixed. Most verbs appear to be spelt according to T&S conventions. However, two verbs, *poomandi* 'to strike'[18] and *boontondi* 'to blow', some pronouns and most of the nouns appear to have come from other sources. It is not clear who sent the Kaurna words to Grey. Perhaps he recorded some himself on a visit to Adelaide in early 1840. Wyatt (1840; 1879) and Williams (1840) do not account for all of the spellings. This material points to the possible existence of another Kaurna wordlist, as yet undiscovered.

Matthew Moorhouse, a medical doctor by training, was appointed South Australia's first full-time Protector of Aborigines from June 1839 until 1857. He lived at Piltawodli and worked closely with Schürmann and Teichelmann, often travelling with them to outlying districts.

According to Schürmann's journals (2 August 1839), Moorhouse opposed the Governor's view, and that of the missionaries, that 'English writing could not be used in the native language, because the fluctuation in the pronunciation may confuse the natives as well as the Europeans'. However, despite this initial opposition, Moorhouse was won over to the 'Adelaide School' and their consistent representation of vowels. Kaurna words recorded in his letters consistently employ T&S spellings.

Teichelmann & Moorhouse (1841) published a joint report which includes a brief sketch of Kaurna grammar, discussed below (p. 95). At Grey's request, Moorhouse (1846) also published on the Ngayawang language from Moorundie on the Murray River, near present day Blanchetown, using T&S as a model. But no works of any substance on Kaurna have been found and Moorhouse's journal has not been located, though a fragment of it appears in a photograph of a page from Cawthorne's sketchbook. The journal might well be a plentiful source of Kaurna language material, for the fragment contains two Kaurna songs not referred to in other Kaurna sources (see below, 'Kaurna songs'). Letters by Moorhouse in the Public Records Office of South Australia contain the names of Kaurna people, some of whom are unknown from other sources.

One letter compares pronouns, number suffixes (dual and plural) and numbers in Kaurna and several other languages. Whilst most Kaurna material in this chart is known from T&S and other sources[9], Moorhouse does give the term *purlaitye purlaitye* 'four', a reduplication of the number 'two', compared with T&S's *yerrabula* 'four' based on the word *yerra* 'expressing the notions of individuality and reciprocity; distinct; different; one another; both' and *bula* 'dual'. The form *purlaitye purlaitye* is also given in a letter written by Klose (29 December 1840). Also of note is the term *pepa meyu* 'judge' (Letter, 8 February 1843). This term has not been sighted in any other source, though the individual words *pepa* 'paper, letter, book' and *meyu* 'man, person' are well attested.[10]

In a letter written on 30 June 1841[11], Moorhouse refers to the land around Lake Bonney as *Mettilittela Yerta* 'Thief Land'. The phrase obviously originated from one of the Kaurna guides accompanying the expedition. Similarly, in a report on a visit to the northernmost settled districts, Moorhouse, who was accompanied by a Kaurna interpreter, reported that Aborigines from the Mount Bryan district said they '*shipi paru padlotti* (longed for sheep's flesh)' when questioned about sheep-stealing (*South Australian Government Gazette,* 26 May 1842: 1). There are also valuable observations in Moorhouse's correspondence about the various languages spoken in the southern regions of South Australia and the use of interpreters and guides, principally Kaurna people from the Adelaide region.

Edward John Eyre is well known in Australian history as an explorer. He came to Australia in 1833 as a pastoralist, and to Adelaide, overlanding stock from NSW, in 1838 and 1839. In 1839 he decided to become an explorer. From 1841 to 1846 he served as the Resident Magistrate and Protector at Moorundie on the Murray River. A full autobiographical account is published in Eyre (1984).

Eyre (1845) is essentially a secondary source, drawing on materials supplied to him and published by the 'Adelaide School'. His journals include a treatise on Aborigines (Eyre, 1845: 147-508) which contains some Kaurna language material, most of which he attributes to Moorhouse, as follows:

- a complete listing of the birth-order names;
- a 45-item wordlist in a chart of comparative vocabulary;
- additional Kaurna words related to culture-specific themes smattered through the text;
- the songs published by T&S.

The birth-order names are especially significant because T&S omitted recording the second born and eighth born children. Eyre's list now serves as the basis for the development of a base-10 number system, outlined in Chapter 6.[12]

Other nineteenth-century primary sources

In addition to materials compiled by the 'Adelaide School', there are a number of lesser sources, mostly short wordlists. This section includes only those which make an original contribution.

M. Gaimard's wordlist was collected in October 1826, but published later in a volume on philology (Gaimard, 1833), along with numerous other languages contacted during the voyage of the *Astrolabe* from 1826 to 1829.[13]

Gaimard's wordlist consists of 168 items. Several are misidentified, and glaring errors were introduced when Gaimard tried to elicit numbers up to 20. Still, most items can readily be identified, and several, such as *mandoout* 'queue d'oiseau' (= 'bird's tail'), were not recorded by other observers. Gaimard's wordlist is analysed in detail in Amery (1998). Its importance lies in its historical value, as the first known recording of the Kaurna language. Its very existence is testament to the travels of some Kaurna people in the precolonial period, and establishes without doubt the linguistic identity of its source.

Charles Robinson's Kaurna wordlist of some 80 entries was recorded on Flinders Island, Tasmania between June 1837 and February 1839 and has only recently been recognised as a Kaurna source (see Amery, 1996d). It was obtained from a Kaurna woman named Kalloongoo (alias Sarah, Charlotte, Windeerer and Cowwerpiteyer) who was kidnapped from the Yankalilla-Rapid Bay area, south of Adelaide. In 1837 she worked as a domestic servant in Robinson's household.

Like the Gaimard wordlist, Robinson's testifies to the early precolonial relationships between the Kaurna and newcomers to their lands. The wordlist and accompanying journal entries establish beyond doubt the identity of Kalloongoo and provide important evidence regarding the linguistic affiliation of the Yankalilla–Rapid Bay region, an area contested in the literature with the publication of Berndt & Berndt (1993). Most of the words are common words attested in other Kaurna sources. However, it does contain several not found elsewhere and provides a new slant on several others. Robinson's wordlist corroborates other evidence pointing to a southern dialect of Kaurna (see detailed analysis in Amery, 1996d).

Edward Stephens is a name that occurs twice in this context. According to Tindale (1935b: 163), the 36 terms for bird species in his papers were 'native names accompanying birds sent to London 27 October 1838 (copied from letter by Edward Stephens to E.G. Wheeler, Manager S. Australian Co. London.)' The words were probably recorded by the Edward Stephens who managed the South Australian Company bank, and who was in the colony early in 1837 (*South Australian Gazette & Colonial Register,* 3 January 1837: 4). Tindale observes that 'these names are all probably Adelaide tribe'. Indeed, counterparts for 13 of the words are readily identified in T&S, Wyatt (1879) and Piesse (1840), despite Stephens' poor transcriptions or errors arising from misreading his handwriting. The English names were not known for nine of the bird species. Should the specimens still survive with the Kaurna names linked to them, this would serve as an invaluable source of Kaurna bird terms. Note that T&S record *trunggu* 'a species of bird', which appears unglossed in Stephens' list as *trown you*.

William Williams, of the Colonial Store Department, arrived in Adelaide aboard the *Africaine* on 13 November 1836. Within three weeks he had met a party of Kaurna, whom he invited back to the settlement at Holdfast Bay. This group visited repeatedly and Williams succeeded in establishing friendly relations with the Kaurna people (Hope, 1968: 116). Williams and James Cronk (also on the *Africaine*) were the first colonists to acquire a working knowledge of the Kaurna language. Williams prepared a wordlist of 377 items plus 28 sentences, published in the *Southern Australian* 15 May 1839 and republished in the *South Australian Colonist* in July 1840 with a few minor typographical variations. Some of the spelling inconsistencies in Williams (1840) are:

- vowels belonging to the phoneme /a/ are written variously as *u, a, o, er* and *ah*;
- vowels belonging to the phoneme /u/ are written variously as *oo, u, ou, o* and *eu*;
- vowels belonging to the phoneme /i/ are written variously as *i, ee, e, ie* and *ey*;
- sounds belonging to the phoneme /k/ are transcribed variously as *k, c, ch, ck, ck-c, c-k*;
- sounds belonging to the phoneme /ty/ are transcribed as *ch* and *tch*.

Years later Williams' wordlist was reprinted in Parkhouse (1923: 59-70) with substantial changes in spelling. For instance, the letter *c* has been regularly replaced by *k* when it represents a velar stop and *oo* has been rewritten as *u*. Williams' wordlist employs spellings based on English intuitions, thus importing many uncertainties which are not present in T&S, as the following examples, with counterparts from T&S and Hercus (1992), illustrate:

Williams (1840)	Williams (1923)	T&S	(Hercus)	Gloss
cud-le	kudle	kadli	katli	'dog'
ci-arr	kiarr	kaya	ka<u>r</u>a	'spear'
cun-doo	kundu	kundo	kuntu	'chest'
cow-e	kaue	kauwe	kawi	'water'
mar-coo	markku	makko	maku	'cloud'
mon-ney	monnei	marni	marni	'good'
poo-you	puyu	puiyo	puyu	'smoke'
hun-nah	ng]'unna	nganna	ngana	'who'
oi-chou	ng]'oichau	ngaityo	ngatyu	'my'
war-rah	warra	warra	warra	'language'

Williams (1839, 1840) either does not hear the initial velar nasal or does not know how to transcribe it, for it is missing from many words or transcribed as *h* on some occasions. In the Parkhouse (1923) version, the initial *ng* has been inserted (e.g. *hoo-yer* has become *ng'uyer* = *nguya* 'smallpox'). Without another point of reference it is difficult to know how to pronounce many words in Williams' wordlists.

Some of the meanings given by Williams are at variance with T&S, as in:

Williams (1840)	Williams (1923)	gloss	T&S or TM	
mee-re	mire	'thunderbolt'	meri	'hail'
tool-tah	tulta	'sister-in-law'	turlta	'sweetheart; girlfriend'

Despite these shortcomings, Williams does include several items not in T&S or TMs, including:

Williams (1840)	Williams (1923)	gloss
ker-kah	kerka	'bream - name of a fish'
pin-charn-ney	pincharnei	'to write' (cf. TM pintyandi 'to make, produce, create; T&S pingyandi 'to raise; make; construct;form &c.)
ta-min-ga	taminga	'gum (white)'
we-nee	weni	'snapper (fish)'
yoo-coo cat-ta	yoku katta	'ship's mast' (cf. T&S yoko 'ship'; katta 'club')

Williams' sentence material is highly unreliable, being more reminiscent of a kind of Pidgin Kaurna or interlanguage variety. There is no evidence of any Kaurna case marking whatsoever. See Simpson (1996) for a full analysis.

Another French observer, **Louis Piesse**, based at Camp Coortandillah, Aldinga, provides a short but nonetheless important wordlist in a letter to the *Adelaide Guardian,* 18 October 1839. It contains 75 items, including terms for birds, ants and marine life not in other sources. Piesse's work was published on the same page as Williams' (1840) wordlist and must be viewed as an addendum to it — as Piesse did, offering to 'add a few names' to Williams' vocabulary (Piesse, 1840: 296). Most of the items in Piesse's list are not in Williams, and the following do not appear to have counterparts in any known Kaurna sources:

ay-cut-tah	'Lowry Parrot'
cut-par-mar-to	'wattle bird'
can-de-out-do	'mawpawk'
paltee-paltee	'species of grass parrot'[14]
buck-o buck-o	'butcher bird'
teen-deen-de	'kingfisher'
bo-ro-tee	'winged ant'
coo-lo-tonne-me	'periwinkle'
cut-tee	'small crab'
ky-chie-ter	'guana'

Like Williams, Piesse failed to transcribe the initial velar nasal. It was often omitted as in *ichi* 'mother' (cf. T&S *ngaityaii* 'my mother'). Just once it was written *h* in *ha-ree* 'blue mountain parrot' (cf. Wyatt *ngerre* 'blue mountain parrakeet'). Within the few verbs provided, there is considerable variation in the verb endings. T&S regularly cite their verbs with a *-ndi* 'Present Tense' affix, whilst Wyatt, like Piesse, is somewhat irregular, with some verbs ending in *-n*, some in *-ne* and others in *-nde*. In this small body of data, there appears to be some correlation between Piesse's and Wyatt's verb endings which causes one to wonder whether T&S regularised their data. Perhaps verb classes existed, defined by the allomorphs above.

Kaurna Sources

Dr William Wyatt arrived in South Australia on 14 February 1837, as a surgeon aboard the *John Renwick*. Wyatt served as South Australia's third part-time Protector of Aborigines from 1837 until 1839. Unlike his successor and the German missionaries, Wyatt did not live at Piltawodli. According to Foster (1990b: 39) he was 'criticised for not 'going among' the Aborigines and for failing to provide information to the public about their culture.' Nonetheless, Wyatt does provide valuable, though sometimes unreliable, information on the Kaurna language. After the German mission sources, it remains the next most important source and includes a sizable number of terms not recorded elsewhere.

A manuscript copy of Wyatt's wordlist, 'Vocabulary of the Adelaide Dialect' (Wyatt, 1840)[15] in the Library of Sir George Grey in the South African Public Library, Cape Town, contains only 67 words, though this is unlikely to represent the extent of Wyatt's knowledge of Kaurna at that time. A more comprehensive paper published later lists approximately 900 Kaurna and Ramindjeri words. The cover page notes that the material was 'principally extracted from his official reports' most of which would have been written when Wyatt served as Protector from 1837 to 1839. Assuming Wyatt's (1840) wordlist in the Grey collection is complete, presumably Wyatt went through his papers and extracted words he had recorded in the early days of the colony. The University of Adelaide Library copy, donated by the author, contains three corrections in Wyatt's own hand, where *n* has been typed instead of *u*. This wordlist was also published in J.D. Woods ed. (1879) without correction of the three typographical errors. Wyatt identifies certain vocabulary items with a subscript $_e$ or $_r$ as Encounter Bay or Rapid Bay words respectively. In 1923, Parkhouse republished Wyatt's paper in three separate wordlists designating them 'Adelaide', 'Encounter Bay', and 'Rapid Bay' with changed spellings, substituting *u* for Wyatt's *oo*.

Wyatt must have been aware of the existence of the work of Williams (1840) and T&S, yet his 1879 wordlist appears to be an independent source, his spellings departing from both T&S and Williams (1840):

Wyatt (1879)	**Williams (1840)**	**T&S**	**gloss**
mayu	*meau*	*meyu*	'man'
ai chu 'I, my'	*oi-chou* 'me'	*ngaityo*	'my'
kadle	*cud-le*	*kadli*	'dog'
kerla 'firewood'	*cur-la* 'fire'	*gadla*	'fire, firewood'
tikkán	*te-carn-ne*	*tikkandi*	'to sit'

Wyatt's (1879) 'Vocabulary of the Adelaide Tribe' comprises 651 items, though several belong to Ngarrindjeri (or Ramindjeri). For instance, Wyatt gives three words for 'I'. Two forms *ai chu* 'I, my' and *aie* 'I' (affix only) correspond with T&S *ngaityo* 'my' and *ngai* 'I'. The latter often appears as the clitic *ai*. However, the third form *anawe* 'I' closely resembles Meyer's (1843: 86) Ramindjeri *ngañ-auwe* 'of me, my, mine' and Taplin's (1879: 131) Narrinyeri 'Mine — *Nganauwe, Anauwe, Anauwurle*'. Several other words and placenames in his 'Adelaide Tribe' wordlist are also Ngarrindjeri:

Wyatt (Adelaide Tr.)	**Meyer (Ramindjeri)**	**Taplin (Yarralde)**	**T&S (Kaurna)**
ngurle 'hill'	*ngurle* 'hill, mountain'	*ngurli* 'hill'	*mukurta* 'hill'
burnowe 'aunt'	*barno* 'aunt'	*barno* 'aunt'	*ngarpadla* 'aunt'
munumbi 'chin'	*numbe* 'point of chin'	*numbe* 'chin'	*nguttoworta* 'chin'
ngérnawe 'you pl.'	*ngunauwe* 'of you pl.'	*ngune* 'ye' (Nom.)	*naako* 'of you pl.'
	ngune 'you pl.'		*na* 'you pl.'
trakin 'to saw or cut'	*drek-in* 'cutting'	*drekin* 'cutting'	*bakkandi* 'to cut'

Wyatt's 'Encounter Bay' wordlist is much shorter than his 'Adelaide Tribe' vocabulary with some 240 items. Most of these 'Encounter Bay' words coincide with Meyer's (1843) Ramindjeri and other Ngarrindjeri sources, but at least 20 (including several personal names) are Kaurna words. Some, notably *kondolle* 'whale; blubber', are shared by Kaurna and Ramindjeri, but several others are most unlikely to be Ramindjeri and appear to have been misplaced by Wyatt. A particularly telling example concerns words associated with the 'rainbow'. In Wyatt (1879) *korunye* 'rainbow' and *ummaiche kombo* 'inner or woman rainbow' are identified as 'Adelaide' but *kombo* 'rainbow' and *mayoo kombo* 'outer or man rainbow' are identified as 'Encounter Bay'. Yet all the elements of these expressions are clearly Kaurna words, having counterparts in T&S. Even Wyatt identified *mayu* 'man' and *ummaiche* 'wife' as Adelaide words. The Ramindjeri words for 'urine', 'man' and 'woman', *kainyar*, *korni* and *mimini* respectively, bear no relationship to their Kaurna counterparts. Meyer (1843: 68) gives *kainge* 'rainbow; so called from their supposing it to be caused by the Supreme Being in making water' thus recognising the connection with urine, being conceptually similar to the terms supplied by Wyatt. Of course, it is possible that these expressions for 'rainbow' were borrowed into Ramindjeri at that time, perhaps in response to a linguistic taboo, then in operation.

Wyatt (1879: 25) lists 17 sentences and a short text at the conclusion of his paper. These sentences are largely devoid of case marking and employ genitive form pronouns *aichoo* (= T&S *ngaityo* 'my') and *ningko* (= T&S *ninko* 'your') irrespective of their case function. See Simpson (1996) for a full discussion. Wyatt's translation of Gawler's speech delivered to the Indigenous people of Adelaide in 1838 (discussed below, p. 98) also survives.

William Anderson Cawthorne was born in London in 1824 and arrived in Adelaide with his family in May 1841 (see Foster, 1991: iv). The young Cawthorne developed friendships with a number of Kaurna people, including Kadlitpinna or 'Captain Jack', and took a keen interest in Aboriginal culture. He painted a number of portraits of Aboriginal people and aspects of their material culture, and hoped to publish a book on 'Native Implements', but this never eventuated. His paper titled 'Rough Notes on the Manners and Customs of the Natives', prepared in 1844, was published in 1926. It includes 51 Kaurna terms referring mostly to material culture including several items such as *kooroo* 'fire-making apparatus' not documented elsewhere. It also includes valuable ethnographic notes and part of a hunting charm that was probably copied (imperfectly) from T&S.

Cawthorne kept 26 volumes of diaries and journals between 1842 and 1859. References to Aborigines, most from the period 1842 and 1846, when

Cawthorne had an active interest in Aboriginal culture, have been compiled by Robert Foster (1991). The journals contain nearly 30 additional Kaurna terms, mostly personal names, a few well-known place names and several other words, mostly found in other sources. Cawthorne's main contribution has been his rich ethnographic and historical notes, particularly the description of Kaurna material culture, complete with illustrations.

Unfortunately, Cawthorne's spellings are particularly unreliable and variable. For example, 'digging stick' is spelt as *katta* (Cawthorne, 1926: 11, 15) ~ *cutta* (Cawthorne, 1926: 7, 24) ~ *gutta* (Cawthorne, 1926: 9) ~ *cuttar* (Foster, 1991: 5) ~ *kutta* (Foster, 1991: 9) ~ *cuttai* (Foster, 1991: 50); 'possum skin drum' is spelt variously as *taparoo* (Cawthorne, 1926: 11) ~ *tapurio* (Cawthorne, 1926: 11) ~ *tarpuro* (Cawthorne, 1926: 13) and 'bag or net used to carry food and possessions' is spelt *wilkatja* (Cawthorne, 1926: 17) ~ *witkalja* (Cawthorne, 1926: 19). Many errors have been introduced into material copied from other sources. Whilst some of Cawthorne's terms for artefacts etc. are genuinely new (ie not attested in other sources), it is difficult to decide in some cases whether they are simply atrocious mistranscriptions or genuine alternative forms for items known by other similar names. In Cawthorne (1926: 27) *wirhalli* 'bier' appears, yet in his journal (Foster, 1991: 81) we find *wirkilta* 'bier'. Are these simply different spellings of the same word, perhaps including typographical errors, or are there in fact two variant forms, perhaps dialectal variants, within Kaurna? Is *magulla* 'stage of initiation' the same as T&S *ngulta* 'a man that has undergone the last tattooing'? Is *tanjalu* 'basket' in fact the same as T&S *taingyedli* 'rush bag; rush'?

Some of Cawthorne's material is clearly original and there is a preference for *c* instead of *k*, *oo* instead of *u*, *ee* instead of *i*, *u* for /a/ and *n* for the initial velar nasal etc. in these original forms. However, Cawthorne copied words and sentences from other sources, leaving the spellings essentially intact as they are in the originals, though many typographical errors have been introduced. Cawthorne introduced several typographical errors in copying six of Williams' (1840) sentences (see Foster, 1991: 82), including *n* substituted for *u* and vice versa, *nn* rewritten as *m* and *t* rewritten as *l*. These are all expected errors arising from misreading the original manuscript.

In summary, Cawthorne is a particularly valuable ethnographic source, especially with regard to Kaurna material culture, but his transcriptions need to be treated with much caution. Cawthorne is the source for a number of Kaurna vocabulary items appearing in George French Angas's *Savage Life and Scenes in Australia and New Zealand*. Angas (1847: 102-107) provides a description of the *Kurdi* dance (see Plate 5) 'thus described by a friend who has frequently witnessed its performance'. His friend was in fact William Cawthorne. In *South Australia Illustrated,* Angas (1846) also provides illustrations of Kaurna artefacts complete with Kaurna labels. The spellings indicate that Cawthorne was again the source. Whilst Angas's illustrations are superb, he adds nothing more to our knowledge of the Kaurna language.

Edward Stephens (a different person from the one discussed earlier) came to Adelaide 'as a lad with [his] parents' (Stephens 1889: 476) in 1839 or soon after. His 282-item wordlist includes 14 phrases and sentences which all have a counterpart from Williams (1840), though the glosses are sometimes slightly different. For example:

Stephens (1889)	Mootanitchee-wangarnee	'cock-crowing'
Williams (1840)	Mut-ta-ni-chie wan-garn-e	'cock crowing'
Stephens (1889)	Hoonanincootourn	'what's the row about'
Williams (1840)	Hun nah nin-co-tow-arn	'What are you quarrelling about?'

Almost all the vocabulary items also have counterparts in Williams (1840). One of the few differences evident is Stephens' *Ichertamaroo* 'first male child' vs. Williams' *Cer-tam-a-roo* '(first child) male' and Stephens' *Pooleearta* 'second daughter' vs. Williams' *War re-er-too* 'second daughter'. Stephens' term for 'second daughter' is not attested in other Kaurna sources and seems to be based on *purlaityi* 'two'. Stephens also introduces the term *werta werta* 'privates' (cf. T&S *worta* 'behind' and *worti* 'tail; penis').

Stephens has organised his wordlist into sections: 'Animals and Birds, &c.'; 'Actions &c.'; 'Time, Number &c', 'Things Various' and 'Parts of the Human Body', perhaps taking Piesse's advice:

> I think also if the names of animals, birds, trees, and of particular places were arranged separately under each head, they would be much easier committed to memory, and render the remainder much easier for reference. (Piesse, 1840: 296)

Stephens does not acknowledge Williams as the source. On the contrary, he claims:

> I have done my best to spell the words so as to convey to the minds of others those sounds which, after the lapse of many years, my memory recalls with so vivid a distinctness, that for a time I again live over the scenes and circumstances of my early life. (Stephens, 1889: 497)

However, his memory could not have been as vivid as he claims, for in changing Williams' spellings he has introduced errors. Whereas Williams' spellings were ambiguous with respect to his usage of the letter *u*, Stephens has often replaced them with *oo*. A few examples of Stephens' spelling changes will illustrate, again using T&S and Hercus (1992) as points of reference:

Williams (1840)	Stephens (1889)	T&S	Nukunu (Hercus)	Gloss
cud-le	kudle	kadli	katli	'dog'
cun-doo	coodoo	kundo	kuntu	'chest'
mur-rah	moora	marra	mara	'hand'

The first example shows that Stephens did not always rewrite Williams' *u* as *oo*. *Kadli* 'dog', of course is a well-known word and presumably Stephens did in fact remember it correctly. In the second, the spelling change is cosmetic, but in the last example Stephens has introduced a fundamental error.

In summary then, Stephens (1889) is not a credible source on the Kaurna language per se, as many errors have been introduced, though the two birth order variants are interesting. Its linguistic contribution is almost wholly subsumed by Williams (1840). The real value of Stephens' work is in the twenty or so pages of ethnographic notes and reminiscences preceding the vocabulary list itself, providing important insights into Aboriginal society during the early years of the colony of South Australia.

Thomas Day 'of Bay Road, Keswick' provides a brief handwritten manuscript entitled 'Memoirs of the extinct tribe of Cowandilla' (Tindale Collection, South Australian Museum). Although it is dated 1902, I have included it here with the nineteenth-century sources because the Kaurna material comes from an earlier period. Day includes a number of Kaurna place names and common vocabulary, and uses spellings which are often quite different from other sources. He also includes several terms from South Australian Pidgin (such as *lubra* 'Aboriginal woman') and *walebil* 'grease' of unknown origins.

Two members of Colonel Light's surveying party, the surgeon Dr John Woodforde and surveyor William Jacob, recorded the Kaurna words *wango* 'a small species of possum', *welta* 'hot' and an exclamation *wurra-dourra* used to express surprise at Woodford's shooting of a bird on the wing (Woodforde Journal, 13 January 1837; Jacob Journal, 14 January 1837). See Amery (1998) for discussion of these sources.

John Stephens (1839) wrote about the 'Adelaide Tribes'. Amongst some useful historical and ethnographic information are a number of Kaurna 'family names' *Atala, Ateon, Ataie, Melanie* and a personal name *Ootinai* said to have been recorded by Gouger, the Colonial Secretary.

In addition to the sources outlined above, Kaurna words are sometimes found in newspaper articles, official reports, letters, journals and memoirs, though they are usually place names and common words adopted into South Australian Pidgin and South Australian English. As such, most are found in other sources such as T&S. Gaol records and police records are a useful source of Kaurna personal names. Place and property names, especially those recorded on early maps, serve as a memory of the language. These are discussed further in Chapter 8.

Kaurna inclusions in comparative wordlists
Comparisons between Australian languages have been drawn since the earliest records, but in the last quarter of the nineteenth century such studies were particularly popular. In 1874 Dr Bleek of Cape Town wrote urging that enquiries be made into the manners and customs of the Aborigines of South Australia (Taplin, 1879: 1). Embedded in the resultant questionnaire distributed throughout South Australia was a wordlist of 70 items (Taplin, 1879: 6). Since the 1870s, Kaurna words have frequently been included in comparative wordlists prepared to illustrate similarities and differences between the languages of Australia and even beyond, with the inclusion of Malay and Kanak from New Caledonia.

With the exception of Earl's short wordlist, which consists of 14 body parts known from other sources but written with independent spellings, all material in comparative wordlists is drawn from other sources which are available in their original form. As these are of little consequence in terms of the revival of Kaurna, they will not be discussed here. For the purposes of language reclamation, secondary sources should be avoided at all costs. Wherever possible, primary sources (see Table 5.3) should be utilised to minimise introduced errors.

Twentieth-century primary sources
After a long period in which the Kaurna people were ignored, an era of renewed interest emerged with the 'discovery' of Ivaritji. She seems to have been first noticed by **Daisy Bates**, who visited Point Pearce in 1919 and talked with her. Bates (Notebook 5c: 76) recorded 25 Kaurna words, mostly kin terms and a few place names. This wordlist, minus one entry, is published in an appendix to Gara's (1990: 101) article on Ivaritji. It corresponds closely to other sources, though *ngangaji* 'mother's mother' corresponds to T&S *ngangaitye* 'mother-in-law' (cf. *kammammi* 'mother's mother'). It also introduces several new terms in relation to marriage, which are not found in other sources.

John McConnell Black, a language enthusiast and member of the Royal Society of South Australia, visited Point Pearce Aboriginal Mission in October 1919. He compiled four short vocabularies from the 'Adelaide Language', Narrunga, Kukatha and Narrinyeri (Ngarrindjeri). Ivaritji, otherwise known as Mrs Amelia Taylor, 'who claims to be the last survivor of the Adelaide tribe' (Black, 1920: 81), was the source for the Kaurna material. Black often corresponded with Daisy Bates and it is likely that he came to know of the existence of Ivaritji through her (see Gara, 1990: 82).

Black's Kaurna wordlist has 66 entries, including eight phrases and about 20 short sentences. Black used a modified form of the International Phonetic Alphabet (IPA) for his transcriptions and made an attempt to explain his system in the paper. His phonetic transcriptions seem to be reasonably accurate and he correctly identifies a series of retroflex consonants, transcribing them with italics [*t*], [*d*], [*n*] and [*l*]. He transcribes two rhotics, '[r] is the rolled or trilled *r*' and '[ɹ] is the Somersetshire (reflexed or inverted) *r*, and is a marked peculiarity of Australian native speech' (Black, 1920: 77). However, modern linguists have identified three rhotics within the Thura-Yura languages.[16] It appears that Black has transcribed the third rhotic, a tap, as [t] as in 'maŋkata'[17] 'girl', transcribed as *mankarra* by T&S and as *mankarra* with a rolled 'r' by Hercus (1992) in Nukunu.

Black does not transcribe interdental consonants, except in the word *waðaŋko* 'whence' where he has transcribed a voiced interdental fricative. Hercus, however, transcribes every instance of 'n' and 't' word initially as an interdental /nh/ and /th/ respectively and there are also many instances of interdentals in medial position. A few examples will serve to illustrate:

Black	T&S	Hercus (Nukunu)	Gloss
ju*rii*la	*yurridla*	*yu̱ri-pila*	'ears' (dual)
diːkanti ~ dikanti	*tikkandi*	*thikatya*	'to sit'
jɛ*li*na	*yerlina*	*yartli*	'male'
kaˈvaiji	*kawai*		'come'
waŋkadli	*wanggadli*	*wangkadli*	'let's talk' (dual)
ka*l*a	*gadla*	*kartla*	'fire; firewood'
mara	*marra*	*ma̱ra*	'hand'
miju	*meyu*	*mi̱ru*	'man'
ŋaiji	*ngai*	*ngayi*	'I'
tidna	*tidna*	*thitna*	'foot'
wara	*warra*	*warra*	'language'

Black's transcriptions are a vast improvement over those of other English observers such as Williams and Wyatt and somewhat of an improvement over T&S, with his transcription of retroflex consonants, the distinction between rolled 'r's and glide 'r's, vowel length and transcription of the velar nasal as [ŋ]. The major shortcoming is his failure to transcribe interdentals which were most likely contrastive in Ivaritji's speech. The brevity of Black's wordlist does not allow adequate evaluation of T&S. Several words, including some common vocabulary, place names and personal names, are not attested in other sources. They are:

ivariti	'misty rain'; personal name
kantara	'basket made of reeds for carrying a baby' cf T&S *taingyedli ~ tainkyedli* 'rush bag'; *kandara* 'veg. resembling radish'
maŋkiti	'finger' cf T&S *marra* 'hand, finger'; *marraangki* 'thumb' (from *marra* 'finger' + *ngangki* 'woman'); *marrayerli* 'forefinger' (from *marra* 'finger' + *yerli* 'father')
ŋanpu	'Port Adelaide' cf T&S *Yertabulti* 'Port Adelaide'
parˈ natatja	personal name
puːlti	'country towards Semaphore' cf T&S *Yertabulti* 'Port Adelaide' (from *yerta* 'country' + *bulti* 'asleep')

Norman Tindale was employed in the South Australian Museum from 1917 until 1965, and made far-reaching contributions to Australian anthropology and archaeology. He was essentially a scientist, commencing in entomology. In 1921, he accompanied an expedition to Groote Eylandt as naturalist. In preparation, he took a crash course in ethnography in 1920 under Baldwin Spencer, from whom he learned the rudiments of linguistic transcription.

On his return to the Museum, Tindale began to take an interest in Aboriginal languages and cultures, including those in the immediate vicinity of Adelaide. He collected previously published papers, letters and old newspaper articles and many of these were pasted into his journals. He also worked first hand with a number of local Aboriginal people, including Ivaritji just before her death in 1929.[18] Tindale also recorded a little information from Alf Spender, a Kaurna man of 'mixed ancestry'. According to Tindale, Alf Spender, son of Lartelare, referred to Ivaritji as *ngammi* 'mother', whilst she called him *kunga* 'son'.[19]

Tindale also questioned Ngarrindjeri men including Milerum (Clarence Long) of the Tangani clan, Albert Karloan (or Karlowan) a Yaralde man,

Reuben Walker and Sustie Wilson of the Ramindjeri clan. According to Tindale (1987: 5) Sustie Wilson's mother was a Kaurna woman. He also obtained information from Robert Mason from Mannum on the Murray River, whose mother belonged to the Peramangk language group of Mount Barker and a Ngadjuri man named Barney Warrior. All of these sources provided some information about Kaurna language and culture.

Tindale compiled several card files on Kaurna, which are still in the South Australian Museum. Although much of this material has been retranscribed from previous publications including T&S, Williams (1839), Piesse (1840), Gell (1841), Wyatt (1879), Stephens (1889) and Black (1920), it also contains additional vocabulary items obtained from local sources, principally Milerum and Karloan (his Ngarrindjeri informants) and several items from Ivaritji.

Tindale employed IPA or a modified phonetic system as outlined in Tindale (1935: 262-265). Like Black, he did not usually transcribe interdental consonants, though he did occasionally record interdental fricatives [θ] and [ð]. He was careful to distinguish between [ng] or [nk], [ŋ] and [ŋg] or [ŋk]. Unfortunately, in retranscribing previously published material, he introduced some errors. For instance, within the same card file, Tindale has 'kaŋariburka "a prolific woman" retranscribed from T&S kangariburka' and on another card 'kaŋgandi "to lead; conduct; accompany; to bear a child; bring forth . . ." from T&S kanggandi'. Both these words have the same root and undoubtedly the *ng* in *kangariburka* should have been transcribed as ŋg. Further evidence is seen in other examples, with 'juŋondi, juŋorendi, juŋoriap:endi "to give; impart; communicate" from T&S *yungondi, yungorendi, yungoriappendi*' on one card while on another he gives 'juŋgul:uŋgul:a "giver; giving" from T&S *yunggullunggulla*'. Again, these words have the same root, which probably should be transcribed [yuŋgu]. Hercus (1992: 34) transcribed *yungkatya,* the Nukunu cognate of T&S *yungondi,* with a nasal + stop cluster. Note that Tindale has also retranscribed T&S's double consonants as long [:], though it is unlikely that this is the case. Tindale also perpetuated errors introduced by Stephens' re-transcriptions of Williams' material. Unfortunately, Tindale's phonetic transcriptions give the appearance that he knows what the pronunciation should be. These examples point to the danger of reforming the spelling system too early. It is better to maintain the ambiguity in written form than to remove it and find out later that it should have been something else.

Tindale's Kaurna card file contains a significant level of Ngarrindjeri material, which is not surprising given that his main informants were Ngarrindjeri people and major movements of people and extensive cultural change had occurred.

The Kaurna placenames card file includes names from a wide variety of sources for locations within Tindale's defined Kaurna territory. Many have been taken directly from maps and historical sources. Tindale provides etymologies, and whilst many appear sound, several are totally fanciful. The most telling example concerns Yatala or Dry Creek. Yatala appears on the earliest maps of Adelaide and a government vessel was named *Yatala* in 1850. Yatala appears as a suburb on an 1889 Military Map. However, Tindale gives the following entry:

′Jatala

Yatala: Dry Creek, 10 Km north of Adelaide. Probably post-contact name arising from the presence of a white man's prison. The name seems to be linked with the verb [′jat:un] 'to steal'.

Moorhouse 1846: 63
Tindale ms. from Mason 1964.

Now [′jat:un] 'to steal' is a Ngarrindjeri word. Meyer (1843: 65) gives 'Yart-in, v.s., stretching out the hand to receive' and Taplin (1879: 136) gives 'Reaching out the hand to receive — Yartin, Yartamin.' *Yatala* itself is attested in Kaurna sources as 'flooded'. For example, T&S (1840: 61) give 'Yertalla, s. water running by the side of a river; inundation; cascade.' Yatala Labour Prison at Dry Creek was not established until 1854. Tindale's Ngarrindjeri origins for Yatala then are absolutely without basis.

On other occasions, Tindale provides several cards and as many as three or four different etymologies for the same name, often including an etymology based on a Ngarrindjeri word or perhaps even a combination of Ngarrindjeri and Kaurna words. One card appears to appeal to a Ngarrindjeri etymology for Yankalilla, based on Ramindjeri *yangaiāke* 'hill' (Meyer 1843: 65). However, Kaurna sources have totally unrelated words *mukurta* 'hill, mountain' or *karnu* 'mountain'. Note the following:

′Jangkaljil:a   (Kaurna Tribe Adelaide, South Australia)
    Yankalilla

Jangkaljil:a 'Yankalilla' Lit. 'Upon the hill' Deriv. [′jangkalja] 'hill' + [íl:a] 'at or upon'
Jangkaljawangk 'Yankalilla' Deriv: [′jangkalja] 'hill' + [′wangk] 'upon'
                                                          (Tindale, n.d.,. Kaurna Card File)

Yet Manning (1986: 237), also citing Tindale as his source, provides a different, but more plausible etymology:

A difference of opinion regarding the origin of the name [Yankalilla] prompted a spate of letters to the Register, each writer giving different versions. (See 10, 13, 16, 17, 20 & 25 February 1928). Professor N.B. Tindale says 'it is derived from the Aboriginal word jankalan, meaning falling' from an incident in the myth of Tjilbruke, whose sister's <nephew's> mummified body began to fall into pieces here, as he was carrying it from Brighton to Cape Jervis for burial.

These examples lead one to be very wary of Tindale's materials as representing the language that was spoken on the Adelaide Plains prior to colonisation. Further, his Kaurna card files include several words commencing with *r*, *l* and *tj* and ending in consonants, which break the phonotactic rules of Kaurna as described by T&S and others. These words can be invariably traced back to Milerum or other Ngarrindjeri sources.

More important than the words themselves are Tindale's ethnographic notes, though it is important always to bear in mind where his information is coming from. Tindale carried out reasonably extensive work in Ngarrindjeri and has recorded and analysed a number of Dreaming stories, some of which are known to have had Kaurna versions belonging to the Adelaide Plains. This aspect will be covered below (pp. 100-104).

Language contact and contact languages

A number of Kaurna words have entered the lexicons of other Indigenous languages. A few, such as *nantu* 'horse' and *wardli* 'house' have been borrowed into a surprising number of Australian languages, as far as Bathurst Island on the other side of the continent (Walsh, 1992). In addition, Pitjantjatjara has borrowed the Kaurna word *mukarta* 'head' in the form *mukata* ~ *mukati* as the word for 'hat'.

Other Kaurna words are shared by neighbouring languages. Some of these are clearly due to diffusion, though it is often difficult to say which language has borrowed a particular word. *Kuntuli* 'whale', *mantirri* 'bush apple, *karrkala* 'pigface' and *kapi* 'tobacco' are examples of words shared by Ngarrindjeri and Kaurna. The latter has undoubtedly been borrowed by Ngarrindjeri from Kaurna, as the word originates from the Kaurna word *kapinthi* 'to vomit'. Other words like Tjilbruke and the name Kaurna itself appear to have been borrowed from Ngarrindjeri in more recent times (see Chapter 1).

Kaurna words are sometimes found in sources on South Australian Pidgin English. Pidgin examples recorded in the latter part of the nineteenth century in locations far removed from the Adelaide Plains reveal that some Kaurna words continued to be used after the language ceased to be spoken regularly. A particularly striking example is the Pidgin word *malanne* (cf. T&S *madlanna* 'no; none; not') recorded by Smith at Rivoli Bay in the south-east of the state in 1864 as follows: 'Me think 'em no more blackfellow grow, only soon die — no more brother — poor fellow me! Brother Jerry and "malanne" (wife) dead — Bobby soon die' (Smith, 1880: 107). It appears from this example that Smith misunderstood *malanne* to mean 'wife'.

In the South Australian Pidgin Data Base being compiled from historical sources by Peter Mühlhäusler and Robert Foster, surprisingly few words of Indigenous origin occur and even fewer have Kaurna origins. The use of *nantu* 'horse' and *wurley* 'house' is of course widespread, but the use of other Kaurna words is rare. Still this remains an area to explore more fully as additional sources come to light.

As discussed in Chapter 1, words from Aboriginal languages continue to be used today in Nunga English, but these include relatively few Kaurna words. Most surviving vocabulary drawn from Indigenous languages appears to come from Ngarrindjeri, Narungga, languages of the West Coast and Western Desert.

Recent compilations of Kaurna material used as resources

In 1982, Howard Groome produced a facsimile edition of T&S, thus raising the profile of the language and providing a ready source for the Kaurna language project to work with. In this section I discuss recent compilations of Kaurna material used as resource materials for Aboriginal Studies, language reclamation activities and teaching programs.

Particular care needs to be taken in the preparation of language materials when the compilers are not familiar with the language. This is a major concern in situations where the language has ceased to be spoken.

In 1989, **Phil Fitzpatrick** at the Aboriginal Heritage Branch of the Department of Environment and Planning produced a selected Kaurna wordlist of almost 700 entries. He cites Gell (1904), Piesse (1840), Stephens (1889), T&S and Wyatt (1879) as sources and claims to have adopted T&S's orthography, even for words taken from other sources (Fitzpatrick, 1989: 3). However, in a number of instances he mixes spelling systems. Numerous typographical errors and erroneous simplifications have been introduced, resulting in increased imprecision (see Amery, 1998: 204-205 for details).

Fitzpatrick's wordlist was useful in the early 1990s, during the early stages of Kaurna revival, because for the first time a Kaurna vocabulary was listed by both Kaurna and English headword. T&S and most other wordlists were organised by Kaurna headword, and it is difficult to look up a word in a list ordered alphabetically in the vernacular, when the vernacular is not known.[20] However, the level of errors means that Fitzpatrick (1989) is not an ideal source. If used, care should be taken to check back to the original sources.

The Kaurna People: Aboriginal People of the Adelaide Plains (EDSA, 1989) is a substantial publication of 266 pages and includes short wordlists on various topics such as the environment, kinship and birth order names, artefacts and foods. The majority of Kaurna words in this publication are drawn from T&S, but several from other sources, notably Cawthorne (1844) and Wyatt (1879), are mixed in without identification. In addition, for some unknown reason, several words from other languages including Diyari and Adnyamathanha have been slipped in. It is impossible to find the source of some vocabulary items such as *kad* 'jew lizard' (EDSA, 1989: 139).

An imprecise guide to pronunciation is given which more or less accommodates T&S spellings. Yet Tindale, Cawthorne and other spellings are employed throughout the book with no explanation of their orthographic conventions, or lack of them, as the case may be. Tindale uses *j* as in IPA for the palatal glide, yet the discussion on p. 60 says to 'Use English pronunciation unless otherwise indicated'. Numerous errors have been introduced through changing glosses and the level of typographical errors is unacceptably high.

For someone interested in the Kaurna language, tracing sources and being sure that the material is as accurate and reliable as possible, *The Kaurna People* is a frustrating source to work with. Specific sources on the Kaurna language are not listed though some acknowledgement is given to T&S and Cawthorne (1844) within the text, but this does not account for all of the putative Kaurna vocabulary. Some Ngarrindjeri words have crept into the wordlists without acknowledgement and the source of some other words cannot be traced. Perhaps another Kaurna source unknown to me exists, though it is more likely that the unknown words have been drawn from other languages or are the result of errors introduced by the compilers.

Jane Simpson and I published a wordlist, together with a brief introduction to the Kaurna language, in Thieberger & McGregor (Eds), *Macquarie*

Aboriginal Words (1994). This made a significant portion of the Kaurna language readily available through Macquarie's wide distribution network. The book has also drawn some international attention. The Kaurna chapter in *Macquarie Aboriginal Words* includes about 500 items drawn predominantly from TMs, supplemented by some items from T&S. Narungga counterparts, where known, are also provided. Thieberger & McGregor also include both an English and a vernacular finder list, enabling comparison across the 17 languages included, and access of specific words.

In 1995, I compiled *Warra Kaurna: A Resource for Kaurna Language Programs*. It included a facsimile of T&S together with a wordlist organised by topic prepared by Jane Simpson and brief 'Notes on Spelling and Pronunciation'. I further revised and expanded the wordlist in 1997. To my knowledge, after students of Kaurna and I have worked intensively with the materials for some time, there are very few introduced errors in these publications. This wordlist is the most comprehensive Kaurna wordlist published to date.

Grammar

Historical sources

There is one main historical source on Kaurna grammar, T&S. Other sources, TMs and Teichelmann (1858) have been written to add to information contained in T&S, whilst Watson, Teichelmann & Moorhouse (1841) and Moorhouse (1843) are papers based on T&S. This single orientation to the description of Kaurna grammar is in many ways fortunate for us in our attempts to reclaim the language. Whilst there are undoubtedly some problems with their analysis, the near absence of competing analyses and conflicting information makes our job much easier.

Fortunately, the analytical skills of the German missionaries were of a high standard. They were trained in philology and the classics. The grammar they produced in the space of 18 months under trying conditions was a remarkable feat. They were aware of certain limitations in their work, but encouraged by Gawler and in response to a perceived need for such a work, they perhaps published earlier than they would have wished.

The 24-page sketch grammar in **Teichelmann & Schürmann** (1840) appears more or less 'complete' with pronoun paradigms, charts of nominal affixes and discussion of verb inflections with examples of their usage. There are indications that Teichelmann and Schürmann tried as best they could to base their analysis entirely on what they actually heard and recorded. Commenting on gaps in the possessive pronoun paradigm they write:

> It may strike the reader to see so many cases wanting in these examples ... All the other cases could have been easily formed according to analogy of the declensions of substantives, had it not been preferred to give only what hitherto has occurred or been met with; there remains little doubt of their existence, inferring from the regularity of the language.   (T&S, 1840: 12)

T&S is the only historical source which provides a grammatical analysis of the language. Other sources provide, at most, only brief generalisations about grammatical structure.

Teichelmann continued working on the language and in 1858 supplied Grey with an annotated copy of T&S in which he made a number of corrections, most prominent of which is his retraction of the Dative case. He writes 'There is no Dative in these <sic> language, because the verbs do not require one'. The putative Dative suffix *-ni* has been deleted throughout, within nominal, pronoun and demonstrative paradigms. He has also made several other minor revisions and contributed some additional explanation in places, but it would appear that in the eyes of Teichelmann 18 years on, the original grammar was still largely intact and accurate.

TMs is essentially a vocabulary, but it contains a number of suffixes and clitics with accompanying explanations, some of which are not found in T&S. These two examples are typical:

> - namalya, -
> This termination is used in forming the modus of a verb, which expresses the continuity of the action.
>
> -anda & -nda, 1. affixed to a personal pronoun it signifies self ngattunda, I myself (am the acting person) excluding other agency. Nindunda thou thyself etc. 2. affixed to possess. pron. ngaityoanda, my own; ninkoanda, thy own etc. 3. yakkoanda, not at all; nurntianda, entirely away.

Some of the other lexical entries also contain a considerable amount of grammatical information. Many are embellished with example phrases and sentences, from which additional insights into Kaurna grammar may be gained. The following example illustrates the level of grammatical material recorded:

> Padlondi,
> 1.to desire, wish, long, covet;
> mai padlond'aii, I long for food,
> padlonintyerla, a desire, one who longs for; - munto p.__ a voluptuous, wanton fellow.
> 2. to die, perish, starve.
> maiitidla kudla padloingko, he is in want of food & will die by himself;
> padlo padlunya, on the road to the grave, going to die; stricken with age'.
> padlunyanna, (a) perishing, dying'. Note from this & other instances it appears that the termination -nya is like the participle in -ing, dying, eating etc. that is the partic. praesens, as boka bokanya, I have rendered, a person who is fond of swimming, a swimmer.
> padli, dead; imperf.
> padletti, having died, he has died,
> padlettianangko, it comes from having died;
> garla padlondi, the fire is dying
> padlo paltandi, to throw to death, to beat out the fire;
> padlo kundandi, to strick <sic>, beat to death;
> padlo appendi, to caus <sic> to die, — perish.

Under the entry for *naa* 'you (plural)', for instance, some of Teichelmann's grammatical reasoning is evident:

> Na, 2nd pers. plur. of the personal pronoun you, ye; affixed to verbs the letter N is dropped & only A. remains, as in parni kawaiinga, come ye hither.
> Na wa wandi! where are you encamping<one line crossed out> naalitya, to you; for you on account of you; naalityangga, with you, at you, in your b.<?>; naandi, only you; none but you. Naako, Gen. & pron. poss. naakoandi, only yours, yours alone; naakulla worlingga, in your house; from this instance it is evidant <sic> that the particles expressing locality, time or other relations may also be affixed to pronouns. Here -lla, because naako is a three syllable, whereas -ngga on two syllables;
> yakko ngaityo yunga kambaritti wort.<?> naako tikkata, my (elder) brother shall not be your cook.

TMs remains a rich source of additional grammatical information, which has not yet been fully utilised. The sentence examples are particularly useful.

Teichelmann (1858) consists of three pages of handwritten notes on Kaurna verbs. Most of the information is already published in T&S, though his discussion of 'continuative verbs' is new and he has collected some instances of previously undiscussed morphology. He again impresses upon the reader the authenticity of his material in the aside 'Observe instances in my phrases, all of which are written down from the mouth of the Aborigines, none formed by myself.' Teichelmann seems to feel the analysis of Kaurna verbs is still incomplete, for in discussing his possible eighth genus 'verba spontania' he says 'all these instances will have to be collected and then compared and examined', and 'in fact, the most attention must be paid to the terminations of the words'.

Teichelmann and Moorhouse (1841) presented a report to the Statistical Society which included a short 5-page sketch of the Kaurna language. Most of the information in this paper is in T&S and TMs. However, it does contain some additional derivations and verbal forms, and some aspects of the grammar are set out with greater clarity in this publication. Teichelmann & Moorhouse (1841) is a useful adjunct to the other sources.

Moorhouse (1843), in a letter to Grey, outlined similarities and differences between the 'Adelaide dialect' and the 'Swan dialect', i.e. Nyungar, spoken in the south-west of Western Australia. He referred to 18 grammatical rules laid down in The Grammar of Western Australia[21], questioning its accuracy in certain respects. In so doing Moorhouse discusses aspects of Kaurna grammar, making several points more explicitly than T&S. The reply was from Governor Hutt, who indicated several differences between Kaurna and Nyungar.

Other sources
A limited number of sentences were recorded by Williams (1840) and Wyatt (1879), from which some grammatical information is recoverable, and a certain amount of morphology is evident in these and other wordlists. These sources are more revealing of the English observers' understandings of Kaurna grammar than of the grammar itself. Grammatical structure recoverable from Williams and Wyatt is often at odds with T&S, demonstrating features of a pidgin. These sources do not add to our understanding of Kaurna grammar.

Some nineteenth century observers outside of the 'Adelaide School' made some fallacious and uninformed comments on Kaurna grammar. Piesse, for instance, says:

> The public do not know instinctively that the verbs are spoken only in the present tense; that almost all nouns are the same in the plural and singular numbers, and that there is no pronoun expressing the third person. It is the want of information on these points that deters many from studying the language. (Piesse, 1840: 296)

Cawthorne echoes these views in an early draft of his published paper (Cawthorne in Foster, 1991: 81).

Black (1920), a more reliable twentieth-century source, includes short sentences which provide some useful points of confirmation and contrast with Kaurna morphology and syntax as recorded by T&S. Black shows that numerals could be used in addition to the dual suffix:

> bulatji, two. (T. and S., purlaitye) This word may be placed before the dual (at least this was done by Amelia), so that a double dual was produced: bulatji kadlila, two dogs; bulatji tappula, two flies; pulatji mijula, two men; bulatji ngangkiila 'two women'
> (Black, 1920: 82)

This was a point of some uncertainty from the German sources, for want of examples. It is also possible that the double marking recorded by Black is due to the advanced stage of attrition of the language.

Grammatical descriptions of neighbouring Thura-Yura languages are very limited. Nonetheless, material compiled by Hercus (1992) on Nukunu and by Black (1920) on Narungga are useful points of comparison. Descriptions of Barngarla grammar (Schürmann, 1844) and Adnyamathanha (Schebeck, 1974; 1976) are more extensive.

Modern sources

In 1965, the linguist Carl von Brandenstein published a paper on the privative suffix in Australian languages, drawing heavily on Kaurna examples taken from T&S. Note that von Brandenstein does not use the term Kaurna, but 'Meiu' (= *miyu* 'man').

Since von Brandenstein's paper, linguists often draw on Kaurna materials in the discussion of grammatical or typological phenomena. Jane Simpson, for instance, has been working on Kaurna for many years. As a student at ANU in the 1970s she wrote several essays on Kaurna, including a comparison between Adnyamathanha, Kaurna and Barngarla phonology, case endings and pronouns (Simpson, 1976). The result of her continuing work, together with insights from my own, will be published shortly (Simpson & Amery, forthcoming). It will contain a detailed analysis of Kaurna phonology, morphology and syntax, and analysis of Kaurna dialectology supplemented with historical and sociolinguistic information. Much of this grammar has been reasonably easy to write, but there are a number of unresolved issues, where the information required to complete the description is lacking.

It is my intention also to write a pedagogical grammar of Kaurna, along the lines of *A Learners Guide to Eastern and Central Arrernte* (Green, 1994), *A Learners Guide to Yankunytjatjara* (Goddard, 1980) and *Wangka Wiru: A Handbook for the Pitjantjatjara Language Learner* (Eckert & Hudson, 1988).

Such a publication would support the teaching of Kaurna. For now though, T&S remains the primary point of reference.

Kaurna texts

The virtual absence of texts is the major shortcoming of T&S and TMs. However, all known Kaurna texts except two were written, transcribed or translated by members of the 'Adelaide School' or their pupils. The German sources include a number of connected sentences or question and answer routines, such as:

> Wadangko padlourlaintya turteanula? Metti biri nindo purla. — Yungki ai padlo — yakko atto metti.
> 'Whence is that jacket? you most likely stole it. — He gave it to me — I did not steal it.'
> (T&S, 1840: 70)

The longest connected text in the phraseology is the following:

> Wortanna ngaityo nungngurruandi manyaurlyo, wodlingga ba waienetti. Yakko ba budnetti manya, burro ai wodlingga tikkaninyidla; madlanna manya budnetti, worltangga ai tikketti wodlingga. Manti ai ingarnetti manyarna wodlingga — nammu ai warrunna, ba budninda manya.[22]

> 'All my moveables become wet by the rain, which could enter into the house. Did it not rain, I should still be sitting in the house; had no rain come, I was sitting warm in the house. I could not foresee the coming rain whilst in the house — now I am outside, the rain just comes.'
> (T&S, 1840: 70)

T&S also provide several song lines (discussed later) and two versions of two short texts, spoken by Mullawirraburka and Kadlitpinna (depicted in Plate 3), in order to illustrate dialect differences:

> KING JOHN
> Natta murriendi adlu; paini paininga adlu yaintya tikki; kutyonillanda tikkaneadlu paru paintyingga, kudyonilla yertangga. Yaintya atto natta kundo puma yerta.

> CAPTAIN JACK
> Natta Padnend' adlu; bukki bukki adlu yentya tikki; kumarnilla yertangga tikkaningadlu paru paintyingga. Yentya atto kundo puma yerta.

> 'Now let us go further; formerly we lived here for some time; otherwere <sic> we will live, upon another district, where meat is at hand. Here I feel now anxious for another district.'

> KING JOHN
> Yakko ninna yerna budnaninditta; nurnti murrendi; kudla tikkandingai, bappa yuwettoai ai.

> CAPTAIN JACK
> Yakko ninna yernta budnaningutta ; nurnti padni; kudla tikka ningai, bappa ngai yiwettoai.

> 'You shall not come hither; go off; I will be alone, else I cannot be circumcised.'
> (T&S, 1840: 72)

TMs includes a number of connected sentences, though none are more extensive than examples already cited from T&S. There are no texts as such.

Wyatt (1879) provides a short text of a Kaurna Dreaming story, just 34 words in all. This text will be discussed in detail (see p. 103). Several other short texts have come to light in the course of my research and are discussed briefly below.

Translated speeches

Governor Gawler's speech to Aboriginal people in Adelaide, 1 November 1838, was translated by Wyatt, the Protector of Aborigines and published in the *South Australian Gazette and Colonial Register,* 3 November 1838. Wyatt's 88 word translation has features indicative of a jargon Kaurna, and is at odds with T&S's grammar on a number of points (discussed by Simpson, 1996: 189-194).

Schürmann's translation of Gawler's address to the assembled Aboriginal people for the Queen's Birthday celebrations in May 1840 was published in the *South Australian Gazette and Colonial Register,* 20 May 1840. This translation, of about 150 words, is a more sophisticated text, employing a greater range of verb morphology and complex sentence constructions. Both speeches, and the circumstances in which they were translated, are discussed by Foster & Mühlhäusler (1996).

Religious texts

A Kaurna translation of the Ten Commandments by Clamor Schürmann was published in the *South Australian Gazette and Colonial Register,* 20 May 1840 (See Plate 10). According to the missionaries they were recited regularly within the school and sometimes in public at official gatherings.

In November 1840, Klose sent to Dresden a page from a copybook written by Kartanya, an 11-year old girl. It consists of three lines as follows, repeated several times on the page (see Plate 6):

> Yeowarnalitya tondari mangaringa;
> <Jehova-to   always worship-IMP(Pl)>
> <'Always worship Jehova.'>
>
> ngadluko pinggalinggala pa;
> <our   creator   3Sg>
> <'He is our creator'>
>
> wakinnaanangko padlu ngadlu tiraappeta.
> <bad-from   3Sg+ERG we protect-FUT>
> <'He protects us from evil.'>[23]

The missionaries apparently produced more Kaurna religious texts, though these have not yet been located. A school prayer written in Kaurna was regularly recited. Klose refers to Bible topics covered in the school program:

> such as the creation, the fall, the flood, the giving of the Commandments; in the New Testament: the birth of Christ, the prodigal son, the resurrection of the young man at Nain and the daughter of Jairus, the suffering and death of the Lord, his resurrection and

ascension, and that he would come again for the judgement. With all of these they are acquainted so far as their language permits, 16 - 18 children came each day.

(Letter to Dresden, 26 April 1842)

I assume these topics were taught in Kaurna because Klose refers to them before he writes of introducing English. In the same letter, Klose elaborates on religious instruction and mentions sending examples of the children's handwriting of Biblical texts:

> With reference to my methods I must apply myself strongly to the language and to the children. The school day begins with singing and prayer. On the first days of the week I repeat what Br Teichelmann has said to the adults and children on the Sunday before. On the rest of the days I tell them a Bible story, repeat and ask about it, but it remains difficult to get answers from the children. After the first hour they have a quarter hour break. In the second they practise arithmetic or I dictate a Bible story or biblical truths which they enjoy writing more than using their own language. With that the morning lessons end.

Letters written by Kaurna children

The earliest known text written by Kaurna authors is a letter written to Governor Gawler by Kaurna children at Piltawodli, dated 15 May 1841[24] (see Plate 9). This letter is a plea to Gawler to stay on in his position as Governor and is signed by nine children, five boys and four girls. Comprising 61 words, it is the longest surviving Kaurna letter.

Two short letters, 25 and 31 words, written in 1843 by two boys, Pitpauwe and Wailtye, both signatories of the 1841 letter, are amongst Klose's papers.[25] The two letters are very similar in form (see Plates 7 and 8). I analyse Wailtye's text below:

> Ngaityo tarruanna
> my   brother-in-law-ALL
> 'To my friends.'

> Ngatto naalityangga paper kaitya. Na ngattaitya ngaityo ngunya waiettinna kaityaninga,
> I+ERG you(pl)-with letter sent   you(pl) me-to my   toy-PL   send-IMP
> 'I am sending you a letter. You have sent me toys.'
> <I have sent you a letter. You send me my toys.>[26]

> ngai   ngunya waietta ngaityo worlingga tauatta tindurna.
> I+NOM play-FUT   my   house-in many   day-PL
> 'I will play in my room for many days.'

> Ngaii   ngunya waieta ngaityo mudli worlinna parni   kaityaninga.
> I+NOM play-FUT   my   thing house-PL towards send-IMP
> 'I will play, send more here.'
> <I will play [with] my household things send here (ie please send more)>

> Wailtyidlo   naako   paper kaitya.
> Wailtyi-ERG you(pl)-GEN letter sent.
> Wailtyi sends you the letter.
> <Wailtyi has sent you the letter>

There are several interesting features. Note the use of the kin term in the salutation 'to my brother-in-law', which Klose translates as 'to my friends'. Also

Wailtyi uses *ngunya waiettinna* 'toys', yet *ngunyawaietti* is known only as 'play; dance; corroboree' in T&S. The affinity is evident through morphological analysis of the word, *ngunya* 'joy' + *wayinthi* 'to move' + *-ti* 'NOML'. So 'toy' is encoded as the 'joy-moving-thing', whereas 'corroboree' is encoded as the 'joy-moving-event'. This is a very important example, adding to our understanding of the use of the nominaliser *-ti*.

A fourth letter written by Itya Maii, the principal signatory of the 1841 letter, was sent to Governor Grey and his wife in 1845. It is housed in Grey's collection in the South African Public Library, Cape Town and was included in Henderson's (1907: 49) biography of Grey. This letter appears to be a short note attached to some watermelons that the children had grown in their garden. I analyse it below:

>   Kambandoanna parnu Yangaroanna
>   <governor-ALL his wife-ALL>
>   The Governor & his Lady
>
>   Pulyonna Ngartunna kaityatti melonilla.   Parnako yertaunangko manketti purlaityi.
>   <black child-PL sent-Past melon-DUAL their   ground-ABL get-Past two>
>   The black children have sent two melons.   Their garden from (they) have taken these two.
>
>   ngaii
>   <I(NOM)>
>   I am
>   ninko panyappi
>   <your younger sibling>
>   your friend

These are the only extant historical Kaurna texts known. Little can be said about original Kaurna discourse structure from them. The speeches, Ten Commandments and hymns are all translations of English or German, and as such reveal little about Kaurna discourse. The few letters known to survive are short. However, they do span a range of purposes. The 1841 letter is basically a protest letter and a plea. Wailtyi's and Pitpauwi's letters are requests, whilst Itya Mai's 1845 letter is a note, though importantly it includes rather formal opening and closing salutations. The texts contain some additional senses of words not otherwise recorded and Itya Mai's note uses the word *Kambando* 'Governor', probably a borrowing from English 'governor', or more likely 'government'. We have used this word in contemporary materials for 'government'.

Kaurna Dreaming stories

The 'Dreaming' is a fundamental part of Aboriginal culture and still holds an important place in the minds of Nungas who might have spent all their lives in an urban area. In the context of Aboriginal Studies in schools, Dreaming stories are highly sought after, almost to the exclusion of everything else.

Unfortunately, few Kaurna Dreaming stories were ever recorded. Most of what is known comes to us from Ngarrindjeri people as recorded by Tindale, the Berndts and others. The German missionaries appear not to have recorded any Kaurna Dreaming stories in the Kaurna language, though they were clearly in a position to do so. Teichelmann indicated in a letter to George French Angas in April 1840 that he had some knowledge of a number of Kaurna Dreaming stories:

> Another opinion is that all the animals have been formerly men and are their ancestors, who by the operation of certain circumstances, turned animals. They personify the celestials' bodies as having formerly lived upon earth and the metamorphosis of which is closely connected with that of their ancestors.
> When the lark and the whale were men, they fought against each other. The lark speared the whale twice in the neck. The whale, finding itself sorely wounded, made its escape, jumped from pain into the sea, became a whale and spouted through the two wounds water to heal them; but in vain, till this very day. The parrot, which has a red belly and yellow-red chest, got in a similar fight, a blow upon his nose, the blood ran down upon chest and belly, and he turning bird, the blood coloured both parts for ever. The emu lost in a fight, if I mistake not, with the eagle, his two arms, therefore in turning bird he got such short wings. Of this sort they have numberless tales of all the animals and also of the celestial bodies.
> (Teichelmann in the *South Australian Colonist*, 1840: Vol. 1, No.18, July 7, 1840: 277)

These accounts are in English and are very brief, making no attempt to tell the full story, though he presumably heard them in the Kaurna language. We have no record that Teichelmann recorded these stories in Kaurna but if he did they have either been lost or remain hidden in some archive or private collection. Fortunately, versions of the lark and whale story are known in Ngarrindjeri, having been recorded by Meyer (1846), Berndt & Berndt (1993: 235-236; 450-451) and Tindale (Journals 20 May 1934).[27] Versions of the parrot and emu stories have not been found in neighbouring languages, though they are familiar themes across Australia (Gale, 2000).

Schürmann refers to other Kaurna beliefs in his letters and journals, and T&S and TMs reveal the nature of Kaurna spirituality through comments in the vocabulary, for example:

> Yura, s. a large snake, or other monstrous and imaginary being. Yura is believed to be the author of circumcision, who first taught it to their ancestors, and who punishes the neglect of it.

Philip Clarke (1990; 1991) has brought much of this material together and further discusses Kaurna cosmology in the context of neighbouring groups in Clarke (1997).

The story of Tjilbruke, recognised as a Kaurna creator ancestor, is known principally from Ngarrindjeri people who worked with both Tindale and the Berndts. The Tjilbruke story was first published in English by W. Ramsay Smith (1930: 331-341), whose unacknowledged source was another Ngarrindjeri man, David Unaipon. Berndt & Berndt (1993: 445-447) and Tindale recorded the story in Ngarrindjeri and have provided us with English translations. Campbell (1985), noting the Ngarrindjeri sources, questions the status of the story in a paper titled 'Is the Legend of Tjilbruke a Kaurna Legend?' Clarke (1991) also notes Ngarrindjeri influences in the story.

However, despite its Ngarrindjeri sources, the Tjilbruke story concerns the creation of sites deep inside Kaurna country and is now a 'core value' for Kaurna people and central to the very existence of KACHA. The Tjilbruke story has been given publicity through the marking of sites in the early 1980s and through its inclusion in Aboriginal Studies materials (EDSA, 1989: 97-101) and the cultural instruction program offered by Tauondi.

Different versions exist. The main source for educational and promotional materials is Tindale (1987), in which Tjilbruke or Tjirbruki is equated with the glossy ibis. But in Unaipon's versions in Ramsay-Smith (1930) and in Berndt and Berndt (1993), Tjilbruke is the blue crane. Tindale (1987) contains a number of Indigenous place names, other vocabulary and snippets of text. Unfortunately, as with the card file, Tindale makes little attempt to distinguish between Kaurna, Ngarrindjeri and other languages or indeed between different varieties of Ngarrindjeri. This is not surprising since Tindale's various sources for the Tjirbruki story had links to the Ngarrindjeri (including Tanganekald, Yaralde and Ramindjeri dialects), Peramangk and Kaurna languages. Tindale gives the following background information:

> Our record of the man Tjirbruki is not complete but gives some insight into the ways of the earlier inhabitants as remembered by present day Aborigines. The account is based, not on direct text material, but has been brought together from conversations with men of four of the tribes over a long period between 1928 and 1964. At first the full import of the Tjirbruki story was not evident to this writer; thus the notes are widely scattered in his journals and in part therefore have been linked together from personal recollections. A firm basis for the story as given here, is the one told to the late H. Kenneth Fry and me on the evening of 14 February 1934 during an extensive field trip on which we had been taken by Milerum of the Karagari clan of the Tanganekald tribe in a survey of his country along the Coorong. Having worked with me for several years, Milerum was a skilled informant. ... It was a long story he had heard at Yankalilla when he was quite young in the early 1880s. The narrators then were using Rapid Bay talk and Milerum attempted to use terms he had heard at that time. There were supplementary discussions thereafter on more than one occasion. (Tindale, 1987: 5)

So Tindale's main informant was Milerum, whose territory is located along the Coorong, some distance from Kaurna country (not adjoining). Ivaritji had died some years earlier, so the account of this Kaurna story necessarily comes entirely from non-Kaurna people. In 1929, Ivaritji had spoken of 'her father's and her own totem, the emu' (Tindale, 1987: 5) though not actually about the story itself.

'Rapid Bay talk' was presumably a variety of Kaurna, as some of the Rapid Bay words identified by Wyatt (1879) are distinctly Kaurna in form, and there are a number of key Kaurna words and place names in Tindale's compilation. However, a great many are of Ngarrindjeri origin, sprinkled throughout the text without identification. Only occasionally when a full sentence or short text is given does Tindale identify it as Tangani or Jaralde (Tindale, 1987: 9) and the song recorded in 1937 by Milerum (Tindale, 1987: 12) is certainly Ngarrindjeri. On one occasion Tindale (1987: 11) tries to draw a distinction between '['ru:we] (lands) and ['paŋkara] (hunting areas)', though I would suggest that *ruwe* in

Ngarrindjeri is equivalent to *pangkarra* in Kaurna. Note the following definitions from historical sources:

pangkarra	a district or tract of country belonging to an individual, which he inherits from his father. (T&S, 1840: 36)
reerwe ~ ruwe	'earth' (Wyatt, 1879: 19) Identified by Wyatt as 'Encounter Bay'.
ruwe	'land' (Taplin, 1879:
ruwe	'land, country, birth-place' (Meyer, 1843: 97)
ruwi	'land, firm earth, country or territory' (Berndt & Berndt, 1993; 358)

There is no suggestion in any source, except Tindale, that *ruwe* is a Kaurna word. Likewise, *pangkarra* does not appear in any Ngarrindjeri sources. It seems that both the Kaurna words *yarta* 'earth; land; soil; country' and *pangkarra* are rendered as *ruwe* in Ngarrindjeri. T&S are quite clear about an ownership dimension in their definition of *pangkarra*. *Ruwe* and *yarta* are given as the respective Ngarrindjeri and Kaurna equivalent terms for 'land' in Taplin's (1879: 143) comparative wordlist.

Some place names in the Tjilbruke story (such as Karika:lingga) are straightforward Kaurna names, attested in T&S and transparent in their meaning. Several (such as Patawilyangk) are clearly Kaurna names, but appear in Tindale (1987) with a Ngarrindjeri locative suffix. Others appear to be Ngarrindjeri, featuring initial r's and l's or ending in a consonant, thus breaking the phonotactic patterns of Kaurna. Similarly, some common nouns like *kardi* 'emu' and *wirra* 'forest' are indisputably Kaurna. They are not attested in the Ngarrindjeri sources and Ngarrindjeri has unrelated words for these items. However, others such as *luki* 'tear' (which contrasts with *miikauwi* in Kaurna) are clearly Ngarrindjeri. Unfortunately, Tindale did not make an effort to distinguish between the origins of the words.

The Munana story told by Kadlitpinna to Wyatt is the only extant Kaurna Dreaming story recorded in the Kaurna language. It is just 33 words including repetitious phrases, originally published in the following form:

> Aichoo ngaicherle erleeta wangan 'Monána aráche kaia pemane, ea pamáne, ea pamáne, boora kaia kurra pemáne, kaia kurra yewáne, kotinne kaia yewáne, kotinne kaia yewáne, boora yerta yewane; Monana kaia tatteene kurra winneen.'

> My father's great-grandfather (or ancestor) said — 'Monana threw many spears, here threw, here threw, by and by a spear upwards threw, the spear above stuck fast, again spear stuck fast, again spear stuck fast, by and by in the ground stuck fast; Monana (by the) spears climbed, above went.' This statement is in the words of Monaicha wonweetpeena konoocha, or 'Captain Jack.' (Wyatt, 1879: 25)

Wyatt's paper was republished in Woods (1879) and again in Parkhouse (1923) in a revised orthography. Schürmann refers to this story in a letter to Angas, 12 June 1839:

> Strange and interesting is the tale of the ascension of Munaina, beings that lived long before them. They threw spears (Kaya) in all directions of the sky, but they fell down to the ground; at last they threw one to the zenith right upwards, which fell not down but

> remained above, then they threw a second which joined the former, sticking with its point in the soft butt end of the other, so a third and so forth, till the pillar reached to the ground and the Munaina climbed upwards. (Schurmann, 1987: 48)

Versions were also published in English by Meyer (1846) and Taplin (1879) who worked with Ramindjeri and Yaralde people respectively. However, longer versions have been recorded this century in Ngarrindjeri, in which the ancestor is identified as Waiyungari who became the planet Mars. In 1934, Tindale worked with Frank Blackmoor, an elderly Ngarrindjeri man, publishing his version of the Waiyungari story in Yaralde and English (Tindale, 1935), whilst the Berndts worked with Albert Karloan publishing his version in Ngarrindjeri and English (Berndt & Berndt, 1993: 228-230; 442-444). The Ngarrindjeri versions are considerably longer and more detailed than Kadlitpinna's Kaurna version published by Wyatt, the latter corresponding to nine lines of a 38-line story recorded by the Berndts.

The seven sisters and Orion. Unfortunately, almost nothing by way of women's stories was ever recorded. The main sources for Teichelmann, Schürmann, Tindale, the Berndts and others were men, so it is not surprising that little should have been recorded. There is little doubt that the 'Seven Sisters' story belonged to the Kaurna. Versions still survive amongst some Ngarrindjeri women, having been handed down orally from one generation to the next. The story is also widespread in the Western Desert and Thura-Yura languages. An Adnyamathanha version was recorded by Mountford (in Tindale, 1935: 142-145) and a brief version was related by the Nukunu man, Harry Bramfield (Hercus, 1992: 16). The Kaurna vocabulary itself indicates the existence of the 'Seven Sisters' story. The Pleiades or Seven Sisters were referred to as *Mankamankarranna* 'the girls', whilst Orion was called *Tinniinyaranna* 'the boys'. In the latter entry T&S provide a little information:

> Tinniinyaranna, s. the Orion, considered by the natives as a group of youths. They are said to hunt kangaroos, emus, and other game, on the great celestial plain (womma), while the mangkamangkarranna dig roots, &c., which are around them.

Pootpobberrie. EDSA (1989) includes an account of the Pootpobberrie story, first published in 1913:

> The outline of this story was told to the writer many years ago by the late James Cronk of Modbury, who came out with Colonel Light and acted as native interpreter to Government officials in early days.
> (signed C.H.H., *Public Service Review*, February 1913: 36)

This seems to be the only surviving record of Cronk's knowledge of the Kaurna language and traditions, which must have been considerable. As the introduction to this material in the Aboriginal Studies resource states:

> This account is probably not a strict 'Dreaming' story. It seems to be a collection of several stories put together by a Kaurna narrator and passed on through the memory of James Cronk ... Included within the story are many interesting pieces of information on Kaurna beliefs. (EDSA, 1989: 78)

The story appears in English, but includes Ngarrindjeri and Kaurna words as the names of the main characters in the story, in the same way that Wyatt's (1879) story appears to use *munana* 'ancestor' as the name of a specific ancestor. Spellings of many words have been changed in *The Kaurna People*.

Dreaming stories in closely related languages

A number of Dreaming stories, known only in English with key Narungga words, have been passed down within Narungga families. However, many concern localised sites on Yorke Peninsula and thus were probably not shared with Kaurna. Similarly, a number of Dreaming stories were recorded from Nukunu people and from other groups about sites in Nukunu country (Hercus, 1992: 13-17). However, a number of the most important Nukunu stories did not extend south to Adelaide. For instance, Port Augusta in Nukunu country marks the start of 'the longest known continuous song-line', the *Urumbula*, which extends north-east to the Gulf of Carpentaria (Hercus, 1992: 13). Songs relating to the Port Augusta section of the song-line have been recorded in Arrernte, though they are about Nukunu country. According to Moonie Davis, a Barngarla man, the *Urumbula* ceremonies 'came right down from the north but not through Adelaide way' (in Hercus, 1992: 16). Numerous Dreaming stories from the Flinders Ranges have been recorded in Adnyamathanha and English (Tunbridge, 1988; Schebeck, 1974). Many are specific to localised sites, though some, such as the 'Seven Sisters' Dreaming, are more general.

Kaurna songs

A number of short Kaurna songs survive in written form, both in published sources and in letters and journals. Several observers also record graphic descriptions of *kurdi, palti* and *ngunyawayiti* song and dance performances, otherwise known in English as 'corroboree'. Unfortunately, apart from an undecipherable recording in the State Library of South Australia said to belong to Adelaide, there are no sound recordings of traditional Kaurna songs.

T&S (1840: 73) record two hunting songs and an initiation song. There is no information about the music or ways in which they were sung. These songs are not reproduced or discussed in detail here out of respect for the sacred material they contain.

Cawthorne (1844: 22) reproduces the English version of T&S's wild dog hunting song practically word for word without acknowledgement, and in *The Legend of Kuperree* (Cawthorne, 1858: verse 113) he misinterprets verbs as nouns by interpreting the Kaurna sentences according to English word order. The original song consistently places the verb last in accordance with preferred word order in Kaurna.

Moorhouse also appears to have recorded Kaurna initiation songs. A fragment from a page of his journal[28] preserves Ngurpo Willo's Palti; it is just two lines, seven words in all, left untranslated, but the vocabulary leads me to believe that it is an initiation song and so it will not be discussed here. The word *ngurpo* is not recorded in Kaurna vocabularies, but appears to be a title. It bears some similarity to T&S's *ngarparpo* 'father-in-law', so perhaps it is a relationship term.

In addition to the traditional hunting and initiation songs which were probably handed down essentially unchanged over many generations, there are four songs in a similar format, which concern recently introduced entities: peas, cattle, roads and Europeans. These appear to belong to a kind of protest song genre, most potently expressed in Ngurpo Williamsie's Palti, also recorded by Moorhouse. I refer to these songs also as 'traditional' Kaurna songs as they appear to have been sung in the traditional style, by contrast with hymns etc. sung to Western tunes.

The two songs recorded by Moorhouse were found by accident among Cawthorne's sketches in the Mitchell Library, Sydney.[29] Ngurpo Williamsie's song runs:

```
Wanti nindo ai kabba kabba }       Ngurpo
where   you I drive - out    }      Williamsie
Ningkoandi kuma   yerta      }
your only   another countries }
```

(PX*D70 f.12 photograph of sketch by W.A. Cawthorne in John Tragenza's Historic Pictures Index held in the Mortlock Library, State Library of South Australia. Original held by the Mitchell Library, Sydney)

This song warrants further analysis. T&S sheds some light on the translation provided:

kabbakabbandi, v.a. to treat harshly or unkindly
kabbandi, v.a. to press as little stones when lying upon them, to send away, to cast out; muiyo kabbandi to hate, to have spite against   (T&S, 1840: 6)

TMs has the following entries:

kabbandi to project, having the tendency to project; to force off, assunder <sic>, as a wedge in splitting; to guard off as in fighting; to hold forth
kabba kabbandi   to send off (a beggar); cast out, etc.

Ngurpo Williamsie's song may be analysed as follows:

```
Wanti     ninthu    -"ai         kapa kapa
where-to  2SgERG    1SgACC       drive out/ send off/ cast out PST PERF

Ninku-anti         kuma   yarta
2SgPOSS- only      another land/country
```

It might be more freely translated as 'Where have you pushed me to? You belong to another country.' The use of the suffix or clitic *-anti* is significant. It signals a notion of exclusivity. In this sentence it implies that 'another country is yours and yours alone'. That is, 'we make no claim on it', the implication being 'why do you make a claim on our land?' This song then is clearly a protest against incursions by Europeans or Murray River peoples into Kaurna lands. It is interesting that several other songs recorded by the German missionaries seem to fit this same genre.

Kadlitpiko Palti[30] consists of a single line:

KADLITPIKO PALTI	CAPTAIN JACK'S SONG
Pindi mai birkibirki parrato, parrato.	'The European food, the pease, I wished to eat, I wished to eat.'
	(T&S, 1840: 73)

This song line might be analysed as follows:
Pinti   mai   pirrkipirrki   parr(a)'athu, parr(a)'athu.[31]
European food peas   chew-I   chew-I
'The European food, the peas, I wished to eat, I wished to eat.'

This song was collected during a five-day hunting trip, as Schürmann notes:

> On this occasion I collected some of the rhymes they used in their own language. The first in the way they told me, is as follows: Waiené numa Burlokka witte (fear the great oxen). Another one — Pinde mai birki-birki (a strange meal are the peas).
> (Schürmann Journal, 9 September 1839)

Interestingly, a little more of the song appears in the published version (T&S, 1840: 73) than in Schürmann's journal. Whilst the song is identified as 'Captain Jack's song' in the published version, it seems that Kadlitpinna was not present on the hunting trip: he was already well known to the missionaries, and would certainly have been mentioned by name if he had been.

Mullawirraburkarna Palti[32] is similarly a short song of two lines:

MULLAWIRRABURKARNA PALTI	KING JOHN'S SONG
Natta ngai padlo ngaityarniappi;	Now it (viz. the road or track) has tired me;
watteyernaurlo tappandi ngaityo parni tatti. (Da capo)	throughout Yerna there is here unto me a continuous road. (T&S, 1840: 73)

This is a somewhat complex and puzzling construction, as follows:

Nata ngai padlu   ngaitya-rni-api
now me it (ERG) weak-INCH-CAUS+PERF
'Now it (viz. the road or track) has tired me';

warti-yarna-urlu   tapanthi   ngaityu parni   tati.
middle-Yarna-that/yon+ERG road-PRES my   toward climb+PERF
'throughout *Yerna* there is here unto me a continuous road.'

Wyatt (1879) gives *yerna yerna* 'undulating ground', but here it seems to serve as the name of a tract of country. Perhaps the sentence means that 'the road passing through Yerna is climbing towards (ie encroaching upon) my [country]'. The road is a further intrusion into Kaurna country, bringing with it Europeans and their animals which destroy traditional food sources. Cawthorne (1858) draws upon this song in verse 49 of *The Legend of Kuperree*, where the Kaurna line *Watteyernorlo Tappande* is followed by Ngarrindjeri *Miny-el-ity an-ambe* 'What is it to me?'

As noted above, Schürmann's journal contains a short song which does not appear elsewhere:

> *Waiené   numa   burlokka witte*
> fear+IMP emotion ox   big
> 'fear the great oxen'

Wayirni is the imperative form of the verb *wayirninthi* 'to fear; be afraid'. *Numa* is glossed as 'right; correct; skillfull; well' but occurs in conjunction with the verb *nakunthi* 'to see' to form the compound *numa nakunthi* 'to like; love'. This latter emotion contrasts with *wadli nakunthi* 'to dislike; hate; detest' where *wadli* is given as 'imperfect; incorrect; bad'. Thus *wayirni numa* 'fear!' is the imperative form of the emotion term. *Purluka* 'ox' is simply borrowed from English 'bullock'. Note that the adjective, *witi* 'large', occurs after the noun to which it refers, in contrast to the more common pattern, with the adjective preceding the noun as in English. It is possible that the Great Ox Song also fits the protest song genre, referring to a large threatening animal which has intruded upon Kaurna lands.

Table 5.1: 'Traditional' Kaurna songs

Song	Source	Length	Topic	Status
Kadlitpiko Palti 'Capt. Jack's Song'	T&S	1 line 5 words	Introduction of European foods — compensation.	? protest song
Mullawirraburkarna Palti 'King John's Song'	T&S	2 lines 9 words	Road from Adelaide to Encounter Bay	? protest song
Great Ox Song	Schürmann Journal	1 line 4 words	Introduction of cattle	? protest song
Ngurpo Williamsie's Palti	Moorhouse Journal	2 lines 7 words	Protest at invasion of Kaurna land	Protest song
Ngurpo Willo's Palti	Moorhouse Journal	2 lines 7 words	Possibly an initiation song	? sacred
Initiation Song	T&S	5 lines 14 words	Initiation song	Sacred
Wild Dog Hunting Song	T&S	9 lines 19 words	Sorcery	Sacred
Possum Hunting Song	T&S	7 lines 14 words	Sorcery	Sacred

Recorded songs that relate to Kaurna country

Tindale recorded the 'Song of Njengari' sung by Milerum, a Ngarrindjeri man, in 1937. Tindale refers to Njengari as a 'kinsman' of Tjirbruki and claims that this song 'may well be the only *matenggauwe* song of the Kaurna that has survived' (Tindale, 1987: 12), noting Meyer's (1843) translation of the term *matenggauwe* as a 'song used by the Adelaide Aborigines'. However, the language of the song, as recorded by Tindale is certainly not Kaurna. None of the words resembles Kaurna in the slightest, whilst the word *ŋareilkundaŋal* 'dance' (= *ngrilkulun* in Taplin, 1879: 128) indicates that the song belongs to a

Ngarrindjeri language. Once again, Tindale seems to draw little distinction between Kaurna and Ngarrindjeri. The song may be about Kaurna country and Kaurna ancestral beings, but it seems to be stretching it to call the 'Song of Njengari' a Kaurna song.

Another song attributed to the people of the Adelaide Plains is in the Mountford collection amongst Adnyamathanha and Arabana songs from the mid-north. Unfortunately, the sound recording is indistinct and there is no transcription of the song. However, none of the words are identifiable as Kaurna and some do not seem to fit expected Kaurna phonological patterns. The singer may be Milerum (Clarence Long), judging by the voice quality (pc Chester Schultz). I strongly suspect that this song, too, was sung in a language other than Kaurna, probably Ngarrindjeri, even though it may relate to Kaurna country.

Ethnography of Kaurna music

There are some interesting ethnographic descriptions of Kaurna *kurdi*, *palti* or *ngunyawayiti* 'play; corroboree'. The German missionaries wrote several accounts of Kaurna ceremonies and include illuminating entries in their vocabularies. Cawthorne took a particular interest in the *palti* and found attending these ceremonies to be a highly exhilarating experience (Cawthorne journals, 30 March 1844). Cawthorne (1844: 8-15) published on Kaurna music and dance in his ethnographic work and also prepared an article for the newspaper titled 'The Native Corroboree' (*South Australian Register*, 16 March 1844). George French Angas (1846; 1847) published vivid accounts based on Cawthorne's work and produced a number of fine paintings. Stephens (1889: 493-495) also provides graphic descriptions.

Chester Schultz has collated and analysed these and other historical accounts in the development of contemporary songs and music in collaboration with members of the Kaurna community. Detailed background notes, including a comprehensive bibliography, were published (Schultz et al., 1999) to accompany modern interpretations of *palti*, based on the historical sources.

A number of Kaurna hymns were written to the tune of German hymns. Perhaps they were translations of the German hymns. Klose included six of these in a letter to the Dresden Missionary Society, 4 January 1843. Fortunately, he named the German melodies to which the Kaurna hymns were sung, enabling the music to be retrieved. Klose indicates that two of these hymns were written by Schürmann, no doubt early in 1840, after the school opened and before Schürmann relocated to Port Lincoln. Certainly Schürmann mentioned the first hymn in his journal[33] in May 1840. According to Klose, the remaining four hymns, which are considerably longer, were written by Teichelmann. The journals and letters of the German missionaries make a number of references to children singing the hymns at the school, in prayer meetings, public performances and even at a funeral at Encounter Bay.[34]

> At the grave some English people were gathered. Here I had my children sing 2 verses of the hymn Burti burlinga <sic> etc. Then the preacher Newland spoke to those present

and consoled Br Meyer on his loss after which the body was consigned to the earth and finally my children sang another verse of the same hymn: Kutteni Kristus budnata etc. and we went back home. The English people in Encounter Bay had never had an opportunity to hear the aboriginal children sing. They were delighted and it encouraged them to support Br. Meyer in everything he undertook with the natives.

(Letter to Dresden, 3 September 1844)

These hymns were evidently popular amongst the children at Piltawodli. Klose records:

Sometimes we hear the children singing a hymn they have learned in school as they leave our houses on the way to their huts, or when they are sitting together on the grass playing. (Letter to Dresden 29 December 1841)

A summary of the hymns is given in the following table:

Table 5.2: Kaurna hymns written in the early 1840s

No.	Author	Verses	Length	Subject
1.	Schürmann	2	19 words	Obedience to God
2.	Schürmann	3	32 words	Before the throne of Jesus
3.	Teichelmann	4	68 words	Redemption
4.	Teichelmann	4	41 words	Christmas carol
5.	Teichelmann	5	88 words	Easter hymn
6.	Teichelmann	3	63 words	Following Christ

Although there are no sound recordings from last century, we have a valuable record of the language, especially that provided by the German missionaries and others in the 'Adelaide School' who shared the same orthography and approach to description of the language. Outside the 'Adelaide School', Wyatt (1879), Williams (1840), Piesse (1840), Cawthorne (1844) and others make valuable contributions. Some Kaurna materials continue to be discovered in archives both here and overseas. Hopefully, additional material known to exist, such as Moorhouse's journal, may turn up one day. Even without new discoveries, available materials provide a solid base for reclamation and development of the Kaurna language, the topic of the next chapter.

Notes

[1] All known secondary sources in the nineteenth and early twentieth centuries are male.
[2] Whilst this letter is dated 19 January 1839, events, such as the hangings, took place months later. Either the letter was commenced then, but not completed until later or the date is wrong.
[3] Note that Schürmann uses *j* instead of T&S *y* in these examples.
[4] Mark Clendon published a commentary on Schürmann's work on Barngarla with University of Adelaide Press in 2015. See http://www.adelaide.edu.au/press/titles/barngarla/
[5] Schürmann (1844) also lists *kurru* 'stick', *midla* 'woomera' and *-nta* 'with' (Instrumental Case). Perhaps the expression meant <'that mob having the word *midla* (like us)'>. *Midla* is shared by both Barngarla and Kaurna.

[6] This expression, *kuya yarta* 'fish country' is reminiscent of the Yolngu expression *guya wäŋa* 'fish country' used in North East Arnhemland, which differs from the English way of expressing this notion. 'Fishing grounds' or 'fishing spot' would be the closest expressions in English.

[7] *kainyani* 'young man arrived at the age of puberty, at which they are painted red, and the beard first plucked out' (Meyer, 1843: 67).

[8] *Poomandi* 'to strike' appears to belong to a different dialect. T&S document *punggondi* 'to strike'.

[9] In fact, Moorhouse repeats the typographical error in *makarta* 'head' where *a* has been inadvertently written instead of *u* in the first syllable. This error has been corrected in the Errata page in T&S.

[10] T&S list *ngaingko* 'an adept; judge; connoisseur; a person knowing anything well'. This term may or may not have been used for a judge in a court of law.

[11] Letterbook, Aborigines Office Adelaide, May 1840 to January 1857.

[12] The Kaurna birth-order names, with the exception of the ninth born, are published in South Africa by Bleek (1871: 97). He acknowledges Moorhouse's Report in Sir George Grey's library as the source, though he also includes forms taken from T&S in brackets where the spellings used in the two sources are at variance.

[13] A short wordlist of the languages from Port Dalrymple in Tasmania and Jervis Bay in NSW, Maori and numerous languages from the Pacific regions is also included within the same volume.

[14] Wyatt (1879: 49) gives *balte balte* 'parrakeet (melopsittacus)' as an Encounter Bay (i.e. Ramindjeri) word, but there is no evidence of other Ngarrindjeri-like features in Piesse's wordlist.

[15] Interestingly, some of the annotations on Grey's copy are written in Arabic script, and the Malay word *orang* 'person' is given correctly as the equivalent of the Ramindjeri word *korne*.

[16] Thura-Yura languages include Kaurna, Narungga, Nukunu, Ngadjuri, Barngarla and Adnyamathanha (see Map II).

[17] Because Black uses italics in his transcription system, I have deviated from my usual practice of using italics for the spelling of non-English words.

[18] Tindale was appointed as Ethnologist at the South Australian Museum in 1928.

[19] The word *kunga* 'son' is not known from other sources. It is now used in modern Kaurna materials.

[20] Learners of Kaurna now have access to electronic vocabulary files which allow one to easily search for an English or Kaurna word.

[21] I am unsure of the author of this grammar; it appears not to be Grey (1840).

[22] T&S provide a footnote for the text: 'Thus a native was speaking, after he had moved all his luggage out of the home, in order to finish it, when he was lying outside, and rain come on unexpectedly.'

[23] These lines were left untranslated. I have supplied interlinear glosses and free translations in brackets <....>.

[24] According to Teichelmann's Diary (15 May 1841) the letter was 'written in their own language by the native girls and signed by those who could write'. O'Connor (1995: 9) has erroneously assumed that Teichelmann wrote the letter.

[25] I am indebted to Reinhard Wendt for locating these letters for me in Leipzig, and to the Lutheran Archives for allowing access to the records.

[26] I have provided a translation in brackets < > because the translation from the German in the line above appears to deviate from the original Kaurna. *Kaityarninga* is an imperative, and is translated as such later, but in this sentence it has been wrongly interpreted as past tense. The error appears to be due to Klose's limited understanding of the grammar rather than a problem in translation by the archivists.

[27] In 1996 Cherylynne Catanzaritti and Buck McKenzie produced a Kaurna song titled *Kondolli* based on this story. In 1997 I wrote and recorded a Kaurna version of the story for the language learning tapes produced for the KL&LE course at the University of Adelaide.

[28] Moorhouse's journals themselves have not been located, though these two songs appear to be in his handwriting on part of a page removed from his journals. The bottom of the page is annotated in a different hand, 'Journal by M. Moorhouse'.

[29] Cawthorne had a close association with the Protector and mentions in his journal (1 November 1844) reading Moorhouse's diary and reports.

[30] Recently this song has been set to music and recorded as part of the Kaurna reclamation project, interpreted as a statement of rights to adequate compensation by Kadlitpinna.

[31] The verbal form *parrato* is referred to as the 'Optative Mood' by T&S (1840: 18) and is a reduction of *parra-* 'to kindle; light; as *kardla parranthi*, to kindle a fire; to chew; to marry' + *ngathu* '1Sg ERG', the first singular ergative pronoun.

[32] In 1995 Mullawirraburkarna Palti was also set to music and recorded by Chester Schultz working together with students of Kaurna language at Inbarendi College.

[33] Unfortunately, the reference to this song was not included in the published version of Schürmann's journals (Schurmann, 1987).

[34] Meyer's baby died at the time Klose visited with seven Kaurna children.

Table 5.3: Kaurna sources making an original contribution

Source	Date[i]	No. of words	Domains	Orthography	Glosses	Addit. Vocab[ii]	Sentences
Gaimard	1826	168	various	'French' spell. e.g. *iouk* = *yuku*	minimal	5 words	no
Robinson	?1837	80	various	'English' spell. *you.co* = *yuku*	minimal	5 words	2
Koeler	1837-1838	150	various body parts	'German' spell *júkka* = *yuka*	minimal; some rich	few words	8 (Pidgin Kaurna)
Williams (1840)	1836-1839	377	all	'English' sp. *yoo-coo* = *yuku*	minimal	ca 30 words	28 (Pidgin Kaurna)
Piesse (1840)	1839	75	fauna; pl. names	followed Williams	varying; spec. locns	26 words	no
Wyatt (1840; 1879)	1837-1839	651	all	'English' sp. *olte* = *ngulthi*	varying	>100 wds 15 places	17 + short text
Earl	1838	14	body parts	'English' sp. *kundi* = *kanthi*	simple	none	no
Stephens	1838	36	birds	'English' sp.	some untransl.	> 20	no
T&S (1840)	1838-1840	**ca 2000**	all	reasonably consistent	extensive	main source	**ca 200 + short texts**
Schürmann Journal	1838-1840	ca 40 + 30 names	culture-specific; religion	similar to T&S; used *j* instead of *y*	rich contextual info.	none	**several + 2 songlines**
Teichelmann Diary	1839-1846	15 wds; 7 names	religion	T&S, but at times used *j* for *y*	in context	none	no
Klose letters	1840-1845	ca 40 7 names 7 grps	numbers, grp names, religion	T&S	rich ethnog. info.	one	**6 hymns 2 letters**
Teichelmann (1857)	1840-1857	**ca 2500**	all	slight modific. of T&S	extensive	?? 600-700 wds	**numerous**
Teichelmann footnotes	1841	**ca 150**	religion	T&S	rich ethno. descript.	enriched glosses	no
Moorhouse correspondence; Journal	1839-?1845	> 50	birth-order names, nouns pronouns	T&S	in context	few birth-order names; *ngurpo*	2 songlines
Cawthorne (1844); diary	1842-1846	51	artefacts	inconsistent *mangno*=*manga*	good descript.	ca 12	no
Stephens (1889).	1840s	few	various	poor *coondee* =*kanthi*	minimal;	two words	no
Day (1902)	?1840s	8 words 7 place names	basic vocab. + pl. names	poor 'English' spellings *cadelcoo*=*karrku*	in context	one word	no
Chittleborough (1906)	1830s-1840s	48	Basic Vocab.	'English' sp. *me-hew* = *miyu*	variable	none	no
Bates	1919	26	kinship	good 'Eng.' sp. *ngappubi* = *ngapapi*	brief	8	no
Black	1920	66	various	modified IPA *miju* = *miyu*	sometimes rich	several pl names	8 phrases 20 sent.
Tindale	1920s	few	various, pl. names	modified IPA *'julti* = *yulti*	rich	few wds, pl. names	few phrases

[i] Date here refers to likely date of collection of Kaurna language material, rather than publication date.

[ii] Kaurna sources are assessed relative to the main sources, T&S.

Table 5.4: Secondary Kaurna sources (in Amery, 2000: 113)

Source	Based on	No. of words	Domains	Sentences	Orthography	Errors
Lhotsky (1839)	Earl 1838	14	body parts	no	'English' spellings	simple
Grey (1840, 1841)	T&S + others	33	nouns, verbs, pronous	no	mixed: T&S + 'Eng.' spellings	one typo
Gell (1842)	T&S (1840)	ca 150	religion	2 songs 1 sentence	T&S	typos
Cawthorne (1844), diary	T&S (1840) Williams	nil	songs	songs 6 sentences	T&S; Williams	many bad typos
Eyre (1845)	Moorhouse T&S (1840)	ca 50	birth order; pronouns; basic vocab.	4 songs from T&S	T&S	perpetuated error in T&S *makarta* 'head'
Angas (1846, 1847)	Cawthorne	45 wds 7 places	culture-specific	no	Cawthorne spellings	one typo
EIM Barry (1887)	? T&S; ? Cawthorne	ca 300	basic vocabulary	no	T&S with minor changes	many typos; bad glosses
Jung (1876)	T&S	65	basic vocabulary	no	minor changes to T&S	typos
Taplin (1879)	Teichelmann	69	basic vocabulary	no	various; mostly T&S	many typos
Curr (1886)	T&S (1840) Wyatt (1879)	ca 180	various	no	T&S and Wyatt	few typos
Stephens (1889)	Williams (1840)	282	various	8	adapted Williams' spellings	typos; wrong subst. of *oo* for *u*
Fraser (1892)	Probably Moorhouse	17	pronouns, numbers	no	adapted T&S (*g = ng*)	two typos
Schmidt (1919)	T&S (1840); + others	ca 70	nouns, pronouns	no	adapted T&S's spellings	some typos
Tindale	T&S (1840); Wyatt (1879); + others	many	various; place names	few phrases	modified IPA	some errors introduced with orthography
Fitzpatrick (1989)	Gell (1904); Piesse (1840); Stephens (1889); T&S (1840); Wyatt (1879)	ca 700	all	no	various. Said to be T&S but has mixed systems. Inconsistent.	typos; reduced glosses; misleading English finder list
The Kaurna People Aboriginal Studies Curriculum (EDSA, 1989)	T&S (1840); Cawthorne (1844); Wyatt (1879); Browne (1897); + ????	> 200	environment, artefacts; kinship; food sources.	no	various. Guide not consistent with spellings.	numerous typos; changed glosses
Amery & Simpson (1994)	Teichelmann (1857); T&S (1840)	500	all	no	T&S	nil known
Amery (1995c)	T&S (1840); TMs (1857)	ca 3000	all	no	T&S	3 typos
Amery (1997)	T&S (1840); TMs (1857); Cawthorne; Wyatt (1879); Williams (1840); Piesse (1840); Robinson (n.d.); Gaimard (1833)	ca 3000 (50 wds from other sources + ca 80 neolog. + prns.)	all	few phrases (sporting domain and time domain)	T&S. Words adopted from other sources adapted to T&S spellings with original spelling given in brackets.	nil known

6
Restoring and Transforming the Kaurna Language

> *This is the seed from which this language grows. Let's make it grow. Language is evolving too ... So I've got no problems about that [developing neologisms/language engineering]. But I still want to know that the guts of those originated from here [Adelaide]...for the future survival of our language then these are the things we need to do if we're going to revive the language. But I've got to know where it comes from.*
> (Katrina Power, interview, 9 December 1996)

The seeds of the language that Katrina refers to are the Kaurna sources described in the last chapter. From these materials our task is to develop a language that meets the needs and aspirations of the contemporary Kaurna community and can be taught in formal language programs. The reclamation of Kaurna involves efforts both to 'restore' the language to its former state and to 'transform' it to meet the needs of the 1990s.

It is too early to describe the 'Modern Kaurna' language comprehensively. Norms of usage are only just beginning to emerge. In this chapter I shall apply the language reclamation method to Kaurna, through an exploration of certain areas of the language and an analysis of current efforts to restore and transform it. To date, most effort has been applied to phonology and lexicon; higher levels such as discourse phenomena remain largely unexplored territory.

The Kaurna language will evolve slowly. It must develop at a pace acceptable to the Kaurna community and in a way that involves Kaurna people centrally. To rush language development would risk alienating the language from the community.

Fortunately, as we saw in Chapter 5, there is one main set of Kaurna resources compiled by the German missionaries and others who followed their methods. These, especially T&S and TMs, constitute the backbone of the Kaurna language. Other sources are appealed to only when these main sources are found wanting. The primary Kaurna sources themselves are interpreted in the light of what we know of closely related languages, and of Australian languages in general. Related languages are utilised in varying ways, seldom directly, to fill gaps and as models for modernisation of the language. Indeed, quite unrelated languages, such as Maori, Hebrew, Cornish, Latin or Esperanto also provide inspiration, as their promoters have been grappling with the issues for much longer.

Recovering the sounds of Kaurna

Phonology cannot be determined directly: there are no sound recordings of the Kaurna language as spoken last century. In order to transform the written records into a spoken form we need to examine the relationship between what we know of the Kaurna sound system and the records compiled by the different observers, each bringing his own language background, linguistic training, ability to hear the language and idiosyncratic spelling conventions to bear in rendering Kaurna into a written form.

Reading and interpreting these old sources can be problematic. In the printed ones, including T&S, there are typographical errors.[1] The secondary sources, such as Schurmann (1987) and the copies of the missionaries' letters and journals, were typed from handwritten originals by people having no knowledge of Kaurna, who introduced many errors. These must be treated with particular caution and, where possible, checked against the originals. Handwritten sources, such as Teichelmann (1857; 1858), letters, journals and government records may be difficult to decipher — particularly names, which lack contextual clues.[2]

For understanding the Kaurna sound system there are four main sources of information:

1. Descriptions of the sounds by the observers themselves. Most simply compiled a wordlist with no explanation of their orthography. However, T&S, Black (1920) and Tindale did attempt to explain their methods of transcription.

2. Comparison of different transcriptions of the same word made by the same observer and different observers.[3] For instance, if one observer writes a vowel *u* and other observers write the same vowel as *er* or *a* it is likely that the vowel is actually [ʌ] as in English 'but' or [a] as in 'Bart'. However, if other observers wrote *oo* or *ou* for this vowel, it is likely to be pronounced [ω] as in 'put'.[4] Donaldson (1995) observed how 18 workshop participants produced 17 versions of the Guugu Yimithirr word *galgaranggurr*, illustrating both differences in the perception of sounds and the different ways people used to write them.

3. Recordings of neighbouring closely related languages. There is a high likelihood, though not guaranteed, that a word recorded in two closely related languages sharing a common sound system (as in Nukunu and Kaurna) will be pronounced the same in these two languages.

4. Remnant phonological patterns within the Nunga community. T&S *kari* [RS *kardi*] 'emu' is pronounced [ga:di] confirming the tap status of the rhotic, as recorded by Hercus (1992). Other words contain distinctive retroflex sounds, indicative of the status of the *t, n* or *l* sound. Whilst this remains a line of further enquiry, there appears to be little in Nunga English or Nunga speech patterns to assist with the pronunciation of Kaurna words. The few known words of Kaurna origins are common words, often shared with Nukunu or transcribed phonetically by Black, so that their pronunciation is already recoverable. However, confirmation of their transcriptions is useful.

Employing these methods, Jane Simpson carried out detailed investigations of Kaurna phonology over a number of years. She posits a three-vowel system for Kaurna, /a/, /i/ and /u/, which themselves are further distinguished for length[5]; there being six phonemic vowels in all. Kaurna consonants appear in Table 6.1:

Table 6.1: Kaurna consonants (from Simpson & Amery, forthcoming)

	bilabial	lamino-dental	alveolar	retroflex	lamino-palatal	velar
stop	p	th	t	rt	ty	k
nasal	m	nh	n	rn	ny	ng
prestopped nasal		dnh	dn	rdn	dny	
lateral		lh	l	rl	ly	
prestopped lateral		dlh	dl	rdl	dly	
semivowel	w				y	
r-sounds tap			r			
trill			rr			
glide				R		

The six places of articulation are justified by language internal evidence alone. Whilst there is evidence from the Kaurna sources for two rhotics, Simpson is forced to appeal to comparative data for the existence of the third. However, she uses the comparative data sparingly, in the main to support rather than posit the above system. Narungga and Adnyamathanha are the languages used most often to support these findings. The reader is referred to Simpson's meticulous work (in Simpson & Amery, forthcoming) for a detailed analysis of Kaurna phonology. Here I shall discuss it merely in the context of reclaiming Kaurna and making use of the historical materials.

Fragments of Nukunu[6], a closely related language, survived into the era of modern linguistics and were tape-recorded by Geoffrey O'Grady, Luise Hercus and Catherine Ellis between 1955 and 1971. They were sufficient for Hercus to analyse the sound system of Nukunu.

However, the Nukunu data itself is limited and was compiled mostly when the language was in an advanced state of attrition. Just 428 entries appear in her main Nukunu vocabulary (Hercus, 1992: 19-34). Most were recorded by Hercus or O'Grady from 'rememberers' of Nukunu. Others are known only from earlier sources such as Tindale or Mountford. Just how much we can rely upon this Nukunu source, especially in matters of phonotactics and frequency of occurrence of sounds in particular environments, is an open question.

Table 6.2: Nukunu consonant system (taken from Hercus, 1992: 3)

['Only the consonants enclosed within boxes can begin a word.']

	labial	velar	dental	palatal	alveolar	retroflex
stop voiceless						rt
stop voiced						rd
stop	p	k	th	ty	t	
nasal	m	ng	nh	nh	n	rn
lateral			lh	ly	l	rl
semivowel	w			y		
r-sounds, tap					r	
trill					rr	
glide						r

I have appealed to Nukunu for two reasons. First, the Nukunu data confirms Simpson's analysis.[7] More important for my purposes is the use I make of Nukunu materials to teach Kaurna phonology[8], which I discuss below (p.121). Throughout this book I use Hercus's conventions for my phonemic transcriptions, rather than Simpson's, where the latter's use of R for the glide (= IPA ɹ) is in conflict with the use of capitals to represent ambiguity (see p.118f).

Modern linguistic studies have also been conducted in Adnyamathanha, spoken further to the north of Kaurna, by Schebeck (1974, 1976), Tunbridge (1985a, 1988, 1991) and McEntee & McKenzie (1992). Whilst Adnyamathanha is more distantly related, it does provide important insights into Kaurna phonology.

T&S attempted to explain the articulation and perception of Kaurna sounds as follows:

1. CONSONANTS.
b, d, g, k, l, m, n, p, r, t, w, y.
With the exception of g and r, they are pronounced exactly as in the English language; g invariably sounds as the same letter in the English words, good, give, &c.; r sometimes sounds as r in English, sometimes rather softer, as in birri, marra, gurltendi, &c.[9] The nasal ng sounds as the same letters in the English words king, living, &c.; and the only difference is that it frequently commences, while in English it only terminates, syllables.

2. VOWELS
a, e, i, o, u.
a	sounds as the same letter in		harp, hard
â	"	"	wall, ball
e	"	"	tell, spell
i	"	"	fish, dish
o	"	"	come, some
u	"	"	full, pull

From this it will be seen that each vowel has one sound merely, except a; the quality of it is the same, but it may be long or short, i.e. its quantity may vary.

3. DIPTHONGS <sic>
ai, au, oi, ui.
ai   sounds nearly as   i   in   wine, or I

au	sounds as		ow	"	now
oi	"		oi	"	oil
ui	corresponds with no English dipthong <sic>; but when u, as it sounds in full, and i, as in fish, are produced rapidly together, the reader will then pronounce this dipthong <sic> correctly.				

(T&S, 1840: 1-2)

This description of Kaurna sounds and their representation is not complete and does not altogether fit with what we know about the sound systems of Australian languages, though some of the comments do allude to expected phonological patterns. Nor do T&S adhere fully to their stated orthographic conventions.

Comparing T&S with Simpson's phonemic analysis of Kaurna and Hercus's analysis of Nukunu[10] reveals a number of points of variance. By way of example I discuss one of the most problematic areas of all — the rhotics. Other problematic areas are discussed in detail in Amery (1998a).

T&S use both *r* and *rr*, but fail to indicate how they differ or how they relate to the variation in the pronunciation of the *r* sounds. Comparison with Nukunu reveals that both *r* and *rr* correspond to all three rhotics in Nukunu /r̠/, /r/ and /rr/. However, T&S's *r* most often corresponds to a tap, whilst *rr* most often corresponds to Nukunu /r̠/ and /rr/. Single *r* before *p* or *k* corresponds to a lateral or a tap. Furthermore, *r* preceding *t, n* or *l* usually indicates retroflexion. Clusters involving a rhotic followed by an alveolar consonant seem not to be permissible, though this possibility cannot be ruled out.

Where a rhotic in one source has been spelt *t* or *d* in another it is almost certainly a tap or trill. Further, a comparison between rhotics in words recorded by T&S and those recorded by Gaimard reveals an interesting pattern. On several occasions *rr* in T&S corresponds to *ll* in Gaimard. In all cases except one where these words have a Nukunu counterpart it is a glide /r̠/. So T&S's *rr* corresponding to Gaimard's *ll* is likely to have been pronounced [r̠]. Thus the phonemic representation of *yurro* 'species of small lizard; skink', transcribed as *ioullo* by Gaimard, is likely to be /yur̠u/.

The spellings of some words in T&S and TMs are not totally consistent:

Table 6.3: Some variant spellings in T&S

Gloss	Variant 1	Variant 2	Explanation
'he; she; it'	*pa*	*ba*	absence of phonemic voicing distinction.
'I' (agent)	*ngatto*	*atto*	'ng' dropped in allegro speech; cliticised
'good'	*marni*	*manni*	retroflexion not always heard
'westerly'	*wonggarta*	*wongarta*	inconsistent transcription of [ŋg]
2nd born +male	*Warritya*	*Waritya*	rhotics written inconsistently
'fire'	*gadla*	*garla*	pre-stopped and non-pre-stopped variants; retroflexion not always heard
'not to stand'	*yuwettoai*	*yiwettoai*	dialectal difference
'head'	*mukarta*	*makarta*	typographical error in *makarta* (see Errata page)

Some inconsistencies are due to introduced typographical errors, which can be identified and eliminated. On other occasions, variation in spelling represents T&S's inconsistent use of their orthographic system in representing the same sound. In some cases, the variation in spelling captures actual variation in pronunciation due to dialectal difference, allegro speech or other intralinguistic variation.

We continued to use T&S's orthography despite its deficiencies, because the vast bulk of Kaurna words were recorded in it. This allowed people to access material directly from the original source and to check their material against it. Constant contact with the main original sources is very important at this early stage, where issues of integrity and authenticity are foremost. It seemed preferable to teach people how to interpret the original sources, and to make intelligent guesses about pronunciation, rather than to change the orthography at that stage.

Alternatives to T&S spelling conventions could include the following:

1. Adoption of a standard Australian orthography based on IPA conventions (cf. Hercus in writing Nukunu). This would eliminate the redundant double consonants and uncertainty about pronunciation. Having adopted Simpson's and Hercus's analysis, we could easily rewrite some Kaurna words phonemically with reasonable certainty. However, for many other words we would simply have to guess at the kind of rhotic, or coronal consonant, or vowel length. Adopting such an orthography would entail committing these guesses to writing. Of course we make the same guesses in the pronunciation of Kaurna words, but there is less chance of errors becoming entrenched orally than in written form.[11]

2. Simpson, Hercus & McEntee use an orthography in which capital letters transcribe consonants where there is some uncertainty about the status of the underlying phonemes. Thus T could be an interdental, alveolar or retroflex stop, /th/, /t/ or /t̠/ respectively; N could be /nh/, /n/ or /n̠/; L could be /lh/, /l/ or /l̠/ and R could be /rr/, /r/ or /r̠/. We would write the word *tirendi* 'to squat' as thiRiNTi for example. This orthography is ideal for purposes of linguistic analysis, as it accurately transcribes areas of certainty and flags areas of uncertainty. However, it would be unwieldy to use as a practical orthography for writing stories and creating language materials where familiar capitalisation conventions are needed.

3. A third possibility might be to ignore vowel length, interdental and retroflex consonants and distinctions between the rhotics. The sound system would then be much more like English, but would reflect pronunciations of most learners and users of Kaurna. Many more homophones and the loss of a distinction between *munto* /munthu/ 'belly' and *mundo* /murntu/ 'anus', for instance, would result.

There is usually even greater uncertainty as to the pronunciation of words drawn from the lesser sources. Still, we can attempt to follow the same methods:

> Step 1: assemble other observers' recordings, if any, of the target word.
> Step 2: assemble corresponding words and their known counterparts in T&S, Hercus (1992) and other sources, to establish the orthographic preferences employed.

Step 3: look at existing words in the language with a similar underlying representation.

A few examples will serve to illustrate the process. Wyatt (1879) recorded *kerta* 'a forest', though T&S never recorded this word.[12] A number of phonemic representations might possibly give rise to Wyatt's spelling, including /kata/, /katha/, /karta/, /ka:ta/, /ka:tha/, /ka:rta/. Nor should we necessarily rule out a high vowel as in /kuta/ etc. or /kita/ etc. at this stage. Fortunately, the word was also recorded by Piesse (1840) and Robinson (n.d.).

Step 1:

Wyatt (1879)		Piesse (1840)		Robinson (nd)	
kerta	'a forest'	*cur-tah*	'scrub, brush, underwood'	*cut.ter*	'shrub'

Knowing these other variant spellings allows us to rule out a high front vowel /i/ in the first syllable. Next we need to ascertain the observer's preferences in writing vowels and T sounds.[13]

Step 2:

Wyatt	Piesse	Robinson	T&S	Hercus	Gloss
kerta	*cur-tah*	*cut.ter*			'scrub etc.'
kertukka			*kartakka*		'shoulder'
Kertányo			*kartanya*	*kartinya*	'1st born+fem'
kerkanya			*karkanya*		'hawk'
kerla		*cull.ar*	*gadla*	*kartla*	'fire'
koora		*cu-rer*	*kura*		'near'
koortukka	*coor-tur-kah*		*kurtakka*		'yg. kangaroo'
kutta			*katta*	*katha*	'digging stick'
Kuttámero			*Kartammeru*		'1st born+male'

More correspondences could be given, but this gives the picture. Every known instance of Wyatt's *er* after *k* transcribes a low vowel, though Wyatt also uses *u* for this same vowel. The known instances where Wyatt writes *rt* correspond to a retroflex stop in T&S and Hercus (1992). So most likely the phonemic representation of the word is /karta/ or /ka:rta/.

Step 3:
T&S list both *karta* 'lap' and Karta 'Kangaroo Island', which probably share the same underlying form. That is, we have three lexemes that seemingly can only differ phonologically on the basis of vowel length in the first syllable, pointing to homophony.

In the majority of cases where the lesser sources contribute words not recorded by T&S there are no corresponding forms recorded by other observers. So we have to do the best we can using Step 2. Sometimes there are other clues to pursue. For example, Williams (1840) lists *me-nin-dah* 'yolk of egg' and *i-e-rah* 'white of egg'.

Williams	T&S	Hercus	Gloss
me-nin-dah			'yolk of egg'
me-no	*minno*	*mirnu*	'wattle'
mee-na	*mena*	*miina*	'eye'
me-poot-tie	*mebutti*	*miina* 'eye'; *puthi* 'hair'	'eyelash'
i-e-rah			'white of egg'
i-char-lie 'friend'	*ngaityerli* 'my father'	*ngatyu* 'my'; *yartli* 'man'	
	ngaiera		'air; sky' cf. Wyatt's *naiara* 'cloud'

In this case, my hunch is that *me-nin-dah* is a compound based on *mii-* or *miina* 'eye'[14], perhaps combined with the root of *tindandi* 'to be narrow; fast; immoveable; to stick fast' (T&S: 46) or *pindapinda* 'bald; sleek' (T&S: 39). We would opt to write the word as *meninda* using T&S conventions. *I-e-rah* undoubtedly commences with a velar nasal as Williams never transcribes them. My guess is that *i-e-rah* is the same as T&S *ngaiera*, the 'sky' or 'cloud' of the egg.[15]

Layout of songs
Songs are often the first contact people have with Kaurna. When words are set to music, it is customary to write the words underneath the notes. How should we break up the words? Should we split the double consonants? Should we adhere strictly to maintaining the integrity of the digraphs? Whilst this is more correct linguistically, will it place an added barrier for language learners? A few examples will illustrate the dilemma:

Alternative 1 (Linguistically correct)	Alternative 2 (English speaker intuitions)	Revised Spelling	English Gloss
ka-mma-mmi	*kam-mam-mi*	kamami	'mother's mother'
pa-rna	*par-na*	parna	'they'
nga-rto	*ngar-to*	ngartu	'child'
ngai-tyo	*ngait-yo*	ngaityu	'my'
i-lya	*il-ya*	ilya	'black snake'
wi-rra	*wir-ra*	wirra	'bush'
mu-dla	*mud-la*	mudlha	'nose'
wa-tte-ya-rna-u-rlo	*wat-te-yar-na-ur-lo*	warti yarna-urlu	'throughout *Yerna*'
ku-rlo	*kur-lo*	kurlu	'female red kangaroo'
yu-nga	*yun-ga*	yunga	'brother'

In some cases (e.g. *il-ya*), hyphenation of the words according to English intuitions may assist in producing a closer approximation to the desired pronunciation. In other cases, (e.g. *kur-lu* and *yun-ga*), it will encourage spelling pronunciations. Splitting the digraphs rl and ng here is like splitting the sh in 'wishing' (ie wis-hing) thus producing a totally wrong pronunciation. To date we have adhered fairly closely to the first alternative. But to follow it requires an understanding of the phonology of the language.

Pronunciation of Kaurna words

In attempting to teach the pronunciation of Kaurna, I have relied heavily on Nukunu and less on language internal evidence and comparisons with Narungga, which is Simpson's method. Since the publication of the *Nukunu Dictionary* (Hercus, 1992), the Nukunu materials have been readily available. I find it easier to explain Kaurna phonology to a group of learners by means of direct comparison between Kaurna and Nukunu cognates than by relying on difficult explanations from language internal evidence. This is not to say that I ignore that evidence or relationships with other languages. Nor does it imply any dispute between Simpson and myself. My main concern is with pronunciation of Kaurna words, whilst Simpson is more concerned with the analysis of the underlying phonological system.

In 1994, I made recordings of a number of Kaurna words that had known Nukunu counterparts on a HyperCard stack to illustrate the sounds of Kaurna. I linked separate cards to the sounds, one listing the phonemes and the other the orthographic symbols employed by T&S. This proved useful for students as they were able to hear the sound and see it written at the same time.

The initial velar nasal, alveopalatal stop, retroflex and interdental consonants are unfamiliar to English speakers, but are acquired without too much difficulty with practice and a little explanation using diagrams of tongue position etc. In Kaurna classes, Nungas seem to have little difficulty in producing initial velar nasals and some have no difficulty in producing rolled r's, which typically cause much difficulty for non-Aboriginal learners. This, no doubt, indicates some residual use of these sounds in the community.

The main problem lies in the uncertain status of *t, tt, d, n, nn, l, ll, r, rr* and *ng* in medial position. Each of these letters or digraphs have been used to write sounds belonging to two and often three distinct phonemes (or sequences of phonemes). Unless there is a direct cognate in Nukunu, or other source, there is no way of knowing which it should be. Attempts are made to teach the correct pronunciation of retroflex and interdental consonants, where this is known, though most of the time they tend to be pronounced as alveolars, as they are in English. All rhotics tend to be pronounced as glides and medial *ng* as a nasal + stop cluster [ŋg].

Fortunately, the pronunciation of Kaurna vowels is, to a large extent, recoverable from T&S. If they write *a, i* or *u* we can be reasonably confident as to the vowel quality. By working back from the Nukunu cognates I was able to posit two simple rules for learners of Kaurna for the pronunciation of *e* and *o*:

    1. If you see e, think [i] except after y when it is pronounced [a].
    2. If you see o, think [u] except after w when it is pronounced [a].

Vowel length is more problematic. Unless there is a cognate in Nukunu or some other language analysed by modern linguists, there seems to be no way of recovering the length distinction. Vowel length is taught in known cases.

'Spelling pronunciations'

Learners of Kaurna are warned against 'spelling pronunciations' but the tendency to 'say them the way they look' is strong. This is the major drawback in the continued use of T&S spelling conventions.

Spelling pronunciations are particularly noticeable in the interpretation of the sequences of letters *er* and *ur*, which tend to be pronounced as [ɜː] as is often the case in English. However, an understanding of the underlying sound system will help to reduce this. For instance, it informs us that the target pronunciation of *kurlu* 'female red kangaroo' should be somewhere in the vicinity of [kurlu] or [gurlu]. The final vowel may have been lowered a little as the spelling *kurlo* indicates, but the pronunciation is unlikely to have been [kəːloʊ] or [kʰəːloʊ] as an English speaker might be tempted to pronounce it.

Carryover of English stress patterns is also a noticeable tendency. For instance, the Kaurna name Medika (drawn from *mitika* 'flower') is heard pronounced [mədíkʌ] rather than [mídɪkʌ] as expected. It is almost certain that Kaurna, like Nukunu, Adnyamathanha etc. regularly stressed the first syllable. Spelling pronunciations and stress placement on the second syllable are more noticeable amongst those who have had little or no contact with Kaurna language programs, and have accessed the words themselves from T&S. But I have noticed a continuing improvement in pronunciation, and a reduction in the frequency of spelling pronunciations amongst learners of Kaurna following further exposure and explanation of the sound system. Learners are generally willing to be guided and corrected in their pronunciation. Indeed, often they seek out correction.

Restoring the lexicon

Lexical resources are being recovered from historical sources and made available to the community and Kaurna programs in Amery (1995c, 1997). It is envisaged that this lexicon will be continually updated with each successive printing of the source. It is based on the vocabularies compiled by T&S and TMs, incorporating words from other Kaurna sources where a counterpart does not exist in the German sources. Spellings of words from other sources have been adapted to T&S conventions: *c* is replaced by *k*, *j* is replaced by *y* or *ty* (depending on the conventions used by the original author); *oo* by *u*; *ee* by *i* etc. For instance, Cawthorne's (1844) *wocaltee* 'shield' has been rewritten RS *wakalti*.

In some cases, T&S and TMs glosses have been refined in the light of other Kaurna sources, related languages or a knowledge of Australian languages generally. For instance, T&S *kangarlta* [RS *kangkarlta*] 'surname' has been reglossed as 'totem' in the light of Tindale's more recent work.

The Kaurna lexicon as drawn from historical sources is probably less than 3000 items. Many words from the language as it was spoken in 1840 were simply not recorded. From our knowledge of more fully documented Australian languages, such as Arrernte (Henderson & Dobson, 1994), Warlpiri (Laughren & Hoogenraad, 1997), Pitjantjatjara (Goddard, 1987) or Walmatjarri (Hudson,

1990) we would expect to find a comprehensive inventory of terms for features of the local environment and words relating to the traditional lifestyle.

In relearning Kaurna in the 1990s, there is probably no purpose in trying to restore the full lexical complexity of the language. The approach we take is to fill gaps as the need arises during the production of Kaurna materials and through teaching the language. Lexical gaps such as 'echidna' clearly need filling immediately. Others, where a generic is available, are less pressing. For instance, *parti* 'grub' will probably suffice in the absence of a detailed inventory of grubs and caterpillars.

Borrowing

Perhaps the most obvious way to fill gaps in the lexicon is to simply borrow words from other languages. Lewis O'Brien (6 June 1995) thought it appropriate to incorporate Narungga words directly into Kaurna because the languages were so close. There is some likelihood that many Narungga terms would have been shared by Kaurna. He also thought it appropriate to incorporate Nukunu, Ngadjuri and Barngarla terms as needed in that order, once the Narungga resources had been exhausted, but not Ngarrindjeri terms, as the languages were quite different.

However, Narungga, Ngadjuri and Nukunu sources are even more limited than the Kaurna sources. So other South Australian languages such as Adnyamathanha and Pitjantjatjara might become lexical resources, taking care to assimilate borrowings into the Kaurna sound system. How acceptable the practice of borrowing is to speakers of the source languages is still unclear.

Borrowing, whilst common in most languages, is not a favoured strategy amongst the Kaurna, who are striving to establish their own identity. Borrowings from English, apart from Indigenous words borrowed into English from other Australian languages, have not been used to fill lexical gaps. Moreover, very few words have actually been borrowed from other Aboriginal languages and used within Kaurna materials. During the seven years spanning this study in which Kaurna has been taught and used to write songs and other materials, just eight words have been incorporated from other Aboriginal languages:

Table 6.4: Borrowings from Aboriginal languages (1990-1997)

Borrowing	Source language	Comments
°*tjintrin*[16] 'willy wagtail'	Narungga *tjintrin*	Used in a song and materials associated with the Tjilbruke Dreaming, EWAC class 1994.
°*watteparu* 'seal' (lit. 'meat in the middle')	Narungga *wadiparu*	Used in the preparation of materials associated with the *Fire from Whale* story, PWAC 1996.
°*nhaalha* 'echidna'	Nukunu *nhaalha*	PWAC class; preparation of materials for KPS and KPECC
°*nyaani* 'sheep'	Nukunu *nyaani* ? from English 'nanny'	Used in the Kaurna translation of *Baa Baa Black Sheep*, 1991.[17]
°*ga* 'and'	Pitjantjatjara *ka*, Yolngu Matha *ga*	EWAC and ECHS programs in 1994.

°*way* 'hey'	Pitjantjatjara *wai*	Used in the translation of Snooky Varcoe's (1990) story *But Dad! (= Way Yerlitta!)*.
°*kuula* 'koala'	Dharuk English 'koala'	Used in the preparation of materials for KPS and KPECC.
°*Marege* [18]'Australia'	Yolngu Matha (orig. from Macassan)	Used in the Easter song *Pingkoalya* Mar. 1997 and in a letter to John Howard, May 1997.

We would expect that Kaurna would have had terms for all but °*nyaani* 'sheep' and °*Marege* 'Australia' in the table above. It is not expected that the Kaurna should have had a name for 'Australia', as such, though they may conceivably have had ways of talking about a larger land mass beyond their own territories. However, there are means available, apart from borrowing, to address the gaps.

Using the language's own resources

Compounding is a simple means of generating new terms from within the language itself. In fact, many compounds were documented by T&S, including terms for natural species such as *karntuwarti* 'scorpion' (lit. 'lightning tail') and *tarnipaitya* 'crab' (lit. 'surf vermin'). Rather than borrow the term *rippuri* 'garfish' from Ngarrindjeri, for instance, it was felt more appropriate to engineer a term based on the appearance of the fish, such as *taa tuwina 'garfish' < *taa* 'mouth' + *tuwina* 'long, stretched, extended'. Compare Narungga *ta:jukuli ~ ta-jukuli* 'flounder' *(Rhombosolea flesoides) lit.,* 'crooked mouth'.

There are several useful suffixes in Kaurna which can be used to derive terms. Some of those recorded by T&S are *–butto* [RS *–purtu*] 'full of' as in *yartapurtu* 'dirty' (lit. 'full of earth'), *-tidli* 'having' as in *yangarratidli* 'married' (lit.'wife-having'), *-tina* 'without' as in *warratina* 'speechless; dumb' (lit. 'speech without'), *-binna* [RS *-pina*] 'inclined to' as in *mingkipina* 'laugher' (lit. 'laugh-inclined to') and *-rli* 'to resemble; -like' can be used to fill gaps in Indigenous domains such as fauna and flora. For instance, instead of borrowing the Nukunu word °*nhaalha* [RS *naalha*] 'echidna', one could derive the word *pitpapurtu lit. 'full of thorns'. The derivation **taamanti tawantarli* 'duck-like beak/lower lip' was used initially in the PWAC class in 1995, but has since been replaced by the shorter and more efficient compound *kauwirlta 'platypus' (lit. 'water possum').

Loan translations

It is also possible to translate words, compounds or phrases from English and Aboriginal languages, to fill lexical gaps. The German missionaries seem to have devised a term for 'hell' in this way: *gadla pinde* [RS *kardla pinti*] is a literal translation of 'fire pit'. Some modern examples are given below.

Loan Translation	Source	Comments
wilto yerlo RS *wirltu yarlu* 'sea eagle'	English 'sea eagle' *wirltu* 'eagle' + *yarlu* 'sea'	Lewis O'Brien consulted me in 1995 to name *Wilto Yerlo*, the Indigenous unit at the University of Adelaide
parriyerta RS *pariyarta* 'Riverland'	English 'Riverland' *pari* 'river' + *yarta* 'land'	Used spontaneously by a Nunga student at KPS in talking about where he and his family came from (September 1997).

marrawitte RS *marawiti* 'octopus' (lit. 'many hands')	Narungga *mar:awitji* *mara* 'hand' + *witji* = *witi* 'much'	Proposed by me in 1996.

Historical/comparative linguistics

Instead of direct borrowing, historical/comparative linguistics can be used to incorporate a word into the language in a form in which we would expect it to have occurred, should the particular word have existed in Kaurna. For example, Adnyamathanha has a number of words to do with hunting methods and implements. Several are identical or cognate with recorded Kaurna words; others do not seem to have been recorded in Kaurna (taken from Tunbridge, 1991: 32):

Adnyamathanha	gloss	Earlier Adnyamathanha[19]	Expected Kaurna reflex
yarru	'wingtrap'	*tharru or *yarru	tharru (tarru) or yarru
vata	'pitfall'	*pata	pata
yadhi ~ yadhi warla	'hide'	*thathi	thathi (tathi)
akitha	'yard'	*kakitha	kakitha

Initial y- in Adnyamathanha often corresponds to th- in Kaurna and v corresponds to p. Vowel initial words in Adnyamathanha correspond to k- in Kaurna. So rather than borrow these words directly from Adnyamathanha, it would make more sense to incorporate them in the forms that occurred before the operation of sound changes in Adnyamathanha. In doing this, we end up with a set of words which are related to, but quite distinct from their modern Adnyamathanha counterparts. In this case, the Kaurna reflex always ends up being the same as the earlier Adnyamathanha form. Of course with another set of languages this will not necessarily follow.

Onomatopoeia

The use of onomatopoeia occurs often in Aboriginal languages, including Kaurna. Consider *kuwa* 'crow', *titititya* 'a species of parrot', *warruwarrukanthi* 'to bark' and *pithapitharni-apinthi* 'to iron linen'. However, onomatopoeia as yet has seldom been used in contemporary Kaurna to fill lexical gaps. The only example that comes to mind is °*yiityi* 'hiss', which might be regarded as both onomatopoeia and borrowing from English, as the English word 'hiss' is itself onomatopoeic. However, there is scope for extending the use of onomatopoeia, particularly for objects (such as birds) or processes which emit a characteristic and distinctive sound.

Case studies

In the subsections that follow, I explore two prominent lexical domains, fauna and marine terms, chosen for their ability to illustrate the principles above. I discuss difficulties which have arisen and how they have been or might be addressed.

A reasonable number of Kaurna terms for fauna have been documented. T&S and TMs make a good start with more than 30 terms for mammals, 15 for reptiles and about 50 bird terms, though some of the glosses are deficient. Other sources also make an important contribution. Williams (1840) and Wyatt (1879) both provide names of several species not recorded elsewhere and their glosses for others help to narrow down the possibilities where T&S's glosses are particularly vague. Wyatt is especially useful in relation to insects and birds. Piesse (1840) has provided no less than seven terms for bird species not recorded elsewhere, including *teen-deen-de* [RS *tiintinti*] 'kingfisher'. Robinson (nd) and Gaimard (1833) both provide several words not recorded elsewhere. In addition to the recognised Kaurna sources, Edward Stephens sent 36 bird names accompanying specimens to London in 1838 (see pp. 81-82). Several of these words are clearly Kaurna, though others[20] bear no relationship to Kaurna words documented in other sources. It is possible that all these words are Kaurna, having been recorded so early. However, they have not yet been included in the Kaurna lexicon (Amery, 1997), as they are somewhat dubious. This remains an interesting sideline to pursue at some time in the future. No English equivalent is given for nine of the terms. If the specimens still remain in England and the names could be linked with them, it could prove a valuable source of terms for species which may even be extinct.

Table 6.5: Prominent lexical gaps in Kaurna fauna terminology

gloss	Narungga	Nukunu	Barngarla	Adnyamathanha
echidna		*nhaalha*		*vakirri* (= porcupine grass)
koala				
platypus				
seal	*wadibaru*		*nengki*	
brolga				*vurrarlka*
willy wagtail[21]	*tjintrin*			
sea eagle	*dit:i*			
ibis				
penguin	*indala*		*tolai*	
gecko	*mungka; wit:a*		[22]	*murnga; waka; wakamilanha*
worm				*vurlkarli* (clearworms); *wityaku̲ru* (tapeworms)

Some of the glaring lexical gaps that remain after compiling all the known Kaurna terms referring to fauna and flora are set out in the table above, together with known counterparts in the most closely related languages.

These lexical gaps have surfaced in various ways. 'Echidna', 'koala' and 'platypus' were needed for picture cards and flash cards being prepared to teach young children. 'Seal', 'willy wagtail' and 'ibis' were used in the preparation of Kaurna Dreaming stories. 'Brolga' was needed in the translation of *Tucker's Mob* in 1991. 'Sea eagle' was requested as the name of the Aboriginal programs unit within the University of Adelaide, named in memory of Gladys Elphick, a prominent Kaurna activist and educationist, 'sea eagle' being her totem. Other terms, such as 'penguin' and 'worm', have not yet been requested, though I envisage that they will be needed, as these items are not easily subsumed under existing Kaurna lexemes.

Presumably Kaurna had terms for all the items listed in the above table. The koala and platypus were known to have inhabited the Adelaide Plains (pc Mike Gemmell, South Australian Museum, September 1997). Some of these lexical gaps have already been addressed by either borrowing the word from another Aboriginal language or by developing a descriptive term.

Table 6.6: Gaps in the fauna domain addressed so far

Animal/bird	Adopted term	Etymology
echidna	°*nhaalha* [RS *naalha*]	borrowed from Nukunu *nhaalha* 'echidna'
koala	°*kuula* [RS *kuula*]	incorporated in its original Dharuk form (Dixon et al., 1990: 72)
platypus	*kauwilta [RS *kauwirlta*]	from *kauwi* 'water' + *pirlta* 'possum'
seal	°*watteparu* [RS *wartipardu*]	from *warti* 'middle' + *pardu* 'meat'; adapted from Narungga *wadibaru* 'seal', which itself perhaps means 'meat in the middle'
brolga	°*brolga*[23]	borrowed directly from English; would have been better to incorporate as *purrarlka*.
willy wagtail	°*tjintrin*	borrowed from Narungga *tjintrin* 'willy wagtail'
sea eagle	*wilto yerlo [RS *wirltu yarlu*]	from *wirltu* 'eagle' + *yarlu* 'sea', a loan translation of English 'sea eagle'.
ibis	*tamandi nurloni [RS *taamanti nurlurni*]	from *taamanti* 'beak' + *nurlurni* 'curved' referring to the distinctive feature of this species.

Marine life — a case study of a lexical domain
By contrast with terrestrial fauna, marine life was very poorly recorded and serves as a particularly striking example of gaps in the lexicon, which are not of course inherent in the language itself. Within Nunga contemporary society, fish still continue to play an important role and terms are needed for the main edible species. Other coastal languages still spoken, such as Djambarrpuyngu (Galpagalpa et al., 1984) or Ndjébbana (Coleman, 1991), show that the lexicon of Australian languages is highly elaborated in this domain. The Djambarrpuyngu wordlist includes 64 head entries for sharks and rays alone. Some of these are synonyms, but there are at least 30 terms referring to different species. The majority of terms are monomorphemic and unrelated to other words in the Djambarrpuyngu lexicon.

T&S and TMs recorded only 12 terms for fish, shellfish and other marine life reflecting their limited experiences and lack of interest in fishing. Many of their glosses are vague, for instance, T&S *yambo* [RS *yampu*] 'a large species of fish'. Other Kaurna sources and cognates in neighbouring languages tell us that *yampu* is in fact the dolphin.

Williams (1839), Wyatt (1879) and Piesse (1840) provide some additional marine terms and further reduce some of the uncertainty. Altogether there are only 16 terms for marine life recoverable from Kaurna sources.

However, Tindale (1935b) recorded more Narungga terms including *awatji* 'estuary catfish', *gulalja* 'Australian salmon' and *kainbara* 'butterfish'. Some Narungga terms are still known and used within the Nunga community (pc Lewis O'Brien), including several not recorded by Tindale.

Only four terms were documented in Nukunu in this domain. Further north, Schürmann (1844) lists about 50 terms for marine life in Barngarla, including 30 fish species. This list includes a number of important species, such as *ngaltai* 'barracouta', not recorded in more closely related languages such as Narungga.

Meyer (1843) includes a number of terms for marine life in his vocabulary of neighbouring but more distantly related Ramindjeri, including the terms *pl˜iye* 'shrimp' and *rippuri* 'gar-fish', which seem not to have been recorded in more closely related languages to the north. Berndt & Berndt (1993: 562-567) also provide a detailed inventory of Ngarrindjeri terms for marine life.

Lexical gaps within the marine life domain are yet to be comprehensively addressed, and there are good reasons why we shouldn't rush into these matters. However, by way of illustration, a possible inventory of Kaurna terms for this domain was drawn up in Amery (1998a: 257f). It draws upon all of the existing Kaurna terms, but also incorporates several from neighbouring Narungga, Barngarla and Ngarrindjeri in that order. It also incorporates a number of compounds, derived terms and loan translations of Narungga terms. Kaurna people, though, may wish to find alternatives to the terms borrowed from other languages. This remains a point for further discussion and language development.

In March 1999, terms for freshwater species of the Adelaide Plains were developed by Lewis O'Brien and myself, with the assistance of Graham Walker of the Native Fish Society, but saltwater fishes have not yet been addressed.

Lexical semantics

A great deal of attention was given to body parts, body products, bodily states and actions. T&S recorded more than 160 terms in this domain including *nepa ~ neparra* [RS *nipa ~ niparra*] 'membrane which keeps the skin to the flesh', *meya* [RS *miya*] 'anterior fontanelle' and *pillapillunna* [RS *pilapiluna*] 'ensiform cartilage'. Words relating to speech, mental processes and feelings were also well documented, no doubt because these terms were useful in their mission to 'Christianise' and 'civilise'. The coverage of many other areas of the lexicon, however, is not so detailed.

One of the most sought after words is a term for 'The Dreaming'. In early 1839 Schürmann had come across the word *munaintyerlo* [RS *munaintyarlu*], which at the time he assumed referred to a creator being. Schürmann was seeking terms and expressions in Kaurna that he could use to talk about God and Christianity. He refers to *munaintyerlo* in a letter:

Munaintyerlo, who of old lived on earth, but who sits now above, has made the sun, moon and stars, the earth and the visible world in general. As soon as I got this name, I substituted it for the hitherto used Jehova, which they could scarcely pronounce. ... If further discoveries do not show that they combine too pagan and absurd ideas with the name Munaintyerlo, I mean to retain it for the name of God.
(Letter, 12 June 1839, in Schurmann, 1987: 46-47)

Later, in a letter dated 3 April 1840 he refers again to *Munaintyerlo:*

The Munaintyerlo is not a Noun proper of a person, as I was then led to believe, but meant only a very ancient being, so that it can be justly said, that the Aborigines have an idea of creation, or that the universe has in very remote times been made by some being, but that they have no distinct notions of that being. (Schurmann, 1987: 91)

Morphologically, the word *munaintyarlu* is complex. The root is *muna* 'before, first', and is used in the expression *muna padni* 'go before', in the compound *muna meyu* [RS *muna miyu*] 'ancestor' (T&S 1840: 25) and in the following derivations:

munangka	'before; first; relative to time' (T&S 1840: 25)
munana	adj. 'former; later; ancient' (T&S 1840: 25)
munana	adj. 'former, ancestor'
munanarna	'plural of munana' (TMs)
munara	adv. 'before'; munara padni 'go before' (T&S 1840: 25)
munambi	not glossed
munaintya	not glossed
munaintyerlo	adj. comp. 'of a very remote time; ancient' (T&S 1840: 25)
munaintyerlo	'sooner than; comparative' (TMs) [i.e. 'earlier']
munaintyerlintya	'superlative to muna' (TMs) [i.e. 'earliest']

Although Wyatt (1879: 33) has *monaincherlo* 'name of a creator' and *monána* 'a man who climbed up to the sky', the word *munaintyerlo* is best considered as a time word. The suffix *-intya* occurs on many demonstratives and temporals with an indefinite function. Pronouns seem to become indefinite when *-intya* is added; as *nguintya* (or *nguntya*) 'some person'; *ngurluntya,* 'some person' (was the agent); *yaintya* 'this, perhaps'; *idluntya,* 'this perhaps' (was the agent) (T&S: 9). The suffix *–rlu* is the Ergative and Instrumental case suffix, but it is also used on temporals, just as the Ergative/instrumental case suffix is used on temporals in Yolngu Matha. Probably the best translation of *munaintyarlu* would be 'in the beginning' and *munaintyarlintya* 'at the very beginning'. This is shown by comparison with other time words as follows:

paininggaintyarlo	comparative of painingga 'formerly, in past time'
kurlaintyarlo	seems comparative form to kurlanna 'the last, hindermost, the present generation, posterity' [i.e. 'more recent, modern']
Wortaintyarlo Sunday budnata.	'At the close of the Sunday I shall come'
(wortaintyarlo 'at the close of' < worta 'last; behind' + -intya 'INDEF'+ -rlo 'TEMP')	

Furthermore, neighbouring languages also use time words for the Dreaming. Thus it would seem reasonable to associate the concept with a time word in Kaurna. Two possibilities were discussed, whether it would be preferable to borrow °*wipma* from Nukunu or to use one of the Kaurna time words. No gloss is provided for *munaintya*, but a likely gloss for it would be 'the beginning; the creation'. Lewis O'Brien (6 June 1995) chose to adopt the latter in preference to borrowing from Nukunu.

The arbitrary assignment of meaning: fungi — a case study
Source glosses are sometimes too vague to be useful. For example, T&S record five terms for fungi. Four of these, *pilge* [RS *pilki*], *taulta* [RS *taulta*], *tangkaiira* [RS *tangkairda*] and *wornkawornka* [RS *warnkawarnka*], are all glossed simply as 'a species of fungus', and contrast with *parnappi* [RS *parnapi*] 'mushroom'. *Pilki* and *taulta* are completely unrelated to any other recorded Kaurna lexeme or referent. *Tangkaira* was used as a female personal name. *Warnkawarnka* appears to be related morphologically to *warnka* 'venereal disease', perhaps referring to 'thrush', a fungal disease affecting the genitals. Perhaps *warnkawarnka* had medicinal properties and was used in the treatment of venereal disease.[24] However, this is a matter of conjecture and doesn't really help in identifying the particular fungus involved. In addition, Piesse records *co-mer-run-kee* [RS *kuma-angki*] 'a large species of fungus', which may be a compound where the second element could be a reduction of *ngangki* 'female; woman'. The first element bears some resemblance to *kuma* 'one; another'. Other than noting these resemblances, little more can be said.

Of the six terms recorded for fungi, only *parnapi* 'mushroom' is useful in the absence of more information. Unless additional meaning is assigned the remaining terms are effectively wasted. Within the domain of fungi, a generic would be useful. Terms for 'toadstool', 'puffball', 'tree fungi' and perhaps 'thrush' and other fungal diseases are probably the most useful in this domain.

Before arbitrarily assigning additional meaning to terms, one should carry out exhaustive comparative research in neighbouring and genetically related languages. Of course, assignment of meaning in this way is fundamentally a matter for the Kaurna community to decide. My role is merely to point out ways in which the Kaurna lexicon might be refined and made more useful.

Extended meanings, nuance, collocations and metaphor
Whilst there are gaps and deficiencies in T&S and TMs, the glosses supplied for some lexical items demonstrate much thought and care. Additional information, glossed phrases etc., serve to indicate the range of meanings of some terms and idiomatic expressions which include the term.

Establishing the denotative meaning of many terms, especially animals or concrete objects, is reasonably straightforward. But even here, animal terms are also used metaphorically. Certain physical features, behaviours or character traits are seized upon to develop metaphors applied to people, machines and ways of doing things. Many languages, typified by English, tend to use these metaphors in a pejorative sense. Whilst the use of animal metaphors is probably universal, they were not documented in Kaurna — probably because of the short time of exposure, since they do exist in other Australian languages better documented.

Not surprisingly, most glosses of concrete nouns give only the primary meaning, though many also give secondary meanings (e.g. *pardi* 'maggot; rice'). We can safely assume that T&S failed to record the full range of senses in which most verbs were used, though some glosses reveal a surprising number of meanings for some verbs. For instance:

> kaityandi [RS kaityanthi]   'to send; to lay eggs; to furnish a spear with quartz'
> paltandi [RS parltanthi]   'to knock; push; throw; beat; pluck off; pull out'

Sentence examples provide occasional additional senses not documented in the vocabulary. TMs gives 'ngatparingaii? [RS ngatparring'ai] "Shall I put me on (the trousers?)" or "shall I enter (the room?)"', providing two quite different contexts in which the utterance is appropriate. In essence Ngatparring'ai? with rising question intonation might mean 'Shall I put myself into (it)?' In other contexts it might mean, for instance, 'Shall I participate (in this venture)?' or 'Will I hop in (to bed)?' or 'Will I get in (the car)?' Exploitation of recorded utterances like Ngatparring'ai? begin to capture the true essence of the Kaurna language as it was spoken last century, and how it can be used in the next.

Language reclamation, then, entails the assignment of additional meanings to documented words. Assumptions need to be made about the range of application of a particular term and the semantic space it occupies relative to other words in the language. Of course, there is a strong de facto pressure from the semantics of English, in the absence of information to the contrary, to assume a similar range of meanings for a Kaurna term as for its English counterpart. For instance, *taapingyanthi* is given as the transitive verb 'to open'. It is obviously a compound formed from *taa* 'mouth' + *pingyanthi* 'to raise; make; construct; form etc.'. T&S (1840: 41) note that *taa* 'is frequently used as a prefix in compound words, implying an opening or aperture or having reference to the mouth'. We used the verb *taapingyanthi* in one of the first workshops to translate the children's song *Open, Shut Them* at a time when we were unaware that it was a compound. *Tartanthi* 'to cover' was used for 'shut'. In retrospect, it is unlikely that *taapingyanthi* and *tartanthi* would be applied to 'opening' and 'closing' the hand. In fact, there is another word *marawaka* 'double hand' and a verb *marawakanthi* 'to hold the double hand'. So, 'shut them (hands)' is probably best realised as *marawakarla!* whilst 'open them!' may be based on an analogous, but unrecorded form. One can imagine that *taapingyanthi* (lit. 'creating a mouth') might well be applied to 'opening a tin' or 'opening a letter', 'opening a purse' etc. but whether or not it applies to 'opening the hand', 'opening one's mind', 'opening one's heart', 'opening a bank account', 'opening a new centre' or 'opening up the land' and other more figurative uses is an open question.

Grammar and syntax

A contemporary grammar of Kaurna is currently being written by Simpson (in Simpson & Amery, forthcoming). Simpson (1995) explains some aspects of the process. The reconstituted grammar of Kaurna is fundamentally an interpretation of T&S, TMs and Teichelmann (1858) in the light of a knowledge of related languages and understandings of Australian linguistics, notably Dixon (1976, 1980), Blake (1987) and Walsh & Yallop (1993).

There is a close alignment between the grammar of Kaurna as outlined by T&S and what we would expect based on modern grammars of related languages. The missionaries document a fairly typical Pama-Nyungan case system. I restrict my discussion here to areas of grammar that have presented particular problems to us as learners and teachers of Kaurna. My concern is with the method of language reclamation, rather than grammatical description and analysis, though the latter is needed of course to undertake the former.

Number

Kaurna is somewhat unusual amongst Pama-Nyungan languages in the extent and frequency by which number is marked on both pronouns and nouns. According to Blake (1977: 4), in languages which mark number by suffixes, this usage is often restricted to certain classes of nominals, perhaps to animate nouns or nouns referring to humans. However, Kaurna appears to use dual and plural suffixes on human, animate and inanimate nouns alike. Note, for instance:

```
      Ngando parnukko bukketidla    katteota   kauwidla?
RS    Nganthu parnuku pukitidla     kati-utha  kauwidla?
      who     her    bucket-DUAL    fetch-will water-DUAL
      'Who will fetch her two buckets of water?'
```

Note that dual number is marked on both the noun *bukketi* [RS *pukiti*] 'bucket' and *kauwe* [RS *kauwi*] 'water' in the discontinuous noun phrase. Here Kaurna makes more use of number marking than English, which treats 'water' as a mass noun. On other occasions Kaurna does not employ number marking in situations where the English translation implies a plural entity as in:

```
      Parndarlo ngatto wodli taieta.
RS    Parntarlu ngathu wardli tayitha,
         brick-INST I+ERG house build-FUT
         'I shall build the house with bricks'.
```

The main problem for us is to know when to mark nouns morphologically for dual and plural. Counting books are amongst the first materials requested. In an expression like 'I see four emus', is the plural marking required on *kardi* 'emu'? There is just one example of a numeral used in a sentence with a nominal: *Purlaitye purlaitye madlurtanna* [RS *Purlaityi purlaityi madlurtarna*] 'Four young ones' (T&S: 66). Here plural marking on the nominal is used in addition to the numeral.

In the expression 'I see two kangaroos', is the numeral *purlaityi* 'two' acceptable in addition to the dual *nanturla* 'kangaroo-DUAL'? In the historical materials there is just one sentence example employing the numeral *purlaityi* 'two':

Painingga purlaityendi meyurla tittappe.
RS Painingka purlaityinthi miyurla titapi.
    'Formerly, only two men have been hanged.'
    formerly two-only   man-DUAL hanged

Dual forms alone predominate, though it is likely that *purlaityi nanturla* is grammatical and the preferred form in the context of a counting book, though *Ngathu nanturla nakunthi* 'I see two kangaroos' is probably more idiomatic.

Naku'athu'rla 'Let me see them' is probably the preferred way of expressing these notions, in a situation where the object is known to both interlocutors. That is, the object is expressed by a third person dual pronominal clitic. Note the sentence *Tidnarla nguiyuatturla* [RS *Tidnarla nguyu'athu'rla*] 'I will warm my feet (dual)' where dual marking appears both on the noun and the verb.

When words like *ngarraitya* 'many' or *tawata* 'many; much' are used, the noun appears both with and without the plural suffix, but there are so few examples that we are unable to draw any firm conclusions.

Word order

Word order is one of the first problems that confronts us as teachers and learners of Kaurna. T&S and TMs give some evidence that, as in other Australian languages, Kaurna word order is flexible, though SOV is preferred for the main constituents of a sentence. However, free word order and the absence of ergative case marking on non-singular pronouns introduces considerable ambiguity in sentences such as:

	ngadlu niwa nakki	cf. niwa ngadlu nakki
RS	ngadlu niwa naki	niwa ngadlu naki
	?'we saw you (two)' OR 'you (two) saw us'	?'you (two) saw us' OR 'we saw you(two)'

No recorded sentences of this type have been found, so it is unclear how the language copes with such ambiguities. We have done so by invoking strict SOV word order. Ambiguities of this kind were probably tolerated in an oral society where agency would have been clear from the context. The functional load borne by plural agents is relatively low. The situation regarding ergative marking on dual or plural nouns is also unclear for want of examples. In preparing Kaurna language learning materials, I have several times used ergative case marking in addition to number marking as in:

Ngartunnarlo ngattaitya wonbanna warramankota.
RS Ngarturnarlu ngathaitya wanparna warramankutha.
    child-PL-ERG me-to   number-PL repeat-FUT
    'The children will repeat the numbers after me.'

(KL&LE Tape Transcripts, p. 44)

However, I have no way of knowing whether this would have been acceptable usage in Kaurna spoken in the nineteenth century.

Some Australian languages allow considerable flexibility of word order within the noun phrase. Pintupi, for instance, allows discontinuous constituents, a feature seemingly shared by Kaurna. Arabana (Hercus, 1994) shows much flexibility within possessive noun phrases but other languages are more constrained.

Note the following pairs of examples from T&S (1840: 24).

	Meyu pulyunnanna [RS Miyu pulyunarna] 'Coloured men'
vs	Pulyunna meyurlo [RS Pulyuna miyurlu] 'A black man (is) the agent'

	Wortanna ngaityo [RS Wartarna ngaityu] 'My moveables'
vs	Ngaityo mudlinna [RS Ngaityu mudlirna] 'My implements'

Tauere marni [RS Tawardi marni] 'Very good' (T&S, 1840: V20)
Gadla tauarikanna [RS Kardla tawardikana] 'To the large fire'
Gadla ngarnda parrando [RS Kardla ngarnta parranthu] 'Make a large fire!'

It seems that an intensifier can either precede or follow the adjective as in:

	paityari marni [RS *paityarri marni*]	'very good'
and	*paityari tauara* [RS *paityarri tawarda*]	'very much, great'
vs	*manni paityaryi*[25] [RS *marni paityarri*]	'monstrous<?> good, morally good'
		(TMs: under *marni*)

We have used both Noun + Adj and Adj + Noun word orders. In early workshops I tended to follow Pitjantjatjara word order, Noun + Adjective. More recently I have often used the opposite as it seems more in accordance with the historical sources.[26] But one has to remember that early observers may have been influenced by word order constraints in English or German, exacerbated by the fact that they had to rely on memory in transcribing sentences.

Tense and aspect

Australian languages typically make a number of tense and aspect distinctions, though in some languages present and past may fall together. Some languages make two or more distinctions between different past tense inflections, often distinguishing between perfect and imperfect aspects (Dixon, 1980: 380). Some languages have a distinctive historical past affix.

In Kaurna, several past tense affixes are documented by T&S. They refer to –*tti* [RS *–thi*] as the 'Preterite or Aorist' and the final vowel change *a, u* -> *i* ~ ø as the 'Perfect'. Eighteen years later Teichelmann (1858) swapped these around. The example sentences are inconclusive and the contexts in which the sentences were uttered are not recoverable. The situation is further complicated by the existence of poorly understood dialectal variants identified by T&S (1840: 16f) in certain verbal affixes. A somewhat arbitrary decision will probably need to be made. For now, the so-called Perfect is used in situations in which the event is complete, finished or definite. The 'Preterite' *-thi* is used for indefinite past notions such as 'used to X' or 'would X' etc.

Pama-Nyungan languages typically have multiple verb conjugations, as many as seven, though some, both in the centre and the south-east, are known to have only one (Dixon, 1980: 280). Diyari (Austin, 1981: 66) and

Adnyamathanha (Schebeck, 1976: 542) are said not to have verb conjugations. In addition, there are often a handful of irregular verbs.

Kaurna seems to have had at least two conjugations on the basis of the 'perfect' inflection, as the vowel alternation *a, u -> i* occurs in some verbs and not in others. The replacement of the final vowel of the root with /i/ is also attested in several languages, including Arabana-Wangganguru and Bägandji (Hercus, 1976: 598) and Djapu, a Yolngu language from North East Arnhemland (Morphy, 1983: 63). In Kaurna, verbs are listed in their present tense form with the suffix *–ndi* [RS *–nthi*]. Unless a verb is used in the past 'perfect' tense in an example sentence, there is no way of knowing whether the final vowel remains or is replaced by *i*. Because of the limited sentence material in the corpus this is the case for many verbs. How then should we form the past 'perfect'? This is another unresolved matter. With some verbs I have left the final vowel unchanged. With other verbs I have changed it to *i* arbitrarily, in the absence of data to guide us.

Allomorphy and dialectal variants

Variant forms of some grammatical affixes present a major headache to the learner or teacher of Kaurna. Some, such as *-nthi*[27] 'Present Tense' are given in a single invariant form by T&S. Most have several variants, some of which are shown in the paradigm charts, whilst others are only recoverable from the sentence examples. The prohibitive suffix presents a bewildering array of variants. T&S (1840: 17) discuss this suffix as follows:

> THE PROHIBITIVE MOOD
> This terminates in urti, rti, ngutti, oti, or tti, in all persons and numbers the same. The general termination is ti, which appears again in its adjectival form and privative signification, tinna; as, warratinna, dumb, deprived of speech; but warratti (viz., tikkainga,) be silent; hold your tongue. All other variations in it belong partly to the dialects, or depend upon the part of speech to which this termination is affixed, as it may be joined to nouns — in which case Europeans must supply an auxilliary verb, of which the language appears destitute; as ngunyaringutti, be not naughty; billyabillyatti (viz., tikkaingwa,) make a less noise; punggourti, do not kill, stab; waietti, do not move, sit still; metteurti, do not steal. What refers to the tenses of this mood, the same applies here that has been said of the imperative.

Whilst the grammar lists five variants, the sentence examples reveal no less than 13 variant forms of this suffix:

> -tti ~ -rti ~ -ti ~ -tte ~ -oti ~ -otti ~ utti ~ -urti ~ -ngutti ~ -nggutti ~ -nggutte ~ -nguti ~ -ngkutti

The forms *-ngutti* etc. which include a velar nasal seem to occur only after *-rri* 'Reciprocal; Reflexive' or *-ni* 'Inchoative'. Thus it is likely that *-ngutti ~ -nggutti ~ -nggutte ~ -nguti ~ -ngkutti* are variants of an allomorph having the phonemic representation /-ngkuti/.[28] However, these forms do not always occur after *-rri* and *-rni*, as the variants *Ngunyaringutti ~Nyunyareutti ~Nunyareurti* 'Don't be naughty!' are recorded.

As for the remaining variants, it is likely that there are at least two different forms, phonemically /-Ti/ and /-uTi/ where the place of articulation of the stop is unclear. On the basis of the historical materials, we cannot tell whether the variants indicate actual differences in pronunciation, that is [-thi] vs. [-rti] vs. [-ti] or whether they are simply spelling variants of the one sound, say [-rti]. The variants may be accounted for by allomorphs associated with verb conjugations discussed earlier. After all, Pitjantjatjara has allomorphs determined by membership of verb conjugation classes which differ in a similar way. Pitjantjatjara present tense affixes are *-nganyi* ~ *-nyi* ~ *-ni* ~ *ni* not unlike a possible /-ngkuti/ ~ /-thi/ ~ /-ti/ ~ /-rti/.

The variation in forms recorded for nominal and verbal affixes probably has multiple causes including phonologically conditioned allomorphy, possible irregular allomorphs, dialectal variation, mishearing, transcription errors and possible stylistic or free variation.

Homophony

The nominal derivational affix *–tti* [RS *–ti*] appears to be homophonous with the prohibitive suffix *-tti* [RS *–rti*] discussed above and the 'preterite' past tense *–tti* [RS *–thi*].[29] There are variant forms of these suffixes, but the dominant form is always spelt the same way *-tti*. It is not clear whether these suffixes are truly homophonous. It could be that one is in fact /-thi/, whilst another is /-ti/ and the third /-rti/, which in fact is the solution that was adopted in 2010 with the introduction of the revised spelling system.

There is a certain amount of pressure to reduce the Kaurna sound system to a single rhotic /r/ and for the alveolar lateral /l/, stop /t/ and nasal /n/ to replace the interdental and retroflex consonants. But this would result in considerable homophony. The alternative is to make a series of largely arbitrary decisions to allocate different consonants to the apparently homophonous suffixes.

Variation

One of the signs of linguistic vitality is the presence of variation. We have just seen evidence in the historical sources of the existence of dialects. They appear to be differentiated lexically and morphologically. Some of these variants are known, but it is seldom clear which variants belong to which dialects. The Kaurna language appears in the sources as something akin to a 'standard', just as English or French might be represented in a school grammar text. However, the source materials do show formal versus casual speech style differences. Whilst there is little contextual information, reduced cliticised pronouns, used in numerous sentence examples in T&S and TMs, are no doubt a feature of a more casual style.

One of the tasks in language reclamation is to rebuild the functional links between the language as it is known in the sources and the people who identify with it. As the language develops new functions to address needs identified by its users, distinctive registers and speech styles will emerge and can be nurtured.

As with other Aboriginal languages, direct equivalents for 'please' and 'thank you' do not exist, a point noted by Klose (Letter, 7 July 1843). However, T&S

noted that the expression *Ngaityo yungandalya!* [RS *Ngaityu yungantalya*] 'Oh my dear brother!'[30] was used where it would be appropriate to express thanks in English. Additional expressions *Ngaityu yakanantalya* 'Oh my dear sister!', *Ngaityayi-alya!* 'Oh my dear mum!' (ie 'Thanks mum'), *Ngaityarli-alya* 'Oh my dear dad!' (ie 'Thanks dad') etc. have since been developed. These expressions have also been used where 'please' is appropriate in English.

In seeking a casual speech style *ngaityalya* was developed as a term equivalent to English 'thanks' as opposed to the more formal *ngaityu yungantalya* used where English might employ 'thank you'. *Ngaityalya* actually arose because learners persistently misanalysed the longer expression *ngaityu yungantalya*:

ngaityu yungantalya	misanalysed as	*ngaityu yungantalya*
my brother-EXCL-dear		thankyou brother-dear
'Thank you'		'Thankyou brother'

As a result of this misanalysis, they shortened the expression to *ngaityu* thinking that *ngaityu* by itself meant 'thank you', whereas it simply means 'my'. After considering this situation for some time I developed the expression *ngaityalya*, which might translate literally as 'my dear' and could be addressed to any person, irrespective of the relationship. In one sense this represents a simplification, but it is a new expression very much in keeping with the existing patterns documented in Kaurna and quite alien to English. Note other expressions in Kaurna such as *nata'dlu* 'now let's' (from *nata* 'now' + *ngadlu* 'us'), an expression difficult to translate directly into English, but one no doubt used in contexts where we might say 'now let's begin', 'let's get on with it', 'let's start', 'let's do it' etc.

In these early stages of Kaurna language revival, learners seek one way of expressing some notion and resist the introduction of variant forms. For instance, they look for a set response to the greeting *Niina marni?* In the initial dialogue I developed in 1991, I used the response *Nii, marni'ai. Niina?* 'Yes I'm good. And you?' This greeting dialogue has been used in teaching programs since then and has caused some confusion. *Nii, marni'ai. Niina?* is often understood as a simple response to the greeting (as opposed to a response + question), uttered with a falling intonation contour. In retrospect I should have used something simpler and more transparent, perhaps just *Marni'ai* 'I'm good', a casual but well-formed response. When people ask me what the 'correct' response should be to *Niina marni?* I respond that a variety of utterances would be appropriate, including *Marni* 'Good'; *Marni'ai* 'I'm good'; *Yaku marni* 'No good' etc. Of course, as beginning language learners, they want to fix on just one, or at the most two simple utterances.

Recapturing the genius of the language

The Kaurna language is being developed in the context of teaching Kaurna in formal language programs, writing speeches, developing language materials such as stories, songs, poems etc., creating signs, finding names and developing expressions for use in the classroom. At this stage, this almost always involves translating from English. Speeches are usually written in English first, then translated into Kaurna.

This imposes restrictions on the style of language adopted. We can seek out more idiomatic ways of expressing thoughts in keeping with the Kaurna language as we know it from the sources and in keeping with what we know of other Australian languages.

Relatively few idiomatic expressions were recorded, but where they do exist, strenuous attempts are made to use them and to construct new idiomatic expressions by analogy. Some examples include:

> parnu tia wortangga tarkaringa [RS parnu tiya wartangka taakarringa]
> 'sing according to his mouth (tooth)'; ie imitate the singer. (T&S, 1840: 58)

> Yellara tadli budna budnai [RS Yalara tadli pudna pudnai]
> 'Just now it began to boil' <lit. 'already spit has arrived'> (T&S, 1840: 72)

It seems that the appropriate thing to say on taking one's leave was:

> Yaintya wandinga; ngai narta padneota. [RS Yaintya wandinga; ngai narta padni-utha]
> 'You remain here; I shall now go' (ie good night) (T&S, 1840: 71)

Whilst recognising the documented expression, I developed a shorter expression *nakutha* 'will see'. *Nakutha*, adopted at first in the form *nakkiota*, is now well known, even beyond those who have participated in Kaurna programs.

Many of the most basic expressions, such as 'Welcome!' or 'How many brothers and sisters do you have?' have to be formulated after much searching for parallel expressions and thinking of a way to express these notions. A seemingly simple expression in English may take hours, days or even weeks before it is rendered in an efficient, appropriate and acceptable way in Kaurna. By default, most expressions are developed as fairly literal translations of English expressions, English being the first language of all Kaurna people and most learners of Kaurna. Reconstituted Kaurna is inevitably heavily influenced by English at the level of idiomatic expression and discourse structure. But efforts are being made to break from English and develop ways of saying things that are compatible with Indigenous Australian languages.

Case study: Pulthurni-apinthu 'Empty the rubbish bin'
In July 1997 I was approached by teachers at KPS for useful expressions they could use in the school. One expression sought was 'Empty the rubbish bin!' This was a puzzle. I really wasn't sure how to encode this notion in an idiomatic way. I thought of various expressions like *Mapa irrkangka parltanthu* 'Throw the rubbish on the heap!' or *Mapatinarninthu!* 'Make (it) become without rubbish!' I rang friends with a good knowledge of Pitjantjatjara to see how these notions were encoded. I discovered that in Pitjantjatjara it would be encoded by a simple imperative *Uldula!* 'Empty (it)!' where the verb *ulduni* 'to empty' is derived from *uldu* 'hollow; empty' as in a hollow tree. I searched further through TMs and came across the following entry:

bulto, seems to signify the mere traces or marks/signs of former existence, of a <sic> formerly having been there. [NOTE: the meaning of this word must not be confounded with tracks, of anything, this is tappa which see.] kurla bulto, the mere marks or traces of; kurla bulto ninna wonggandi, you speak in the air, i.e. no body is there, or listens to you; maii bulturna, (they are) empty or without food; tea kurla bulto, empty of tea; worli bulto, a forsaken place, where a hut has been; parnu worli bultungga, upon his former place, in his forsaken house; ningko bultungga, after you (following), or in place of you; ningko bulto, after you, behind; buki bitti pa padni, bulto burro. Long since he is/has gone, the mere signs (of his having been here). meyu bulto, perhaps the traces of once human existence.

bulto purrunna, the fresh mark (of his etc.); bultounungko or bultounangko, from the place (coming); ningko - ngaityo tidna bultoarra, in thy or my footsteps; (going), follow after.

bultarrappendi, to draw along a mark e.g. with a lead pencil, which an other has prescribed.

bulturnendi, 2. 'to disapear <sic>', 1. to be absent, away, gone; kutteni ba bulturni, she was gone again, had again absconded;

bulturnendai tauaninyanna, I shall go away, because they have chided, scolded (me).

[NOTE Observe the way in which the because is given in the termination of the verb, as also to express the tense. This you will have to deduce in all the phrases;]

bulturniappendi, 'to cause to — to permit to abscond'; the idea of secretly in this and the preceding must be kept in view.'

It seems that the notion of 'empty' is encoded by this word *pulthu*, which focuses on the 'traces' or 'signs' of something having been there before. When the tea cup is empty, the focus is on the last drops in the bottom. When the rubbish bin is empty, presumably the focus is on the signs of rubbish having been there previously, gum stuck to the side for example. It is likely then that saying something equivalent to 'Empty the rubbish bin!' would have been *Pulthurni-apinthu!*, literally 'make the contents become traces!' Note, however, that according to the entry above, the verb *pulthurni-apinthi* means 'to cause ... permit (someone) to abscond' (in secret). So Teichelmann encountered this word in a very different context from the one in which we intend to use it. But if we understand its morphology and semantics, the two situational usages are compatible. It probably has a more general meaning 'cause to disappear', which may be applied to a person or a thing.

I present *pulthurni-apinthu!* 'Empty (it)!' by way of example of the process by which we can begin to recapture the genius of the Kaurna language and learn to express ourselves in a way that is closer to the original idiom than is achieved by literal translation of English expressions. There is scope for much more work of this kind as we, as learners and researchers of Kaurna, become more familiar with the grammar, vocabulary and expressions recorded.

Discourse features

Very little is known about Kaurna discourse structure because of the paucity of texts. Wyatt's (1879) short text telling of a Dreaming ancestor throwing spears into the sky illustrates a reiterative discourse structure found commonly in other Australian languages.

There is great potential in modelling Kaurna texts, especially Dreaming texts, on languages such as Pitjantjatjara or Warlpiri. Unfortunately, texts in

Adnyamathanha, a more closely related language, are not readily available though they certainly exist in unpublished form.

To date, almost all contemporary Kaurna texts have been developed as translations of English texts. Letters have been modelled to some extent on those written by Kaurna children in the 1840s. A group letter written to Prime Minister Howard in June 1997 used a phrase taken directly from the 1841 letter to Governor Gawler. Others use the same closing formula as employed in Itya Maii's 1845 letter to Governor Grey. However, the development of a truly Indigenous Kaurna discourse remains largely unexplored territory. As Kaurna discourse develops, discourse patterns present in Nunga English may be drawn on, or texts in other Australian languages might be more closely examined.

The reintroduction of aspects of traditional culture

We saw in Chapter 5 that very little material relating to Kaurna Dreamings was actually recorded in the Kaurna language, though snippets of stories relating to Kaurna country were recorded in English and Ngarrindjeri. Despite the paucity of materials, the Dreaming has occupied a central place in Kaurna language revival, as evidenced by songs and projects.

Kaurna language revival activities operate hand in hand with attempts to reintroduce other aspects of traditional culture[31], though many of these attempts also take place independently of language-related activities and predate language revival activities. The Kaurna word parranthi according to T&S (1840: 38) means 'to kindle; light; as gadla parrandi [RS kardla parranthi], to kindle a fire; to chew; to marry; as yangara parrandi [RS yangarra parranthi]'. Nunga people tell me that the use of parranthi for both lighting a fire and marrying is because of the use of fire in marriage, which they talk about as 'firestick weddings'.[32] In contemporary Nunga culture, de facto relationships not formalised with a marriage ceremony are sometimes referred to as 'firestick weddings', a marriage without legal status under Australian law.

There are indications in the Kaurna lexicon that smoke was important in Kaurna rituals, including funerals, 'weddings' and initiations. The KACHA-sponsored 'Reviving the Dreaming' project is investigating these matters.

Kinship

Kinship occupies a central place in Nunga society. Nunga English kinship terms are used in different ways from standard English: 'Auntie' and 'Uncle' are terms of high respect; 'Gran' or 'Granny' is used for both grandparents and grandchildren, reflecting the affinity between *kamami* 'mother's mother' and *kamilya* 'daughter's daughter' in Kaurna. The terms 'brother' and 'sister' are frequently used far beyond the nuclear family in Nunga society. It is not surprising then that kinship terms, such as *ngarrpadla* 'auntie', *kauwawa* [sic][33] 'uncle', *yunga* 'brother', *yakana* 'sister' and *kamami* 'mother's mother' were amongst the first Kaurna words to be relearnt and are used often by members of the Kaurna community, gaining currency beyond the small group of active language learners in the formal programs.

Modules on Kaurna kinship were amongst the first to be developed and taught in Kaurna programs (see SSABSA, 1996b: 36-46). Students have been encouraged to research their family trees and to apply Kaurna kin terms and birth order names to their relatives. Feedback indicates that they found this to be a highly meaningful task through which they not only learnt Kaurna language but also discovered things about their families that had been previously unknown to them.

T&S and TMs did a reasonably good job in documenting Kaurna kinship, given their limited exposure to the language and the virtual absence of anthropological materials. Their documentation of this area begins to reveal the complexity of Kaurna kinship. They correctly identified the four distinct grandparent terms and reciprocal grandchild terms, and recorded some terms for in-laws, step-relations, persons whose close relatives had died and terms for 'my mother' and 'your mother' as distinct from the general term for 'mother'. However, there are gaps and uncertainties. They were unable to provide specific glosses to several terms they collected and failed to document some terms, for example cousins and great grandparents, sought by Kaurna people today.

Expressions for talking about kinship are badly needed. Fortunately the expression *Ngai nindo kuma panyapi pinggandi.* 'You make me, too, your brother' was documented (T&S: 67). I developed other expressions, such as *Ngana ngai niinani?* 'What am I to you?', *Ngaityu taikurtirna yarapurla* 'There are four in my family', *Ngadli purlaityi ngarturla kangkanthi* 'We have two children' and *Ngai marnkutyi yakanatidli* 'I have three older sisters.'

Interest in reviving the language of kinship is accompanied by a desire to reinstitute the kinship roles and responsibilities through which discipline and social order are maintained. Again, the language is seen as but one part of a wider cultural phenomenon.

Kaurna in the twenty-first century

To this point I have discussed the interpretation of historical sources and efforts to restore Kaurna to what we might imagine it to have been when it was spoken on a daily basis in the nineteenth century. However, restoration of the language alone, even if that were possible, is not sufficient to meet the needs of Kaurna people today. There is also a sense in which the language must be transformed and 'updated' if it is to function into the twenty-first century (see Amery, 1998). We noted in Chapter 2 that language revival necessarily entails transformation (see Fettes, 1997; Dorian, 1994; Bentahila & Davies, 1993). Harlow (1993) notes that:

> there is ... widespread acceptance of the position that there needs to be such expansion of the domains of use of Maori if it is to survive. For people to want to speak Maori, especially children for whom it is at least a first equal language, they must be able to use it to speak about what interests them, not just topics which are seen as uniquely Maori.

It is probably not necessary that Kaurna be equipped to talk about 'anything under the sun'. It does not need, and probably never will need, terminology for talking about the inner workings of a rocket engine or a set of expressions and protocol used by air-traffic controllers. However, words are needed to talk about aeroplanes, helicopters and probably rockets because they are a part of everyday life.[34] More importantly, we need terms for everyday objects in locations in which the language is being used. In addition, Kaurna people are wanting to talk about notions like 'identity', 'culture', 'reconciliation' and a 'vision for the future' in the Kaurna language.[35] Whilst these are not strictly 'new' as Kaurna people have always had a culture and an identity, and no doubt people have been reconciled with each other following disputes and were able to talk about a vision for the future, the sense in which these words are being used today is new. There are no ready-made terms for these concepts in the historical materials and there probably never were terms for them as such, at least not as nominals as they are encoded in English. The term 'reconciliation', for instance, within the context of Aboriginal Affairs in the 1990s has an associated political agenda, and a burgeoning literature and press coverage. It is concerned with a specific political and social movement working towards bringing Indigenous and non-Indigenous Australians together, developing mutual understanding of our history, making reparation for past injustices, respecting and resolving our differences and working towards a common future.

Neologisms

The German missionary, Klose, observed:

> To create or coin new words is for us not possible as we do not have sufficient command of the language. This could well be possible, because they will give any and everything a name even though they may never have seen it.   (Letter, 29 December 1840)

New terms created by Kaurna people themselves provide the basis for creating neologisms for talking about life in the 1990s. With the exception of religious terms such as *kardlapinti* 'hell' (lit. 'firepit') and Schürmann's attempt to use *Munaintyarlu* for 'God', the missionaries appear to have taken a 'hands-off' approach to the Kaurna language. For us, unlike Klose, coinage of new words is possible, indeed it is a necessity.

Fortunately, T&S and TMs documented scores of new terms for introduced concepts and material culture. I have discussed the processes by which new concepts were incorporated into Kaurna in the nineteenth century in some detail in Amery (1993), when we had added only a few new terms to the language. Since then, scores of neologisms, a base-10 number system, terms for the quantification of time, some mathematical terminology and sporting terminology have been developed.

In an earlier section (pp. 122-130 above) I discussed processes by which lexical gaps can be filled. These same strategies can be employed to develop neologisms, though some processes seldom used to fill gaps referring to Indigenous features now come to the fore. Unfortunately, neighbouring languages provide scarcely any neologisms. Few are recorded in published Adnyamathanha sources (McEntee & McKenzie, 1992). Recent dictionaries of Australian languages, for example Zorc (1986), Goddard (1987), Henderson & Dobson (1994), Hudson (1990) and Lee (1993) do demonstrate ways in which languages that are still spoken on a daily basis incorporate new concepts though they do not take a central place in these sources. Often no word appears for common everyday objects such as 'table' or 'fork' let alone 'computer' or 'telephone'. Typically such 'strong' or 'viable' languages as Yolngu Matha, Tiwi, Arrernte or Pitjantjatjara borrow words for new concepts directly from English, sometimes assimilating them into the sound system of the language. But increasingly these borrowings are unassimilated or only partly assimilated, and though frequently used by speakers of these languages, they have been largely ignored in the compilation of dictionaries as they are foreign and not thought of as part of the language. Neologisms developed from within the resources of the language itself tend to be older words incorporated at a period when there were more monolingual speakers.

Several articles have been written on neologisms in Australian languages: O'Grady (1960), Simpson (1985) and Amery (1986b). Dixon et al. (1990), drawing mainly on the sources just mentioned, and Black (1993) in an insightful article titled 'New Uses for Old Languages', address the issue in a broader context. Black points to the importance of language change:

> As a culture or language stops keeping up with the changes in daily life it becomes increasingly less useful and less likely to survive. To 'maintain' a culture or language it seems that you often have to let it change or even help it to change.   (Black, 1993: 218)

In my capacity as a trainer of Aboriginal Health Workers in Arnhemland I produced a booklet titled *Yolngu-Matha for use by Members of the Health Profession in North East Arnhemland* (Amery, 1986a). It included vocabulary and expressions for diagnosis and treatment, medical procedures and a range of medical equipment as used by Yolngu healthworkers. The wordlists include many borrowings from English together with derivations, compounds and extended meanings. By contrast with my Kaurna work, in Arnhemland I simply recorded terms already in use. I was not involved in the coining of any of the terms compiled in that source.[36] Granites & Shopen (1987) developed new expressions in Warlpiri in the domain of motor car maintenance. A community development agency in north-east Arnhemland has been researching areas such as systems of government, law and native title (ARDS, 1993a; 1993b). They draw on traditional concepts encoded within Yolngu Matha and extend those concepts to new situations that have arisen in the modern world. That is, they are applying traditional concepts of government, law and land tenure to Commonwealth and state laws and systems of government now imposed upon Yolngu. Despite these few promising studies, the means by which Aboriginal languages change, develop and adapt to the modern world is a much under-researched area in Australian linguistics.

The following table provides examples of neologisms incorporated into Kaurna, together with their etymologies. All were developed by me (usually in the context of a workshop or class) except for *kuu 'room' (Lewis O'Brien) and *warri 'airconditioner' (PWAC students, 1996). This table is by no means complete, but serves to illustrate the processes.

Table 6.7: Examples of Kaurna neologisms developed in the 1990s

Neologism	Gloss	Etymology	Process
*kuu	'room'	kuu 'shelter'	semantic extension
*warri	'airconditioner'	warri 'wind'	semantic extension
*tura	'photo; picture'	tura 'shadow'	semantic extension;
*turarna	'movies'	tura 'shadow' + -rna 'pl'	analogy with Yolngu Matha
*wadnawadna	'law'	wadnawadna 'inquest'	semantic extension
*mukarntu	'computer'	mukamuka 'brain' + karntu 'lightning'	reduced compound
*tipumarngu	'switch'	tipu 'spark' + marngu 'anything round and hard, as a button'	compound
*tampithirkanthi	'to read'	tampinthi 'to know; recognise; be aquainted with' + tirkanthi 'to know; understand; learn'	compound verb
*markati	'pencil'	markanthi 'to trace; guess'	nominalisation -ti
*karrikarriti	'aeroplane'	karrinthi 'to fly'	nominalisation + reduplication
*tirkalirkala	'student'	tirkanthi 'to learn'	Agentive nominaliser -la[37] + reduplication.
*warnupaltha	'nappy'	warnu 'buttocks' + -paltha 'covering'	-paltha derives clothing items
*yailtya	'concept; belief'	yailtyanthi 'to believe; think'	Backformation
*ngutu	'knowledge'	Ngutu-atpanthi[38] 'to teach'	Backformation

In the context in which Kaurna is being used, borrowings, especially from English, are strongly resisted. Rather, there is a strong preference to develop neologisms in keeping with the word-forming processes documented in the historical sources (see Amery, 1993). Semantic extension, compounding and derivations are mostly employed. In addition to word-forming processes listed in this table, there are other devices, such as reduplication and a range of suffixes, which have not yet been exploited.

Abstract nouns

In our early efforts, the nominaliser -ti was used to derive abstract nouns such as *taaparriti 'opening' from taaparrinthi 'to open' (opening of Yaitya Warra Wodli, 26 February 1993) and *nakuti 'vision' from nakunthi 'to see' (in Nakkotti Yangadlitya 'Vision for the Future' conference theme, 7 April 1995). However, it is more likely that *nakuti would translate as a thing used for looking with, such as 'binoculars' and *taaparriti might be better applied to a 'can opener'.[39] Backformation, using the bare root of the verb *naku may be preferable to encode concepts such as 'vision', and is now the preferred means of forming abstract nouns.

Borrowings from English

Only about 20 English borrowings are recorded in the Kaurna sources. These are discussed in Amery (1993). More loans may have been used but deliberately purged from the nineteenth-century vocabularies, just as modern dictionaries of Australian languages seldom reflect the actual level of usage of loanwords.

In modern times a mere handful of terms have been borrowed from English. They are preferably assimilated into the Kaurna sound system, being more acceptable if they are not easily recognised as borrowings. Assimilated loans are as follows:

Borrowing[40]	Source Word	Comments
°yiityi	hiss	Used in the writing of a song, 1995.
°Yiitya	Easter	Used in terms for public holidays (Amery, 1996c); song *Pingkoalya*, 1997.
°Yimitpi	MFP	Request for Kaurna name
°Kityamitya	Christmas	Used in translation of *The Twelve Days of Christmas*, 1996. The term *Yiuwa warnirntu* (lit. 'Jehova's Birthday') was not used as it didn't fit the music.
°Yingkilityi	English	Used in Kaurna teaching programs.

The phrase *marni weekender* 'have a good weekend' was used by students at PWAC during 1995 and 1996 prior to the development of the Kaurna names for days of the week and the expression *Marni milirntu warta!* 'Have a good weekend!' (Amery, 1996c: 14). However, it is now no longer used.

Place names and English personal names are of course used in Kaurna conversation and translation exercises. In my translation of *Tucker's Mob* (Amery, 1992a) I borrowed 'marble', 'lily', 'brolga' and 'read'; the last has since been replaced with *tampithirkanthi 'to read'. 'Pizza' and 'chops' were used as they are pronounced in English by James Parkin in Kaurna songs written in 1995. None of the English borrowings could yet be described as being widely known and integrated into the Kaurna language.

The role of other Australian languages
Almost all new terms have been formed using the resources of the Kaurna language itself. However, other languages do play a role. For instance, the term *tura 'photo; picture; movie', an extension of *tura* 'shadow', was developed knowing that Yolngu Matha uses *wungili* 'shade; shadow; picture; image etc.' in this way. Whilst we have not yet developed a term for 'bicycle', Adnyamathanha provides a useful model in *mika wiri,* literally 'bat wing'. By analogy we could develop the term *maityuwampi, a reduction of *maityu maityu* 'bat' + *wampi* 'wing'. Tiwi uses *pipirriwini* 'dragonfly' for 'helicopter' (Lee, 1993: 113). *Puntuntu 'helicopter' (from Wyatt's *pondo ondo* 'large dragonfly') is the Kaurna counterpart. Few of these calques have actually been adopted into Kaurna, but obviously other Australian languages provide a good source of inspiration for the development of neologisms using existing Kaurna words in new ways.

Incorporating neologisms into Kaurna: an evolutionary process
Like Ben Yehuda's early neologisms in Hebrew and the adoption of new terms in Maori, contemporary Kaurna neologisms are created on an ad hoc basis in response to requests, a specific task at hand such as translating a song, or on the spur of the moment when a word is needed.

The first neologisms were created in June 1990 in the context of a Kaurna language workshop held at KPS. Josie Agius, a workshop participant, noticed the word *tikathikati* 'chair' in the vocabulary and its relationship to *tikanthi* 'to sit'. We used the word *tikathikati* as a teaching point in the workshop, breaking it down into its component parts and noting similarities with other words such as *pakipakiti* 'knife' derived from *pakinthi* 'to cut'. It was a natural progression within the workshop context to derive *padnipadniti 'car' from *padninthi* 'to travel' and *karrikarriti 'aeroplane' from *karrinthi* 'to fly'. These then were the first two neologisms created in the Kaurna language in modern times. *Padnipadniti was taken up immediately and used in Snooky Varcoe's story *Wai Yerlitta!* [RS *Wai Yarlita!*]' But Dad!' (Varcoe, 1990).

In 1991, Lewis O'Brien, a Kaurna Elder working at the University of South Australia, posted Kaurna signs, some of which use old words in new ways (e.g. *kuu* 'shelter' for 'room'). Early in 1993 the Aboriginal Education Unit in DECS requested the Kaurna text for a number of signs. Some incorporated neologisms including *inparriti 'meeting' < *inparri-* 'meet' + *-ti* 'NOML' and *turaturarnti-apiti 'photocopier' < *tura* 'shadow' -> 'image' + REDUP + *-rnti* 'VERB' + *-api* 'CAUS' + *-ti* 'NOML'.

With the implementation of the Year 11 Kaurna course in 1994, a number of new terms, such as *tarralyi parkana 'whiteboard' < *tarralyi* 'board' + *parkana* 'white', which are associated with classroom use, have been implemented. Throughout 1995 and 1996, more neologisms were added through student projects and in the development of teaching materials for the PWAC program.

In the revised edition of the *Warra Kaurna* textbook printed in early 1997, neologisms were identified with an asterisk *. These included number, maths and sporting terms, and an additional 18 neologisms, mostly concrete objects.

Throughout 1997 additional neologisms were created. I prepared a list of 28 classroom objects in response to a request from teachers at KPS, specifically for the Year 8 Program at Fremont-ECHS. Whilst some had been in use for some time and some were revisions of terms previously used, I also developed a significant number of new terms in fulfilling the request (see Amery, 1998b: 286f. for details). The pace at which neologisms are developed and adopted is gathering momentum, as demand increases with expanding uses of the language (see Chapter 8), and in response to the needs of the formal teaching programs.

Kaurna numbers, maths and quantification of time

Kaurna, like the majority of Australian languages, has a minimal number system consisting of words for 'one', 'two', 'three; a few' and 'many'. Additional numerals were sometimes constructed as combinations of these. Klose remarked on this in the context of teaching arithmetic at Pirltawardli:

> ... I began giving instruction in arithmetic. But here I encountered considerable difficulty, as they have no words for figures, apart from one and two. KUMA is the word for one and PURLAITYE for two. Three they express as PURLAITYEKUMA, four PURLAITYE PURLAITYE and so on to 7 or at the most 8. Then it is: TANATA TANATA[41] <sic> which means: a large number. (Letter, 29 December 1840)

This base-two number system, whilst quite logical, would become unwieldy very quickly. In response to new circumstances, many Australian languages, such as Yolngu Matha, have borrowed the English number system wholesale (see Walker & Ross, nd). Occasionally numbers have been engineered.

Kaurna, like a number of other South Australian languages, has distinctive birth order names, which fortuitously count progeny up to the ninth born. I used the roots of the birth order names, *irrka* 'heap', *partu irrka* 'big heap, *tawata* 'many' and *wiwurra* 'a multitude' as raw materials to develop a base-10 number system in 1996.

In addition, new terms were devised for basic mathematical operations, including addition, subtraction, multiplication and division using the words *yara* 'distinct; different; one another; both'; *murrma*, the root of the verb *murrmarninthi* 'to decrease; grow less'; *tawatantinthi* 'to multiply; increase in number' and *wirrumanthi* 'to divide; part in two' respectively. Fractions were encoded as X/Y-LOC using the locative suffix attached to the denominator following the iconic principle, for example *purlaityi marnkutyila* 'two thirds'. Finally, a series of terms for the quantification of time, days of the week, months of the year, public holidays and expressions for 'Happy Birthday' etc. were developed.

Sports terminology

In early 1997 Lester Rigney, also a sports educator, worked with me to develop a range of expressions for use in sports. Sport is a core aspect of Nunga life, there being several Nunga sporting teams, some of which now bear Kaurna names (see Chapter 8). Lester looked specifically at Australian Rules football, netball and basketball, with a view to introducing these expressions first into KPS. We developed terms for the sports themselves, player positions, scoring terms and frequently used commands and expressions specific to these sports.

Most of these terms are loan translations, including the term for cricket using *yartapirriti* 'cricket' referring to the insect. In addition, several terms for animals were extended to football positions. For example, *tarka* 'a large species of kangaroo' was extended to 'ruck'. Some of this terminology has been used already within the KPS program.

Authenticity and integrity

Kaurna language enthusiasts express a strong desire for authenticity and integrity. But what is an authentic 'modern' Kaurna? We have seen that the current practice in producing Kaurna texts has been to begin with an English text and attempt to translate it into Kaurna. This method necessarily incorporates many literal translations of English expressions. In this way Kaurna is rapidly converging towards English. With greater knowledge of Kaurna grammar and increased familiarity with the few existing Kaurna texts, however, we are able to resist English influence to some extent.

Is an authentic Kaurna language one that draws upon Nunga English, the variety of English that currently embodies contemporary Nunga cultural values and serves as the vehicle of Nunga identity? Or is an authentic Kaurna one that is modelled on idioms, metaphors and ways of speaking encountered in other Australian languages? The latter is a difficult undertaking that requires an in-depth knowledge of other Australian languages, above and beyond the knowledge of those involved in the reclamation of Kaurna, including myself. One possibility that remains largely untried and untapped would be to work intensively with a native speaker of an Australian language, such as Pitjantjatjara or Warlpiri, to tap distinctively Australian ways of expressing certain notions that involve a range of metaphors, idioms and ways of thinking about the world different from those found in English. Of course there is no guarantee that Kaurna would have expressed these notions in the same way as Pitjantjatjara, but there is a somewhat greater likelihood because of the greater affinity between the languages.

Attitudes towards the creation of neologisms

So far, the reaction towards newly created neologisms has been overwhelmingly positive. A number of Kaurna people seem ready and willing to invent and use new terms. Their comments demonstrate an awareness of language change as a process occurring in all languages. However, some have reservations. One Kaurna person, when confronted with recently engineered terms in an initial session of exposure to Kaurna and the historical sources, commented 'I know I'm being silly. I just need time to think about it. I don't feel right about changing the language. I understand the process. You don't have to say any more. I just need time' (Field Notes 4 March 1994). Snooky Varcoe, a Nunga language specialist who has been teaching Kaurna since 1990, responded:

> I used to feel like that a couple of years ago. It's not the problem with the language. It's the problem with us. We've been brought up to think that our languages are rubbish and simple. We've been brought up to think how our languages should be, just a leftover from the past. (Field Notes, 4 March 1994)

In developing the base-10 Kaurna number system, I drafted a 14-page discussion paper which I sent out in September 1996 to a number of Kaurna individuals, to staff at KPS and to KACHA. It was not feasible or timely to bring people together to discuss the issues, so this seemed the best way to go about it. I had been sitting on the proposal for a year or so and had discussed the matter informally with several Kaurna people over that period. I was aware that this was a rather 'brazen' act for a non-Aboriginal linguist. Instituting a base-10 number system was far more intrusive than suggesting a few neologisms or suggesting how a word might have been pronounced. This was a matter of deliberately altering the underlying conceptual system underpinning the language.

But the proposal was warmly received. Two Kaurna Elders, Phoebe Wanganeen and Lewis O'Brien, rang me the same day they received the proposal (Field Notes, 24 September 1996). Auntie Phoebe was very keen to see the numbers taught immediately and encouraged me to make a tape so that people could learn them in their own homes. Lewis was also very happy with the proposal, but raised a few minor concerns. In particular, he did not like my use of the word *kuinyunta* 'bringing death; lethal; dangerous; forbidden; sacred' with *tirntu* 'day' in the neologism **kuinyunta tirntu* 'holiday'. He felt that the word *kuinyunta* should be reserved for other things of a sacred nature. I promptly dropped **kuinyunta tirntu* from the proposal, using instead **ngunyirntu* 'holiday' from *ngunya* 'joy; pleasure' + *tirntu* 'day' and **ngunyirnturna* 'holidays'.

The Kaurna base-10 number system, maths terminology and other new terms are currently taught within the KPS program. By all accounts the system works well. Teachers also see that it is important for their students to develop some understanding of the process of lexical expansion, and an awareness of themselves as participants in an innovative process where both they and their teachers are learners and are at times searching for new words together.

Lewis O'Brien is generally recognised by the Kaurna community as one of the main authorities in language matters. He is keen to use the Kaurna language's own resources in the creation of new terms where these are needed. Transformation is an underlying philosophy, a central Kaurna concept, which is appealed to by Lewis, Georgina Williams and others. In lectures and public addresses Lewis refers to the Inchoative suffix *-rninthi*, citing examples of its use in transforming one thing into another, for example *nanturninthi* becoming a kangaroo'. Georgina Williams sees herself as one who actively promotes drawing on linguistic and cultural heritage, and transforming and adapting it for use in the present (pc 8 May 1998). So the creation of neologisms sits comfortably within their personal philosophy.

In Lewis's view, using Kaurna roots is far preferable to borrowing words from other languages, even closely related languages such as Nukunu. This view is also strongly espoused by Maori, who avoid loans from English, though calquing on foreign languages is frequent. Maori lexical expansion draws primarily on Maori roots, precisely because of its status and position vis-à-vis English. Harlow points out that for Maori to borrow English terminology is tantamount to an 'admission of defeat' whereas '[t]o preserve the language as a living means of communication entails preserving it in opposition to, and distinct from, English' (Harlow, 1993: 104).

Similarly, the whole reason for pursuing Kaurna language reclamation is in support of the establishment and recognition of a distinct Kaurna identity. For that reason, Kaurna must appear quite distinct from English. But the process has to be kept within reasonable bounds: creating too many neologisms too fast has the potential of alienating the custodians of the language.

Authenticity vs. simplicity
Pitted against a desire to develop a language with the full range of complexity expected in a Pama-Nyungan Australian language is the desirability of developing a language which is not overly difficult for learners to acquire.

Should we indeed forget about the distinction between the rhotics, forget about the distinction between interdental, alveolar and retroflex consonants and ignore vowel length? In reconstructing Kaurna grammar, we could invoke verb classes and complex aspectual distinctions within the verbal affixes, as this is the kind of complexity we would expect in a Pama-Nyungan language. However, it may be preferable to ignore this complexity and opt for a simple and regular distinction between past, present and future tense. This would certainly enable easier acquisition of Kaurna.

Hebrew language revivalists were faced with a similar dilemma over vague tense and aspect distinctions. Modern Hebrew is now characterised by a simpler past vs. present vs. future tense system (Kutscher, 1982: 190).

However, suggestions of simplifying Kaurna grammar have received a lukewarm response (PWAC session, August 1997). At this stage learners of Kaurna would rather grapple with the full range of complexity evident in the sources, than knowingly learn a simplified grammar.

Language reforms

Over the last seven years a number of early mistakes have been corrected and improvements made to earlier forms and expressions. In the process of translating songs, stories, speeches etc., I often introduce corrections and changes, much to the annoyance and frustration of language learners. However, sometimes the 'errors' remain. I have pointed out to several groups of Kaurna learners that T&S probably got it wrong when they used *kauwawa* for 'uncle' (see earlier section on kinship). But this term already has wide currency within KPS, families of children attending the school and beyond, and it would be too confusing to change it now. The language teacher Cherie Watkins, and others, rationalise this situation with the observation that 'all languages change anyway'.

In the adoption of new names, neologisms, expressions etc., Lewis O'Brien (pc August 1997) suggested that we should research all the available information and then make a decision and stick to it, for better or for worse, even if it proves not to have been the best decision. For my own part, I welcome corrections and continual refinements as we come to understand the materials better. In view of this, for some time I resisted pressure to produce a set of language learning tapes. It is much easier to correct pronunciation whilst the delivery is oral and written work is limited to ephemeral handouts. Once the language is recorded and published, as in the set of tapes produced for the KL&LE course, it becomes fixed. If these tapes are actually used to learn the language, it will be more difficult to introduce corrections and reforms. But this view must be tempered against the needs of language learners and early users of the language who have already learnt words and expressions.

I tend not to worry about pronunciation too much. It is more important to encourage people to use the language. Too much correction could be counterproductive and discourage people from 'having a go'. Every now and then I might have a session about 'spelling pronunciations', but spelling pronunciations are an enduring fact of life in a situation where the language is being learnt primarily from written records and where there is little opportunity to hear the language spoken. However, for an 'authentic' Kaurna in the eyes of the wider community, especially native speakers of other Australian languages, strenuous efforts should be made to acquire distinctive retroflex and interdental consonants, to pronounce words with Australian vowels (not English vowels such as [æ]) and to ensure that stress is placed regularly on the first syllable.

In this early phase of Kaurna language revival, practically all Kaurna language spoken is highly monitored. Thought is put into the construction of each utterance. Speeches, songs and a variety of language materials are carefully translated to the best of our ability. Whilst this situation persists, there is room for corrections. However, once the expressions become internalised and are produced as a more automatic response, there will be less room for revision.

Should the situation ever eventuate, where Nunga children grow up speaking the language from birth or from an early age, it is to be expected that the language will expand[42] and develop many features not in accord with the grammar of nineteenth-century Kaurna as we know it from the historical sources. It is likely that reanalyses of grammatical categories, changes in word order constraints and perhaps considerable lexical and semantic borrowing from English will occur.[43] If and when that time comes, it is entirely possible that there might be fierce resistance by adults who had learned more conservative forms from the historical materials and formal Kaurna courses. This is an issue we can only speculate on.

It is already apparent that there are some differences of opinion within the Nunga community as to what constitutes an 'authentic' Kaurna. For some there is a considerable level of faith and trust placed in the German mission sources and on their interpretation by linguists such as myself and Jane Simpson. For others, however, there is considerable suspicion of the involvement of non-Aboriginal people to the point where the language is stigmatised as a 'white creation'. The politics of Kaurna language revival are discussed further in Chapter 10.

Development of Kaurna language materials

Groome & Irvine (1981: 6-7), in an Aboriginal Studies booklet, incorporated a double-page spread of a scene depicting traditional Kaurna life with speech balloons filled with well-chosen sentences from T&S to create dialogue. However, there was no attempt to construct new sentences.

A number of new Kaurna texts which use the language in novel and creative ways have been written since 1990 in conjunction with workshops and teaching programs. See Amery (1998a: 295) for details.

A more extensive project (Amery, 1992a) involved a request from the Aboriginal Education Unit to produce a translation of the children's book *Tucker's Mob*, by Christobel Mattingley (1992), mentioned earlier in the discussion of English borrowings. The Kaurna text, of about 20 pages complemented by attractive colour pictures, is a fairly literal translation of the English and includes a number of complex sentence constructions. It is not for sale, but has been distributed to interested schools.

To date, all texts created by students of Kaurna are written first in English, then translated into Kaurna. Students are encouraged to translate their text as far as they can by themselves. They search for the required vocabulary and attempt to structure their own sentences. Then Cherie and/or I assist by correcting the grammar and making suggestions for restructuring. No Kaurna narratives have yet been published commercially. However, this is an important area that needs to be addressed both for providing good quality materials for the Kaurna programs and for increasing the profile of the language.

In addition to the above, a number of short texts have been produced as resource material for the Kaurna programs. Other texts have been generated from time to time within the teaching programs.

Contemporary Kaurna songs

The current revival of Kaurna began with a 'Songwriters Workshop' at Tandanya in early 1990, which resulted in a songbook and tape (Ngarrindjeri, Narrunga & Kaurna Languages Project, 1990), of which seven of the 23 songs made use of Kaurna words. This is believed to be the first creative use of the language since the death of Ivaritji in 1929. These songs, written primarily for children, employ various combinations of English, Kaurna and other Nunga languages. They range from the simple insertion of a few words to songs written entirely in Kaurna.

During 1991-1994, several songs were written in workshops, including translations of well-known nursery rhymes and children's songs and a Kaurna version of the *Kookaburra* song, titled *Ngungana*. It incorporated nine new verses to the same tune about a range of other animals indigenous to the Adelaide Plains.

In the latter half of 1995, Chester Schultz, Snooky Varcoe, Cherie Watkins, myself and students from the Kaurna program at PWAC and KPS worked on a collection of 25 songs (Schultz et al., 1999). Most of these songs are more complex than those in the 1990 songbook. Kaurna songs continue to be written at a steady rate, often in response to contemporary events or needs of the Kaurna teaching. See Amery (1998a: 297-301) for details.

Kaurna hymns

In Chapter 5 we saw that T&S translated six German hymns into Kaurna. Fortunately, Klose noted the melodies, recoverable from Lutheran hymnbooks, to which the hymns were sung. Since 1995 a number of Christmas carols and English hymns have been translated and there is interest in pursuing this further. Veronica Brodie suggested that we produce a Kaurna hymnbook using the nineteenth-century hymns as the core, supplemented with translations of hymns such as *Tatayaingki-alya* 'The Old Rugged Cross', which are well-known and loved. The translation of hymns into Kaurna has reignited a tradition laid down in the 1840s. Perhaps Kaurna hymns will play an important role in Nunga Christianity in Adelaide in the future.[44]

Language-learning materials

In the last decade some attempts have been made to devise appropriate language-learning materials for the contemporary context. In 1991, nursery rhymes and worksheets were collated into a photocopied booklet and the expressions recorded on tape. Modules of work have been developed in association with the teaching programs. The most serious attempt yet to develop Kaurna language learning materials are a series of Kaurna lessons with accompanying tapes which we developed in conjunction with the KL&LE course at the University of Adelaide (Amery et al. 1997). The lessons are designed to run over 13 weeks, the duration of the KL&LE course. Each is based on a theme, beginning with a text and followed by a series of exercises. These are mostly substitution exercises, but cloze exercises, comprehension questions, open-ended questions and vocabulary matching exercises are also included. The course is designed partly to promote some basic linguistic and communicative competence, focusing on frequently used functions (greetings, leavetakings, introductions, commands and requests etc.). But communicative competence is not the only aim. Other themes, such as 'A Kaurna "Dreaming" Story: Tirritpa and Kuntuli', 'Kaurna country' and 'Kaurna foods' were included to give students insight into Kaurna heritage and Kaurna culture.

Trial of these tapes has shown that the level of language is sometimes beyond the reach of a beginning learner. But it is not intended that all the material be immediately accessible; some texts are designed for listening, rather than the acquisition of active competence in the structures and forms introduced. These tend to be longer, with some in excess of 100 words. Other texts are reasonably short. Lesson 1, for instance, has just 33 words, mostly short utterances.

Summary and conclusions

Over the last few years the Kaurna sources have been assembled and a composite lexicon compiled. Although a Kaurna language planning authority is yet to be established, contemporary Kaurna is a highly planned language, based around our interpretation of the historical sources. At the present time there is a strong desire amongst learners of Kaurna to maintain the full range of grammatical complexity gleaned from the Kaurna sources. But no learner or 'speaker' of Kaurna can yet be considered fluent in the sense of being able to conduct a conversation about everyday matters as they do in English. Kaurna is still in the early stages of development. Expressions for talking about many aspects of everyday life have yet to be developed. However, the sources are not as meagre as might at first sight appear. Deeper insights are emerging as we continue to work with the material. It provides a good basis from which we can develop and transform the Kaurna language for use into the twenty-first century.

Notes

[1] Austin & Crowley (1995) identify and describe common printing errors. Confusion between 'u' and 'n', where the printing block has been inadvertently flipped upside down by the print setter, is often encountered in older sources.

[2] Troy (1995) alerts us to some of the problems encountered in reading old sources which use characters such as ʃ for 'ss' and certain handwriting styles not normally employed today. Lower case 'u' and 'n' can be impossible to tell apart. Depending on the style of handwriting and the level of care with which it has been produced, there can be a fair amount of guesswork involved.

[3] Austin & Crowley (1995) employ this method to posit underlying forms for Tasmanian, Gamilaraay and Bundjalung words working with a range of poor quality transcriptions.

[4] I have used a modified IPA, a system which mirrors Hercus's phonemic analysis of Nukunu. Most of the time I have used broad phonetic transcriptions, writing just three vowel symbols [a], [i] and [u] in line with the phonemic analysis.

[5] Whilst length appears to have been phonemic in Kaurna, long vowels were probably marginal within the system, occurring relatively infrequently and only in initial syllables.

[6] Unfortunately, early records of Nukunu are extremely scant. Far less is known of Nukunu than of Kaurna, but it is evident that they share many common words, a common sound system and similar grammars.

[7] Whilst Simpson's chart may look different from Hercus's their underlying phonologies are almost identical. Hercus distinguishes between voiced and voiceless retroflex stops, but the former occurs in just one word *kurdi* 'phlegm' in Hercus's data and is so marginal that I ignore it. Simpson has included prestopped nasals and laterals in her chart of Kaurna consonants, whereas Hercus has omitted them, but still notes that they occur, often in free variation without prestopping (Hercus, 1992: 6). In Nukunu, /m/ can also be prestopped.

[8] In relying on the Nukunu materials so heavily, I have assumed that the Kaurna and Nukunu sound systems are identical. At the most there could only be very minor differences.

[9] The way this sentence reads, one would expect that the rhotics in these three words would all be pronounced as a 'soft' glide [ɹ], rather than a tap or trill. The examples given here are curious. *Birri* 'fingernail' and *marra* 'hand' are common Australian vocabulary. The rhotic in *birri* [RS *pirri*] is rolled, in *marra* [RS *mara*] it is a glide whilst the *r* in *gurltendi* [RS *kurltinthi*] presumably indicates a retroflex lateral.

[10] Because many words are shared by Kaurna and Nukunu, I have used the Nukunu cognates as my main method of calibration of the Kaurna materials, rather than T&S's own description of the sounds. By lining up the Kaurna-Nukunu cognates the accuracy and consistency of T&S's transcriptions can be tested to a far greater extent than by relying on internal evidence alone.

[11] In Chapter 5 we saw that Tindale introduced errors through rewriting T&S spellings in a modified IPA.

[12] Perhaps *kerta* [RS *karta*] is a southern dialectal alternative to T&S *wirra* 'wood, forest, bush'.

[13] I use upper case T, following Simpson, Hercus & McEntee (see pp. 118-119 above), when the status of the underlying phoneme is uncertain. It might be /th/, /t/ or /rt/.

[14] Note that in Indonesian 'fried egg' is *telur mata sapi* (Lit. 'egg [like a] cow's eye').

[15] Kaurna people have reacted favourably to this etymology (pc Lewis O'Brien, Georgina Williams & Cherie Watkins, 8 May 1998).

[16] I have identified borrowings with ° and neologisms with * inserted before the word as in Amery (1997). * is also used on p. 124 to identify hypothetical earlier Adnyamathanha forms in accordance with established usage in identifying proto-language forms.

[17] The English borrowing *sheepi* is used in T&S (1840: 8) and *sheepe* in Wyatt's translation of Gawler's speech in 1838, though we were not aware of this in 1991.

[18] In creating a Kaurna song about the 'Easter Bilby' a term was needed for Australia. I used Marege, a word familiar to Yolngu in north-east Arnhemland, which was used by the Macassans to refer to the Australian continent during their annual visits to the northern coastline.

[19] Barngarla and Nukunu counterparts have not been identified. As these words were recorded in Adnyamathanha only, there is no way of knowing whether they were part of proto-Thura-Yura.

[20] A good example of this is *cia-cow kutu* 'laughing jackass', a distinctive bird species difficult to confuse with others. *Cia-cow kutu* is totally dissimilar to *ngungana* documented by T&S.

[21] Ngadjuri has *'witjililki* 'Willy Wagtail' (Berndt & Vogelsang, 1941: 10), whilst Diyari has *'tindri'tindri*, which shows a closer relationship with the known Narungga word *tjintrin*.

[22] Schürmann (1844) recorded five lizard species terms, though none can be identified as 'gecko'.

[23] In the translation of *Tucker's Mob*, I borrowed 'brolga' directly from English. In retrospect it would have been better to adopt the word close to its original form, *burralga* in Kamilaroi

(Dixon et al., 1990: 87), which is shared by languages across to Lake Eyre and cognate with Adnyamathanha *vurrarlka*. It makes sense to incorporate the term as *purrarlka* knowing that there is some possibility that Kaurna had this term, though observers failed to record it.

[24] Peter Mühlhäusler (September 1997) made this suggestion.

[25] The variations in spelling are not typographical errors, but occur within TMs.

[26] Mühlhäusler (1986) investigates word order of noun phrases in Tok Pisin, noting that it and a number of other pidgins and creoles have mixed systems (Adj - N and N - Adj) which defy any simple explanation.

[27] Other variant forms of this affix are recorded by other authors, however. Wyatt (1879) uses *-nde ~ -ne ~ -n* and sometimes records more than one variant with the same verb root.

[28] We saw that T&S were inconsistent in their representation of /ngk/ as *ng ~ ngg ~ ngk*.

[29] Of course, in English the plural -s (/-s/ ~ /-z/ ~ /-´z/) is homophonous with the possessive -'s and the verbal suffix -s. Note 'too many cooks' vs. 'the cook's trousers' vs. 'he cooks'.

[30] Yolngu speakers in North East Arnhemland employ similar expressions: *gumurr-djararrk* 'My dear!' and *marrkapmirri* 'dear; beloved' (Zorc, 1986) in similar circumstances.

[31] Similarly, Indigenous peoples in North America are also reviving old traditions and cultural practices in conjunction with their languages. For instance, the Esselen in California have revived sweat lodge ceremonies in conjunction with a daily prayer in the Esselen language (pc David Shaul, 1995). The Huron, too, are engaged in relearning old Huron songs in their 'long house' (pc, e-mail Linda Sioui, 8 September 1997).

[32] Veronica Brodie's grandfather, Jacob Harris, is said to have been the last of the Ngarrindjeri at Raukkan married in a 'fire-stick' wedding (pc Steve Hemming, September 1997; see Brodie, 2002). The ceremony involves crossed fire-sticks and the wife carries her fire sticks to the husband's camp. In 1991 a version of the 'fire-stick' wedding was reinstituted at the wedding of Kym and Cindy Poole (Proctor & Gale, 1997: 46).

[33] Kauwawa is given by T&S as 'uncle', but Wyatt has kou wou wa 'cousin' and kouánu 'uncle'. We have since followed Wyatt and now use kauwanu 'uncle' and kauwawa 'cousin'.

[34] It is interesting to see the extent to which language modernisation has been taken in Maori. A database of new and technical terms is maintained on the web, which includes terms for 'DNA', 'electron', 'proton', 'neutron' and nearly 600 terms in the computing domain (http://www.nzcer.org.nz/kimikupu/, accessed April 1998). Harlow (1993) notes that Maori now has extensive scientific terminology, including elements in the periodic table. Hebrew, as the national language of Israel, has undergone extensive lexical development this century in many domains. Alloni-Fainberg (1974) discusses Hebrew terms for 'Parts of the Car'. See also Fellman (1873, 1974, 1976), Kutscher (1982) and Saulson (1979) for a detailed discussion of the modernisation of Hebrew.

[35] Few abstract nouns are recorded in the Kaurna sources. As in other Australian languages, these notions were probably expressed in different ways.

[36] At a later date I was directly involved in the development of one Yolngu term, however, *gulang djäkamiriw rerri* 'AIDS' (lit. 'defenceless blood disease'). This term emerged from my discussions with Yolngu healthworkers in my attempts to begin some AIDS awareness and AIDS education.

[37] The nominaliser *-la* can be used productively to derive terms for most occupations.

[38] *Ngutu-atpanthi* 'to teach' is itself a compound; the second element is *ngatpanthi* 'to put into'.

[39] The semantics of *-ti* are broad. Most often it derives a concrete object or instrument which performs the action specified by the verb, though this is not always the case. *Ngunyawayiti* formed from *ngunya* 'joy; pleasure' + *wayinthi* 'to move; flow; turn; do' + the nominaliser *-ti* is given as 'play; dance; *corrobberee* <sic>', confirmed by other sources. However, in letters sent to Germany in 1843, Pitpauwe and Wailtyi used the word in its plural form, spelt *ngunyawaietinna* and *ngunya waiettinna* respectively, for 'toys' (Klose's papers: K47-K50). In *yarrurriti* 'rent; tear' formed from *yarrurrinthi* 'to tear', *-ti* derives a noun which is the result of the action. On the basis of the majority of examples, one might predict that it should mean 'ripper' or something that tears things. *Marniti* 'grease; a boy greased and painted with red ochre'

derived from *marnirrinthi* 'to grease' and *marni* 'fat' shows that it derives the substance used to perform the action, as well as the stage of initiation resulting from the application of the substance. In some instances, there seems to be no difference in meaning with or without the suffix as in *wampi ~ wampiti* 'wing of a large bird; for instance, an eagle'. Whilst *-ti* performs a range of functions, its use for post-invasion phenomena consistently derives concrete objects closely associated with the verb.

[40] All of these English borrowings, except for *yiityi* 'hiss', are introduced concepts quite foreign to Kaurna of the early nineteenth century.

[41] *Tanata tanata* is undoubtedly a misreading of *tauata tauata* [RS *tawata tawata*] by the Leipzig Mission archivists who provided the Lutheran Archives in Adelaide with a typescript version of Klose's handwritten letters. I have not yet been able to view the originals which remain in Germany.

[42] This expansion would be similar to creolisation, except that the process starts with interlanguage varieties, rather than a pidgin.

[43] Changes are evident in the speech of Warlpiri children (Bavin & Shopen, 1991) under the influence of English. We would expect that even more far-reaching changes would occur in Kaurna spoken by children growing up in an entirely English-speaking environment.

[44] Jane Simpson (pc 17 June 1998) notes that in Warumungu, spoken around Tennant Creek, the only material spontaneously translated has been hymns, hence their importance for language maintenance. Linda Sioui informs me that the Huron in Quebec City still get together to sing the Huron Carol (de Brébeuf, 1990) translated into Huron in the seventeenth century.

7

Kaurna Language Programs

This project is really important for everybody because it is renewal. And reclaiming our language is also reclaiming our heritage. I actually thought that we'd lost our language. I can't speak a word of Kaurna at all. But I heard Cherie and Rob one day speaking it and I was over the moon about it. I was so proud to think that these people are bringing our language back to us and I think it will be a great thing in the future.

(Fred Warrior, Payneham Youth Centre, 27 March 1996)[1]

In the absence of much knowledge of the language within the community, formal language programs serve as the powerhouse for Kaurna language revival. This is recognised by KACHA and the Kaurna community. Most of the Kaurna language activity emanates from, or is closely associated with, formal language learning programs; these also provide a venue for use of the language and give it a role and a purpose. Most importantly, the language programs serve to develop the language skills of the teachers, which over the space of a few years have developed significantly.

In this chapter I trace the origins of Kaurna language programs, focusing on Kaurna language ecology within the education sector, and discuss issues critical to their delivery and success. My primary motivation in discussing Kaurna language programs is to investigate their place within, and relationship to, the revival of Kaurna.

Precursors of Kaurna programs in the education sector

Kaurna language programs followed interest in and teaching of other aspects of Kaurna culture within Aboriginal Studies programs, and the teaching of other Indigenous languages within Kaurna country. The introduction of the Languages Other Than English (LOTE) program also boosted interest in local languages.

A number of Kaurna people, including Lewis O'Brien, Alice Rigney, Georgina Williams and the late Gladys Elphick were intimately involved in the development of the innovative Aboriginal Studies curriculum now offered widely within South Australian schools, thus ensuring that Kaurna perspectives were included.

Ellis & Houston (1976) carried out much research into Kaurna culture and history with a view to producing resources for school programs. Their research fed into the development of later publications. In 1988, the Education Department of South Australia (EDSA) published eleven short booklets to resource Aboriginal Studies courses in primary schools. Kaurna culture, Dreaming stories and history have an important place in these booklets, along with those of Pitjantjatjara, Adnyamathanha, Ngarrindjeri, Narungga and some other South Australian groups. However, apart from the inclusion of a few salient words, languages are given little coverage. Soon after, a more substantial resource aimed at junior secondary programs was published (EDSA, 1989), containing more Kaurna language; but as we saw in Chapter 5, it is still restricted to a number of short specialised wordlists. However, the Tjilbruke and Pootpobberrie Kaurna Dreaming stories did gain currency within the school system, as a result of the Aboriginal Studies curriculum, prior to the Kaurna language programs.

Aboriginal language programs returned to Adelaide schools (for the first time since 1845)[2] in 1986, with the introduction of Pitjantjatjara from the far north-west of South Australia, far removed from Kaurna territory. Pitjantjatjara was chosen for a number of reasons: it is a viable language spoken by several thousand people including children; it is easily the 'strongest' Aboriginal language in South Australia and is perhaps the best known within Australia; Pitjantjatjara was taught at the South Australian College of Advanced Education (SACAE), having been introduced into the tertiary sector in 1968[3]; there were several teachers with the necessary knowledge and skills; and Pitjantjatjara language teaching materials were available.

Before the mid-1980s, languages no longer spoken were not taken seriously by education providers in South Australia. Some Kaurna Elders, who are now staunch supporters of Kaurna language programs, viewed Kaurna as a lost cause and actually promoted the introduction of Pitjantjatjara programs to Adelaide schools (pc Greg Wilson).[4] Many Kaurna people were not then aware of the existence of Kaurna language resources such as T&S, or, if they were, they did not realise its potential for the teaching of Kaurna. Many ignored it on first inspection because they did not understand the spelling conventions. Even common words seemed unfamiliar or looked wrong.

The Pitjantjatjara programs in the Port Adelaide region proved to be very popular and served as the vehicle or trigger for the use of the Nunga students' own languages. Students began to use words drawn from Ngarrindjeri and Narungga openly in the classroom and playground (pc Greg Wilson, 24 September 1996). The Pitjantjatjara programs served to legitimise the use of Nunga languages, the use of which had previously been discouraged within the school system[5], paving the way for language revival programs.

The first language revival activity in the Adelaide region involved Ngarrindjeri and Narungga. Little thought was given to Kaurna, though Georgina Williams expressed an interest at a very early stage. In about 1985, she approached the School of Australian Linguistics (SAL), at Batchelor in the Northern Territory, for assistance in reviving her language. However, a minimum of six students were required. Other Kaurna people were not interested or able to travel to Batchelor at that stage, and SAL could not offer a course for one student (pc Georgina Williams, 3 June 1996). Georgina seemed to be a lone Kaurna voice at the time.

A group of Ngarrindjeri students, however, were able to take linguistics courses at SAL, in 1985. A list of Ngarrindjeri words still actively known within the community was compiled and a practical orthography was devised with the late Steve Johnson. Two years later Brian Kirke[6], teaching Pitjantjatjara at SACAE, produced a Ngarrindjeri language kit (Kirke, 1987) aimed at Aboriginal Education Workers (AEWs) using the orthography devised at SAL. This kit was produced to assist the teaching of Ngarrindjeri within kindergarten and school programs.

The following year Brian Kirke produced a Narungga Language Kit. He also conducted a number of Language Teaching Methodology workshops for AEWs and others intending to use the kits. However, Brian did not pursue the Kaurna language and little interest was shown in it at that stage. My involvement with language revival in South Australia actually began in 1988 with an invitation from Brian Kirke to participate in several workshops held at the Underdale campus of SACAE, Raukkan and the Ngurlongga[7] Nunga Centre.

Language ecology in the education sector

The teaching of languages in Australian schools has traditionally been restricted to classical European languages, which were offered to a minority of students (Mercurio & Amery, 1996). In the 1980s the education sector embraced language education for all students and broadened the range to include Asian languages, especially Chinese, Japanese and Indonesian. In the early 1990s minority languages were increasingly given a place in the school system. By 1993, 34 languages were accredited at senior secondary level in South Australia; Indigenous languages were completely left out[8] (Mercurio & Amery, 1996: 37), although Aboriginal Studies was introduced. Concurrently, the plight of Aboriginal students in schools was taken more seriously through the introduction of AEWs and Aboriginal Education Resource Teachers (AERTs), and Indigenous teachers were entering the workforce in greater numbers. These changes to education policy had important indirect effects on Indigenous languages.

The introduction of languages other than English (LOTE)

During 1986 Joseph Lo Bianco prepared the federal government's *National Policy on Languages,* recommending that 'students in every Australian school ... be offered soundly-based, continuous and serious programs for learning a second language' (Lo Bianco, 1987: 120), preferably for the duration of their school careers. This became official national language policy (DEET, 1991: 61), and specific targets were proposed:

> 1. By the year 2000, the proportion of Year 12 students studying a language other than English will increase to 25%.
> 2. By the year 2000, all Australians will have the opportunity to learn a language other than English *appropriate to their needs*. [my emphasis] (DEET, 1991: 62)

Prior to the release of the official Commonwealth government policy, South Australia had already prepared a state languages policy which stated that 'all students [will] have the opportunity to study a LOTE by 1995' (EDSA, 1986).

In 1989, EDSA embarked on the Languages Other Than English Mapping and Planning Project (LOTEMAPP) to prepare for the introduction and resourcing of LOTEs in all South Australian schools by 1995.

The planned introduction of compulsory LOTEs into South Australian schools actually gave Aboriginal languages a significant psychological boost, even though Aboriginal languages were barely present within the LOTEMAPP proposals. The fact that Nunga students were being forced to learn a LOTE stimulated many Nunga parents to question the policy and assert their right to their own languages. I know of one Nunga woman who, in 1989, would go up to the school whenever the Indonesian class was offered and remove her child from the program, saying 'If he can't have his own language, he's not going to learn that foreign language'. Many Nungas were heard to voice similar concerns.

Indigenous language activists in a sense have had to push their way in. Initially, there was some resistance and even antipathy from within the LOTE sector to the participation of Indigenous languages, which were regarded as the responsibility of Aboriginal Education and outside the scope of LOTE. This attitude is still encountered occasionally but, fortunately, no longer prevails. Indigenous languages are gaining increasing recognition and support within the Education Department and there seems to be a genuine commitment on both sides of politics to begin to address Indigenous issues. In the 1998 allocation of the top-up Mother Tongue Development salaries, 5.0 out of 15 or 20 salaries were allocated to Indigenous languages. A total of 0.4 salaries were allocated to Kaurna programs, divided between three schools (pc Greg Wilson, October 1997). Some funds are also allocated for training teachers of Indigenous languages. Whilst these funds are still insufficient to address the needs of Indigenous languages, this represents a vast improvement on the previous situation and does enable meaningful programs to be established.

The National Aboriginal Languages Program (NALP)
NALP was the first national initiative to support language maintenance activities for Australia's Indigenous languages. It was established by the Commonwealth as a result of Lo Bianco's (1987: 118) recommendations.[9] Previously, language programs were run on goodwill and one-off grants.

The NALP/LOTE Local Languages Program 1989-1990
In 1989, funds were obtained from NALP for programs in local languages. Josie Agius, a senior, respected and experienced AEW of Kaurna descent, and Kathryn Gale, a qualified teacher with experience in bilingual Aboriginal schools in the Northern Territory and in the north-west of South Australia, were employed as project officers. Snooky Varcoe with Ngarrindjeri and Narungga connections and Liz Rigney, a Ngarrindjeri woman, were recruited by Greg Wilson through his contact with them as parents of Nunga students involved in the Pitjantjatjara programs. They had a strong interest in teaching Aboriginal languages in schools and were employed part-time with LOTE Mother Tongue funding allocated to the Adelaide Area. At the same time the Southern Area,

based at Noarlunga, also obtained a LOTE Mother Tongue salary for Aboriginal language programs, which was used to employ myself as Teacher Linguist.[10] Personnel employed under these various funding arrangements all banded together to create a meaningful project, knowing they had no means of continuing beyond the end of the financial year.[11]

The NALP/LOTE funded Aboriginal language project worked across three languages, Ngarrindjeri, Narungga and Kaurna. Relatively little attention was paid to Kaurna in 1989, but it was included at the insistence of Josie Agius, as it was the language belonging to Adelaide itself.[12] Consultations with Nungas in the Southern Region (as recorded in my diary) favoured the introduction of Pitjantjatjara or Ngarrindjeri programs, though a number did not mind which language, so long as it was an Aboriginal language. I had gone, accompanied by an AEW, to visit at least a dozen Nunga parents identified by the AEWs and school principals. Interestingly the LOTE officer within the Southern Region viewed the Aboriginal Languages Project in his region as a Kaurna project: 'He thought it was looking at the language of the local Adelaide Plains people, ie Kaurna. Had no idea of Ngarrindjeri, Narrunga aspect' (Amery, diary, 22 August 1989). However, there was no mention of Kaurna in the Job and Person Specification, which mentioned 'proficiency in an Aboriginal language, preferably Ngarrindjeri and/or Pitjantjatjara'.

The project ran workshops and consulted with the local Aboriginal community and schools regarding the feasibility of introducing Aboriginal language programs. I ran a series of in-service sessions for AEWs and Aboriginal language workers. I included Ngarrindjeri, Narungga and Kaurna, though my main focus was on Ngarrindjeri at that time. The NALP project culminated in the Songwriters Workshop held early in 1990 (see Chapter 6). In retrospect, the production of the songbook and tape was a very good move. It created a tangible stand-alone item that could be utilised in the absence of further funding for a language program.

Much was achieved in a short time through the NALP project. Consultation with the community and general awareness-raising was documented in the Project's Final Report and a number of interviews were documented on video. There was a demonstrable grassroots interest in local Nunga languages; the NALP project had touched a chord within the Nunga community.

The role of the Aboriginal Education Unit

In August 1989 a working party was set up by the Aboriginal Education unit to draft a South Australian Aboriginal Languages Policy. It met over a period of three and a half months, culminating in a 23-page draft proposal written principally by myself. Kaurna is given only scant attention; in fact, in reference to the NALP/LOTE funded project, Kaurna was not mentioned:

> More recently (1989) work commenced training personnel and developing curriculum for the eventual implementation of Ngarrindjeri and Narrunga programs within Metropolitan Adelaide. A high level of interest has been shown in these programs by Aboriginal children, parents and schools. (Williams et al., 1989: 3)

However, Kaurna was placed on a continuum of South Australian Aboriginal languages (Williams et al., 1989: 4) and was one of nine languages listed with language-specific references (Simpson, n.d. and T&S). Many more references were cited for Pitjantjatjara, Yankunytjatjara, Adnyamathanha, Arabana, Ngarrindjeri and Narungga, which were the main languages focused upon in the document. In fact, it urges that statistics be compiled in relation to Pitjantjatjara, Kukatha, Adnyamathanha, Arabana, Ngarrindjeri and Narungga. Significantly, Kaurna and Barngarla are not mentioned in this context. Certainly in my mind, Kaurna was not a serious contender in the establishment of language programs. My views were based largely on consultations conducted with Nunga parents, AEWs and school principals in mid-1989.

When it became evident that nothing could be achieved in the Southern Region because of the unwillingness of the Director to employ Nungas to work with me to set up language programs, I was transferred to the Aboriginal Education Unit. For the remaining few months of my contract I continued to work with the NALP project, but also began to work on strategies to continue and consolidate Aboriginal languages within the education system. I continued to work on the draft Aboriginal languages policy and began negotiations with the LOTE sector regarding the funding of Aboriginal language programs. A formal submission was prepared. These attempts are described and analysed in detail in Amery (1989).

This work did not bear immediate fruit, though it could be argued that it did prepare the ground for future developments. The submission for funds from the LOTE sector was not successful. Nor was Aboriginal Education willing to allocate any funds to continue work with Aboriginal language revival. A fundamental problem existed. The Aboriginal Education section saw Aboriginal languages as being primarily a LOTE responsibility; accordingly, they were unwilling to commit Aboriginal Education funds for Aboriginal language programs, a move perceived as letting the LOTE sector 'off the hook'. On the other hand, the LOTE sector saw Aboriginal languages as an Aboriginal issue and part of the responsibility of Aboriginal Education. There was, and still is, a reluctance on the part of the LOTE sector to move on Aboriginal languages for fear of 'treading on toes' politically within the Nunga community.

With this gulf between the two sectors, nothing much happened. Many of the initiatives, such as the NALP program, were funded by Commonwealth sources and were able to operate independently. I have long argued that Aboriginal languages should be able to draw from both sectors (Amery, 1992b: 46). After all, many other languages draw from the LOTE sector and the government of the home country in the funding of advisory and curriculum development positions, exchange visits and provision of materials and resources. Aboriginal languages should be funded in the same way.

The gulf is still there, though they are beginning to work together, in the understanding that Aboriginal Education has responsibility for the politics of Aboriginal languages, while LOTE has primary responsibility for the implementation of programs. And there is a growing commitment within LOTE to support the implementation of Aboriginal language programs, following the relocation and appointment of Greg Wilson to the Languages and Multiculturalism Team, and the appointment of Guy Tunstill in 1998 to develop the Aboriginal languages curriculum.

The Australian Indigenous Languages Framework (AILF)

The AILF project, commencing in 1992, worked towards the introduction of Aboriginal and Torres Strait Islander languages into senior secondary studies. AILF was a federally funded national curriculum project and I was its first project officer, based at SSABSA during 1993-1994. The AILF project developed a framework that actively promoted diversity and attempted to include all Australian Indigenous languages irrespective of the extent to which they were spoken or had been documented (see Mercurio and Amery, 1996). A number of distinct program types were developed. AILF programs consist of two components: the Australian Languages component which looks at the broad picture of Australian languages, and the Target Languages component which focuses on a particular language. Within the Target Languages component, programs are required to consider not only the specific language but also the languages of the region (see SSABSA, 1996a). In this way AILF takes an ecological perspective.

In the course of the development of the AILF project, I developed a rough Kaurna program for Years 11 and 12 for discussion by the National Steering Committee[13] during 1993. Discussions were held with schools and the community about introducing a Year 11 AILF program. Inbarendi College, being an umbrella organisation for six high schools, was in a good position to pool resources and support the introduction of a new program. Additional federal funds were obtained to mount a pilot project.

In 1994 the AILF Year 11 program at Inbarendi College was launched. The first semester was spent in recruiting staff, assembling resources, formulating the Year 11 program and the learning of Kaurna by the teachers themselves; Snooky Varcoe at EWAC, Cherie Watkins at ECHS, and Jennifer Simpson, classroom teacher supporting both programs.[14] I worked as consultant linguist in assembling resources, offering advice, checking Kaurna language materials and teaching some aspects of the course, such as phonology and Kaurna grammar. The teaching programs at EWAC and ECHS did not actually commence until Semester 2, July 1994.

Kaurna occupies a central place within the AILF project. It was amongst the first Australian Indigenous languages to be taught in accredited courses at senior secondary level (along with Eastern Arrernte, Gupapuyngu, Yorta Yorta, Antikirinya and Pitjantjatjara/Yankunytjatjara). The reclamation of Kaurna is described in some detail in Chapter 9 of the AILF textbook (SSABSA, 1996c) and other chapters have additional Kaurna examples. Interviews with members of the Birko Warra Kaurna teaching team, including greetings in Kaurna, are included on the accompanying CD-ROM. A 35-page description of the Kaurna program, including modules of work and resource material, was published (see SSABSA, 1996b). Additional Kaurna examples are included within the

Specimen Assessment Instruments (SSABSA, 1996b: 198-201), while comments from students of the Kaurna program appear on pages 9-10.

South Australian Secondary School of Languages (SASSL)

SASSL, as the name suggests, is a specialist secondary school engaged in the teaching of languages. It has special responsibility for languages, such as Vietnamese, that fall beyond the list of priority languages promoted by DETE. It offers many courses on-site, at nearby Adelaide High School, but increasingly, SASSL is a service provider, supplying teachers and resources to mount specialist language programs in a range of high schools across the state.

In 1996 Sylvain Talbot, Principal of SASSL, agreed to allocate one full salary to the teaching of Aboriginal languages in South Australia. SASSL consulted with schools, communities and language groups across South Australia to devise a plan for SASSL involvement in teaching Indigenous languages. Following a series of meetings in 1996 between representatives from PWAC, Fremont-ECHS, KPS, Newton Curriculum Centre and Linguistics at the University of Adelaide, SASSL decided to support the teaching of Kaurna at PWAC (Year 11) and at Fremont-ECHS as a 10-week language module within the existing Aboriginal Studies course at Year 8 level from 1997 onwards. SASSL, as a complementary provider, is increasingly seen as the body through which Aboriginal language programs will be taught in secondary schools.

Aboriginal Languages Standing Committee

A number of matters were raised at the Inbarendi Warra Kaurna Reference Committee meetings in 1996, which could not be addressed at the school level, so an Aboriginal Languages Standing Committee was established in late 1997. This committee includes senior DETE departmental officers and representatives from other stakeholders within Aboriginal affairs and the tertiary sector. The terms of reference are as follows:

> the Standing Committee will monitor and advise on:
> - the development and delivery of Aboriginal languages in the context of the implementation of the Languages Plan 1998-2007
> - teacher recruitment and placement issues
> - issues related to the participation of Aboriginal language and cultural specialists in programs
> - the operation of Aboriginal languages teaching teams
> - the development of curriculum materials to support the different program types
> - teacher training/retraining pathways
> - other matters determined in the course of its operation
>
> The Working Party would expect to achieve the following outcomes:
> - the identification and documentation of needs for Aboriginal languages across the State
> - an audit of current programs
> - the medium to long term resources implications for staffing, curriculum development and professional development
> - the setting of realistic time frames for implementation
>
> (Attachment 1, letter of invitation to participants from Jim Dellit, Executive Director Curriculum Services, DETE, 12 November 1997)

The establishment of the Committee marks a growing recognition within DETE of the existence of Indigenous languages programs, and their special requirements which need to be addressed at the highest levels. Its membership will ensure that the Committee has the power to address these matters.

Kaurna language programs

Map 7.1 Location of Kaurna language programs, 1990-1997

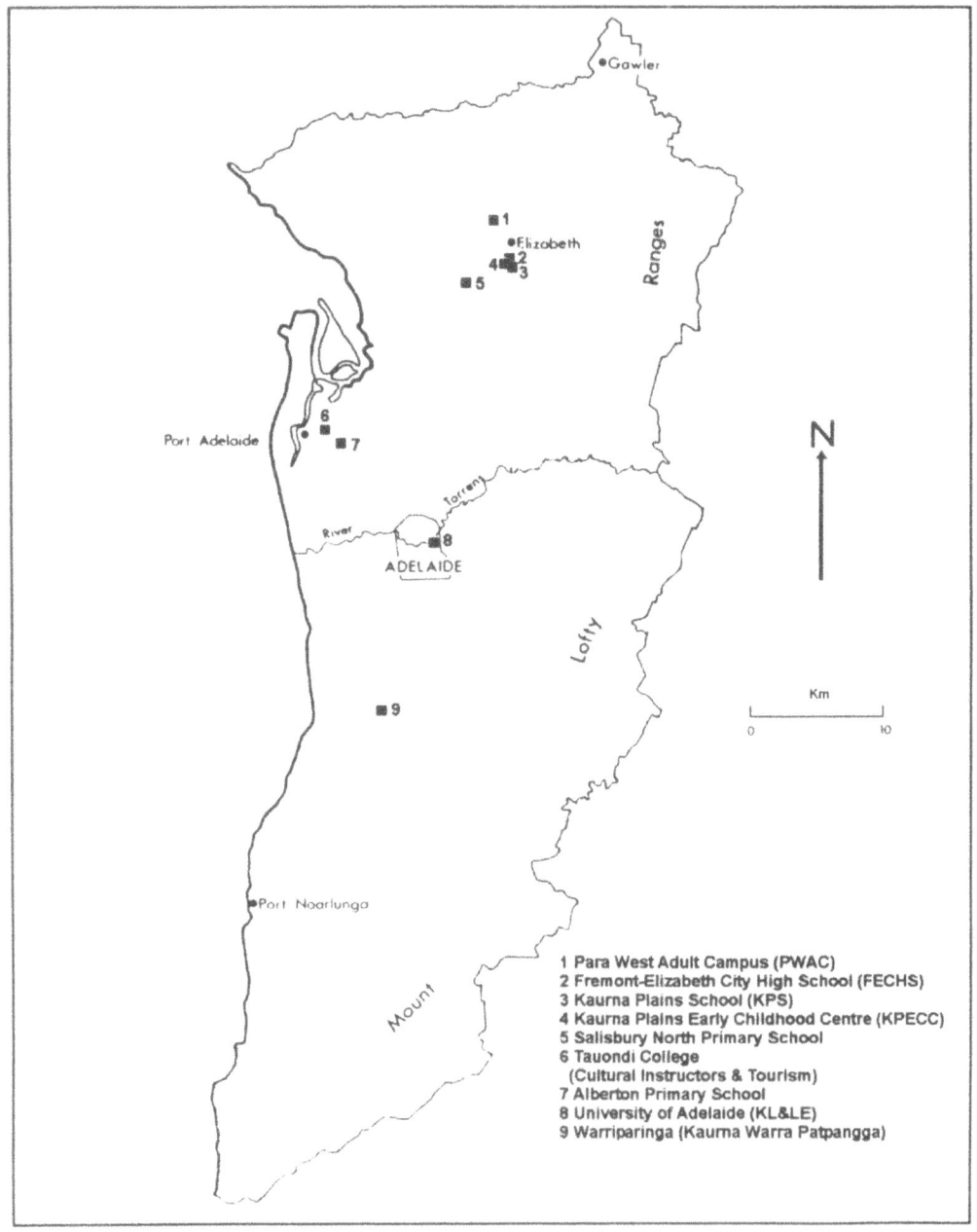

1 Para West Adult Campus (PWAC)
2 Fremont-Elizabeth City High School (FECHS)
3 Kaurna Plains School (KPS)
4 Kaurna Plains Early Childhood Centre (KPECC)
5 Salisbury North Primary School
6 Tauondi College
  (Cultural Instructors & Tourism)
7 Alberton Primary School
8 University of Adelaide (KL&LE)
9 Warriparinga (Kaurna Warra Patpangga)

Kaurna language activities within the education sector began slowly, with little financial support and no guarantee of ongoing funding. However, the first workshops provided a vision for what might be possible working with the historical Kaurna sources. They also inspired the establishment of a Kaurna LOTE program within KPS in 1992, which was introduced despite the system.

Five years later, Kaurna language programs had been established at all levels of education, including early childhood, primary, junior secondary, senior secondary, adult, TAFE and tertiary level programs. Despite this wide range of activity, the actual number of students of Kaurna is still relatively small, perhaps 250 in all in 1997. However, the programs have gained a certain level of status and respectability, and financial support which was previously denied. More recently, DETE has been more forthcoming with funding and support for Kaurna programs, but the major initiatives in schools were established by means of external funding. Given the centrality of education programs in Kaurna language reclamation, a more detailed description and analysis is warranted.

Table 7.1: Kaurna language programs: a chronology

Date	Event
1980	**Warriappendi Alternative School named.** First known use of a Kaurna word by Kaurna people for public naming purposes
1985	**Georgina Williams calls for revival of Kaurna as a spoken language.** Assistance sought from SAL
1988	Alice Rigney (KPS) met with David Tassell (Aboriginal Education Unit) about Kaurna language programs[15]
1988	Introduction of Aboriginal Studies materials containing some Kaurna words
1989	Publication of *The Kaurna People*
1989	NALP/LOTE funded local languages program (awareness raising activities)
Dec. .1989	Kura Yerlo workshop (display of Kaurna materials)
1990 -	**Kaurna Plains Early Childhood Centre** (Kaurna songs, visual aides, words and expressions)
Mar. 1990	**Songwriters workshop**, Tandanya (five Kaurna songs)
Jun. 1990	Workshop, Kaurna Plains School (K, N & Ng --> K)
1991	Two-week CSO Workshop, Aboriginal TAFE.
Jun. 1991-Dec.1991	Monthly CSO workshops run by Snooky Varcoe (worked on development of Kaurna language materials)
Jan 1992 -	**Kaurna LOTE began, Kaurna Plains School**
1992	One-week workshop, KPS
1993	One-week workshop, KPS
1993 - 1996	AILF project. (Kaurna exemplar materials and resources)
1993 -	**Kaurna course at Tauondi** (Community College)
Jul. 1994 – Dec. 1995	**Year 11 program ECHS** (accredited under AILF)
Jul. 1994 -	**Year 11 program EWAC -> PWAC** (AILF program)
1994 - 1995	Series of seven PDTAL workshops
1995	TAFE Accreditation of Aboriginal Language unit based on Kaurna course, Tauondi
1996	Kaurna at Smithfield Plains PS (Cherylynne Catanzaritti)
Apr. 1996 – Oct. 1996	**Kaurna Warra Patpangga** course at Warriparinga
May 1996	Half day Workshop with KPECC
1996	QW Language Revival project (video & book)
Aug. 1996	Teaching Aboriginal Languages Conference (2 days)
Oct. 1996	Teachers from KPS released to participate in PWAC program (training as Kaurna language teachers)

Jan. 1997 –	SASSL takes over delivery of PWAC program
Jan. 1997 –	SASSL assists in Yr 8 program, Fremont-ECHS
1997 –	**Yr 8 program, Fremont-ECHS** (for all students within Aboriginal Studies program)
12 Feb. 1997	Programming for Aboriginal Language Renewal and Reclamation Conference (one day)
Jun. 1997	Teaching Aboriginal Languages Conference (two days)
Jul. 1997 –	Kaurna sessions at Salisbury North PS (Cherie Watkins)
Jul. 1997 –	**'Kaurna Language and Language Ecology'** Linguistics Unit introduced, University of Adelaide
1998	Karrendi PS
1998	Reintroduction of Yr 11 program, Fremont — ECHS

There has been growing interest in Adelaide schools in establishing Kaurna language programs as the language becomes more familiar through public performance. Negotiations are taking place (1999) towards the introduction of a Kaurna program at Salisbury HS.

There are numerous links between programs in the early childhood, primary, secondary, TAFE and tertiary sectors. Teachers delivering programs in one sector are themselves students in other programs. Those involved in the delivery of Kaurna programs typically work across a range of programs. Cherie Watkins, for instance, teaches or has input into programs across the entire spectrum, in many different locations.

Descriptions of the Kaurna programs appear in appendices in Amery (1998, Vol. 2). Here I shall identify common emerging themes and differences between the programs. I am interested particularly in investigating the relationship between the programs and the broader Kaurna language movement.

Programs aimed at adults are absolutely crucial in the revival of Kaurna because teachers of Kaurna have to learn the language themselves. Adult programs have been delivered by a range of education providers and funding bodies. Whilst initial activities in 1989 focused on awareness-raising and songwriting, workshops over the next two or three years tried to develop basic linguistic skills and some vision of what might be possible. From these uncertain beginnings, Kaurna gained a firmer footing with the introduction of the Kaurna LOTE program at KPS. Since 1994, Kaurna programs for adults have been institutionalised within Inbarendi College and Tauondi. At Inbarendi College Kaurna is embedded within the senior secondary SACE (South Australian Certificate of Education), whilst at Tauondi it is an integral part of the TAFE accredited Cultural Instructors and Tourism course. Kaurna was further institutionalised at the tertiary level in 1997 with the introduction of the 'Kaurna Language & Language Ecology' (KL&LE) course within Linguistics at the University of Adelaide.[16] So the Kaurna language has made rapid gains in status over this eight-year period.

Adult programs have always focused on developing materials for use with children. Initial language programs focused on phonology, pronunciation and orthography issues. These have since receded into the background as learners become more familiar with T&S's orthographic conventions. Initial workshops also aimed at developing linguistic understandings. This has been maintained in subsequent courses through overt teaching, worksheets and exercises. However, with the exception of the KL&LE course, Kaurna linguistics has also become less of a priority. Increasingly, attention has been directed towards developing competence in the language.

Teacher training and in-service

Kaurna programs provide training for practising and would-be teachers of Kaurna. Many of the participants are themselves delivering Kaurna programs in their own schools and teaching situations. DETE has released teachers to participate in the course at PWAC and the University of Adelaide with the express purpose of preparing them as teachers of the Kaurna language. There have also been workshops and in-service programs focusing on language teaching methodology in which the Kaurna teaching teams have participated.

Professional development was also provided by the AILF project during the piloting of Kaurna programs in 1994 and 1995. Since then some support has been provided by DETE through a network of Aboriginal language programs and in-service activities. Professional development activities have played an important role in giving members of the teaching team a view of themselves as part of a wider movement. They can draw inspiration from other programs, whilst at the same time gain useful skills.

Curriculum development

When we began teaching Kaurna in schools, there was a complete absence of any Kaurna curriculum. T&S was the only Kaurna resource available for the first activities and workshops. There were, however, curriculum documents of a more general nature relating to the teaching of languages in schools. I was aware of the Australian Language Levels (ALL) Project (Scarino et al. 1988) but did not find it particularly useful for our purposes.

In mounting Kaurna language programs we were pioneering new areas, in terms both of the language itself and the type of program. We had to create our own resources and develop our own programs. Existing curriculum resources, while of some use, ignore crucial parameters, such as identity issues and the special relationship between language, land and place. Emphasis is placed on communication in the narrow sense, a skill not central to Kaurna programs.

The early 1990s saw the development of national curriculum designed to guide the teaching of languages in schools. Though the LOTE Statement did recognise Indigenous language revival programs as a part of the LOTE area of learning, the special needs of these languages were not taken into account by the LOTE Profiles, which 'describe the progression of learning typically achieved by students during the compulsory years of schooling' and 'provide a common framework for reporting student achievement' (Curriculum Corporation, 1994: 1). The Profile document makes it clear that 'the outcomes of all LOTE learning focus on communicating in LOTE' (Curriculum Corporation, 1994: 2) but contradicts itself by observing that 'as the content of the strands is based on communicating in LOTE, it will not apply to classical languages or to some

Aboriginal and Torres Strait Islander reclamation and language-awareness programs' (Curriculum Corporation, 1994: 3). Consequently, the LOTE Profile document, whilst it is supposed to guide all language teaching, has been largely ignored in the development of Kaurna programs.

Development of Kaurna curriculum at Kaurna Plains School

Like many Aboriginal language programs taught in schools, there was little opportunity for extensive preparation prior to the implementation of the Kaurna program at KPS. It was initiated in 1992[17] through sheer determination by Auntie Alice Rigney, assisted by Snooky Varcoe. In subsequent years the program was implemented by the Kaurna focus teacher, Pilawuk White, followed by James Parkin, with little input from outside. Staff at KPS in 1996 described their programming as follows:

> The Pitjantjatjara and Yankunytjatjara LOTE syllabus frameworks and adapted outcomes from the Western Australian Framework for the teaching of Aboriginal languages in primary schools guide teaching and learning and form a basis on which planning, programming, record-keeping, assessing and reporting can take place.
> ...
> There is no specific syllabus framework to guide the program on matters of content, teaching approaches and the like, but a range of themes are used to cover the seven years of learning. (DECS, 1996: 63)

In 1997, individual classroom teachers took increasing responsibility for implementation of the Kaurna program. They pursued themes, such as number, kinship, fauna etc. that complemented their overall teaching program, and were assisted by input from Cherie Watkins. The Kaurna language is integrated with other activities, such as art, music and sport, and taught in conjunction with other areas of the curriculum, especially cultural studies and society and environment. Teachers strive for an integrated holistic approach to curriculum.

There is still no Kaurna curriculum as such at KPS, but there is a much larger range of resources available for teachers to construct their own programs. Many of these have been created by the teachers themselves. Songs have always been a major component within the KPS program. Some have been written by teachers with input from students. Others have been written in workshops or in the adult programs. A Kaurna songbook and tape has just been published (Schultz et al., 1999). Other songs are 'floating around' on handouts. The creation of the KPS school song in mid-1997 has added another boost to the program.

Senior secondary Kaurna curriculum

In contrast to the KPS program, considerable thought and planning went into the implementation of Kaurna programs at senior secondary level, through the AILF Framework document (SSABSA, 1993). Kaurna was used as a hypothetical exemplar program (SSABSA, 1993: 52-60) and a weekly planner for Year 11 and 12 was drafted. The actual program was much more task-oriented than this draft planner, which was largely grammar-driven. Still, it served a useful purpose in sketching out a range of topics and tasks, some of which were used. The program implemented in July 1994 followed the AILF Framework, especially the Assessment Plan. After trialling the program in 1994 and 1995, the 'Warra Kaurna Detailed Program', as it was taught in 1994, was published along with two sample modules of work (see SSABSA, 1996b: 22-55). I have prepared numerous worksheets and translation exercises for the PWAC program. Many of these are also used in the Tauondi program and other programs.

DETE support for the development of Kaurna curriculum

Kaurna school programs, like most other revival programs in Australian Indigenous languages, arose within the context of a specific school in a specific community, with little departmental support. In the early 1990s, EDSA funded the development of Pitjantjatjara/ Yankunytjatjara second language curriculum to support the programs offered in metropolitan schools (DECS, 1994). As noted earlier, these documents have been of some use to teachers of Kaurna. However, it was not until the establishment of the Indigenous languages advisory position that any support was forthcoming for the development of Kaurna curriculum, or indeed, language revival curriculum.

Systemic support of language revival programs began sensibly with attempts to document the current situation and to draw this information together in the form of an Aboriginal Languages Handbook. This document is still under development, though an early draft was printed in 1996. Also in 1996, a Language Renewal and Reclamation Project was launched to investigate the relationship between the LOTE Statement and Profile and these kinds of programs, focusing on Kaurna and Ngarrindjeri. A preliminary draft identifies reasons for the establishment of the Project. These included a recognition of the inappropriateness of the Profiles for Indigenous languages[18], problems encountered by teachers and the 'the DECS requirement ... that by 1997 all R-10 language programs will be assessing and reporting in terms of the LOTE statement and profile' (DECS, 1996: 11, DETE, 1998: 4-5).

The project got underway in 1996 and produced a video (DECS, 1997) and a book (DETE, 1998). It included a unit planner proforma specifically developed for renewal and reclamation programs and an example of a completed proforma for the Year 8 Kaurna program at Fremont-ECHS (see DETE, 1998: 46-48). The project filmed interviews with a number of teachers of Kaurna and filmed classrooms at KPECC, KPS and Tauondi. Cherie and I were engaged as consultants to the Project. As a follow-up, Greg Wilson coordinated a one-day Programming for Aboriginal Language Renewal and Reclamation conference on 12 February 1997 in which participants, including the Kaurna teaching team, were instructed in the use of unit planning proformas and program planning.

In late 1997, Indigenous languages programs were obliged to participate in the Scope and Sequence project, initiated by a directive from DETE. The intent, apparently, was to develop a resource on the worldwide web that language teachers could use to organise and plan their teaching programs. DETE required curriculum officers to draft documents (at short notice) which specified the scope of the programs and the progression of learning throughout the years of schooling for each individual language. Curriculum in each language was to be specified relative to the LOTE Profile (Curriculum Corporation, 1994). The linguistic dimensions were specified in terms of language awareness, functions and notions, grammar and text types for each band level according to the four main skills: listening, speaking, reading and writing. Whilst this is a relatively straightforward task for most languages offered in South Australian schools, it was not so self-evident for Indigenous language programs. Two one-day workshops, involving representatives from Indigenous languages programs were held to investigate the issues, and as a result the curriculum development for Kaurna was drawn up.

Centralised language planning, epitomised in the LOTE Profile, is driven by the needs of second language programs and does not take into account the special needs of revival programs for languages such as Kaurna. Fortunately, the Language Renewal and Reclamation project and the Scope and Sequence project have provided the opportunity for those involved in the teaching of Kaurna in schools to reflect on their programs and on the need for planning. This has been very useful in identifying and articulating the special needs of these programs and in raising awareness of them within DETE.

There will be a need to produce a Kaurna curriculum document comparable to the Pitjantjatjara/Yankunytjatjara curriculum documents sometime in the future, but it is perhaps wise not to rush into such a venture. The curriculum needs to be workable in terms of the situation at KPS and the available Kaurna resources. It would be better perhaps if it were written with the hindsight afforded by a decade of language teaching.

Approaches and methods

Involvement of the Kaurna community in Kaurna programs is crucial. Community involvement is sought to oversee the programs and to provide advice and direction. The AILF project advocates the setting up of a program reference committee on which local Indigenous representation is maximised. Within the school sector, Alice Rigney, Principal of KPS (1987-1997), has been the mainstay for the programs. A significant amount of consultation and negotiation with key members of the Kaurna community also took place prior to the introduction of Kaurna into the university. Kaurna Elders and representatives of KACHA have been engaged in the delivery of programs as guest speakers on issues of Kaurna identity, epistemology, Dreamings, culture and heritage.

In mounting Kaurna programs we have been 'sailing uncharted waters'. We have had to do the best we can with the limited resources at our disposal and within the limitations of our own skills and knowledge. Few teachers of Kaurna are well prepared for the task. Language specialists, such as Cherie Watkins, are not qualified teachers and so do not have a background in program planning and teaching methods. Nor am I a trained teacher, though I have completed a graduate diploma in continuing education, which included some English as a Second Language teaching methodology.

A team approach is vital in the teaching of a language reclamation program, at least in the early stages, until there are trained Nunga teachers with an in-depth knowledge of Kaurna. Senior secondary Kaurna programs were introduced through the teaming of language specialists with a trained teacher and linguist. Ideally, much of the teaching of the program is performed by the Nunga language specialist. They should be the ones who 'call the shots' and bear the primary responsibility for what is taught and the way in which it is taught. The classroom teacher's role is administrative, organising excursions etc. and planning the lesson beforehand with the language specialist. The teacher should provide support and training to facilitate good teaching practice. The role of the linguist is to assemble the language materials, to evaluate and interpret them, to put them into a more useable and accessible form where appropriate, to assist in the preparation of resources for the language programs and to support the acquisition of Kaurna by the language specialists.

It is very hard to live up to this ideal of role differentiation. In practice I have been involved in a significant amount of up-front teaching in the programs, particularly on aspects of phonology and grammar, but also in aspects of Kaurna history and geography. The bulk of the content of the adult program, as it is currently taught at PWAC, has been generated by me, including almost all of the written worksheets and documentation which have been used effectively by Cherie within the Tauondi program.

These programs have been asking a lot of the language specialists, who are themselves learning Kaurna and are often just one step ahead of the students. However, the team approach in this situation is also another form of on-the-job training for the language specialist: one of the best ways of ensuring one learns a language is through having to teach it.

Teaching methodology

Because the language is being re-learnt from historical sources, literacy is a major focus. In this regard, language reclamation programs, such as Kaurna, differ from most other language programs, where oral language skills are primary. Revitalisation programs stress listening, speaking, reading and writing in that order.[19] Reclamation programs, by necessity, more or less reverse this order. In the absence of anything much to listen to, or read, production skills are emphasised over reception skills.

An eclectic approach is taken to language teaching methodologies in the teaching of Kaurna. Elements of many well-known methods, including Grammar-Translation, Audiolingual, Total Physical Response, Direct Method and Community Language Teaching are evident in the programs. A considered approach for the teaching of Kaurna will be discussed in detail in Chapter 9.

Content and materials

In the first Kaurna language programs we were totally dependent on the historical materials. T&S remains the mainstay of all Kaurna programs. We prefer to maintain a direct link with the historical materials, in the interests of maintaining the integrity and authenticity of the language. Exercises are based directly on words, sentences, songs or texts recorded in the historical materials.

The choice of content in Kaurna programs is an important, and sometimes contentious issue. We have always tried to allow identity issues and developments within the community to determine content. The language is not taught in isolation, but hand-in-hand with aspects of Kaurna culture and heritage. The identity of Kaurna students is reinforced. For Cherie Watkins it 'is not just about learner development, but also teacher development, language development, culture development. And there are issues of identity and heritage that come into the whole thing' (Cherie Watkins in *Warranna Purruna* (RS *Warrarna* Purruna) video, DECS, 1997).

We try to use the language as a key to understanding the history, the environment, the Kaurna culture and the Kaurna people.[20] We try to choose themes accordingly, and themes which will be of interest to the students. Thus, kinship, local place names, Dreaming stories, contact history, naming practices and historical texts have been prominent topics[21], along with some communicative language teaching.

Students learn about the geography and history of the Adelaide Plains and about neighbouring languages and cultures and their links to Kaurna. Of course Kaurna is not unique in teaching language and culture together. In the Kaurna context, the importance of this approach is heightened by the need to appeal to cultural understandings in order to make sense of the historical records themselves and, conversely, the linguistic records provide important insights into understanding Kaurna culture. The same can be said of history and geography. On the one hand the Kaurna language provides important insights into early contact history and the nature of the physical environment of the Adelaide Plains in the mid-nineteenth century. The lexicon and some place names afford insights into the dominant fauna, flora and topography.

Conversely, a knowledge of early South Australian colonial history and geography from other sources aids in the interpretation of the early language records.

In addition, some effort is made to teach history through the language itself, by looking directly at extant Kaurna texts (for example the letters written by Kaurna children) and in the translation exercises. Sentences such as RS *1850rlu, Moorhouserlu Kaurna miyurna Poonindie-ana kaitya*, 'In 1850, Moorhouse sent Kaurna people to Poonindie', are given by way of example to illustrate case marking. Students are then asked to translate into Kaurna a series of English sentences such as 'In the 1820s George Bates and John Anderson took Kalloongoo from Rapid Bay to Kangaroo Island', telling of the movements of a Kaurna woman kidnapped by sealers. Conversely, students are asked to translate a series of Kaurna sentences telling of the movements of Kaurna people who accompanied sealers to King George Sound, WA in 1825.

A number of Kaurna songs recently written and recorded are actually based on texts from the historical materials. For instance, RS *Pirrkipirrki* 'Peas' (Schultz et al., 1999: 42-47) is an embellishment of *Kadlitpiko Palti* 'Captain Jack's Song' (T&S, 1840: 73) and RS *Yarna Tapa* (pp. 36-39) is based on *Mullawirraburkarna Palti* 'King John's Song' (T&S, 1840: 73). RS *Palti Makanthi* 'Thigh Shaking Dance' (pp. 70-73) is based on the sentence *Wārpunna wiltarninga, meyunna, nganta makketitya*. 'Men, let your bones be strong so as to shake well (as at the native dance)' (T&S, 1840: 71).

Whilst the Kaurna language courses, especially those aimed at adults, include much material which could best be described as Kaurna Studies, the focus of these courses is still always language (Warra Kaurna). The Kaurna language is used as the key to provide insights into aspects of Kaurna history and culture, whereas other disciplines such as history and anthropology are used to contextualise and make sense of the Kaurna language materials themselves. It is a constant two-way process. Kaurna Studies are inseparable from the Kaurna language. The students recognise the value of this approach, as indicated in feedback and course evaluations, which I will discuss later.

However, this approach to the choice of content is in conflict with centralised planning. Through the LOTE Statement and Profile, ALL Guidelines and the Scope and Sequence project, there is a certain pressure to choose content that conforms to a LOTE formula or template that applies across all languages. This was certainly the case with the content for the Year 8 Kaurna programs as requested by SASSL. The themes specified, 'me and my world' from the student's perspective, numbers, days of the week, months of the year and colours, simply replicate a formula applied to any LOTE that makes no effort to draw on the unique aspects which will give students an understanding of the Kaurna people or culture.

As mentioned earlier, Kaurna language reclamation began with the Songwriters Workshop in 1990. The songs written then made use of the very first new Kaurna sentences generated in the modern period. Songs have continued to play a very important role in all Kaurna programs; they are an especially important medium through which to introduce the language to children of preschool and primary school age, and also work well with adults, who are keen to learn them, both for themselves and in order to teach their children and grandchildren. However, songs do not work so well with adolescent students who are more self-conscious and less attracted to the kind of songs that have been produced.

A highlight of the 1991 workshop was the translation of a number of popular nursery rhymes and children's songs chosen by the workshop participants. These included *Twinkle Twinkle Little Star, Baa Baa Black Sheep, Open Shut Them, A Sailor Went to Sea, Hickory Dickory Dock* and *I Wiggle My Fingers*. All the translations of these rhymes and songs were done in the workshop. Aspects of Kaurna grammar were explained as we went. We used a book of Malay songs and nursery rhymes for inspiration, looking to see how they had translated culturally-loaded verse of this kind. Participants enjoyed translating and singing the songs and took them back to their centres, where they have proved to be very popular.

In 1995, a singing group was formed at PWAC. It performed at a number of public events and served to motivate students beyond the language course itself. It brought students together and developed a sense of camaraderie. In semester 2, at the direction of Snooky Varcoe, the group became heavily involved in the recording of the tape *Kaurna Paltinna* (RS *Kaurna Paltirna*) (Schultz et al., 1999). Practice and recording sessions, sometimes amounting to a dozen or more 'takes' were very effective in developing Kaurna competence through sheer repetition.

At KPS, the entire school always sings the school song in Kaurna to welcome visitors and, at the conclusion of the assembly, the host class sings the RS *Niina marni* song to the classes leaving who respond accordingly. When I attended the school assembly on 28 November 1997, the children sang no fewer than eight Kaurna songs. Most impressive was their performance of RS *Makanthi Wapinthu!*, a Kaurna adaptation of Hokey Pokey. Instead of 'Do the hokey pokey' the Kaurna song says RS *makanthi wapinthu!* 'Do the *makanthi*.[22] The children were totally involved in the performance, singing the song at the top of their voices and giving a lively and skilful performance of the *makanthi*. They clearly loved it.

The Alberton School Choir[23] sings Pitjantjatjara songs, but recently, in recognition of the Kaurna people and Kaurna lands, they also sing Kaurna songs in public. In March 1997, Alberton PS engaged Snooky Varcoe to teach the choir his song RS *Munaintya Warrarna* 'I Can Hear the Voices of the Dreaming', which they sang at the Multicultural Education Coordinating Committee (MECC) Expo. Snooky has since accompanied the Alberton School Choir on several occasions, and at one event they also sang RS *Mingki Tirntu Warni* 'Happy Birthday' to Peter Coombe, a well-known children's musician who was the guest of honour. In November, Snooky accompanied the choir singing two new songs, RS *Yartapuulti* 'Port Adelaide' and RS *Nguyanguya Murra'dlu* 'Reconciliation' on the themes of unity and working together for the official opening of the Port Adelaide Visitor Information Centre on 9 November

1997. Snooky wrote these songs especially for the occasion, and taught them to the school choir one week prior to the event.

Songs are also a useful means of promoting the language through one-off activities. Snooky Varcoe, Josie Agius, Cherie Watkins, Jamie Parkin, myself and others have used songs in one-off activities in schools, as parents or special guests. For instance, in 1995 Snooky Varcoe and I ran a session at Highgate PS for the combined Year 3 classes of which my daughter was a member. We introduced ourselves in Kaurna, sang a number of Kaurna songs and taught the children several Kaurna expressions. Later that year, I attended the Year 3, school camp as a parent helper and ran a series of elective Kaurna sessions in which I taught some Kaurna songs, vocabulary and expressions. The children were exceptionally receptive and keen and volunteered to sing the songs at the camp concert.

New songs and new Kaurna translations of songs are still appearing at a steady rate. Over the period 1990-1997, more than 50 Kaurna songs (see Chapter 6) have been written or translated from English, usually as a group exercise in class. Several Kaurna hymns have also been revived.

A key strategy employed in Kaurna language programs has been to engage students in the production of Kaurna language materials to promote the language and to feed into other programs. This is also a good way of motivating adult learners. Adult students have been encouraged to produce simple story books for the programs at the KPECC and KPS. They have also produced board games, card games, posters and a variety of other material. These are checked for grammatical accuracy prior to their release for use as Kaurna language resources.

Cherie Watkins has produced a series of booklets for KPS designed to teach vocabulary in specific domains such as body parts, numbers, colours, kinship, etc. Other teachers and childcare workers also produce their own resources. As mentioned earlier, some language learning tapes have also been recorded. There are now a fair number of unpublished Kaurna language materials in circulation. In 1999 KPS is planned to produce a series of Kaurna readers by translating some of the children's favourite story books. I translated several short books of their choosing, but this was not taken further. The only materials available for purchase prior to 2000 were the two songbooks, the *Warra Kaurna* textbook (Amery, 1997) and the readings prepared for the KL&LE course.

In 1989 Jane Simpson began creating electronic files of the Kaurna sources and immediately made these files available to myself and to the Kaurna language projects. Her primary motivation was to expedite comparative linguistic research into the languages of South Australia, but she also wanted to provide a resource for the fledgling Kaurna language project in Adelaide. She began by keyboarding TMs, which at that time existed only as a handwritten manuscript.

As mentioned earlier, during 1994 I created several HyperCard multimedia stacks which combine sound, text and graphics. The Kaurna Sounds and Spellings stack was modelled on the orthography section of Nick Thieberger's Australian Languages Stacks produced by AIATSIS. I also created a stack based around ten sentences taken from T&S. I recorded these sentences together with a question and a set of multiple choice answers. Snooky Varcoe drew an illustration for each sentence which was scanned into the stack. With the commencement of the Year 11 Warra Kaurna program in Inbarendi College in 1994, the school purchased ten Macintosh laptop computers onto which the Kaurna vocabulary files were loaded. In 1994 and 1995 the laptops were used across both Inbarendi programs.

Multimedia remains a potentially useful and largely untapped technology that could work well with a group of computer-literate language learners. In 1999 Lewis O'Brien and I commenced work on creating a Kaurna language archive using e-mail and multimedia programs on IBM laptops on loan from Ngapartji Multimedia Centre. We intend to create sound recordings for all the vocabulary items, phrases and sentences which appear in the historical sources, together with new expressions. This work may result in a CD-ROM being made available to the community and schools.

Assessment of student performance within KPS is conducted informally. This can be done as classes are small in size. Oral skills are observed through children's use of requests such as RS *Marni'ai kudnawardli-ana padnita?* 'May I go to the toilet' or spontaneous utterances, such as RS *Warrarti!* 'Be quiet!' or RS *Tika!* 'Sit down!' Children are often heard using expressions such as these to other children in the class. Listening and comprehension skills are likewise assessed through observation of behavioural responses to commands (pc Kevin Duigan, December 1997).

The assessment of Kaurna language proficiency in the senior secondary programs is conducted more formally with an increased emphasis on written work. Written assessment has revolved around the creation of Kaurna language materials or translation exercises from Kaurna to English or vice versa. There is a strong practical focus in the assessment tasks, in line with the assessment schema written into the Australian Indigenous Languages Framework (SSABSA, 1996a: 33). Initially, the oral assessment consisted of one-on-one oral tests of vocabulary items, question and response or pre-prepared dialogue. This proved to be extremely time-consuming for the teacher and somewhat stressful for the students. Since then, assessment of the oral component has been done in-situ. For instance, recording of songs, performance of songs in public, delivery of speeches, giving a Kaurna lesson within a primary school or early childhood centre or running a session within a Kaurna language workshop have all counted towards the assessment of the oral component.

Assessment of the KL&LE course at the University of Adelaide has been based primarily on a set of practical linguistic exercises which give students hands-on experience with the historical materials, as well as an essay, video review and a tutorial presentation. Kaurna oral/aural language skills are not assessed, at least not in the course as it was taught in 1997. Assessment tasks for this course are similar to the kinds of tasks set for other linguistics courses, such as 'Foundations in Linguistics' taught at the University of Adelaide.

Evaluation

Thorough evaluation of Kaurna language programs in schools has not yet been undertaken. The usual means of evaluating LOTE programs in schools, by measuring student performance in 'strands' which focus exclusively on communication, have been seen to be inappropriate (see p. 162).

Teachers of Kaurna programs need to be concerned, not only with learner development, but with their own development and with the development of the language itself, something which other mainstream programs do not need to bother with. In fact, I would argue that teacher development and language development are far more important than learner development at this stage, as long as learners' interest and enthusiasm are maintained and cultivated. Communicative competence in Kaurna should be judged relative to the context in which the Kaurna language is being used. At the moment, it is more important to expand and develop this wider context and the language itself, than worry too much about student performance, which otherwise operates in a vacuum.

Having said this, it will be apparent that the long-term success of the programs depends on their relationship with the Kaurna community, and the broader Nunga community. I believe that the school programs should be judged primarily by the attitudes of the students themselves, and the attitudes of teachers, as well as the degree to which the programs are accepted and supported by the parents, the community and the education system. According to these criteria, the Kaurna programs have been successful.

In September 1992, the Education Review Unit (ERU) conducted a review of KPS, which stressed the importance of the teaching of Aboriginal languages and cultures in the school program:

> For parents, students and staff the highlight of the school was the focus on Aboriginal cultures and languages. This was seen as developing pride, self-esteem and a sense of identity in the students. As one parent said:
> 'This school has helped my children identify who they are and what they are, and as an Aboriginal parent that makes me feel proud'.
> A number of parents commented on how their understanding of the cultures and languages had improved by being involved with their children and this had improved communication and relationships within the family. (Wilmshurst, 1992: 4)

According to the ERU review, the Kaurna program received universal support from students, parents and staff at the school. In social and cultural terms, the program has been extremely successful. Educational outcomes such as the development of communicative competence are something of an unknown quantity. Certainly James Parkin, teacher of Kaurna language at KPS from 1993 to 1996, was not overly impressed by language proficiency outcomes:

> ... in terms of language proficiency, it's a grind ... I reckon I've still got, after four years, kids who can say 'Um I think RS Ngai wardli-ana padninthi <hesitant> means 'I'm going to school'... That's being a bit unfair. A few kids know more than that, but not many. And few of them would volunteer. You know, it's a bit of a shame job really to use Kaurna amongst themselves. They use the language that's asked of them in terms of greetings and being quiet and all that, but that's all. (Interview, 28 November 1996)

At the same time, however, he acknowledged the value of the program in terms of identity, culture and developing a sense of history amongst the children.

A comprehensive report was compiled following the completion of the initial Kaurna courses at Inbarendi College in 1994 as an AILF pilot project (Smiles & Simpson, 1995). This was not an independent evaluation, but more a product of critical reflection on the part of two non-Aboriginal members of the team identifying strengths and weaknesses of the program. The teacher's report noted that 'students were finding the 'pace' of the lessons too fast. New language was introduced before they felt confident with the work they had already covered' and that 'the students found the section on the Kaurna Sound/Spelling System and Grammar difficult' (Simpson, 1995: 1). For this reason, in 1995 I downplayed the formal teaching of grammar and phonology only to find that students subsequently demanded that more attention be given to these areas.

Informal evaluation of the course by teachers and the program's reference committee has been ongoing. Informal feedback in 1997 revealed that all students had gained substantially from the course and felt it to be positive and constructive. However, students repeatedly requested that more structure be built into the sessions. They wanted to know exactly what was going to be covered and they wanted more grammar, verb paradigms, case suffixes, grammar translation, rote learning and more overt teaching of sounds and spellings.

One of the students, Klynton Wanganeen, wrote a 1000-word critique of the course as part of his adult education course at the University of South Australia. He was generally favourable in his assessment concluding:

> The classroom sessions were structured in such a manner that there was flexibility in the delivery of subject matter, opportunities for students to practice what they learnt, each session was an extension of the previous session and students had the opportunity to reflect on the sessions through their journal.
> . . . The bottom line is that the Kaurna language course is delivered in a highly effective and efficient manner.   (Wanganeen, 1997: 6)

Klynton went on to make four recommendations to improve the course:

> • There needs to be more oral interaction in Kaurna Language introduced into the classroom activities to expand on the introductions that already take place. Some basic oral questioning and answering in Kaurna Language introduced in the second term would improve the ability of the students to speak the language better.
> • The journals be written in English first and translated into Kaurna as homework would overcome current problems of students doing homework instead of participating in group discussions and would probably make the journal more meaningful.
> • Journal to be handed in and assessed on a fortnightly basis.
> • Students should submit a project proposal for confirmation to avoid having students completing similar projects.   (Wanganeen, 1997: 5-6)

Klynton's recommendations are generally sound, though students at this level would probably be ill-equipped to translate their journals into Kaurna. Insistence on this could stifle their capacity to engage in critical reflection in the journal and they might feel overwhelmed and burdened. However, there is certainly scope to use more Kaurna language in their journals than takes place at present.

A formal evaluation of the 'Kaurna Language & Language Ecology' course at the University of Adelaide was conducted in 1997 with over two thirds of the students returning the questionnaires. This formal evaluation produced a very favourable result, students seeing the unit as challenging and relevant. None of the students evaluated the subject or the teaching negatively and most gave it a resounding endorsement. Many students commented on the value of an ecological approach to language revival. The comments written by six of these students in relation to Question 23, 'What were the best aspects of this subject, and why?' are cited below:

> Gave excellent insights into Kaurna culture past and present. It was wonderful having Lewis, Georgina & Cherie in the class giving their observations, opinions and sharing their stories. This subject has been a real eye opener ... The best subject I have done in my university career. A very relevant subject for our times.
>
> Very challenging and particularly that the written work is very relevant — proper 'hands on' development of skills rather than artificial exercises.
>
> I gained a lot of knowledge about things I would never have known — all of it of local knowledge & issues. The input from the Kaurna community was also good ...
>
> The subject matter, especially the focus on the people and their opinions. It was in this that the language came to life. Here that we could see its importance to the people.
>
> The fact that you are dealing with subject matter that is happening now — therefore a sense of dynamism. Also the access the subject provides to non-Indigenous students to learn about Kaurna, and more generally, Aboriginal culture.
>
> 1. Listening to the Kaurna people.
> 2. Learning the relationship between the language and the land.
> 3. Learning about the cultural significances embedden <sic> in the language.
> 4. the other students — their interest & enthusiasm.

By all accounts the initial KL&LE course in 1997 was considered an outstanding success, though it could benefit from a little 'fine tuning'. Several students made useful suggestions. One major issue that needed clarification concerned the place of language learning in the course. In order to better cater for the needs of students in 1998, I split the two tutorial groups, with one focusing on learning the language while the other focuses on language issues. The former is aimed at people from the Kaurna community and those involved with teaching Kaurna. Each student is required to develop a module and teach it to the students within the tutorial group. The other group is assessed by presentation of a tutorial paper.

Formal evaluations and direct feedback are two means of judging a course, but there are many others. Attendance, participation, involvement in extracurricular language-related activities, work produced by students, all give an indication of the effectiveness of the program.

Enrolments, attendance and student retention

Members of the Kaurna community are encouraged to participate as students in the programs, though attempts to involve them have met with limited success. In all, probably no more than 40 Kaurna adults have been involved as students in the various programs and workshops offered between 1989 and 1997. However, *all* Kaurna language programs have involved some Kaurna people as students. The majority of students in some programs were Kaurna people. In others, such as the KL&LE course at the University of Adelaide, input from the relatively small number of Kaurna people auditing the course has been significant and extremely valuable. Non-Aboriginal students are left in no doubt about the attachment Kaurna people have to the language and the authority they exercise over it. Students valued the input from Kaurna people, some pinpointing this as the highlight of the course.

Some Kaurna people, whilst having a keen interest in the language and a desire to revive it, have no interest in participating in a formal language program. They would prefer to keep it within their own families and organisations. Some would prefer to learn the language in the privacy of their own homes, no doubt in an attempt to avoid 'loss of face'. Kaurna people who have learnt Kaurna in the formal programs have employed the language in various ways for their own purposes and in their own work situations. Whilst we have been moderately successful in involving Kaurna people in the courses, there is room for more input and involvement. The success not only of the Kaurna programs, but of the revival of Kaurna itself hinges on this.

The Kaurna course at EWAC, as it was then known, commenced with 14 students, nine of whom completed the SACE requirements. Almost all were retained, though some did not complete all of the assessable tasks. Few students have ever enrolled in the Warra Kaurna program at PWAC in order to obtain a SACE certificate. Typically they enrol specifically for the Kaurna language.

Enrolments in the adult program at Inbarendi College have fluctuated over the three and a half years to the end of 1997, ranging from a healthy 18 to a marginal five or six. The most exciting, vibrant groups, in semester 2, 1994, and semester 1, 1997, were boosted by certain Kaurna extended families, those of Josie Agius and Alice Rigney respectively. Student retention within this program has generally been good, far exceeding retention rates found in most other courses at PWAC. Significantly, a number of students have returned year after year to continue doing the course. Whilst we have been reasonably good at retaining students in the PWAC course, we have not been very good at recruiting new students. This has been a major shortcoming of the program. However, DETE is increasingly taking notice of the Kaurna programs and has implemented measures which may prove crucial in ensuring their long-term survival and development. DETE has supported the attendance of KPS teachers in the PWAC program, thereby improving the quality of the KPS program itself. At the same time, the teachers' attendance has bolstered numbers in the PWAC program, thus improving its viability. I have suggested that AEWs and AERTs working in Adelaide Metropolitan schools, and elsewhere in Kaurna country, should be encouraged, even required, to study some Kaurna language. This would greatly enhance their performance in their work roles, whilst at the same time guaranteeing a solid student base for the PWAC program now run by SASSL. These are the kinds of measures needed to ensure the re-establishment of a viable Kaurna language ecology.

Student numbers at Tauondi have remained at an acceptable level, as Graph 8.1 (overleaf) shows. On the other hand, the Kaurna course at Warriparinga, run exclusively for KACHA and the Kaurna community, could be judged a failure in terms of student numbers. By August 1996, the Warriparinga course had been reduced to one Nunga student, together with a non-Aboriginal student not enrolled. This drastic reduction in student numbers had been due largely to internal conflicts within the Kaurna community. On 19 August the course was suspended until it could be discussed at the Annual General Meeting of KACHA held on 11 October, though the issue was never raised. I was requested again in 1999 to recommence the Warriparinga course.

Even though this course was short-lived, had few participants and attendance was erratic, it served a useful purpose. It allowed me to develop a closer relationship with KACHA and with a number of Kaurna individuals such that they now feel more comfortable in approaching me for assistance in drafting and translating Kaurna speeches. Several participants became involved in the KL&LE course introduced into the University of Adelaide in 1997.

Graph 7.1: Enrolments and graduates of Tauondi Kaurna course, 1993-1997

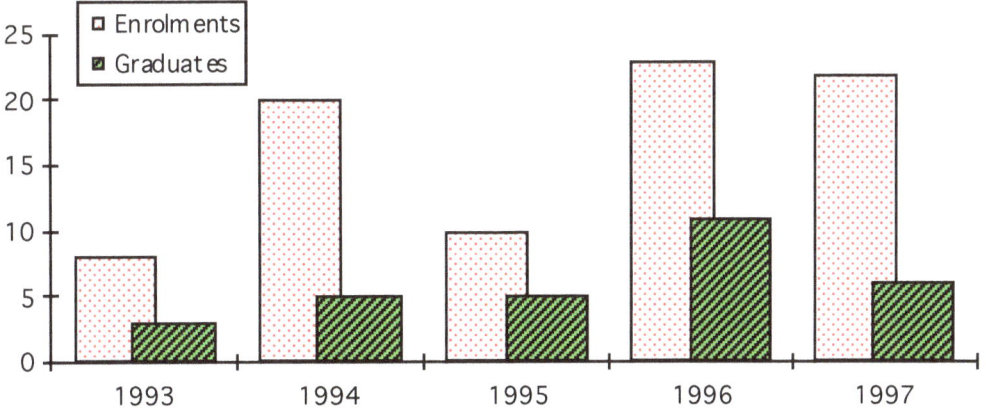

Kaurna is offered to all students at KPECC and KPS. Students have generally participated eagerly in the programs and, significantly, their enthusiasm for the language has grown. Young children, especially, relate well to the programs. Vicki Hartman, a long-serving teacher at KPECC, explains 'our children in particular really love learning an Aboriginal language. They're so proud of their identity. And Aboriginal songs and words are the first things they'll often use' (on Warranna Purruna video, DECS, 1997). In recent times the children seem to have taken much greater ownership of the program, especially with the introduction of the school song which they helped write in mid-1997. Kaurna songs are now sung with great gusto, with the Kaurna versions sung louder than the English. The children's enjoyment of Makkandi Wappendo! (RS Makanthi Wapinthu!) has already been noted (p. 168).

The Kaurna program at Fremont-ECHS is compulsory for all students in Year 8, most of whom are non-Indigenous. Some fail to see the relevance or importance of learning Kaurna. This is due in part to a disinclination to learn languages per se, rather than learning Kaurna in particular. However, most students are willing to participate in these programs and even become quite involved in the courses.

The Kaurna program offered at Salisbury North PS is offered on a withdrawal basis and attendance is strictly according to parental desire and approval. Parents of Nunga children may choose for their child to participate in the Kaurna or Ngarrindjeri program or neither; almost all Nunga children choose to participate, and some parents wish them to have access to both languages, which is difficult logistically (pc Cherie Watkins, December 1997), but reflects the level of desire for Kaurna and Ngarrindjeri programs.

Of course there is a fundamental difference between adult programs, where the students are there because they want to be, and many compulsory primary and junior secondary programs. The Tauondi program falls somewhere in between, as the Kaurna language course is a compulsory component of the Cultural Instructors and Tourism course. With this element of compulsion, not all students readily accept having to learn Kaurna — understandably, because many come from other areas, including interstate. However, these concerns, once addressed, are usually put aside.

In the strictly voluntary program at PWAC, most students have attended regularly, though attendance has fluctuated at times due to illness or other commitments. Many of the students work full-time and have family commitments, but have nonetheless demonstrated a high level of dedication and perseverance.

Feedback

Students' comments in the younger years of schooling indicate a high degree of engagement with the subject matter, as shown by the following examples taken from interviews conducted on video by Jenny Burford in 1997:

> My name's Travis [Varcoe] and I'm 9 years old and I talk Kaurna and I reckon it's great talking Kaurna. And in the classroom when you go to the toilet you've got to say RS Marni kudnawardli-ana padni'ai.[24] And I come from Ngarrindjeri.

> My name's Trisha Agius. And I've been learning Kaurna language for six years. It's really good that I'm learning it and I feel good that I'm learning my culture and that I can teach my kids when I grow up.

My interview with James Parkin (28 November 1996) provided different insights into how the program was received by the students at KPS. He assessed student reaction to the program as follows:

> The kids are bored with learning it ... They see the point in learning Kaurna, the importance for cultural business and their heritage ... But there's a difference in saying 'Yes, I reckon it's really important that we learn Kaurna language' and sitting down and learning Kaurna language ... But they do it and they learn it and they like the trips and they like the songs and games and participate in all those things pretty happily. Every now and then they'll say, you know, 'What's the use of learning Kaurna?' But at the same

> time people like Trisha Agius will very proudly display her Kaurna speech and read it out and take all the accolades that come with that. And other kids look on enviously ... The little kids are especially keen. Some kids, like Kahlia Power, who is Alma's granddaughter, Katrina's daughter, she is especially, but all little kids are really proud of how much they know, what they're learning and the significance of it. Kahlia came back from Alberton. She was there briefly. She says 'They don't teach Kaurna down there. They're just learning Pitjantjatjara.'

James had had a difficult period at the school and was probably somewhat 'burnt out' when I spoke with him just prior to his departure. He prefaced his interview with 'Oh, it's the wrong time to ask'. Nonetheless, his views provide an important balance to other perhaps over-optimistic views expressed.

Older students and adults, of course, are able to provide much more comprehensive feedback. This has been obtained through informal conversation and questioning of students, questionnaires and students' journal entries. There has been a certain amount of spontaneous comment. Students find the content areas covered highly relevant, particularly kinship, Kaurna place names, Kaurna Dreaming stories and aspects of Kaurna history, especially the excursion to RS Pirltawardli. Auntie Alice writes:

> This was the most fascinating visit to Piltawodli to actually 'feel' where our people began this journey into the invader's world ... To be able to walk the paths of the ancestors in this land of the Kaurna was very significant for me because I felt so much pain in my soul/spirit.   (Alice Rigney, journal entry 25 February 1997)

Some participants in the PWAC course in 1997, however, were more critical of the teaching methods. At times the sessions were not well prepared and some felt that the course was not sufficiently challenging.

Growth of programs

It was only a few years ago that the Kaurna language was dismissed out of hand by those working in the Education Department and also to a large extent within the Nunga community itself. It was largely unknown. Those who had heard of Kaurna generally dismissed it as 'dead' or 'extinct' or simply too far gone to do anything with. Indeed, my own involvement with Aboriginal languages in South Australia was initially with those where more had survived in the community.

The steady growth of Kaurna programs, from one-off workshops in 1990-1991 to established LOTE programs is in itself a strong indicator of success. Though initially dismissed, these programs have also gained recognition from DETE. For instance, the Kaurna LOTE program did not qualify for Mother Tongue Development (MTD) funding when it was first established in 1992. Now, the program is at the forefront of the Department's efforts to break new ground in the development of curriculum supporting the revival of Indigenous languages and has received a significant level of support of various kinds.

Mark Williams, Coordinator of Aboriginal Education, recognised the growth of Aboriginal language programs 'with minimal resources' (Aboriginal Languages Standing Committee meeting, 10 December 1997). Kaurna programs, along with Pitjantjatjara/Yankunytjatjara and Ngarrindjeri programs, have been at the centre of these developments. Accompanying the growth in the number of programs, there has been a steady growth in the number and range of resources, including songs, games, story books and other teaching aids.

The growth and expansion of Kaurna programs within the education sector is one major indicator of success. The programs have gone a long way towards raising the profile of the Kaurna language to a point where it is now taken seriously in many quarters, and has gained some local and national media attention. The language programs have afforded much greater recognition of the Kaurna people and their culture.

Kaurna programs pioneering language reclamation

The teaching of Aboriginal languages in Adelaide was pioneered by the introduction of Pitjantjatjara programs, followed by Ngarrindjeri and Narungga. Currently, however, Kaurna programs are leading the way in some sectors. Kaurna programs pioneered the way for the introduction of Aboriginal languages into Tauondi. Kaurna, and Pitjantjatjara/Yankunytjatjara were the first languages to be introduced into senior secondary studies.

The Year 11 Kaurna program, using AILF as a vehicle, is seen as a model for language reclamation and, as such, is sought after in a number of current publications including the AILF textbook and supporting materials, a DEET (1995) promotional brochure, an Applied Linguistics course at the Northern Territory University (Amery, 1996b), and DETE curriculum (DECS, 1996; DECS, 1997; DETE, 1998). Descriptions of the Kaurna program and language teaching methodology have also been published in current publications on the teaching of Aboriginal languages (see Varcoe, 1994; Amery, 1994) and Aboriginal sociolinguistics (Amery, 1995a). Kaurna language programs and language reclamation have been promoted at conferences including the Modern Language Teachers Association (Amery, 1992b), the Australian Linguistics Institute, the Australian Linguistics Society (Amery, 1996a) and the South Australian Anthropological Society, as well as within various courses and programs offered at the University of Adelaide, Flinders University, the University of South Australia and the Northern Territory University.

A full analysis of the Kaurna programs themselves is beyond the scope of this study. The Kaurna programs in the education sector have made remarkable progress over the last decade, increasing in number and type. They have been institutionalised to a certain extent, and are gaining more support, but they remain vulnerable, particularly because they are dependent on a small number of individuals.

Schools cannot revive the language by themselves. Successful language revival ultimately depends on the community and building links with the formal programs, which are the powerhouse for reclamation at the present time. But the renaissance of Kaurna language and culture has its roots within the Kaurna community. The current re-emergence of Kaurna identity is essentially independent from what happens in schools, though it is strongly reinforced by the programs. The implementation of the Kaurna programs in schools was timely, picking up on trends already occurring within the community. The next chapter investigates the use of Kaurna within the Nunga community and in wider society.

Notes

[1] Fred, vice-chair at the time, spoke on behalf of KACHA at the consultation session for the Language Renewal and Language Reclamation project, which had a major focus on Kaurna language programs in schools.

[2] In July 1845, the Kaurna language ceased to be used in schools with the closure of Piltawodli (RS Pirltawardli).

[3] In 1968 Pitjantjatjara was offered through the Department of Continuing Education at the University of Adelaide (Edwards, 1995: 6). Pitjantjatjara has been offered continuously within the tertiary sector from 1968 up to the present.

[4] Lewis O'Brien (13 October 1997) tells how he and Greg Wilson toured around schools. 'We told them all to speak Pitjantjatjara.' The Nunga response was 'Why can't we learn our own?' In Lewis's view, the direction has come from the community and that is what is important.

[5] There are many reports from the 1950s and 1960s of Nunga students having been punished for using their languages at school (Tom Trevorrow, talk at Camp Coorong 19 September 1996). One still occasionally hears reports that the use of vernacular words and Nunga English, as a non-standard English variety, is discouraged in school contexts.

[6] In 1985, inquiring into why so few Nunga students were enrolling, Brian was told that Pitjantjatjara was not their language, it was from the north of the state. Nunga students expressed an interest in having access to their own languages which prompted Brian to pursue language revival activities (pc Brian Kirke, 1989).

[7] The Ngurlongga Nunga Centre used the spelling Ngurlongga, in accordance with Tindale's questionable etymology of the word, based on the Ngarrindjeri word *ngurle* 'hill'. It is more likely that Noarlunga is derived from the Kaurna RS *nurlu* 'curvature, corner' in reference to Horseshoe Bend, a prominent landmark on the Onkaparinga River in the vicinity of the Old Noarlunga as it is known today.

[8] They were not accredited until 1994, through the AILF project.

[9] Lo Bianco recommended the allocation of $6 million over three years, though only $2.5 million was actually forthcoming over the period 1987-1990 (House of Representatives ... , 1992: 77).

[10] The LOTE salaries from the SA Education Department unexpectedly dried up at the end of 1989, having been in effect for just one semester.

[11] The federal NALP program was drawing to a close; 1989 was the final year of funding. The LOTE Mother Tongue salaries had also effectively dried up, as far as Aboriginal languages in the metropolitan area were concerned.

[12] Josie approached Georgina Williams in 1989, inviting her participation in the project. However, Georgina declined as she had misgivings about teaching Kaurna within the school system, because in her view the language should remain within the community (pc Georgina Williams 3 June 1996). Josie herself had expressed these reservations to me back in 1989, perhaps reflecting Georgina's views.

[13] Several Kaurna people were represented on the AILF National Steering Committee including Alice Rigney, Principal of KPS, Josie Agius, former project officer with the NALP project, and Paul Hughes, then Coordinator of Aboriginal Education in South Australia.

[14] Jennifer was then a student in the Graduate Diploma of Applied Linguistics offered by Northern Territory University, and had previously taught Pitjantjatjara.

[15] I was unaware of this development until Alice Rigney drew it to my attention in February 1998.

[16] This course was funded by 'soft' money generated from overseas students and was established, again, despite the system, through the support of Prof. Peter Mühlhäusler. An ongoing funding source is still being sought.

[17] Alice Rigney had, however, given thought to introducing Kaurna language years earlier. In 1988 she held discussions with David Tassell at the Aboriginal Education Unit to this end.

[18] Despite repeated representations from Greg Wilson, myself and others, the drafting of the National LOTE Profile failed to accommodate the Indigenous Australian languages in revival situations.

[19] Some revitalisation programs, such as the Kungarrakany and Larrakiya program taught in Darwin in 1995 are restricted to listening and speaking, as their communities are ideologically opposed to committing them to writing.

[20] Aird (1991) describes the importance of the Yugambeh language in reconstructing cultural heritage in South East Queensland.

[21] This is also true of the Ganai program at KODE campus, Gippsland, which is also centred on a Dreaming trail, Dreaming stories and other aspects of Koorie culture (pc e-mail Lynette Dent 17 June 1998).

[22] The RS *makanthi* is a distinctive dance movement, described in the literature and painted by Cawthorne, where the dancer stands with legs apart and rhythmically shakes the thighs.

[23] Alberton PS in the Port Adelaide area has a high proportion of Aboriginal enrolments. In 1993 they adopted Pitjantjatjara as the school LOTE program, offered to all children regardless of their linguistic and cultural background. Previous to this, Pitjantjatjara had only been offered to Nunga students at Alberton on a withdrawal basis.

[24] On the video tape this Kaurna utterance was spoken fast and fluently; faster than his English.

Key Historical Figures

Plate 1: Clamor Schürmann
(courtesy Lutheran Archives)

Plate 2: Christian Teichelmann
(courtesy Lutheran Archives)

Plate 3: Kadlitpinna 'Captain Jack'
(courtesy South Australian Museum)

Plate 4: Ivaritji (Amelia Taylor)
(courtesy South Australian Museum)

Kaurna Ceremonies

Plate 5: The *Kuri* (RS *Kurdi*) and *Palti*
(courtesy South Australian Museum)

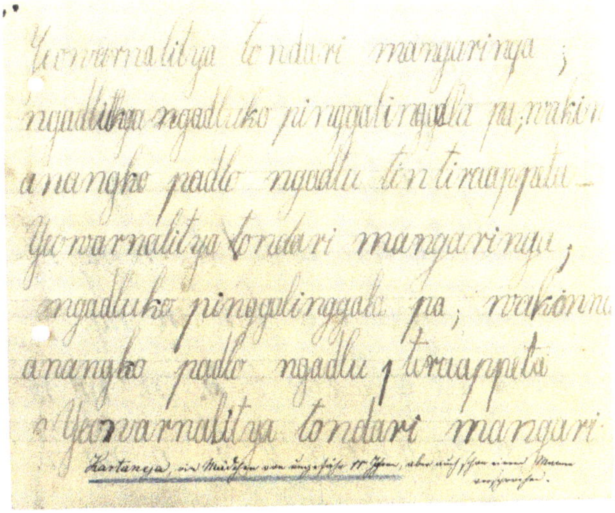

Historical Kaurna Texts

Plate 6:
A page from Kartanya's copybook, 1840

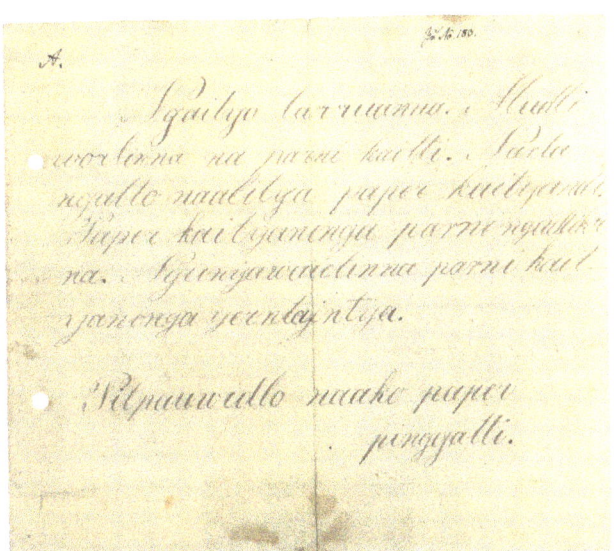

Plate 7:
Letter written by Pitpauwi, 1843

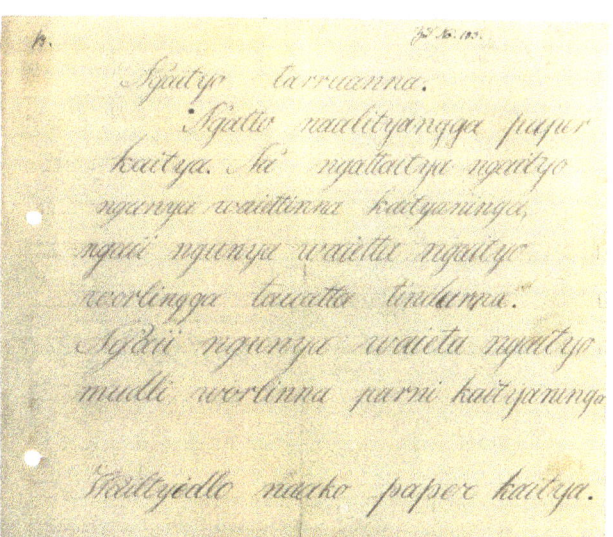

Plate 8:
Letter written by Wailtyi, 1843

Images courtesy of Barr Smith Library, University of Adelaide

Historical Kaurna Texts

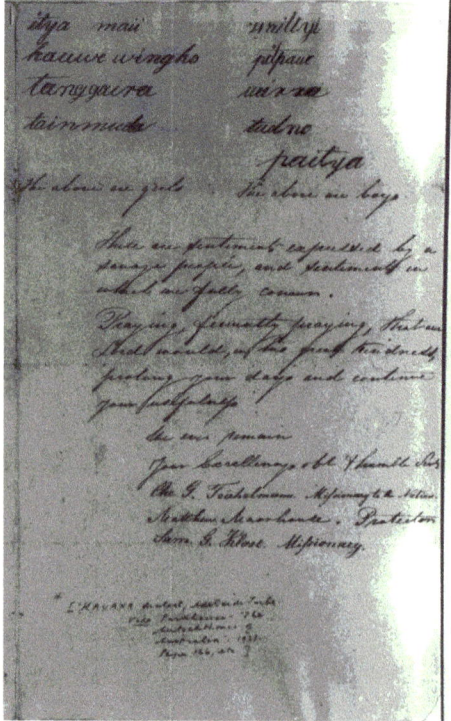

Plate 9:
Group Letter
written to Gawler
(penned by Itya Maii), 1841
(images courtesy of State Library of South Australia)

Texts Produced by Missionaries

THE COMMANDMENTS.

Tarata itto warrarna Yowa pudlotti, wangi ba.

1. Ngai Yowa, atto ninna pingyatti; kuma Yowa ngai taikurri yailtyaûrti.

II. Yowarna tura pingyaûrti yakkoakarr-anangko, yakko yerta anangko, yakko yerlo-anangko; turarna mikangga mamba tartarta tikkaûrti. Ngai Yowa, atto ninna pingyatti, marngubi na ai, wakinnanna ai paiereota; maraninna, ngai numa nakkoanna, warranna aityo yurrekaityanna, tangka waierendai par-nakko.

III. Yowarna narri madla pudloriappeûrti; Yowadlo yakko kudnunna yailtyaota par-nakko narri madla pudloriappinanna.

IV. Yowarna tindo mukkabando, kuinyundappindo ba; yerrabula purlaitye tindurna mudliitya worpulaingki; kudyunurlo tindoûrlo Yowarna tindo, mudliitya worpulaeûrti. Yerrabula purlaitye tindurna Yowadlo karra, yerta, yerlo, purrudye pingyatti, kudyunurlo tindurlo ba kudla tikketti; namurtya padlo kudla kuinyundappi.

V. Ninkerli, ninkainuma nangando, ninra nurntikki purruna tikketinna yertangga.

VI. Padlokundaûrti.

VII. Kuma yangarra wandiapeûrti.

VIII. Metteûrti.

IX. Ninko nepo marta martaûrti.

X. Ninko nepukko wodli, parnu yangarra, parnu bullokke, parnu nanto, parnukko purrudye mudlinna, manga mangaûrti.

THE GOVERNOR'S ADDRESS.

Pulyonna meyunna!

Itto warranna (wa na yellara yurre kaitya) yowarna yerlterittinna, padlo pinkyatindo, yerta, parkanna meyunna, pulyonna meyunna, kutyoanna mudli-wodlinna purutye vowadlo pinkya.

Yaintya warranna tindo partanna yurre kaityaninga, mukabaninga.

Na mette-urti.

Tanaringutti, pungoringutti, yerra padlokundaringutti, yerra padlokundaringutti.

Wakwakkunna naakunna padlokunda-urti.

Yangaranna naakunna numma nangainga, taua-urti, kabbakabba-urti, wonda-urti parna. Yowarna takutya, Yesus Christus numma nangainga, parnu padlo nintyerlanna tikkainga.

Tindo partanna pa naalityangga waiendi.

Padlo na wakinna partannunangko tirra pe uta, marni ngarraitye na padlo yunggo uta.

Kopardabinnanna tikka-urti, Kopurlurlo na kuma'pi war angkearndappe-uta, padloappe-uta.

Woditanpanga tikkainga, *Mullawirra burka* (King John,) *Kadlitpinna* (Captain Jack), *bukartiwillo*, kutyoanna meyunna turraturrauna.

Na wadlappanna tieta, parkanna meyunna taikurri taieta, ngando marnko uta.

Ngarraitye turcki tidlinna waiinga *Mullawirra burka*, *Kadlitpinna*, kutyoanna meyunna turraturraua.

Ngarraitye parngutta, cabbage, turnip, kutyoanra maiinna igatpaninga. Encounter Bay Bob mai yerta padlondi, Karromarranend'ai parnu warrarlo ngatto pa yungoûta, na kutyoanna meyuona yerta kokata, ngatto na yunggo-uta.

Mr. Moorhouse, Mr. Teichelmann Mr. Schürmann, parnakko warranna yurrekaityaninga, wappeninga, parna, na padlondi.

Itto warranna na wappe-uta, na ngunye-uta; parkanna meyunna, pulyonna meyunna, yunyayungawortanna kumangka tikkata.

Plate 10: Ten Commandments and Gawler's speech, 1840
(images courtesy of State Library of South Australia)

The Main Players in the 1990s

Plate 11: Lewis O'Brien and Georgina Williams KL&LE launch

Plate 12: Nelson (Snooky) Varcoe teaching Kaurna at KPS, 1992

Plate 13: Dr Alitya Wallara Rigney at KL&LE launch, 1997

Plate 14: Cherie Warrara Watkins, steps of Parliament House, 1996

Plate 15: Alma Ridgway and Vicki Hartman, 1996

Learners of Kaurna in the 1990s

Plate 16: First Kaurna Workshop, KPS, 1990

Plate 17: Nola foster and children out the front of KPS

Plate 18: Tauondi students on excursion

Plate 19: Julie Hodgkinson and children at KPS

Plate 20: Nelson Varcoe and PWAC singers, 1995

Plate 21: Kevin Duigan, Cherie Watkins and KPS children, 1997

Kaurna in Situ in the 1990s

Plate 22: Singing group in Tarntanyangga (Victoria Square)

Plate 23: Smoking ceremony at PWAC

Plate 24: Kevin Duigan and KPS children, 26 May 1999

Plate 25: Nelson Varcoe at Journey of Healing, 26 May 1999

Plate 26: Lester Irabinna Rigney, 26 May 1999

CKLR Team

Plate 27: Kaurna radio shows team, 2010:

Steve Gadlabarti Goldsmith
Rob Amery
Jamie Ngungana Goldsmith
Jack Kanya Buckskin
Christine Brown
Katrina Karlapina Power
Dr Lewis Yerloburka O'Brien
Rod Midla O'Brien

Plate 28: CKLR team

Paul Finlay
Gerhard Rüdiger
Rob Amery
Steve Gadlabarti Goldsmith
Jack Kanya Buckskin
Taylor Tipu Power-Smith

Plate 29: Kaurna media team (Steve and Taylor) on location at Brighton

Plate 30: Jack Kanya Buckskin and daughter Mahleah Kudlyu

KWP Memorable Events

Plate 31:

KWP Members,
4 December 2014
Steve Gadlabarti Goldsmith
Jack Kanya Buckskin
Rob Amery
Dot Goldsmith
Trevor Tirritpa Ritchie
Taylor Tipu Power-Smith
Gerhard Rüdiger
Chester Schultz
Dr Lewis O'Brien (front)
Dr Alitya Rigney (front)

Plate 32:

Signing of MoU between KWP and the University of Adelaide, 2013:
Dr Lewis O'Brien
Prof Warren Bebbington
Dr Alitya Rigney

Plate 33:

Return of Kaurna letters from Germany
Signing of MoU between KWP, Lutheran Mission, Leipzig and the University of Adelaide
Dr Altiya Rigney (KWP)
Martin Habelt (LMW)
Dr Lewis O'Brien (KWP)
Rev. Hans-Georg Tannhäuser (LMW)
Paul Wilkins (UofA BSL)
2013

Students of Kaurna in the Twenty-first Century

Plate 34:

Kaurna TAFE Certificate III course, 2012
Mary-Anne Gale (Coord.)
Cherie Warrara Watkins
Taylor Tipu Power-Smith
Frank Wanganeen
Rob Amery (Ling.)
Dr Lewis O'Brien
Stephen Goldsmith
Dr Alitya Rigney
Garth Agius
Jenny Wright
Jack Kanya Buckskin
Trevor Tirritpa Ritchie

Plate 35:

TAFE Certificate III graduates, December 2013:
Dr Alitya Rigney
Dr Lewis O'Brien Jenny Wright
Garth Agius
Frank Wanganeen

Plate 36:

University of Adelaide Kaurna Summer School Warriparinga Excursion with Jack Kanya Buckskin & Stephen Goldsmith, January 2013

Kaurna in the Public Domain

Plate 37: Steve Gadlabarti Goldsmith at Kaurna Learner's Guide launch, Tandanya, December 2013

Plate 38: Jack Kanya Buckskin and *Kuma Kaaru* dance troupe

Plate 39: Kaurna street signs

Plate 40: Kaurna Coast public artwork

Plate 41: Tindo solar bus

Plate 42: Kaurna graffiti art under Southern Expressway

8

Kaurna in Society

As long as you see steps all the time, you see time doesn't matter ... if we're starting to greet each other, then we start running meetings with it, then we've openings at your conferences, that's starting. All those things are fitting in. Every year you find extensions, and they're starting to multiply.
(Lewis O'Brien, interview transcript, 28 October 1997)

This chapter focuses on the social aspects of Kaurna language reclamation, specifically the situations in which Kaurna is being used and the underlying purposes for its use. All aspects of Kaurna society and language revival are embedded within a dominant English-speaking culture. Kaurna people are currently establishing niches within this monolithic society. There has been a growing recognition of the value of multiculturalism in Australia, though multicultural Australia has been dominated by migrant groups; on this level, too, it has been necessary to seek out niches and fight for recognition. When people think about using Aboriginal languages, there is still strong pressure to turn to Pitjantjatjara, which is comparatively well known. The Kaurna are heavily outnumbered by the Ngarrindjeri and other groups in their own country, so the Kaurna have to fight for recognition on many fronts and many levels.

Within this context, the Kaurna people and Kaurna language enthusiasts have made significant gains. In Chapter 7 we saw that the Kaurna language is now taught in accredited programs at all levels of the education system, from early childhood to university studies. In this chapter, we shall see that it is gaining a higher profile in public domains, though it still plays only a small role. Most Adelaideans would probably confess to never having heard of the Kaurna people or language, let alone having heard the Kaurna language spoken.

Names and naming

Although names may seem an insignificant aspect of language use, Kaurna names remain one of the few areas of continuity. Many of the names on a map of the Adelaide plains are Kaurna; others that appeared on early maps of the area, even before colonisation, have been lost, though there are now proposals to reinstate them.

There has been a long-standing practice within the non-Aboriginal community of adopting 'Aboriginal words' to name suburbs, streets, railway sidings, properties, houses, boats, businesses, clubs and occasionally even persons. For most of this century little notice was taken of the source language and so Kaurna words were sometimes used well outside Kaurna country, while numerous words from other parts of Australia were brought in. Since the 1990s, however, there has been a new awareness of the need to use words from the appropriate language and to consult and negotiate with communities for permission to use them, though there are still many violations of this Indigenous protocol.

Map 8.1: Prominent Kaurna names appearing on current maps (with Revised Spelling in brackets; updated with assistance of Ash Starkey)

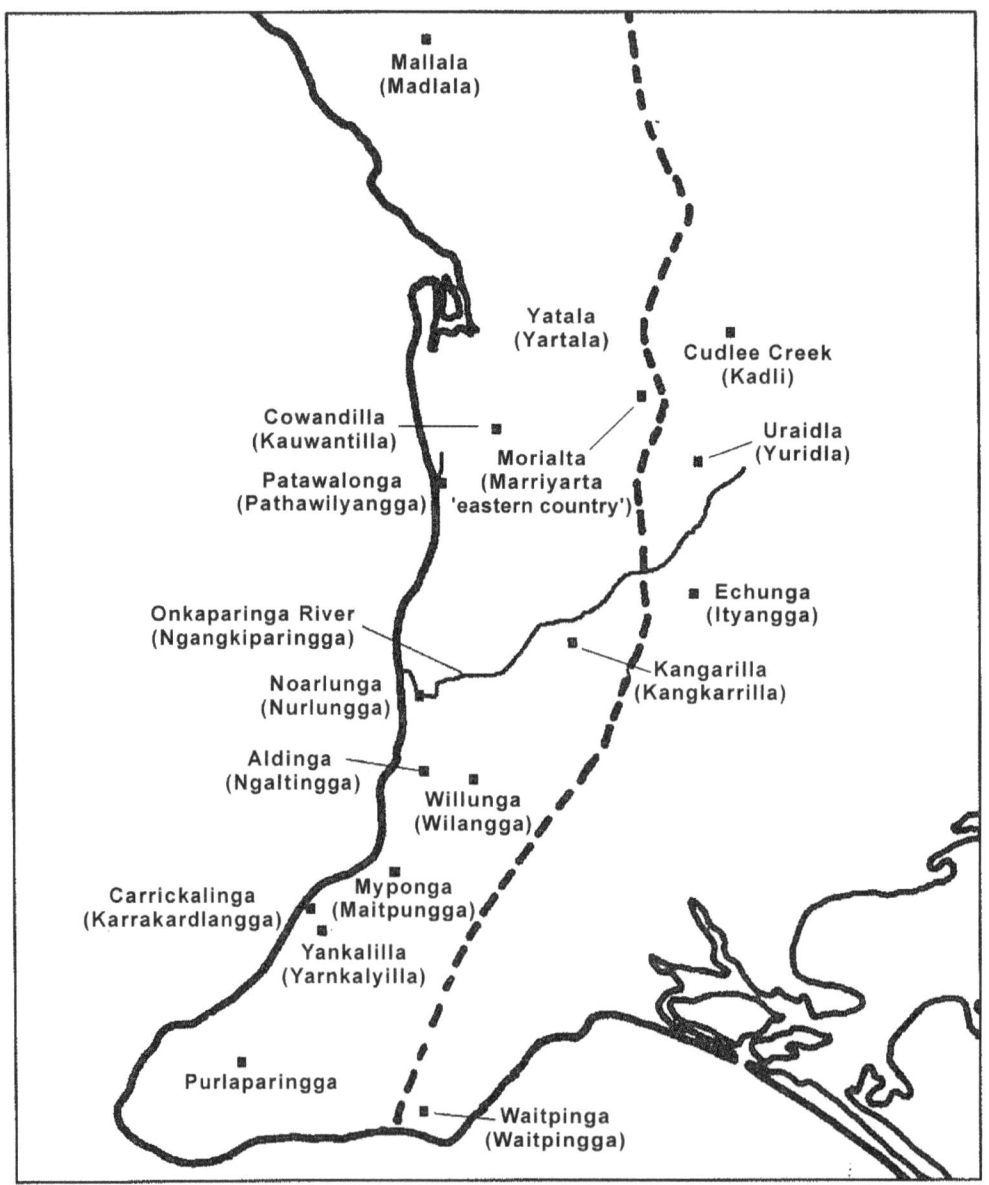

Interesting and complex though this topic is, I am more concerned here with the use of Kaurna names within the Indigenous community and the relationship between this use and the revival of the language.

The application of new Kaurna names by members of the Kaurna community heralded a renewed interest and activity in the language, predating Kaurna language courses and language revival programs by some years. The naming of Warriappendi Alternative School[1] in 1980 was perhaps the earliest use of a Kaurna name, for a public institution, instigated and promoted by Aboriginal people in the modern period. Leila Rankine, herself a Kaurna descendant, proposed the name on the basis of research conducted in the archives by Peter Buckskin, another Aboriginal person (pc Greg Winner, 14 May 1996). The Kaurna Plains Football Club and Tukatja[2] (later changed to KPECC) were also established in the early 1980s. The Nunga community is increasingly interested in drawing on their linguistic heritage for names of Aboriginal organisations, educational institutions and government bodies dealing with Aboriginal people or issues, and sometimes also for personal names and other private purposes, such as computer passwords. This practice represents the earliest stage of the current linguistic and cultural revival, and has widespread support within the Kaurna community. Whilst the use of Kaurna names might be called 'window-dressing', it does much, especially when combined with other language use and awareness-raising activity, to promote recognition of the Kaurna people and the Kaurna language.

Kaurna names in the public sector

There has recently been a renewed interest in sectors of the non-Indigenous community and in government, in using Kaurna names, not just because they sound nice, but because of a genuine desire to recognise the Kaurna people as prior occupants and owners (RS *mathanya*)[3] of the Adelaide Plains. There is a growing recognition of the central place of Indigenous peoples and their cultures in the fabric of the nation. Accordingly, the state government instituted a Dual Naming policy in 1991[4], whereby Indigenous communities can put forward proposals for the use of Indigenous names alongside existing ones. It has been suggested, for instance, that Port Adelaide should be known as both Port Adelaide and RS Yartapuulti. This may well be officially adopted at some point in the near future.[5]

At first, Kaurna names were applied in recognition of the Kaurna people, with good intentions, but without consulting Indigenous communities. With increased awareness of and respect for Indigenous protocol KACHA, Kaurna Elders, Tandanya, the Museum, the Aboriginal Education unit, KPS, Tauondi and other organisations now receive numerous requests from members of the public, government agencies, even large corporations, requesting suitable names for specific purposes and/or permission to use these names. Most requests come from the Indigenous community. More than 60 requests have come to me during 1993-1997 for suggestions, advice or confirmation,[6] quite apart from the numerous other requests directed to and addressed by a range of Elders, which I may never hear about. I provide advice but encourage the enquirer to check back with KACHA or Kaurna Elders for permission to use the name.

The pace of adoption of Kaurna names is accelerating, largely due to their promotion by Kaurna people working within the public sector with the support of the community. Local government authorities are increasingly paying attention to local Aboriginal history and to the reconciliation process. Several parks have been given Kaurna names. For instance, in April 1997 a new wetlands reserve was named Tartonendi (RS Tarturninthi) by the Marion City Council and a plaque erected reading 'Tartonendi. This Reserve is named Tartonendi, which is a Kaurna word meaning 'transforming the land into wetlands'. The Kaurna people are the original inhabitants of the Adelaide Plains.'

At the request of the Adelaide City Council, as part of the reconciliation process, I developed a naming proposal, which suggested Kaurna names for the 29 parks within the parklands and for the seven city squares. A set of naming principles was developed, which promoted the use of the few recorded original names. Additional names proposed related to a particular plant species found in the area or known to have existed there, or referred to current use of the park. For example, Park 02 was named Padipadinyilla [RS Pariparinyilla] 'swimming place' because of the Aquatic Centre there. I also proposed that the squares and four high profile parks be named after prominent nineteenth-century Kaurna individuals, such as Mullawirraburka [RS Murlawirrapurka] 'King John', and that the golf course greens at Piltawodli [RS Pirltawardli] on Park 01 could be named after Kaurna children and adults who were known to have lived there. These names have yet to be officially adopted.[7]

Restructuring and forced amalgamations of local councils has provided the opportunity for introducing new names. Kaurna names have been proposed by councillors or residents with an active interest in Aboriginal issues, but it seems that in every case these have lost out against more conventional English labels, often on the grounds that the Kaurna word is 'too difficult to pronounce'.[8]

Kaurna names are also being adopted for a range of government agencies which deal with Indigenous peoples, including health, welfare[9] and community services.

Kaurna names in the education sector

The naming of Warriappendi Alternative School, as mentioned earlier, was perhaps the first instance in the modern period of Kaurna people turning to their ancestral language as a source of names. However, Warriappendi was not the first school to gain a Kaurna name. A number of schools are named after towns, suburbs or streets in which they are located or, in the case of Wirreanda HS which was named in 1977,[10] after a nearby property. Karrendi Primary School was named in 1979 after *karrendi* [RS karrinthi] 'to fly', probably because of its proximity to Parafield Airport. Karrendi was supplied and approved by the Geographical Names Board in 1978, seemingly without any Aboriginal involvement (pc John Simmons; Liz Blinko, 14 May 1996).

In 1986, in the year of South Australia's Jubilee celebrations, the sporting teams of Highgate PS were given the names *conanda* 'north', *patpa* 'south', *maree* 'east', *wongarta* 'west' from a wordlist[11] the Principal, Gary Hildebrand, came across in the State Library of South Australia (pc Gary Hildebrand, 11 October 1996). Less than a decade later many of the children associated the words with animals embossed with them on the banners. Thus *conanda* was thought to mean 'swan', *patpa* was equated with 'platypus', *maree* with 'kangaroo' and *wongarta* with 'frill-neck lizard'. It is amazing how quickly the meaning of names is lost, as this example demonstrates. Staff and students in the 1990s had no idea of the source language for their team names.

A number of educational institutions in Adelaide now bear Kaurna names. Inbarendi College was established in about 1987. The Aboriginal Community College changed its name to Tauondi[12] in 1995 in recognition of the Kaurna people. A few educational institutions with Kaurna names, such as Tauondi or KPS, were established exclusively for Aboriginal students, but in most, Aboriginal students are a small minority. Some, such as Inbarendi College, adopt Kaurna names because they actively promote Aboriginal Studies programs and specialist programs for Aboriginal students. Several use Kaurna names extensively to refer to specific courses, programs or events. All three universities in South Australia make use of Kaurna names. The USA led the way in its Faculty for Aboriginal and Islander Studies, prompted by Lewis O'Brien who was employed at the university from 1991 until 1993. The use of many names and signage (discussed later) can be traced back to Lewis.

Aboriginal organisations and clubs
Since the early 1980s, many Aboriginal organisations based in Adelaide have been given Kaurna names. These include bodies concerned with land, politics, heritage and culture, community centres, sporting clubs, youth groups and businesses. Most have been given Kaurna names upon their establishment, but some older organisations have actually been renamed out of respect for the land-owning group. In the last 15 years, scores of Aboriginal organisations in Adelaide have been given Kaurna names by Kaurna people, often, though not always, seeking my advice for a particular Kaurna expression. A brief selection follows, where in all but the first example my advice was sought:

- Kura Yerlo 'near the sea', an Aboriginal community centre at Largs Bay named by Lewis O'Brien in 1986.
- Yaitya Warra Wodli 'Indigenous language place', the South Australian Aboriginal Language Centre opened in 1993. Named by Snooky Varcoe.
- Narna Tarkendi 'the door is open', Australian Indigenous Performing Arts Coalition launched in February 1995. Named by Katrina Power.
- Paruparruappendi 'to place oneself in an attitude of challenge', Northern Metropolitan Basketball team. Named by Pearl Nam in 1995.
- Tarni Burkanna 'people belonging to the surf', Nunga Boardriders Association, Moana. Named in July 1996 by Georgina Williams.

Currently there is a strong tendency to give Kaurna names to Aboriginal organisations in Adelaide, though this practice is by no means universal. When the Aboriginal Health Service shifted premises in 1993, it was renamed Nunkuwarrin Yunti, the name being drawn from Ngarrindjeri. Occasionally names incorporate both Kaurna and Ngarrindjeri words in an effort to include both groups. This happened in the case of Patpa Warra Yunti[13], the ATSIC

Personal names

W.A. Cawthorne was probably the first European to make use of Indigenous personal names in South Australia. Cawthorne's journal entry of 5 July 1854 gives some insight into contemporary attitudes regarding the use of Kaurna names:

> ... A very fine baby, a boy. We are going to give him a native name, Witto Witto, or Mullewirra, or Woowoodteyedloo. Some laugh, some scorn and some commended, but I intend having my own way. Charles Mullewirra Cawthorne. Mullewirra being the name of King John, the chief of Adelaide. (in Foster, 1991: 59)

In the end he settled on Charles Witto Witto[15], from Kaurna *wito wito* 'a tuft of feathers worn as an ornament by young men on the fore part of the head'. Cawthorne named two other children Florence Wadhillo and Nhudlo (see Foster, 1991: v, vi), though I can't be certain which languages the other names are taken from. Perhaps Cawthorne is the only European ever to officially use Kaurna names as personal names. I know of no other case. However, a student of KL&LE reported that she was approached by a non-Indigenous expectant mother for a Kaurna name. The mother was advised against it and subsequently dropped the idea after a bad dream (pc Beverley Mitchell, August 1997).

More significantly, in recent times a number of Nunga children have been officially given Kaurna names. Perhaps one of the first was Kudnarto Watson, daughter of Aboriginal lawyer and activist Irene Watson. Kudnarto was born in 1986, the bestowal of her name thus predating any of the formal Kaurna language courses. The name was suggested by Georgina Williams in memory of her Kaurna ancestor. At that time, neither Georgina nor Irene was aware that Kudnarto referred to the third born female child. The girl to whom the name was applied was in fact second born.

A number of Kaurna children born in the 1990s have been given Kaurna names and several Kaurna people with older children have told me that if they were to have children now, they would definitely name them with Kaurna names. Perhaps these are the beginnings of the reintroduction of Kaurna names into the Kaurna community.

One prominent Nunga family, descendants of the Ngadjuri man Barney Warrior, still retain the Warrior surname. It is now almost certain that this is an anglicisation of the birth-order name *Warriya* 'second born + male'. Barney's second name was spelt Waria by Berndt & Berndt (1993). With newfound awareness of the etymology of this name, serious consideration is being given by Josie Agius and other descendants to changing the spelling by deed poll so that it is clearly Nunga in appearance. Kaurna birth-order names are now promoted and used within the Agius family association (pc Garth Agius, 1996).

Students engaged in the Kaurna language courses are encouraged to take Kaurna personal names in addition to birth order names, at least for use within the language course. Whilst this practice was introduced for pedagogical reasons, Kaurna people have found it an especially meaningful aspect of the programs. Nunga students have often adopted the name of their totem where this is known, probably in line with traditional practices. It is likely that personal names, being drawn from nature, signified a totemic affiliation. Where the totem is not known, names are often chosen because the person feels an affinity with a particular animal, or maybe just likes the sound of the name. Others have chosen names based on character traits or occupations. One Kaurna student in the first class held at Inbarendi in 1994 gave herself four Kaurna names: Karro 'blood', being the translation of her English name Emma; Kari 'emu' as that was her totem; Wartoitpinna[16] 'parent of *warto* "wombat"', her son's totem; and Manmarra 'moonshine' because she liked its sound and meaning.

Some Kaurna adults have expressed an intention to officially change their names to Kaurna names by deed poll. Some have used their adopted Kaurna names beyond the language learning situation. Lester Rigney, for instance, uses his Kaurna name, Irabinna 'warrior', on his calling card, answering machine, conference papers and in a variety of other forums. For him, and a number of others, adopted Kaurna names have become an integral part of personal identity, much more than a tag for the purposes of language learning. Lester is one who has expressed an intention to officially adopt his Kaurna name.

Non-Aboriginal learners of Kaurna are, sensibly, unlikely to use their Kaurna names beyond the language learning context. Indeed, in the current climate, to do so could be construed as misappropriation of the language and most learners are sensitive to this. I, too, have had second thoughts about promoting the adoption of Kaurna names by non-Aboriginal learners. Perhaps the use of birth-order names, without the adoption of personal names or totems would be more acceptable. However, Georgina Williams (pc 22 November 1997) replied to my misgivings that she favours the adoption of animal names by non-Indigenous learners, together with a willingness to take a special interest in and responsibility for that animal species to ensure its preservation. This is a modern extension of traditional practices associated with totems. I know of one instance where a poet has adopted a Kaurna pseudonym, Kurraki Munato 'white cockatoo; third-born+female' (O'Connor, 1995: 122). Oddly, this female birth-order name was adopted by a male. The use of this Kaurna pseudonym was quite independent of the Kaurna programs and only came to my notice in March 1998.

Several Kaurna people, not surprisingly, have given their pets Kaurna names. Auntie Pearl Nam named her dog *Ngaityo kadli* 'my dog'. In 1996 Katrina Power named her kitten *Milte* 'red', Paul and Naomi Dixon named their pet magpie *Kurraka* 'magpie', whilst Georgina Williams named her dog *Marni Kadli* 'good dog'. There could well be much more of this kind of naming activity of which I am unaware, both among Kaurna people and others.

In 1996, a request from the Adelaide Zoo was directed to Paul Dixon, then Chair of KACHA, for Kaurna names for newly born native animals at the zoo. Whilst this was welcomed by Paul, it seems that with turnover of personnel, both at the zoo and within KACHA, the request has not been acted upon.

The use of Kaurna names is widespread and has been the enduring aspect of Kaurna language use, providing continuity between the past and the present.

Kaurna people are increasingly taking control of the use of their language for naming purposes. Some demand exclusive rights to the use of Kaurna names, others are keen to share the language, promote it within the wider community and use it as a means of fostering reconciliation, a theme taken up in Chapter 10. Controlling the naming process is a powerful means by which the Kaurna community can exercise their authority, reassert their presence and strengthen their culture, especially if this is done in combination with other activities.

The public function of Kaurna

Since the early 1990s, the public profile of Kaurna has been increasing. Public exposure to the Kaurna language before that was limited to archival materials, place names and mention in some publications on archaeology and Aboriginal Studies materials. Reference to the Kaurna language was minimal. Since 1990, the language has been used in a wide variety of ways and is now much more accessible to the general public, especially those interested in Aboriginal affairs and Indigenous issues. Increasingly, Kaurna language is used as a political tool in the struggle for justice. It is also being used in the reconciliation process through the delivery of speeches, singing of songs and other forms of cultural expression.

While much of this activity is directly associated with the formal Kaurna language programs, the use of oral Kaurna in public and the first posting of Kaurna signage was commenced in 1991 by Lewis O'Brien, independently of these programs. Individuals not directly associated with the programs, and who use Kaurna language in public, continue to emerge.

Kaurna speeches

The delivery of speeches of welcome to Kaurna country is now commonplace, almost established protocol at the openings of public events in Adelaide, particularly those related in some way to Aboriginal affairs. Major events such as the Adelaide Festival of Arts, which has wide public appeal, have given recognition to the Kaurna people; for example, they were included in *Flamma Flamma* at the opening of the Festival in February 1998.[17] Lewis O'Brien, Kaurna Elder, and Georgina Williams, Kaurna senior woman, both gave Kaurna speeches to a capacity audience of 30,000 in Elder Park.

Events at which Kaurna speeches are given range from these large public festivals and international conferences to smaller, more localised gatherings such as events occurring within KPS or Inbarendi College which are open to the public.

Kaurna in Society

Graph 8.1: Kaurna speeches in public, 1991-1997

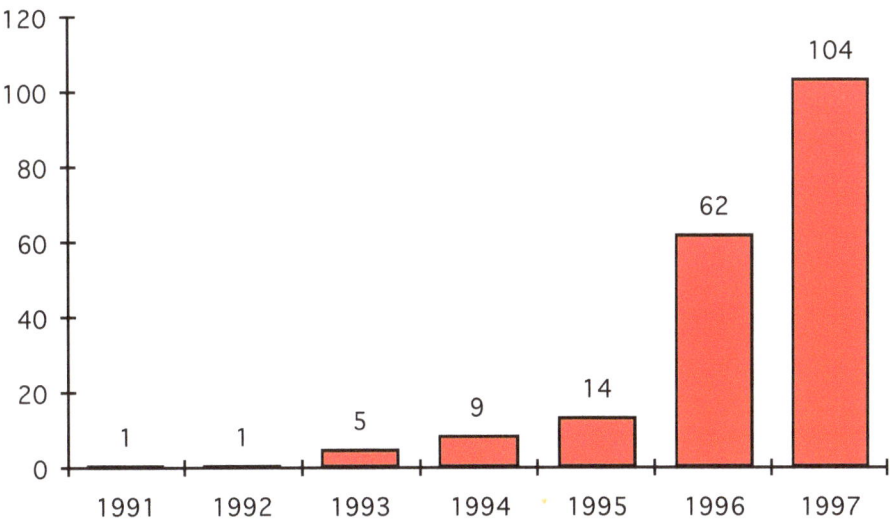

Contemporary Kaurna public speeches began in 1991 when Lewis O'Brien delivered a short speech introducing the Unaipon Lecture held under the auspices of the University of South Australia. In 1992 he extended a Kaurna welcome to world-renowned environmentalist David Suzuki at a public lecture in the Entertainment Centre, Hindmarsh. Concurrently, at the Kaurna workshops held in June 1991, 1992 and 1993, I had devised dialogues and speeches in order to demonstrate that the language could be used in extended ways to express a range of ideas. During the workshop at KPS in 1993, I was asked by the Principal, Alice Rigney, if I could develop a short welcome speech in Kaurna that staff and students could use when visitors came to the school. This was the result:

> Welcome to Kaurna Country   (Revised Spellings)   23/6/93

Ngangkirna, miyurna!
Naa marni purrutyi?
Ngai nari _____. Ngai yaitya miyu, _____ pirrku-unungku. Martu-itya wakwakurna'dlu ngai wangkanthi.
Pangkarra ia, Kaurnaku yarta, maiyarta. Kaurna pangkarra Crystal Brookunungku kauwantila, Cape Jervisana patpangka, karnurna paintyila marrikurlu.
Marni naa (niina) pudni iangka, ngadluku yartangka, inparritya ngadlu-ityangka. Kaarumarrarninga!
Narta ngadlu palti tarrka-utha, kurdi ngunyawai-utha naani (niinani).
Ngaityu yungantalya, yakanantalya.

Ladies and gentlemen.
Welcome! (i.e. how are you all)
My name is _____. I'm an indigenous person from the _____ group. I'm speaking on behalf of all of us students here.
This is Kaurna country, good country. Kaurna country extends from Crystal Brook in the north to Cape Jervis in the south and this side (to the east) of the hills.

> It's good that you are able to come here to meet with us. We hope you enjoy yourselves. We are now going to sing some songs and perform some dances for you.
> Thank you.

Some of the elements of this speech had already been developed in previous workshops. Greetings, leave-takings and introductions were explored and developed during the 1991 workshop, where Snooky Varcoe and I performed a short dialogue we had developed and rehearsed beforehand.

In all workshops and courses since 1991, I have included an element of extended oral language delivery, either as a monologue or a dialogue in order to show that Kaurna can be used to convey information, and that it can perform many of the same functions as other languages.

One of the first lengthy speeches delivered in public, outside the context of a workshop or seminar, was Snooky Varcoe's at the opening of Yaitya Warra Wodli (YWW) in February 1993. It was written in English by Snooky, then translated by me into Kaurna. Snooky welcomed the then Premier of South Australia, Lyn Arnold, Minister of Aboriginal Affairs, Kym Mayes and the federal member for the seat of Port Adelaide, Rod Sawford. The speech included a particularly moving paragraph (in Revised Spelling):

> Kardla Kaurna miyurna Mikawamangga painingkiana yaku ngadlinthi. Warltu ngadluku muinmurninthi miitarninthi. Ngadlu wingku palta paltarrinthi ngadluko warra. Ngadlu tadlanyarna padlunthi warra wangkanthi. Ngadlu yurirna padlunthi warra yuringkarninthi. Ngadlu mukamukarna wingku taakanthi muka Kaurnarli. Ngadlu padlunthi mukapanthi warra Kaurnaku.
>
> Ngadlu kuntu pungkurrinthi. Ngadlu tudnu pidnanthi iaku. Ngadluku tangkuinya taninthi.
>
> The campfires of the Kaurna people on the plains around Port Adelaide have long since gone out, but we can still feel the warmth in our hearts. We long for our languages again. Our tongues long to say the words. Our ears want to hear the words. Our brains still think as Kaurna brains. We want to remember the Kaurna language.
>
> Our hearts are heavy; we have long been waiting for this occasion. Our dreams are becoming a reality.

The final line of this speech includes the words RS *Ngadlu kuntu pungkurrinthi* 'Our hearts are heavy', an expression taken directly from the 1841 letter written by Kaurna children to Governor Gawler. Elements of Snooky's YWW speech have been used on a number of occasions since. The paragraph quoted above was included on a six-minute loop tape recorded for the *Ruins of the Future* installation built for the Festival of Adelaide in 1996.

Most speeches have been delivered by people closely associated with the Kaurna language courses. Many have been given by Snooky Varcoe and Cherie Watkins, both language specialists employed to teach Kaurna at Inbarendi College, KPS and Tauondi. Lewis O'Brien consults me by phone on the formulation of many speeches to tailor the content to the specific event. Another Kaurna Elder, Josie Agius, uses what she learnt as a language worker and student in the Inbarendi Year 11 program to deliver well-received speeches. Georgina Williams has emerged as another frequent user of Kaurna language in public since her involvement in the Kaurna courses at Warriparinga and the University of Adelaide. Though I have worked with all of them, they soon grasp the skills to construct their own speeches for future events based on elements previously learned. Two students of KPS, Nathan Kite and Trisha Agius[18], have delivered speeches at large public events with considerable eloquence and fluency.

Finally and importantly, several people who have had no direct contact with the Kaurna programs have used elements of Kaurna speeches developed in those programs to address gatherings. Typically they are tutored beforehand by other Nungas skilled in the delivery of Kaurna speeches. Lester Rigney began giving Kaurna introductions in all his introductory and guest lectures at Flinders University in 1996[19], having learnt the expressions from Lewis O'Brien and members of his own family. Both Katrina Power and Simon Lampard greeted people in public speeches in 1995 with the phrase RS *Niina marni*, a neologism first developed in the 1991 workshop. In September 1993, Muriel Van Der Byl used phrases including RS *marni niina pudni* (lit. 'It's good that you came'), a neologism developed in previous Kaurna workshops for 'welcome', and RS *ngaityu yakanantalya* lit. 'Oh my dear sister' for 'Thank you', developed by analogy with the phrase *ngaityo yungandalya* 'my brother! (i.e. I thank you)' (T&S: 23). On 30 March 1997, Edmund Wanganeen appeared on ABC TV news delivering a Kaurna speech at a reconciliation march. At the time, Edmund was unknown to me. It seems that he had 'picked up' some Kaurna from Lewis O'Brien and others and had been using Kaurna words, such as RS *panpapanpalya* 'conference', in the Northern Metropolitan Aboriginal Council (NMAC) newsletter for some time previous to this. This is early evidence that the revival of Kaurna is beginning to have a life of its own, independent of the formal language programs.

Over the period 1991-1997, I have noted 18 adults and five children (students from KPS) deliver Kaurna speeches in public and the number of individuals making Kaurna speeches is gradually increasing year by year. Once started, most, but not all, continue the practice.

Graph 8.2: Number of individuals giving Kaurna speeches in a given year

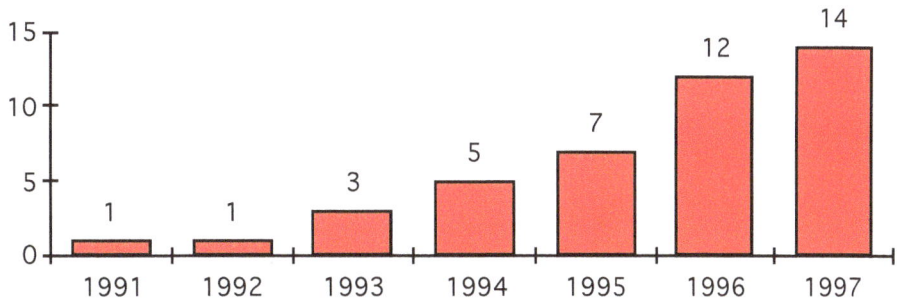

Kaurna speeches are being delivered more often and are getting longer. While many are still read, some speeches are now given without reference to notes.

With practice, delivery is becoming fluent. Many of the phrases and expressions are becoming familiar, so that someone like Cherie Watkins can prepare a speech appropriate for a particular event with minimal notice. Several Kaurna people report that giving Kaurna speeches is an excellent way to learn and develop fluency in the language (pc Georgina Williams; Eileen Wanganeen).

Public performance of Kaurna songs

The performance of Kaurna songs in public has been a major strategy in the promotion of Kaurna. Possibly the first time this was done in modern times was in June 1992, when Alice Rigney appeared on *The Bookplace* show on Channel 7 and sang *Kammammi's Lullaby,* written in the Songwriters Workshop in 1990. Kaurna songs are usually sung in public by children from KPS or by adult learners from PWAC and their teachers. Since 1997, the Alberton PS choir, tutored by Nelson Varcoe, has performed at a number of major events. Mostly, Kaurna songs are sung at celebratory in-house events, such as those associated with NAIDOC week, though sometimes they reach a much wider audience.

Kaurna songs are often sung simply as a celebration of Aboriginality, Kaurna culture and the Kaurna language. Snooky Varcoe, Cherie Watkins, Kathy Burgemeister and Veronica Brodie have sung for the enjoyment of residents at the Nunga Elders Village, Davoren Park. They are also sung as part of the struggle for recognition of Aboriginal rights at conferences, rallies, marches and other gatherings, sometimes impromptu, though mostly pre-arranged (see Plates 21 and 22). The subject matter of some recent songs reflects this struggle, in particular *Nguyanguya murr'adlu* 'Reconciliation'.[20]

Kaurna songs and hymns are also gaining some currency within church circles, as in the very moving memorial service for the late Dr Catherine Ellis, Cherie Watkins and Veronica Brodie sang *Tattayaingkialya* 'The Old Rugged Cross' in St Peter's Cathedral, North Adelaide. Dr Ellis, an ethnomusicologist, had had a long association with Aboriginal people, and with these two women in particular. She was instrumental in setting up the Centre for Aboriginal Studies in Music (CASM), so this was a most fitting tribute to her life.

A number of Christmas songs and carols have also been translated into Kaurna. Two were sung to a large gathering at a Carols by Candlelight service in 1996. Three women, Cherie Watkins, Veronica Brodie and Kathy Burgemeister, have been particularly active in promoting Kaurna songs and are sometimes joined by others at numerous rallies, political and church events. Nelson Varcoe continues to write Kaurna songs and perform in public. Many of his songs are written specifically for particular events. KPS students are also called upon to sing Kaurna songs at large public gatherings. In May 1999, Nelson set Ngurpo Williamsie's protest song (see Chapter 5) to music; KPS students sang a number of songs, including one of the hymns translated in the 1840s and their 'Welcome to Land' song, to a large crowd at the Journey of Healing reconciliation event. See Plates 24, 25 and 26.

Kaurna songs have been sung in public on at least 50 occasions since 1992, and, like the speeches, have increased markedly in frequency.

Graph 8.3: Performance of Kaurna songs in public, 1992-1997[21]

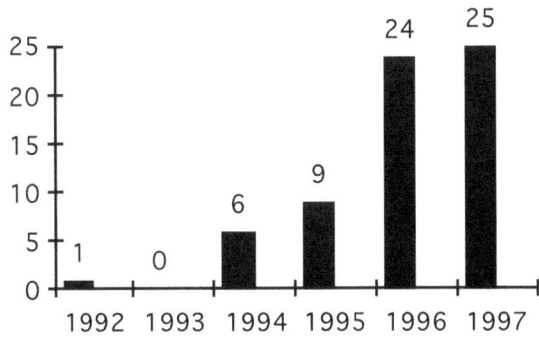

Dance, ceremony, drama and film

There is enormous potential for the use of Kaurna in the performing arts. Although little has yet been done, there is a strong desire to develop this area more fully.

In 1995, two pieces, *Ngadluko Palti* 'Our Song and Dance' and *Palti Makkandi* 'Thigh Shaking Dance', were written as part of the Kaurna songbook project. These songs, intended to accompany dance routines, have been recorded on tape, including introductions, exclamations and interjections in Kaurna to be sung out during the performance. However, the dances themselves have never been choreographed or performed. Kaurna people (pc Lester Rigney; Karl Telfer) have expressed a desire for this kind of performance.

A young Kaurna man, Joseph Williams, was one of the founding members of the Bapu National Indigenous Dance Company. After four and a half years with Bapu in Canberra, Joseph returned to Adelaide and formed a group of young Kaurna male dancers, the Tjilbruki Dance Group. They first performed at the Warriparinga Open Day in January 1996, when several Kaurna words, including RS *kardi* 'emu', were uttered.

The Tjilbruki dance group has performed at numerous events including the Victor Harbor Folk Festival in September 1996, where they proved very popular. The composition of Kaurna dance troupes seems to be very fluid. Sometimes Joseph and his brother Karl Telfer perform alone. Other times they involve other young Kaurna boys and sometimes girls. Karl also joins up with accomplished dancers including Steve and Brian Goldsmith, formerly of the Ngarrindjeri Narungga Dreaming dance troupe who performed in the 1995 Adelaide Festival; Andrew Lindsay, a Ngarrindjeri man who has been involved in the delivery of the Cultural Instructors and Tourism course at Tauondi for many years; and Yäpuma, a Yolngu man from North East Arnhemland. Karl, however, is the one who carries the Kaurna language input, by way of introductions, Kaurna song lines and interjections.

Joseph and Karl both want to include much more Kaurna language in their performances, and Karl in particular is making increasing efforts to do so. His introductory speech is highly fluent and spontaneous. He has worked with me on developing Kaurna songs and is keen to pursue a career in the performing arts drawing on his Kaurna heritage. There is considerable demand for professional Aboriginal dance troupes at major cultural events and conferences[22] and there is room for much development in this area.

The Kaurna community is also beginning to develop ceremonial functions drawing on elements of Kaurna traditions as recorded in the writings of missionaries, anthropologists and other observers. Smoking ceremonies have been performed in a ritual cleansing of premises after untoward events, or on the opening of a building. See Plate 23. These ceremonies are accompanied by the utterance of key phrases such as RS *Wakinha tuwila nurnti padni!* 'Bad spirits be gone!'

There is also interest in reviving some elements of traditional funeral practices and other aspects of Kaurna culture and ritual. Clearly the Kaurna language can play an important role here. It will be interesting to see how this area develops as people take hold of their heritage and traditions and forge a new culture which addresses contemporary needs.

There is great potential for the use of Kaurna in drama and film, though this has not yet been realised. Role plays have been used within school programs. In 1997, the Warra Kaurna class developed a script for a short play which traced the history of the Kaurna language (see Amery, 1998: 367). The play relies on the languages that the various parties would have naturally spoken. Aboriginal characters primarily use Kaurna, Europeans primarily use English, though there is also the use of Kaurna by sealers, missionaries and Protectors when they act as interpreters, translators and intermediaries. The use of English in this way has the added advantage of keeping the audience informed about the events unfolding. However, there is plenty of scope for the inclusion of Kaurna utterances in situations where their meaning is evident from the context. It was intended to perform this play at the end-of-year graduation, but this proved to be beyond the resources of the group.

However, at the Journey of Healing reconciliation event in May 1999, students from Emmanuel College re-enacted the reading of the Ten Commandments and parts of Governor Gawler's speech in Kaurna. They only had a few weeks to prepare, but the Aboriginal students performing the Kaurna lines were enthusiastic, with more students volunteering for the parts as time went by.

For some years now, I have wanted to see the production of a film based on the publications and journals of the Lutheran missionaries, on much the same lines as the script outlined above. This would be a long-term project. To be done properly, it would need to unfold over a period of years. Production of a film of this kind could serve as an additional, external motivation for Kaurna people to learn and use the language in the same way that *Dances with Wolves* performed that function for the Sioux. A number of Kaurna people are interested in these ideas, and are quite capable of performing major roles in such a film, provided they are given sufficient time and support to come to terms with these roles and the Kaurna language requirements.

Kaurna language in published materials

The preparation of Kaurna stories and other texts was discussed in Chapter 6. A number of publications, such as this book, also now bear Kaurna titles. Another example is Sheridah Melvin's 1992 report commissioned by the Aboriginal Community College on the learning needs of the local Aboriginal population (Gray, 1993: 57). This was entitled *Tauondi — Breakthrough* and Gray himself adopted *Tauondi* in the title of his publication. Two years later Tauondi was officially adopted as the new name of the College.

At least nine contemporary newsletters from various institutions or groups in South Australia bear Kaurna names, often the same name as the organisation or program distributing them. The earliest publication, *Tarndanya*, the newsletter of Adelaide Bushwalkers, dates back to 1948. The others are more recent and are all associated with Aboriginal organisations or programs. Some elements of Kaurna language are beginning to be used in these and other newsletters and ephemera. *Wadu*, the newsletter of KPS, typically opens with a letter from the Principal or her representative, which begins 'Na marni ...' (Greetings) and ends with 'Nakkota'[23] (See you later) and is signed by 'Ngarpadla Alitja' (Auntie Alice). The Kaurna language content in *Wadu* is not extensive, but the editor in 1996, Julie Hodgkinson, herself a student in the EWAC Kaurna course in 1994, attempted to include what she could. Some other Nunga newsletters make similar sporadic use of Kaurna, especially greetings.

Kaurna letters

On 3 June 1997, the Warra Kaurna class at PWAC drafted a group letter to Prime Minister John Howard in response to his failure to apologise on behalf of the nation to the 'stolen generations'. As mentioned earlier, this letter in Kaurna and English was modelled on the letter written to Governor Gawler in 1841 by children attending the Piltawodli school. The phrase *ngadlu kundo punggorendi* 'Our hearts are heavy' was drawn from the earlier letter. A copy of the 1841 letter was faxed to John Howard along with the newly written letter. Two days later the PWAC letter was read to the Teaching Australian Languages in Schools conference attended by Rob Lucas, then state Minister for Education.

Placards

During a professional development workshop held in Port Augusta during NAIDOC week in 1994, participants prepared placards in various languages for the annual NAIDOC Day march. The Kaurna placards featured phrases (here in Revised Spelling) such as:

Tampinthu Yaitya Warrarna!	Recognise Indigenous Languages!
Warraparna Kaurna	Speak Kaurna
Warra Kaurna tawardi marni	Kaurna language is really good
Ngutu-atpanthu Yaitya Warrarna!	Teach Indigenous Languages!

During the march itself, some slogans were chanted and recorded for Umewarra Radio, the local Aboriginal broadcaster in Port Augusta. The following year, these same placards and slogans were used in the Aboriginal Focus Week march in Adelaide.

Kaurna signage

This ranges from permanent official signage to ephemeral signs at events such as open days. Some of the first Kaurna signs to appear were *Ninna Marni* (RS *Niina marni*) 'Welcome' on the outside of the front door at KPS and *Nakkiota* (RS *Nakutha*) 'See you later' on the inside, together with signage on the toilets, following the Kaurna language workshop in 1990.

In 1992, Lewis O'Brien, then working at the University of South Australia, organised the placing of Kaurna signs within the Faculty of Aboriginal and Islander Studies at the Underdale Campus. This includes one major sign with all words and their meanings placed in a prominent position in the front foyer, supplemented by individual signs on the doors of various rooms. The following year, Paul Hughes, the Aboriginal Education Coordinator, himself a Kaurna descendant, instructed Greg Wilson to look into the posting of Kaurna signage within the Aboriginal Education Unit. I was asked to make suggestions, which were adopted. In the course of preparing these signs I consulted with Lewis O'Brien who was delighted to see that others were following his lead.

Many Kaurna signs were prepared for the EWAC Open Day on 6 September 1995 at the request of Auntie Edie Carter, AEW at the school. Signs needed for various displays included many proper names not easily translated, and so not all of the requests were fulfilled. At the Warriparinga Open Day on 27 January 1996, a number of Kaurna signs were prepared by KACHA with Cherie Watkins' advice. These included:

Kundanye (RS Kuntanyi)	cordial
Murki Turra (RS Murki Tura)	face painting
Meyu (RS Miyu)	Gents
Ngangki (RS Ngangki)	Ladies
Palti (RS Palti)	Dances

In schools, signs are posted in the teaching areas where Kaurna courses are held, to reinforce language learning and attempt to create a language-rich environment. Some students report that they have signs all around their house to help them learn common expressions and the names of everyday objects.

Murals and installations

Several murals and installations have incorporated elements of the Kaurna language. Murals including Kaurna text have been proposed for the Echo Tunnel in Belair National Park and installations for the South Australian Museum and Adelaide City precincts. We can expect to see much more use of Kaurna in this way in the future.

A mural entitled *Yerrakartarta*[24] was created by Milika or Darryl Pfitzner, a Kukatha artist from the Gawler Ranges on the Eyre Peninsula, and located within the Adelaide Plaza, North Terrace. The mural, unveiled on 1 February 1995 (*Advertiser*, 7 February 1995: 14), incorporates a number of Kaurna words and a sentence taken directly from T&S (1840: 67):

Natta atto nanga; yakko atto bukki nakki
RS *Narta-athu nanga; yaku-athu puki naki*
'Now I know (or understand) it; formerly I did not know'

Pfitzner has altered the translation slightly to more idiomatic English for the 1990s, 'I know it now. Before I didn't' and simply added the phrase 'Kaurna yerta 'This is Kaurna country". On the four main ceramic mural panels a number of Kaurna words and several Ngarrindjeri words label figures and features. All words used on Panel 4 are drawn from Ngarrindjeri, whilst those on panels 1, 2 and 3 are drawn from Kaurna.[25] Pfitzner's work is an important aspect of the public face of the Kaurna language and one of the few sites outside educational institutions where Kaurna text of more than single words is publicly displayed. Pfitzner consulted Kaurna Elders over the Kaurna language content of his mural (pc Lewis O'Brien, May 1996).

An installation in *Ruins of the Future*[26] incorporating some Kaurna songs and spoken Kaurna was designed for the 1996 Adelaide Festival. A six-minute loop tape, with Kaurna songs and a short text, played continuously throughout the Festival. The tape was recorded by Cherie Watkins and myself, though Fred Warrior, as Deputy Chair of KACHA, was present during the recording session giving his approval and support to the way in which the project was carried out. It was felt that there should be both male and female voices on the tape. A written text was incorporated into the sign explaining the installation as follows:

> BULTO TARKARIKO
> Martuityangga Kaurna meyunna ngadlu wanggandi 'Marni na budni pangkarra Kaurnaanna.'
> Yurringgarninga warranna bukkiunungko, birko Kaurna pintyandi. Warranna bukkiunungko warranendi tarkarirlo.
> RS PULTHU TARRKARRIKU
> Martu-ityangka Kaurna miyurna ngadlu wangkanthi 'Marni naa pudni pangkarra Kaurna-ana.'
> Yuringkarninga warrarna puki-unungku, pirrku Kaurna pintyanthi. Warrarna puki-unungku warrarninthi tarrkarrirlu.
>
> RUINS OF THE FUTURE
> The Kaurna people welcome you to their country. Listen to the voices of the past as they rebuild the Kaurna nation. The words of the past are being transformed into the future.

Ephemera

Kaurna ephemera has included a postcard produced by KPS with the Kaurna greeting *Ninna Marni?*, Christmas cards and T-shirts which feature Kaurna names and phrases. For the Aboriginal Focus Week celebrations held at PWAC in 1996 numerous Kaurna badges were made. They included birth order names; common animals, birds, plants and other words used as names; common or catchy expressions such as *Ninna Marni?* 'Hello', *Paitya* 'Deadly!', *Ngai Purle* 'I'm a star' and slogans or messages such as *Tampendo Yaitya Warranna!* 'Recognise Indigenous Languages' and *Warrabarna Kaurna!* 'Speak Kaurna!'. These badges proved to be popular amongst children and adults alike and were also distributed at the Tauondi Open Day.

Media coverage

Kaurna language programs have received some coverage in the media, initially on the *7.30 Report* on ABC TV in 1992 in a program addressing Aboriginal education issues and KPS. The introduction of the KL&LE course at the University of Adelaide was covered in the University of Adelaide's newspaper the *Adelaidean*, the Adelaide *Advertiser* and the *Australian* national newspapers and *DECS Press*, and also in radio interviews. Media coverage of local events has occasionally broadcast snippets of Kaurna speeches of welcome. *Lateline* (7 May 1998) on ABC TV included a short segment on Kaurna revival in its program on World English. The Kaurna letters returned from Germany (discussed in Chapter 5) gained considerable coverage on local and national ABC TV and radio news and current affairs programs in May 1998, whilst Ngurpo Williamsie's song gained media coverage in the *Australian* newspaper (May 1999) and on a number of radio stations, including the BBC.

Radio and TV broadcasts in the Kaurna language are probably a long way off, though other language movements demonstrate that they could prove to be a powerful positive force for increasing the vitality of the language.

Telephone answering machines
A number of Kaurna language specialists, individuals and institutions have recorded Kaurna greetings and leave-takings on telephone answering machines. This is another good way of increasing awareness of the language through public exposure.

Internet
In the early 1990s Nick Thieberger, then working at AIATSIS, posted information on the internet concerning the Aboriginal Studies Electronic Data Archive (ASEDA), which contains several files on Kaurna including T&S, TMs and other sources (http://www.aiatsis.gov.au/ased_abt.htm). In 1996, the Kaurna community was consulted by Thieberger's successor Dave Nathan, about posting a Kaurna dictionary and Kaurna language materials directly on the internet, as distinct from the ASEDA posting, which only provided information, not the materials themselves.

Discussion with the Kaurna community (Warriparinga, 29 April 1996) formed the opinion that it would be a good idea to establish a Kaurna Home Page which provided information about the community and its cultural and heritage programs, and maybe some short modules in the Kaurna language. But it was decided it would be a mistake to put the dictionary or comprehensive Kaurna materials on the internet. If people wanted that material, then they should have to pay for it. The Kaurna community wants to maintain some form of control over their linguistic and cultural heritage, whilst at the same time letting other people know that they exist.

More and more messages in Kaurna are being posted on the web. The KPS website posted a message from Alice Rigney on her retirement at the end of 1997, with an introduction in Kaurna. It also uses Kaurna instructions, for example *kawai* 'come in' and *muinmonendi* 'to continue' to move around the site.[27] Kaurna welcomes appear on a number of websites including that of the University of South Australia (dated 7 April 1998), Yunggorendi at Flinders

University and Port Arts. We can confidently predict that more Kaurna will appear on the web in the near future.

Cultural tourism

Cultural tourism offers a marvellous avenue for the use of Kaurna language. Excursions to sites of cultural significance have been an important adjunct to Kaurna language programs and provide a venue for the use of Kaurna very different from that of the classroom.

Aboriginal cultural tourism is rapidly expanding in the 1990s due particularly to demand from overseas tourists to see something uniquely Australian. Aboriginal culture serves as a major attraction at a number of well-known international tourist destinations, such as Uluru, Kakadu, Bathurst Island and Injinoo (Cape York). Some airport shops, in locations such as Alice Springs and Darwin, now deal exclusively in Aboriginal artefacts, art, music and literature (including literature written in or about Aboriginal languages).

Domestic interest in the cultures indigenous to Australia is also growing, especially in the cities. Adelaide is no exception, as a visit to the South Australian Museum, Tandanya and various Aboriginal art galleries will confirm. An emerging literature directed primarily at the tourist industry is exemplified by Philip Jones's (1996) book *Boomerang: Behind an Australian Icon*. The South Australian Tourist Commission distributes a glossy 16-page booklet with the support of ATSIC and the Department of State Aboriginal Affairs titled *The South Australian Aboriginal Tourism Experience*, which includes two pages on 'Adelaide and The Plains', in which the Kaurna people are acknowledged. While this booklet begins with a short text in Pitjantjatjara, apart from the place names Tandanya and Para Wirra, the Kaurna language is entirely absent. Cultural tourism has tended to focus on 'remote' and 'exotic' locations.

Kaurna cultural tourism

Kaurna cultural tourism has its roots in the efforts of Robert Edwards of the South Australian Museum and other members of the Tjilbruke Track Committee to promote public recognition of the Indigenous heritage of the Adelaide plains. A public appeal was established for funds to 'signpost Tjilbruke's Track with a series of sculptures and plaques' with the aim of making it:

> ... a permanent memorial to the proud people who lived on the Adelaide Plains before white man usurped his land ... a monument to the culture of the Kaurna tribe of Aborigines ... <and> a fascinating tourist attraction — an ideal one day outing along some of the State's most magnificent coastline for overseas and interstate visitors — and for ourselves. (Sunday Mail, 13 February 1971)

The article concludes: 'It will add romance and fascination to a well-blazed tourist route.'

From these beginnings, when cultural tourism was a non-Aboriginal venture by well-meaning people and Aboriginal people had little control over their own affairs, Kaurna people have, to a large extent, taken control of Kaurna cultural tourism, even though some of the activity takes place within institutions, such as the museum, national parks and local councils. Aboriginal organisations, like

Tauondi College and Tandanya are centrally involved in many of the initiatives, both within and outside their own organisations. Some activity is organised within the Kaurna community itself and almost all players in Kaurna cultural tourism at the time of writing acknowledge the custodial role of KACHA, and actively seek to involve members of the Kaurna community.

KACHA is aware of the potential for cultural tourism. At a meeting of the Blackwood Reconciliation Group at Belair National Park on 14 October 1996, Ricky Poole spoke of an offer from an Asian developer to embark on a joint venture with KACHA to the tune of $10 million to develop a major cultural tourist venture. However, KACHA, whilst not rejecting such proposals outright, is not wanting to rush into them, fearing that their cultural integrity could be compromised. Pressure from developers has caused or exacerbated divisions within the Kaurna community.

Of major cultural significance are a range of archaeological sites, such as Greenfields, an ancient burial site unearthed on 20 March 1992 (see *Advertiser*, 24 June 1995: 10), and sites of known occupation in colonial times, such as the Lartelare site at Glanville (see Brodie & Melvin, 1995). Interpretive centres have been proposed for both the Greenfields and the Lartelare sites, and they are to be included in heritage tours.

Many sites are located in the last remaining relatively untouched areas of bush along the coast and in the national parks dotted around Adelaide. Some are located on private property, such as Wirrina Cove, a tourist resort south of Adelaide. Others are like Piltawodli in the city, altered beyond recognition, but still important. The Botanic Gardens, the South Australian Museum and Tandanya are also main venues for Kaurna cultural tourism.

The national parks, especially Belair, are popular destinations for local, interstate and overseas visitors. Kaurna cultural tourism within these parks has been limited. Recognition of the Kaurna people, though minimal, is found in most of the management plans of the various parks. Cultural tours have not yet been instituted by the National Parks and Wildlife Service, though a number of employees, supported by community groups, are attempting to develop the cultural tourism dimensions of some parks in consultation with KACHA. The parks are an important venue for excursions organised by the Kaurna language programs.

Kaurna in Society 223

Map 8.2: Kaurna sites of cultural significance in the metropolitan area

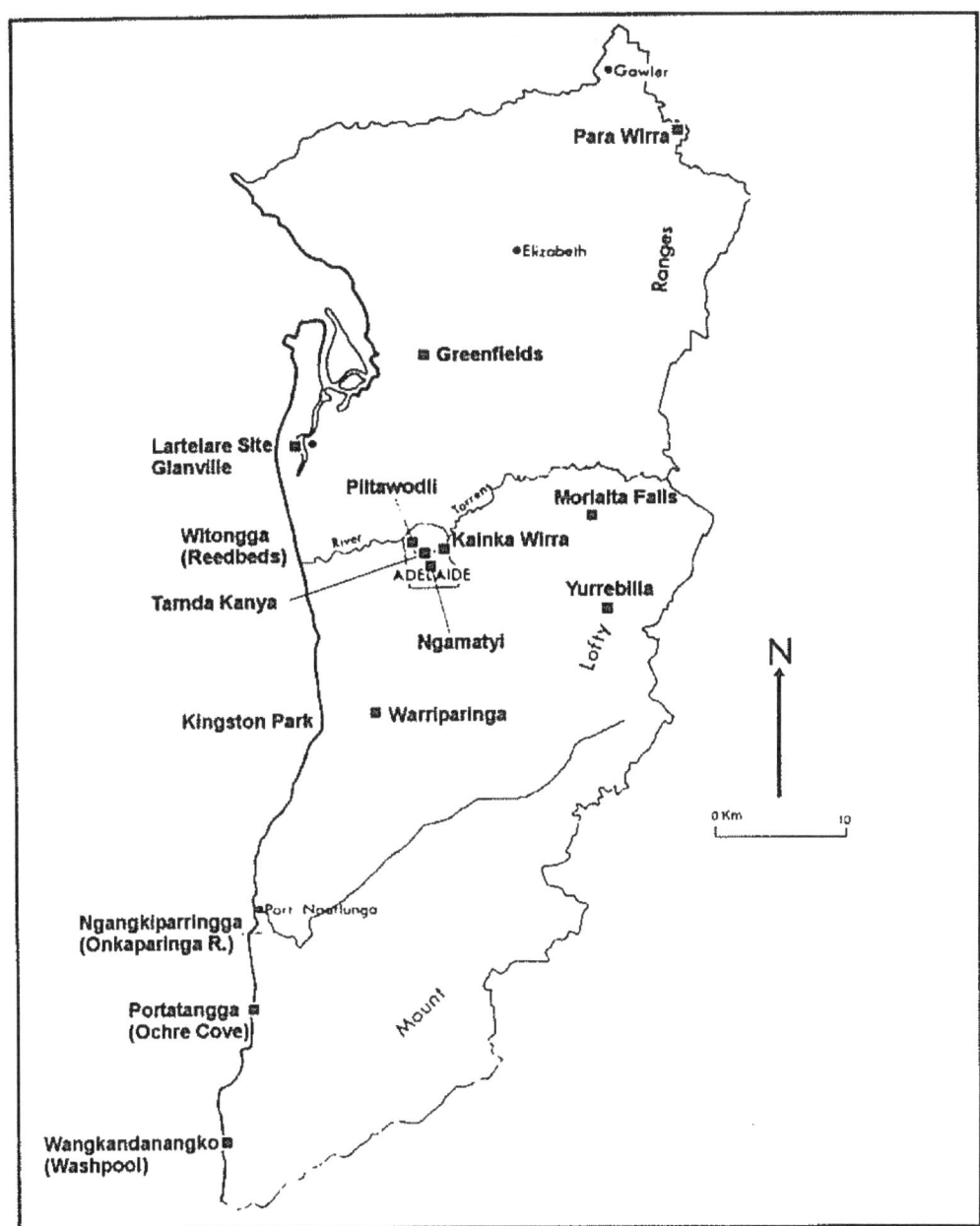

The remainder of this section documents developments in Kaurna cultural tourism, particularly the role played by the Kaurna language. Cultural tourism activities are interrelated: plans for the development of Kaurna trails are often made in conjunction with proposals for the establishment of interpretive centres; tours typically make use of existing trails and interpretive centres and may involve a number of agencies.

Kaurna trails and Kaurna sites

The Tjilbruke Trail, marking the beginnings of Kaurna cultural tourism, was laid out before there was much interest in the Kaurna language and before Kaurna language programs had been established. Documentation of the Tjilbruke Trail includes place names and personal names, but that is the limit of Kaurna language input. There is no Kaurna language signage on the trail itself. Other proposals do, however, plan to incorporate the Kaurna language in more significant ways, through the placement of signage and interpretive panels. The Piradli Trail, proposed for Belair National Park, is one such significant proposal.

The Tjilbruke Trail was marked with a series of cairns, and a sculpture by John Dowie, a non-Aboriginal sculptor, was erected at Kingston in 1972. Articles and booklets were published, notably Ross (1984), and the Tjilbruke Trail became a major component of Aboriginal Studies programs in schools (see ASTRU, 1985; EDSA, 1989: 97-101).

Malcolm Lane, a Nunga ranger of Ngarrindjeri and Kaurna descent, recognised the untapped potential of Aboriginal heritage within Belair National Park to promote reconciliation and understanding of Aboriginal culture and issues. He began working on a proposal to develop a Kaurna walking trail, obtaining the name Piradli from staff at the South Australian Museum, who drew on Tindale's materials. Malcolm's proposal was already well formed when he gave me a copy for comment in mid-1995. It included a plan to erect 17 interpretive signs, each with about half a page of text. The signs included more than 50 salient Kaurna words. I made suggestions for increasing the Kaurna language content and drafted a possible 10-line Kaurna text with English translation that might be placed on one major diglot sign at the start of the trail. Meetings have been held with the Blackwood Reconciliation Group, the National Parks and Wildlife Service and Representatives of KACHA to discuss the proposal, but no progress has been made. Four years on, the project is now 'on hold'.

More modest 'in-house' trails, such as the PWAC Tirkandi Food and Medicine Garden, established by the 1994 Community Studies class, have been more successful. Signage and an accompanying booklet titled *Tirkandi Food and Medicine Plants* were produced, which included 15 or so Kaurna words. Most appear to have been taken from T&S, though *wocalti* 'shield' most likely came from Cawthorne (1844). The sources for *coora* 'South Australian Blue Gum', *minnokorra* 'bulrush' and *minnokoora* 'cat-tail bulrush roots' are unknown. Signage also included the Tjilbruke story, a map of Kaurna territory and a brief history of the Kaurna people in addition to hunting and gathering practices. The booklet incorporated Snooky Varcoe's poem *Warrabarna Kaurna* 'Let it be Spoken', with an English translation.

Kaurna trails have also been proposed through local government initiatives. A Kaurna employee of the Adelaide City Council, Dot Davey (pc December 1996), has a vision of establishing a Kaurna trail through the city of Adelaide, especially along the Torrens River, identifying places of significance to Aboriginal people. She is keen to tell the general public about the Kaurna heritage of the area and the early contact history through a series of markers, signage, commemorative plaques and 'talking totems' or listening posts. She wants to place signs of welcome, in the Kaurna language, on all the major arterial entrances to the city. Dot is also keen to inform her own people: 'Our kids need this history', she told me. She is acutely aware that the young need to feel good about themselves and their people, and one way of achieving this would be to make Kaurna heritage more visible in this way.

Interpretive centres and displays
There is comparatively little Kaurna language on public display. As well as the *Yerrakartarta* mural and other art works discussed in the last section, there is a little signage in Stage 1 of the Warriparinga Interpretive Centre project opened in October 1997, and some place names, personal names and other salient vocabulary in other displays. There have been proposals to make much more extensive use of the Kaurna language to include words, phrases, texts and sound recordings, but few of these plans have been realised. In 2000, a plaque was placed at Piltawodli, which begins with Ngurpo Williamsie's song and features an image of Pitpauwe's handwritten letter (see Chapter 5).

The South Australian Museum established a small exhibition of Kaurna material culture, featuring almost all Kaurna material held by the museum.[28] As mentioned previously, there are plans to expand the Aboriginal Cultures gallery in a way that might include a major exhibition of Kaurna language. Preliminary discussions with Philip Jones canvassed the setting up of listening posts with tape-recordings of the language, and presenting contemporary Kaurna culture, with information about the current Kaurna language revival. As a central, high profile location, the South Australian Museum offers considerable potential for the use and promotion of the Kaurna language.

Plans are underway to establish an interpretive centre on the Warriparinga site, on the Sturt River, where an understanding of Kaurna heritage issues and Kaurna culture will be promoted. In 1994 the City of Marion, with input from KACHA, prepared a design which incorporated a number of key Kaurna symbols. The roof represented 'tjirbruki spirit – glossy ibis in flight' whilst other aspects of the architecture represented 'brukunga – tjirbruki's body – pyrites – fire; lu:ki[29] – tjirbruki's tears – rainwater cascade; warra pere – gully winds – river – earth wall; rocky outcrop – river – catchment hills'. A year later, a further plan for the Warriparinga site (see Playfair, 1996) included a Landscape Concept Plan in the form of a map, which features 'Karra Wirra ['redgum forest']; Kaurna Cultural Centre; Kaurna Cultural Walks; Kaurna Food Trail Walks and Fire Stones'. Stage 1 of the Warriparinga Project, *Tjirbruki narna arra' ngatpandi* 'Entering through the Tjilbruki Gateway', was opened on 30 October 1997 by Garth Agius and Vince Copley representing KACHA and the Kaurna people, Colin Haines, the Mayor of Marion City Council, Lowitja O'Donoghue and the Governor General, Sir William Deane (see *Advertiser,* 31 October 1997: 11). A commemorative board with Kaurna text and an information kit with five tastefully produced brochures which contain key Kaurna terms were produced. In mid-1999 text for a set of signs explaining the significance of a series of sites at Warriparinga was translated into Kaurna, though the signs are yet to be erected.

An interpretive centre with touchscreen displays and backlit panels was established in January 1997 at Mt Lofty Summit overlooking Adelaide. Panels include information on the Urebilla and Tjilbruke Dreamings as well as Ivaritji (spelt Iveritji on the panel). Few Kaurna words are included. The Urebilla story talks of '*Jureidla,* the two ears of the great ancestral giant Urebilla (pronounced Yura-billa)'. It is unfortunate that Tindale's spelling, *Jureidla,* is used without explanation. Will visitors link the word with the nearby town in the Adelaide Hills which appears on the maps as Uraidla?[30] People will be inclined to pronounce the j as in 'judge', whereas Tindale used it according to IPA conventions. The level of awareness of the Kaurna language in a new display such as this leaves a lot to be desired.

Tours and excursions

Some Kaurna people see cultural tourism as playing a major role in their community through the provision of employment opportunities and self-sufficiency. In 1994, Paul and Naomi Dixon's ambitious plans to develop a Kaurna Heritage Tour, Warriparinga Tour and Tjilbruke Tour were published by the Salisbury, Elizabeth, Gawler *Messenger* (19 October 1994: 5). Between them the tours would cover an area from Cape Jervis to Crystal Brook and offer jobs to 150 Indigenous people. The article quotes Paul Dixon: 'we have the only Dreaming trail intact so close to a major city in the world ... The only reasons we are going into tourism is to help preserve our heritage and to create employment for Kaurna people'. Two years later, despite little progress, Paul and Naomi were still enthusiastic about cultural tourism. The tours are yet to commence in an organised way.

However, cultural tourism remains firmly on the agenda of KACHA, as their ongoing participation in the Warriparinga project and other initiatives demonstrates, but with a clear recognition of its hazards. Paul Dixon explains the importance of site protection: 'obviously you can't take millions of tourists down to a site without putting something back in ... That's why it has taken the time it has taken, because it's that line between site protection and showing the sites off' (Interview, 21 November 1996).

Local family groups are being encouraged to take responsibility for sites within their area. But there are strong pressures from government to run cultural tourism in a more centralised fashion. Georgina Williams (KL&LE lecture, 11 September 1997) expressed disquiet about recent moves by the South Australian government to put $11 million into an Aboriginal cultural museum in a centralised location in Adelaide at the expense of ignoring local initiatives.

Tauondi — cultural instructors and tourism course

Tauondi is the main provider of organised Kaurna cultural tourism. It has long recognised the importance of promoting Aboriginal culture and heritage, both in schools and the community. The college grew from a submission put forward by John Morley in 1969 proposing 'the establishment of a more formal educational programme for Aboriginal adults' (Gray, 1993: 5). His proposal was directed at providing some training for teacher aides who would be 'an affirmation that Aborigines are a unique people with a unique and important contribution to make to Australian society' (Gray, 1993: 5). His submission stated that at the time he was 'unaware of any educational situation in which Aboriginal children are taught their own heritage, rich though it is in custom, thought, music, art and craft' (in Gray, 1993: 5).

The Aboriginal Studies Teaching Resource Unit (ASTRU) was established in 1975, just two years after the College, to 'promote a more positive understanding of the diversity of Aboriginal people and their culture by visiting schools and community groups. It was an area of race relationships which the College pioneered and which has probably reached over 100,000 people' (Gray, 1993: 9). ASTRU published a 66-page booklet, *The Kaurna Seasonal Trail Excursion Teacher's Handbook*, in 1985 complete with maps, diagrams and worksheets.

In 1988, the Cultural Instructors' Course was set up to prepare Aboriginal people to participate in teaching the Aboriginal Studies curriculum. In 1994, Snooky Varcoe started teaching the Kaurna language at Tauondi, as part of this course. In 1995, the Cultural Instructors' Course became the TAFE accredited Certificate in Aboriginal Cultural Instruction and Tour Guiding and included a unit titled Aboriginal Language, in which Kaurna is taught. Tauondi has recognised the importance and centrality of Aboriginal languages in Aboriginal cultural tourism by establishing the language unit as one of the core units of the course.

The Kaurna language taught in this course is oriented towards specific needs of Kaurna tour guides, with little attention to teaching grammar. Emphasis is placed on introductions, leave-takings and other basic expressions, and naturally there is a strong focus on vocabulary in the domains of fauna, flora, artefacts, ochres and other terms related to the natural environment. The course also emphasises Kaurna Dreaming stories and songs. It is practical in orientation, and students are required to demonstrate their language skills by running tours in a variety of venues, including the Tjilbruke Trail, Botanic Gardens, Adelaide Zoo and other locations.

Although primarily an education provider, in 1998 the college established a tour-guiding business, the Tauondi Cultural Agency, to provide employment for graduates of the course. The Agency runs tours within Cleland Wildlife Park, the Adelaide Zoo and the Botanic Gardens, but plans to extend them. Other locations, such as Predator Park, have also expressed interest. On the tours in Kaurna country, tour guides introduce themselves in Kaurna, and use salient vocabulary in their explanations of Kaurna culture and history.

Kaurna cultural tours are also run by individuals or small groups using varying amounts of Kaurna language. The Nendi[31] cross-cultural awareness program was established by Lester Rigney in 1993. Lester works with Aboriginal and non-Aboriginal kids deemed to be 'at risk', who are needing a direction in life. He facilitates camping trips along the Tjilbruke Trail, which include Kaurna songs and some use of the Kaurna language.

Christine Wilkinson, a former AEW and student of the Kaurna language program at EWAC in 1994, began working as a tour guide in the Botanic Gardens. In 1996, she registered her own tour-guiding business with the Kaurna name *Wirra Mai* 'bush food'. Christine incorporates a certain amount of Kaurna in her tours, including a greeting and the names of various plants and foods.

Since 1988, a non-Aboriginal naturalist, Waldo Bushman, has been running regular bush walks through the Mt Lofty foothills, commencing at Glenunga in the eastern suburbs. He chose the name *Pilyabilya* 'butterfly' from Williams' (1840) wordlist for these walks. Waldo has taken a particular interest in Kaurna bush foods and gives a slide show presentation in which he uses the Kaurna names of a number of plant species.

Language use within the Kaurna community

A number of Kaurna people have participated actively in formal language learning activities, delivering speeches in public, using Kaurna words for naming purposes, singing Kaurna songs and, to some extent, using the language with each other in social interaction. This section discusses the last of these cases.

The spontaneous use of Kaurna language within the Kaurna community is still fairly minimal, though people are beginning to use elements of the language in various ways for their own purposes. Importantly, there are signs that use of these elements is beginning to spread beyond those who have participated in formal language learning programs. The greeting *Niina marni?* and leave-taking *Nakutha!* are most widely used. Some use them on a regular basis, both on the telephone and face to face. Kinship terms, such as *yunga* 'older brother', *yakana* 'older sister' or *ngarrpadla* 'auntie' are often a part of the conversation. Conversational routines are still fairly minimal, but the Kaurna elements are gradually expanding. Some e-mail communications between Lester Rigney, Lewis O'Brien and myself are conducted at least partly in Kaurna. The limiting factor is time. The salutation, greetings, leave-takings, kinship terms etc. are automatic, but the rest takes time, both to formulate and decipher at the other end. As we are busy people, often the use of Kaurna in the main message falls by the wayside, as in Lester's message:

> Date: Wed, 4 Jun 1997 12:12:22 +0930
> To: ramery@arts.adelaide.edu.au (Rob Amery)
> From: Lester.Rigney@flinders.edu.au (Lester Rigney)
> Subject: Re: NGAI TIAKURTINNA <sic>
>
> Yungalya Pilta,
>   I have sent your email around to the mob. Yes, your attachment Document worked. I agree, the letter to Gawler by our mob would benefit our point of view and locate our struggle in the context of a long history of activism.
> Paitya! Nakkota!
> Ngai Irabinna Kudnuitya, ninko yunga.

Kaurna in Society 229

On occasion I have formulated entire e-mail messages in Kaurna, for some of which I provide an English translation and other sentences I leave for Lester or Lewis to work out.

E-mail is a useful medium with which to begin to use the language. There is more time to formulate a response than in face-to-face interaction and to look up the books if need be, yet the response is, or can be, almost immediate. For those who lack confidence face-to-face, e-mail provides a useful means of practising the language in a non-threatening and face-saving way.[32] E-mail offers another way in which the dispersed Kaurna community can unite[33] and, though few Kaurna people have access to it yet, it has great potential.

Early in 1997, two Nunga learners of Kaurna engaged in a friendly fax exchange about a football match on the previous weekend. One message in the rivals' exchange read:

> Narungga inggani Raukkan tidnaparndo ngunyawaiendi.
> <'Narungga asked Raukkan [to] play football'>[34]
> Narungga worndandi, Narunggarlo Raukkan worniworninya.[35]
> <'Narungga is soaring, Narungga beat Raukkan/ Raukkan is easily beaten'>
> Narungga purtendi, Raukkan murka kopaiendi.
> <'Narungga is rejoicing; Raukkan is crying.'>
> Score: Narungga 23 goals 12 points; Raukkan 11 goals 9 points.
> (FAX message 1 April 1997 from Klynton Wanganeen to Vicki Hartman)

Though both sought my help, the text above was produced unassisted by Klynton, who had only participated in a formal Kaurna program for a few weeks. Much of the grammar is correct, though two different verbal suffixes are needed.

Some parents of children at KPS are learning Kaurna words and expressions from their children. One of them, Katrina Power, reflects on this in her interview:

> [I know more Kaurna] since my child has been going to the Nunga school [KPS] than I knew in my whole life. So I encourage her. We all speak as much as we can. We always refer to Kaurna words or Narungga words. We try to apply it as much as possible ... We've just got a little kitten. It's Milte, means 'red' ... I know colours. But these are all from the kids. And Ngungana [the Kookaburra Song] ... I know songs and stuff like that. But they're all from my kids. My kids are teaching me ...

> R: Have you learnt some of your Kaurna from a book or is it all directly from the kids?
> K: Yeh, mum and the kids, mum and the kids. I've never learnt anything Kaurna from a book. And Uncle Lewis. Uncle Lewis has been great. I love learning like that. . .

> R: So you use a bit of the language at home. At work here [Tandanya]?
> K: Yeh ... if we want to be discreet, you know, talking about someone we talk in language [LAUGH] so that the person referred to can't understand [LAUGH]. But there's no Board minutes in Kaurna yet, but we'll work on that.   (Interview, 9 December 1996)

Similarly, Lester Rigney learnt some Kaurna words, expressions and songs from other members of his immediate and extended family, and only subsequently enrolled in a formal Kaurna course, along with four other family members:

> So that's how I know these words, through mum, just talking generally and through singing in my family and my nieces and nephews speaking the language from the Kaurna school ... Even my own sister comes home and you can't stop her from repeating Kaurna language all the time and talking and trying to get her kids to listen and talk. Powerful stuff. And the songs, as we drive over to Point Pearce we sing the songs because mum and Eileen start singing and the kids start singing and so we're singing in the bus. And you can't help but be marinated in the language. (Interview, 20 November 1996)

As indicated in these interviews, songs are important in some Kaurna families. The spiral-bound songbook we produced in 1990, which included six Kaurna songs, has reportedly fallen apart through use in some cases. Kathy Burgemeister, a Kaurna person who has been involved continuously in Kaurna programs at Inbarendi College and Tauondi since mid-1995, responded to the question *What Kaurna words/phrases/songs do you use outside of the Kaurna classes?* as follows:

> All the songs we have learnt so far. The greetings. The Kaurna relationship terms. I have Kaurna names stuck on most things in my home and everyone now uses the Kaurna words. I find I am more confident about sharing the language and history as each week goes by. (Response to questionnaire, PWAC, 10 August 1996)

Since then, Kath reports a further increase in the use of Kaurna in her household, to the point where she claims it is becoming a 'second language', with many words, phrases, questions and replies in Kaurna being used. The children are no longer satisfied with mere words and want to know how to express notions using longer phrases. If Kath doesn't know, they expect her to find out from Cherie Watkins. The use of Kaurna in the home is reinforced by attendance at KPS. Roxanne, in Year 1, uses Kaurna to ask questions like *Wanti ngadlu padnendi?* 'Where are we going?' Often she feels no need to translate into English. Brendon, one-year old in 1997, listens and mimics Kaurna expressions and responds to Kaurna words and commands. Not surprisingly, he is growing up pronouncing Kaurna words without any apparent difficulty. As Kath puts it 'the kids are so natural with the language now. It's just like second nature' (pc Kath Burgemeister, 4 November 1997).

Some other Kaurna families use known Kaurna words within English, particularly in the context of child-rearing (Paul & Naomi Dixon interview, 21 November 1996). Some of these words, such as *tidna* 'foot', *mara* 'hand' and *kudna* 'poo' are original retentions, having been handed down within the Nunga community, while others have been acquired more recently. There could be much more informal use of Kaurna in Kaurna households and between different members of the community than I am aware of; there is certainly considerable enthusiasm. Developments on this front must be viewed from the perspective of a long time frame.

Summary and discussion

In this chapter I have made a thorough attempt to document all the situations in which the Kaurna language is being used, the media through which it is conveyed and the purposes for which it is being used. I can confidently say that I have documented the majority of instances of usage of the language, both oral and written, over the period 1990-1997[36] (see Amery, 1998 for details). There are few other spoken languages for which this would be possible.

The Kaurna language is 'awakening'[37] as Cherie Watkins, Alice Rigney and other Kaurna people would say. During the 1990s, it has developed from a language that was restricted to the written mode, known only from historical sources and some place names, to one which is being used to express an increasing range of notions relevant to Kaurna life today. In the process, it is gaining a range of new words and expressions.

Over the period 1990-1997 there has been strong growth in many areas. The number of Kaurna speeches is increasing exponentially, from just one in 1991 and 1992 to more than 100 in 1997; songs sung in public have increased from one in 1992 to 25 in 1997, and new songs continue to be generated at a steady rate. There is also strong growth in the use of Kaurna names by Aboriginal organisations, sustained interest and a new sensitivity amongst government agencies and the non-Aboriginal population. A limited number of Kaurna language publications such as song books and story books have also appeared. Other publications have included salient Kaurna words and acknowledged the source language. However, much remains to be done in this area.

The present indications are that the Kaurna language is still at the beginning of a period of growth and development. The language movement continues to gather activists, adherents and supporters. Kaurna is being taken more seriously in many quarters, within both Aboriginal and non-Aboriginal society. Viewed in another way, however, Kaurna still has a long way to go — most residents of Adelaide are still totally unaware of the Kaurna people, let alone the language. Perhaps in ten years' time this situation will have changed.

The greatest challenge, however, is to extend the domains of language use away from the formal Kaurna programs and staged use in public, where it is reasonably well established, back into the Kaurna community.

Notes

[1] Manning lists 'Warriappendi the name of a school at Glandore. Aboriginal for 'to seek' or 'to find'' (1986: 223), obviously drawing on T&S, without acknowledgement.

[2] The name Tukatja was probably identified as Narungga. The word is shared by both Kaurna and Narungga and is still known and used within Nunga English. The spelling Tukatja deviates from known Kaurna and Narungga sources.

[3] *Mattanya* 'owner; proprietor, master' (T&S: 21). Territory, or *pangkarra* is defined as 'a district or tract of country belonging to an individual, which he inherits from his father' (T&S: 36).

[4] Geographical Names Act, Section 8, Subsection 5.

[5] However, Dual Naming legislation applies only to geographical features. If Port Adelaide were to be known officially as Yartapuulti, this would require a name change.

[6] Many of my suggestions have been taken up. Others have fallen by the wayside.

[7] It is not clear why the naming proposal is taking so long. An in-principle motion was passed in early 1997.

[8] This charge was levelled at the Adelaide City Council place-naming proposal in *The Advertiser* (10 February 1997) in an editorial opinion titled 'Unsayable Adelaide'.

[9] In March 1998, I was approached by the Aboriginal Child Care Agency (ACCA) for a new name that more accurately reflected the operations of the agency and acknowledged Indigenous

peoples and Indigenous protocol. I suggested *Martuitya* 'on behalf of' and a theme *Martuitya taikurtinnako: wadlowadlondi kumangka* 'On behalf of families: sharing the load'.

[10] Wirreanda is not necessarily a Kaurna name, even though it appears to be analysable as *wirra* 'forest' + *yarnta* 'large, wide'. Cooper (1962: 37) lists a meaning 'place of big trees' compatible with this analysis. However, Manning (1986: 232) refers to Wirreanda in the Hawker district, established in 1877, as being derived from *wirra* 'gum tree' and *ando* 'rock wallaby', an etymology consistent with Adnyamathanha (Tunbridge, 1991: 61). Perhaps the old property in the Morphett Vale area could have been named after this place in the Flinders Ranges. Perhaps the names are quite independent, and it does have Kaurna origins.

[11] Whilst these terms are readily identifiable as Kaurna direction terms, the identity of the wordlist Hildebrand referred to remains obscure. He thought the list might have been Wyatt's. However, Wyatt's wordlists in their various forms (Wyatt, 1840, 1879, 1923) all use k-initial spellings. Yet the word *conanda* for 'north' perpetuates Wyatt's typographical error corrected by him (*konanda* -> *kouanda* 'north') in the copy of his paper (Wyatt, 1879) lodged in the Barr-Smith Library. Further, the word for 'west' seems to have been omitted by Wyatt (1879). Maybe there is yet another wordlist in the State Library with which I am unfamiliar.

[12] *Tauondi* [RS taunthi] 'to penetrate; break through'; *tau* 'hole'.

[13] Patpa Warra Yunti is formed from the Kaurna words *patpa* 'south' and *warra* 'language' and the Ngarrindjeri word *yunti* 'together', and was conceived as 'talking together in the south'.

[14] Yunggorendi Mande is formed from the Kaurna word *yunggorendi* 'to give to each other' and the Ngarrindjeri word *mande* 'house', in reference to a place of learning.

[15] A plaque in memory of Charles Witto Witto Cawthorne is embedded in the North Terrace pavement.

[16] In retrospect this probably should have been Wartongangki 'mother of *Warto*'. However, we were not aware then that the *-itpina* suffix referred only to the father.

[17] The opening ceremony also included a Kaurna float and Kaurna dancers. A photograph of Karl Telfer at the event appeared in the press (*The Advertiser*, 28 February: 1, 14), although he wasn't named.

[18] I have not worked directly with these KPS students, though I have been consulted by their teachers on occasion for advice.

[19] In 1997, Lester enrolled in the PWAC Kaurna program. As a result he has extended his Kaurna introductions and they become more complex.

[20] This song was included in the choir program in 1998 (SAPSMS, 1998), learnt by approximately 15,000 schoolchildren and sung to sizable audiences in the Festival Centre.

[21] There may well have been more occasions than this. It is likely that I am unaware of some events at which Kaurna songs were performed in public, though I suspect that most are included in this graph.

[22] In 1997, Karl attended an Indigenous Cultural Festival in France where he performed Kaurna dances, and in May 1999, he visited the United States.

[23] In early editions of *Wadu* this word is spelt *Nakkiota*, but in later editions is spelt *Nakkota* in line with reforms introduced, at the prompting of Lewis O'Brien in early 1995.

[24] T&S (1840: 61) translate *Yerrakartarta* as 'scattered; disorderly; without design; at random'

[25] The names of characters in the Tjirbruki story, including the name Tjirbruki itself, may in fact have their origins in Ngarrindjeri, but the characters are universally accepted as Kaurna ancestral beings.

[26] The *Ruins of the Future* installations were designed by architecture students in a design competition run by the Adelaide Festival of Arts. Designers were instructed to draw inspiration from plans laid down for the city of Adelaide by William Light who surveyed the city in 1836.

[27] I was not aware of the use of Kaurna on these websites until I undertook a netsearch for 'Kaurna' on 17 May 1998, which gained 57 hits. A similar search six months earlier resulted in far fewer hits, whilst in 1995, references to ASEDA were the only result. A similar netsearch on 25 May 1999 using Infoseek generated 88 hits, whilst Looksmart resulted in 388 hits.

[28] Unfortunately, very few Kaurna artefacts remain, so the exhibition of Kaurna culture is very small, but it does include some salient vocabulary.

[29] *Lu:ki* 'tear' is a Ngarrindjeri word known both from contemporary usage (see SAL Wordlist, 1985) and historical sources (Meyer, 1843; Taplin, 1879). Compare with *miikauwi* 'tear' in Kaurna. Kaurna words never commence with a lateral according to nineteenth-century sources.

[30] Certainly the visitor information desk was not aware of the connection when I rang on 4 November 1997.

[31] The name, Nendi, chosen by Lester in consultation with Lewis O'Brien, comes from the inchoative suffix 'to become; be transformed into'.

[32] A number of Kaurna people have told me that they would prefer to learn the language themselves at home, rather than in a formal course. Perhaps e-mail between kin or close family members or friends would suit some of these people.

[33] The dispersed Huron nation, now located in Quebec, Oklahoma, Detroit and Kansas, maintains contact through the internet, forming a 'Cyber Nation' (pc Linda Sioui, e-mail 23 May 1998).

[34] The glosses provided in < > brackets are mine. They were not included in the original fax.

[35] This line does not really make sense, as *worniworninya* 'easily beaten in a fight' is not a verb. *Narunggarlo* should be omitted.

[36] If current trends continue, it will become increasingly difficult to make this claim. In 1998 and 1999, I heard of many occasions and find many uses of the Kaurna language of which I had no prior knowledge. There must be many more of which I am unaware.

[37] This metaphor has some international currency as the title of Collis ed. (1990) shows: *Arctic Languages: An Awakening*.

9
Kaurna Language Revival: The Formulaic Method

> *... our dream would be to see it a bit of a bilingual language, I mean a dual language, where a lot of Kaurna people actually speak English and Kaurna as well. Now that's the ideal, where I'd like to see Kaurna is actually used as an everyday language not just for tourism or for heritage matters, but for day to day life.*
> (Paul Dixon, Chair of KACHA, interview transcript, 21 November 1996)

A revival of Kaurna as a spoken language?

There is a hope and a desire on the part of many Kaurna people to see Kaurna reinstated as a spoken language in the home and the community alongside English. This desire is clearly articulated by a number of Kaurna people at the centre of the revival movement. Jenny Burford questioned Auntie Alice Rigney on this point at length:

> JB: So do you think that Kaurna language will be spoken as a first language by future generations of Kaurna people?
> AR: Well, that would be the ideal, eh. That's what I would dearly love to see.
> JB: So you see it as an ideal. Do you see it as a realistic ideal?
> AR: I would like to say yes to that, because there's enough information around ... and there's enough good resources, human resources, when you look at the linguist we teach, work with and I think it could be a reality. (Interview, 29 October 1997)

Lewis O'Brien answers the question even more confidently:

> LO'B: Well I want everyone to be able to talk and greet each other in the language and hold conversations and developing it right to its fullest extent. That may take time, but it's worth a go at ... And I think people are seeing that it's worth it, to have a go at, for lots of reasons.
> JB: So do you see it as your hope that it will eventually be spoken as a first language?
> LO'B: Yep, I do. And I think it's important to do that. Because otherwise if you don't, well you may as well go with the flow, and then just be an Australian in the general term.
> (Interview with Jenny Burford, 28 October 1997)

Both Auntie Alice and Uncle Lewis have worked with the Kaurna language intensively over a number of years and participated in formal Kaurna language programs. So they are talking from considerable personal experience of the language reclamation process.

In the context of a long time frame, in a world in which he envisages that the basic necessities of life will be taken care of, Lester Rigney, too, is optimistic:

> So in a hundred years' time, if we can quell some of those things, I think Kaurna will boom. It will boom far more than I think linguists and our people give it credit.
> (Interview with Jenny Burford, 21 October 1997)

In the short term, however, Lester is a little more cautious and guarded in his predictions for the future. He sees the use of Kaurna restricted to a limited number of fixed expressions within English, such as greetings and frequently used questions:

> So do I think Kaurna language will be spoken as a first language of future generations? Sadly I don't think so, because there's been too much open wounds and damage done. I think that its only avenue is that it becomes a command use type of language, whereby we use it in a similar vein to Aboriginal English in simple commands interspersed with English. You know, 'Niina marni sister, how are you? What are you up to?' Because I think that's the only way that it can, that it will eventuate.
> (Lester Rigney, interview with Jenny Burford, 21 October 1997)

To see Kaurna spoken again on a regular basis is probably a universal desire among Kaurna people. However, they are under no illusion that the task will be easy, or will happen overnight. But is it really possible for Kaurna to be revived in this way? Or is it, as Dixon (1989, 1997) says, 'an impossible dream'? I believe that in theory it would be possible. There is no linguistic reason preventing Kaurna from developing to a point where it can be used for whatever purposes Kaurna people wish. However, there are many obstacles of a social kind to be overcome. Much will depend on the will of the Kaurna community in the long term and the support structures that can be put in place.

In terms of achieving this ultimate goal, or even the lesser goal of establishing Kaurna as an auxiliary language, it is worth considering a range of approaches to language revival. While we can contemplate the long-term future, it is probably of more use to focus on more immediate goals that are achievable.

Approaches to language revival

Several approaches to language revival have important lessons for the Kaurna situation, but not one fully meets the needs and aspirations of the Kaurna community and the Kaurna language as it is now situated.

Language immersion is generally accepted as the ideal way to learn a language, particularly in early childhood. French immersion programs in Canadian schools have proved very successful (Cummins & Swain, 1986: 55-56). However, these programs, mounted in a major world language, do not translate easily into the language revival context.

Kohanga Reo '*Language Nests*'

Innovative language immersion programs pioneered in New Zealand have made substantial progress in the revitalisation of Maori.[1] In 1982, the now well-known *Kohanga Reo* 'language nest' movement was initiated, linking the grandparent generation, who still spoke Maori, with the preschoolers. Between 1981 and 1989, 500 Kohanga Reo were established, catering for about 8000 children. By 1995, more than 14,000 children were enrolled in these programs (Keegan, 1997: 15). These 'language nests' have produced hundreds of fluent Maori-speaking children. Despite the success of the Kohanga Reo, in 1990 Richard Benton warned that the language was still on the brink of imminent extinction, even though there are now at least as many fluent speakers of Maori as there were in the 1880s and 1890s, and many more New Zealanders have some knowledge of Maori compared with last century. The problem lies in the demographic profile. Half of the fluent Maori speakers were over 60 in 1990. Whilst there are a good number of preschool children with demonstrable fluency, only a small proportion of the generations in between are fluent Maori speakers.

Unfortunately, few children emerging from the Kohanga Reo have an opportunity to continue their education in Maori and consolidate what they have acquired. The Kohanga Reo have given rise to some bilingual Kaupapa Maori schools, but in 1990 less than 2% of Maori children attended these schools. The situation has improved since (see Keegan, 1997: 18), but still less than 20% of Maori children have access to any form of Maori immersion education. There is an acute shortage of Maori-speaking teachers. The Kohanga Reo have created a demand for adult language classes, giving rise to the Te Atārangi movement, so that parents can learn and support their children's Maori language development.

The Kohanga Reo 'Language Nest' approach has been hailed as an outstanding success and has been successfully replicated in Hawai'i where it is known as Punana Leo 'Language Nest' (Schütz, 1994: 365-369). In 1992 there were 131 children between the ages of three and five enrolled in Punana Leo programs. They hear and speak only Hawai'ian for ten hours a day, five days a week.

The 'Master-Apprentice' method (Hinton, 1994)
Hinton (1994), whilst recognising the outstanding success of the Maori and Hawai'ian language nests, questions their applicability to the languages of California:

> Despite the inspiring nature of the Hawaiian program, the number of speakers and even of people who might ever be interested in speaking a given language is so small for each of the California languages that the idea of training hundreds or thousands of children to speak one seems unthinkable. In California, teaching even one child to speak is a great feat.
> (Hinton, 1994: 229)

Instead, she proposes a Master-Apprentice method which she claims is more suited to the Californian situation where the languages are no longer used on a daily basis. In the Master-Apprentice method, an older fluent speaker is paired with a motivated young adult keen to learn the language on a full-time basis. The pair spends about four months together with their living expenses funded so that they can devote all their time to language learning. The apprentice accompanies the master participating in a range of activities including traditional pursuits such as hunting, the making of traditional crafts or participating in ceremonies, and non-traditional activities such as fixing a car, going to the store etc. At least 20 hours per week are spent actively learning the language.

Both the 'Language Nest' and 'Master-Apprentice' approaches are based on the principles of language immersion. In the Kaurna situation, language immersion is impossible for us to achieve, at least in the early stages of language reclamation. Still, there are lessons to be learnt. We can strive to create immersion-like experiences, but until the teachers of Kaurna programs gain more fluency in the language and there are more situations in which learners can hear, see and use Kaurna, immersion is simply not achievable.

I was asked by Paul Dixon, then Chair of KACHA, at a meeting of the committee held at the end of 1995 if I thought it would be possible for them to conduct their meetings in Kaurna. I responded by preparing a short tape with an accompanying transcript of a number of Kaurna expressions that I believed would be useful in a meeting context. Expressions were chosen that were not too difficult to learn. I advocated the use of short utterances such as RS *Watu!* 'Agreed', RS *Ngana wangki?* 'Who said?' RS *Warrarti!* 'Be quiet!', which could be dropped into what was otherwise English conversation. In the earliest stages, the learning of just one expression each week would be a useful start. As long as everyone makes the effort to learn it and use it then it will become established as a habit, an accepted normative use within KACHA or within the community. Once people get into the habit of learning and using the new expressions and feel comfortable with them, I would anticipate that the rate of incorporation of new expressions into the speech repertoire would increase.

Prompted by Paul's request, and drawing on my experiences and observations of Kaurna language use at KPS and in the community, I have proposed what I call the Formulaic Method for language revival.

The Formulaic Method

The 'Formulaic Method' entails the staged introduction of well-formed utterances. By contrast with language immersion, or Hinton's 'Master-Apprentice' method, this method, particularly in the early stages, involves the use of vast amounts of English with just a little Kaurna. However, I propose to introduce only grammatically well-formed and complete utterances which draw to a maximal extent on Kaurna grammar as we know it from the nineteenth-century sources.

Initially, I propose that minimal one-word utterances that can stand alone as questions, responses, commands, greetings, leave-takings and the like should predominate in the repertoire taught and used. Words which are short, easy to pronounce, easy to remember and, most importantly, carry a high functional load are introduced first. We might begin by teaching the word RS *paitya* 'deadly'. 'Deadly!', meaning something like 'terrific!' or 'super!', is a frequently used utterance that distinguishes Nunga English from mainstream Australian English. As it stands alone, children can drop it into their speech and use it at the appropriate time. The expression RS *paitya!* can be used often and is easily pronounced. RS *Kurukarri!* 'Shame!' is another expression which draws on Nunga English, where the expression 'Shame job!' is an entrenched defining feature of the social dialect, uttered (often in jest) when someone steps out of line, does something outrageous or breaks cultural mores.

Swearwords and insults also serve as self-contained expressions. Several 'opprobrious terms', as T&S called them, were recorded in the German sources. Additional loan translations of some mild English obscenities, such as RS *kudnapurtu* 'full of shit', were introduced at KPS in 1997 and 1998 and have served as a strong motivating factor, with students finding their own friendly insults. Staff at KPS report that their introduction has been empowering for students at Fremont-ECHS and has had something of a calming effect. Students can say things in their own language without teachers and students in the mainstream school getting upset. The introduction of these kinds of terms might also work well in the context of reintroducing the language into the Kaurna community, but as yet is untested.

Other useful one-word expressions that stand alone and can be used often in answer to questions might include (RS):

nii	'yes'	*marni*	'good'
yaku	'no'	*madlana*	'none; nothing'
wuintyi	'maybe'	*muinmu*	'more; again'
ku	'OK'		

Pronouns, too, especially *ngai* 'me', *niina* 'you', *pa* 'he, she, it' are useful as single word responses in certain contexts, although there are certain grammatical complexities, with the need to distinguish between Nominative and Ergative cases and singular and dual number.

Question words are very useful one-word expressions and should be introduced early. In Kaurna they include:

ngana	'who'	*waa*	'where'
ngaintya	'what'	*wanti*	'where to'
nganaitya	'why'	*wathangku*	'where from'
wamina	'what's up? what's wrong? what's the matter?'		

Simple commands are also useful as high frequency stand-alone expressions. But here again there is some complexity, with the need to distinguish between singular, dual and plural addressees. Useful singular imperatives include:

Tika!	'Sit down'
Karrikarri!	'Stand up!'
Parni kawai!	'Come here!'
Nurnti padni!	'Go away!' etc.

In the context of the classroom, additional plural imperatives are also very useful, as are negative imperatives, not distinguished for number. They include:

Yuringkarninga!	'Listen!'	*Warrarti!*	'Be quiet!'
Parni Nakuinga!	'Look here!'	*Pilyapilyarti!*	'Quieten down!'
Tikainga!	'Sit down!'	*Wayirti!*	'Don't move!' etc.

These kinds of expressions were amongst the first sought by teachers and childcare workers in the very first Kaurna workshop in 1990.

In addition, the greetings *Niina marni?* (Sg.) and *Naa marni?* (Pl.) and response *Marni'ai*, welcome *Marni niina pudni* (Sg.) and *Marni naa pudni* (Pl.), leave-taking *Nakutha* 'will see (ie goodbye)', thanks *Ngaityalya!* and apology *Yakalya!* 'I'm sorry' should be introduced first because of their high functional load, even though some of these expressions are a little longer.

I encourage people to use these expressions in preference to English whenever and wherever appropriate within the conversation, and to use them as often as possible. Initially, the interlocutor should feel under no pressure to respond in Kaurna, nor should the speaker expect a response in Kaurna. The expressions need to be incorporated into the conversation as natural and automatic elements of the speech event.

Once the basic one-word expressions are known and used confidently, longer and longer expressions can be introduced in succession. Useful examples are as follows:

Padni'adlu!	'Let's go!'
Parni ngatpa!	'Come in!'
Wanti niina?	'Where are you going?'
Warru-ana padni!	'Go outside!'
Ngana wangki?	'Who said?'
Ngai kuma.	'Me too.'
Naawi X?	'How many X?' (e.g. *Naawi miyurna?* 'How many people?')
Ngai taityu!	'I'm hungry!'
Niina purli?	'Have you had enough?' (T&S 'Are you satiated?')
Maimpi?	'Do you want something to eat?'

Even longer expressions that could usefully be introduced fairly early include:

Ngai kudnawardli-ana padninthi.[2]	'I'm going to the toilet.'
Ngai wardli-ana padninthi.	'I'm going home.'
Ngai titawardli-ana padninthi.	'I'm going to the shops.'
Marni milirntuwarta!	'Have a good weekend.'
Pakadla parni-apinthu!	'Pass the salt!'
Nala-alati ngadlu padninthi?	'When are we going?'

Of course the usefulness of particular expressions will depend somewhat on the individual's situation, whether they intend to use the language at home, within KACHA meetings, at school, Nunga social gatherings or on the football field etc.

The formulaic method entails building up a stockpile of speech formulas of increasing complexity that will gradually replace English in conversation. This method sits well with the ways in which Kaurna is currently being used. Most Kaurna language, including longer pieces like speeches, is learnt and used as speech formulas. Within speeches, certain phrases such as *Martu-ityangka Kaurna miyurna ngai wangkanthi* 'I am speaking on behalf of the Kaurna people' are frequently used.

A theoretical basis for the Formulaic Method

Applied linguists such as Corder (1973) have looked at the question 'What does it mean to know or speak a language?' within the context of teaching foreign languages or English as a second language. Traditionally, the answer to this question focused on grammar and lexicon, ignoring subtler questions of idiomatic usage and 'ways of talking' (Grace 1987: 92). This grammar-lexicon model of language, as Pawley (1985: 85) refers to it, whilst accounting for much linguistic behaviour is deficient in a number of ways.

Communicative competence[3] involves more than the ability to construct grammatical sentences. Rather it entails the ability to use language appropriately. In addition to 'linguistic competence' it includes paralinguistics, cultural knowledge and other more peripheral aspects.

Pawley (1985: 87-88) identifies a range of 'ordinary language-users' understandings of what it takes to know a language' distilled from anecdotes of what they say about learning and using languages. They are as follows:

> a) grammaticality,
> b) pronunciation of consonants and vowels,
> c) musical conventions: intonation, stress and rhythmic patterns, voice quality, modulations of volume, etc.
> d) productive fluency: conforming to norms of tempo, structure and quantity for chunking utterance elements into fluent units,
> e) hearing fluency: being able to decode fluent speech,
> f) idiomaticity: the selection of familiar, nativelike ways of saying things as opposed to things that are merely grammatical,
> g) lexical knowledge: including the ability to distinguish between those expressions that are lexicalised (standard designations) and those that are ad hoc descriptions,
> h) contextual appropriateness: saying the right thing at the right time,
> i) coherence: saying things that make sense in terms of normal understandings of the world shared by a particular speech group, and in terms of standard procedures of inference,
> j) inference: being able to make sense of ordinary discourse: to work out conversational implicatures, to understand the communicative intentions of particular utterances,
> k) creativity, of various kinds, including:
> i) phonological — making up new word forms, ii) syntactic, iii) semantic,
> iv) contextual — apt matching of expression with situational context in a non-routine way. A distinction (not sharp) may perhaps be drawn between rule-governed creativity and special kinds of creative use of language in which conventions are broken or manipulated to achieve special effects; as in Pig-Latin, puns, metaphors, etc.

Pawley & Syder (1983) argue that fluency is achieved by learning a vast number of preformed 'chunks' of language in the form of 'lexicalized sentence stems'. As this is a somewhat radical departure from traditional notions of language and language learning I quote them in detail:

> fluent and idiomatic control of a language rests to a considerable extent on knowledge of a body of 'sentence stems' which are 'institutionalized' or 'lexicalized'. A lexicalised

sentence stem is a unit of clause length or longer whose grammatical form and lexical content is wholly or largely fixed; its fixed elements form a standard label for a culturally recognized concept, a term in the language. Although lexicalized in this sense, most such units are not true idioms but rather are regular form-meaning pairings. The stock of lexicalized sentence stems known to the ordinary mature speaker of English amounts to hundreds of thousands. In addition there are many semi-lexicalized sequences, for just as there is a continuum between fully productive rules of sentence formation and rules of low productivity, so there is a cline between fully lexicalized formations on the one hand and nonce forms on the other.

(Pawley & Syder, 1983: 191-192)

They go on to provide many examples of these 'lexicalized sentence stems', and in another paper, Pawley (1991) gives a detailed analysis of the complexity involved in being able to 'talk cricket'. Other authors (e.g. Kuiper & Haggo, 1984) have analysed speech events such as livestock auctions, race calling and oral poetry, where remarkable feats of oral language fluency are required. This fluency is achieved by a good command of speech formulas. (See also Pawley, 1992.)

The formulaic approach draws on the insights afforded by the research of Grace, Pawley and Syder cited above. It is clear that reviving languages from written records is more than learning the vocabulary, internalising the rules of grammar and memorising the corpus of sentences contained in the historical sources, even though this is all that is available. Relatively few preformed 'chunks' exist and in most cases we do not have a good sense of the contexts in which the recorded utterances were said. Conversational routines, speech formulas, idioms, ways of talking about things and of expressing ideas need to be developed. In so doing, language conventions are established. This makes acquisition of Kaurna doubly hard because this repertoire of preformed 'chunks' of language has to be built up bit by bit. The Kaurna language learner needs to acquire these preformed 'chunks' just as learners of any other language do.

Addressing lexical gaps and developing neologisms is the more obvious end of a wider spectrum of language development, many aspects of which are subtler and more difficult to pinpoint and describe.

Introducing the language into the Kaurna community

The formulaic approach, outlined above, is as yet largely untested. Despite showing some interest, KACHA is yet to introduce Kaurna expressions into their meetings in a systematic way. The Kaurna sports terminology and expressions developed by Lester Rigney in 1997 have been partially utilised by some classes at KPS, but are yet to be embraced by a Nunga sporting team. Some speech formulas have been introduced at KPS, but the classroom is an artificial situation. Several Kaurna people are gradually introducing an expanding range of fixed expressions into their speech, but this is happening on an ad hoc basis using their own initiative.

In 1999, submissions were prepared to fund a series of workshops which would bring teachers from KPS together with members of the Kaurna community and myself as linguist to systematically develop a range of high-frequency expressions for use within specific domains, beginning with parent/caregiver <—> infant/child interaction. It is proposed to compile these expressions in a booklet which would serve as something of a 'manual for raising your child speaking Kaurna'. But these plans are yet to be realised and the formulaic method has not yet been implemented on a systematic basis. However, it has been accepted on an ideological level by key Kaurna language enthusiasts who wholeheartedly backed the proposal to hold the series of workshops. Basically it is a logistical problem of bringing people, who otherwise lead busy lives, together to engage in this activity.

Perhaps the greatest failure of the formal Kaurna language programs has been an inability to attract many Kaurna people as active learners and participants in the programs. Over the eight year period 1990-1997, only about 40[4] Kaurna adults have ever accessed any of the formal language learning courses. This is despite very positive and supportive comments made by Kaurna Elders and members of KACHA.

The desire to introduce the language into the Kaurna community is an issue which concerns Kaurna language enthusiasts, such as Lester Rigney, who observed:

> ... if we are going to reclaim Kaurna language, it must not just go with the school, right? like the goonyas have done. We've got to have a mechanism in our structures whereby there is a whole group learning. Let's dream for a possibility. Why isn't language taking place in the community? ... Why isn't there a community aspect of trying to get these things up and running? Why aren't Aboriginal organisations taking on the language acquisition ... it's only done at schools and universities.
> (Interview with Jenny Burford, 21 October 1997)

Fishman (1991: 408) points to the relative difficulty of establishing the language at the grass roots level:

> It is obviously harder to build Xish families, neighbourhoods and communities than to establish Xish schools, publications or non-print media. However, the former immediately provides a base for intergenerational continuity and a point of departure for stages that come after it and can be supported by it, whereas the latter do not because they are too restricted in time and place and have no daily, intimate, socialization foundation underlying them. At best they can contribute to the 'spirit' necessary for such a foundation to be laid, but they do not lay it themselves.

The difficulty in actively involving Kaurna people is due, I believe, to a multiplicity of reasons. There are some obvious logistical problems. Kaurna people are dispersed widely across Adelaide and may live some distance away from the venues where Kaurna language is offered. Many do not own motor vehicles, relying on public transport. The Kaurna course at PWAC is run in the evening and is located on the northern fringe of the metropolitan area. It is simply inaccessible for most Kaurna people. Some students rely on others for transport. One student's non-attendance may result in several not attending. Also, a number of Kaurna people, who might otherwise be involved in programs, work full time and have family commitments after hours.

However, there are subtler reasons, many of which reflect the relatively poor participation rate of Aboriginal people in the education process (see SSABSA, 1998). Some older members of the Kaurna community have expressed a wish to be able to learn and speak Kaurna, but consider themselves too old to be able to learn. There is perhaps an unwillingness to participate in language classes for fear of being 'shown up' by younger learners. Age, of course, is not a barrier in itself, it is simply perceived to be so by some. People may feel insecure about the fact that they are not able to speak their own language. This is highlighted by the fact that some non-Aboriginal people, such as myself, have a much greater knowledge of their language than they do. Coupled with this is a reluctance to learn from a non-Aboriginal person. This is a factor which has been mentioned to me on a number of occasions (see discussion on the role of linguistics in Chapter 10), and one which is probably very important in explaining the relatively low rates of participation. The Kaurna people who do actively participate are often those operating within the education system or who have experience in working alongside non-Aboriginal people.

Kaurna language activities tend to revolve around a handful of people, as noted by Lester Rigney:

> I think that the Kaurna reclamation is almost personality driven. And if tomorrow Ngarrpadla Cherie, Mum and Rob were to go, touch wood, I think that the whole process would fall. So we're not good at training new ones to come through.
>
> (Interview with Jenny Burford, 21 October 1997)

The credibility of the teachers[5], and their own personal networks and associations with the community, are often pivotal in determining who is attracted to the courses. Kaurna people tend to get involved in activities or issues as families, not individuals. The involvement of family members may encourage others to attend. On the other hand, the presence of some families may inhibit or preclude the attendance of others.

There is perhaps a reluctance to learn the language in public. A number of Kaurna people have requested tape recordings for use at home, to avoid embarrassing themselves in public (cf. p. 172 above). Some do in fact spend considerable time perusing the Kaurna materials in private. Perhaps it would be a good idea to produce a 'Teach Yourself Kaurna' kit using a multimedia computer program, video tapes or cassette tapes. This could give people at least some familiarity with Kaurna, thus raising their confidence to the point of being willing to participate actively in a course of study. Part of my motivation for producing the language learning tapes for the KL&LE course was to be able to make this material available, at low cost, to members of the Kaurna community. These tapes have not yet been widely disseminated due to non-resolution of the copyright issue.[6]

Whilst many Kaurna people acknowledge the importance of learning the language, it is not the highest priority for most. KACHA itself has been more concerned with material culture and non-linguistic aspects of cultural heritage. KACHA is a small organisation which is concerned with Kaurna heritage issues, representing Kaurna interests across the entire region, from Crystal

Brook to Cape Jervis. The committee has had pressing concerns, such as the Southern Expressway, forced upon them. In October 1996, KACHA was dealing with no fewer than 31 developers (Ricky Poole, Blackwood Reconciliation Group Meeting 14 October 1996). In this atmosphere of rapid change, language issues are a much lower priority.

Of all the Kaurna programs ever run, attendance has been poorest within the course actually set up at the request of Kaurna people, for Kaurna people. The Kaurna Warra Patpangga program at Warriparinga was located on the Kaurna people's 'home turf' at the then location of the KACHA office. Despite the availability of funding with support from TAFE, this course ceased, because of non-attendance, within just five months of its establishment. It was never restarted. This non-attendance was primarily due to internal conflicts and division within the Kaurna community.[7] The program was placed 'on-hold' until matters could be resolved at the KACHA Annual General Meeting. Unfortunately, language matters were never raised at the AGM, being eclipsed by constitutional issues and other matters. Again, it is largely a matter of priorities.

There is a big gap at times between an individual's expressed intention to become actively involved in learning the language, and actually following it through. In addition to the 40 or so Kaurna people formally involved at one time or another, there are others who have said that they would come along or would like to. I can only assume that other things have come up or that they don't 'get their act together', or that when it comes down to it, it is just too hard and potentially too much loss of face. As Dixon (1997: 111) rightly points out, 'a language is a difficult thing to learn, other than as a young child, and requires application and concentration'. Most Kaurna people have had only limited exposure to other languages and many have had limited success with formal education processes.

The Kaurna language movement is not yet a mass movement with widespread appeal to the general Kaurna population. It is restricted to a small, but growing body of language enthusiasts. Only time will tell if it will ever gain the critical mass required for its use on an everyday basis alongside English in a truly bilingual community.

Despite the desire to see the language used once again in the home and the community, not too much progress has been made yet. Again, there is something of a gap between intentions and actions. Identity politics and internal factional politics within the Nunga community, and the response of particular individuals and families, are likely to be the major factors in determining the extent to which the Kaurna community replaces English with Kaurna for instrumental and communicative purposes. These are themes taken up in the next chapter.

The formulaic approach and the painstaking language reclamation process that underpins it in the context of languages 'no longer spoken' are not, however, the only options for language revival. Alternative approaches have been developed, which are considerably easier to implement and are more in keeping with the ways in which people actually use elements of their ancestral languages within Nunga English.

'Artificial pidgins' and Ngarrindjeri 'language renewal'

Jay Powell, working with Quileute in the north-west of the United States, advocates the development of what he refers to as an artificial pidgin formed by the incorporation of Quileute words, one by one, into English sentence structure. Powell (1973: 6-7) provides the following example to illustrate his method:

> Increasing vocabulary size allowed rapid progress from
> > Give me half that candy.
> to Give me half that lape',
> to hes me half sa' lape'
> to hes me tala'a sa' lape'
>
> a lopsided sentence according to Quileute syntactic structure but a functional statement full of real Quileute words that could be understood by members of the in-group.

Whilst Powell's approach is a deliberate strategy in the revival of Quileute, a somewhat similar result is occurring in an ad hoc fashion in the context of Ngarrindjeri language revival. Within that community, some people claim to speak Ngarindjeri, but the language they speak is in fact a kind of re-lexified English. Ngarrindjeri programs taught at Murray Bridge High School and other locations also seem to be heavily dependent on English grammar. Word order is strictly SVO (Subject Verb Object), following English word order. English sentences tend to be translated word for word, even to the extent of using Ngarrindjeri case suffixes as separate words in translating English prepositions.[8] English expressions tend to be translated literally, even when it is apparent from the sources that Ngarrindjeri used a different idiom. And there is a concerted rejection of involvement of linguists in the development of the language.

In the production of the video *Warranna Purruna* [RS *Warrarna Purruna*]: *Pa:mpi Tungarar: Living Languages*, a Ngarrindjeri text was written by Rhonda Agius, which was published in the booklet accompanying the video (DETE, 1998: Preface). That text is substantially a one-to-one, isomorphic translation of the English version, where nominal case suffixes are used as independent words, functioning as prepositions. A variety of means are used to cope with words like 'the', 'a', 'an', 'or' and 'and', which are typically absent in Australian languages. Verbs always appear in their present tense citation form and the interrogative *yange* 'where?' appears to have been used for 'were'. A poem entitled *Ikay Ruwe — This Land* was also published by Rhonda Agius in *Tauondi Speaks from the Heart* (Procter & Gale, 1997: 6), which demonstrates the same features.

The strength of Agius' approach is the ease by which the language can be constructed and used. It allows individuals and communities to revive their languages themselves, without having to first acquire an in-depth knowledge of linguistics and the grammar of Aboriginal languages. Unlike language reclamation, there is no need to engage the services of a linguist or outsiders. This has the obvious advantage that it is much easier to maintain control over the process. So long as people feel happy with the resultant language, which seems to be the case with Ngarrindjeri, this appears to be a useful approach in these circumstances.

Nor is the approach taken by Agius without historical precedent. Nissaya Burmese as reported by Burling (1970: 181-184) is a variety of Burmese that has developed from the translation of Pali religious texts. Initially, an interlinear gloss, whereby each Pali word was given a Burmese equivalent underneath, was used as an aide to learning the foreign Pali texts. This pattern persisted for hundreds of years. However, around 1800 the texts began appearing in Nissaya Burmese without the original Pali text. As such, Nissaya Burmese no longer functions as an aide to learning Pali, but is an independent language in its own right. Its grammar is almost pure Pali, whilst the lexicon is drawn entirely from Burmese. Because it is still associated with religion, Nissaya Burmese is the high status variety of Burmese, whilst everyday Burmese which maintains its original indigenous grammar is held in low regard. Written Burmese and literary forms are heavily influenced by Pali grammar.

In another well-known case from the Indian subcontinent, three languages, Urdu, Marathi and Kannada, the first two drawn from Indo-Aryan whilst the latter belongs to the unrelated Dravidian language family, have developed a common grammar in the village of Kupwar (Gumperz & Wilson, 1971), where speakers of the two languages have lived side-by-side for centuries. Yet their lexicons have remained distinct. According to Foley (1997: 389f) 'it may not be far off the mark to say that Kupwar residents actually speak just one language, with three different lexicons.' So for members of Kupwar village, ethnic identity is maintained through the lexicon whilst grammatical differences have been ignored.

Other modern languages, particularly those varieties spoken by the Western-educated elites, are also showing rapid convergence with English, both in lexicon and grammar. Foley (1997: 415) discusses the case of Modern Thai in which the high status form has incorporated many European features, partly as a result of King Rama VI having translated Shakespeare into a highly anglicised form of Thai.

So the deliberate 'pidginisation' approach taken by Powell in Quileute and the unplanned 'language renewal' introduced in Ngarrindjeri by Agius and others are but additional examples of a more widespread phenomenon that sometimes occurs in situations of intense language contact. However, this Ngarrindjeri 'language renewal' is a fundamentally different approach to that taken in language reclamation in the Kaurna situation, which seeks to draw on the grammar of the language as it was spoken at the time of colonisation, and to capture the essence of the language in its original form. It should be recognised, though, that both Modern Ngarrindjeri and Modern Kaurna are major departures from the traditional languages. Both are undoubtedly heavily influenced by English. In Modern Kaurna, this influence is primarily at the level of discourse and idiom whereas in Modern Ngarrindjeri, the influence of English extends down into the syntax and grammar.

The formulaic approach is similar to Powell's 'artificial pidginisation' in that both methods promote a staged, gradual introduction of the target language into conversation or text which is otherwise English. However, the two methods differ sharply in that in Powell's approach, words from the target language are deliberately introduced into English sentences, whilst in the formulaic approach only well-formed utterances which preserve the original grammar of the target language are acceptable.

The relationship between minority and majority languages

One of the most important parameters in the language ecology of reviving languages is that of the relationship between the minority languages undergoing revival and the dominant majority languages with which they are forced to coexist. Language revival is about expanding functions and domains of use of a language, and of course increasing the numbers of speakers of the language. We have seen that, in the Kaurna case, this involves carving out niches within English and Nunga English which are currently used for all purposes within Nunga society.

In Nunga English words drawn from Indigenous languages are inserted in English sentences as in, for example, 'Go and wash your *marra*s (hands)!' or '*Nakkun* that *kathari korni* over there!' (look at that handsome man over there). Ngarrindjeri language renewal, and Quileute language recreation as Thieberger (1988b) refers to it, build on this pattern of language use. This contrasts markedly with the Formulaic Approach whereby only well-formed Kaurna expressions are introduced into English conversation. For the language to develop with integrity, only well-formed expressions, I believe, should be promoted in conjunction with English.[9]

Whilst both Powell's artificial pidginisation and my formulaic approach advocate the gradual introduction of the target language into English discourse, the 'Language Nest' and 'Master-Apprentice' models advocate the total exclusion of English, at least for certain periods of the day or week, or even more extended periods. As Hinton (1994: 242) says 'the single biggest challenge' facing the Master-Apprentice teams is 'leaving English behind while developing the habit of speaking in the language'. She strongly discourages the use of two languages in her 'Eight Points of Language Learning' where she urges both teachers and apprentices not to use English:

Teachers	Apprentices
2. Don't use English, not even to translate	2. Don't use English, not even when you can't say it in the language. Find other ways to communicate what you want to say.

Hinton (1994: 243)

We have found through experience that insistence on the total exclusion of English, even for short periods, stifles conversation and serves as a major demotivating factor. It is simply too difficult for beginning learners of Kaurna to engage each other in Kaurna only, even for half an hour. Further, it is difficult for us as teachers to continue to use Kaurna in an animated impromptu manner responding to the situation at hand. Often we have to stop and think how to say something, or worse still, stop to devise new expressions.

Steven Harris (1990: 80), writing from the perspective of bilingual education programs in Indigenous languages in the Northern Territory where two languages are employed, argues for strict separation between English and Indigenous languages. Code-switching has often been viewed as a sign of language breakdown and is generally discouraged in these programs. However, in the context of language reclamation, code-switching can be viewed in a more positive light to reintroduce a language in an easier and less threatening way than having to know a lot of language before being able to use it.

Harris makes a distinction between 'code-switching', which 'involves the conscious changing between two languages within a discourse for stylistic, humorous or authority-seeking purposes [which are] neither random nor of roughly equal proportions', and 'code-mixing', 'the unconscious use of two languages within the same phrase or sentence on what appears to be a random basis'. Harris regards 'code-switching' as legitimate, but sees 'code-mixing' as an indicator of '"pidginisation" and the ultimate death of a traditional language' (S. Harris, 1990: 80). Whilst I do not agree with Harris's characterisation of 'code-switching' as conscious and 'code-mixing' as unconscious, his general distinction between them is useful for our purposes. 'Code-switching' is preferable to 'code-mixing' in terms of modelling patterns of language use. If vernacular words are dropped into a sentence or discourse structure that is otherwise English, people may learn new individual lexical items, but they will gain little appreciation of a distinctive grammar that is organised on different principles from English. However, code-switching in Harris's terms is a deliberate strategy to be pursued and promoted in the formulaic approach.

The formulaic approach, as outlined here for Kaurna, would seem to be generally applicable in situations where a 'sleeping' language is to be revived. It sits well both in terms of the ways in which we learn and use languages in general, and with the functions that a newly emergent 'awakening' language first acquires. This method is likely to have more appeal to the average community member than a highly structured approach, such as grammar-translation, and seems to be the only feasible communicative approach in a situation in which there are no fluent speakers.

Notes

[1] Maori and Hawai'ian, whilst suffering serious decline and shrinkage of domains of use since colonisation, never ceased to be spoken. Efforts to revitalise Maori started in the 1970s. At the Young Maori Leaders' conference in Auckland in 1970, a motion that 'Maori should be in all preschools and schools' was debated and passed. Shortly afterwards the Ngā Tamatoa was formed 'to push for Māori rights, for education, land and language' (Te Hemara, 1993: 189). Hana Te Hemara started a 'Petition for the Teaching of Māori Language in Schools'. The petition, bearing 42,000 signatures, was presented to Parliament on 14 September 1972, the day being declared 'Maori Language Day', to become 'Maori Language Week' the following year.

[2] This expression has been introduced into KPS and its use is enforced by the students themselves. If a new child comes to school, another child whispers the expression in their ear, but until the child utters the expression, they are not permitted to go (pc Cherie Watkins; Kevin Duigan, 1998).

[3] A fundamental distinction is that between 'linguistic competence' and 'communicative competence', originally conceived by Hymes in 1966 (Hymes, 1972: 269) as a major rethink of Chomsky's 'competence' vs. 'performance' dichotomy and Saussure's 'langue' vs. 'parole'. According to Saville-Troike, 'Hymes repeatedly emphasises that what language is cannot be separated from how and why it is used, and that considerations of use are often prerequisite to recognition and understanding of much of linguistic form' (Saville-Troike, 1989: 3). See also Gumperz (1972).

[4] Though small, 40 is a significant number within the context of the Kaurna population. The number of adults who actively identify as Kaurna probably numbers several hundred.

[5] Cherie Watkins, who does much of the teaching of Kaurna across a variety of programs, has won considerable respect from all Kaurna people for her language abilities, gained through persistence and hard work since 1994.

[6] It has proved difficult to bring the parties together to discuss the issues. We need to establish who owns the tapes and how these ownership rights should be exercised before tapes are sold.

[7] This conflict was in no way due to dispute over the language. Rather it concerned the leadership of KACHA and differences over management of Kaurna heritage. The conflict resulted in one section of the community preferring to stay away.

[8] Use of the Kaurna suffix -*unangku* 'from' was also observed in use as a preposition in a speech of introduction by one Ngarrindjeri participant in the Journey of Healing on 26 May 1999.

[9] Having argued against the use of Kaurna words within English sentences, I should note that a number of songs produced by staff and students at KPS and by students at PWAC have introduced Kaurna words in this way. Whilst I do not encourage this practice, I do see some merit in it. At least children learn the words and their meanings in this way, whereas with a song written entirely in Kaurna, they might learn it off by heart but not fully appreciate its meaning, or indeed be able to associate individual words with specific meanings.

10

Sociopolitical Dimensions of Kaurna Language Revival

> *Language is power. If we don't have that power base we are continually going to become Anglicised.*
> (Alice Rigney, in Warranna Purruna video, DECS, 1997)
>
> *[L]anguage reclamation is a part of the Aboriginal decolonisation of Australia.*
> (Lester Irabinna Rigney, Interview with Jenny Burford, 21 October 1997, adapted by Lester 6 March 1998)

Having seen the ways in which the Kaurna language is being used in teaching programs within the Kaurna community, and in the public domain, let us now look at what drives this activity. Why do some people invest so much time and energy in the language movement?

Of course there are multiple and constantly changing reasons, but a number of common themes emerge. Participation in Kaurna programs and use of the Kaurna language is fundamentally an 'act of identity' for Kaurna people. Questions of personal and group identity underpin the need to make a public statement to the world about the survival of the Kaurna people. Identity issues underpin the struggle for empowerment and the need to understand Kaurna history and Kaurna culture. These are central concerns for most, if not all, who are actively involved.

For a number of Kaurna people, their engagement with the Kaurna language is intensely personal, with its own inbuilt rewards. As Lewis O'Brien says (Interview, 28 October 1997):

> It's all those things you find out, see, it's those extensions you're building on, and that's what I see is so beautiful about this ... You get rewarded. See, it's a personal reward ... So that you feel better in yourself ... You think 'Gee! That's incredible!' It's all that sort of mix of things. But that takes a long time and that doesn't matter. That's irrelevant.

For Lewis, study of the Kaurna language is primarily an intellectual pursuit; for him, the language reveals much about the way Kaurna people thought and viewed the world. These conceptual understandings often resonate with Lewis's childhood memories of stories he heard from the old people when he was growing up at Bukkiyana.

Lewis has been poring over the Kaurna sources for many years, even prior to the establishment of Kaurna programs, trying to match up the records compiled by the missionaries with his childhood memories. His engagement seems to parallel the actions of several Indigenous Californians who are working with notes recorded by the linguist, J.P. Harrington. Ernestine McGovran, for instance, is pursuing Chumash through the records of her grandmother's speech recorded by Harrington (Hinton, 1994: 227), so that for both Lewis and Ernestine pursuit of their languages is a very personal quest. The Kaurna language has become so much a part of Lewis that he seems certain to continue to learn and use it for the rest of his life, irrespective of the fortunes of the language amongst the rest of the Kaurna community or within the wider community.

Whilst Lewis is to some extent 'off doing his own thing', as some others in the Kaurna community would say, at the same time he works tirelessly to promote the language in his own and the wider community, as evidenced by the number of speeches he has delivered and his active engagement in Kaurna courses, even though he is retired. He frequently delivers lectures in tertiary level courses or in public forums on Kaurna epistemology, in which he is intensely interested. He makes a point of discussing certain Kaurna words and concepts such as the Inchoative suffix *–nendi* [RS *–rninthi*], *yerra* [RS *yara*] 'expressing the notions of individuality and reciprocity', *yerrakartarta* [RS *yarakartarta*] 'scattered; disorderly; without design; at random', *banbabanbalyanendi* [RS *panpapanpalyarninthi*] 'to hold a conference or a meeting', *kumangka* 'together' and *taikurrendi* [RS *taikurrinthi*] 'to be mixed; together'.

For Kath Burgemeister, the language has been a means of finding her roots and reconnecting with her heritage. The Kaurna language has become a major part of her life and that of her family (see pp. 7 and 202).

Beyond these personal issues, a study of the Kaurna language, and language ecology, affords numerous insights into aspects of Kaurna culture and early contact history on the Adelaide Plains. This is recognised by learners of Kaurna and by those who promote its revival. A focus on place names, culture-specific lexemes and the few remaining snippets of text which have survived from the nineteenth century resonates well with Kaurna people.

As Auntie Alice says:

> Our language is linked to our land. It is intrinsic to culture. The two are very strongly connected. Our language gives us the clues that tell us about our environment, the meaning for our existence. (Alice Rigney in *Warranna Purruna* video, DECS, 1997)

Lewis, and others, see the Kaurna language not only as a means of understanding aspects of Kaurna culture, but as a means of retrieving the culture: 'To me the overall aim is to get the people speaking, get their self esteem back and get the culture back through language' (Lewis O'Brien, interview, 8 December 1997).

For some the language has become important only after a long period of searching and learning about Kaurna history and other aspects of Kaurna

culture. The language offers the possibility of extending and deepening this knowledge. Paul Dixon, a former chairperson of K
ACHA, explains:

> Now that we've been involved in heritage for quite a while now, we can see that the language component of it is a vital bit of it. You can only grow so far without the language ... I'd like to see a lot more Kaurna descendants getting involved in the language. Because they're brought up speaking English as their first language, which is nothing wrong with that, but I mean to be able to speak both languages would be ideal. You know, we've all got a bit of mix of both. I think we can speak English OK. Now we've just got to get the Kaurna business right. It'll just make the cream on the top, if I can put it that way. (Paul Dixon, interview transcript, 21 November 1996)

As Kaurna begins to be used in combination with other aspects of Kaurna culture, such as song and dance, the language is increasingly used to celebrate the survival of the Kaurna people. It is obvious to any observer of the children at KPS, either in public or in the classroom, how much they enjoy singing songs in their own language, the language of the country in which they live (see pp. 167-168).

The considerable pride in the language and its use in public is to a large extent a celebratory activity. Kaurna speeches are now given at most large Nunga events in Adelaide, in both recognition and celebration of the survival of Kaurna people and culture. The excitement generated by the reclamation of Kaurna is obvious in a number of interviews, as when Katrina Power, Chairperson of Tandanya, spoke about the rebirth of the Kaurna language:

> ... there's a new spirit involved here. It's a great period of reclamation. And you know, I don't want to give off the idea that there's any kind of fabrication or anything like that in this context, because the fact is that we know the basic stuff. Now we're building on it and we're growing. It's like we're learning to talk again. I can't say enough how exciting that is. (Katrina Power interviewed by Anna Gillen, Radio 5UV, 23 April 1997)

Lester Rigney also talks with feeling and passion about the use of Kaurna language within his family.

For some, such as Alice Rigney, the Kaurna language has become a means not only of strengthening their own identity, but of nurturing future generations in their personal and cultural identity. She expresses her motivations as follows:

> Well, I reckon it's really important for me, particularly, because when I listen to Kaurna language I believe that I can feel myself being deeply involved in part of my past. Because, you see, I didn't really believe that there was a language as such around. And when I listen to it, it just gives me so much power within myself and, because it's something that belongs to me and my group from my mother's side, from the Kaurna people, and I just think it's absolutely wonderful. Because it is part of me that I never knew existed and although I heard bits and pieces, you know, when I lived on Point Pearce, but nothing as concrete as this. So it's really important to me to be able to reclaim part of that history that belongs to me and my future kids and the future generation of my group.
>
> I believe that this is something that we have to hand on to our children, and their children, because every bit of every part of culture and language that we can reclaim, we have to do that. Because in order to be able to be strong in our identity, we have to be

> able to come to terms with reclaiming what was, so that what we can ensure for the future is going to be around. Because I would like my great grandchildren to be able to speak fluently in the language. You know, because there's some potential for tourism, for job opportunities, but just for themselves, to be able to reaffirm culture and language for ourselves.
> (Alice Rigney, interview, 29 October 1997)

All of the Kaurna adults actively involved in the language movement have a strong desire to pass the language on to their children and to their 'grannies'.[1] Many of them work within the education sector and use the knowledge gained through formal courses in their own workplace or schools attended by their own children. Others attempt to pass on some of the language within their nuclear family and family networks. The desire to pass the language on to younger siblings and the next generation is even a reason cited by children at KPS:

> My name's Trisha Agius. And I've been learning Kaurna language for six years. It's really good that I'm learning it and I feel good that I'm learning my culture and that I can teach my kids when I grow up.
> (Trish Agius, video shot by Jenny Burford, KPS, August 1997)

> I can speak to my nanna and pappa and I want to teach my kids when I grow up.
> (girl from KPS, voiceover on *Warranna Purruna* video, DECS, 1997)

While most, if not all, Kaurna people learn Kaurna primarily for themselves and for their own people, there is also a sense in which they learn and use the language to reach out to the wider community. In this regard the Kaurna language movement is intensely political, not in a partisan or party political sense, but in the sense of fighting for Indigenous rights and changing the balance of power within society. The language is used to challenge and change preconceived notions (about the Kaurna language and people being 'extinct'), to promote understanding of the Kaurna people and their culture, to fight for recognition and promote reconciliation.

For Lester Rigney, perhaps the primary purpose for engaging in the reclamation of Kaurna is in the liberation struggle for his people and as a tool for decolonisation. Georgina Williams describes herself as a 'warrior woman' with a lifelong mission to 'wake up the people' and reinstate traditional cultural values (see video of the launch of KL&LE, University of Adelaide, 1997).

Kaurna people have a long history of struggle against oppression and racism and many, such as the late Gladys Elphick, the late Mary Williams and her daughter Georgina Williams, were at the forefront of the Aboriginal Rights movement of the 1960s and the 'Tent Embassy' in Canberra in the early 1970s.[2] Kaurna people have worked both within and outside the system in this struggle. Kaurna language reclamation has become an integral part of this longstanding fight for justice and recognition and it is the community leaders and activists at the centre of this struggle for justice who are most active in the language movement. These themes are taken up in more detail below ('The struggle for recognition', pp. 229ff.).

Some Kaurna people learning Kaurna do so, at least in part, for more practical reasons. It provides them with skills useful in the area of cultural tourism or the means to pursue a job teaching the language. Cherie Watkins began learning Kaurna on the job as a language teacher (cf. p. 158), but it has now become a very personal quest, giving her a new direction in life. She explains in the AILF textbook:

> Being involved in teaching Kaurna language has given me a new lease of life — in fact it has turned my life around — at the age of 55 I have developed a voracious appetite to learn more of this language that has been lost to me for so long. My culture is being returned to me via the language. My horizons have been widened.
> (Cherie Warrara Watkins, in SSABSA, 1996c: 201)

Her daughter Cherylynne Catanzaritti, one of the first adult students in the program at Inbarendi College, has used her language skills to obtain work at KPECC and at Smithfield Plains PS.

Others have become involved in learning the language primarily through music and dance performances as we saw in the case of Karl Telfer (see p. 190). The Kaurna language is already a strong element in Karl's performances, though he wants to build on it and develop it over a long period to strengthen a career in the performing arts (pc Karl Telfer, 1997; 1998). Snooky Varcoe's involvement with Kaurna began with his language work within school programs, and continues primarily through music and songs.

Whilst the number of Kaurna people actively engaged in learning Kaurna is small, their level of commitment is high. Most have continued to use the language for their own personal purposes and in the public arena. A number are engaged in teaching it. Many have developed an intense, enduring relationship with the Kaurna language.

Almost all public use of Kaurna is by Kaurna people themselves. However, a number of non-Aboriginal people, in addition to myself, are engaged in language revival activities, learning and teaching Kaurna. They do so primarily in a supporting role at the direction of Kaurna people, some as part of their work as teachers at KPS. A few learn and use the language at home as spouses or partners of Kaurna people. Others learn it out of interest and a desire to understand the local Indigenous language, culture and local history. Some students may have begun learning Kaurna purely out of curiosity and self-interest, but in so doing have come to understand and support the Kaurna people's struggle for recognition.

There is, however, some difference of opinion over access to the language by non-Aboriginal people, which will be discussed in more detail in the section 'Whose language is it?' (pp. 234ff.).

Beyond the motivations of individual participants in the Kaurna language movement are specific issues and events which help to illuminate the contemporary language ecology in which Kaurna is embedded. First I will investigate Kaurna identity more fully. I focus specifically on the role that the Kaurna language is now playing in shaping and giving voice to that identity.

The construction and reconstruction of identity

Since the 1967 referendum and the Self-Determination policy of the 1970s, Aboriginal society has been regrouping and redefining itself. Initially this redefinition took the form of forging a new positive Aboriginality in the face of negative stereotypes and categories forced onto Aboriginal people by mainstream society. Indigenous peoples had internalised these stereotypes to varying degrees. Previously, many individuals were forcibly removed from their families at a young age, cut off from their people, their culture, their land, their way of life and their language. Some Aboriginal people even grew up believing that they were something else. For instance, the well-known Aboriginal writer, Sally Morgan, from Western Australia, grew up thinking that she was Indian only to 'discover' her Aboriginality as an adult (Morgan, 1987).[3] Some Kaurna people, and others involved in the Kaurna language revival efforts, were amongst the 'stolen generations'. For them, it was a matter of getting back in touch with their own Aboriginality. For instance, the late Naomi Dixon[4], whilst always aware of her Aboriginality, only became aware of her Kaurna ancestry in about 1990, through the South Australian Museum's Family History Project coordinated by Dr Doreen Kartinyeri.

As the Aboriginal rights movement has matured, Aboriginal peoples have moved beyond simply forging a new Aboriginality, though this is a continuing concern. People have moved to reclaim their individual and group identities and their associated cultures.[5] Attempts are being made to re-establish links with the land and to reconnect with the past in meaningful ways for the present and for the future. Kaurna identity is not so much an identity of resistance, as Nunga identity is often portrayed (see Hollinsworth, 1992). Rather, it is a proactive, creative resurgence of identity, rooted in the past, but very much a reality of the present. Kaurna people are defining themselves and transforming their society into the way they want to be. No longer are they willing to be defined by others or satisfied in defining themselves predominantly in opposition to the mainstream. Increasingly they are in control of who they are and their own destiny.

Jordan, writing in the 1980s, downplays the role of anthropological writings and Nunga languages in the construction of identity. Note that she is specifically referring to Adelaide Aboriginal people:

> For most Aboriginal people, however, the writings of anthropologists have little immediate impact. Rather, it is enough to adhere to a somewhat vague, unspecific knowledge of the remote past that is a form of sedimentation of knowledge passed on from generation to generation. Thus the older urban Aborigines may refer to 'secrets' that they possess (though they do not possess the language). They may stand in awe of tradition-oriented people and, in an inchoate way, they may appreciate the coherence of the culture of that group. Nevertheless, the tradition-oriented culture does not provide urban dwellers a model with which they can readily identify in their daily lives, although they ally themselves with causes (such as land rights) which pertain to tradition-oriented people. (Jordan, 1988a: 118)

This observation may well have been correct at the time and could still be true for many Aboriginal people living in Adelaide. However, it is my experience that numbers of Nungas here are searching for a detailed knowledge of the past, of 'forgotten' culture and language, and are prepared to turn to the writings of anthropologists, missionaries, explorers, pastoralists and colonial officials in pursuit of this knowledge. Some decades ago, Berndt (1970: 6) observed that 'even in a highly industrialized city like Adelaide, the survival of the past is significant to the present.'

Jordan ignores the role of language in the construction of Aboriginal identities in Adelaide, though, in the same paper, acknowledging its centrality for the Sami (Jordan, 1988a: 127). Yet she was writing just at the time when Adelaide Nungas were beginning to voice concern for ancestral languages. Three years before, a group of Ngarrindjeri students had travelled to Batchelor in the Northern Territory and interest had been expressed in reviving Kaurna. By 1988, the SACAE (now University of South Australia) was engaged in Ngarrindjeri and Narungga language revival activities.

The parameters of Kaurna identity are formally set out in KACHA's criteria for membership as stated in its constitution:[6]

> 5. MEMBERSHIP
> 5.1 Membership of the association is based on a traditionalist model; members must be Kaurna Aboriginal people belonging to Kaurna family clan groups.
> 5.2 Those persons who are recognised as Kaurna Aboriginal people will be one[7] or all of the following:
> a) descendants of Kaurna Aboriginal people
> b) members of a Kaurna family clan group
> c) a person who acknowledges himself or herself as a Kaurna person
> d) a person who is recognised and accepted by the Kaurna community as such;
> 5.3 Each family will be responsible for maintaining their own family records, a copy of which will be held by the association.
> 5.4 It will be the responsibility of the association to ensure that each family clan group will be helped where necessary in the development and maintenance of its own family clan group records.
> 5.5 K.A.C.H.A. Inc. will keep a registry or data base of all family clan records.
> (KACHA, 1994: 4-5)

At the Annual General Meeting held in October 1996, 22 extended family groups, or 'family clan groups' as they are referred to in the Constitution, were represented. However, KACHA does not represent everybody who claims to be Kaurna. In early 1996, a small but vocal minority made an unsuccessful attempt to establish a rival Kaurna heritage committee. In addition, there are a number of Kaurna people, secure in their own Kaurna identity, who prefer to remain aloof from KACHA politics. Probably other Kaurna families remain unrepresented in this way.

The re-emergence of Kaurna identity is focused primarily on genealogies and family ties, sites and territory, and aspects of material culture associated with these sites. Those who have links to the people of the Adelaide Plains are coming together to forge the new Kaurna nation. Genealogy or 'blood lines' remains the primary criterion for establishing one's Kaurna identity. There is some dispute within the community about the accuracy of published and unpublished genealogies assembled by the Family History Project (Kartinyeri,

1989; 1990) at the South Australian Museum and by anthropologists (Berndt & Berndt, 1993; Tindale papers), which sometimes conflict with oral tradition. Added to this are questions about the identity of various 'Kaurna' ancestors and their place of origin. As a result, claims of Kaurna identity are often disputed, though Aboriginality itself is seldom brought into question. People are still in the process of sorting out who they are in terms of affiliation to language group, land and cultural traditions.

Within the Kaurna community there is a major line of cleavage between those with strong ties to Raukkan, and the main body of people who relate more to Bukkiyana. Those with ties to Raukkan are often seen by others to belong to the Ngarrindjeri. Added to this, there is a more recent Northern Kaurna and Southern Kaurna split, based primarily on modern residence patterns in the northern or southern suburbs. At one stage these two groups were having separate meetings about heritage matters, though they still remained under the umbrella of KACHA.

Despite the passage of more than 150 years of postcolonial history, Nunga kinship networks are still surprisingly strong and resilient. Extended family networks can be extensive. Allegiance to the extended family is a powerful force for cohesion within the network, but may also exacerbate divisions within the developing Kaurna community.

The Kaurna renaissance is taking place in the wake of the destructive government policies of the past which saw Aboriginal people as second class citizens and actively suppressed their languages and cultures. It is not surprising that factions and conflict should arise in the process of undoing the acts of racism and oppression.

Now, when the Kaurna are increasingly recognised, governments and private companies are spending money on consulting fees and site surveys in an effort to inveigle approvals for their various schemes from KACHA. These consultations are putting considerable pressure on a community that is small and inexperienced compared to the large corporate interests they are forced to deal with. Pressure from developers is diverting the energy and attention of the Kaurna community away from language and cultural revival, which some Kaurna do regard as more important.

Many Kaurna people, perhaps the majority, have always kept an intact sense of Aboriginal or Nunga identity, in contrast to the 'stolen generations', who often came from more remote areas in the north of the state. Alice Rigney says:

> I went to an all-girls school in town, and one of the students that came down from the country — I'm not sure where she fitted in the scheme of things in relation to identity as an Indigenous person. — And I remember talking to this student and saying 'Where I come from I feel really strong about who I am' because I knew my mother was an excellent teacher for me. And I had strong black female role models like Kath's mother and Georgina's mother and they were strong women. And I gained strength from that. So my identity was strong.
> (Discussion Panel at launch of KL&LE, University of Adelaide, 31 July 1997)

During the mission era, many Nungas who are now Elders and leaders in their communities tried to hang on to what remained of their languages and cultures, though in many cases they were denied access to it by mission and government authorities and even by their Elders. A few, especially those whose appearance allowed them to pass as some other nationality, denied their Aboriginality in the face of strong pressure by the dominant society. Some Kaurna people were fostered out to white homes and cut off from their people and their culture. In the main, however, Kaurna people grew up with a history and certain traditions which separated them from mainstream society. Along with their history and culture, a deep sense of injustice, hurt and pain has been inherited by Nunga people. The descendants of Kudnarto, for instance, have known of the wrongful repossession by the government after her death of the block of land that had been granted to her. People have felt aggrieved at having been pushed around and moved from place to place, robbed of their successful farming ventures at Poonindie and Bukkiyana. And they are ever mindful of the loss of their lands, cultures, traditions and languages as the result of colonisation. All this they know first-hand from oral tradition. The historical record merely confirms these basic facts and fleshes out the details.

Nunga identity has been an identity of resistance. It was an identity forged in a situation where people from many different places and cultures were forced together on the missions. Lester Irabinna Rigney gives his view of the development of Nunga English in this context:

> ...Aboriginal people and particularly Kaurna people and Narungga have resisted using English as a form of colonisation. The way that they have resisted is using Aboriginal English which was a combination of the many different language groups that were forced together on the missions. So to give them a sense of power and control they use this Aboriginal English to decode messages, to speak without the dominant culture hearing or listening, as a way to power and control.
>
> (Interview with Jenny Burford, 21 October 1997)

Nunga English gave voice to Nunga identity and could be described in Smolicz's terms as a core value. Whilst some Nungas attached an element of shame to Nunga English as a non-standard variety, certainly by the 1980s most Nungas used Nunga English with pride.

With the emergence of distinct identities, Kaurna, Narungga, Ngarrindjeri etc., there is a new resistance to Nunga English, precisely because it mixes words from different Aboriginal languages. Lester Irabinna Rigney explains:

> ... Aboriginal English, as far as I know and my use of it, is a whole interspersed of Ngarrindjeri, Narungga, Adnyamathanha you see ... Kaurna doesn't belong there. Kaurna belongs as a whole new entity so when you use those Kaurna words you know you're using Kaurna, although it might be Kaurna English OK. But you're using Kaurna words. You're not using Aboriginal English. You're using pure Kaurna with English.
>
> [JB: So in a sense you'll actually be getting more specialised forms of Aboriginal English so that Ngarrindjeri will be speaking Ngarrindjeri Aboriginal English and the Kaurna people will be speaking Kaurna Aboriginal English.]
>
> Ne! <yes> ... and those languages should only be spoken in those countries, which will give you a whole new presence because when you are reviving customary law you will

revive it according to your language rules, so you can use Ngarrindjeri English, Kaurna English and then start to recreate that sort of stuff.

(Interview with Jenny Burford, 21 October 1997)

For some Nungas, it seems that the possession of a distinctive variety of Nunga English, whilst valued, is not sufficient for the development of a complete sense of identity. Snooky Varcoe, for instance, talks of the Kaurna language 'filling a gap':

> I find doing this language revival and teaching very challenging and rewarding in so many ways. It brings back fond memories of my childhood. It also gives me a sense of fulfillment, a gap in my personality that has not been fulfilled, a sense of identity complete. I've wasted so many years of my life doing nothing, but now I want to do something useful for my people, my children, and future generations. This program is creating so much interest among the Aboriginal community and settlements. I wonder why it has not been started years ago. My people want to stand up and be counted, it gives them pride and a sense of direction.
>
> (Nelson Varcoe, 1989 quoted in Amery, 1995: 74)

Increasingly Nungas are searching for their roots and exploring their heritage in an attempt to 'fill the gap'. A transitional stage with two competing views has emerged: on the one hand, many Nungas are still very attached to Nunga English, feeling it to be 'their language'. For them, Kaurna is something 'new' and 'foreign', even something imposed from outside via their children attending a school program or created and promoted by white linguists.[8] This view contrasts sharply with that of the Kaurna language activists who portray Nunga English as the product of colonisation and a hangover from the mission era, in contrast to Kaurna, which is their 'own' language, possession of which is empowering and liberating.

Since Kaurna language programs were introduced into the education sector in the 1990s, the Kaurna language has had a much higher profile, serving as a marker of Kaurna identity. However, it must also be said that although KACHA (1994: 2) recognised the Kaurna language in its constitution (Object 3.6, 'To monitor and influence the use of Kaurna historical elements, culture and language and prevent any inappropriate use of such information'), it comes as a lower priority than the identification and protection of sites and other aspects of material culture which are addressed by a number of additional more specific clauses. Even until comparatively recently, the leadership of KACHA had not really taken the language seriously. The enthusiastic comments of its Acting Chairperson, Fred Warrior, about language reclamation early in 1996 have already been quoted (Chapter 8, epigram) but they were prefaced by his acknowledging: 'I'm not much into education and all that. I'm more into heritage.' Later in 1996, Paul Dixon suggested the formation of several subcommittees, including 'a) Heritage; b) Music, Dance, Art; c) Language; d) Community Issues' under the auspices of KACHA in recognition of the need to carry out more detailed work in these areas. There has been more talk recently of the need to hold meetings and workshops to work out directions for the development of the language. It is clear that the language is becoming more important in the minds of more Kaurna people and that it is becoming a somewhat higher priority within KACHA.

At the same time, it remains true that for many Kaurna people knowledge of or even interest in the language is not essential for establishing or maintaining Kaurna identity, but is more like a bonus. They may well feel sincerely Kaurna, but the possibility of knowing the language adds 'the cream on the top', as Paul Dixon puts it (p. 221 above).

In general, however, the Kaurna language is increasingly serving as a focus of Kaurna pride, even though most Kaurna may have little knowledge of the language themselves. The Kaurna community is keen to promote the language visibly through signage and audibly through the public performance of song and the delivery of speeches. Increasingly, it seems, Kaurna language is becoming one of the 'main props' or 'pillars' of Kaurna identity. At KPS, children take pride in being able to use Kaurna, albeit in limited ways. The school song, which they helped to write in Kaurna and English in May 1997, is now a focus for this pride. They reportedly sing the Kaurna version with greater feeling and volume than the English version (pc Kevin Duigan; Cherie Watkins, September 1997). KPS staff claim that the Kaurna version of the song is more meaningful and powerful than its English counterpart.

Lester Irabinna Rigney conveys something of the strength and depth of feeling about the contribution of the language for his identity in the following excerpts:

> Kaurna language means to me an opportunity to start to dialogue between my people in a language that is our own. I find it frustrating talking and communicating in English which is a language that is foreign to this country. And I'm really frustrated in using the language of the oppressor because it does not espouse my world view.
> ...
> I also feel powerless without Kaurna language. I feel that my identity is not fulfilled. So Kaurna language to me fulfils and reaffirms my identity. Reconnecting Kaurna makes me whole and affirms in me who I am.
> ...
> And so to rediscover language is then to rediscover, reaffirm and celebrate Kaurna and Narungga culture. But, for me, it will also give me an ability to communicate in my own language, which for me is paramount.
> ....
> I see my own family who just love Kaurna language, you can see the pride in their faces when they speak this. The sense of identity, the sense of ownership. The sense that this is the part that I've always been longing for. The part that's been missing that I've been looking for that I've found. (Interview, 20 November 1996)

There is little doubt that for Lester, Alice, Lewis and others, Kaurna language is a main pillar of their identity, though it probably cannot yet be described as a 'core value' for Kaurna society as a whole.

The struggle for recognition, empowerment and reconciliation

As well as having value and significance for individuals and for the Kaurna people as a distinctive group, the Kaurna language is also a means of renegotiating power relations outside the group. Underpinning the vast majority of current uses of Kaurna, both in school programs and the public domain, is its use as a medium of cultural expression. The primary use of Kaurna is not for communication: English and Nunga English already perform that function in the Kaurna community. Rather, use of Kaurna language is another means, alongside dance, art and other forms of cultural expression, by which Kaurna people can make their existence known.

The Adelaide City Council placenames proposal is also seen to further the cause of recognition of the Kaurna people. As Auntie Doris Graham said, when questioned about the importance of using Kaurna names, 'Well they're the owners of the soil. They never have anything, no-one's been recognised from the Kaurna Plains people of those days, and I think it's nice' (Doris Graham interviewed by Jenny Burford, 27 October 1997).

Different Kaurna people use and promote the language in different ways to this end. Some, like Lewis O'Brien, wish to see Kaurna names proliferate and the language used more and more, both by Kaurna people and others. Interstate businesses could use Kaurna words, for instance, so long as the Kaurna people were consulted. Increasingly, businesses are expected to pay for the use of Kaurna names. Others, like Georgina Williams, prefer to use the language in more sparing and challenging ways. When Georgina constructs a Kaurna speech, it is to express ideas from the heart, which will challenge people's preconceived ideas. She is not content to give people what they want to hear.

On a much broader front the Kaurna language is part of the whole struggle for recognition of Indigenous peoples' rights. As I write, Australia is suffering the aftermath of a heated political debate about Native Title. Most of those actively using, teaching and learning Kaurna are also actively involved in this wider struggle. Kaurna speeches have been given and Kaurna songs sung at a number of public meetings and rallies held in support of the Mabo and Wik decisions (see pp. 233-234) and in support of the Kumarangk Coalition's stand on the Hindmarsh Island Bridge issue (p. 232). An impassioned Kaurna speech was delivered by Cherie Watkins at the South Australian opening of the National Inquiry into the Separation of Aboriginal Children from their Families. A letter was written in Kaurna and English, which was sent to the then Prime Minister John Howard in protest at his refusal to apologise to the 'Stolen Generations' (see Amery, 1998a, Vol. 2: 115). So there is a sharp political edge to the Kaurna language movement.

The Kaurna language is seen as a means of bringing about reconciliation, not only between Indigenous and non-Indigenous Australians, but also between Kaurna people themselves. This was clearly articulated on 31 January 1997 by Veronica Brodie at a meeting of Kaurna Elders. Veronica made the point that Kaurna people come from two different areas, Raukkan, the heart of the Ngarrindjeri nation, and Bukkiyana, the centre of the Narungga nation; they therefore have somewhat different histories and allegiances, whilst also having links with Kaurna people and Kaurna country through the ancestors. The Kaurna language is seen by Veronica as something that all these people have in common, that can help to build bridges between the two groups and forge one Kaurna people and one Kaurna nation.

By means of its use in school-based and tertiary language programs, and its use in renaming the landscape and institutions, the Kaurna language is also seen as a tool to bring about reconciliation between the Indigenous and non-Indigenous community. This is something that Auntie Alice Rigney promotes strongly: 'In reclamation programs there is a sharing of power. Access by all to language is reconciliation. This sharing I believe helps to overcome racism because of the understanding this brings' (*Warranna Purruna* video, 1997). The Kaurna language serves as a key to gaining insights into local history, the local environment and the local culture of the people of the Adelaide plains. It is difficult, if not impossible, to teach reconciliation head on. By means of insights gained through the language, however, people can gain an appreciation and respect for Aboriginal culture and Aboriginal people.

This holds true, not just for Kaurna of course, but for all of Australia's Indigenous languages, as articulated in the Australian Indigenous Languages Framework:

> It is hoped that the study of and about Australian languages will contribute to a breaking down of barriers between Aboriginal and Torres Strait Islander and non-Aboriginal societies by encouraging respect for Australian languages and the cultures in which they are embedded. A knowledge of and about Australian languages could contribute to the emergence of a unique Australian identity. (SSABSA, 1996a: 3)

So there is a very personal identity agenda and a wider cultural agenda operating within the Kaurna community, a still wider educational agenda aimed primarily at Nunga children and adults but extending out into sympathetic sections of the non-Aboriginal community, and a more far-reaching political agenda reaching out to the wider community, which underpin the use and social functions of Kaurna in the 1990s.

The sociopolitical backdrop for Kaurna language revival

The Kaurna are a dispossessed people. As Georgina Williams pointed out in her address at the Colebrook reunion[9], the Colebrook site in the Adelaide Hills is the only piece of Kaurna land currently under Aboriginal control, and, even so, not directly under the control of the Kaurna.[10]

The Kaurna have, however, achieved a measure of recognition and are consulted by government departments and developers over sites of significance threatened by development. The Southern Expressway and Wirrina Cove, for instance, are major developments over which protracted negotiations have taken place through which the Kaurna have gained some concessions. Because Kaurna land includes the Adelaide metropolitan area, the surrounding fertile plains and adjoining coastline, the Kaurna gain more recognition than they otherwise would. The special relationship of the Kaurna to the Adelaide Plains is gaining increasing public recognition, especially from other Aboriginal people. It is accepted protocol, now, for interstate visitors such as Mick Dodson, Marcia Langton or Evelyn Scott (all high-profile Aboriginal leaders) to begin their speeches with an acknowledgement of the Kaurna people as the original landowners.

More attention has been directed towards Aboriginal languages by governments of all persuasions in recent times. In 1987 the Federal Government allocated $3 million dollars towards language maintenance activities under the National Aboriginal Languages Program (NALP) (see pp. 156f.). This funding has been continued under the Aboriginal and Torres Strait Islander Languages Initiatives Program (ATSILIP). Under a previous South Australian Labor Government, Mike Rann, as Minister for Technical and Further Education and Minister for Aboriginal Affairs, spoke at the national Aboriginal Languages Conference held at Tandanya in December 1991 of the need 'to save and revive Aboriginal languages in South Australia' (Rann, 1992: 71) and of the relevance of this linguistic heritage to both Aboriginal and non-Aboriginal people. In line with the Minister's recommendations, a language centre, Yaitya Warra Wodli, was established in 1993. DETE now supports 49 language programs in nine languages, offered to 1719 students in 39 South Australian schools.[11] These include the Kaurna programs at Inbarendi College. Governments are certainly more receptive and sensitive to the needs of Indigenous peoples like the Kaurna than they were, even just a few years ago.

However, despite these positive developments, recent events (discussed below) have created an atmosphere in which Aboriginal people perceive their basic human rights as being denied. They are being marginalised and at times vilified. Australian society is becoming more polarised on these issues, with an accompanying increasing hostility towards Aboriginal people and Aboriginal affairs.

Paradoxically, these events have served to strengthen Aboriginal identity and to harden the resolve of Kaurna people to rebuild their nation and their culture, including the language. A softer approach to language and culture by the federal government may be a trade-off for their hardline stance on land matters — a partial compromise which directs some additional resources to those areas which do not pose a direct threat to the economic interests of the rich and powerful.

The Hindmarsh Island Bridge saga

One dispute over development which has bitterly divided the Ngarrindjeri community (see Varco in Hart, 1997: 241) is the Hindmarsh Island Bridge affair: a long-running battle, fought in State and Commonwealth Parliaments, the High Court and the media[12], between developers' intentions to build a bridge to the island and attempts by the local Ngarrindjeri to stop them.

Hindmarsh Island is within Ngarrindjeri lands, but some Kaurna people, having both Ngarrindjeri and Kaurna ancestry, are directly involved in the dispute. Two women in particular are at the forefront in both the movement to stop the bridge and the struggle for recognition of Kaurna language and heritage. Veronica Brodie[13] was the only Ngarrindjeri woman to give evidence for the existence of 'women's business' on Hindmarsh Island during the course of the Royal Commission, and was also an Elder on the Executive of KACHA. Cherie Watkins, working as Kaurna language specialist since 1994, has also been prominent within the Kumarangk Coalition (an anti-bridge collective).

One of the themes that emerged from the Hindmarsh Island Royal Commission and associated media coverage was the denial of the right of the Ngarrindjeri to a dynamic, changing culture. Much weight was placed on verification of beliefs according to their documentation by anthropologists and missionaries. If the culture had not been documented, it was as if it did not exist. The only culture Ngarrindjeri people were entitled to was some static, rarified account appearing in the historical record, any deviation from which was deemed a 'fabrication'.

Now, for the Kaurna who are attempting to rebuild their society, by recreating their Dreamings and reviving their language on the basis of very limited oral history and documentation, the implications are obvious. As Hemming (1996: 25) observes:

> This allegation of fabrication has seriously undermined the position of Aboriginal people in 'settled' Australia as inauthentic, weakening potential native title claims.

As we saw in Chapter 6, in reclaiming Kaurna we are changing the language, both deliberately and unintentionally. Some of these changes that have been introduced, such as the base-10 number system, are a radical departure from the language as it was spoken last century. We must be prepared then to address the charge that Kaurna of the 1990s is a 'fabrication'. These issues of authenticity and integrity are constantly in our minds as we rebuild the language. The charge that 'Kaurna is a whitefella creation', referring to the role both of the German missionaries and myself, has been raised on several occasions from individuals outside the language movement.

The 'stolen generations'

The issue of the 'stolen generations', children who were forcibly removed from their families to be fostered or institutionalised, continues to wound Indigenous people. Many Kaurna families were spared, living the hard but relatively stable life of the missions at Point Pearce and Point McLeay.[14] Others were members of the stolen generations, and some of these have since rediscovered their families and now identify strongly as Kaurna people. Government policy is blamed for the loss of identity, culture and language.

A National Inquiry into the Separation of Aboriginal and Torres Strait Islander Children from Their Families was established in 1995 and its findings published under the title *Bringing Them Home* (Commonwealth of Australia, 1997). Fortuitously, the report was tabled in Federal Parliament concurrently with the national convention in Melbourne of the Council for Aboriginal Reconciliation. The report was the topic of vigorous and emotional debate in parliament, the Prime Minister steadfastly refusing to apologise on behalf of the nation for the misguided policies of the past. The issue gained significant publicity in the Australian media and also drew some international attention.

The report also addressed the issue of linguistic and cultural loss and restitution. Two recommendations are of relevance:

> Language, culture and history centres
> Recommendation 12a: That the Commonwealth expand the funding of Indigenous language, culture and history centres to ensure national coverage at regional level.
> Recommendation 12b: That where the Indigenous community so determines, the regional language, culture and history centre be funded to record and maintain local Indigenous languages and to teach those languages, especially to people whose forcible removal deprived them of opportunities to learn and maintain their language, and to their descendants. (Commonwealth of Australia, 1997: 300)

The Council for Aboriginal Reconciliation was established in 1991 by an Act of federal parliament, which received the unanimous support of both houses. The vision adopted by the Council is of: 'A united Australia which respects this land of ours; values the Aboriginal and Torres Strait Islander heritage; and provides justice and equity for all' (Council for Aboriginal Reconciliation brochure *Reconciliation and Its Key Issues*). The 1990s were designated the Decade for Reconciliation. Following extensive consultation with Indigenous peoples throughout Australia, the Council prepared a submission to the Government in early 1995. A summary version was subsequently published (Council for Aboriginal Reconciliation, 1996).

We have seen in Chapters 7 and 8 that the Kaurna language revival movement is regarded as operating very much in the interests of reconciliation. It provides insights into Kaurna culture, people and history. As we have seen, many, if not all, involved in the Kaurna language movement have participated in reconciliation events.

Since the establishment of the Reconciliation Council, a number of events have occurred that have polarised Australian society. In early 1996, a Liberal/National Party government was elected, as was the controversial and outspoken Member for Oxley, who was expelled from the Liberal Party just prior to the election for her extreme views. On being elected, the Prime Minister and the Minister for Aboriginal Affairs failed[15] to adequately counter the extreme views of the Member for Oxley under the guise of supporting freedom of speech and the end of 'political correctness'. This failure allowed this little-known bigot to become the focus of increased racist activity. The extreme right attempted to capitalise on her fame to gain support and legitimacy.

The former Prime Minister John Howard, himself, frequently talks of rejecting a 'black arm-band' version of history and would like to deny that the present government or the present generation bears any responsibility for the past, yet at the same time he promotes pride in Australia's history and the efforts of the 'Australian pioneers', including the squatters who seized the land illegally.

In the wake of the historic Mabo decision of June 1992 when the High Court of Australia finally overturned the doctrine of *Terra Nullius* and recognised Indigenous Australians' sovereign rights to their lands, the mining and pastoral industry lobbies have swung into action. The Wik decision, which affirmed the rights of the Wik peoples to an interest in leasehold land, has further fuelled this opposition. (See Bachelard (1997) for an excellent discussion of Wik, Mabo and the Ten-Point Plan — a set of amendments to the Native Title Act, passed in 1998.)

Whilst these matters have no direct impact on the Kaurna, for it is unlikely that they would be able to satisfy the criteria for a successful land claim, repercussions from the Wik and Mabo decisions have a major influence in defining the political climate in which the Kaurna programs operate in the late 1990s. Attitudes are hardening and views on Aboriginal affairs are becoming increasingly polarised (see Johnson, 1996). However, this merely serves to galvanise the Indigenous community. These topics are a frequent focus of informal conversation and discussion amongst adult participants of Kaurna language courses and are clearly among the factors motivating them to pursue a knowledge of their ancestral language and culture. Many students talk of gaining an increased inner strength through an in-depth knowledge of their language.

Whose language is it? Ownership and copyright issues

One of the major issues impinging on the future of Kaurna is the issue of ownership and copyright. There is a tension between wanting to see the language used and recognised on the one hand, and maintaining control over it and keeping it within the Kaurna community on the other. As might be expected, there are major differences of opinion on this question.

As for non-Indigenous Australians, the majority are quite ignorant of and indifferent to the Kaurna language. However, an increasing number do recognise Indigenous languages, such as Kaurna, as Australia's unique heritage, and in a sense part of their heritage, too. Then there is the 'new age' fringe who would wish to appropriate Indigenous knowledges, and those who appropriate Aboriginal identities as their own[16], though not necessarily intending to be exploitative. Finally there are those, such as Leon Carmen (alias 'Wanda Koolmatrie'), who have willingly and shamelessly exploited and falsely created an Aboriginal identity for commercial gain (see Koolmatrie, 1994; Hosking, 1997; *The Advertiser,* 13 March 1997: 1, and 15 March 1997: 10, 29).

Certainly concerns over ownership and copyright issues, and a lack of clear direction resulting from an inability to resolve these issues, is one of the main limiting factors in the public promotion and use of the Kaurna language, and ultimately in the revival of the Kaurna language itself.

According to Australian law, the issue of copyright is clear. Kaurna historical materials are in the public domain and there are no legal restrictions as to what people can do with them. Despite this, the Kaurna community believes that the language belongs to them and that they have moral rights to it as Indigenous cultural property. They are totally united on this point. There is a growing movement within Indigenous communities to assert their rights over these materials and to insist on certain protocol in relation to their use. Brown, drawing on cases from around the world, identifies the differing perspectives on cultural information taken by Indigenous societies relative to Western legal systems. According to Brown:

> The assumptions that inform this emerging [Indigenous] perspective can be summarised as follows:
> 1. An ethnic nation — a people, in other words — can be said to have enduring, comprehensive rights in its own cultural productions and ideas. These include the right to exercise total control over the representation of such productions and ideas by outsiders, even in the latter's personal memoirs, drawings, and fictional creations.
> 2. A group's relationship to its cultural productions constitutes a form of ownership. This ownership may be literal — that is, based on some comprehensive definition of cultural or intellectual property — or metaphorical, reflecting universal recognition that in moral terms a group 'owns' the ideas and practices that it holds dear.
> 3. Cultural information pertaining to ethnic minorities that was gathered in the past by anthropologists, missionaries, government administrators, filmmakers, and novelists is by definition so contaminated by the realities of colonial power that it cannot meet (today's) standards of informed consent. This information may therefore be quarantined or subjected to severe access restrictions when and if its subjects deem its presence in the public domain offensive. (Brown, 1998: 194-195)

In Australia, Indigenous cultural and intellectual property copyright issues have begun to be addressed in an ATSIC-funded, AIATSIS-commissioned discussion paper (Janke, 1997), which puts forward a series of proposals for the reform of Australian copyright laws. Language issues are not addressed in detail in this paper, though they certainly are included in the definition of 'Indigenous Cultural and Intellectual Property' (Janke, 1997: 7), and the report advocates the recognition of 'the right to control the use of ... the particular language which may be intrinsic to cultural identity' (Janke, 1997: 8). The only specific reference to language use regards Indigenous words and names used by non-Indigenous businesses as trademarks and brand names (Janke, 1997: 28; 34). Should these reforms be accepted, the general public would no longer be at liberty to do what they liked with the Kaurna historical materials.

A submission prepared in 1994 by Fourmile, for an inquiry on Indigenous intellectual and cultural property rights, distinguishes between 'cultural property' and 'cultural resources', the latter being 'the product of interactions between Indigenous and non-Indigenous people (most notably explorers, researchers, missionaries, and administrators)' (Fourmile, 1994: 11-12). In this sense the Kaurna language consists almost entirely of 'cultural resources', not only in relation to the historical resources, but also in relation to new language materials generated. According to Fourmile's categories, the Kaurna language is very much a 'shared heritage' to which, she argues, 'neither party should enjoy exclusive rights' (Fourmile, 1994: 12).

As we have seen in Chapter 6, new materials, such as songs, story books, HyperCard stacks and language learning tapes, contain recently developed words, phrases and expressions not found in the historical materials. Who should own or hold copyright over these materials? As it stands at the moment, according to copyright law, the author of the materials or the author's employer, in the case of curriculum materials, owns these materials. The right of the Kaurna community is simply not recognised. In the case of Kaurna language materials, many are currently generated by myself, often in conjunction with others, colleagues or students of Kaurna.

Ownership and copyright issues have been raised with KACHA, with members of the Kaurna community, with education providers and with students of the Kaurna language. The issues are yet to be resolved satisfactorily, mainly because the copyright laws do not cover the rights demanded by Indigenous peoples. In the meantime, I have placed on record with KACHA an undertaking 'to pay all royalties resulting from the publication and sale of Kaurna language materials back into the Kaurna language programs'[17] (letter from R. Amery to David Branson, Chair KACHA, 8 August 1995).

A discussion on these issues was held with the 1997 KL&LE class and, as a result, a submission was prepared for the ATSIC inquiry (Janke, 1997) in which we urged the writers to take into account a wider range of language-related issues and activities. We raised two problematic case studies for consideration: the Kaurna language learning tapes and transcripts produced for the KL&LE course, and the Kaurna translation of *The Kookaburra Song*. We recommended that rights over language materials be recognised at several levels, so that group rights over the language itself are recognised concurrently with the rights of institutions over language materials prepared under their auspices, together with the recognition of individual intellectual property rights in their creation. We also urged that 'the process of translation be given due recognition as a creative endeavour which involves intellectual property rights'. Our concerns were included in the final report (Janke, 1998: 20-23).

A number of requests have been received from the Kaurna community for taped language learning materials and I am keen to sell the materials produced at the University of Adelaide for a nominal fee. However, I am reluctant to do so until the copyright issues are resolved and we work out some arrangement as to who owns the tapes. The ambiguities in this area are a considerable stumbling block.

Indeed, some Kaurna people (pc Georgina Williams & Karl Telfer, November 1997) have called for the copyrighting of the entire Kaurna language, word by word, as contained in the historical sources, under the Heritage Act. Even if copyrighting of the language in this way were possible, what of the status of neologisms, songs and Kaurna language materials created since 1990?

The sensitivity within the Kaurna community over non-Aboriginal and non-Kaurna access to the Kaurna language[18] causes questions to be raised as to how much of the language should be made available and what restrictions should be placed on its use, at least until adequate protection and safeguards are put in place (Georgina Williams in Reilly, 1997: 2). Karl Telfer does not believe that non-Aboriginal people should be allowed to learn the language, because in his view, the language itself is sacred (Reilly, 1997: Appendix 1: 2). Some people feel that too much has been given away already and believe that teaching the Kaurna language to non-Kaurna people somehow takes it away from the Kaurna people. This belief stems from a view of the language as a 'cultural artifact', as discussed in Chapter 3, as if it were the same as a wooden artefact that can't be in two places at the same time.

In 1996, when Kaurna was taught at Warriparinga within the Kaurna community, some local non-Aboriginal residents expressed interest in learning it (Paul Dixon, Interview transcript, 1996), but it was decided to keep the language within the Kaurna community. Other Kaurna people see sharing the language as a means of achieving reconciliation and increasing understanding of Aboriginal history and culture. They view themselves as a 'sharing' society. At the same time, they would like to see their own children have access to it first and not see it taught to non-Aboriginal students at the expense of their own. Both Lewis O'Brien and Alice Rigney acknowledge that the Kaurna community, and the number of learners of Kaurna emerging from within that community, is not sufficient to sustain Kaurna programs which are strictly in-house. They recognise that co-opting non-Aboriginal people into the Kaurna programs, both as learners and in the delivery of programs, is a necessary step. Auntie Alice explains in her interview with Jenny Burford:

> JB: So that would suggest that you have quite a positive impression of non-Indigenous people learning the language? You don't have any problems with that?
>
> AR: No, no I don't. But in the beginning, you know, I thought that it would have been just for the group who the language belongs to. At the beginning. But again it comes down to numbers and monies and all those other things that go with it, whether that's the way it's going to be taught.
>
> JB: So it's a pragmatic choice that non-Indigenous people are involved ... you're faced with a choice of ... well if we don't let other people in to boost the numbers, then we don't have the language?
>
> AR: That's right.
>
> JB: It's better to have the language, than it is.
>
> AR: Yes. That's right. ... we're on about this coming together, working together, and there are lots of people who are as passionate about this as I am. You are too. And if we work together we can show people that it can happen, and it can be successful. But we need to all get in and do it together, you know, because the world is just getting smaller and smaller and we need to do our bit, eh, to make it a good world to live in for the next generation who comes through.

In the same way, Lester Irabinna Rigney sees alliances created with non-Indigenous people as a crucial part of the liberation struggle for Kaurna reclamation. Nevertheless, Lester, Lewis, Alice and others are absolutely certain about who should be in control of the process: the Kaurna community.

In the mounting of the KL&LE course, I was aware that the majority of students would be non-Aboriginal. I had some misgivings about attempting to teach the Kaurna language with an emphasis on communication. There seemed to be little point: who would the students use the language with? What would they gain from it? However, I did prepare a set of language learning tapes with both Kaurna and non-Aboriginal students in mind, choosing topics which I thought would provide useful insights and a broad appreciation of the language and the contexts in which it is being used. The tapes were available for students to pursue if they wished, but the course did not revolve around them, nor was this aspect assessed. Rather, I have emphasised developing some understanding of Kaurna linguistics through practical exercises and developing understandings of the process of language reclamation and Kaurna language ecology, both historical and contemporary. I have made a point of drawing attention to issues of protocol and etiquette, beginning the course with a panel discussion on the topic between Kaurna Elders.

As it turned out, much less emphasis was given to actual language learning than had originally been planned, in response to concerns raised by Georgina Williams about non-Aboriginal people having access to the language. According to Helen Reilly who interviewed Georgina in the final weeks of the course:

> She (Georgina) doesn't believe that the Kaurna Language & Language Ecology course is the right thing to do at present and believes that any such course should be subject to the direct control of KACHA. Georgina regarded my suggestion that the course could teach about language reclamation with reference to Kaurna language materials but without the language learning component as being worth consideration. (Reilly, 1997: 7)

On the other hand, others in the Kaurna community (pc Alice Rigney, November 1997) have expressed some disappointment that more language learning was not included in the course.

Transportability of programs

We saw in Chapter 7 that education providers like to have programs neatly packaged and well-resourced so that anyone can pick them up and teach them anywhere. They do not like the programs to depend on a particular individual. While this is sound thinking on the part of the education provider who wants to be able to resource programs and ensure continuity, it runs contrary to the way things are done in Nunga society and might actually be counterproductive.

Mainstream society institutes checks and balances through regulations and documentation. Nunga society, on the other hand, maintains its authority and control to a large extent through relationships. The way the Kaurna people deal with ownership and copyright issues is by establishing a relationship with the people who deliver the programs and entrusting them to do so with respect. This also ensures they know where the programs are taught and to whom.

Some Aboriginal individuals and communities maintain their control and ownership over the language by refusing to write anything down and by insisting that programs are absolutely dependent on the individual. This was certainly the case with Kungarakany and Larrakiya taught in Darwin by Janama Robbie Mills. According to Mills (speaking at the PDTAL workshop, 5-7 December, 1995), when he departed the program would stop by design.

Does the Kaurna community lose or gain the language through its promotion within the wider society and through non-Aboriginal people learning it? This is a difficult question and not one to be passed over lightly.

On the one hand, having more people using the language, irrespective of whether they are Kaurna or not, helps to build up a momentum and extend its spheres of influence, which in turn provides more feedback and reinforcement for the learners of the language. More interest and more learners generally means more resources devoted to the enterprise. This is the rationale that Lewis

O'Brien appeals to when he promotes the use of Kaurna names within the wider community:

> People objected in the beginning when I was doing it [giving permission to non-Aboriginal people to use Kaurna words] and then they suddenly see the sense of it because it's really bringing the language into the fore and it's making people use it and then they have to address it and then indirectly you are bringing the language into use, which is a good thing. Because then everyone's using it and they know the reason for using that word. They've learned that word and that's useful in itself.
> (Lewis O'Brien, interview with Helen Reilly, 10 November 1997)

On the other hand, it is easy to see how the language could be appropriated by the non-Aboriginal community and be taught and used without reference to the Kaurna community, particularly if the language were packaged according to a predetermined LOTE formula. Such a program might consist of modules on 'My World' from the perspective of the student, 'Numbers', 'Colours' and other favoured topics within school programs. Such topics could easily be taught without reference to the Aboriginal community, or anything that leads students to recognise the Kaurna people or the links between the language they were learning and the country in which they lived. The program could be packaged with a set of accompanying print, audio, video and multimedia resources that could indeed be picked up and taught by anyone with a language teaching background. Given a favourable political climate, they could even be distributed and implemented in every primary school and high school in Adelaide. But that would not necessarily further the interests of the Kaurna community.

However, if the modules were developed in a way that involved the Kaurna community in the production of multimedia resources and the content were chosen to highlight the links between the language, the Kaurna people, the Adelaide Plains and local environment, early contact history and Kaurna culture (both 'traditional' and contemporary), then it might indeed be a good thing if it were taught in every school in Adelaide and even if, by necessity, it was taught in some schools by non-Aboriginal teachers.

But if too many non-Aboriginal people gain a knowledge of the language before the Kaurna people do, potentially it could cause a negative, defeatist reaction. Certainly there is a fear that non-Aboriginal students could perform better in Aboriginal language programs than Aboriginal students owing to previously acquired study skills and home situations that are more supportive of learning.[19]

Much may be gained by providing the wider community with access to the Kaurna language and Kaurna language programs. If the language is in the public sphere it is a constant reminder of the survival of the Kaurna people. However, links need to be constantly made back to the Kaurna community.

The 1992 South Australian Aboriginal Languages Workshop leading up to the establishment of Yaitya Warra Wodli, the South Australian Aboriginal Language Centre, took a strong position on asserting Indigenous ownership and control over Indigenous languages. This is reflected in the press release formulated at the conclusion of the two-day workshop at which Kaurna people were present:

> Aboriginal people want
> — what has been taken away, is to be given back to the rightful owners, and
> — to re-establish both the ownership and control of our languages and cultures.
> (SAAETAC, 1992: 24)

Kaurna people are united in their desire to maintain ownership and control of their language, but with different ends in view. Auntie Alice Rigney states:

> Permission must always be given to others to use our language. We must own this process. In reclamation programs there is a sharing of power. Access by all to language is reconciliation. This sharing I believe helps to overcome racism because of the understanding this brings.
> (In *Warranna Purruna* video, DECS, 1997)

Georgina Williams on the other hand has expressed the view that:

> Kaurna shouldn't be taught to non-Kaurna people mainly because of unresolved problems of potential exploitation and commodification of the language. 'Copyright protection of the language is essential, and not giving things away that can become the copyright of other people'
> ... She [Georgina] thinks the language should be protected before it is shared.
> (Interview with Georgina Williams, paraphrased by Helen Reilly, 12 November 1997)

A number of Kaurna people are now calling for a broad round of discussions about the future of the language and the associated ownership and copyright issues.

I view the expression of concern about ownership and copyright issues as a very positive development: Kaurna people are demonstrating a preparedness to work with linguists whilst at the same time taking ownership and control of the process. There are potential dangers, however. Legalistic approaches have the potential to stifle Kaurna language activity and could turn away useful allies. In the final analysis, these are issues which the Kaurna people must work out for themselves.

There are some concerns that the revival is moving too fast, that there is perhaps an over-emphasis on the formal delivery of Kaurna programs within schools or in the tertiary sector, and over the possible divisions that this may cause within the community. There is recognition of the need for engaging a linguist, though some would rather see Kaurna people themselves acquire linguistic skills than rely on non-Indigenous input (Reilly, 1997: 8).

The role of linguistics

We have seen in Chapter 6 that language reclamation is essentially a linguistic approach to language revival. It brings a range of linguistic skills and analyses to bear on the remaining materials in order to create a language which is as compatible as possible with the language as we know it from the sources, and with what we know and would expect from a study of related languages and Australian languages generally.

Assistance from linguists in the Kaurna program is generally well received and acknowledged by some as essential. Lewis O'Brien, when questioned about the role of linguists and linguistics, replied:

> Well, at this time it's very important to us, because if we're going to revive we can't do it without that [linguists and linguistics]. You've got to have, like I mentioned before, that basic structure. You know like we were talking before, you know verbs and nouns. You've got to know all that grammatical thing, you've got to know all the ins and outs of those sorts of things to be able to do it. It'll take us years to be able to do that and in the meantime we'll lose this impetus. I reckon that at this stage in our revival ... it's always important to work with someone else. We always get extensions from that — what they do, what you do. And then you build on that. And I think that's marvellous to do it that way. (Interview, 8 December 1997)

Or as Lester Rigney explains:

> Aboriginal people must draw on Indigenous and non-Indigenous movements. Non-Indigenous specialists must be included in the Kaurna struggle for language. Now this might mean that linguists jump on board, and anthropologists and archaeologists. Whether they be white is OK in its infancy, but the most important thing is that Kaurna peoples must own the language. So, yes, non-Indigenous peoples can be involved with it, as long as they're guided by the Kaurna people.
> (Interview with Jenny Burford, 21 October 1997)

Cherie Watkins, who began working in Kaurna programs in 1994 and now teaches Kaurna across a variety of programs, depends on the input of a linguist 'in the grammatical structure of the language and explanations of some of those things that I don't quite understand' (in Warranna Purruna video, DECS 1997). As the revival of Kaurna proceeds, the contribution that linguists can make, including specific techniques, such as comparative linguistics, is increasingly recognised. Auntie Alice expresses her feelings about this:

> ... and the linguists look at, you know Rob will look at Nukunu and see how they can, they have a look at words and then they change them to suit a particular nation. I reckon that's really great. (Interview with Jenny Burford, 29 October 1997)

There is evident support for the role of linguistics in Kaurna reclamation by those directly involved, but, as we have seen, the number of Kaurna people in the formal programs is not large. The attitudes of most of the Kaurna population towards the central involvement of non-Aboriginal linguists in the teaching and development of their language is hard to assess. Undoubtedly there is an element of suspicion and unease among some who choose to keep their distance and not get involved. Indeed, as observed earlier, some Nungas regard the language as 'a whitefella creation' and some find it very hard to learn their language from a non-Aboriginal person. Lester Irabinna Rigney, himself very supportive of my involvement, notes these feelings:

> Where you learn these languages are only at institutions where our mob have to pay ... our language is taught in institutions that are driven by non-Indigenous personalities and white linguists. Now that's a real difficult concept for Indigenous peoples to swallow.
> (Interview with Jenny Burford, 21 October 1997)

But these sentiments are seldom voiced openly, at least not to me. It is difficult to assess how widespread or how deeply they are held by members of the Kaurna community.

Recognition of input from linguists is evident in a number of ways. Some people will openly acknowledge the value of this approach. Kaurna people frequently contact me for assistance in constructing speeches, translating songs and other forms of expression in the Kaurna language. Those most proficient in using Kaurna, such as Cherie Watkins, are now able to use their own initiative to express themselves, but still like to check their texts with me for correct grammar. Kaurna people involved in the programs generally accept correction from me and often actively seek it. This has become an accepted part of the Kaurna programs and of the language movement itself within the community.

Language engineering or modernisation, such as the base-10 number system and the use of neologisms, have been warmly received in the school programs and within the community. Some Kaurna people direct naming enquiries my way or ask for assistance in addressing such enquiries. On the other hand, Kaurna people are ready to volunteer information about specific words we should avoid because of interlinguistic taboo, or advise on dealing with sensitive issues, such as men's or women's business. I try to address these concerns and incorporate suggestions made.

This all points to a fairly healthy, constructive relationship between myself, as linguist, and the Kaurna community. Their willingness to embrace linguistics contrasts with attitudes held by the neighbouring Ngarrindjeri community, who generally seem to distrust linguists and any advice about the linguistic structure of Ngarrindjeri. These differences in attitudes are reflected in the report of the Aboriginal Languages Workshop, which I did not attend, in which the 'Kaurna-Narrunga' were the only group to mention linguists in the development of their five year plan (SAAETAC, 1992: 15). They spoke of 'defin[ing] the role of linguists', 'develop[ing] criteria for linguists' and recommended that the work of linguists 'be under the control of Kaurna and Narrunga groups'. Mention of any role for linguists or non-Aboriginal resource people was conspicuously absent from plans put forward by the Ngarrindjeri group (SAAETAC, 1992: 17).

The rise of Kaurna to some prominence has shifted the locus of power within Nunga politics to some extent. Before the 1990s, other groups had dominated Nunga politics in Adelaide due to their numerical superiority and strong spokespeople. With the return of aspects of customary law and respect accorded to traditional landowners, the position of the Kaurna has improved relative to other groups and there is understandably some resentment. Linguistic rivalries, therefore, as an important ingredient in the contemporary language ecology and with potentially far-reaching effects on the shape of things to come, warrant further discussion here.

Competition with neighbouring Ngarrindjeri and more distant but well-known Pitjantjatjara is a motivating factor for learning and using Kaurna. The Kaurna people are aware that other groups tend to dismiss them because they don't speak their own language, as Frank Wanganeen (a Kaurna man) explains:

> Traditional people view Kaurna people as meaningless because they're not able to speak their language. They don't know any of the culture or their Dreaming or their environment. They're out of touch with themselves. I think it's important that you always have at the back of your mind that you know within yourself, yeh, I can speak it. That it's who I am as a Kaurna person that I can speak it ... It's just a matter for your own personal self because so much has been taken away. It's good to maintain something, I mean you know it's always there. It's part of a rich culture that Aboriginal people have. It's part of the jigsaw that needs to be put back.   (Interview, 17 October 1996)

This is a view echoed by many others. The constant reminders by the Pitjantjatjara, Ngarrindjeri and other groups of the extent of Kaurna people's loss of language and culture has the effect of generating interest in Kaurna. Vince Branson, another Kaurna man, also cited this as a major factor stimulating his interest in learning Kaurna:

> I get sick of jumping on buses and you hear all these Vietnamese people and all these Greeks and ... Wherever they come from, they're all talking in the languages. And if I was sitting down and if I had four or five fellas that speak Kaurna, we'd be rattling it off like crazy, you know. Shut 'em right up. They'd think 'Hey! What these fellas talking about?' you know ...
> You hear the same thing like when you travel on the bus from Alice Springs down to Adelaide, right? We jumped on there with a couple of watis [initiated men] heading down to Coober Pedy there. And they was just rattling off. Everyone on the bus, everyone was just looking at them. They knew they were the centre of attention. They was just giggling away, laughing. I'm sure they was talking about everyone on the bus there you know. Every time I looked around they were going for it. They started rattling you know. Oh, deadly!   (Interview, 15 November 1996)

On the one hand, awareness of other languages stimulates interest and provides a living model of what it would be like for the Kaurna to be able to speak their own language. Kaurna people, like Vince, are clearly envious of other groups. Possession of one's own language and an ability to speak it in public is clearly seen as a desirable thing. On the other hand, local linguistic rivalries pose a serious threat to developments in the Kaurna language. They need to be carefully managed so that one language is not privileged at the expense of others and so that individuals are strengthened and empowered.

Increasingly the assertion is made, while pointing out that it would be quite unacceptable to teach Kaurna in Pitjantjatjara country or Ngarrindjeri country, that only Kaurna should be taught in Kaurna country.[20] NSW Koories have implemented a policy to that effect, that only local languages should be taught in NSW schools. That is, Indigenous languages should not be transported away from their place of origin. Accordingly, there is considerable disquiet that Bundjalung from northern NSW is being taught in Victoria at Monash University.

However, the Aboriginal population in Adelaide is diverse — a diversity reflected in the student population at KPS and Tauondi. The allegiance to ancestral linguistic identities is strong and becoming stronger. Just as there has been some resistance to Pitjantjatjara programs and the use of Pitjantjatjara names in the metropolitan area by Kaurna people, so, too, there is some resistance by other groups to the development of Kaurna programs. Language groups to the north and west have a perception that Kaurna has cornered DETE funds and is 'getting everything' (pc Chris Warren; Greg Wilson, 1997). It seems that the success of the Kaurna programs is generating jealousies amongst other language groups. Some adult students at Tauondi who do not have direct links with the Kaurna community have resented having to learn the language in order to become cultural instructors and tourism operators (pc Cherie Watkins, 1997; Kevin O'Loughlin, 1999).

Whilst children of varying linguistic backgrounds at KPS seem happy to be learning Kaurna, and to date parents have been supportive of the Kaurna program[21], Lester Irabinna Rigney is concerned that it might create schisms within the Nunga community:

> Kaurna language strengthens Aboriginal identity, well that's coming from the old model of identity. If a person is learning Kaurna and that child is Narungga/Adnyamathanha descent, how really does it strengthen their identity? In actual fact it is doing the reverse. You see? Because you're instilling a whole new value and ideological system, because with language comes values and customs and beliefs. Even if you don't acknowledge it, it's in the language. So if you're teaching all of these separate communities the Kaurna language, then in fact you're overriding Narungga/Adnyamathanha culture and belief through the language.
>
> ...
>
> Let's look at six years down the track. Will we eventually have a group of students who have graduated with Kaurna that can speak some Kaurna. Well, what will that do to their parents? What will it do to their identity, particularly if they're from another group.
>
> (Interview with Jenny Burford, 21 October 1997)

These are very real concerns. With rising ethnic consciousness, we can expect that there will be greater resistance to compulsory Kaurna programs from students affiliated to other language groups, which is likely to rise in proportion to the success of the programs. It is important therefore, within an ecological model, to ensure that Kaurna programs are implemented in a way that also includes other languages. Cherie Watkins makes an effort to draw on students' linguistic and cultural backgrounds and encourages students with a knowledge of another Aboriginal language to make comparisons between their own language and Kaurna (personal observation; pc Cherie Watkins, December 1997).

Languages can exist side by side. One language need not be a threat to another — indeed programs in one language can support programs and development in another. We saw earlier, however, how rivalry with or envy of other languages has served as an important motivating factor and inspiration for Kaurna.

Following initial approval from the Nunga community, our main preoccupation in the early 1990s, in mounting Kaurna programs, was with resources and access to funds. Nunga politics was in the background. Now, although resources and funding remain a concern, the impact of Nunga politics is a much more important consideration.

In our enthusiasm for the language, we went ahead and did things, such as the adoption of Kaurna names by students or screen-printing a Tjilbruke T-shirt, where now we would be much more careful to consult more widely. Little thought was given to copyright issues when we produced the songbook in 1990. Now, copyright has become a major issue whenever we produce Kaurna materials, one that has yet to be adequately addressed. Much more serious consideration is now given to questions of who should have access to the language, and to protocol and etiquette in the use of Kaurna. Some round table discussions on future directions for the language are urgently needed.

As the language becomes politicised, we might expect to see some people distance themselves from it. Whilst some people thrive on conflict, others withdraw totally. We see that some Cornish people, otherwise enthusiastic about all manner of things Cornish, distance themselves from involvement in the language movement because of disagreements over orthography and the varieties of Cornish promoted by different factions.

Mühlhäusler warns against the politicisation of languages and language movements:

> In a lot of societies there is [a connection between politics and language]. And the general impression I've gained is that if you package language with party political issues, it's a deadly recipe. You'll lose the language because people feel excluded. Any language in any society should include people of different opinions, different religious beliefs, different aims, different ambitions, different age groups. Languages should be there to unite, not to divide.
> (Interview with Margaret Meadows, 2NF Radio, Norfolk Island, 6 October 1997)

These sentiments are echoed by others, for example in the North American context McCarty et al. (1997: 101) suggest that 'internal politics are best set aside for the benefit of the language restoration work at hand'.

Factionalism and in-fighting are common in language revival movements around the world, or, as Fishman (1991: 406) puts it, 'beliefs, resources and actions do not always come together in unproblematic ways'. So far, divisions within the Kaurna language movement have not been major, but the potential is there. Despite their differences, Kaurna people have been generally united in their support for the language reclamation efforts and do see the language as a means of uniting people across the various factions and family alliances within the Kaurna community.

Notes

[1] 'Grannies' is a Nunga English term referring to one's grandchildren.

[2] Aboriginal people felt that they were strangers in their own land, not represented in government or served by government institutions; so they set up a 'Tent Embassy' on the lawns of Parliament House to inform the public and serve as a focus for protests in the struggle for land rights. It remained in situ for two and a half decades.

[3] Sally Morgan was not one of the 'stolen generation'. Rather 'Aboriginality' was suppressed within her family in the era when she was growing up, in order to prevent the children from being taken away.

[4] Naomi was a central figure in KACHA affairs and the Warriparinga site in the mid-1990s.

[5] Typically, the reclamation of individual and group identities is centred on language groups. For many who have been totally cut off from their past, boundaries of the language group they identify with are simply those defined by Tindale (1974).

[6] The criteria laid down by KACHA for recognition as a Kaurna person mirror the Commonwealth definition: 'An Aboriginal person is defined as a person who is a descendant of an indigenous inhabitant of Australia, identifies as an Aboriginal, and is recognised as Aboriginal by members of the community in which she or he lives' (Jonas et al. 1993: 2).

[7] There has been criticism of the drafting of this constitution by some members of the committee, who have called for a tightening up of this clause so that all criteria are required. If it is only required that 'a person acknowledges himself or herself as a Kaurna person' there is a concern that it leaves the way open for anyone to claim membership.

[8] Lester Rigney has observed something of a backlash within the community whereby disparaging comments have been directed at the Kaurna language (interview with Jenny Burford, 21 October 1997).

[9] The Tjitji Tjuta – 'Colebrook Kids' regathering and reconciliation event was held on the site of the Colebrook Training Home, Eden Hills on 1 June 1997.

[10] The site is owned by the Aboriginal Lands Trust of SA, which has plans to develop it for recreational and cultural purposes.

[11] 'Aboriginal Language Programs 1999', paper prepared by Greg Wilson, tabled at the Aboriginal Languages Standing Committee meeting on 16 September 1999.

[12] For details see the findings of the Royal Commission (Stevens, 1995) and an alternative report based on the same transcripts prepared by Greg Mead (1995). A special edition of the *Journal of Australian Studies* (Number 48, 1996) titled *Secret Women's Business: Hindmarsh Island Bridge Affair* publishes a series of essays which cast doubt on the Royal Commission's findings.

[13] Veronica has been fighting for recognition and access to the site of the former CSR factory at Port Adelaide where her great grandmother, Lartelare, was born in 1851 (see Brodie, 2002). A research report was prepared for the Lartelare Homeland Association by Sheridah Melvin (Brodie & Melvin, 1994).

[14] But here, too, families were disrupted by goverment policies. Men often had to leave the missions for extended periods to find work. Those perceived as being able to 'fit in' to white society were granted exemption from the Aborigines Protection Act, thus becoming honorary whites, whereupon 'consorting' with other Aboriginal people was prohibited. Consequently, they were not allowed back on the missions and reserves without a permit.

[15] The Prime Minister belatedly moved with more direct criticism of Hanson in 1998 after the electoral interests of the Liberal Party in Queensland were threatened.

[16] Indeed, one PWAC student who has been learning Kaurna since 1995, an artist born in Germany, has adopted an Aboriginal name, Moona Nookenbah. Whilst not Kaurna, it is immediately recognisable as an Aboriginal name. According to a newspaper report she 'considers herself part of the Aboriginal community and uses elements of Aboriginal mythology in her work' (*Eastern Courier*, 15 October 1997: 19). Not everyone in the Kaurna community is happy with her use of Kaurna words and phrases in her works of art.

[17] Royalties from *Macquarie Aboriginal Words* are paid to KPS and used to support Kaurna language programs through the production of materials and the hiring of language instructors. Proceeds from the sale of songbooks, textbooks and course materials are returned to help fund some courses and to fund further print runs of materials.

[18] Some Kaurna people would like to restrict the language to the Kaurna community in much the same way that some Pueblo Indian communities have done in New Mexico and Arizona. However, these same people realise the reality of their current situation and recognise that a sharing of the language is the only way forward.

[19] These concerns were raised by a number of respondents to the AILF consultation (Report of the National Consultation on the AILF, November 1993 - February 1994: 15).

[20] It is still commonplace for people to think of only Pitjantjatjara when it comes to Indigenous languages, without giving any thought to the possibility of teaching Kaurna.

[21] Many Nunga parents are keen to see that their children have access to an Indigenous language, even if it is not their own. This is true not only of Nunga parents at KPS, but also of the Nunga parent body at Alberton PS where Pitjantjatjara is offered, at Mansfield Park PS where a Ngarrindjeri program operates, at Salisbury North PS, which offers both Ngarrindjeri and Kaurna, and elsewhere throughout the Metropolitan area.

11

Into the Twenty-first Century: Developments since 2000

> *[P]eople like Jack, Kaiya, Jamie...they can sit there together and have a great yarn together [in Kaurna], which gives me great pride. They're all young fathers now, young parents teaching their own language, Kaurna.... They're going to have something special that we didn't have growing up around Point Pearce or Raukkan [and that] is that background in language. They'll grow up with that and it'll be second nature to them*
> (Stephen Gadlabarti Goldsmith, interview with Rob Amery, 3 December 2014)

The previous chapters have documented, analysed and discussed the reclamation and the earliest stages of Kaurna language revival. In this chapter I provide a brief snapshot of some of the main developments in the reclaimed Kaurna language and within the Kaurna language movement since 2000. On the one hand, a number of Kaurna people, some of whom played a significant role in the re-introduction of Kaurna, have passed on and others have retired. On the other hand, several young people have become involved and some others have become much more active. Jack Kanya Buckskin began learning Kaurna in mid-2006 and is now easily the most proficient and fluent Kaurna speaker and the main teacher of the Kaurna language (see Amery & Buckskin, 2012). Non-Aboriginal supporters, too, have come and gone, though there have been some long-term stayers, such as Chester Schultz, who was instrumental in the very first songwriter's workshop in 1990. Chester has been researching Kaurna placenames for KWP since 2007 and completed his own projects *Dancing Ngutinai* in 2002 and *Songs with the Nungas* in 2006.

Significantly, I have had the opportunity to travel to Germany several times since 2010 and was able to see the home towns of Teichelmann and Schürmann, the institutions where they undertook their training and the churches in which they, and missionaries Klose and Meyer, were ordained. I have sighted first-hand the correspondence they sent to Germany and the handwritten letters and copybook pages from the Kaurna children Ityamaii, Pitpauwi and Wailtyi. Kaurna representatives, Ngarrpadla Alitya Rigney and Karl Winda Telfer, and Ngarrindjeri woman, Verna Koolmatrie, also had the opportunity to visit the archives of the Dresden Mission Society, now located in the Francke Stiftungs (Francke Foundations) in Halle, near Leipzig. Ngarrpadla Alitya, Karl, Verna and I were accompanied through Germany in August 2011 by Gerhard Rüdiger, who subsequently worked for KWP in an administrative and research role. We were invited to participate in the 175-year anniversary celebrations of the formation of the Dresden Mission Society in Dresden. We also had the opportunity of seeing the collection of hundreds of birds that Teichelmann had sent from Adelaide to Altenburg in 1842. For a more extensive account of this visit see Amery (2012). Since 2010, I also had opportunities to meet with the Schürmann family, including descendants of Clamor Schürmann who travelled from Australia to Osnabrück in 2012 for the 500 anniversary of surviving records of the family.

Kaurna sources

As mentioned in the Preface to *Warrabarna Kaurna!*, since the completion of the PhD, an additional early German source was obtained from Berlin by Heidi Kneebone. A ship's doctor, Hermann Koeler visited South Australia between mid-October 1837 and late April 1838. He published a list of approximately 150 words and eight Pidgin Kaurna sentences, together with observations on the customs of the Kaurna people and the state of the colony. This source is a significant find, adding several words to the known lexicon and helping to refine knowledge of the meanings and pronunciation of some words. The Pidgin Kaurna sentences appear to correlate closely with sentences recorded by Williams and Wyatt (analysed by Simpson, 1996), providing further confirmation of the existence of a Pidgin Kaurna language. See Zweck (2006) for an English translation and Amery & Mühlhäusler (2006) for an analysis of Koeler's papers and Kaurna wordlist.

In 2001, I became aware of another short wordlist (just 52 common words of which 50 are actually Kaurna) compiled by an early colonist J. Chittleborough who grew up as a child with Kaurna children. He published his memoirs in *The Advertiser*. Chittleborough (1906) does not yield any words that have not been documented by others and features a number of errors, but it is an additional primary source with different spellings to those used by others.

In the course of his placenames research, Chester Schultz investigated the correspondence of Stephen Hack. In a letter written in 1837, Schultz found a phrase and a sentence written in Pidgin Kaurna complementing Pidgin Kaurna sentences of Wyatt (1879), Williams (1840) and Koeler (1842).

There have also been some other promising leads, which, unfortunately, have not increased our knowledge of the Kaurna language. Lois Zweck from the Lutheran Archives became aware of correspondence between Teichelmann and Hans Conan von der Gabelentz with reference to having sent a wordlist. Dr Emig in charge of the Thuringen State Archives in Altenburg suggested that there might be material in Russia. Sure enough, James McElvenny found a copy of T&S that was annotated by Protector Matthew Moorhouse that had been taken by the Russians as war booty from von der Gabelentz's private library in his castle of Poschwitz on the outskirts of Altenburg. I was hopeful that this annotated copy of T&S might yield additional material and insights into the Kaurna language, but it appears that Teichelmann had incorporated all of Moorhouse's comments into his TMs 1857 manuscript prior to sending Moorhouse's copy of T&S to Altenburg.

We were hopeful that further research in the German archives might unearth additional documents. There is mention in the writings of the Dresden missionaries of several documents, including a school prayer, a farewell letter to Mr Forster and translations of 'Biblical truths', such as the story of Jairus. Despite an extensive search by Gerhard Rüdiger in 2012, no trace of these documents has yet been found.

Restoring and transforming the Kaurna language

Our understanding of the Kaurna language has greatly increased over the last one and a half decades. Lexical gaps are slowly being filled as the need arises. With the writing of a learner's guide between 2005 and 2013 many new terms for household objects, fishing equipment and football were incorporated (Amery & Simpson, 2013). Importantly, metalinguistic terminology, such as *wapiwarrarla karrpa* 'complex sentence' (lit. two-verb sentence) and *yitpiwarra* 'meaning' (lit. seed word), were adopted for the chapter headings. These were developed in the context of a TAFE course run specifically for Kaurna people in 2012-2013.

Issues of authenticity and integrity have come to the fore with a series of National Sorry Day posters appearing with unexplained pseudo-Kaurna forms for concepts of 'recognition', 'respecting', 'righting' etc. (see Amery, 2013).

Intensive research into Kaurna placenames has been conducted, initially by myself (Amery, 2002), and more recently meticulous and detailed research by Chester Schultz (forthcoming a; forthcoming b). In 2000, I prepared a section which translated or adapted placenames of Ngarrindjeri form into Kaurna (Amery, 2000) for a booklet *Footprints in the Sand* produced by the Holdfast Bay Reconciliation Group (Allen, 2000).

In line with the formulaic method, a range of useful expressions have been developed in several specific domains, beginning with the context of childrearing (Amery & Gale, 2000) and talking with children (Amery & Simpson, 2013: 74-79). This was followed by funeral protocols, including translation of funeral liturgy and the Lord's Prayer, translation of familiar and well-loved hymns, such as *The Old Rugged Cross,* such that Kaurna people may conduct an entire funeral in the Kaurna language should they so choose (Amery & Rigney, 2006; Amery & O'Brien, 2007).

Useful expressions were also developed in the domains of football and fishing (see Amery & Simpson, 2013: 84-92). These two domains of language use were targeted for several reasons. First, both fishing and football are popular activities amongst many Kaurna people. Football is an activity in which the Kaurna language can have an important instrumental function within an English-speaking society. If a Kaurna football team is able to use a wide range of expressions spontaneously it can implement strategies without the opposing team understanding, thus potentially giving them something of an advantage.

Expressions needed tend to be short and formulaic, thus they are easy to learn, but if they are to be effective they need to be well-rehearsed, rapid-fire and spontaneous, which are useful skills in developing full fluency. Fishing expressions are also often short and easy to learn, but in contrast to football, there is mostly plenty of time to formulate what one wants to say, unless there happens to be a fish on the line. Fishing is a pastime that one engages in with family or mates. The situation is relaxed and one characterised by silence. Many of the expressions, such as *Kuya payanthi?*, 'Are the fish biting?' require a minimal response. For these reasons, fishing is a particularly easy activity in which to begin using the Kaurna language.

Another domain where words and expressions have been developed is cycling. Development of the Kaurna language in this domain was stimulated by the *Maityuwampi* Cycling for Culture fundraiser for the Kaurna language movement held in October 2013.

Revised Kaurna Spelling (2010)

Of major import to the form of the reclaimed Kaurna language is the spelling reforms adopted in 2010.[1] For some twenty years, we had used T&S spellings and words drawn from other sources (Williams, 1840; Piesse, 1840; Wyatt, 1879 etc.), where there was no counterpart in T&S or TMs, were adapted using T&S-like spelling in the revisions of the Warra Kaurna wordlist. For instance, wocaltee 'bark shield' was adopted as wakalti (Amery, 1995: 14) and murrangá yoo 'freshwater tortoise' as marrangayu (Amery, 1997: 25) [RS marangayu].

I have long been aware of the deficiencies of T&S spellings, see (Amery, 2000: 117-120) but have found them to be workable, and importantly they allow the reader to easily find the words in the original source material (T&S and TMs). When Jack Kanya Buckskin came to teach the Kaurna language, naturally less familiar with the historical and comparative materials than I, it was difficult for him to know whether t's, n's and l's were interdental, alveolar or retroflex, or whether the rr was rolled or glide, and where the vowel should be lengthened. He wanted to be able to tell from the spelling how each and every Kaurna word should be pronounced. The uncertainty was also frustrating his students. A spelling revision was also strongly encouraged by other linguists, Mary-Anne Gale and Jasmin Morley. Kaurna Elders Kauwanu Lewis O'Brien and Ngarrpadla Alitya Rigney were a little reluctant at first but were persuaded by the cogent arguments put forward. I also saw that it was time to adopt spelling reforms, knowing full well the amount of work that this would entail. The Kaurna Learner's Guide had already been written using T&S spelling and copies of a Prototype version had been circulated, but it had not been published. So a major revision was required, culminating in the Amery & Simpson (2013) publication.

Revised Spelling (RS) was introduced following vigorous discussion at a number of KWP meetings throughout 2010. I took a PowerPoint presentation prepared for the Kaurna Learner's Guide and produced several versions of spelling revisions to show people how the language would actually look if these revisions were adopted. These were also demonstrated at a workshop at Kaurna

Plains School with teachers and members of the School Council. The Revised Spelling system that was eventually adopted included some modifications that deviate from a strictly phonemic spelling system. Notable amongst these modifications is the spelling of initial interdental stops and nasals as *t* and *n*, but *th* and *nh* elsewhere. This is because there is no alveolar/interdental contrast word-initially and an initial *th* would cause a greater degree of mispronunciation amongst English speakers with no understanding of the Kaurna spelling system. The locative suffix is spelt *–ngga* and *–illa* in placenames, as they are familiar to many people in this form, as opposed to *–ngka* and *–ila* on common nouns. Thus there is a contrast between Nurlungga 'at Noarlunga' versus *nurlungka* 'on the bend', though they are exactly the same word and pronounced in exactly the same way.

At the time Revised Spelling was accepted by KWP, we were in the middle of producing Kaurna radio shows. I immediately revised the spellings in the scripts we were using and I saw how easily the participants adapted to the new spelling and were able to read the scripts without difficulty, despite some considerable prior familiarity with T&S spelling. Jack Buckskin also reports the ease with which he has been able to introduce Revised Spelling with his students. All participants of the Kaurna TAFE Certificate III course offered in 2012 are very familiar with the Revised Spelling and the contrast with T&S spelling.

Revised Spellings have been introduced through naming and translation requests to KWP since September 2010 and have been adopted by the Adelaide City Council for placenames within their jurisdiction. Existing signage will remain, however, until they need replacing when Revised Spelling will be employed.

All Kaurna language materials produced by KWP from now on, will of course employ Revised Spelling. The flagships for introducing Revised Spelling the second edition of the *Kaurna Alphabet Book* (Buckskin et al., 2013), *Kulurdu Marni Ngathaitya!*, the Kaurna Learner's Guide (Amery & Simpson, 2013), the Kaurna Dictionary (Morley & Amery, forthcoming) and increasingly the *Kaurna Language Learning Series* YouTube channel (http://bit.ly/kaurna). Revised versions of existing resources, such as *Kaurna Paltinna* (Schultz et al., 1999), *Kaurna Palti Wonga* (Amery & Rigney, 2006) and *Warra Kaurna* will be forthcoming.

There is, however, some opposition to the Revised Spelling, with some people expressing the view that there was insufficient consultation. Because T&S spellings have been in use for two decades in some public signage and in Kaurna language learning materials, these spellings have become very familiar and, as to be expected, some Kaurna people have developed an attachment to these spellings, even though when people like Tim Hughes and Auntie Gladys Elphick first saw the T&S spellings they did not relate well to them (p.c. Lewis O'Brien). The RS *kardi* 'emu' presumably would have made much more sense to them than T&S *kari* because they heard the *rd* as a d-sound rather than an r-sound. Unfortunately, some think that by changing the spelling, the substance of the Kaurna language is changed. Whilst Kaurna words should be pronounced the same, irrespective of the spelling system employed, there is the consideration of spelling pronunciations, discussed in Amery (2000: 121-122). If anything, Revised Spelling should help to reduce 'English pronunciations'.

Kaurna language programs

The teaching of the Kaurna language within schools continues. Many more programs could be commenced but for the want of teachers of the language. Cherie Warrara Watkins, the main teacher of Kaurna language during the 1990s retired. In the meantime, Jack Kanya Buckskin took on the teaching of Kaurna in a range of programs (see Amery & Buckskin, 2012) and more recently Taylor Power-Smith has been teaching Kaurna at Gilles Street Primary School in the city since 2014.

The Department of Education and Childhood Development (DECD) compiles statistics for the numbers of students studying Aboriginal languages in South Australian schools. In 2014 (the most recent statistics available), there were reportedly 610 students (down from 1150 in 2011) studying Kaurna in government schools, 159 Indigenous students (257 in 2011) and 451 non-Indigenous students (cf. 893 in 2011). There were six Kaurna language programs offered (cf. 11 in 2011) and all of these were located in the Adelaide metropolitan area, mostly in the northern and western suburbs. At the same time, 445 students (160 Indigenous and 285 non-Indigenous) were studying Pitjantjatjara in four metropolitan schools whilst two additional programs offered Ngarrindjeri in the Adelaide metropolitan area for 45 Indigenous students. Much of the decline in numbers of programs and students studying Kaurna is due to Jack Kanya Buckskin's withdrawal from the school sector and movement into the adult education sector at Tauondi College.

I adapted the tertiary-level Kaurna linguistics course, which was introduced first at the University of Adelaide in 1997, and offered it at the University of South Australia from 2002 to 2004 under the title 'Kaurna Language and Culture', initially as a semester-length course and then as an intensive summer school. After my return to the University of Adelaide I offered 'Kaurna Language and Language Ecology' there again, first as a summer school with low enrolments. In 2009, it became 'Reclaiming Languages: a Kaurna Case Study' (see Amery, 2012), which was offered again as a Summer School in January 2013 and 2015 with a significant level of input from a range of Kaurna people, especially Jack Kanya Buckskin. There are approximately 25-30 enrolments in the course as it is now taught.

With the retirement of Greg Wilson from DECS in 2011 the department used salary savings to support community-based Aboriginal language programs to develop resources and expertise to assist the teaching of these languages in schools. KWP was seen by DECS to be the best conduit for working with the Kaurna community on the Kaurna language. Since 2011, DECS (now DECD) entered into formal partnerships with KWP and KWK to support the training and professional development of Kaurna language teachers and the development of Kaurna language curriculum and Kaurna language resources. Jasmin Morley was employed through the University of Adelaide to write a Kaurna language curriculum, working together with Kaurna Plains School (KPS). DECD also supported the publication of the Kaurna Learner's Guide and the Kaurna TAFE course (see below).

In order to address the acute shortage of teachers of Aboriginal languages Mary-Anne Gale developed a TAFE Certificate III course 'Learning an Endangered Aboriginal Language' and a Certificate IV course 'Teaching an Endangered Aboriginal Language'. The Certificate III course was taught first to a group of Ngarrindjeri students at Murray Bridge in 2010-2011 and Wirangu students on the West Coast also in 2011. Throughout 2012 and early 2013, the Certificate III course was taught to a group of Kaurna students, with nine graduating and several others completing some course components. These students comprise the core of the Kaurna language movement. Comprehensive reports (Gale, 2012a, 2012b, 2012c, 2012d, 2013) were written for each of the intensive week-long workshops. Several students, who have placements in schools and teaching programs, commenced the Certificate IV course in late 2013. Jack Kanya Buckskin and Taylor Power-Smith have since completed their Certificate IV in 'Teaching an Endangered Aboriginal Language (Kaurna)'. However, much more needs to be done in this area of training and professional development.

Kaurna in society

The Australian National Census asks a question 'Do you speak a language other than English at home?' followed by a question asking the respondent to nominate the language they speak. Until 2001 the number of people who responded 'Kaurna' was not compiled, but rather subsumed in the category 'Eastern Aboriginal nec'. In the 2001 Census there were 29 people who claimed to speak Kaurna at home, whilst in the 2006 census there were 34. There has been a 118% increase in the 2011 census (Office for the Arts Indigenous Languages Support (ILS) Fact Sheet, 2013: 4) and Kaurna is one of the few languages in Australia where speaker numbers are increasing with 48 recorded in the 2011 census.[2] Of course census figures are self-reportage and claims to speak Kaurna at home cannot be a claim to speak the language fluently and exclusively in the same way that Dinka or Vietnamese might be spoken at home. However, as indicated in the quote by Steve Goldsmith at the beginning of this chapter, there are now three young Kaurna men, Jack Kanya Buckskin, Jamie Ngungana Goldsmith and Kaiya Agius, who are able to conduct a conversation and joke around in Kaurna without having to resort to English and Jack is raising his two young children as bilingual Kaurna-English speakers.

The use of Kaurna in the public domain has increased significantly since 2000. The giving of Kaurna speeches of Welcome to Country by Kaurna people continues unabated. Non-Indigenous people are now encouraged to give an Acknowledgement of Kaurna country in the Kaurna language and some prominent individuals have done so, including the ex-Premier of South Australia, Linn Arnold, the Vice Chancellors of the University of South Australia and the University of Adelaide, former Adelaide City Lord Mayor, Stephen Yarwood amongst others.

Kaurna language is also incorporated into cultural performance by three Kaurna dance troupes all of which bear Kaurna names: *Paitya* 'deadly' lead by Karl Winda 'owl' Telfer, *Taikurtinna* 'family' led by Steve Gadlabardi 'native bee' Goldsmith and *Kuma Kaaru* 'one blood' led by Jack Kanya 'rock' Buckskin. These three Kaurna dance troupes are frequently engaged to perform at conferences and public events including the annual Adelaide Festival of the Arts, Spirit Festival, Blak Nite and NAIDOC Week. A riveting performance was given by *Taikurtinna* and *Kuma Kaaru* at Pirltawardli on the occasion of the visit of Rev. Volker Dally, Director of Leipzig Lutheran Mission[3] on 27th July 2013.[4] These performances began with a fluent introduction in Kaurna. Jack Kanya Buckskin also gave a rendition of a song with Kaurna words, but modelled upon traditional Yolŋu style *manikay* (song) through his close association with Yolŋu friends visiting Adelaide.

There is a strong demand for Kaurna names across many sectors of society with an estimated 1000 names having been adopted since 1980. A surprisingly wide array of entities now bears Kaurna names including rivers and other geographical features, walking trails, parks and reserves, streets, buildings, rooms, businesses, products, organisations and units within organisations, programs, conferences, a solar bus, a tram, a patrol boat, an emergency beacon, a frost chamber, a wheat variety and an allele. Not surprisingly, the adoption of Kaurna names by Kaurna people, the giving of Kaurna names to their children and the naming of pets is much increased.

The Adelaide City Council Kaurna place-naming initiative developed in 1996-1997 (discussed in Chapter 8) was progressively implemented (see Amery & Williams, 2002). Karrawirra Pari (River Torrens) was officially dual-named in November 2001. The park names were progressively adopted over a number of years with installation of signage for most parks in 2004, whilst dual naming of the city squares was finally adopted in 2012. The Adelaide City Council Kaurna naming initiative has been a standout for the use of Indigenous names within an urban environment within Australia (see Hodges, 2007: Amery & Rigney, 2006).

A number of public art initiatives which include the Kaurna language have also been completed since 2000. Notable amongst these have been the redevelopment of the Adelaide Festival Centre concourse in 2002, the *Tappa Parruna* <sic> (Journey of Life) public art created by Kaurna artist Karl Winda Telfer working in collaboration with Gavin Malone and completed in 2006.

Tastefully executed graffiti art also appeared under the Southern Expressway bridge near Warriparinga that includes the words *Marni naa budni Warriparinga* 'Welcome to Warriparinga'.

Kaurna on the web

In 1995, a web search for the word 'Kaurna' yielded just one hit, that of the AIATSIS electronic archive (ASEDA) mentioned in Amery (2000: 194). Over the next few years Kaurna acknowledgements and welcomes began to appear on a number of websites over the next few years. Since then, there has been an explosion of Kaurna language on the web. A Google search for 'Kaurna' now yields 183,000 hits[5] and a search for many other Kaurna terms now also results in numerous hits where previously they would not have been found. For instance, *pangkarra* 'territory', now yields 11,300 hits (including a pasta range, wines and a landscaping company in NSW). Of course, many Google hits are duplicated. Nonetheless the Kaurna language now has a substantial and varied presence on the worldwide web.

In 2003, I obtained a small grant from the Adelaide City Council (ACC) for a project titled 'Kaurna Language in the City', which documented the use of Kaurna language within the City of Adelaide, including the placenames adopted by ACC. This information was posted on the ACC's own webpages (http://www.adelaidecitycouncil.com/community/reconciliation/kaurna/place-naming/), including graphics and sound files.

In 2005, KWP established its own webpages, hosted by the University of Adelaide (www.adelaide.edu.au/kwp) to provide basic information about the Kaurna language, resources and the Kaurna language movement. The Kaurna language itself (Kaurna wordlists etc.) and minutes of KWP meetings are password-protected, which is made available to Kaurna people.

The Kaurna Placenames website (www.kaurnaplacenames.com), a collaborative project between the Kaurna Heritage Board and its Tappa Iri Agreement with the four southern councils, City of Onkaparinga, City of Marion, City of Holdfast Bay and Yankalilla Council, together with the South Australian state government Geographical Names Unit and KWP, was launched in July 2006. This website displays Kaurna placenames on Google Earth, together with a sound file for pronunciation, meaning and location[6] displayed in a pop-up box (Amery & Buckskin, 2014).

A sister database was developed, which maps new Kaurna names in the public domain adopted since 1980. These names and text included in public artworks etc. are also mapped on Google Earth with different icons to show which names were approved by KWP, which were approved by a Kaurna person outside KWP and others which are questionable (see Amery, 2010).

In 2014, the University of Adelaide (Ghil'ad Zuckermann and Rob Amery) embarked on the production of a Massive Open Online Course (MOOC) on Language Revival with one full week devoted to a case study of Kaurna. This opened up the opportunity to interview a number of Kaurna people, and others, about their journey in the Kaurna language movement and KWP/KWK has the rights to use this raw footage in ways they see fit. The Language Revival MOOC was launched in July 2015 running over five weeks with over 4000 students enrolled worldwide coming from more than 140 different countries. See https://www.edx.org/course/language-revival-securing-future-adelaidex-lang101x

Media coverage

The Kaurna language movement gained some media coverage throughout the 1990s (discussed in Amery, 2000: 193-194). Sporadic media coverage has continued in the local, national and international media. Our visit to Germany in 2011 gained some coverage in German newspapers, radio and television, especially in Osnabrück, Clamor Schürmann's home town. In 2013, sparked by a story run by the BBC in January, Spiegel online ran a story which was then picked up by Swiss National Radio, who interviewed Jack Buckskin and me by phone. The Kaurna language has gained considerable publicity through Jack Buckskin's 2011 Young South Australian of the Year Award and finalist for Young Australian of the Year. In 2012, young Indigenous Central Australian filmmaker Dylan McDonald produced an hour-long documentary on Jack Buckskin and his efforts to teach and re-introduce Kaurna. The film includes interviews with his family and with Steve Gadlabardi Goldsmith, Lutheran Archivist, Lyall Kupke and myself. It also includes footage of KWP meetings in progress and Jack teaching Kaurna in schools and at Warriparinga. The film, titled *Buckskin*, won the Foxtel Documentary Award at the Sydney Film Festival in June 2013.

International profile

In addition to the international media coverage, discussed above, Kaurna language reclamation efforts have gained some international profile within academic circles as a result of the publication of *Warrabarna Kaurna* and a number of positive reviews (Lund, 2000; Johnson-Weiner, 2001; Walsh, 2001; Clarke, 2001; Loether, 2002; Bowern, 2003), and through invited lectures and presentations at various international universities and conferences.

International Conference Presentations and Invited Lectures:
- In June 2004, I presented a paper titled 'Kaurna language reclamation and the Formulaic Method' presented at the Stabilising Indigenous Languages (SIL) conference, University of California at Berkeley. This paper was subsequently published (Amery, 2009).
- In November 2004, I was invited as the Lansdowne Scholar to the University of Victoria, British Columbia, Canada where I presented 'Kaurna language reclamation: Lessons learned from attempts to re-introduce the Indigenous language of the Adelaide Plains' in addition to lectures on endangered Indigenous Australian languages and Indigenous languages in education.
- In July 2005, KWP supported Dennis O'Brien's attendance of the Linguistics Society of America (LSA) Linguistics Institute at Harvard University where he presented 'Waking up and ancient language: Reclaiming Kaurna of the Adelaide Plains, South Australia'.
- In October 2007, Jack Buckskin and I attended the Foundation for Endangered Languages (FEL) conference at the University of Malaya, Kuala Lumpur. See Amery & Rigney (2007).
- In March 2009, I presented at the Language Documentation and Conservation conference at the University of Hawai'i at Manoa, Honolulu (Amery, 2009).
- In June 2010, Jack Buckskin and I were invited to run a three-day workshop 'Strategies for re-introducing languages no longer spoken' at InField, University of Oregon, Eugene. Jack was also an instructor in the Language Activism Workshop along with other Indigenous instructors from Kenya and the US. We also presented a paper 'Mapping Names and the Use of Indigenous Languages on Google Earth: Recent innovations in Kaurna, the language of the

Adelaide Plains, South Australia'. at the Stabilising Indigenous Languages (SIL) conference there.
- From October 2010 until February 2011, I served as a guest professor at the University of Cologne, Germany, giving a series of lectures on Australian Indigenous Languages and an advanced course 'Why Bother with a Dead Language? Reclaiming Kaurna, the language of the Adelaide Plains, South Australia'.
- In October 2010, I presented to the Pacific Network conference at the University of Cologne.
- In November 2010, I was invited by the Manx Language Foundation to give the annual Ned Madrell lecture titled: 'Mapping Names and the Use of Indigenous Languages on Google Earth: Recent innovations in Kaurna, the language of the Adelaide Plains, South Australia' during Manx Language Week.
- In December 2010, I presented a seminar on mapping Kaurna placenames within Afrikanistiks at the University of Cologne.
- In December 2010, I presented at a seminar at the University of Leiden, The Netherlands.
- In January 2011, I presented at the School of Oriental and African Studies (SOAS), University of London.
- In August 2011, I gave a guest lecture 'Kaurna Language Reclamation: Attempts to re-introduce the Indigenous language of the Adelaide Plains and the work of Kaurna Warra Pintyandi (KWP)' at the University of Leipzig, Germany.
- In August 2012, I presented at an international Sociolinguistics Symposium at the Freie Universität, Berlin: 'The Re-introduction of a 'sleeping' language: Kaurna, the original language of Adelaide, capital city of South Australia'.
- In August 2013, Jack Buckskin and I presented 'Having it Both Ways: Towards recognition of the Kaurna language movement within the community and within the university sector.' at the Foundation for Endangered Languages (FEL) conference at Carleton University, Ottawa.
- In October 2014, I was invited to give a keynote address 'A New Lease of Life: 25 years of reclaiming and re-introducing a forgotten language in metropolitan Adelaide, South Australia' at the 10th International Symposium on Taiwanese Languages and Teaching at Chengkung University in Tainan, Taiwan.
- In September 2015, I presented a workshop on Australian Indigenous Languages and Kaurna language revival at the Universitas Syiah Kuala, Banda Aceh, Indonesia and a seminar on 'Re-introducing a Sleeping Language, Kaurna' at Australian Corner language centre, Banda Aceh.

Kaurna language reclamation efforts have been cited by a number of high profile linguists as a case of successful language revival (see Evans, 2014: 330-331). World-renowned linguist David Crystal (2000: 162) makes the following comments in relation to reclaimed Kaurna:

> the revived language is not the same as the original language, of course; most obviously, it lacks the breadth of functions which it originally had, and large amounts of old vocabulary are missing. But, as it continues in present-day use, it

will develop new functions and new vocabulary, just as any other living language would, and as long as people value it as a true marker of their identity, and are prepared to keep using it, there is no reason to think of it as anything other than a valid system of communication.

Sociopolitical dimensions of Kaurna language revival

Kaurna Warra Pintyanthi (KWP)

During the 1990s, I received some requests for Kaurna names and translations. I addressed these as best I could. Some of these requests, as noted previously (Amery, 2000: 241), came from, or were referred on to me by, Kaurna people. But there were other requests from the general public. As a non-Indigenous linguist, I felt uncomfortable about addressing these requests. Sometimes I would liaise directly with Kauwanu Lewis O'Brien or would tell people that they really should consult with a Kaurna person and ask for permission. But I was often unsure whether they followed it up or not. For this reason, the Kaurna language movement continued to meet on a monthly basis at the conclusion of the funeral protocols workshops in November 2002. This committee soon became known as Kaurna Warra Pintyandi (KWP) or Kaurna Warra Pintyanthi in Revised Spelling, Kauwanu Lewis O'Brien and Ngarrpadla Alitya Rigney became the signatories and I convened the committee. KWP, its formation and operations are discussed in some detail in Amery & Rigney (2007) and Amery & Buckskin (2013). KWP has met on a monthly basis since its formation, holding its 143rd meeting in January 2015, whereupon subsequent meetings were convened by Kaurna Warra Karrpanthi (KWK) (see below).

Through KWP, a means was established whereby requests for Kaurna names, translations and information about the Kaurna language could be addressed by a group of Kaurna people, linguists, educators, researchers, Kaurna language activists and supporters. Anything up to 15 or so requests might be addressed at the monthly KWP meetings. Following the meeting a Kaurna person (e.g. Taylor Tipu Power-Smith) records a sound file of the Kaurna words and sends it to the requestor, together with the relevant section of the minutes, the KWP logo and invoice, where appropriate. For many years, such requests were addressed free of charge and still today requests from members of the Kaurna community, reconciliation movement etc. are still not invoiced. For a few years we suggested that the requestor consider making a donation to support the work of KWP. Then in August 2006, a schedule of fees was adopted by KWP and invoices were issued: $100 for education providers, $200 for local government and $500 for businesses with room for negotiation. There has been some criticism of the commodification of Kaurna language, with the accusation sometimes levelled at KWP that money received is going into the pockets of individuals. KWP receives no funding from the University. The funds raised through providing a service to address requests went some way towards a part-time salary for a KWP administrative assistant and to cover meeting costs. KWP runs largely through voluntary effort.

KWP meetings also became a place to discuss, report on and make decisions about Kaurna language projects. KWP has executed a number of

Commonwealth-government funded projects beginning with a Mentoring project where Kaurna man Dennis O'Brien was employed.

The Consolidating Kaurna Language Revival Project (2012-2015)

In February 2012, two grant applications were submitted to the Indigenous Languages Support (ILS) program, one to finance a KWP Secretariat and the other to produce YouTube clips and Kaurna radio shows. The funding body combined these two applications into the Consolidating Kaurna Language Revival (CKLR) project and funded it over three years. This enabled the employment of two key Kaurna people, Jack Kanya Buckskin as Kaurna Language Coordinator and Steve Gadlabarti Goldsmith as Kaurna Media Production Officer. In addition, Paul Finlay was employed as Kaurna Media Mentor and Gerhard Rüdiger as Kaurna Administration Coordinator, all with 0.4 positions (two days per week). Steve and Paul have been busy producing film clips as Kaurna language learning resources with Jack Buckskin as the speaker/teacher. A Kaurna Language Learning Series channel has been established on YouTube (go to http://bit.ly/13iLQi7). During Kaurna Language Week in October 2014, the CKLR media team launched the Pirltawardli Puppet Show, which has proved to be very popular and a great way to introduce the Kaurna language.

Kaurna Language Project (2015-2017)

Additional Commonwealth funds were secured in August 2015 to continue the work of the Kaurna media team and Kaurna placenames research at the University of Adelaide for another two years. A Kaurna language camp is also planned. Additional puppets, beginning with Ngungana 'kookaburra' (Katrina Power), are being added to the repertoire of the Pirltawardli Puppet Show. The work of the Kaurna media team was showcased at the Puliima conference in Melbourne in October 2015.

Table 11.1: KWP Projects funded by Commonwealth Government Grants (2005-2015)

Jun. 2005–Sep. 2008	Strengthening Community Involvement in Kaurna Language Revival	$20,000
Sep. 2005–Sep. 2006	Kaurna Learner's Guide	$63,000
	Kaurna Phonology Project	$30,028
2006–2007	Kaurna Postcards	$20,000
2006–2009	Kaurna Language Database	$20,000
Jul. 2010–Oct. 2013	Kaurna Learner's Guide Redesign and Publication	$22,517
Jul. 2010–2013	Kaurna Radio and Downloads	$44,177
Jul. 2011–Dec. 2013	Kaurna Dictionary	$53,000
2012–2015	Consolidating Kaurna Language Revival	$420,000
2015–2017	Kaurna Language Project	$300,000

The relationship between KWP and the University sector

As mentioned above, KWP was formed in 2002. At the time I was working within the Unaipon School at the University of South Australia (UniSA) where I introduced the 'Kaurna Language & Culture' course, which I had developed previously at the University of Adelaide. Following lengthy negotiations with UniSA a Memorandum of Understanding (MoU) was signed by DVC International Prof. Ian Davy, Kaurna Elders Lewis Yerloburka O'Brien, Alitya Wallara Rigney and myself. This MoU vested ownership of all Kaurna course materials with the Kaurna community as represented by O'Brien and Rigney. Upon my resignation, UniSA reassigned my intellectual property rights to O'Brien and Rigney without consulting them or myself. All three of us wrote to UniSA on 1 August 2006 reiterating that the agreement of 14th May 2003 was still current. The MoU included the clause:

> *Courses offered by the University based on the Course Materials licensed to the university under Item (2) may only be delivered by Dr Amery unless consent in writing is obtained from the Kaurna community through Mr O'Brien and Dr Rigney or their nominees.*

Upon my return to the University of Adelaide in 2004 I tried to negotiate a similar agreement. I opened up discussions with the university legal team at Adelaide Research and Innovation (ARI). The first draft of a MoU was developed on 3 February 2006. A MoU was finally signed on 2 September 2013 by the Vice Chancellor, Prof. Warren Bebbington and Drs Alitya Wallara Rigney and Lewis Yerloburka O'Brien on behalf of KWP. Amongst other things, the MoU commits the University to teach and research the Kaurna language, to promote the language and continue to work with KWP. KWP was also granted special permission to use its own branding within the University of Adelaide environment.

Incorporation

The CKLR project was KWP's window of opportunity to put structures in place to make the Kaurna language movement sustainable over the long term. A first step in this direction has been to form an incorporated body, Kaurna Warra Karrpanthi (KWK) 'supporting Kaurna language', to support the work of KWP inside the University.

For many years now, incorporation of KWP had been considered, but as an academic with little administrative support, I have been reluctant to take this path. The CKLR funding and the employment of Gerhard Rüdiger gave us the opportunity to lay the groundwork for incorporation, which was in fact a stated goal of the application for the funding received (Ref. the Business Plan). On 5 September 2013, the inaugural meeting of Kaurna Warra Karrpanthi (KWK) was held. The meeting was attended by six Kaurna people and five non-Kaurna people, whilst another six Kaurna people and one non-Kaurna person sent in their apologies as they were not able to attend because of illness, bereavement, car trouble and other engagements. Five directors were nominated and all accepted: Dr Alitya Wallara Rigney, Dr Lewis Yerloburka O'Brien, Katrina Karlapina Power, Rod O'Brien and Trevor Tirritpa Ritchie. Katrina Power was elected Chairperson, Rod O'Brien, Vice Chairperson and Trevor Ritchie, Secretary and KWK was subsequently registered as an incorporated body through the Office of the Registration of Indigenous Corporations (ORIC) on 24 October 2013.

From February 2015, KWK has met each month at Tauondi College, Port Adelaide, to address requests for Kaurna names, translations and information that had previously been dealt with by KWP. A MoU has been drafted between Tauondi and KWK such that Tauondi might become the initial point of contact for KWK business and provide an office for KWK operations.

Whilst the usage of the Kaurna language has increased considerably and the public has a much greater awareness of it, the Kaurna language movement is still fragile and vulnerable. It is still heavily dependent on a small handful of individuals and is still trying to develop a mechanism whereby the many demands from the public might be addressed. However, this language movement, despite its small size, has demonstrated a certain resilience. I have some confidence that despite the obstacles and challenges that might be encountered, Kaurna people and their supporters will rise to the challenge and find a way through.

References

Crystal, David (2000). Language Death. Cambridge: Cambridge University Press.

Evans, Nicholas (2014). *Wenn Sprachen Sterben und was wir mit ihnen verlieren*. Nördlingen: C.H. Beck.

Notes

[1] The revised spelling system itself is outlined in the Prologue to this book and explained further in the Kaurna Learner's Guide (Amery & Simpson, 2013: 28-35).

[2] The figures in the spreadsheet downloadable from http://caepr.anu.edu.au/Indigenous-language-usage.php include 22 speakers of Kaurna in 2006, which conflicts with the previous figure of 34 obtained.

[3] In 1848, the Liepzig Mission became the successor of the Dresden Mission Society.

[4] October 2013 marked 175 years since the arrival of the Dresden Missionaries in South Australia.

[5] This includes 33,800 hits for the singer Kaurna Cronin, but as he originates from Adelaide, it would seem that the name he has adopted also relates to the name for the people of the Adelaide Plains.

[6] Essays, sometimes up to 30 pages or more, by Schultz on specific Kaurna placenames have been uploaded on the KWP website (www.adelaide.edu.au/kwp).

12

Summary and Conclusions

We need to promote whatever is left of language for our kids, because that strengthens them in relation to the job they have to do in the future. I can't stress enough, that identity is crucial for Indigenous survival in this country. If we let it lapse in one form or another we will not survive as whole people. So it's crucial that we marry the culture, the language and the identity to become the strength of the future.
(Ngarrpadla Alitya Rigney, Discussion Panel at Launch of KL&LE unit, University of Adelaide, 31 July 1997, recorded on video)

This study has traced the fortunes of the Kaurna language from its historical roots to its current incipient revival. There are two main periods in the development of Kaurna as we know it, the mid-nineteenth century and the 1990s onwards. In between these two periods little was documented and the language was scarcely used. In the words of Kaurna people themselves, the language was 'sleeping'.

Initially, the Kaurna language was valued — Kaurna language skills acquired by sealers and some colonists were envied by others. The colonists and missionaries used the language for certain official and religious purposes and a school program operated between 1840 and mid-1845. This initial positive embracing of Kaurna was exceedingly short-lived. The Kaurna language was soon 'written off', even by those who had recorded it and invested considerable time and energy promoting it. Within two or three decades following colonisation, the Kaurna people were said to be 'extinct' or to 'no longer exist'.

However, the Kaurna people have regrouped and are rising again as a distinctive people and a social and political force within Adelaide, and within South Australian Aboriginal affairs. The founding of Adelaide, the heart of the colony of South Australia, brought about the rapid demise of the Kaurna language. Now, paradoxically, the fact that the seat of government and the urban and commercial heartland of the state are embedded in Kaurna territory provides a political forum and a purpose for the use of Kaurna within the public domain that otherwise would either not exist or have far less impact. The Kaurna language is a powerful tool that the Kaurna people can use to fight for recognition and to celebrate their survival. The Kaurna programs are a means by which we can forge a genuine reconciliation between Kaurna people and the majority population within which they live.

Because of my role in the Kaurna language movement, and my relationship with the Kaurna language enthusiasts, I have taken a partisan stance in this work. I make no apology for this. I believe it is important for linguists to be able to engage actively with a social movement they believe in. This book shows how the language reclamation approach, which has been adopted in the revival of Kaurna in the 1990s, draws heavily on the discipline of linguistics. A range of linguistic techniques are brought to bear on the language data recorded in historical sources to build a clearer picture of the language as it was spoken in the mid-nineteenth century. The Kaurna sources themselves are analysed and compared with each other and with neighbouring languages, both closely and more distantly related.

The historical sources, especially the German mission sources T&S and TMs, are the foundation of the Kaurna language as it is being revived today. However, a knowledge of related languages and understandings of Australian languages in general enable us to fill gaps in the historical record and to adapt the language to cope with life in the twenty-first century. Neologisms are created as the need arises during workshops and courses, in the development of language materials, or in the writing of speeches or other forms of expression in the language or in the context of addressing requests for Kaurna names or translations. Kaurna language revival goes hand in hand with the revival and re-creation of other aspects of Kaurna culture, such as fire-making[1], smoking ceremonies, music, song and 'traditional' dance forms, Dreaming stories and the manufacture of artefacts such as shields, clubs, canoes and woven baskets.

My work challenges linguists to rethink widely held ideas of what is possible in language revival. Whilst it is exceedingly difficult to revive so-called 'dead' or 'extinct' languages, the Kaurna case shows that it may not be impossible, as many linguists believe. Nor is the Kaurna case a total aberration or enigma, as we can see by the many cases of language revival, 'constructed' languages and other deliberate language planning measures. These varied entities, most of which do not closely parallel the Kaurna situation, nonetheless do share common elements with Kaurna.

This study also challenges commonly held notions about the very nature of language itself as a 'natural' phenomenon. Linguistic orthodoxy has often disregarded, ignored or disparaged linguistic entities that fail to measure up to their criteria of 'natural' language. However, the very notion of language as 'natural' is based on a myth, a misconception about the ways in which languages are formed, are maintained and change. This myth ignores or downplays deliberate measures speakers use to create, change and transform their languages.

This discussion has viewed language from an ecological perspective. The Kaurna language is a microcosm in which to view the development of a language. Until a few decades ago, the Kaurna language was almost completely restricted to the status of an historical artefact, a language without a speech community. Its revival involves the rebuilding of this speech community and the development of functional links between the language and those who identify with it. The Kaurna language, at this stage of its development, operates on such a small scale relative to other languages that we can see more clearly these ecological principles at work. This study has documented the situations in which Kaurna is being used since the 1990s, and analysed the purposes for its use. In the Kaurna study, we can view the very earliest stages of the formation of a speech community and the shaping of a language ecology that supports the reclaimed language of a small Indigenous minority dispersed within a dominant English-speaking society. This development, taking place over more than 25 years now, has been extensively documented through comprehensive KWP/KWK minutes and a series of academic papers. A further detailed study, a sequel to this book, is planned for the future.

Whilst we can measure and identify certain parameters, there are many more that operate in realms beyond our powers of perception and observation. Even in such a reduced microcosm, where virtually all the language users are known and much of the language use is known and describable, we simply cannot accurately predict the outcomes of revival efforts. We can, however, identify certain trends in its development and crucial factors likely to have a major bearing on eventual outcomes.

At this juncture, it is worth considering the major themes that are likely to aid our assessment of the Kaurna situation and future prospects.

The language revival cases investigated reveal that a considerable amount of time is usually required before a language which has ceased to be spoken for regular communicative purposes again takes root within the speech community as the vernacular. In the Cornish case it took almost a century before the first bilingual Cornish-English speaking children emerged. And still Cornish is largely restricted to a relatively small number of language enthusiasts scattered around the globe. In the case of Hebrew, where there was widespread knowledge of the language which continued to be used in restricted domains, efforts to revive the language as a spoken tongue bore little fruit during the first few decades of activity in Palestine. It is now, of course, a regular everyday language within the state of Israel, now spoken by some millions of people.

Relative to these revival movements, Kaurna is in its infancy. Against this time frame, much has been achieved in a quarter century since the initiation of Kaurna language revival activities and programs. Kaurna people are generally aware that Kaurna will not be revived overnight and the key individuals involved are in it 'for the long haul', having taken note of the Hebrew and Cornish experience (pc Ngarrpadla Alitya Rigney, March 1998).

Progress in the revival of Kaurna has far exceeded my expectations for a language with limited documentation, no sound recordings and little known within the community and where that community was dispersed and fragmented. But we had to wait some 15 years before the appearance of Jack Kanya Buckskin, the first to really internalise the Kaurna language, be able to impart that knowledge and raise his own children as Kaurna speakers. This is portrayed magnificently in the documentary *Buckskin*.[2]

Outsiders have a role, as Robinson (1997: 109) observes:

> Those who would develop the language in some way or work against its disappearance are most often outsiders. Their actions are interventions in a community to which they do not belong; they may bring with them useful skills and resources, and in doing so introduce new dynamics of power and culture.

Whilst Robinson is referring primarily to previously unwritten languages in 'traditionally-oriented' societies in the Pacific or Latin America, where the Summer Institute of Linguistics (SIL) is especially active, his observations are nonetheless pertinent to the Kaurna situation. We have seen the catalyst role played by Steve Hemming, Meredith Edwards, Howard Groome and others in the development of Aboriginal Studies curriculum and the inclusion of Kaurna perspectives. These professionals brought with them research skills and writing skills. The very act of engaging with the Kaurna community in research has focused attention on particular areas and provided impetus for developments within the community.

So, too, in Kaurna reclamation, I, as a non-Aboriginal linguist, have been a catalyst for the establishment of Kaurna programs and for much of the use of Kaurna within public forums and the Kaurna community, and for the particular form that the revived Kaurna language takes. I do not control or own these processes, but nonetheless this linguistic input is a central element in the language ecology, without which the Kaurna language simply would not have developed as it has, or be used to the extent that it is. Now, however, the Kaurna language is developing a life of its own[3], and most of the use of the Kaurna language now, no longer has any direct input from me.

Successful language revival efforts with which I am familiar almost invariably have this catalyst element of skills brought from outside the community. This can be seen in the Esselen case, and in the work done by Leanne Hinton with other Californian languages. In Australia, we see this catalyst effect repeatedly in the cases of Djabugay, Nyungar, Yorta Yorta, Awabakal, Gumbaynggir, Gamilaraay-Yuwaalaraay and Wiradjuri, to name but a few. The most dynamic and successful Aboriginal Language Centres have seen fit to employ linguists, who are almost always non-Indigenous, in recognition of the skills they offer.

Where language revival movements have rejected input from outsiders, developments have been less impressive and plans often not put into practice, through a want of expertise and not knowing where to start. There is little to show for the 11 years of Yaitya Warra Wodli's existence[4] largely due to their unwillingness to engage with linguists. In Amery (2000: 249), I wrote about the slow pace of development in Wampanoag in Massachusetts and closer to home with Ngarrindjeri from the Lower Murray and Coorong due to the reluctance of engaging linguists. I am pleased to report here, some 15 years on, that both Wampanoag & Ngarrindjeri have enjoyed considerable success with the input of linguists Ken Hale and Norvan Richards into Wampanoag[5] and Mary-Anne Gale for Ngarrindjeri (Gale et al., 2012). Ngarrindjeri language revival has been spurred on in part by seeing the success of Kaurna language revival efforts. A little competition can be very motivational and productive. Revival activities in Ngarrindjeri commenced some years before those in Kaurna with input from Brian Kirke, who had been a teacher of Pitjantjatjara. With Kirke's departure, little development took place until the involvement of Gale in 2002 when Ngarrindjeri people were finally prepared to grapple with the complexities of traditional Ngarrindjeri grammar.[6] In the intervening years the use of

Ngarrindjeri words was calqued onto English structures in the absence of linguistic skills and understandings.

Successful language revival comes from within the language community. Much depends on the relationship between linguists and the language community (see Amery, 2014), on the successful transfer of linguistic skills and understandings and the development of acceptable 'power sharing' arrangements. Key individuals within the Kaurna community have embraced specialists, such as myself. Over the last quarter century, my relationship with the Kaurna community and language enthusiasts has grown and matured, so that we all have a much greater understanding of what we can expect from each other in terms of knowledge, skills and expertise. I believe that considerable mutual respect has resulted (see Amery & Rigney, 2007; Amery & Buckskin, 2014).

No matter how sound the approaches of linguists and language planners, successful language revival can only be achieved if these 'resonate' with the community and their desires and aspirations. Catalysts are important, but the substance of revival comes from within. I have sought to tailor Kaurna language development according to trends or events occurring within the community. Focus on particular domains and topics has come from schools and community members. I have attempted to reinforce and expand these trends.

Neologisms in the historical sources were first brought to my attention by Auntie Josie Agius. A reduced form for expressing 'thanks' was introduced by Eileen Wanganeen. The word for 'soap', *tadlipurdi* (Lit. foaming stone) quickly replaced my proposed *wiltaitpurla* (Lit. hard oil) after Kauwanu Lewis O'Brien gave the matter some thought overnight (Amery & Gale, 2000: 22). *Wiltaitpurla* was used for 'butter' instead. Similarly, Steve Gadlabarti Goldsmith replaced my suggestion of *murlapiti* (Lit. dry making thing) with the reduplicated form *murla-murla* (Lit. dry-dry) as the word for 'towel' (see Amery & Simpson, 2013: 214-215). *Murlapiti* became used for 'clothes dryer' instead, which is a much more elegant solution. Over the last few years, Jack Kanya Buckskin has come up with his own terms for golf[7], playing cards (poker) and for alcoholic beverages without any input from me. Increasingly, Kaurna people are shaping their own language in line with their own needs and aspirations.

There must be a desire to relearn and revive a language. In the case of a dormant language, this desire is often only kindled after the individual has had direct experience with the language itself — one reason why the process takes so long. Language revival is a social process which must take its place alongside other things happening in the community, which may be viewed as more important. It would appear that the revival of Huron, as envisaged by Linda Sioui, has not progressed far because of lack of support from the community and the education sector.

The role of Kaurna Elders, especially Kauwanu Lewis Yerloburka O'Brien, Ngarrpadla Alitya Wallara Rigney and Ngarrpadla Josie Agius, in initiating the use and teaching of Kaurna, should not be underestimated. The working relationship forged between these Elders and the education system, and their commitment and perseverance, have inspired non-Aboriginal people within the system. A genuine collaboration has emerged, to the extent that some others in the Kaurna community, more sceptical and suspicious of the system, have seen fit to join in.

Whilst Kaurna Elders have been crucial in initiating and supporting Kaurna language revival, it is the younger generation who are now forging ahead with the language. The most knowledgeable and most proficient speakers of Kaurna are all under 30 years of age, and in some cases were first exposed to the Kaurna language at school. Now children are being raised as at least semi-native speakers. It will be interesting to see how the language develops as these children mature and interact with each other as siblings.

Successful language revival goes hand in hand with cultural revival. Cornish language revival was accompanied by the revival of the Gorsed, the reinstatement of the bards and a renewed interest in things Cornish. The nearest parallel language revival movements to Kaurna are probably found in North America. They, too, point to the centrality of cultural revival within language revival efforts, as in the case of Esselen and Huron, where sweat lodge ceremonies and long house traditions (respectively) have been reinstated. In California, attempts being made to revernacularise Classical Nahuatl[8] (as described by Tezozomoc et al., 1997) have grown from the performance of Danza ceremonies. Groups of Mexicans in California are turning to Nahuatl, one of the original languages in which Danza was performed, as a means of 'recovering an original culture' (Tezozomoc et al., 1997: 69). The Danza ceremonies are accompanied by a series of lectures on aspects of traditional culture based on archival research. The teaching of the language appears to be totally embedded in the teaching and performance of other cultural practices. Tezozomoc et al. (1997: 73) see 'spirituality and language' as the 'requirements ... for reacquiring a lost culture'. Noting that 'most language reversal projects have met with the problem of not being able to reach enough people and then stagnating', the Danza movement addresses the issue by travelling on a circuit from California to Texas to Mexico, disseminating songs, grammar books and exercises as they go. The Danza for some has become a total way of life. There seem to be parallels between the Danza and what the Williams family, especially Karl Telfer, are trying to accomplish. As we saw in Chapter 11, there are now three Kaurna dance troupes, all with Kaurna names, who inject considerable Kaurna language into their performances through song, chant and the spoken word. Significantly, such 'traditional' dance is very popular amongst the youth with numbers of young men and boys dancing alongside their Elders and somewhat older mentors.

Even Esperanto, which was instituted to transcend cultures and nations, owes its success, in large part, to the development of an 'Esperanto culture', which shares many of the trappings of other cultures — flag, songs and a set of shared norms, values and beliefs. It even sees itself as an 'ethnic' movement (Carlevaro, 1989: 185). Children whose first language is Esperanto grow up with a dual identity, an international 'Esperanto identity' and the local national or ethnic identity.

The development of language and culture in tandem, and adopting a holistic approach, is an important aspect of shaping the language ecology. We have seen that Kaurna people view the language as one component of a much larger whole. But significantly, the Kaurna language is seen as the key to understanding and reclaiming an array of knowledges and cultural practices.

Timing has undoubtedly been a crucial factor in the success of Kaurna programs. In the late 1980s and 1990s a particular set of circumstances and individuals came together. Expressions of Kaurna identity and interest in Kaurna heritage were already developing in the community. Furthermore, Nungas had recently gained some control and influence over education processes for their children, especially with the establishment of KPS in 1986. The Songwriters Workshop in 1990 fortuitously brought together a range of talented individuals who succeeded in establishing a 'vision' of what might be possible. The importance of the 1990s as the National Decade for Reconciliation and 1993 as the International Year of the World's Indigenous Peoples in changing attitudes within the broader community, and possibly also in the allocation of funds to projects such as AILF, should not be overlooked. The wider community became more aware of Indigenous issues and protocols as a result, providing openings for expressions of Kaurna identity and survival through the use of the Kaurna language in public.

The public domain serves as a major forum for the use of Kaurna, by virtue of the fact that Kaurna is the language of Adelaide, the capital of South Australia. The use of Kaurna in speeches, performance, signage, public artwork and naming is burgeoning and in high demand.

One of the main reasons why the reclamation of Kaurna has been so successful in these early stages is because we got on with the job of writing songs, setting up Kaurna programs, developing and using the language and producing Kaurna language resources in a relative state of naivety and unpreparedness. A consultation process was conducted in 1989, before the initiation of language revival activities, and Kaurna people were involved from the very beginning. But we did not wait until every problem had been sorted out or until we had every Kaurna person enthusiastically behind the undertaking. If we had waited for that, undoubtedly Kaurna language revival activities would never have commenced.

To a large extent we felt our way. We had to look up even the most basic of words. The construction of the first Kaurna sentences and the writing of the first Kaurna songs back in 1990 was a slow laborious process. The important thing was that we got on and did it together. When the language specialists, Nelson Varcoe and Cherie Watkins, began teaching Kaurna they had little knowledge of the language and little preparation. Yet they took the plunge and applied themselves to the job. This is also true of Jack Kanya Buckskin who threw himself into learning and teaching Kaurna to adults through the School of Languages and students at Adelaide High School, KPS and Salisbury High School after only one year of exposure. For Taylor Tipu Power-Smith, too, who in her own words was 'conned' by her mother Katrina Karlapina Power to participate as an English-language voice in the Kaurna radio shows we were making in 2010, has also taken the plunge and applied herself to teaching Kaurna and making Kaurna language resources.

Similarly, with the public delivery of Kaurna speeches: Kaurna people have not waited until they could speak fluently before using the language in public. For some, their initiation was to read a prepared speech in public with only minimal opportunity to practise beforehand. These first speeches were, naturally, stilted and the delivery faltering. But the secret of success is that the people have had the conviction and the confidence to 'have a go' and not to be discouraged. It is remarkable how quickly they gain confidence and develop fluency and familiarity with established patterns after delivering only a few speeches.

Persistence is another major factor. The language specialists, Cherie and Nelson, have persevered in grappling with the grammar and developing their Kaurna language skills, contributing far more than a job demands. Nelson no longer teaches Kaurna language, but he has continued his involvement in the revival through his main love — music, song-writing and performing. Nelson's creative skills and talents have made an enormous contribution. The students, too, have persisted. Some have re-enrolled semester after semester. Others have continued to use the Kaurna they learnt in their own work situations, local schools and in their local networks. For a number of Kaurna people, the Kaurna language has become a major force in shaping their lives over several decades now.

Capacity-building has been a particular focus and a number of young Kaurna people have been employed over the years at the University of Adelaide and mentored on-the-job, as well as through participating in and running Kaurna language classes and workshops. Particularly important here has been the accredited training provided through the TAFE Cert III and Cert IV courses. Several Kaurna people have expressed the need for ongoing workshops of this nature, as without them, they feel that their language skills are growing 'stale'. We are planning a Kaurna language camp for Easter, 2016 and follow-up camps or weekends to provide an opportunity for key families and individuals in the Kaurna language movement to consolidate and utilise their Kaurna language knowledge and skills.

The existence of KPS under the direction of Ngarrpadla Alitya Rigney, a Kaurna Elder of considerable stature within the community and very committed to the Kaurna language, has been extremely important. In the early years, KPS provided a focus for the language and a nurturing enclave. Elements of the language took root within the homes of at least some children attending KPS. The program has provided an additional reason for establishing senior and junior secondary programs within Inbarendi College. Ngarrpadla Alitya's strong character and vision for the language has inspired many, within her own family, the community and education circles, to embrace Kaurna.

In the 1990s, Kaurna language revival was, to a large extent, driven by formal language programs in the education sector, especially KPS, and I have previously described these formal programs as 'the powerhouse for Kaurna language revival' (Amery, 2000: 153). This is no longer the case. As the Kaurna language movement consolidates and matures, the relative importance of the education sector and formal language programs in driving Kaurna language revival, has declined considerably. Even in absolute terms, the Kaurna language is less vibrant now at KPS than it was during the 1990s. Children at KPS in the 1990s, or those who had attended then, were reportedly more knowledgeable of and fluent in Kaurna than children at KPS today where the current focus is placed on the National Assessment Program — Literacy and Numeracy (NAPLAN) results, which are dependent on English literacy, not Kaurna. However, Kaurna language revival was never wholly dependent on the formal programs. An expressed desire to revive Kaurna as a spoken language by members of the Kaurna community predates the language programs in schools. The commitment to the language by certain Kaurna people transcends these programs or what others might do with the language.

Also crucial to success has been the level of support from the Kaurna community for the language programs, and for the use of the Kaurna language in public forums. Many Kaurna people, including the Elders, those in the school system and those active in KACHA, are very supportive and speak of the use of Kaurna with admiration and pride. The late Veronica Brodie, speaking at the inaugural meeting of the newly combined Port Adelaide Enfield Council, remarked:

> It's a beautiful language and we, through the help of one of our linguists, that's Rob Amery, has taken up the very hard task of teaching the Kaurna language. And it's being taught at a special school at Elizabeth. And so we're breaking out everywhere. We're coming to life. We're bringing it to life. It's great! It's fantastic! What it means to have something of your own culture. And hopefully it will be made, it already has, the curriculum in schools where not only French, German, Japanese will be learnt but ... Kaurna language. Because we believe that one day it will be the number one language.
> (Port Adelaide Enfield Council Meeting, 7 August 1996)

Similarly, the late Phoebe Wanganeen, another Kaurna Elder, voiced her support:

> And I'd like, myself, to see the Kaurna language taught in every school wherever there are Aboriginal children. Because it's most important. We've lost so much in the past and it's about time that our kids be given the chance to speak their own language.
> (Consultation session, DECS Project, Language Renewal and Language Reclamation Programs relative to the LOTE Statement and Profile, 27 March 1996)

Since the publication of Amery (2000), the centre of gravity of the Kaurna language movement has shifted away from the formal Kaurna language programs to the community and the tertiary/adult education sectors. Through the University of Adelaide, Commonwealth Government resources have been granted to support capacity building within the Kaurna community and Kaurna language resource development. Initially, funding was modest, but since 2012, Commonwealth funding has been more significant, to the tune of $140,000 to $150,000 per year. This has facilitated the formation of a small team of part-time workers, including several key Kaurna people (there have never been any full-time workers employed within the Kaurna language movement).

Kaurna is emerging as an auxiliary language, used in addition to English, for a range of specific purposes that promote Kaurna identity and celebrate Kaurna survival. Its role in public speeches of welcome, and in the performance of songs, appears to be already well established and its future in cultural tourism on the Adelaide Plains is promising. School programs, though vulnerable, are growing in number and strength. There is every likelihood that Kaurna will again be used in association with the performance of ritual and ceremonies which draw upon what is known of traditional ceremonies. Indeed, there has already been some use of the language for these purposes.

Kaurna language revival began in 1990 with the production of a resource, *Narrunga, Kaurna and Ngarrindjeri Songs*, followed by the *Warra Kaurna* wordlist (Amery, 1995, 1997) and *Kaurna Paltinna* songbook (Schultz et al., 1999). With advances in technology, the cassette tapes produced with these songbooks have been digitised and the books reprinted. Resource production has been a major focus for the Kaurna language movement with alphabet books (Watkins & Gale, 2006; Buckskin et al., 2013), funeral protocols book (Amery & Rigney, 2006) and Kaurna Learner's Guide (Amery & Simpson, 2013) being major innovative projects which have involved the community intimately in their development. As technology changes, so does the nature of resource production with the appearance of phone apps and video clips on YouTube. The introduction of the *Pirltawardli* puppet show has been a major innovation that proves to be very popular with audiences of all ages, but particularly young children. Perhaps even more important than the resources themselves, is the process of developing and creating the resources, which is where people develop their knowledge and skills and where new terms and expressions are forged.

Will Kaurna emerge as a fully functional language spoken in the home for everyday purposes? The prospects of this happening seemed unlikely, but, as we have seen, some families are beginning to use Kaurna to express a range of notions through phrases and sentences, not just words, and are actually conversing in Kaurna. Several children are growing up experiencing Kaurna as a first language, alongside English. However, as Kauwanu Lewis O'Brien points out, preoccupation with this question is not necessarily helpful. For him it is the journey that is important, rather than the endpoint. Clearly there is a deep commitment to the language, on the part of a number of individuals, which will ensure its place in the future in some form or another.

The fortunes of the Kaurna language increasingly depend on Nunga politics rather than perhaps more obvious parameters such as demography, pedagogical issues, availability of language resources, funding constraints and so on. When we commenced with the reclamation of Kaurna in 1989-1990, political considerations were not such an issue, precisely because few Nungas took very much notice of or actively identified with the Kaurna language as it is known in the historical sources. The politics of Kaurna language revival are now much hotter, and that in itself is probably a measure of its success. The outcomes will be highly dependent on the actions and positions taken by key individuals.

Some Kaurna people are concerned that the revival of Kaurna is going too fast, without people really having a chance to reflect on the progress made and the changes implemented. Increasingly people are calling for discussions on ownership and the current direction of the language movement. Whilst Georgina Williams and others are almost asking for a cessation of Kaurna language activities, until the ownership and copyright issues can be resolved and until protections and safeguards are built in, others such as Lewis O'Brien see this as a backward step that would result in a loss of momentum.

Since 2000, there have been considerable advances in the development of organisational structures for the Kaurna language movement with the formation of KWP in 2002 and KWK in 2013. KWP and KWK have provided forums where Kaurna language projects can be planned, reviewed and progressed and where the public can engage with Kaurna people over Kaurna language matters, including requests for names, translations and information. KWP and KWK have cemented the collaboration between linguists and other specialists with Kaurna members. Significantly, a formal record is kept of decisions made. Through KWP, and even more so through KWK, Kaurna people are increasingly taking control of the Kaurna language movement.

As I have pointed out, the Kaurna language has become such an important aspect in the lives of some Kaurna people that I believe the language movement will be able to resist negative developments. There may be temporary setbacks, but fundamentally I believe that the language has a bright future, at least within the parameters laid down for it as an auxiliary language. It remains to be seen to what extent the language becomes part of the everyday speech repertoire of members of the Kaurna community, though there have been considerable developments here, way beyond my expectations, especially over the last decade.

Warraparna Kaurna
'Let Kaurna be Spoken'

Notes

[1] Karl Winda Telfer has perfected the traditional art of making fire (through rubbing sticks (*kuru*) together) by experimenting with various materials. His skills are frequently called upon at large public events, and go hand in hand with the use of Kaurna language.
[2] See http://buckskinfilm.com/
[3] Whilst I have worked intensively with a number of Kaurna people in translating, recording and practising their first Kaurna speeches, these same people are now in a position to construct their own speeches and feel no need to seek assistance. Similarly, once 'off the ground', the school programs operate with little outside input from me.
[4] Yaitya Warra Wodli, established in 1993, was South Australia's Aboriginal Language Centre. It was funded by the Commonwealth Government, but proved to be a dismal failure (McConvell et al., 2001) and was eventually defunded in 2004.
[5] See *We Still Live here Âs Nutayuneân*, a 56-minute documentary by Anne Makepeace produced in 2010, for a vivid and moving portrayal of the success of Wampanoag language revival efforts.

[6] In fact, Ngarrindjeri has far more historical resources and residual knowledge within the community, so has great potential for language revival.

[7] See https://www.youtube.com/watch?v=1hINOP-4v0I for a YouTube video clip which utilises these golfing terms.

[8] Classical Nahuatl, the language of the Aztecs, was said to have been 'extinct" by 1833 (Grimes, cited in Tezozomoc et al., 1997: 57), though many related languages are still spoken in Mexico.

Bibliography

Abley, Mark (1992, 7 August). The prospects for the Huron language. *Times Literary Supplement*: 4.

Agius, Josie (1994). Josie Agius interviewed by Caterina Caruso. In Rosie Egan (Ed.), *Angkiku Bulto — Women's Paths* (pp. 20-24), compiled by Port Adelaide Girls High School students. Queenstown, SA: Port Adelaide Girls High School.

Agius, Josie & Peter Gale (1994). *Narrunga and proud of it*. Adelaide: The authors.

AILF Project (1993, 1996). See SSABSA.

Aird, Michael (1991). The reconstruction of cultural heritage. *Ngoonjook, Batchelor Journal of Aboriginal Education* 6: 61-62.

Aitchison, Jean (1991). *Language change: Progress or decay?* (2nd ed.). Cambridge: Cambridge University Press.

Alloni-Fainberg, Yafa (1974). Official Hebrew terms for parts of the car: A study of knowledge, usage and attitudes. In Joshua A. Fishman (Ed.), *Advances in language planning* (pp. 493-517). The Hague: Mouton.

Amery, Rob (1986a). *Yolngu-Matha for use by members of the health profession in North East Arnhemland (Gumatj Dialect)*. Nhulunbuy: NT Health.

Amery, Rob (1986b). Languages in contact: The case of Kintore and Papunya. *Language in Aboriginal Australia* 1: 13-38.

Amery, Rob (1989). A case study of the establishment of a language revival program within the formal education system. Unpublished research paper. University of New England, Armidale, NSW.

Amery, Rob (1992a). *Maikoko birko*. [Kaurna translation of *Tucker's Mob*.] See Mattingley (1992).

Amery, Rob (1992b). Retrieving cultural and linguistic heritage: Revival and resurrection of Aboriginal languages. In *9th National languages conference: Conference proceedings*. Darwin: Modern Language Teachers Association.

Amery, Rob (1993). Encoding new concepts in old languages: A case study of Kaurna, the language of the Adelaide Plains. *Australian Aboriginal Studies* 1: 33-47.

Amery, Rob (1994). Heritage and second language programs. In Hartman & Henderson (Eds), pp. 140-162.

Amery, Rob (1995a). It's ours to keep and call our own: Reclamation of the Nunga languages in the Adelaide region, South Australia. *International Journal of the Sociology of Language* 113: 63-82.

Amery, Rob (1995b). Making use of historical language materials. In Thieberger (Ed.), pp. 147-164.

Amery, Rob (Ed.) (1995c). *Warra Kaurna: A resource for Kaurna language programs*. Adelaide: Inbarendi College.

Amery, Rob (1996a, July). Language reclamation: The interaction between linguistic and social processes in the restoration of languages no longer spoken. Paper presented at the Australian Linguistics Society Conference, Canberra.

Amery, Rob (1996b). Topic 5 'Language reclamation' & Topic 6 'Language awareness in South Australia'. In EAL551 'Teaching Australian Indigenous Languages' study guide (pp. 145-192). Darwin: Northern Territory University.

Amery, Rob (1996c). Kaurna numbers, maths and the quantification of time. Unpublished paper, in KL&LE Readings, Vol. 1.

Amery, Rob (1996d). Kaurna in Tasmania: A case of mistaken identity. *Aboriginal History* 20: 24-50.

Amery, Rob (Ed.) (1997). *Warra Kaurna: A resource for Kaurna language programs*. Rev. and expanded. Adelaide: Inbarendi College.

Amery, Rob (1998a). Warrabarna Kaurna! Reclaiming Aboriginal languages from written historical sources: Kaurna case study. Unpublished doctoral dissertation (2 vols.), University of Adelaide.

Amery, Rob (1998b). Sally and Harry: Insights into early Kaurna contact history. In Simpson & Hercus (Eds), pp. 49-87.

Amery, Rob (1998c). Case study 3.1. In DETE (1998), *Towards successful language learning in schools: A collection of case studies* (pp. 85-90). Adelaide: Department of Education, Training & Employment.

Amery, Rob (2000). *Warrabarna Kaurna: Reclaiming an Australian Language.* Swets & Zeitlinger: Lisse, The Netherlands.

Amery, Rob (2000). The First Lutheran Missionaries in South Australia and their contribution to Kaurna language reclamation and the reconciliation movement. *Journal of Friends of Lutheran Archives,* No. 10, October 2000: 30-58.

Amery, Rob (2001). Round Pegs in Square Holes: Formalising the teaching of Australian Indigenous languages. In the *MLTASA Newsletter*, Spring 2001. Paper presented at the AFMLTA Conference, Canberra, 7-10 July 2001.

Amery, Rob (2001). Language planning and language revival. In *Current Issues in Language Planning* 2(2&3): 141-221.

Amery, Rob (2002). Indigenous language programs in South Australian schools: Issues, dilemmas and solutions. Paper prepared for the NSW Board of Studies. March 2002.
http://www.boardofstudies.nsw.edu.au/aboriginal_research/pdf_doc/indig_lang_sa_amery.doc

Amery, Rob (2002). Weeding out spurious etymologies: Toponyms on the Adelaide Plains. In Luise Hercus, Flavia Hodges and Jane Simpson (Eds), *The land is a map: Placenames of Indigenous origin in Australia* (165-180). Canberra: Pacific Linguistics.

Amery, Rob (2002). Marginalised relics or dynamic modern languages? Emerging issues when Australia's Indigenous languages modernise. *Babel* 37(2): 10-15; 37-38. Paper presented at the Indigenous Languages Panel, *AFMLTA* conference, Canberra, 10 July 2001.

Amery, Rob (Ed.) (2003). *WARRA KAURNA: A Resource for Kaurna Language Programs*. 3rd ed. revised and expanded. Kaurna Warra Pintyandi, c/- University of South Australia. Reprinted September 2005, Image & Copy Centre, The University of Adelaide.

Amery, Rob (2004). Beyond their expectations: Teichelmann and Schürmann's efforts to preserve the Kaurna language continue to bear fruit.[iii] In Walter F. Veit (Ed.) *The struggle for souls and science. Constructing the Fifth Continent: German missionaries and scientists in Australia.* Strehlow Research Centre, Alice Springs: Occasional Paper No. 3: 9-28.

Amery, Rob (2004). Early Christian missionaries — Preserving or destroying Indigenous languages and cultures? Commissioned paper written for *Holy Holy Holy* exhibition, Flinders University, 2004. In Vivonne Thwaites (Ed.), *Holy Holy Holy* (36-45). Flinders University City Gallery.

Amery, Rob (2009). Phoenix or relic? Documentation of languages with revitalization in mind. *Language Documentation & Conservation (LD&C)* 3(2), December 2009. Online at: http://nflrc.hawaii.edu/ldc/

Amery, Rob (2009). Kaurna language reclamation and the Formulaic Method. In Wesley Y. Leonard & Stelómethet Ethel B. Gardner (Eds), *Language is life. Proceedings of the 11th Annual Stabilizing Indigenous Languages Conference* 10-13 June 2004, at University of California at Berkeley. Report 14, Survey of California and other Indian Languages (pp. 81-99). Online at: http://linguistics.berkeley.edu/~survey/resources/publications.php

Amery, Rob (2012). Four Dresdners in South Australia in the early-mid nineteenth century: a lasting legacy for Kaurna, Ngarrindjeri and Barngarla peoples. *Zeitschrift für Australienstudien* 26.

Amery, Rob (2012). Taking to the airwaves: A strategy for language revival. In M. Ponsonnet, L. Dao & M. Bowler (Eds), *Proceedings of the 42nd Australian Linguistic Society Conference — 2011.* Australian National University, Canberra, 5-6 December 2011. ANU Digital Collections. http://hdl.handle.net/1885/9280

Amery, Rob (2013). Authenticity and correction of errors in the context of language reclamation. *History and Philosophy of the Language Sciences.* http://hiphilangsci.net/2013/08/28/authenticity-and-the-correction-of-errors-in-the-context-of-language-reclamation

Amery, Rob (2013). A matter of interpretation: Language planning for a sleeping language, Kaurna, the language of the Adelaide Plains, South Australia. *Language Problems and Language Planning* 37(2): 101-124.

Amery, Rob (2014). Reclaiming the Kaurna language: A long and lasting collaboration in an urban setting. *Language Documentation and Conservation* 8: 409-429. (*The Role of Linguists in Indigenous Community Language Programs in Australia,* special issue edited by John Henderson). http://hdl.handle.net/10125/4613

[iii] This paper is based on an earlier paper entitled "The first Lutheran missionaries in South Australia: Their contribution to Kaurna language reclamation and the reconciliation movement" which was published in the *Journal of Friends of the Lutheran Archives* No. 10, October 2000: 30-58.

Amery, Rob (2014). A new lease of life: 25 years of reclaiming and re-introducing a forgotten language in metropolitan Adelaide, South Australia. 2014 Tâi-Uân Gí-giân Kap Kàu-hàk Kok-tsè Hàk-sut Giân-thó-huē: *Proceedings of the 10th International Symposium on Taiwanese Languages and Teaching.* Tainan, Taiwan: Chengkung University. Vol. 1: 1.1 - 1.26 (invited Keynote address).

Amery, Rob (2015). Kaurna. In Nicola Grandi & Livia Körtvélyessy (Eds), *Edinburgh handbook of evaluative morphology* (423-429). Edinburgh: Edinburgh University Press.

Amery, Rob (forthcoming). The trail of discovery of Kaurna Language source material. To appear in a Special Issue of the *Australian Journal of Linguistics* edited by Ian Green.

Amery, Rob (forthcoming). The application of Dual Naming to Kaurna toponyms. Australian National Placenames Survey 2011 Workshop, Adelaide, 2 September 2011.

Amery, Rob & Jack Buckskin (2012a). A comparison of traditional Kaurna kinship patterns with those used in contemporary Nunga English. *Australian Aboriginal Studies* 1: 49-62.

Amery, Rob & Jack Buckskin (2012b). Handing on the teaching of Kaurna language to Kaurna Youth. *Australian Aboriginal Studies* 2: 31-41.

Amery, Rob & Jack Kanya Buckskin (2013). Having it both ways: Towards recognition of the Kaurna language movement within the community and within the university sector. *Proceedings of FEL XVII Endangered Languages Beyond Boundaries: Community Connections, Collaborative Approaches, and Cross-Disciplinary Research.* The Seventeenth Conference of the Foundation for Endangered Languages: Ottawa, Canada, October 2013.

Amery, Rob & Mary-Anne Gale (2008). Language Revival in Australia. In William McGregor (Ed.) *Encountering Aboriginal Languages: Studies in the History of Australian Linguistics* (339-382). Canberra: Pacific Linguistics.

Amery, Rob & Mary-Anne Gale (2014). They came, they heard, they documented: The Dresden missionaries as lexicographers. Australex Adelaide: Endangered Words, and Signs of Revival, 25-28 July 2013. http://www.adelaide.edu.au/australex/publications/amery_and_gale.pdf

Amery, Rob & Peter Mühlhäusler (2006). Koeler's contribution to Kaurna linguistics. In Peter Mühlhäusler (Ed.), *Hermann Koeler's Adelaide: Observations on the language and culture of South Australia by the first German visitor* (25-48). Unley, SA: Australian Humanities Press.

Amery, Rob & Dennis O'Brien (2007). Funeral liturgy as a strategy for language revival. Chapter 34 in Jeff Siegel, John Lynch & Diana Eades (Eds), *Linguistic description and linguistic applications: Studies in memory of Terry* Crowley (457-467). Amsterdam: John Benjamins.

Amery, Rob & Alice Wallara Rigney with Nelson Varcoe, Chester Schultz & Kaurna Warra Pintyandi (2006). *Kaurna Palti Wonga — Kaurna Funeral Protocols.* Book, CD & Sympathy Cards. Adelaide: Kaurna Warra Pintyandi.

Amery, Rob & Alitya Wallara Rigney (2007). Collaborative language revival — the work of Kaurna Warra Pintyandi (Adelaide Plains, South Australia). *FEL XI Working Together for Endangered Languages: Research Challenges and Social*

Impacts. The Eleventh Conference of the Foundation for Endangered Languages, Kuala Lumpur, Malaysia. Rumah University, University of Malaya 26-28 October 2007 (paper delivered by Rob Amery & Jack Buckskin 26 October 2007).

Amery, Rob & Lester Irabinna Rigney (2006). Recognition of Kaurna cultural heritage in the Adelaide Parklands: A linguist's and Kaurna academic's perspective. *Proceedings of The Adelaide Parklands Symposium 10 November 2006: A balancing act: past — present — future*. Adelaide: University of South Australia, 12-26.

Amery, Rob & Jane Simpson (1994). Kaurna. In Thieberger & McGregor (Eds), pp. 144-172.

Amery, Rob & Jane Simpson (2013). *Kulurdu Marni Ngathaitya! Sounds good to me! A Kaurna learner's guide.* Kent Town, SA: Wakefield Press, in association with Kaurna Warra Pintyanthi.

Amery, Rob, Cherie Watkins & Lester Rigney (1997). Tape transcripts. A series of weekly lessons with accompanying tape for self-instruction. Prepared for the Kaurna Language & Language Ecology course, University of Adelaide.

Amery, Rob & Georgina Yambo Williams (2002). Reclaiming through renaming: The reinstatement of Kaurna toponyms in Adelaide and the Adelaide Plains. In Luise Hercus, Flavia Hodges & Jane Simpson (Eds), *The land is a map: Placenames of Indigenous origin in Australia*, 255-276. Canberra: Pacific Linguistics.

Angas, George French (1846). *South Australia illustrated*. London: Thomas McLean.

Angas, George French (1847). *Savage life and scenes in Australia and New Zealand*. London: Smith, Elder.

ARDS (1993a). Mägayamirr — a system of government. Information paper no. 2. Nhulunbuy, NT: Aboriginal Resource and Development Services.

ARDS (1993b). Political structures of government. Information paper no. 3. Nhulunbuy, NT: Aboriginal Resource and Development Services.

ASTEC Key Centre (1987). *Narrunga language word lists*. Underdale: SA College of Advanced Education.

ASTRU (1985). *The Kaurna seasonal trail excursion teachers' handbook*. Aboriginal Studies Teaching Resource Unit. Port Adelaide: Aboriginal Community College.

Austin, Peter (1981). *A grammar of the Diyari language of north-east South Australia*. Cambridge: Cambridge University Press.

Austin, Peter & Crowley, Terry (1995). Interpreting old spelling. In Thieberger (Ed.), pp. 53-102.

Bachelard, Michael (1997). *The great land grab: What every Australian should know about Wik, Mabo and the ten-point plan*. South Melbourne: Hyland House.

Baldauf, Richard (Ed.) (1995). *Backing Australian languages: Review of the Aboriginal and Torres Strait Islander Languages Initiatives Program*. Deakin, ACT: National Languages and Literacy Institute of Australia.

Barry, Sir Redmond (Ed.) (1887). Exposition internationale Melbourne: Vocabulaire des dialectes des aborigènes de l'Australie, 1886-7. EIM wordlist. Melbourne.

Bates, Daisy (1919). Typescripts, correspondence, photographs etc. (11 vols.). Folio 6/III/5k, Barr Smith Library, University of Adelaide. [The Kaurna wordlist is Appendix 1 to Gara (1990: 101)].

Bavin, Edith & Tim Shopen (1991). Warlpiri in the 80s: An overview of research into language variation and child language. In Romaine (Ed.), pp. 104-111.

Beard, H. (1991). *Latin for all occasions: Lingua Latina occasionibus*. London: Angus & Robertson.

Bentahila, Abdelâli & Eirlys E. Davies (1993). Language revival: Restoration or transformation. *Journal of Multilingual and Multicultural Development* 14(5): 355-374.

Berndt, Ronald & Catherine Berndt, with John Stanton (1993). *A world that was: The Yaraldi of the Murray River and the Lakes, South Australia*. Carlton, Vic.: Melbourne University Press at the Miegunyah Press.

Berndt, Ronald M. (1970). Introduction. In R.M. Berndt (Ed.), *Australian Aboriginal anthropology* (pp. 1-18). Nedlands, WA: University of Western Australia Press, for AIAS.

Berndt, R.M. & T. Vogelsang (1941). Comparative vocabularies of the Ngadjuri and Dieri Tribes, South Australia. *Transactions of the Royal Society of South Australia* 65(1): 3-10.

Bindon, Peter & Ross Chadwick (1992). *A Nyoongar wordlist from the south west of Western Australia*. Perth: West Australian Museum.

Black, J.M. (1920). Vocabularies of four South Australian languages, Adelaide, Narrunga, Kukata, and Narrinyeri with special reference to their speech sounds. *Transactions of the Royal Society of South Australia* 44: 76-93.

Black, Paul (1993). New uses for old languages. In Michael Walsh & Colin Yallop (Eds), *Language and culture in Aboriginal Australia* (pp. 207-223). Canberra: Aboriginal Studies Press.

Blake, Barry (1977). *Case marking in Australian languages*. Canberra: Australian Institute of Aboriginal Studies.

Blake, Barry (1987). *Australian Aboriginal grammar*. London: Croom Helm.

Blake, Barry (1991). Woiwurrung, the Melbourne Language. In R.M.W. Dixon & Barry J. Blake (Eds), *The handbook of Australian languages* (Vol. 2, pp. 30-122). Melbourne: Oxford University Press.

Blanke, Detlev (1987). The term 'planned language'. *Language Problems & Language Planning* 11: 335-349.

Blanke, Detlev (1989). Planned languages — a survey of some of the main problems. In Klaus Schubert (Ed.), *Interlinguistics. Aspects of the science of planned languages* (pp. 63-87). Berlin: Mouton de Gruyter.

Bleek, W.H.I. (1872). On the position of the Australian languages. *Journal of the Anthropological Institute* 1: 89-104.

Bobaljik, J.D., Rob Pensalfini & Luciana Storto (Eds) (1996). *Papers on Language endangerment and the maintenance of linguistic diversity*. MIT Working Papers in Linguistics, 28. Cambridge, Mass.: MIT Press.

Bradshaw, Joel (1995). How and why do people change their languages? *Oceanic Linguistics* 34(1): 191-201.

von Brandenstein, C.G. (1965). Ein Abessiv im Gemein-Australischen. *Anthropos* 60: 646-660.

Brauer, Alfred (1956). *Under the Southern Cross: History of the Evangelical Lutheran Church of Australia*. Facs. ed. 1985. Adelaide: Lutheran Publishing House.

British Parliamentary Papers (1841). *First and second reports from the select committee on South Australia together with the minutes of evidence, appendix and index*. Colonies, Australia Vol. 2. Facs. ed. 1968. Shannon: Irish University Press.

Brock, Peggy & Kartinyeri, Doreen (1989). *Poonindie, the rise and destruction of an Aboriginal agricultural community*. Netley, SA: Aboriginal Heritage Branch, Department of Environment and Planning and South Australian Government Printer.

Brodie, Veronica (1991). Veronica Brodie. In Murphy (Ed.), pp. 114-118.

Brodie, Veronica (2002). *My side of the bridge: The life story of Veronica Brodie (as told to Mary-Anne Gale)*. Adelaide: Wakefield Press.

Brodie, Veronica & Melvin, Sheridah (1994). Kudlyo the Black Swan Dreaming: Veronica Brodie and the continuity of Kaurna history at Glanville and Le Fevre Peninsula. Unpublished research report prepared for the Lartelare Homeland Association.

Brown, Michael F. (1998). Can culture be copyrighted? *Current Anthropology* 39(2): 193-222.

Browne, J.H. (1897). Anthropological notes relating to the Aborigines of the lower north of South Australia. *Transactions of the Royal Society of South Australia*, 21: 72-73.

Brunato, Madeleine (1973). *Worra and the Jilbruke Legend*. London: Frederick Muller.

Buckskin, Jack Kanya, Mary-Anne Gale, Rob Amery, Cherie Warrarra Watkins & Jane Wilson (2013). *Kaurna Alphabet Book Second Edition*. Adelaide: Kaurna Warra Pintyanthi, University of Adelaide.

Bull, J.W. (1884). *Early experiences of life in South Australia*. Adelaide: Sampson, Law, Marston & Co.

Burling, Robbins (1970). *Man's many voices: Language in its cultural context*. New York: Holt, Rinehart & Winston.

Bynon, T. (1977). *Historical linguistics*. Cambridge: Cambridge University Press.

Campbell, Valerie (1981). Archaeology of the southern Adelaide region: Introduction. *Journal of the Anthropological Society of South Australia* 19(8): 1-5.

Campbell, Val (1983). Moana revisited. *Journal of the Anthropological Society of South Australia* 21(8): 5-6.

Campbell, V.M. (1985). Is the legend of Tjilbruke a Kaurna legend? *Journal of the Anthropological Society of South Australia* 23(7): 3-9.

Cantoni, Gina (Ed.) (1996). *Stabilising indigenous languages*. Centre for Excellence in Education Monograph. Flagstaff: Northern Arizona University.

Carlevaro, Tazio (1989). Planned auxiliary language and communicative competence. In Klaus Schubert (Ed.), *Interlinguistics: Aspects of the science of planned languages* (pp. 173-187). Berlin: Mouton de Gruyter.

Cawthorne, W.A. (1842-1859). Literarium diarium (journals). Mitchell Library, Sydney.

Cawthorne, W.A. (1844). Rough notes on the manners and customs of the natives. MS notes, SA Archives Department.

Cawthorne, W.A. (1858). *The legend of Kuperree or, The red kangaroo. An Aboriginal tradition of the Port Lincoln Tribe*. Adelaide: Alfred N. Cawthorne.

Cawthorne, W.A. (1926). Rough notes on the manners and customs of the natives. *Proceedings of the Royal Geographical Society of Australia (SA Branch)* 27, 1-31.

Chittelborough, J. (1906). 'Primitive Adelaide' in *The Register*, 27/28 December 1906 [article includes a short Kaurna wordlist].

Chomsky, Noam (1982). *Some concepts and consequences of the theory of government and binding*. Cambridge, Mass.: MIT Press.

Clarke, Philip A. (1990). Adelaide Aboriginal cosmology. In Gara (Ed.), pp. 1-10.

Clarke, Philip (1991). Adelaide as an Aboriginal landscape. *Aboriginal History* 15(1): 54-72.

Clarke, Philip A. (1994a). Contact, conflict and regeneration: Aboriginal cultural geography of the Lower Murray, South Australia. Unpublished doctoral dissertation, University of Adelaide.

Clarke, Philip A. (1994b). The historical origins of contemporary Aboriginal language in southern South Australia. Draft manuscript, 15 August 1994.

Clarke, Philip A. (1997). The Aboriginal cosmic landscape of southern South Australia. *Records of the South Australian Museum* 29(2): 125-145.

Clarke, Philip A. (1998). The Aboriginal presence on Kangaroo Island, South Australia. In Simpson & Hercus (Eds), pp. 14-48.

Cockburn, Rodney (1990). *South Australia. What's in a name?* (Rev. ed.). Adelaide: Axiom. Original work published 1908.

Coleman, Carolyn (1991). Progress report: The production of encyclopaedic 'resource packages' at Maningrida CEC. *NT Bilingual Education Newsletter* 91, 46-54.

Collis, Dirmid R.F. (Ed.) (1990). *Arctic languages: An awakening*. Paris: UNESCO.

Commonwealth of Australia (1997). *Bringing them home. Report of the national inquiry into the separation of Aboriginal and Torres Strait Islander children from their families*. Canberra: Human Rights and Equal Opportunity Commission.

Comrie, Bernard (1981). *Language universals and linguistic typology*. Oxford: Basil Blackwell.

Comrie, Bernard, Stephen Matthews & Maria Polinsky (Eds) (1996). *The atlas of languages: The origin and development of languages throughout the world*. London: New Burlington Books.

Cooper, H.M. (1962). *Australian Aboriginal words and their meanings* (4th ed.). Adelaide: South Australian Museum.

Cooper, Robert L. (1989). *Language planning and social change*. Cambridge: Cambridge University Press.
Corder, S.P. (1973). Applied linguistics and language teaching. In *The Edinburgh Course in Applied Linguistics: Volume 2*. Oxford: Oxford University Press.
Cordes, Dean (1983). *The park at Belair: A social history of the people whose struggles and visions gave South Australia the national parks and wildlife service we cherish today*. Vol. 1: *The pioneering decades*. Adelaide: The author.
Corsetti, Renato (1996). A mother tongue spoken mainly by fathers. *Language Problems & Language Planning* 20: 263-273.
Coulmas, Florian (1997). A matter of choice. In Martin Pütz (Ed.), *Language choices: Conditions, constraints, and consequences* (pp. 31-44). Amsterdam: John Benjamins.
Council for Aboriginal Reconciliation (1996). *Going forward: Social justice for the first Australians*. Canberra: Australian Government Printing Service.
Crawford, James (1996). Seven hypotheses on language loss: Causes and cures. In Cantoni (Ed.), pp. 51-68.
Crowley, Terry & Dixon, R.M.W. (1981). Tasmanian. In R.M.W. Dixon & Barry J. Blake (Eds), *Handbook of Australian languages* (Vol. 2, pp. 394-421). Canberra: Australian National University Press.
Crystal, David (1994). *An encyclopedic dictionary of language and languages*. (First published by Blackwell 1992). Harmondsworth: Penguin.
Crystal, David (2000). Language death. Cambridge: Cambridge University Press.
Cummins, Jim & Merrill Swain (1986). *Bilingualism in education*. London: Longman.
Cumpston, J.S. (1970). *Kangaroo Island 1800-1836*. Canberra: Roebuck Society.
Curriculum Corporation (1994). *Languages other than English — a curriculum profile for Australian Schools*. Carlton, Vic.: Curriculum Corporation.
Curr, E.M. (1886). *The Australian race: Its origin, languages, customs, place of landing in Australia and the routes by which it spread itself over that continent*. 4 Vols. Melbourne: Government Printer.
David, Stephen (1997, 15 March). The living word. Who said Sanskrit is a dead language? Not the people of this Karnataka village. *India Today*, 7.
Day, Thomas (1902). Memories of the extinct tribe of Cowandilla natives. MS, Tindale Collection, South Australian Museum.
de Brébeuf, Fr Jean (1990). *The Huron carol*. Illustrated by Frances Tyrrell. Trans. J.E. Middleton. London: Deutsch.
Denison, Norman (1977). Language death or language suicide? *International Journal of the Sociology of Language* 12: 13-22.
DECS (1994). Yankunytjatjara Stage A — Years R-2. Syllabus for second language learners at junior primary level. Department for Education and Children's Services, South Australia.
DECS (1996). Indigenous languages in South Australian preschools and schools. Department for Education and Children's Services, South Australia [Incomplete Draft].
DECS (1997). *Warranna Purruna — Pa:mpi Tungarar — living languages*. Video. Department for Education and Children's Services, South Australia.

DEET (1991). *Australia's language: The Australian language and literacy policy.* White Paper. Canberra: Australian Government Publishing Service.
DEET (1995). *Alive and deadly. Reviving and maintaining Australian Indigenous languages.* Commonwealth Department of Employment Education and Training, and Social Change Media. Leichhardt: Social Change Media.
DETE (1998). *Warranna Purruttiappendi* — reviving languages — living languages: Renewal and reclamation programs for indigenous languages in schools. Department of Education Training and Employment, South Australia.
Dick, Galena Sells & McCarty, Teresa L. (1997). Reclaiming Navajo: Language renewal in an American Indian community school. In Nancy H. Hornberger (Ed.), *Indigenous literacies in the Americas: Language planning from the bottom up* (pp. 69-94). Contributions to the Sociology of Language 75. Berlin & New York: Mouton de Gruyter.
Dixon, R.M.W. (Ed.) (1976). *Grammatical categories in Australian languages.* Canberra: Australian Institute of Aboriginal Studies.
Dixon, R.M.W. (1980). *The languages of Australia.* Cambridge: Cambridge University Press.
Dixon, R.M.W. (1989). The original languages of Australia. *VOX 3*: 26-33.
Dixon, R.M.W. (1991). The endangered languages of Australia, Indonesia and Oceania. In Robert H. Robins & Eugenius M. Uhlenbeck (Eds), *Endangered languages.* Oxford: Berg.
Dixon, R.M.W. (1997). *The rise and fall of languages.* Cambridge: Cambridge University Press.
Dixon, R.M.W., Ramson, W.S. & Mandy Thomas (1990). *Australian Aboriginal words in English: Their origin and meaning.* Melbourn: Oxford University Press.
Donaldson, Tamsin (1995). What word is that? In Thieberger (Ed.), pp. 43-52.
Dorian, Nancy, C. (1987). The value of language-maintenance efforts which are unlikely to succeed. *International Journal of the Sociology of Language* 68: 57-67.
Dorian, Nancy, C. (1994). Purism vs. compromise in language revitalization and language revival. *Language in Society* 23: 479-494.
Dulicenko, Aleksandr D. (1989). Ethnic language and planned language. In Klaus Schubert (Ed.), *Interlinguistics: Aspects of the science of planned languages* (pp. 47-61). Trends in Linguistics Studies and Monographs 42. Berlin: Mouton de Gruyter.
Dulichenko, Aleksandr D. (1988). Esperanto: A unique model for general linguistics. *Language Problems and Language Planning* 12(2): 148-151.
Dutton, Tom, Malcolm Ross & Darrell Tryon (Eds) (1992). *The language game: Papers in memory of Donald C. Laycock.* Pacific Linguistics, Series C-110. Canberra: Australian National University.
Eades, Diana (1982). You gotta know how to talk ... Information seeking in South-East Queensland Aboriginal society. *Australian Journal of Linguistics* 2: 61-82.
Eades, Diana (1983). English as an Aboriginal language in South East Queensland. Unpublished doctoral dissertation, University of Queensland.

Eades, Diana (1988). They don't speak an Aboriginal language, or do they? In Ian Keen (Ed.), *Being Black: Aboriginal cultures in settled Australia* (pp. 97-115). Canberra: Aboriginal Studies Press.

East, J.J. (1889, 16 July). The Aborigines of south and central Australia. Paper read before the Field Naturalists' Section of the Royal Society. Pamphlet, Mortlock Library of South Australia.

Eastman, Carol M. (1979). Language resurrection: A language plan for ethnic interaction. In Howard Giles & Bernard Saint-Jacques (Eds), *Language and ethnic relations* (pp. 215-222). Oxford: Pergamon Press.

Eastman, Carol M. (1984). Language, ethnic identity and change. In J. Edwards (Ed.), *Linguistic minorities, policies and pluralism* (pp. 259-276). London: Academic Press.

Eastman, Carol M. & T.C. Reece (1981). Associated language: How language and ethnic identity are related. In *General Linguistics* 21(2): 109-116.

Eastman, Carol M. & Roberta F. Stein (1993). Language display: Authenticating claims to social identity. *Journal of Multilingual and Multicultural Development* 14(3): 187-202.

Eckert, Paul & Hudson, Joyce (1988). *Wangka Wiṟu: A handbook for the Pitjantjatjara language learner*. Underdale: South Australian College of Advanced Education.

EDSA (1986). *Languages policy*. Adelaide: Education Department of South Australia.

EDSA (1989). *The Kaurna people: Aboriginal people of the Adelaide plains*. Adelaide: Education Department of South Australia.

EDSA (1990). *The Ngarrindjeri people: Aboriginal people of the River Murray, lakes and Coorong*. Adelaide: Education Department of South Australia.

Edwards, Bill (1995). Teaching an Aboriginal language at university level. *Babel* 30(2): 4-11, 38.

Edwards, John (1984). Language, diversity and identity. In J. Edwards (Ed.), *Linguistic minorities, policies and pluralism* (pp. 277-310). London: Academic Press.

Edwards, John (1985). *Language, society and identity*. Oxford: Blackwell/ Deutsch.

Edwards, Robert (1972). *The Kaurna people of the Adelaide plains*. Adelaide: South Australian Museum.

Ellis, P. Beresford & S. Mac A'Ghobhainn (1971). *The Problem of language revival*. Inverness: Club Leabhar.

Ellis, P. Beresford (1974). *The Cornish language and its literature*. London: Routledge & Kegan Paul.

Ellis, R.W. & C. Houston (1976). *The Aboriginal inhabitants of the Adelaide plains: A resource series in Aboriginal studies*. Adelaide: Aboriginal and Historic Relics Advisory Board.

Evans, Nicholas (2014). *Wenn Sprachen Sterben und was wir mit ihnen verlieren*. Nördlingen: C.H. Beck.

Eyre, Edward John (1845). *Journals of expeditions of discovery into Central Australia, and overland from Adelaide to King George's Sound, in the years 1840-1841*. London: T. & W. Boone.

Eyre, Edward John (1984). *Autobiographical narrative of residence and exploration in Australia 1832-1839*. Ed. with introduction and notes by Jill Waterhouse. London: Caliban Books.

Fellman, Jack (1973). *The revival of a classical tongue: Eliezer Ben Yehuda and the modern Hebrew language*. Contributions to the Sociology of Language 6. The Hague: Mouton.

Fellman, Jack (1974a). The academy of the Hebrew Language: Its history, structure and function. *International Journal of the Sociology of Language* 1, 95-103.

Fellman, Jack (1976). Language planning in Israel: The Academy of the Hebrew Language. *Language Planning Newsletter* 2(2): 1, 6.

Fettes, Mark (1996). The Esperanto community: A quasi-ethnic linguistic minority? *Language Problems & Language Planning* 20: 53-59.

Fettes, Mark (1997). Stabilizing what? An ecological approach to language renewal. In Reyhner (Ed.), pp. 301-318.

Fettes, Mark (in preparation). The linguistic ecology of education. Unpublished doctoral dissertation, Ontario Institute for Studies in Education, University of Toronto.

Fishman, Joshua (1991). *Reversing language shift*. Clevedon: Multilingual Matters.

Fishman, Joshua A. (Ed.) (1993). *The earliest stage of language planning: The 'first congress' phenomenon*. Contributions to the Sociology of Language 65. Berlin: Mouton de Gruyter.

Fitzpatrick, Phil (1989). *Warra 'Kaurna: A selected wordlist from the language of the Kaurna People of the Adelaide plains*. Adelaide: Aboriginal Heritage Branch, Department of Environment and Planning.

Foley, William A. (1997). *Anthropological linguistics: An introduction*. Malden, MA: Blackwell.

Forster, Peter G. (1982). *The Esperanto movement*. Contributions to the Sociology of Language 32. The Hague: Mouton.

Foster, Robert (1990a). The Aborigines' location in Adelaide: South Australia's first 'mission' to the Aborigines. In Gara (Ed.), pp. 11-37.

Foster, Robert (1990b). Two early reports on the Aborigines of South Australia. In Gara (Ed.), pp. 38-63.

Foster, Robert (Ed.) (1991). *Sketch of the Aborigines of South Australia: References in the Cawthorne Papers*. Adelaide: Aboriginal Heritage Branch, SA Department of Environment and Planning.

Foster, Robert (1993). An imaginery dominion: The representation and treatment of Aborigines in South Australia. Unpublished doctoral dissertation, University of Adelaide.

Foster, Robert (1998). Tommy Walker walk up here ... In Simpson & Hercus (Eds), pp. 191-220.

Foster, Robert & Mühlhäusler, Peter (1996). Native tongue, captive voice. The representation of the Aboriginal 'voice' in colonial South Australia. *Language & Communication* 16(1): 1-16.

Fourmile, Henrietta (1994). *Submission to the inquiry into Aboriginal and Torres Strait Islander culture and heritage*. Submission prepared on behalf of the Office of the Aboriginal and Torres Strait Islander Social Justice Commissioner. Canberra: House of Representatives Standing Committee on Aboriginal and Torres Strait Islander Affairs.

Fraser, John (Ed.) (1892). *An Australian language as spoken by the Awabakal, the people of Awaba or Lake Macquarie (near Newcastle, NSW). Being an account of their language, traditions, and customs*, by L.E. Threlkeld (1834). Rearranged, condensed and edited with an appendix by John Fraser. Sydney: Charles Potter, Government Printer.

Gaimard, M. (1833). Vocabulaire de la langue des habitans du Golfe Saint-Vincent. In M.J. Dumont D'Urville, *Voyage de découvertes de L'Astrolabe 1826-1827-1828-1829: Philologie*. Paris: Ministère de la Marine.

Gale, Fay & Wundersitz, Joy (1982). *Adelaide Aborigines: A case study of urban life 1966-1981*. Canberra: Development Studies Centre, ANU.

Gale, Fay (1959). The role of employment in the assimilation of part Aborigines. *Proceedings of the Royal Geographical Society, South Australian Branch*, 49-58.

Gale, Fay (1962). Aborigines of South Australia. *Pacific Viewpoints* 3: 103-104.

Gale, Fay (1970). The impact of urbanization on Aboriginal marriage patterns. In R.M. Berndt (Ed.), *Australian Aboriginal anthropology* (pp. 305-325). Perth: University of Western Australia Press for AIAS.

Gale, Fay (1972). *Urban Aborigines*. Canberra: ANU Press.

Gale, Mary-Anne (1997). *Dhangum djorra'wuy dhäwu: A history of writing in Aboriginal languages*. Underdale: Aboriginal Research Institute, University of South Australia.

Gale, Mary-Anne (2000). Poor bugger whitefellas got no Dreaming: The appropriation and representation of Dreaming narratives as published texts [working title]. Unpublished doctoral dissertation, University of Adelaide.

Gale, Mary-Anne (2012a). Summary Report TAFE Certificate III 'Learning an Endangered Aboriginal Language (Kaurna Language)' workshop held at the University of Adelaide, 10-14 April & 25 April 2012.

Gale, Mary-Anne (2012b). Summary Report TAFE Certificate III 'Learning an Endangered Aboriginal Language (Kaurna Language)', workshop held at Relationships Australia SA, Hindmarsh, 9-13 July 2012.

Gale, Mary-Anne (2012c). Summary Report TAFE Certificate III 'Learning an Endangered Aboriginal Language (Kaurna Language)' workshop held at Wilto Yerlo University of Adelaide, 24-28 September 2012.

Gale, Mary-Anne (2012d). Summary Report TAFE Certificate III 'Learning an Endangered Aboriginal Language (Kaurna Language)', workshop held at Relationships Australia SA, Hindmarsh, 17-21 December 2012.

Gale, Mary-Anne (2013). Summary Report TAFE Certificate III 'Learning an Endangered Aboriginal Language (Kaurna Language)' workshop held at Port Adelaide TAFE, 15-19 April 2013.

Gale, Mary-Anne, Eileen McHughes, Phyllis Williams, Verna Koolmatrie (2012). Lakun Ngarrindjeri Thunggari: Weaving the Ngarrindjeri Language Back to Health. *Australian Aboriginal Studies* 2: 42-53.

Gale, Peter (1991). 'Nunga and proud of it'. Aboriginal languages in Adelaide: From the loss of 'mother-tongue' to language revival. Unpublished honours thesis, Flinders University.

Galpagalpa, J., Wanymuli, D., de Veer, L. & Wilkinson, M. (1984). *Dhuwal Djambarrpuyngu dhäruk mala ga mayali'- Djambarrpuyngu wordlist*. Yirrkala, NT: Literature Production Centre.

Gara, Tom (1986). Burial customs of the Kaurna. *Journal of the Anthropological Society of South Australia* 24, 6-9.

Gara, Tom (1990). The life of Ivaritji ('Princess Amelia') of the Adelaide tribe. In Gara (Ed.), pp. 64-104.

Gara, Tom (Ed.) (1990). *Aboriginal Adelaide,* special issue of *Journal of the Anthropological Society of South Australia* 28, 1.

Gara, Tom (1998). The life and times of Mullawirraburka ('King John') of the Adelaide Tribe. In Simpson & Hercus (Eds), pp. 88-132.

Gargett, Kathryn & Susan Marsden (1996). *Adelaide: A brief history*. Adelaide: State History Centre.

Gell, John Philip (1841-1842). The vocabulary of the Adelaide Tribe. Typescript, South Australian Museum, as published in the *Tasmanian Journal of Natural Science, Agriculture, Statistics, &c.* 1: 109-124 [Appears as 1841 in Tindale's card file].

Gell, John Philip (1904). South Australian Aborigines — the vocabulary of the Adelaide Tribe. *Proceedings of the Royal Geographical Society of Australasia, South Australian Branch* 61, 61-78.

Gibbs, R.M. (1995). *A history of South Australia* (Rev. ed.). Blackwood: Southern Heritage.

Goddard, Cliff (1980). *A learner's guide to Yankunytjatjara*. Alice Springs: Institute for Aboriginal Development.

Goddard, Cliff (1987). *A basic Pitjantjatjara/Yankunytjatjara to English dictionary*. Alice Springs: Institute for Aboriginal Development.

Goddard, Cliff (1992). *Pitjantjatjara/Yankunytjatjara to English dictionary* (2nd ed.). Alice Springs: Institute for Aboriginal Development.

Goddard, Ives (1973). Philological approaches to the study of North American Indian languages: Documents and documentation. In Thomas A. Sebeok et al. (Eds), *Linguistics in North America*. Current trends in linguistics 10. The Hague: Mouton.

Golden, Bernard (1987). Conservation of the heritage Volapük. *Language Problems & Language Planning* 11: 361-367.

Gouger, Robert (1838). *South Australia in 1837 in a series of letters with a postscript as to 1838* (2nd ed.). London: Harvey & Darton.

Gouger, Robert (1898). *The founding of South Australia as recorded in the journals of Mr Robert Gouger, first Colonial Secretary*. Ed. Edwin Hodder. London: Sampson, Low, Marston.

Grace, George (1981). *An essay on language*. Columbia, South Carolina: Hornbill Press.

Grace, George (1987). *The linguistic construction of reality*. London: Croom Helm.

Graetz, Joyce (1988). *An open book: The story of the distribution and production of Christian literature by Lutherans in Australia*. Adelaide: Lutheran Publishing House.

Graham, Doris & Graham, Cecil (1987). *As we've known it: 1911 to the present*. Underdale: ASTEC, South Australian College of Advanced Education.

Gray, Mike (1993). *Tauondi: A record of the Aboriginal Community College's first 20 years*. Adelaide: Lutheran Publishing House, for the Aboriginal Community College.

Green, Jenny (1994). *A learner's guide to Eastern and Central Arrernte*. Alice Springs: IAD Press.

Grey, George (1840a). *A vocabulary of the dialects of South Western Australia*. London: T. & W. Boone.

Grey, George (1840b). Philology in the library of His Excellency Sir George Grey. South African Library, Cape Town.

Grey, George (1841). *Journals of two expeditions of discovery in North-West and Western Australia, during the years 1837, 38, and 39*. Vol. 2. London: T. & W. Boone.

Groome, Howard & Irvine, Jan (1981). *The Kaurna, first people in Adelaide*. Largs Bay, SA: Tjintu Books.

Gumperz, John (1972). Sociolinguistics and communication in small groups. In J.B. Pride & Janet Holmes (Eds), *Sociolinguistics* (pp. 203-224). Harmondsworth: Penguin.

Gumperz J. & R. Wilson (1971). Convergence and creolization: A case from the Indo-Aryan-Dravidian border. In Dell Hymes (Ed.), *Pidginization and creolization of language* (pp. 151-167). Cambridge: Cambridge University Press.

Gunson, Niel (Ed.) (1974). *Australian reminiscences & papers of L.E. Threlkeld, missionary to the Aborigines 1824-1859*. Canberra: Australian Institute of Aboriginal Studies.

Haas, Mary R. (1951). Interlingual word taboo. *American Anthropologist* 53: 338-344.

Haas, Mary (1975). Problems of American Indian philology. In Herbert H. Paper (Ed.), *Language and texts: The nature of linguistic evidence* (pp. 89-106). Ann Arbor: University of Michigan.

Hale, Ken (1992). On endangered languages and the safeguarding of diversity. *Language* 68(1): 1-3.

Hale, Ken (1996, November/December). The next 35 years in linguistics. *The Sciences*, 8.

Hall, Robert A. Jr (1950). *Leave your language alone.* Ithaca, NY: Doubleday Anchor.

Harkins, Jean (1994). *Bridging two worlds: Aboriginal English and crosscultural understanding.* St Lucia: University of Queensland Press.

Harlow, Ray (1993). Lexical expansion in Maori. *Journal of the Polynesian Society* 102: 99-107.

Harré, Rom, Jens Brockmeier & Peter Mühlhäusler (1999). *Greenspeak: A study of environmental discourse.* London: SAGE Publications.

Harris, John (1990). *One blood. 200 years of Aboriginal encounter with Christianity: A story of hope.* Sutherland: Albatross Books.

Harris, Rhondda (1999). Archaeology and post-contact Indigenous Adelaide. Unpublished honours thesis, Flinders University of South Australia.

Harris, Roy (1980). *The language makers.* London: Duckworth.

Harris, Stephen (1990). *Two way Aboriginal schooling: education and cultural survival.* Canberra: Aboriginal Studies Press.

Harry, Ralph (1992). Esperanto after 100 years. In Donald Broadribb (Ed.), *Presenting Esperanto* (pp. 6-9). Sunnybank, Qld: Australian Esperanto Association.

Hart, Max (1997). *A story of fire, continued: Aboriginal Christianity.* Blackwood, SA: New Creation Publications.

Hartman, Deborah & Henderson, John (Eds) (1994). *Aboriginal languages in education.* Alice Springs: IAD Press.

Hassell, K.L. (1966). *The relations between the settlers and the Aborigines in South Australia, 1836-1860.* Adelaide: Libraries Board of South Australia.

Haugen, Einar (1972). *The ecology of language.* Stanford: Stanford University Press.

Hawker, James Collins (1899). *Early experiences in South Australia.* Adelaide: E.S. Wigg & Son.

Heath, Jeffrey (1978). *Linguistic diffusion in Arnhem Land.* Canberra: Australian Institute of Aboriginal Studies.

Heath, John (1982). The Awabakal Aboriginal Cooperative. In Jeanie Bell (Ed.), *Language planning for Australian Aboriginal languages* (pp. 124-126). Alice Springs: Institute for Aboriginal Development.

Hemming, Steve (1989). The South Australian Museum's Aboriginal Family History Project. *Records of the South Australian Museum* 23: 147-152.

Hemming, Steve (1990). 'Kaurna' identity: A brief history. In Gara (Ed.), pp. 126-142.

Hemming, Steve (1996). Inventing ethnography. *Journal of Australian Studies* 48: 25-39.

Hemming, Steve & Philip A. Clarke (1992). *Aboriginal people of South Australia.* Canberra: Council for Aboriginal Reconciliation and the Aboriginal and Torres Strait Islander Commission.

Hemming, Steve & Rhondda Harris (1998). Tarndanyungga Kaurna yerta. A report on the Indigenous cultural significance of the Adelaide Parklands. Adelaide parklands management strategy prepared for the Kaurna Aboriginal Community Heritage Committee, Hassell Pty Ltd & Adelaide City Council.

Henderson, George (1907). *Sir George Grey, pioneer of Empire in southern lands*. London & New York: J. M. Dent & E.P. Dutton.

Henderson, John & Veronica Dobson (1994). *Eastern and central Arrernte to English dictionary*. Alice Springs: IAD Press.

Hercus, Luise (1976). Arabana-Wangganguru and Bagandji. In R.M.W. Dixon (Ed.), *Grammatical categories in Australian languages* (p. 398). Canberra: Australian Institute of Aboriginal Studies.

Hercus, Luise (1992). *A Nukunu dictionary*. Canberra: The author.

Hercus, Luise (1994). *A grammar of the Arabana-Wangkangurru language Lake Eyre Basin, South Australia*. Pacific Linguistics, Series C-128. Canberra: Australian National University.

Hercus, L.A. & V. Potezny (1999). 'Finch' versus 'Finch-water': A study of Aboriginal place-names in South Australia. *Records of the South Australian Museum* 31(2): 165-180.

Hill, D.L. & S.J. Hill (1975). *Notes on the Narangga Tribe of Yorke Peninsula*. Adelaide: Lutheran Publishing House.

Hinton, Leanne (1994). *Flutes of fire: Essays on California Indian languages*. Berkeley, Calif.: Heyday Books.

Hinton, Leanne (1996). Breath of life — silent no more: The native California language restoration workshop. *News from Native California* 10: 1.

Hoenigswald, Henry M. (1960). *Language change and linguistic reconstruction*. Chicago: University of Chicago Press.

Hollinsworth, David (1992). Discourses on Aboriginality and the politics of identity in urban Australia. *Oceania* 63(2): 137-155.

Hope, Penelope (1968). *The voyage of the Africaine: A collection of journals, letters and extracts from contemporary publications*. South Yarra, Vic.: Heinemann Educational.

Hosking, Sue (1997, 21 April). The Wanda Koolmatrie hoax: Who cares? Does it matter? Of course it does! *Adelaidean* 2: 6.

House of Representatives Standing Committee on Aboriginal and Torres Strait Islander Affairs (1992). *Language and culture — a matter of survival. Report of the inquiry into Aboriginal and Torres Strait Islander language maintenance*. Canberra: Australian Government Publishing Service.

Howchin, Walter (1934). *The stone implements of the Adelaide Tribe of Aborigines now extinct*. Adelaide: Gillingham.

Howitt, A.W. (1904). *The native tribes of South-East Australia*. London. Facs. ed. 1996. Canberra: Aboriginal Studies Press.

Hudson, Joyce (1990). *Walmajarri — English dictionary*. Darwin: Summer Institute of Linguistics.

Hudson, Richard (1981). Some issues on which linguists can agree. *Journal of Linguistics* 17(2): 333-343.

Hymes, Dell (1972). On communicative competence. In J.B. Pride & Janet Holmes (Eds), *Sociolinguistics* (pp. 269-293). Harmondsworth: Penguin.

Ihimaera, Witi (Ed.) (1993). *Te Ao Mārama — Regaining Aotearoa: Māori writers speak out*. Vol. 2: *He Whakaatanga o Te Ao — The reality*. Auckland: Reed Books.

Inglis, Judy (1961). Aborigines in Adelaide. *Journal of the Polynesian Society* 70(2): 200-218.
The Invasion Diary Collective (1986). *The White Invasion Booklet*. Torrensville, SA: White Invasion Diary Collective.
Jacob, William (1837-1838). MS Journal, Mortlock Library of South Australiana.
Jaensch, Dean (Ed.) (1986). *The Flinders history of South Australia. Political history*. Netley, SA: Wakefield Press.
Janke, Terri (1997). *Our culture, our future: Proposals for the recognition and protection of Indigenous cultural and intellectual property*. Canberra: Australian Institute of Aboriginal and Torres Strait Islander Studies.
Janke, Terri (1998). *Our culture: our future: Report on Australian Indigenous cultural and intellectual property rights*. Prepared for the Australian Institute of Aboriginal and Torres Strait Islander Studies and the Aboriginal and Torres Strait Islander Commission. Surry Hills, NSW: Michael Frankel & Co, Solicitors.
Janton, Pierre (1977). *L'espéranto. Que sais-je?* (2nd ed.). Paris: Presses Universitaires de France.
Jeffers, Robert J. & Ilse Lehiste (1979). *Principles and methods for historical linguistics*. Cambridge, Mass.: MIT Press.
Johnson, Jeanette (1996). *Unfinished business. Australians and reconciliation*. South Melbourne: Brian Sweeney & Associates.
Johnson, Howard (1898-1900) [Narungga Vocabulary]. Published in a series of articles appearing in *The Pioneer of Southern Yorke Peninsula,* 26 December 1930; 9 January 1931; 16 January 1931. Rpt. Tindale (1936).
Johnson, Steve (1987). The philosophy and politics of Aboriginal language maintenance. *Australian Aboriginal Studies* 2: 54-58.
Jolly, Lesley (1995). Waving a tattered banner? Aboriginal language revitalisation. *Ngulaig* 13, 1-29.
Jonas, Bill, Marcia Langton & AIATSIS staff (1993). *The little red, yellow & black (and green and blue and white) book. A short guide to indigenous Australia*. Adelaide: Australian Institute for Aboriginal and Torres Strait Islander Studies on behalf of the Council for Aboriginal Reconciliation.
Jones, Philip G. (1995). Obituary: Norman B. Tindale 12 October 1900 - 19 November 1993. *Records of the South Australian Museum* 28(2): 159-176.
Jones, Philip G. (1996). *Boomerang: Behind an Australian icon*. Adelaide: Wakefield Press.
Jordan, Deirdre F. (1984). The social construction of identity: The Aboriginal problem. *The Australian Journal of Education* 28(3): 274-290.
Jordan, Deirdre F. (1988a). Aboriginal identity: Uses of the past, problems for the future. In Jeremy Beckett (Ed.), *Past and present: The construction of Aboriginality* (pp. 109-130). Canberra: Aboriginal Studies Press. Rpt. in Jordan (1989, pp. 41-58).
Jordan, Deirdre F. (1988b). Rights and claims of Indigenous people: Education and the reclaiming of identity. The case of the Canadian natives, Sami and Australian Aborigines. In Tove Skutnabb-Kangas & Jim Cummins (Eds),

Minority education: From shame to struggle (pp. 189-222). Clevedon: Multilingual Matters.

Jordan, Deirdre F. (1989). *Aboriginal peoples: Autonomy, education and identity.* Batchelor, NT: Educational Media Unit, Batchelor College.

Jung, C.E. (1876). Zur Kenntnis südaustralischer Dialekte. *Mitteilung des Vereins für Erdkunde zu Leipzig* 4: 68-75.

KACHA (1994). Kaurna Aboriginal Community and Heritage Association incorporated rules. MS.

Kaldor, S. & I.G. Malcolm (1982). Aboriginal English in country and remote areas — a Western Australian perspective. In R.D. Eagleson, S. Kaldor & I.G. Malcolm (Eds), *English and the Aboriginal child.* Canberra: Curriculum Development Centre.

Kartinyeri, Doreen (1983). *Rigney Family genealogy, Point McLeay.* Adelaide: Aboriginal Research Centre, University of Adelaide.

Kartinyeri, Doreen (1989, 1 October). *Perna Adjunda Rudkee ('King James Rodney').* Tandanya Opening Day Souvenir Program. Adelaide: Tandanya.

Kartinyeri, Doreen (1990). *The Wilson Family genealogies.* Vols. 1-3. Adelaide: South Australian Museum.

Kaurna Plains School (1995). *Kaurna Plains School R-12: Introducing our school.* Underdale: Aboriginal Research Institute, University of South Australia.

Keegan, Peter (1996). *The benefits of immersion education. A review of the New Zealand and overseas literature.* Wellington: New Zealand Council for Educational Research.

Keegan, Peter (1997). *1996 Survey of the provision of Te Reo Maori.* Wellington: New Zealand Council for Educational Research & Ministry of Maori Development.

Kennedy, William Bruce (1989). *Lutheran missionary to the Aborigines: Pastor Christian Gottlöb Teichelmann 1807-1888, his family, life & times.* Coolangatta: The author.

Kerr, Donald (1997, 7 April). Sir George Grey and Australia. Unpublished MS: talk hosted by the State Library of South Australia.

Kirke, Brian (1987). *Ngarrindjeri yanun* [Language kit.] Underdale: South Australian College of Advanced Education.

Klose, Samuel (1840-1845). Correspondence. Original MSS in German held by the Lutheran Archives, Leipzig. Typescript copies and English translations held by the Lutheran Archives, Adelaide.

Koerner, Konrad (1997). Linguistics vs. philology: Self-definition of a field or rhetorical stance? *Language Sciences* 19(2), 167-175.

Koolmatrie, Wanda (*pseud*.) (1994). *My own sweet time.* Broome, WA: Magabala Books.

Krauss, Michael (1992). The world's languages in crisis. *Language* 68(1): 4-10.

Krauss, Michael (1996). Status of Native American language endangerment. In Cantoni (Ed.), pp. 16-21.

Kühn, Wilhelm (c1880). Narungga Vocabulary No. 67 — Yorke's Peninsula. In E.M. Curr (1886). Rpt. in Narrunga Language Kit. Underdale: SACAE, 1987.

Kuiper, Koenraad & Douglas Haggo (1984). Livestock auctions, oral poetry and ordinary language. *Language in Society* 13: 203-234.
Kutscher, Eduard Yechezkel (1982). *A history of the Hebrew language*. Jerusalem: Magnus Press, Hebrew University.
Kwan, Elizabeth (1987). *Living in South Australia: A social history*. Vol. 1, *From before 1836 to 1914*. Adelaide: South Australian Government Printer.
Labov, William (1972). *Language in the inner city: Studies in the Black English vernacular*. Philadelphia: University of Pennsylvania Press.
Ladefoged, Peter (1992). Another view of endangered languages. *Language* 68(4): 809-811.
Landau, Jacob M. (1993). The first Turkish language congress. In Fishman (Ed.), pp. 271-292.
Large, Andrew (1985). *The artificial language movement*. Oxford: Blackwell.
Laughren, Mary & Robert Hoogenraad (Eds) (1997). Warlpiri wordlist. Warlpiri — English. Unpublished MS and electronic data file for limited distribution.
Le Page, R.B. & Andrée Tabouret-Keller (1985). *Acts of identity: Creole-based approaches to language and ethnicity*. Cambridge: Cambridge University Press.
Lee, Jenny (1993). *Ngawurranungurumagi Nginingawila Ngapangiraga: Tiwi-English dictionary*. Darwin: Summer Institute of Linguistics.
Lenfer, Anouchka (1993). Aboriginal heritage sites in urban environments: A study of issues relating to Kaurna heritage sites in metropolitan Adelaide. Unpublished master's dissertation, University of Adelaide.
Lhotsky, John (1839). Some remarks on a short vocabulary of the natives of Van Diemen Land; and also of the Menero Downs in Australia. *Journal of the Royal Geographical Society of London* 9: 157-162.
Liddy, Peter (1993). *The Rainbird murders 1861*. Adelaide: Peacock.
Linn, Rob (1991). *Cradle of adversity: A history of the Willunga District*. Blackwood, SA: Historical Consultants.
Lo Bianco, J. (1987). *National policy on languages*. Canberra: Australian Government Publishing Service.
Maguire, Gabrielle (1991). *Our own language: An Irish initiative*. Clevedon: Multilingual Matters.
Malcolm, Ian G. & Susan Kaldor (1991). Aboriginal English — an overview. In Romaine (Ed.), pp. 67-83.
Manning, Geoffrey H. (1986). *The romance of place names of South Australia*. Adelaide: The Author.
Maori Language Commission (Te Taura Whiri i te Reo Maori) (1996). *Te Matatiki: Contemporary Maori words*. Oxford: Oxford University Press.
Martin, Jim (1990). Language and control: Fighting with words. In Walton & Eggington (Eds), pp. 12-43.
Mathews, R.H. (1900). Divisions of the South Australian Aborigines. *Proceedings of the American Philosophical Society* 39: 78-93.
Matthews, Stephen & Maria Polinsky (1996). Epilogue: Language loss and revival. In Bernard Comrie, Stephen Matthews & Maria Polinsky (Eds), *The atlas of languages* (pp. 210-215). London: New Burlington Books.
Mattingley, Christobel (1992). *Tucker's Mob*. Norwood, SA: Omnibus Books.

Mattingley, Christobel & Ken Hampton (Eds) (1988). *Survival in our own land: 'Aboriginal' experiences in 'South Australia' since 1836*. Adelaide: Wakefield Press.

McCarty, Teresa L., Akira Y. Yamamoto, Watahomigie, J. Lucille & Zepeda, Ofelia (1997). School–community–university collaborations: The American Indian Language Development Institute. In Reyhner (Ed.), pp. 85-104.

McConvell, Patrick, Rob Amery, Mary-Anne Gale, Christine Nicholls, Jonathan Nicholls, Lester Irabinna Rigney & Simone Ulalka Tur (2002). 'Keep that Language going!' A needs-based review of the Status of Indigenous languages in South Australia. A consultancy carried out by the Australian Institute of Aboriginal and Torres Strait Islander Studies for the Aboriginal and Torres Strait Islander Commission, South Australia.

McEntee, John & Pearl McKenzie (1992). *Adña-mat-na English dictionary*. Adelaide: Nobbs.

McKay, Graham (1996). *The land still speaks: Review of Aboriginal and Torres Strait Islander language maintenance and development needs and activities*. Commissioned Report No. 44, National Board of Employment, Education and Training. Canberra: Australian Government Printing Service.

Mead, Greg (1995). *A royal omission: A critical summary of the evidence given to the Hindmarsh Island Bridge Royal Commission with an alternative report*. Adelaide: The author.

Mercurio, Antonio & Rob Amery (1996). Can senior secondary studies help to maintain and strengthen Australia's Indigenous languages? In Bobaljik, Pensalfini & Storto (Eds), pp. 25-57. Paper originally presented at the World Indigenous Peoples' Conference on Education, Wollongong, December 1993.

Meyer, H.A.E. (1843). *Vocabulary of the language spoken by the Aborigines of the southern and eastern portions of the settled districts of South Australia*. Adelaide: James Allen.

Meyer, H.A.E. (1846). *Manners and customs of the Aborigines of the Encounter Bay Tribe: South Australia*. Xerographic facs. Adelaide: State Library of SA.

Ministry of Education Western Australia (1992). *Framework for the teaching of Aboriginal languages in primary schools*. Perth: Ministry of Education.

Moorhouse, M. (1840, 14 January). Protector's Report. In Report of the Colonisation Commissioners for South Australia, 1842. *British Parliamentary Papers*, Papers Relating to Australia 1842-44. Vol. 7. Colonies: Australia (pp. 322-324). Facs. ed. 1969. Shannon: Irish University Press.

Moorhouse, M. (1840-1857). Protector of Aborigines Out letter book, 21 May 1840 to 6 January 1857. State Records, Adelaide.

Moorhouse, M. (1843). Letter to Sir George Grey sent from Adelaide May 1st, 1843 and replies to Moorhouse's Inquiries from J. Hutt, Governor of Western Australia. Original in Sir George Grey's Collection, Auckland Public Library.

Moorhouse, M. (1846). *A vocabulary and outline of the grammatical structure of the Murray River language spoken by the natives of South Australia from Wellington on the Murray, as far as the Rufus*. Adelaide. Facs. ed. 1962. Adelaide: Libraries Board of South Australia.

Morgan, Sally (1987). *My place*. Fremantle: Fremantle Arts Centre Press.

Morphy, Frances (1983). Djapu, a Yolngu dialect. In R.M.W. Dixon & Barry Blake (Eds), *Handbook of Australian languages* (pp. 1-188). Canberra: Australian National University Press.

Mühlhäusler, Peter (1986). Bonnet blanc et blanc bonnet: Adjective-noun order, substratum and language universals. In Pieter Muysken & Norval Smith (Eds), *Substrata versus universals in Creole genesis* (pp. 41-55). Amsterdam: John Benjamins.

Mühlhäusler, Peter (1992). Preserving languages or language ecologies? A top-down approach to language survival. *Oceanic Linguistics* 31(2): 163-180.

Mühlhäusler, Peter (1994). Babel revisited. *UNESCO Courier*: 16-21.

Mühlhäusler, Peter (1996a). *Linguistic ecology: Language change and linguistic imperialism in the Pacific region*. London: Routledge.

Mühlhäusler, Peter (1996b). On the effectiveness of language maintenance programs. In R. Baldauf (Ed.), *Backing Australia's languages: Review of the Aboriginal and Torres Strait Islander Languages Initiatives Program*. Deakin, ACT: National Languages and Literacy Institute of Australia.

Mühlhäusler, Peter (1996c). Review of Tove Skuttnab-Kangas and Robert Phillipson (Eds), *Linguistic human rights: Overcoming linguistic discrimination*. *Lingua* 99: 253-267.

Mühlhäusler, Peter (Ed.) (2006). *Hermann Koeler's Adelaide: Observations on the language and culture of South Australia by the first German visitor*. Unley, SA: Australian Humanities Press.

Mullarney, Maire (1987). The departure of Latin. *Language Problems & Language Planning* 11(3): 356-360.

Murphy, Catherine (Ed.) (1991). *Of ships, strikes and summer nights. Oral histories from the Port Adelaide community*. Port Adelaide: Community Arts Centre.

Nahir, Moshe (1977). The five aspects of language planning. *Language Problems and Language Planning* 1: 107-123.

Ngarrindjeri, Narrunga and Kaurna Languages Project (1990). *Narrunga, Kaurna & Ngarrindjeri Songs*. Elizabeth, SA: Kaurna Plains School.

Oates, W.J. & L.F. Oates (1970). *A revised linguistic survey of Australia*. Canberra: Australian Institute of Aboriginal Studies.

O'Brien, Lewis (1990). My education. In Gara (Ed.), pp. 105-125.

O'Brien, Lewis (1991). Lewis O'Brien. In Murphy (Ed.), pp. 104-107.

O'Brien, Lewis & Georgina Williams (1992). The cultural significance of the Onkaparinga River. *Kaurna Higher Education Journal* 2: 67-70.

O'Connor, Luisa (1995). Kudnarto. Unpublished typescript, p. 130.

O'Connor, Luisa (1998). Kudnarto. In Simpson & Hercus (Eds), pp.133-157.

O'Grady, Geoffrey (1960). New concepts in Nyangumada: Some data on linguistic acculturation. *Anthropological Linguistics* 2(1): 1-6.

Pandharipande, Rajeshwari (1996). Language shift with maintenance: The case of Sanskrit in India. In Shivendra K. Verma & Dilip Singh (Eds), *Perspectives on language in society* (pp. 182-205). Delhi: Kalinga Publications.

Parkhouse, T.A. (1923). *Reprints and papers relating to the Autochthones of Australia*. Woodville, SA: The author.

Parkhouse, T.A. (1936). Some words of the Australian Autochthone: An experiment in Australian etymology. *Mankind* 2(1): 16-19.

Paulston, C.B., Pow Chee Chen & Mary C. Connerty (1993). Language regenesis: A conceptual overview of language revival, revitalization and reversal. *Journal of Multilingual and Multicultural Development* 14(4): 275-286.

Paulston, C.B. (1994). *Linguistic minorities in multilingual settings: Implications for language policies*. Amsterdam: John Benjamins.

Paulston, C. B., Pow Chee Chen & M.C. Connerty (1994). Language regenesis: language revival, revitalization and reversal. Addendum to Paulston (pp. 91-106).

Pawley, Andrew (1985). On speech formulas and linguistic competence. *Lenguas Modernas* 12: 84-104.

Pawley, Andrew (1991). How to talk cricket: Linguistic competence in a subject matter code. In R. Blust (Ed.), *Currents in Pacific linguistics: Papers on Austronesian languages and ethnolinguistics in honour of George Grace* (pp. 339-368). Series C-117. Canberra: Pacific Linguistics.

Pawley, Andrew (1992). Formulaic Speech. In W. Bright (Ed.), *Oxford international encyclopaedia of linguistics*, Vol. 4 (pp. 22-25). Oxford: Oxford University Press.

Pawley, Andrew & Frances Hodgetts Syder (1983). Two puzzles for linguistic theory: Nativelike selection and nativelike competence. In Jack C. Richards & Richard W. Schmidt (Eds), *Language and communication* (pp. 191-226). London: Longman.

Piesse, Louis (1840). Letter to the Editor of the *Adelaide Guardian* dated 18 October 1839. *The South Australian Colonist* 1(19): 296.

Playfair, Roger (1996, February). *Some ecological suggestions for the development of the Warriparinga site*. Resource Monitoring and Planning, Marion City Council, Adelaide.

Plomley, N.J.B. (Ed.) (1966). *Friendly mission: The Tasmanian journals and papers of George Augustus Robinson 1829-1834*. Hobart: Tasmanian Historical Research Association.

Plomley, N.J.B. (1976). *A Word-list of the Tasmanian Aboriginal languages*. Launceston: The Author.

Plomley, N.J.B. (Ed.) (1987). *Weep in silence: A history of the Flinders Island Aboriginal settlement*. Hobart: Blubber Head Press.

Pope, Alan (1989). *Resistance and retaliation: Aboriginal-European relations in early colonial South Australia*. Bridgewater, SA: Heritage Action.

Powell, Jay V. (1973). Raising pidgins for fun and profit: A new departure in language teaching. *Proceedings of the Pacific Northwest Conference on Foreign Languages* 17, 40-43.

Powell, Jay V. (1976, February). Preparing a second language program for teaching a Washington Indian language. Lecture to Language Learning Colloquium, University of Washington.

Praite, R. & J.C. Tolley (1970). *Place names of South Australia*. Adelaide: Rigby.

Procter, Jo & Mary-Anne Gale (Eds) (1997). *Tauondi speaks from the heart: Aboriginal poems from Tauondi College*. Port Adelaide: Tauondi College.

Rabin, Chaim (1976). Language treatment in Israel: Especially the development and spread of Hebrew. *Language Planning Newsletter* 2(4): 1, 3-4, 6.

Ramsay-Smith, W. (1930). *Myths and legends of the Australian Aboriginals.* London: Harrap.

Rann, Mike (1992). South Australian Aboriginal languages. *Kaurna Higher Education Journal* 2: 71-73.

Reilly, Helen (1997). Untitled final essay [on issues of control and ownership of the Kaurna language], KL&LE course, University of Adelaide.

Reyhner, Jon (Ed.) (1997). *Teaching Indigenous languages.* Centre for Excellence in Education monograph. Flagstaff: Northern Arizona University.

Richards, E. (Ed.) (1986). *The Flinders history of South Australia: Social history.* Adelaide: Wakefield Press.

Richards, Jack C. & Theodore S. Rodgers (1986). *Approaches and methods in language teaching: A description and analysis.* Cambridge: Cambridge University Press.

Rigney, Alice (1994). Alice Rigney interviewed by Christina Harkness, transcribed by Rosie Egan. In Rosie Egan (Ed.), *Angkiku bulto — women's paths* (pp. 60-64). Compiled by Port Adelaide Girls High School Students. Queenstown, SA: Port Adelaide Girls High School.

Rigney, Alice & Iswaran, Pathma (1996). *Te Reo Maori: Visit to Aotearoa.* Elizabeth: Kaurna Plains School.

Rigney, Lester (1994). *Nendi, goal setting for vision.* Adelaide: Accompany Outdoors.

Rigney, Lester (1995). Indigenous Australians: Addressing racism in education. A conversation with Lester Rigney. *Dulwich Centre Newsletter* 2: 5-15.

Rigney, Lester (1996a). *Racism and physical education: A critical Indigenist analysis of the senate standing committee's report on physical and sport education.* Unpublished master's dissertation, University of South Australia.

Rigney, Lester (1996b, 10 February). A Narungga future: Our past is our strength to our future. Opening address at the historical Narungga Nation Ceremony.

Robins, R.H. & E.M. Uhlenbeck (Eds) (1991). *Endangered languages.* Oxford: Berg.

Robinson, Clinton D.W. (1997). Developing or destroying languages? What does intervention do to linguistic vitality? *Notes on Sociolinguistics* 2(3): 109-126.

Robinson, George Augustus (n.d.). Papers held in Mitchell Library, Sydney. A7085(6). Rpt. Amery (1996d).

Romaine, S. (Ed.) (1991). *Language in Australia.* Cambridge: Cambridge University Press.

Ross, Betty (Ed.) (1984). *Aboriginal and historic places around metropolitan Adelaide and the south coast.* Adelaide: Anthropological Society of South Australia.

SAAETAC (1992). *Proceedings of the South Australian two day Aboriginal languages workshop, Adelaide 2nd and 3rd June.* Adelaide: South Australian Aboriginal Education and Training Advisory Committee.

SAL (1985). Ngarrindjeri wordlist. Unpublished typescript, School of Australian Linguistics, Batchelor, NT.

Sandefur, John (1983). The Quileute approach to language revival programs. *Aboriginal Child at School* 11(5): 3-16.
Sapinsky, Tania H. (1997). *Language use and language attitudes in a rural South Australian community*. Unpublished master's dissertation, University of Adelaide.
SAPSMS (1998). *Festival of music 1998*. Adelaide: South Australian Public Schools Music Society.
Sasse, Hans-Jürgen (1992). Theory of language death. In Matthias Brenzinger (Ed.), *Language death: Factual and theoretical explorations with special reference to East Africa*. Contributions to the Sociology of Language 64. The Hague: Mouton de Gruyter.
Saulson, Scott B. (1979). *Institutionalized language planning: Documents and analysis of the revival of Hebrew*. Contributions to the Sociology of Language 23. The Hague: Mouton.
Saville-Troike, Muriel (1989). *The ethnography of communication: An introduction*. (2nd ed.). Oxford: Blackwell.
Scarino, A., D. Vale, , P. McKay & J. Clark, (1988). *Australian language levels guidelines, books 1-4*. Canberra: Curriculum Development Centre.
Schayer, Herr (1844). Über Sprache, Sitten und Gebräuche der Urbewohner von Süd-Australien [On the language, customs and practices of the original inhabitants of South Australia]. Gesellschaft für Erkdkunde zu Berlin. Monatsberichte über die Verhandlungen, pp. 189-195. Translation of Gell (1841-1842).
Schebeck, Bernhard (1974). *Texts on the social system of the At^{y}n^{y}amatana people with grammatical notes*. Pacific Linguistics, Series D–21. Canberra: Australian National University.
Schebeck, Bernhard (1976). Thangu and Atjnjamathanha. In R.M.W. Dixon (Ed.), pp. 516-550.
Schmidt, Annette (1990). *The loss of Australia's Aboriginal language heritage*. Canberra: Aboriginal Studies Press.
Schmidt, Wilhelm (1919). *Die Gliederung der australischen Sprachen: Geographische, bibliographische, linguistische Grundzüge der Erforschung der australischen Sprachen*. Wien: Druck und Verlag der Mechitharisten-Buchdruckerei.
Schultz, Chester (1999). Kaurna historical and musical notes. In Schultz, Varcoe & Amery (Eds), pp. 79-120.
Schultz, Chester (forthcoming). 'Ask the right question, then look everywhere: Finding and interpreting the old Aboriginal place-names around Adelaide and Fleurieu Peninsula.' Australian National Placenames Survey 2011 Workshop, Adelaide, 2 September 2011.
Schultz, Chester (forthcoming). Feet on the Fleurieu.
Schultz, Chester, Nelson Varcoe & Rob Amery (Eds) (1999). *Kaurna paltinna: A Kaurna song book*. Elizabeth, SA: Kaurna Plains School.
Schürmann, Clamor W. (1838-1853). Journals. Copies of originals in German held by Lutheran Archives Adelaide. English translation held by Anthropology section, South Australian Museum, Adelaide.

Schürmann, Clamor W. (1844). *A vocabulary of the Parnkalla language. Spoken by the natives inhabiting the western shores of Spencer's Gulf. To which is prefixed a collection of grammatical rules, hitherto ascertained.* Adelaide: George Dehane.

Schurmann, Edwin A. (1987). *I'd rather dig potatoes: Clamor Schurmann and the Aborigines of South Australia 1838-1853.* Adelaide: Lutheran Publishing House.

Schütz, Albert J. (1994). *The voices of Eden: A history of Hawaiian language studies.* Honolulu: University of Hawai'i Press.

Schwab, Jerry (1988). Ambiguity, style and kinship in Adelaide Aboriginal identity. In Ian Keen (Ed.), *Being Black: Aboriginal cultures in 'settled' Australia* (pp. 77-95). Canberra: Aboriginal Studies.

Schwarz, Silvia (1995). *Sociolinguistic aspects of the Latin language.* Unpublished honours dissertation (Latin and Linguistics), University of Adelaide.

Shopen, Timothy (Ed.) (1985). *Language typology and syntactic description.* Vol. 3, *Grammatical categories and the lexicon.* Cambridge: Cambridge University Press.

Simpson, Jane (n.d.). A grammar of Kaurna. Incomplete unpublished MS made available to Kaurna programs in 1989.

Simpson, Jane (1985). How Warumungu people express new concepts. *Language in Central Australia* 4: 12-25.

Simpson, Jane (1992). Notes on a manuscript dictionary of Kaurna. In Dutton, Ross & Tryon (Eds), pp. 409-415.

Simpson, Jane (1995). Making sense of the words in old wordlists. In Thieberger (Ed.), pp. 121-145.

Simpson, Jane (1996). Early language contact varieties in South Australia. *Australian Journal of Linguistics* 16(2): 169-207.

Simpson, Jane & Luise Hercus (Eds) (1998). *History in portraits: Biographies of nineteenth century South Australian Aboriginal people.* Monograph 6. Canberra: Aboriginal History inc.

Simpson, Jane (1998). Aboriginal personal names on the Fleurieu Peninsula at the time of the invasion. In Simpson & Hercus (Eds), pp 1-13.

Simpson, Jane & Rob Amery (forthcoming). *A grammar of Kaurna.*

Simpson, Jennifer (1995). Evaluation of the Year 11 Warra Kaurna Program developed under the Australian Indigenous Languages Framework (AILFI) Project. Teacher's Report. In Smiles & Simpson (n.p.).

Sioui, Linda (1996). Is there a future for the Huron Language? In Jacques Maurais (Ed.), *Quebec's Aboriginal languages: History, planning, development* (pp. 250-255). Clevedon: Multilingual Matters.

Sissons, Jeffrey (1993). The systematisation of tradition: Maori culture as a strategic resource. *Oceania* 64(2): 97-116.

Skutnabb-Kangas, Tove & Jim Cummins (1988). *Minority education: From shame to struggle.* Clevedon: Multilingual Matters.

Skutnabb-Kangas, Tove & Robert Phillipson (Eds) (1994). *Linguistic human rights: Overcoming linguistic discrimination.* Berlin: Mouton de Gruyter.

Smiles, Ruth & Jennifer Simpson (1995). Inbarendi College, Kaurna Language Program, 1994 final report. Submitted to DEET, Australian Indigenous Languages Framework Trial, Inbarendi/Augusta Park Pilot Project, March 1995.

Smith, Christina (1880). *The Booandik Tribe of South Australian: A sketch of their habits, customs, legends, and language*. Facs. ed. 1965. Adelaide: Libraries Board of South Australia.

Smolicz, J.J. (1981). Core values and cultural identity. *Ethnic and Racial Studies* 4(1): 75-90.

Smolicz, J.J. (1984). Minority languages and the core values of culture: Changing policies and ethnic response in Australia. *Journal of Multilingual and Multicultural Development* 5(1): 23-41.

Spolsky, Bernard (1995). Conditions for language revitalization: A comparison of the cases of Hebrew and Maori. *Current Issues in Language & Society* 2(3): 177-201.

SSABSA (1993, November). *Australian Indigenous Languages Framework National Consultation Document*. Wayville, SA: Senior Secondary Assessment Board of South Australia.

SSABSA (1996a). *Australia's Indigenous Languages Framework*. Wayville, SA: Senior Secondary Assessment Board of South Australia.

SSABSA (1996b). *Australia's Indigenous languages in practice*. Wayville, SA: Senior Secondary Assessment Board of South Australia.

SSABSA (1996c). *Australia's Indigenous languages*. Ed. David Nathan. Wayville, SA: Senior Secondary Assessment Board of South Australia and Wakefield Press. With CD-ROM.

SSABSA (1998). Report of Aboriginal students and the SACE. Report on research conducted for SSABSA by Yunggorendi First Nations Centre for Higher Education and Research, Flinders University. Wayville, SA: Senior Secondary Assessment Board of South Australia.

Stephens, Edward (1838, 27 October). Letter to E.G. Wheeler, Manager, South Australian Co. London. In Tindale (1935b), pp. 163-164.

Stephens, Edward (1889, 2 October). The Aborigines of Australia. Being personal recollections of those tribes which once inhabited the Adelaide plains of South Australia. Read before the Royal Society of NSW.

Stephens, John (1839). *Land of promise*. London: Smith, Elder.

Stevens, Iris (1995). *Report of the Hindmarsh Island Bridge Royal Commission*. Adelaide.

Taplin, Rev. George (1864). *Lessons, hymns & prayers for the native school at Point MacLeay*. Adelaide: Aboriginal Friends Association.

Taplin, Rev. George (1873). *The Narrinyeri*. Rpt. in Woods (Ed.) (1879).

Taplin, Rev George (1879). *The folklore, manners, customs, and languages of the South Australian Aborigines*. Adelaide: Government Printer.

Te Hemara, Hana Jackson (1993). Interview with Donna Awatere-Huata. In Ihimaera (Ed.), pp. 188-190.

Teichelmann, C.G. (1839-1846). Christian G. Teichelmann Diary 1839-1846 and Letters from and to him 1838-1853. Original MSS in German held by the

Lutheran Archives, Leipzig. Typescript copies and English translations held by the Lutheran Archives, Adelaide.

Teichelmann, C.G. (1841). *Aboriginals of South Australia: Illustrative and explanatory note of the manners, customs, habits and superstitions of the natives of South Australia.* Adelaide: Committee of the SA Wesleyan Methodist Auxiliary Missionary Society.

Teichelmann, C.G. (1857). Dictionary of the Adelaide dialect. MS 4 vo. pp. 99 (with double columns). No. 59, Bleek's Catalogue of Sir George Grey's Library dealing with Australian languages, South African Public Library.

Teichelmann, C.G. (1858). Of the verb. MS 8vo. pp. 3. No. 57, Bleek's Catalogue of Sir George Grey's Library dealing with Australian languages, South African Public Library.

Teichelmann C.G. & M. Moorhouse (1841). Report on the Aborigines of South Australia. Presented to the Statistical Society in Adelaide. *Register* (Adelaide), 8 January 1842. Rpt. Foster (1990b).

Teichelmann, C.G. & C.W. Schürmann (1840). *Outlines of a grammar, vocabulary, and phraseology, of the Aboriginal language of South Australia, spoken by the natives in and for some distance around Adelaide.* Adelaide. Published by the authors at the native location. Facs. ed. 1962. Adelaide: Libraries Board of South Australia. Facs. ed. 1982. Adelaide: Tjintu Books. A copy annotated by Teichelmann sent to Grey in 1858, held in the Sir George Grey Collection, South African Public Library, Cape Town.

Telfer [now Williams], Georgina (1984). Elderly, disadvantaged, disabled: I. *The Aboriginal Health Worker* (South Australian ed.) 8(3): 22-24.

Telfer, Karl (1997). Wiltarninga. In Procter & Gale (Eds).

Tezozomoc, Danza Azteca Huehueteotl, & Danza Azteca Tenochtitlan (1997). Revernacularizing classical Náhuatl through danza (Dance) Azteca-Chichimeca. In Reyhner (Ed.), pp. 56-76.

Thieberger, Nicholas (1988a). Aboriginal language maintenance: Some issues and strategies. Unpublished master's dissertation, Latrobe University, Melbourne.

Thieberger, Nicholas (1988b). Language programmes for tradition or for today. In Barbara Harvey & Suzanne McGinty (Eds), *Learning my way : Papers from the National Conference on Adult Aboriginal Learning* (pp. 81-90). Mt Lawley, WA: Institute of Applied Aboriginal Studies, WACAE.

Thieberger, Nicholas & William McGregor (Eds) (1994). *Macquarie Aboriginal words.* Sydney: Macquarie Library.

Thieberger, Nicholas (Ed.) (1995). *Paper and talk: A manual for reconstituting materials in Australian indigenous languages from historical sources.* Canberra: Aboriginal Studies Press.

Thomason, S.G. (1982). Historical linguistics. Unpublished MS.

Threlkeld, L.E. (1834). *An Australian grammar, comprehending the principles and natural rules of the language, as spoken by the Aborigines, in the vicinity of Hunter's River, Lake Macquarie, &c. New South Wales.* Sydney. Rpt. Fraser (Ed.).

Thurston, William R. (1982). *A comparative study in Anêm and Lusi.* Pacific Linguistics, Series B – 83. Canberra: Australian National University.

Thurston, William R. (1987). *Processes of change in the languages of north-western New Britain*. Pacific Linguistics, Series B – 99. Canberra: Australian National University.

Thurston, William R. (1989). How esoteric languages build a lexicon: Esoterogeny in West New Britain. In Ray Harlow & Robin Hooper (Eds), *VICAL 1: Oceanic languages, papers from the Fifth International Conference on Austronesian Linguistics* (pp. 555-579). Auckland: Linguistic Society of New Zealand.

Tindale, Norman B. Assorted papers, Tindale Collection, South Australian Museum.

Tindale, Norman B. Kaurna place names card file, Tindale Collection, South Australian Museum.

Tindale, Norman B. Kaurna vocabulary card file, Tindale Collection, South Australian Museum.

Tindale, Norman B. Permangk vocabulary card file, Tindale Collection, South Australian Museum.

Tindale, Norman B. (1935a). Legend of Waijungari, Jaralde Tribe, Lake Alexandrina, South Australia and the phonetic system employed in its transcription. *Records of the South Australian Museum* 5(3): 261-274.

Tindale, Norman B. (1935b). Notes on the Kaurna or Adelaide Tribe and the natives of Yorke Peninsula and the middle north of South Australia. Unpublished journal, Tindale Collection, South Australian Museum.

Tindale, Norman B. (1936). Notes on the natives of the southern portion of Yorke Peninsula, South Australia. *Transactions of the Royal Society of South Australia* 60: 55-69.

Tindale, Norman B. (1940). Results of the Harvard–Adelaide Universities anthropological expedition, 1938-39. Distribution of Australian Aboriginal Tribes: A field survey. *Transactions of the Royal Society of South Australia* 64: 140-232.

Tindale, Norman B. (1974). *Aboriginal tribes of Australia: Their terrain, environmental controls, distribution, limits and proper names*. Berkeley: University of California Press.

Tindale, Norman B. (1987). The wanderings of Tjirbruki: A tale of the Kaurna People of Adelaide. *Records of the South Australian Museum* 20: 5-13.

Tonkin, Humphrey (1987). One hundred years of Esperanto: A survey. *Language Problems & Language Planning* 11: 3, 264-282.

Toolan, Michael (1996). *Total speech: An integrational linguistic approach to language*. Durham: Duke University Press.

Towler, David J. & Porter, Trevor J. (n.d.). *The hempen collar: Executions in South Australia, 1838-1964. A collection of eyewitness accounts*. Norwood, SA: Wednesday Press.

Troy, Jakelin (1994a). Melaleuka: A history and description of New South Wales Pidgin. Unpublished doctoral dissertation, Australian National University.

Troy, Jakelin (1994b). *The Sydney language*. Produced with the assistance of the Australian Dictionaries Project and the Australian Institute of Aboriginal and Torres Strait Islander Studies. Canberra Aboriginal Studies Press.

Troy, Jaki (1995). Reading old sources. In Thieberger (Ed.), pp. 35-42.

Tunbridge, Dorothy with Coulthard, Annie (1985). *Artefacts of the Flinders Ranges*. Port Augusta: Pipa Wangka.

Tunbridge, Dorothy (1985a). Language as heritage: Artefacts of the Flinders Ranges. *Journal of the Anthropological Society of South Australia* 23(4): 7-13.

Tunbridge, Dorothy (1985b). Language as heritage: *Vityurna* (dried meat) and other stored food among the Adnyamathanha. *Journal of the Anthropological Society of South Australia* 23(7): 10-15.

Tunbridge, Dorothy (1985c). Language as heritage: Flora in place names, a record of survival in the Gammon Ranges. *Journal of the Anthropological Society of South Australia* 23(8): 3-15.

Tunbridge, Dorothy (1988). *Flinders Ranges Dreaming*. Canberra: Aboriginal Studies Press.

Tunbridge, Dorothy (1991). *The story of the Flinders Ranges mammals*. Kenthurst, NSW: Kangaroo Press.

Van Heerden, Etienne (1991). Reclaiming language. *Iowa Review* 21(2): 9-14.

Varcoe, Nelson (1990). *Wai Yerlitta!* But Dad! Unpublished MS, Adelaide.

Varcoe, Nelson (1994). Nunga languages at Kaurna Plains School. In Hartman & Henderson (Eds), pp. 33-39.

Varcoe, Nelson (1998). Reconciliation. In *Festival of Music 1998*. Adelaide: South Australian Public Schools Music Society.

Walker, Alan & Joyce Ross (n.d.). Gumatj Wordlist: Part Two. Unpublished typescript, Yirrkala, NT.

Walsh, Michael (1992). A nagging problem in Australian lexical history. In Dutton, Ross & Tryon (Eds), pp. 507-519.

Walsh, Michael & Yallop, Colin (Eds) (1993). *Language and culture in Aboriginal Australia*. Canberra: Aboriginal Studies Press.

Walton, C. & Eggington, W. (Eds) (1990). *Language: Maintenance, power and education in Australian Aboriginal contexts*. Proceedings of the Cross Cultural Issues in Educational Linguistics Conference held at Batchelor College, 1987. Darwin: Northern Territory University.

Wanganeen, Eileen (1987). *Point Pearce: Past and present*. Researched by Narrunga Community College. Adelaide: Aboriginal Studies and Teacher Education Centre, SACAE.

Wanganeen, Klynton (1997). A critique of the Warra Kaurna course taught at PWAC, Semester 1, 1997. UFU 039 negotiated studies assignment, University of South Australia, Underdale.

Wardhaugh, Ronald (1987). *Languages in competition*. Oxford: Blackwell/ Deutsch.

Warriparinga Consultant Team (1995). *Warriparinga Interpretive Centre conservation & management plan*. Adelaide: City of Marion.

Watkins, Cherie Warrara & Mary-Anne Gale (2006). *Kaurna alphabet book*. Elizabeth: Kaurna Plains School.

Weatherstone, John (1843). Vocabulary of native dialect spoken by natives of the <illeg> tribes of natives on the Murray River, South Australia. MS, Methodist Missionary Archives, School of Oriental and African Studies, London.

Webb, Noel Augustin (1936-7). Place names of the Adelaide Tribe. In *Municipal Year Book* (pp. 302-310). Adelaide: City of Adelaide.

Williams, Georgina (1986). 'Wailing spirit' and 'Coming home'. In The Invasion Diary Collective (Eds), pp. 21 and 26.

Williams, Georgina (1997). 'Georgina Williams', 'The crossroads', 'In-sanity' and 'Coming home'. In Procter & Gale (Eds), pp. 57-61.

Williams, Mark, Wilson, Greg, Gale, Kathryn & Amery, Rob (1989, December). Draft Proposal for an Aboriginal Languages Policy. MS, Enfield: SA Aboriginal Education Curriculum Unit.

Williams, R.F. (c1986). *To find the way: Yankalilla and district 1836-1986*. Yankalilla, SA: Yankalilla and District Historical Society.

Williams, William (1839). *A vocabulary of the languages of the Aborigines of the Adelaide district, and other friendly tribes, of the province of South Australia*. Adelaide: A. McDougall.

Williams, William (1840). The language of the natives of South Australia. *South Australian Colonist* 1(19): 295-296.

Williams, William (1923). A vocabulary of the language of the Aborigines of the Adelaide district. In Parkhouse (1923), pp. 57-70.

Wilmshurst, John (1992). *Report of the review of Kaurna Plains School*. Adelaide: Education Review Unit, Education Department of South Australia.

Wilson, Greg (1996). 'Only Nungas talk Nunga way': A preliminary description of Aboriginal children's English at Alberton, South Australia. Unpublished master's dissertation, University of New England, Armidale.

Woodforde, John (1836-1837). Journals. Mortlock Library of South Australiana.

Woods, J.D. (Ed.) (1879). *The native tribes of South Australia*. Adelaide: Government Printer. Rpt. Parkhouse (1923).

Wyatt, William (1840). Vocabulary of the Adelaide dialect. Copied from Mr Wyatt's Vocabulary at Adelaide, April, 1840. Sir George Grey's collection, South African Public Library, Cape Town.

Wyatt, William (1879). Some account of the manners and superstitions of the Adelaide and Encounter Bay tribes. In Woods (Ed.), pp. 157-181. Original MS with corrections in Barr Smith Library Special Collections, University of Adelaide.

Wyatt, William (1923). Some account of the manners and superstitions of the Adelaide and Encounter Bay Aboriginal tribes with a vocabulary of their languages, names of persons and places etc. Rpt. from J.D. Woods (Ed.), in Parkhouse (1923), pp. 16-56.

Zorc, David (1986). *Yolngu-Matha dictionary*. Batchelor, NT: School of Australian Linguistics.

Index

Aboriginal and Torres Strait Islander Languages Initiatives Program (ATSILIP), 263
Aboriginal Education Unit, 166, 176-177, 181, 205, 218
Aboriginal languages: *see* Australian Indigenous languages
Aboriginal Languages Handbook, 185
Aboriginal Languages Standing Committee, 179, 199, 278
Aboriginal Studies Teaching Resource Unit (ASTRU), 244, 227
'Aboriginality', 12, 15, 81, 214, **255-258**
Aborigines Act (1911-1962), 79, 80
Adams family 7; Adams, Tom (husband of Kudnarto) 7, 9, 72
'Adelaide School' of linguists, 86, 90-92, 110, 124
'Adelaide Tribe', 3-5, 56-57, 73, 75, 89, 90, 92, 95-96, 99, 100; *see also* Kaurna
Afrikaans, 17
Agius, Garth, 209, 225
Agius, Josie, 161, 175-176, 196, 201, 208, 212, 299
Agius, Rhonda, 245
Agius, Trisha (student KPS), 198-199, 213, 253
AIATSIS, 169
Aitchison, Jean, 19
Alberton Primary School, 14, 190, 199, 214
Amery, Rob, 5, 19, 38, 52-53, 57-59, 88, 92, 99, 143, 157-158, 166-168, 174, 177-178, 200, 230, 268, 280-293, 299, 303-304
Ammondt, Jukka, 21
Anêm (PNG), 49
Angas, George Fife, 62, 65, 68, 87, 118
Angas, George French, 97, 114, 123
archaeological sites, 222-223
Armstrong, John, 7-8
Arnhemland, 51, 124, 150, 158, 169-170, 215
assimilation policy, 12, 63, 72, **81**
Austin, Peter, 35, 149, 169
Australian Indigenous languages; *see also* Kaurna

Adnyamathanha, 5, 36, 105, 117, 118, 122, 130, 131, 137, 138, **140**, **141**, 149, 155, 157, 160, 173, 177
Antikirinya, 17, 178
Arabana, 122, 148, 150, 177
Arrernte, 118, 137, 158
   Eastern, 110, 178
Awabakal, 65, 298
Barngala, 5, 17, 68, 89, 109, 118, 124, 125, 138, **141**, **143**, 170, 177
Bundjalung, 275
Butchulla, 51
Diyari, 35, 105, 149, 170
Djabugay, 298
Djambarrpuyngu, 142
Gumbaynggir, 298
Gupapuyngu, 178
Guugu Yimithirr, 129
Kukatha, 14, 100, 177
Kungarakany, 202, 270
Larrakiya, 202, 270
Narungga, 2, 3, **5**, 7-9, **14-15**, 17, 46-47, 73, 79-80, 104, 106, 109, 118, 125, 130, 136, 138-143, 173-177, 200, 231, 256, 258, 261, 276
   affinity with Kaurna **5**, 138
Ndjébbana, 142
Ngadjuri, 5, 85, 102, 125, 138, 170
Ngarrindjeri, 2, 4, 6, 14-15, 46, 51, 89-90, 95-96, 100-105, 114-118, 138-139, 143, 167, 173-174, 198, 200, 208, 215, 219, 256-258, 261-264, 275-276, 183, 285-286, 298-299
   and 'language renewal', 245-246
   Ramindjeri dialect, 68, 89, 90, 95-96, 102-103, 115, 117, 143
   Tanganekald, Yaralde dialects, 115
Ngayawang, 3, 6, 17, 86, 91
Nukunu, 3, 5,17, 98, 100-102, 109, 117, 118, 125, 129-134, 138-139, 141-144, 169, 178
   relationship with Kaurna, 129-133, 145
   sound system, 130-131, 136
Nyungar, 17, 35, 90, 108, 298
Pama-Nyungan group, 17, 147, 149, 164, 165
Parnkalla (Barngarla), 68

Index

Peramangk group, 6, 17, 102, 115
Pintupi, 148
Pitjantjatjara, 6, 15, 36, 46, 104, 110, 137-138, 149, 151, 153-154, 158, 163
   in SA schools, 173-174, 176-178, 181, 184-186, 190, 199-202, 203, 231, 275-6, 279, 285, 298;
      Sydney language, 2, 35
         Thura-Yura subgroup, 5, 100, 109, 117, 125, 170
         Tiwi, 158, 160
         Walmatjarri, 137
         Warlpiri, 137, 154, 158, 163, 171
         Western Desert, 6, 17, 104, 117
         Wiradjuri, 299
         Woiwurrung (Melbourne), 35
         Yankunytjatjara, 110, 177-8, 184-6, 200
         Yolngu Matha, 138-9, 144, 158-60, 162
         Yorta Yorta, 178, 298
Australian Indigenous Languages Framework (AILF), 47-51, 55, 178, 181, 183, 185, 187, 194, 200-201, 254, 279, 301
Barker, Capt. Collet, 59
base-10 number system (Kaurna), 81, 139, 143, 145, 241
Batchelor (NT), 173, 256
Bates, Daisy, 57, 80, 85, 100, 126
Baudin, Nicolas, 57
Belair National Park, 73, 218, 222, 224
Bentahila, Abdelâli, 27, 48
Ben Yehuda, Eliezer, 37, 52, 160
Berndt, Ronald and Catherine, 4-6, 12, 85, 92, 114-7, 143, 208, 256
Birko Warra Kaurna teaching team, 178
birth-order names, 91-92, 126, 208-209
   and numbers, 162
Black, John McConnell, 85, 100-102, 109, 125, 129
Black, Paul, 158
Blackmoor, Frank, 117
Blake, Barry, 35, 36, 146, 147
Bleek, Dr Wilhelm, 83, 99, 124
borrowing, 51, 138-144, 158-60, 164, 166
Bramfield, Harry, 117
Brandenstein, Carl von, 96

Branson, Vince, 268, 276
Breton, 26, 54
Bringing Them Home, 264
Brock, Peggy, 72, 73, 79
Brodie, Veronica, 8, 12, 78, 79, 167, 214, 222, 261, 263, 303
Bromley, Capt. Walter, 64
Buckskin documentary 297, 305
Buckskin, Jack Kanya 280, 283-292, 297, 299, 301, 304
Buckskin, Peter, 205
Bukkiyana (Point Pearce), 5, 7, 9, 12, 17, 57, 73, 78-82, 250, 257-258, 261
Burford, Jenny, 198, 234
Burgemeister, Kath, 8, 214, 230, 251
Burmese, Nissaya, 246
Bushman, Waldo, 228
Californian languages, 26, 170, 236, 251, 298, 300
Camp Coortandillah, Aldinga, 94
Campbell, V.M., 77, 83, 115
Cape Jervis, 4, 8-9, 58-59, 103
Carter, Edie, 218
CASM, 214
Catanzaritti, Cherylynne, 125, 182, 254
Cawthorne, W. A., 56, 63, 65, 91, **96-97**, 105, 109, 119, 121-124, 125, 126-127, 137, 202, 208, 232
   diaries and journals, 96-97
   Legend of Kuperree, 119
ceremony, 13, 33, 54, 90, 118, 122, 155, 170, **215-216**, 232, 237, 296, 300, 304
   smoking ceremonies, 13, 155, 216, 296
Chittleborough wordlist, 281
Christianising and 'civilising', 61, 64-78, *passim* 86, 143
Clare district (SA), 7-8, 11, 72
Clarendon (SA), 4, 79-80
Clarke, Philip, 14, 57-8, 115
Cock, Robert, 61-62
Colebrook Training Home, 262, 279
colonisation and Aboriginal people, 6, 9, 59, **61-65** *passim*, 77, 85, 103, 203, 246, 258-259
computer languages, 28
Comrie, Bernard, 23, 36
Cooper (sealer), 60
Cooper, Mary, 81
Cooper, Robert L., 26
Copley, Vince, 225

copyright, 50, 52, 55, 243, **266-268**, 270, 273, 278, 305
Cornish, 22, 25-258, 39, 46, 54, 128, 278, 297, 300
corroboree: *see* song and dance
Cronk, James, 60-61, 64, 93, 118
Crowley, Terry, 35, 169
Crystal, David, 35, 291
'cultural resources', 267; *see also* copyright
cultural tourism, 3, 13, 41, 221-228, 253, 304
culture, Indigenous, 262-265
   destruction of in SA, 48, 71, 73, 76, 80, 257-258, 274-275
   material, 96-97, 157, 225, 244, 256, 259
   reintroduction of, 155-156, 224-225, 251-252, 254, 296
Cumpston, J.S., 58
Curriculum; *see also* LOTE:
   Aboriginal languages, 176-80, 183-186, 199, 303
   Aboriginal studies, 12, 172-173, 227, 298
   Kaurna language curriculum, 183-186, 285-286; *see also* Kaurna language programs
Damin (Mornington Island), 29
dance, 215-216
Dancing Ngutinai, 280
Davey, Dot, 224
Davis, Moonie, 118
Day, Thomas, 99
Deane, Sir William, 225
Denison, Norman, 23
Dick, Galena Sells, 19
dictionaries, 35, 38, 51, 88, 157-159, 220, 284, 293
Dictionaries for Reconciliation, 51
discourse phenomena, 113, 128, 153-155, 240, 247-248
diseases, European, 7, 43, 56, 74-76 *passim*
Dixon, Naomi, 11, 209, 226, 230, 255
Dixon, Paul, 13, 209-210, 226, 230, 237, 252, 259, 260, 269,
Dixon, R.M.W., 20, 26, 29, 235, 244
Donaldson, Tamsin, 129
Dowie, John, 9, 224
drama, 215-216
Dreaming, 9-13, 43, 114-8
   and Kaurna language revival, 154-155, 168, 173, 188
   term for, 143-144

Dreaming stories; *see also* Tjilbruke, 103, 114-148, 173
   few recorded in Kaurna, 114-115
   Munana, 116, 118
   Pootpobberrie, 117, 173
   Seven sisters and Orion, 117-178
   Urebilla, 226
Dresden Missionary Society, 65, 70-72, 88-9, 111-112, 123, 280-282
Dulicenko, A.D., 29-31 *passim*
e-mail and Kaurna, 200-201
Eastman, Carol, 47-48
Ebenezer (mission), 69-70
ECHS, 178, 181; *see also* Fremont-ECHS
Eckert, Paul, and Hudson, Joyce, 110
Edwards family, 9
Edwards, John, 20, 26, 48
Edwards, Robert, 57, 221
Ellis, Catherine, 130, 214
Ellis, P. Beresford, 26
Ellis, R.W., 172
Elphick, Gladys, 8, 9, 12, 18, 85, 141, 172, 253, 284
Emma (Emue), 8, 59, 76
Encounter Bay, 68, 70, 76, 89-90, 95-96, 116, 122-123
   'Encounter Bay' people, 3, 5-6
   'Encounter Bay Bob': *see* Tammuruwe Nankanere
English: exoteric language, 49
   replaces Kaurna, 77-78
ephemera, Kaurna, 84, 165, 217-219
Esperanto, 28-31, 45-46, 128, 300-301
Esselen, 170, 298, 300
Everett, Jim (sealer), 50
EWAC, 138, 178, 181, 196; *see also* PWAC
Eyre, Edward John, 89, 91-92
fauna terms, 139-142, 184, 189, 227
Fellman, Jack, 37-38
Fettes, Mark, 27, 44, 46, 48, 156
film, 190-191
'firestick weddings', 155
Fishman, Joshua, 24-26, 39, 242, 244, 278
Fitzpatrick, Phil, 105
Flinders Is (Tas), 92
Flinders, Matthew, 57
Formulaic Method in language revival, 234, **237-242**, 282-283, 289
Foster, Robert, 53, 83, 85, 92, 98
Fremont ECHS, 179, 181-182, 185, 198, 238; *see also* ECHS

Index

Gaimard, M., 65, 92, 126, 132, 141
  first recording of Kaurna, 92
Gale, Fay, 81-82
Gale, Kathryn, 175
Gale, Mary-Anne, 19, 282-283, 286, 298, 304
Gale, Peter, 46-47, 82
Gara, Tom, 80, 100
Gawler (SA), 4, 79
Gawler, George, Governor, 63-66 *passim*, 86-87, 96, 106
  children's letter to, 72, 112, 212, 217
  speech translated into Kaurna, 68, 96, 111
Gell, John Philip, 90, 102, 105, 127
Glanville, Laura, 8
Glenelg, Lord, 62
Glenelg (SA), 60
Goddard, Cliff, 110, 137, 157
Goddard, Ives, 34
Goldsmith family, 9
  Steve and Brian, 215
Goldsmith, Stephen Gadlabarti, 280, 286-287, 289, 292, 299
Gouger, Robert, 59-61, 63, 83, 99
Graham, Doris, 10, 261
grammar, 25, 36, 87-88, 106-110, 146-155, 194, 237, 240
  abstract nouns, 159
  allomorphy, 150-151
  historical sources for, 106-110
  of Kaurna, 36, 106-110, 146-151, 165
  in Ngarrindjeri 'language renewal', 245-247
  number, 147-148
  tense and aspect, 149-150
  Pama-Nyungan case system, 147
  word order, 148-149
Green, Jenny, 110
Grey, Capt. George, Governor, 2, 69-70, 77, 86, 88, 90-91, 107-108, 127
  library of, in Cape Town, 95, 113
Groome, Howard, 104, 166, 298
Haas, Mary R., 32, 34
Hack, Stephen, 281
Hale, Archdeacon Horatio, 7, 71-72
Hale, Ken, 24, 46, 298
Harlow, Ray, 38, 156, 164
Harrington, J.P., 251
Harris, Rebecca (Kumai), 85
Harris, Steven, 248
Harry (Kaurna man, 1820s), 57-59
Hartman, Vicki, 197, 229

Haugen, Einar, 44, 50, 52
Hawai'ian, 236, 248
Heath, Jeffrey, 51
Hebrew, 22, 23, 25-26, 28, 37-39, 46, 52, 160, 165, 297
Henderson, John, and Dobson, Veronica, 137, 157
Hercus, Luise, 5-6, 93, 98, 100-102, 109, 117-8, 129-136, 148, 150
Highgate Primary School, 191, 207
Hindmarsh Island bridge, 263-264
Hinton, Leanne, 236-237, 247, 251, 298
Hoenigswald, Henry M., 36
Holdfast Bay, 59-60, 93, 282, 288
Houston, Carol, 172
Howard, John, 155, 217, 261
Hudson, Joyce, 137, 158
Hughes family, 9
Hughes, Paul (KP), 218
Huron, 26, 170-171, 299-300
Hutt, John, Governor of WA, 108
HyperCard: in teaching phonology, 136, 191, 267
identity, 81-82, 250, 254-260
  and language, 31, 43, 47, 82, 183, 258-260, 274-275, 282, 284-287, 303-305
  and missions, 81-82, 257-258; *see also* Kaurna language
Ido, 29
immersion method, 235-237
Inbarendi College, 30, 52, 178, 182, 192, 194, 196, 207, 211-212, 230, 254, 263, 302
Indigenous Languages Support (ILS), 287, 293
Indigenous rights: *see* rights
Indonesian, 174-175
Inglis, Judy, 81
Interlingua, 29
Internet, and Kaurna, 220, **288**
invasion, European, 56, 61, 74, 122
Irish, 20, 26, 47
Itya Maii (Piltawodli student), 113, 155
Ityamaiitpinna ('King Rodney'), 8, 80
Ivaritji (Amelia Taylor), 1, 4, 8, 57, 80, 85-86, 100-102, 115-116, 167, 226
Jacob, William, 99
Japanese, 49, 174, 309
Johnson, Steve, 174
Jones, John (sealer), 58
Jones, Phillip, 221, 225

Jordan, Deirdre, 48, 53, 82, 255-256
Journey of Healing, 214, 216
KACHA: *see* Kaurna Aboriginal Community and Heritage Association
Kadlitpiko Palti, 120
Kadlitpinna ('Captain Jack'), 64, 76, 87, 96, 110, 116, 120
Kalloongoo (Cowwerpateyer, Windeera, Charlotte, Sarah), 8, 59, 76, 92, 189
Kangarilla (SA), 79
Kangaroo Island, 8, 57-60, 134, 189
'Kapunda Tribe', 75
Karloan (Karlowan), Albert, 4, 101-102, 117
Karrendi Primary School, 182, 206
Kartinyeri, Doreen, 7, 8, 72-3, 79, 255-256
Katharevousa, 46, 52
Kaurna Aboriginal Community and Heritage Association (KACHA), 5, 10, 11, 13, 43, 115, 155, 163, 172, 187, 197, 205-206, 210, 218-219, 222, 224-226, 234, 237, 239, 241-244, 256-257, 259, 263, 268, 270, 303
    Constitution, 256
    'Reviving the Dreaming' project, 13, 155
Kaurna community, 193, 196-197, 200-201, 205, 209-210, 215-216, 220, 228-231, 268-272, 279, 284-286, 291-294, 303-305,
Kaurna hymns and prayers, 68, 77-78, 86, 89, 113, 119, 123-124, 126, 167, 191, 214, 282
Kaurna language
  access to, 198, 229, 242, 254, 262, 267-273, 277-278
  'artificial', 30-31
  'authentic', 54, 162-166, 188, 283
  borrowing and, 51, 114, 138-139, 142, 144, 158-160, 166
  borrowing from, 90
  colonists' knowledge of, 60-61, 64-65
  and copyright, **266-268**, 270, 273, 278, 305
  dialectal variants in, 4, 87, 92, 97, 110, 132-133, 149-151
  esoteric 49-50
  genius of the, 152-154
  and identity, 31, 43, 47, 53, 183, 188, 194, 250-1, 258-260, 274-275, 284-287, 303-305
  Indigenous rights and, 16, 27, 43, 253, 261, 266-270, 253, 293
  loss of, 71-78, 258, 264-265, 276
  Modern, 27, 30, 128, **156-168**, 246
  neighbouring languages and, 2-3, 5, 7, 32-33, 36, 43, 104, 109, 114-115, 129, 142-145, 157, 188, 298-299
  oral transmission of, 85-86
  'ownership' of, 49-50, 52, 266-268, 270, 272-273, 293, 305
  Pidgin, 77, 94, 104, 108, 126, 282
  as political tool, 210, 253, 261, 296
  in public use, 203, 210, 250, 261, 286-287, 295-296, 298, 301
  and reconciliation, 190, 206, 210, 213-214, 216, 224, 261-262, 265, 269, 273, 282, 291, 295
  revival, reclamation of, 1, 12, 16, 37, Ch.6, Ch.7, Ch.8, Ch.9, Ch.10, Ch.11, Ch.12
  social use of, 228-230, 235, 252, 261, 278
  sounds of: *see* phonology
  spoken, 27, 31, 215-217, 219, 221, 254, 278, 297-299, 301-305
  teaching, 3, 12-13, 16, 135-136, Ch. 7 *passim*
  teaching in, 65, 71, 111-113
  translations into, 87, 96, 111, 113, 123, 138, 141, 155, 160, 162, 166-167, 190-192, 268, 282, 284, 291, 294, 296, 305
Kaurna Language & Language Ecology (KL&LE), University of Adelaide, 168, 182-183, 191-192, 195-197, 220, 243, 253, 268-269
Kaurna language programs, 1; *see also* Fremont–ECHS, KPECC, KPS, PWAC, Tauondi), 106, **Ch. 7**, 210, 220-222, 224, 234, 242, 259, 268, 271, 285-286, 302-303
  assessment in, 179, 185, 192
  evaluation of, 193-195
  Kaurna Warra Patpangga, 181, 244
Kaurna people
  and colonists, Ch. 4 *passim*
  'extinct', 9, 12, **56-57**, 73, 78, 99, 253, 296

Index 343

identity, 8-9, 11, 15, 53, 56, 80, 82, 164, 187, 200, 254-257, 259-260, 301, 304
population numbers and profile, 4, 56, 59, **74-77**, 81-82
sociopolitical history, Ch. 4 *passim*, 253-5, 261-266
survival, 22, 56-57, 78, 250-252, 256, 271, 295, 301, 304
Tarndanya clan, 8
territory, **4-5**, 7-8, 74-75 102, 224, 295
traditions and culture, 7, 12-15, 85, 128, 216, 258
destruction of, 7, 48, 73, 78
Kaurna People, The (EDSA), 12, 71, 105, 115, 117-178, 127, 173
Kaurna Plains Early Childhood Centre (KPECC), 181, 185, 191, 197, 205, 254
Kaurna Plains School (KPS), 139, 153, 161-165, 167, 179-184, 190-194, 211-214, 218-220, 229-230, 238, 241-242, 252-254, 260, 276-277, 286, 301-303
language programs 180-182, 184, 187, 190-194, 197-199; *see also* Kaurna language programs
school song, 184, 190, 197, 260
Kaurna texts, **110-113**, 116-117, 154-155, 162, 166, 189
letters, 57, 99-100, 137, 166, 191, 193
Kaurna Warra Karrpanthi (KWK), 285, 288, 291, 293-294, 297, 305
Kaurna Warra Pintyanthi (KWP), 280-281, 283-285, 288-294, 297, 305
Keegan, Peter, 38, 236
King George Sound (WA), 57-59 *passim*
'King John': *see* Mullawirraburka
kinship terms, 99, 105, 138, 163, 200
Kirke, Brian, 174, 298
Kite, Nathan (student KPS), 213
KL&LE: *see* Kaurna Language & Language Ecology
Klausner, Josef, 37
Klose, Samuel, 65, 69-71, 75, 77-78, 86, 89, 91, 111-113, 123, 125-126, 151, 157, 161, 171, 280
and Kaurna beliefs, 70, 89
and Kaurna hymns, 89, 123, 167
and Kaurna letters, 112-113
Kneebone, Heidi, 35, 281

Koeler, Hermann, 126, 281
Koerner, Konrad, 34
KPECC: *see* Kaurna Plains Early Childhood Centre
KPS: *see* Kaurna Plains School
Kudnaipiti, 67
Kudnarto, 7, 8, 11, 71-72, 208, 258
Kumai (Rebecca Harris), 85
Kumarangk Coalition, 261, 264
Kura Yerlo, 207
Kura Yerlo Workshop, 181
Labov, William, 53
'lame', 52-53
land rights: *see* rights
Lane, Malcolm (Nunga ranger), 224
Language Renewal and Reclamation project, 185-186
language:
and culture, 4, 13, 19, 32, 46, 66, 102, 155-156, 189, 200, 203-205, 215-216, 262, 266, 276, 287, 296, 301
as cultural artefact, 29, 42, 50-52, 268
'dead', 'extinct', 116, 19, 20-24, 31, 34, 199, 296
linguists' attitude to, 14, 20, 22-28, 31, 34
ecological approach to, Ch. 3 *passim*
modernisation, 30, 37-38, 128, 275
'natural' v. 'artificial', 29-31, 245-247
and ownership, 44, 49-50, 52, 266-273, 293, 305
planning, 22, 28, 38, 45, 50, 52, 54, 168, 186, 296
politicisation of, 278
renewal, 20, 44, 245-247
restriction of access to, 51
revitalisation, 20, 188, 236
'sleeping', 1, 20, 47, 248, 295
symbolic v. communicative, 3, 27, 47-48
'theft' of, 51
typology, 32, 36
variation or change in, 151-152
vitality, 151, 220
language ecology15, 33, **41-44**, 50, 61, 88, 172, 174, 197, 247, 251, 254, 270, 275, 198-199, 296, 301
language immersion, 235-237
language learning, 195, 228, 237, 240-243, 247, 270, 284

language-learning materials, 168, 268, 284, 292
    tapes, 165, 168, 191, 243, 267-270, 304
language policy: colonial, 50, 63, 174
    South Australian Aboriginal Languages policy, 176-177
language programs, Ch. 7 *passim*
    government involvement in, 2, 175, 263
    and Kaurna revival, 177, 292, 303
language reclamation, 1, 19-40 *passim*; 41-42, 44, 48, 52, 100, 124, 128, 146, 151, 163-164, 178, 181, 187-190, 200, 203, 237, 243-244, 248, 252-253, 273-275 281, 296-299, 301, 304
    applied to Kaurna, 1-2, Ch. 6 *passim*
    borrowing 38, 51
    casual speech, 151-162
    historical sources used in: *see* sources
    methods for, 20, 31-39, 147, 163, 187-192
    neologisms and, 37-39, 54, 139, 157-159
    transformation, 27, 43, 128-129, 156, 164, 168, 282-283, 296
    related terms, 19-20
language revival, 23-26, 41-43, 45-48, 50-52, 166, 172, Ch. 7 *passim*, 234-240, 256, 272-273, 295-298
    Dreaming stories and, 11-13, 141, **155**, 168, 188, 296
    ecological approach to, **Ch. 3** *passim*, 172, 182, 195, 247, 251, 259, 270, 275, 296-305
    formulaic approach to: *see* Formulaic Method
    intergenerational transmission and, 24-26, 41, 48, 242
    idiomatic expressions and, 145, 153-154, 240-241
languages:
    artificial, 28-31, 46
    auxiliary, 22, 29-31, 235, 305-306
    'endangered', 24, 46, 289-290
    esoteric, 49-50
    exoteric, 49-50
    planned, 31, 168
    universal, 31; *see also* Esperanto
Languages Other Than English (LOTE), 172, 174-178, 183-186, 189, 193, 199
    Kaurna LOTE, 181-182, 199, 271, 303
    profiles inappropriate to Kaurna, 184, 186, 189, 193, 271
Lartelare, Rebecca, 7, 8, 101, 222
Latin, 20-21, 28, 30, 87, 128
Latino Sine Flexione, 29
Lee, Jenny, 158, 160
lexical case studies, 140-146, 142-144, 158-60
lexical semantics, 143-146
lexicon, Kaurna, 126-127, 137-146
    body terms, 99, 126-127, 143
    and borrowing, 138-40, 142-144, 158-160
    compounding, 139, 159, 143-146
    fauna terms, 139-142
    fish terms, 142-143
    fungi, 145
    onomatopoeia, 140
    range of meaning in, 145-146
Liddy, Peter, 75
Light, Col. William, 59
Lindsay, Andrew, 215
Lindstedt, Jouko, 28
linguistics: historical/comparative, 25, 32-35, 140, 274
linguists: Indigenous people's attitudes to, 51, 245, 259, 273-275, 298, 303
    in language reclamation and revival, 42, 51-53, 136, 166, 274-275, 283, 289-291, 296-299, 305
    obligations, 53-54
Lo Bianco, Jo, 174-175
LOTE: *see* Languages Other Than English
Lutheran Archives, Adelaide, 33, 70, 90, 125, 171, 281
Mac A'Ghobhainn, S., 26
Maityuwampi Cycling for Culture fundraiser, 283
Manning, Geoffrey, 103, 231-232
Maori, 20, 38-39, 45, 128, 156, 160, 164, 170, 248
    Kohanga Reo, 236
Maria (Kaurna woman, 1840s), 72
Mason, Robert, 102-103
Master-Apprentice method, 236-237, 247
Mathews, R.H., 5
maths terms, 161, 164

Index

Mattingley, Christobel and Hampton, Ken, *Survival in Our Own Land*, 9, 61, 79, 80; *see also Tucker's Mob*
McCarty, Teresa L., 19, 278
McEntee, John, 131, 133, 157, 169
media coverage, 220, 289
Melvin, Sheridah, 217
Meyer, H.A.E., 69, 70, 86, 89-90, 95-96, 103, 114, 116-117, 122-125, 143, 280
Milerum (Clarence Long), 101-103, 115-116, 122
Miller, Fred, 78
Mills, Janama Robbie, 270
Milte-widlo, 63
Miru languages, 5
missionaries, 13, 33, 52
   German, 65-71, 75-78, 86-91, 106-108, 111-114, 120-124, 128-129, 139, 147, 157, 216, 251, 256, 264, 267, 280-282, 295
   and language preservation, 65-66; *see also* Teichelmann, Schürmann, Klose
missions, 79-82; *see also* Bukkiyana, Raukkan
Monaitya, 72
Moorhouse, Matthew, 6, 63, 65, 72-74, 86, 90-91, 103, 106, 108, 119, 126-127, 281-282
   letters, 91
   lost journal, 91, 119, 122
Morgan, Sally, 255, 278
Moriarty, John, 10
Mortlock Library, SA, 33, 119
Mountford, Charles, 117, 122, 130
Mühlhäusler, Peter, 35, 49-50, 104, 111, 278, 281
   Linguistic Ecology, 44
Mullawirraburka ('King John', 'Onkaparinga Jack'), 3, 64, 77, 87, 110-111, 206
Mullawirraburkarna Palti, 120, 122, 125, 189
multiculturalism, 203
multimedia resources, 191-192, 243, 271
Munaintya (the Dreaming), 144, 157, 190
munaintyerlo, 143-144
Munaitya Wattiwattitpinna, 66-67
Munana Dreaming story: *see* Dreaming stories
murals and installations, 218-219, 225
Murray Mouth (SA), 58, 59

Murray River people, 6-7, 71-72, 76, 78, 102, 120
   impact on the Kaurna, 76
Murrell, Joseph (sealer), 57
Museum of South Australia: *see* South Australian Museum
music, 122-124
Nahir, Moshe, 26
Nahuatl, 300, 306
Nam, Pearl, 207, 209
names; *see also* place names, **203-210**, 217-218, 261, 288, 306
   birth-order names (*qv*), 91-92, 98, 105, 126, 156, 162, **208-209**
   totem, 137, **209**
Naragansett, 26
Narungga, 2-3, 5, 7-9, 12, 14-15, 46-47, 79-80, 109, 118, 130, 136, 138-143, 173-177, 258
National Aboriginal Languages Program (NALP), 175-176, 201, 263
   NALP/LOTE Aboriginal Languages program, 175-7, 181
National Parks of South Australia, The, 73
National Parks and Wildlife Service, 122, 124
National Sorry Day posters, 282
Native School Establishment, Kintore Ave (1845), 71-72
Native Title debate, 43, 264-265
Navajo language, 19, 39
neologisms, 21, 32, 54, 128, 157-165, 241, 268, 275, 296, 299
Newton Curriculum Centre, 179
Ngarrindjeri Narungga Dreaming dance troupe, 215
Ngarrindjeri people (Kukabrak), 2-9, 12, 14, 46, 51, 57-58, 73-74, 76, 79-81, 85-89, 95-96, 100-105, 121-122, 173-177, 198, 200, 203, 219, 245-247, 256-258, 261, 263-264, 275-276, 279-280, 282, 285-286, 298-299
   source for Kaurna Dreaming stories, 114-118
Ngayawang, 6, 76
   grammar and vocabulary of, 86, 91
Ngurlongga Nunga Centre, 201
Ngurpo Williamsie's Palti, 119, 122, 214, 220, 225
Nobbs, Chris, 35
Norwegian, 46, 52

Nukunu people, 5, 117-118
numbers, 91, 92, 148, 161-163, 191
Nunga community, 1, 3, 6-11, 16, 203, 205, 208-210, 228-231, Ch. 10, 255-260, 281, 287-288, 292-295, Ch.12
   identity, 2, 117, **255-260**
   kinship networks, 257
Nungas and sport, 162, 241
Nunga English, **13-15**, 32, 44, 104, 129, 155, 162, 238, 245, 247, 258-259, 261
   attitudes to, 15, 258-259
   relationship with Kaurna, 14-15, 129
   with other groups, 15, 104
Nyungar, 17, 35, 90, 108, 298
O'Brien, Dennis, 282, 289, 292
O'Brien, Lewis, 3-12, 15, 138-139, 143-144, 158, 161, 163-165, 172, 192, 195, 203, 207, 210-213, 218-219, 228-229, 234, 250-251, 260-261, 269, 271, 274, 283-284, 291, 293-294, 299, 304-305
O'Brien, Rod, 194
O'Donaghue, Lowitja, 225
O'Grady, Geoffrey, 130, 158
Occidental, 29
'Onkaparinga Jack': *see* Mullawirraburka
orthography, 34-35, 86-88, 105, 117, 124, 16-17, 129, **133**, 174, 182, 191, 278
   of the 'Adelaide School', 86, 124
   using IPA, 133, 174
Parkhouse, T.A., 93, 95, 117
Parkin, James, 160, 184, 191, 193, 198
Paugusett, 26
Paulston, Christine Bratt, 19-20, 22
Pawley, Andrew, 240-241
Pequot, 26
Permangk people ('Mt Barker Tribe'), 6, 17
Pfitzner, Darryl (Milika), 218-219
Phillips, James, 79
philology and language reclamation, 31, **34-35**, 42, 92, 106
phonology, 27, 109, 128
phonology, Kaurna, 129-137, 292
   consonants, 130-132
   stress, 137, 166, 240
   vowels, 131, 136-137
Pidgin: 'artificial', 245-247
   Kaurna, 77, 94, 126, 281

New South Wales, 2
Quileute, 52, 245-247
South Australian, 99, 104
Piesse, Louis, 65, 93-94, 98, 102, 105, 109, 126, 134, 141-142, 145, 284
Piltawodli ('Native Location'), 64-66, 69-71, 74, 77, 86, 89-90, 95, 112, 123, 199, 206, 214, 222, 225
Piradli Trail, 224
Pirltawardli Puppet Show, 293, 305
Pitpauwe, Pitpowie (Piltawodli student), 72, 112-113, 171, 225, 281
place names, 2, 6, 66, 88-89, 97, 99-101, 115-116, 126-127, 188-189, 210, 224, 280-282, 284, 288, 290, 292
   Tindale's card file of, 102
Point McLeay Aboriginal Mission: *see* Raukkan
Point Pearce Aboriginal Mission: *see* Bukkiyana
Poonindie, 7, 71-73, 77-80, 258
Pope, Alan, 57, 61, 63, 72, 74-75
Port Adelaide, 7-8, 78-79, 101, 173, 190-191, 205, 212, 294, 303
Port Augusta (SA), 118
Port Lincoln (SA), 68-69, 71, 73, 89
Port Philip (Vic.), 8, 76
Portatangga ('Ochre Cove'), 77
Portland (Vic.), 8
Powell, Jay, 52, 245-247
Power, Katrina, 39, 47, 128, 199, 207, 209, 213, 229, 252, 292, 294, 302
Power-Smith, Taylor Tipu, 285-286, 291, 301
Presley, Elvis, 21
pronunciation, 102, 105-106, 129-130, 132-133, 135-137, 165, 182, 281, 284-285, 288; *see also* phonology
'Protector' of Aborigines, 34, 61-65, 72, 79-80, 90-91, 95, 111, 281
Provençal, 26
Pulthurni-apinthu! 153-154
PWAC, 167, 179, 181-183, 185, 187, 190, 196-199, 214, 217, 219, 242, 249, 279; *see also* EWAC, Inbarendi
   Tirkandi food and medicine garden, 224
Quileute 'artificial pidgin', 52, 245-247
racism, 16, 18, 253, 257, 262, 273
Rainbird Murders, 75

Index

Ramindjeri people, 3-6, 68, 89-90, 95-96, 102-103, 115, 117
Rankine, Leila, 205
Rapid Bay (SA), 5, 59-60, 92, 95, 115-156, 189
'Rapid Bay talk', 116
Rathjen, Cynthia, 35
Rathoola, 7-8, 72
Raukkan (Point McLeay), 6-7, 9, 12, 73, 76, 78-82, 170, 257, 282
reconciliation, 69, 157, 190, 206, 210, 213-214, 216, 222, 224, 244, 253, 260-262, 264-265, 269, 274, 277, 241-243, 252-253, 232, 233, 279
    Council for Aboriginal Reconciliation, 265
reserves, 64, 80-81, 84; *see also* missions
rhotics, 100, 130, 132-133, 136, 164, 169; s*ee also* phonology
rights: of citizenship, 81
    Indigenous, 16, 19, 48, 50, 80, 210, 253, 255, 261, 263, 265
    intellectual property, 267-268, 293; *see also* copyright
    land, 61, 255-256
    linguistic, 50, 52, 266-268
Rigney, Alitya (Alice) Wallara, 12, 172, 181, 184, 187, 196, 199, 211, 214, 217, 220-221, 231, 234, 250-253, 257, 260, 262, 269-270, 280, 283, 291, 293-295, 297, 299, 302
Rigney, Lester Irabinna, 13, 15, 19, 85, 162, 213, 215, 227-229, 232, 233, 235, 241-243, 250, 252-253, 258, 260, 269, 274, 277, 279
Rigney, Liz, 175
rivalry, linguistic, 277, 298
Rivoli Bay (SA), 104
Robe, F. H., Governor, 71
Robinson, Charles: wordlist, 65, 92, 126-127, 134, 141
Robinson, Clinton, 297-298
Robinson, George Augustus, 84, 92
Rüdiger, Gerhard, 281-282, 292-293
Ruins of the Future, 212, 219, 232
Salisbury High School, 182, 301
Salisbury North Primary School, 182, 198, 279
Sally (Kaurna woman c. 1820s), 57, 59
Sansbury family, 9
Sanskrit, 20-21
Sasse, Hans-Jürgen, 22-23, 39
Schayer, Herr, 90

Schebeck, Bernhard, 109, 118, 131, 149
School of Australian Linguistics (SAL), 173
Schultz, Chester, 122-123, 125, 167, 184, 189-190, 280-282, 294
Schurmann, Edwin A., 88, 129
Schürmann, Clamor, 65-70, 77, 86-90, 106, 111, 114, 117, 123-124, 126, 143, 280-281, 289
    interpreter to Gawler, 68
    journals, 88-89, 122, 126
    knowledge of Kaurna, 67-68,
    and *munaintyerlo*, 143-144, 157
    relations with Indigenous people, 67-68
    song collector, 120-122
    Vocabulary of the Parnkalla Language, 89
Schwarz, Silvia, 21
sealers and whalers, 57-60, 295
    and Aboriginal women, 57-59, 84
    impact on the Kaurna nation, 75, 84
    as interpreters, 59-60, 64
Shopen, Timothy, 36, 158, 171
Short, Bishop, 72, 83
signage, in Kaurna, 41, 207, 210, **218**, 224-225, 260, 284, 287, 301
Simpson, Jane, 77, 86, 88, 94, 96, 105-106, 109, 166, 191, 283-285
    and Kaurna grammar, 146
    and Kaurna phonology, 130-133, 136
Simpson, Jennifer, 178
Sioui, Linda, 26, 170, 171, 233, 299
smallpox, 74-75, 93
Smith, Christina, 104
Smith, W. Ramsay, 115
sociopolitical pressures and language, 44, 50-51, 250-254
Solomon, George (husband of Rathoola), 7, 72
Solomon, John, 73
song and dance, 215, 252
    Kuri, Palti and *Ngunyawaietti*, 97, 118-120, 122-123, 189-190, 215
songs, Kaurna, 88, 91, **118-122**
    modern, 14, 160, **167**, 181, 189, 190-191, 197, 214-216, 219, 228, 230, 232, 261, 301
song books, 191, 231, 279, 304
    Kaurna Paltinna, 190, 284, 304
    Songs with the Nungas, 280
Songwriters' Workshop, Tandanya, 167, 176, 181, 189, 214, 301

sources for Kaurna language revival, Ch. 5 *passim*
   primary sources, 87-104, 126
   secondary sources, 105-106, 127
South Australian Act, 61-62
South Australian colony: ideals of, 59-61
South Australian Company, 61, 92
South Australian Museum, 3, 9, 10, 12, 14, 35, 99, 101-102, 142, 218, 221-222, 224-225
   Family History Project, 7, 255-256
South Australian Secondary School of Languages (SASSL), **179**, 182, 189, 197
speeches, public, 41, 51, 66, 77, 87, 111, 152-153, 165-166, 192, 197, **210-215**, 220, 228, 231, 240, 251-225, 260-261, 263, 275, 286, 296, 301-302, 304, 305
Spencer, Baldwin, 18, 101
Spender family, 9
   Alf (Lartelare's son), 85, 101
   George, 7-8
Spolsky, Bernard, 26, 41
sporting terms, 157, 161-162
Stephen, George, 62
Stephens, Edward (of the SA Company), 92-93, 141
Stephens, Edward, 56, 93, **97-99**, 102, 105, 123, 126-127
Stephens, John, 99
'stolen generations', 81, 217, 255, 257, 261, 264
Sutherland, Captain, 58
T&S, 3, **87**-98 *passim*, 101-103, **106-107, 110-111**, 118-119, 120-122, 126-127, 129, 136-157
   and Kaurna phonology, 131-133
   inconsistencies in, 129, 132-133
   main source of Kaurna grammar, 106-107, 110, 128, 188
   record of songs, 118-119
Talbot, Sylvain, 179
Tammuruwe Nankanere ('Encounter Bay Bob'), 3, 68
Tandanya (national Aboriginal Cultural Institute), 7-8, 14, 167, 181, 205, 221-222, 229, 252, 263
Tandanya (Kaurna name for Adelaide), 14, 84, 221
Tangkaira (mother of Ivaritji), 8, 145
Taplin, Rev. George, 17, 84, 95-96, 99, 103, 116-117, 122, 127, 233

Tarnda Kanya site, 77, 84
Tasmania, 8, 17, 50-51, 57-59, 61, 63, 84, 92
Tasmanian Aboriginal Centre, 50-51
Tasmanian Languages, 35, 124, 169
Tassell, David, 181, 202
Tauondi Community College, 43, 115, 181-182, 185, 187, 197-198, 200, 205, 207, 212, 215, 217, 219, 222, 226-227, 230, 243, 276-277, 285, 294
Taylor, Amelia: *see* Ivaritji
Te Taura Whiri i te Reo Maori, 38
Teichelmann, C.G., 3, 56, 63, 65-70, 77-78, 85-91, 106-108, 123-124, 126-127, 129, 280-282
   diary, 68, 89, 126
   and Dreaming stories, 114, 117
   Kaurna vocabulary (*see* TMs), 87-88
   Kaurna grammatical notes, 87-88, 146; *see also* T&S
   knowledge of Kaurna, 69
   Moorhouse and, 91
   moves to Happy Valley, Morphett Vale, 69-70
   relations with Kaurna people, 68-69
Telfer, Karl, 12-13, 215, 232, 254, 268, 280, 287, 300, 305
Ten Commandments translated into Kaurna, 68, 87, 111, 113, 216
'Tent Embassy', 253, 278
terra nullius, 62, 265
territory, 43, 74-75, 224, 256, 288, 295
Thieberger, Nicholas, 191, 220, 247
   and McGregor, W., *Macquarie Aboriginal Words*, 105-106
Thomason, S.G., 22-23
Threlkeld, L.E., *An Australian grammar*, 65, 83, 87
Thu<u>r</u>a-Yu<u>r</u>a subgroup, 5, 100, 109, 117, 125
time, terms for, 157, 161-162
Tindale, Norman, 1, 4, 7, 12, 17, 51, 74, 84-85, 92, 101-103, 112, 126-127, 224, 226, 257, 279
Aboriginal Tribes of Australia, 4
   card files, 102-103
   and Dreaming stories, 114-117
   ethnographic notes, 103
   songs recorded by, 122
   unreliability of, 102-103, 169, 201

Index

Tjilbruke (Tjirbruki): Kaurna creator ancestor, 115, 122, 225
Tjilbruke Dreaming, 9-11, 14-5, 103-104, 115-116, 173
    trail, 9-10, 13, 18, 221, 223-224, 227
Tjilbruki Dance Group, 215
TMs, 3, 70, 86, 88, 94, 110-111, 114, 119, 126-128, 132, 137, 140, 142, 144-146, 148-149, 151, 153, 156-157, 170, 282-283, 296
    electronic version, 191, 220
    grammatical information in, 106-108
Tok Pisin, 52, 170
Torrens River (Adelaide), 74, 244
Trask, Larry, 28-29, 39
Troy, Jakelin, 2, 35
Tucker's Mob translated into Kaurna, 141, 160, 166, 170
Tuitpurro, 67
Tunbridge, Dorothy, 118, 131, 140, 232
Tunstill, Guy, 178
Turkish, 28, 46
Umewarra Radio, 217
Unaipon, David, 115
University of Adelaide: Linguistics, 179, 192, 200, 285-288, 292-3, 302-303; *see* KL&LE
Uraidla (SA), 226
Urebilla Dreaming, 226
Urumbula (song line), 118
Van Der Byl, Muriel, 213
Van Heerden, Etienne, 19, 39
Varcoe, Nelson (Snooky), 163, 167, 175, 178, 181, 184, 190-192, 200, 207, 212, 214, 224, 227, 254, 259, 301
    '*Wai Yerlitta!* But Dad!', 138, 161
Vietnamese, 179, 276, 286
Volapük, 30, 46, 269
Wailtyi (Piltawodli student 1840s), 112-113, 171, 280
Waiyungari (ancestor), 117
Walker, Reuben (Ramindjeri man), 102
Walkerville school for Murray River children, 71, 78
Walsh, Michael, 104, 146, 289
Wampanoag (Natick, Massachusett), 26, 298, 306
Wanganeen, Edmund, 213
Wanganeen, Eileen, 214, 299
Wanganeen, Frank, 275

Wanganeen, Klynton, 194, 229
Wanganeen, Phoebe, 163, 303
Wardhaugh, Ronald, 22, 27
Warra Kaurna: A Resource for Kaurna Language Programs, 106, 161, 191, 304
Warranna Purruna: Pa:mpi Tungarar: Living Languages video, 245
Warrette (Emma Pritchard), 79, 84
Warriappendi Alternative School, 181, 205-206, 231
Warrior (Warria), Barney (Ngadjuri man), 102, 208
Warrior, Fred, 5, 172, 219, 259
Warriparinga, 13, 181, 197, 213, 215, 218, 220, 225-226, 244, 269, 278, 287, 289
Watkins, Cherie Warrara, 1, 13, 47, 165, 167, 178, 182, 184, 187-8, 191, 198, 212, 214, 218-219, 230-231, 254, 260-261, 264, 274-275, 277, 285, 301, 304
Watson, Irene, 208
Watson, Kudnarto, 208
Weatherstone, John, 6, 86
Welsh, 26
White, Pilawuk, 184
Wilkins family, 7-8
    John, 7, 18
Wilkinson, Christine, 227
Williams, Georgina Yambo, 8-13, 18, 56, 77, 81, 164, 172-174, 169, 181, 195, 201, 207-210, 213-214, 226, 253, 257, 261-262, 268, 270, 273, 287, 305
Williams, Joseph, 215
Williams, Mark, 199
Williams, Mary, 253
Williams, William, 60, 64-65, 90, **93-95**, 98-99, 101-102, 124, 126-127, 134-135, 141-142, 228, 281, 283
Wilson family, 9, 18
    Sustie, 102
Wilson, Greg, 14, 173, 175, 178, 185, 201-202, 218, 277, 279, 285
Woodforde, John, 99
Woods, J.D., 56, 95, 117
wordlists, comparative, 99, 116
wordlists, Kaurna, 57, 87-106
World Indigenous Peoples Movement, 43
Wyatt, William, 3, 62-65, 85, 90, 93-96, 101-102, 105, 108, 111, 116,

121, 124-127, 134, 141-142, 154, 160, 169-170, 232, 281, 283
  Dreaming story recorded by, 14, 111, 116-168
  orthography, 134
Yaitya Warra Wodli (YWW), 159, 207, 212, 263, 271, 298, 305
Yallop, Colin, 146
Yankalilla (SA), 18, 57-59, 76, 92, 115, 288
  etymology of, 103
Yäpuma (Yolngu dancer), 215
Yaralde people, 6, 101, 115, 117
Yiddish, 30
Yorke Peninsula, 4-5, 14, 72, 118
Zorc, David, 157, 170

Electronic Index

This book is available as a free fully-searchable ebook from
www.adelaide.edu.au/press

www.ingramcontent.com/pod-product-compliance
Lightning Source LLC
Chambersburg PA
CBHW040509110526
44587CB00047B/4408